EVER
CLOSER
UNION?

To Wendy and Conor

EVER CLOSER UNION?

An Introduction to the
European Community

Desmond Dinan

Lynne Rienner Publishers ■ Boulder, Colorado

ACD -9905

Published in the United States of America in 1994 by
Lynne Rienner Publishers, Inc.
1800 30th Street, Boulder, Colorado 80301

Library of Congress Cataloging-in-Publication Data
Dinan, Desmond, 1957–
    Ever closer union? an introduction to the European Community /
Desmond Dinan.
        p.   cm.
    Includes bibliographical references and index.
    ISBN 1-55587-357-X (hc) (alk. paper)
    ISBN 1-55587-388-X (pb) (alk. paper)
    1. European Economic Community. 2. European federation.
I. Title.
HC241.2.D476   1994
337.1'42—dc20   93-37612
                                                          CIP

Printed and bound in the United States of America

∞   The paper used in this publication meets the requirements
    of the American National Standard for Permanence of
    Paper for Printed Library Materials Z39.48-1984.

Contents

Tables

Acknowledgments

Having taught courses on the European Community (EC)—the core of the European Union established by the Maastricht Treaty—for a number of years, I wanted to write an introduction to the subject for students, academics, and policymakers about to begin work on the EC, as well as for interested lay readers. Above all, I sought to provide a comprehensive, readable synthesis of the Community's history, institutions, and policies, based on accessible (hence, for my audience, mostly English-language) sources. Lynne Rienner, who has done so much to advance EC studies in the United States, had the same idea, as did Peter Doyle, director of press and public affairs of the EC's delegation in Washington. I am extremely grateful to both for their encouragement. Indeed, this book was made possible in part by a generous research grant from the Delegation of the Commission of the European Communities in the United States.

From the outset, I worked closely with Jamie Coniglio, librarian at George Mason University's International Institute and one of the most knowledgeable people in the United States—or anywhere else, for that matter—about the EC's voluminous publications. Many thanks to Jamie for her professionalism and patience, and for her ability to find elusive material.

I am also grateful to the staffs of the EC Commission Library in Brussels and the College of Europe's Library in Bruges.

Two research assistants provided invaluable help. First, Adrian Murcia helped me organize and tackle the project. Then, when Adrian made good on his threat to study Spanish in Madrid, Veronica Fennelly materialized out of nowhere and threw herself wholeheartedly into the project. I don't know how I could have begun the book without Adrian, or how I could have finished it without Veronica.

A number of people read the text and provided indispensable (and mostly constructive) criticism. First and foremost was Sir William Nicoll,

EC Fulbright Fellow at George Mason University in 1991–1992. Despite numerous, far more pressing demands on his time—including revision of his own book on the Community—Bill read the entire manuscript carefully and commented copiously. Tony Wallace, also at George Mason University, was equally unstinting with his insights and erudition. I am grateful to a number of other colleagues at George Mason University, notably John Moore and John Paden.

Others who gave generously of their time and expertise to comment on all or part of the manuscript include Cesira d'Aniello, Council of Ministers; Jonathan Davidson, EC Delegation, Washington, DC; Wendy Moore (my wife), U.S. Mission to the EC; David Neligan, Council of Ministers; Neill Nugent, Manchester Polytechnic; Willy Patterson, Edinburgh University; and Mark Tokola, U.S. Mission to the EC.

My father, Jack Dinan, a retired copyeditor, had the misfortune to visit us when the proofs arrived. I'm sorry for him, but pleased for me, that his trip to Brussels turned into a busman's holiday.

Last but not least, I should mention Conor, our 1992 Euro-baby, who kept me sleepless but sane during an otherwise trying time.

D.D.

Introduction

The European Community (EC) directly affects the daily lives of most of its twelve member states' inhabitants. Travelers stand in "EC citizen" lines at airports, clutching burgundy-colored EC passports. Students participate in EC-sponsored university exchange agreements. Farmers depend on the EC's Common Agricultural Policy (CAP) for their livelihoods. Businesspeople examine the latest rules and regulations from the EC's headquarters in Brussels before devising manufacturing and marketing strategies. Millions of unemployed Europeans take EC-funded training courses. Throughout the Community, women enjoy equality in the workplace because of landmark decisions in the EC's Court of Justice.

The Community has rarely been out of the news since the mid-1980s, when it launched a program to establish a single market—in which goods, people, capital, and services could move freely across member states' frontiers—by the end of 1992. The single market program, in turn, revived interest in Economic and Monetary Union (EMU), a long-cherished Community objective. Events in 1989 and 1990—revolution in Eastern Europe, the collapse of the Berlin Wall, and German unification—focused attention also on European Political Union (EPU), including a common foreign and security policy. By incorporating both EMU and EPU, the 1992 Maastricht Treaty was a decisive step on the road to "ever closer union," an aspiration first expressed thirty-five years previously in the Treaty of Rome, the European Community's founding charter.

Under the terms of the Maastricht Treaty, a European Union now officially exists (indeed, the formal title of the Maastricht Treaty is the "Treaty on European Union"). The Union established by the Maastricht Treaty is based on three pillars: amendments to the treaties that founded the European Coal and Steel Community (ECSC), the European Economic Community (EEC), and the European Atomic Energy Community (Euratom); a Common Foreign and Security Policy; and cooperation in the

1

sphere of justice and home affairs. Of the three communities, the EEC is by far the most important. Moreover, the Maastricht Treaty officially replaced the term European Economic Community with the more familiar European Community, a term already widely used to describe both the EEC individually, and the EEC, ECSC, and Euratom collectively. The EC is the essence of the new European Union.

The EC's pervasiveness tends to obscure its uniqueness and relative newness. The voluntary sharing of sovereignty by nation-states—the ever closer union envisioned in the treaties of Rome and Maastricht and implicit in the term "European integration"—is unprecedented in modern history. Before World War II, the kind of European Community with which we are so familiar today was a pipe dream. Nations jealously guarded their sovereignty (national authority) and cooperated only on the basis of intergovernmental agreement. Less than fifty years ago, France and Germany were implacable enemies.

The change in political opinion and behavior that brought the EC into existence owed much to the destructiveness of World War II and the virulent nationalism that preceded it, as well as the complexity of economic, social, and political life that followed. To a great extent, the EC was a security system for Western Europe. Its first manifestation, the European Coal and Steel Community (ECSC), emerged in 1952 in response to an urgent need both to rehabilitate defeated Germany and to allay understandable French security concerns, all in a radically altered international economic environment. Coal and steel lay at the core of both countries' economic systems and war-making potential. By establishing a supranational entity to manage the coal and steel sectors, the ECSC's six member states (France, Germany, Italy, Belgium, the Netherlands, and Luxembourg) became so closely intertwined that a future war between them soon appeared unthinkable and impossible.

For Jean Monnet, a senior French official who pioneered the idea of sectoral economic integration, the ECSC was not an end in itself but part of a process that would culminate in a European federation transcending the nation-state.[1] Such a goal was inherent in the word "community," which distinguished the new arrangement from traditional forms of intergovernmental collaboration and international organization. The ECSC was supranational as well as transnational: It engaged in activities that cut across national boundaries and included a High Authority (the forerunner of the European Commission) with power to make decisions at a level above that of national governments.

Integration indeed progressed. The functionally broader European Economic Community (EEC) followed in the wake of the ECSC, and initially it prospered politically as well as economically. But French President Charles de Gaulle's inflexible opposition to supranationalism caused a reassessment of earlier, optimistic thinking about the supposedly inexorable nature of European integration. Ideological and political battles in the mid-1960s emphasized an apparent dichotomy between intergovernmentalism and supranationalism, between the supposed decline of the nation-state and the putative rise of a European federation.

In reality, intergovernmentalism and supranationalism are not irreconcilable; rather, they jointly characterize the European Community. Community member states are willing to share sovereignty in certain areas because, quite simply, it is in their national interest to do so. Put negatively, in an age of rapid technological and commercial change, national governments are unable to act independently to maximize their citizens' welfare. Although willing to share sovereignty, however, governments retain as much political control as possible.[2] Hence the Community's peculiar institutional and legislative structure: In very few cases the European Commission (the Community's executive body) has sovereign authority, but in most areas it is relatively powerless; in some cases government ministers are willing to be outvoted in the Council of Ministers (the Community's decisionmaking body); in others they retain a national veto over proposed Community decisions.

The 1986 Single European Act (SEA) is a striking example of how member states reconcile intergovernmentalism and supranationalism in relation to the Community's functional scope and institutional structure. By the mid-1980s, the Community had enlarged from the original six ECSC member states to include the United Kingdom, Denmark, Ireland, Greece, Portugal, and Spain. Earlier in the decade, ideological, technological, and economic developments convinced member states to achieve a single, barrier-free market by the end of 1992 and to buttress the Community marketplace in associated areas, such as social, environmental, and industrial policy. Although the SEA broadened the Community's functional scope, it did not extend the Community's activities beyond the obligations of the Treaty of Rome. Similarly, member states agreed to enhance the Community's limited supranational authority only to the extent necessary to achieve the SEA's goals.

The 1992 Maastricht Treaty saw an extension of Community competence, most notably in the area of EMU. Member states considered EMU a corollary of the successful single market program and wanted to end de facto German dominance of the existing European Monetary System (EMS). Their response was a supranational structure for monetary policymaking in the Community worthy of a federalist such as Jean Monnet.

By contrast, the Common Foreign and Security Policy (CFSP) enshrined in the Maastricht Treaty clearly shows the limits of supranationalism. Not least because of German unification, governments concurred during the Maastricht negotiations on the necessity of closer foreign policy and security cooperation. But they failed to share national sovereignty over those areas. Thus, the high political issues of foreign, security, and, ultimately, defense cooperation were consigned to a separate "pillar" outside the Community system, subject to intergovernmental agreement.

The fate of the Maastricht Treaty also demonstrated the limits of European integration. In 1993 the single market reached completion. Simultaneously, however, growing popular concern about further loss of sovereignty and about secretive and undemocratic decisionmaking in Brussels— compounded by creeping economic recession, the high cost of German unification, and intense frustration over the Community's inability to broker a lasting cease-fire in Yugoslavia— shook confidence in the Community's future. Failure to ratify the Maastricht Treaty by the end of 1992 epitomized for many a deep Community crisis.

Clearly there is much popular concern about policy formulation and decisionmaking in the Community. People in the Community perceive a huge democratic deficit: The Commission, headquartered in Brussels, appears remote and democratically unaccountable, and national governments seemingly run the Community like a cartel. The crisis revealed genuine concern about further loss of national sovereignty, proving that popular acquiescence in a major transformation of the Community system cannot be taken for granted. In response, the Community developed the imprecise principle of "subsidiarity" (a federalist-type doctrine to delineate the proper level at which decisions should be made—either in Brussels or in national capitals) and promoted openness and transparency in the Community's legislative process.

At the heart of the ratification debacle lay doubts about the Community's relevance in the post–Cold War world. What was the EC's feasibility and utility in a radically altered international environment? From the outset, the Community had considered itself synonymous with "Europe." With the Cold War over, could the Community foster a sense of pan-European solidarity and a genuinely all-European integration? Despite the Commission's leadership of the Eastern European assistance effort, by 1992 the Community's *Ostpolitik* seemed to have lost direction. The opening of enlargement negotiations with Austria, Sweden, Finland, and Norway in 1993 raised the perennial question of whether "wider" would also mean "weaker."

It is easy to exaggerate the Community's difficulties in the post-Maastricht period, although serious problems undoubtedly exist. Yet the notion of a Community in crisis could be misleading and need not be entirely disadvantageous. The history of the Community's development is a history of overcoming crises: the crisis of German reconstruction in the late 1940s, leading to the European Coal and Steel Community; the European Defense Community crisis in the mid-1950s, leading to the "relaunch" of European integration; the crisis of declining competitiveness and decisionmaking paralysis in the 1970s and early 1980s, leading to the SEA; and the crisis of German unification in the late 1980s, leading to the Maastricht Treaty.

Whether or not the Maastricht ratification crisis triggers the kind of revival and transformation that followed other crises in the Community's history, the political and economic setbacks of 1992 and 1993 hardly represent a threat to the Community's survival. There is no talk of dismantling the single market or of systematically rolling back existing levels of integration. Moreover, the Community has a long list of applicant and potential-applicant countries waiting to open enlargement negotiations or to apply for membership. A more pertinent concern relates to the Community's functional scope: Will it finally become a "high politics" Community? Regardless of the impact of economic recession and currency turmoil on EMU, is there sufficient popular support for a single European currency? Will member states use the planned 1996 treaty negotiations to bring the CFSP squarely within the Community framework? Will they give substance to the "eventual" Common Defense Policy?

Whatever happens, the EC will continue to have a direct impact on the everyday lives of over 300 million people. The Community is an inextricable part of the political process, economic organization, and social structure in Western Europe today. For that reason alone, it is imperative to understand why the Community exists, how it came about, what it does, and how it works. Accordingly, this book attempts to provide a comprehensive introduction to the Community's history, institutions, and policies so that readers will appreciate the full extent, complexity, and significance of European integration, and realize the extraordinary impact that the Community has had, and continues to have, on political, social, and economic developments inside and outside its borders.

NOTES

1. For a theoretical explanation of Monnet's goals and aspirations, see Ernst Haas, *The Uniting of Europe: Political, Social and Economic Forces, 1950–57* (Stanford: Stanford University Press, 1958); Leon Lindberg, *The Political Dynamics of Economic Integration* (Stanford: Stanford University Press, 1963); and Leon Lindberg and Stuart Scheingold, *Europe's Would-Be Polity* (Englewood Cliffs, NJ: Prentice-Hall, 1970).

2. On the relationship between supranationalism and intergovernmentalism in the Community's history, see Alan Milward, *The European Rescue of the Nation State* (Berkeley: University of California Press, 1992).

PART I

History

1

Reconstruction, Reconciliation, and Integration, 1945–1957

Rondpoint Schuman (Schuman Circle) is the site in Brussels of the European Commission headquarters. *Schuman* is also the name of the subway station located there. In the station, between the usual advertisements and notices, there is an unusual poster. It depicts two men, Jean Monnet and Robert Schuman, standing together "at the beginning of the European Community (9 May 1950)." The date in parentheses is the day on which Schuman, then foreign minister of France, announced an unprecedented plan to place "the whole of Franco-German coal and steel production under a common High Authority, within the framework of an organization open to the participation of the other countries of Europe."[1] Monnet was the brains behind the novel French initiative.

It is difficult to appreciate today the boldness and prescience of Schuman's proposal. The intervening decades have virtually obliterated our awareness not only of the depth of distrust toward Germany in the immediate postwar years but also of the importance of coal and steel for European reconstruction, let alone prosperity, at that time. Schuman's short, simple statement outlined a strategy to reconcile German economic recovery and French national security. Moreover, by accepting the recently established Federal Republic as an economic equal and handing over responsibility for both countries' coal and steel industries to a supranational authority, the Schuman Plan gave substance to the hitherto vague notion of European unity and integration. Thus, the Schuman Declaration resulted first in the European Coal and Steel Community (ECSC) and later in the European Atomic Energy Community (Euratom) and the European Economic Community (EEC). Schuman Day is now celebrated annually

9

on May 9 in Brussels, Luxembourg, and Strasbourg as the birthday of what has become collectively known as the European Community (EC).

The Community holiday and the solemnization of the Schuman Plan have contributed to a myth about the movement for European unity. The poster commemorating Schuman Day bolsters what can be called the "official history" of European integration, which depicts Monnet and Schuman as visionaries who soared above the squalor and squabbles of postwar Europe, pointing the way to the promised land of peace and prosperity along the prudent path of economic and political integration. Without doubt, Monnet and Schuman *were* men of vision who sincerely believed in the virtues of integration and the necessity of European unity. But the declaration of May 9 owed as much to narrowly defined national interest as to broadly based international altruism and was rooted as much in the experience of the interwar years as in the apparently unique circumstances of the postwar world. Just as the Schuman Declaration was itself the product of clever political calculation, so, too, were the institutions to which it ultimately gave rise the result of intense international bargaining.

JEAN MONNET AND THE EUROPEAN MOVEMENT

At the time of the Schuman Declaration, Monnet was director of the French Modernization Plan. As its name implies, the plan was designed to overhaul the French economy, which had shown signs of serious sickness well before the damage and dislocation of World War II. General de Gaulle, leader of the provisional government formed immediately after the liberation, realized that France could never become great again barring a radical economic revitalization. Without improving its performance and competitiveness, France would be unable to satisfy the domestic demands for economic growth on which the postwar political consensus rested; nor would it be able to play a leading role in the emerging international order. Keenly aware of the need to increase national production, improve productivity, boost foreign trade, maximize employment, and raise living standards, de Gaulle charged Monnet with achieving these formidable objectives at the head of the newly established economic planning office.[2]

Despite his unconventional background, Monnet was an ideal choice. Then in his late fifties, he had spent a lifetime working in the private and public sectors in France and abroad. During both world wars, Monnet served as an Allied economic planner in the United States. His experiences there, admittedly forged on the anvil of wartime emergency, convinced him of the potential of peacetime economic planning. Monnet's energy, imagination, ability, and faith in the future of France greatly impressed de Gaulle. Nor was he encumbered by political baggage. Atypically for a Frenchman who had matured in the intensely ideological twenties and thirties, Monnet had no party affiliation. Inasmuch as he was politically motivated, it was by the remorseless ideology of efficiency.[3]

In addition to developing a belief in the value of economic planning, Monnet had acquired overseas a commitment to international cooperation in general, and to economic integration in particular, as the only means by which conflict in Europe could be avoided. In an August 1943 note to the French Committee of National Liberation in Algiers, Monnet claimed that there would be no peace in Europe "if States reestablished themselves on the basis of national sovereignty with all that this implies by way of prestige politics and economic protectionism." Instead, Monnet argued, "the States of Europe must form a federation or a 'European entity,' which will make them a single economic entity."[4]

Although such sentiments may seem radical in retrospect, they were by no means unusual at the time. On the contrary, during and immediately after World War II public figures and political pundits on both sides of the Atlantic outdid themselves in their advocacy of European integration. Repugnance against the slaughter of two European civil wars in as many generations and the economic depression and political extremism of the intervening years fueled popular support for a reorganization of the international system. Words such as "integration," "union," and even "supranationalism" were bandied about as panaceas for Europe's ills. The popular and political mood gave rise in the late 1940s to the European movement (with a lowercase *"m"*; the European *M*ovement was a specific group within the broader movement), a loose collection of individuals and interest groups ranged across the political spectrum, from the noncommunist left to the discredited far right, that shared advocacy of European unity.[5]

The intellectual ancestry of the European movement may have stretched into antiquity, but its immediate roots lay in the interwar years. In 1923 an Austro-Hungarian aristocrat, Count Coudenhove-Kalergi, buoyed by the success the previous year of his book, *Pan-Europa,* launched an organization of the same name. Inspired as much by the devastation of the Great War as by the emergence during it of a powerful United States and a menacing Soviet Union, Pan-Europa quickly acquired an ardent following, not least amongst influential politicians. The zenith of the pan-European movement was a stirring speech by Aristide Briand, then French foreign minister, before the League of Nations in 1929. But the lofty ideals of European unity were soon swept aside by the flood tide of fascism in the 1930s. It took the bitter experience of defeat and occupation in 1939 and 1940 for pan-European ideas to revive and flourish in European minds.[6]

The resistance movement, itself a loose collection of individuals and groups opposed to Axis occupation, took up the cause of European unity as one plank of a proposed radical reorganization of postwar politics, economics, and society. Resistance literature, secretly circulated in occupied Europe, espoused the goal of international cooperation and integration as a basis for future peace and prosperity. Altiero Spinelli, a fervent federalist and a leading player in what eventually became the European Community, drafted a manifesto in 1940 and 1941 for a "free and united Europe" while imprisoned on the Italian island of Ventotene. Following his release after Mussolini's ouster, Spinelli traveled secretly to Switzerland for a meeting of European resistance representatives. Out of that meeting, held in Geneva in June and July 1944, came the "Draft Declaration of the European Resistance," which included a call for a "Federal Union among the European peoples."[7]

The legacy of the prewar "Pan-Europa" and the wartime resistance movement generated a groundswell of support for European unity in the early postwar years. Politicians as diverse as Konrad Adenauer (a German Christian Democrat), Leon Blum (a French Socialist), and Anthony Eden (an English Conservative) espoused the cause of economic and political integration. One politician above all others came to personify the European movement: Winston Churchill, then Europe's best-known and most popular statesman. Renowned especially for his inspiring oratory, which had boosted British spirits during the dark days of 1940 and 1941, Churchill raised European morale by calling for a "United States of Europe" in a speech in Zurich in September 1946.[8]

But Churchill advocated a more limited and cautious form of European integration than did many of his continental colleagues. The United Europe Movement, which Churchill launched in May 1947, promoted what became known as the "unionist" position, as distinct from the more radical "federalist" position of Spinelli and his Union of European Federalists. Differences between the unionists and federalists, based on political, geographical, and cultural considerations, came to the fore at the Congress of Europe, a glittering gathering of over six hundred influential Europeans from sixteen countries held in The Hague in May 1948. Both sides agreed only on the desirability of European unity and on the need to institutionalize that ideal by establishing an international organization with a parliamentary body. For the unionists, that body would be merely a consultative assembly bound to defer to a committee of government ministers. For the "federalists," by contrast, the parliamentary body would be a constituent assembly charged with drafting a constitution for the United States of Europe.

What emerged from the acrimonious Hague congress and from follow-up negotiations in late 1948 and early 1949 had the appearance of a compromise but was in fact a capitulation to the minimalist unionist position. The ensuing Council of Europe was a far cry from what the federalists had initially wanted. Although pledged "to achieve a closer union

between its members in order to protect and promote the ideals and principles which constitute their common heritage and to further their economic and social progress," the Council of Europe did little more than exchange ideas and information on social, legal, and cultural matters.[9] Only
in one important area, that of human rights, did the Council of Europe distinguish itself. The council's Court of Human Rights, often confused with
the European Community's Court of Justice, is vital for the protection and
promotion of civil liberties throughout Europe today. Apart from its
human rights agenda, the council enjoyed a brief resurgence in 1989 during the revolution in Eastern Europe, when public attention once again focused, as it had forty years earlier, on the possibility of establishing pan-
European institutions.

In most other respects, the council accomplished little. Despite
spirited efforts by some of its members subsequently to advance the federalist agenda, notably during the European Defense Community and
European Political Community initiatives of the early 1950s, the Consultative Assembly of the Council of Europe soon turned into a caricature of
a windy debating chamber. Nevertheless, the Assembly's contribution to
the history of the European Community is far from negligible. For one
thing, its numerous debates and resolutions kindled the concept of European integration, especially in the mid-1950s, when the defeat of the proposed European Defense Community had demoralized the European
movement. For another, the Assembly socialized an entire generation of
European politicians, particularly British parliamentarians (who had little
exposure during the war to the intellectual ferment of the resistance movement). Roy Jenkins, president of the European Commission in the late
1970s, is one of those British politicians who "contracted European
fever," and a high proportion of his fellow Labour Party delegates to the
Assembly went through "a brief [Council of Europe] induction course."[10]

In one more respect, the Council of Europe had an indirect impact
on the development of the future European Community. Its member states
wanted to locate the council away from a national capital to symbolize
European reconciliation, and they settled on Strasbourg, a frequently
fought-over city on the border between France and Germany. Later, the
European Community placed its Parliament there also. As the European
Community revived and flourished in the 1980s, many members of the
European Parliament (MEPs) regretted the choice of Strasbourg, nearly
three hundred miles from the Commission and the Council of Ministers'
secretariat in Brussels, as the Parliament's seat. For them, Strasbourg
came to symbolize not Franco-German reconciliation but the obscurity
and relative unimportance of their own institution.

Almost alone amongst influential Europeans at the time, Monnet
stood aloof from the European movement of the postwar years and from
the Council of Europe that emerged from it. Monnet's detachment was

due not to doubts about European unity but to disdain for the populism and pontification of the movement and its constituent parts. Monnet was an elitist and a pragmatist. His road to European unity would follow the unglamorous path of functional integration. Close cooperation between countries in specific economic sectors, Monnet believed, held the key to overcoming national sovereignty and ultimately achieving European federation. Decisions to implement functional economic cooperation would be taken not by six hundred delegates at the Congress of Europe but by powerful politicians in the privacy of their government ministries.

Monnet loved aphorisms. "Nothing is possible without men; nothing is lasting without institutions" was one of his favorites.[11] Another one—"People only accept change when they are faced with necessity, and only recognize necessity when a crisis is upon them"[12]—offers a clue to Monnet's modus operandi. At a decisive moment during World War II, Monnet saw a unique opportunity to act. With France on the verge of military defeat and political capitulation in June 1940, Monnet proposed to Prime Minister Churchill an "indissoluble union" between both countries. By offering common citizenship, forming a joint government, and pursuing a single war strategy, Monnet hoped to strengthen French Premier Reynaud's flagging position, encourage French forces in North Africa to continue the war within the Alliance, and lay the foundation for future European union.[13]

The failure of the extraordinary June 1940 initiative represented, in Monnet's mind, a huge opportunity lost. The lessons were obvious: Only great crises move men to act against their cautious political instincts; only a future crisis would provide the necessary push for European integration.[14] Moreover, the episode taught Monnet something about Churchill. Although he had brought the offer to the British cabinet's attention, the prime minister had been skeptical, if not hostile, from the outset. Thus, it must have irritated Monnet to see Churchill emerge after the war as the mouthpiece of the European movement. That alone might have convinced Monnet to find other ways to pursue his cherished goal of European integration.

Uninvolved in the federalist or unionist movements, Monnet devoted his considerable energy in the immediate postwar years to drafting the Modernization Plan. To a great extent, given his conviction that Europe could not be united unless France was resurgent, the plan was an indispensable component of Monnet's strategy for European integration. In pursuit of that elemental purpose, Monnet toiled with a troupe of young disciples to transform the ailing French economy. Based on lengthy consultations with employers, workers, and consumers, Monnet's team set production targets, foreign trade goals, and employment objectives. Few were ever met, but the plan instilled badly needed confidence and a sense of mission in French society, both of which helped the country achieve an enviable economic recovery (although not by later German standards).

In the meantime, no catalytic crisis had occurred to allow Monnet to seize the moment and push for European integration. However, two ominous situations greatly alarmed European governments and fueled the European movement. The first was the state of the European economy after six years of invasion and occupation, blitzkrieg and aerial bombardment. World War II was the most costly conflict in modern history, and its destructiveness has been well documented. Perhaps the most surprising aspect of the war, however—precisely because of the technological and strategic innovations unleashed during it—was that six years of incessant fighting had not caused even greater physical damage and destruction. The war's major material impact was less on industrial plant than on infrastructure, compounded by shortages of raw materials and skilled labor. Both Monnet and Robert Marjolin, his assistant in the Modernization Plan, mention in their memoirs that there was less material destruction in France in 1945 than either had expected to find on their return from exile. By Monnet's assessment, "industrial capacity had remained at about 80% of its pre-war level."[15] Wartime demolition of roads, bridges, canals, dikes, and docks posed a more formidable challenge to postwar planners than did the destruction of factories and plant.

The task of economic recovery was doubtless daunting, but it could be undertaken without radically revising the international system and undermining the authority of the nation-state. Although the unprecedented extent of material destruction during World War II was certainly a factor in the growth of the postwar movement for European integration, it was not, Monnet realized, serious enough to trigger a political reaction of the kind that would cause European countries to pool their sovereignty in a unique, supranational entity. Nor was the collapse of the Grand Alliance and the emergence of the Cold War sufficient by itself to produce the desired result.

Like the destructiveness of World War II, the origins and development of the Cold War are well known. As hostility between the erstwhile Allies intensified, Western European governments grew increasingly alarmed, not as much about the prospect of direct Soviet attack as about the more realistic prospect of internal communist subversion. Communist parties were popular in Western Europe immediately after the war and fared well in early postwar elections, especially in Italy and France. They owed their popularity to the corresponding unpopularity of capitalism—a reaction against the economic depression and the outbreak of war at either end of the thirties. More important, communist parties reaped the electoral rewards of their participation in, and often leadership of, the wartime resistance movement. So, too, did they benefit from wartime admiration in Europe and the United States of the Soviet Union's heroic stand against Nazi Germany, a struggle led by the indomitable "Uncle Joe" Stalin.

In 1946 and 1947, the French Communist Party shared power with the Christian Democrats and the Socialists, and the Italian Community Party seemed on the verge of an outright election victory. As relations between the Soviet Union and the Western powers deteriorated, relations between indigenous communist parties and their noncommunist counterparts similarly degenerated. In May 1947 Paul Remadier, the French premier, ousted the Communists from government; in Italy, U.S. money and Christian Democratic scaremongering helped keep the Communists in opposition. Although communism remained popular with large numbers of people, electoral support waned as the Cold War intensified, notably after the February 1948 communist coup in Czechoslovakia and during the Berlin blockade of 1948–1949. Nevertheless, the economic consequences of the war, exacerbated by a summer drought in 1946 and an ice-bound winter in 1947, seemed to offer ideal conditions for the revolutionary communist parties to exploit.

The emergence of the Cold War and its domestic political repercussions contributed to the growth of the European movement, whose rhetoric stressed the need for the countries of Europe, once at the center of the international system, to join together to assert their position in an increasingly rigid bipolar world. As the Cold War intensified and the Iron Curtain descended abruptly to divide the continent, integration became a means by which Western Europe could defend itself, in close collaboration with the United States, against the external Soviet threat and the internal communist threat. Moreover, Western Europe's relative economic weakness and supposed political vulnerability drew the United States deeper into the continent's affairs and turned Washington into a zealous champion of European integration.

THE MARSHALL PLAN AND EUROPEAN INTEGRATION

Probably the best-known U.S. international initiative ever, the Marshall Plan was the main instrument used by the United States to encourage European integration.[16] But the Marshall Plan—or the European Recovery Program, as it was formally called—had many origins and objectives, all of them interconnected. One was humanitarian. William L. Clayton, U.S. assistant secretary of state for economic affairs, painted a harrowing picture of a devastated Europe upon his return from a fact-finding mission in May 1947.[17] Famine and starvation appeared imminent, especially in occupied Germany, where economic recovery had barely begun. Elsewhere in Europe the situation was by no means as bad, but Clayton understandably concentrated on the worst cases he had witnessed. Clayton's renowned report led directly to a far more famous event: General George

Marshall's Harvard commencement speech of June 5, 1947, in which the U.S. secretary of state pledged wholehearted U.S. support for European postwar reconstruction.[18]

Healthy economic and political self-interest also guided the U.S. undertaking. Fear of an imminent economic recession, similar to that which followed the cessation of hostilities in 1918, was one such motivation. Without economic growth in Europe, U.S. exports would stagnate and decline, and the United States itself would follow Europe into depression. But the U.S. economy depended much less on exports to Europe in the late 1940s than it does today. Thus, the export argument alone would not have sufficed to convince a skeptical Congress to give substance to General Marshall's speech in the form of massive financial assistance.

A less immediate but nonetheless palpable concern about economic security, coupled with powerful political and strategic arguments, finally made the difference. Twice in the previous thirty years, the United States had become involved militarily in Europe's wars, and hundreds of thousands of American lives had been lost. Despite its strong emotional appeal, isolationism had patently failed. Apart from the emerging consensus that postwar U.S. security depended on increasing international involvement, the onset of the Cold War provided a powerful incentive for the United States to play a leading part in European affairs. A future resurgent Germany, however unlikely in 1947, may have posed a serious threat to U.S. security, but the immediate danger seemed to come from the Red Army in the East and local communist parties in the West.

Americans and Europeans agreed about the problem and the prescription. The direct Soviet threat could best be countered by immediate U.S. intervention—as in Greece in 1947—and military alliance building and leadership—as in the case of NATO two years later. The indirect communist danger, by contrast, could best be defused by restoring Western Europe to sound economic health. The United States would play the role of pharmacist, dispensing large doses of drugs in the form of badly needed dollars. On both sides of the Atlantic, the prescription emphasized the importance of integration for future peace and prosperity in Europe.

The lessons of the interwar years had led U.S. officials and policymakers, like their European counterparts, to endorse postwar integration. A small number of influential Americans had been swayed by the teaching and writing of Coudenhove-Kalergi, who spent World War II at New York University.[19] Others, who would play a pivotal role in the formulation and implementation of U.S. policy toward Western Europe in the late 1940s and early 1950s, became close friends of Jean Monnet in Washington. With Monnet, "the *eminence grise* of the Wise Men of American foreign policy," they discussed the limits of national sovereignty and advantages of supranationality.[20] Also, they applied to war-torn Europe the lessons of modern U.S. history. Just as the United States had grown strong and prosperous by promoting interstate commerce and establishing a single market, so, too, could Europe. In that simple, straightforward way, European integration became an essential part "of a grand design for remaking the Old World in the likeness of the New."[21]

The Marshall Plan occupies a special place in the historiography of the Cold War. Some revisionist historians see in it an effort by the United States to acquire an empire in Europe by design; others argue that Europe's economic weakness allowed the United States to acquire an empire there by default.[22] For their part, many contemporary Europeans were well aware of the dangers of relying too much on U.S. economic largess and military protection, and perceived European integration as a means of asserting the continent's independence. Similarly, perhaps paradoxically, many contemporary Americans looked to European integration, which the Marshall Plan was supposed to enhance, as a way of obviating the necessity for future U.S. intervention in the Old World.

Historical controversy also surrounds the extent to which the Marshall Plan assisted Europe economically, even the extent to which Europe needed such aid in the first place. Alan Milward, a leading English economic historian, argues that the economic crisis of 1947 amounted to a shortage of dollars for the purchase of U.S. capital goods, urgently required to maintain the already impressive economic recovery of Europe.[23] Even if that is the case, points out Michael Hogan, a U.S. historian, "the payments crisis, after all, portended a serious crisis in production that would come with the collapse of critical dollar imports."[24] Hogan offers the judicious assessment that the Marshall Plan "facilitated essential imports, eased production bottlenecks, encouraged high rates of capital formation, and helped to suppress inflation, all of which led to gains in productivity, to improvements in trade, and to an era of social peace and prosperity more durable than any other in modern European history."[25]

Disputes about the significance of the Marshall Plan for postwar U.S. foreign policy and about the impact of Marshall aid on Europe's postwar recovery are related to an equally important question: What part did the Marshall Plan play in fostering European integration? Again, Milward takes the heretical view that the Marshall Plan failed dismally to break down national barriers.[26] Neither Marshall's stricture that participating countries must act together to devise and present to the United States a common recovery program as a prelude to establishing European unity, nor the enormous influence and wealth of the United States, could overcome the reluctance of European governments to cooperate closely, let alone share sovereignty. By effectively excluding the Soviet Union and its satellite countries in Eastern Europe, the Marshall Plan at least ensured that integration would be confined to Western Europe. But the degree of integration attained was far from what U.S. planners had sought.

For all their platitudes about integration, European governments were not yet willing to turn rhetoric into reality. To meet the prerequisite for Marshall Plan assistance, they established the Organization for European Economic Cooperation (OEEC), an umbrella body to solicit U.S. funds. But the OEEC was too large and diverse to act as an institutional instrument of integration. Its eighteen members varied greatly in size, population, and economic well-being. Perhaps more important, widely differing political cultures and wartime experiences made the prospect of agreement on integration extremely remote. Thus, the OEEC failed to live up to its foster parents' expectations.[27] Instead, shortly after the EEC began functioning in 1958, the OEEC turned into the Organization for Economic Cooperation and Development (OECD), the Paris-based body for international economic research and analysis.[28]

Like the contemporaneous Congress of Europe, the OEEC triggered debate on European integration, but it produced a paucity of tangible results. For all their interest in integration and European unity, governments remained reluctant to take concrete steps to surrender some of their sovereignty. Yet the Marshall Plan indirectly caused the cataclysmic crisis that Monnet knew was necessary to prompt the French government to act. Because it involved the reconstruction of Western Germany as part of the reconstruction of Western Europe, the Marshall Plan set the stage for a series of diplomatic decisions that would gradually rehabilitate the former enemy, much to the consternation of Germany's neighbor to the west. The threat to France's own economic recovery and security was immense. Here was a crisis that Monnet could exploit to the full.

Even as the United States and Great Britain revised their harsh policies toward Germany, France stuck stubbornly to a number of severe strictures. Germany would be demilitarized, decentralized, and deindustrialized. France had suffered grievously from German militarism and expansionism, far more than either Britain or the United States.[29] The humiliation and horror of World War II—defeat and occupation, deportation and enslavement, pillage and destruction—would not quickly be forgotten. France had salvaged some of its honor through the resistance movement and by raising an army in 1944 that participated in the final stages of the national liberation and the subsequent invasion of Germany. Denied a place at the negotiating table in Yalta and Potsdam, France at least won the right to occupy a small part of the vanquished Third Reich. The gradual softening of British and U.S. occupation policy served only to strengthen French determination to stick to a rigid course. Not surprisingly, France refused to merge its occupation zone into the newly established Anglo-American "Bizonia" in May 1947.[30]

For all his remonstrations about integration and reconciliation, even Jean Monnet was not unaffected by the rampant Germanophobia that swept France at the time. Moreover, Monnet had predicated his plan for

French economic modernization upon a punitive policy toward Germany. Coal and steel, the two key industrial sectors in mid-twentieth-century Europe, lay at the heart of the Modernization Plan. Postwar French policy toward Germany sought both to win control over the coal-rich Saar, which France then administered, and to prevent the economic recovery of the Ruhr. Not only had the Ruhr become a synonym for the evil German military-industrial complex, but its resuscitation would threaten France's own economic revival. Monnet based his economic planning squarely on the assumption that Ruhr coal would be available to fuel French steel mills, whose increased output would find buyers in displaced German markets. German economic rehabilitation, if it came before full implementation of the Monnet Plan, would greatly imperil France's economic fortunes and, by extension, France's international stature.

As long as the Soviet Union was somehow involved in formulating Allied policy toward Germany, France had a good chance of thwarting Britain's and the United States' increasingly benign approach. Although there had never truly been four-power cooperation on Germany, the Western Allies were reluctant to break openly with the Soviet Union, hoping perhaps to avert an irrevocable collapse of the Grand Alliance. To try to negotiate a postwar settlement or at least to maintain the fiction of Allied unity, the foreign ministers of Britain, France, the United States, and the Soviet Union met periodically. The breakdown of the Moscow meeting of foreign ministers in March 1947 proved decisive. Thereafter, the Anglo-Americans increasingly acted unilaterally in the West and the Soviet Union pursued its own policy in the East.

French difficulty in adhering to a repressive policy came to a head in early 1948. The Ruhr lay within the British zone of occupation, and France was not party to Anglo-American planning in Germany. As long as France remained outside Bizonia, Paris could only watch angrily as London and Washington gradually loosened the Ruhr's economic shackles. Pragmatism briefly triumphed when France agreed to cooperate with Bizonia in an effort to influence Anglo-American policy from within. During the subsequent London Conference of the Western Allies, which led eventually to the merger of the French zone and Bizonia into the Federal Republic of Germany, France pressed for the establishment of the International Ruhr Authority as a vehicle of controlling industrial production there.

The Federal Republic of Germany, conceived in the Western Allies conference and born in September 1949, lacked many attributes of sovereignty. Apart from accepting limits on foreign policy and a complete absence of defense policy, the new German state had to acquiesce in the existence and operation of the International Ruhr Authority. But French hopes that the authority would serve French interests by maintaining strict controls on Ruhr production soon proved unrealistic. Realizing that the

Ruhr was the industrial heartland (or, to use the metaphor current at the time, the "spark plug") of Europe,[31] the United States pushed more and more for German industrial recovery as a vital prerequisite for European economic recovery. By the same token, the United States appreciated the implication of that policy for Paris and understood the need to involve France fully in bringing about a durable European economic and strategic settlement. Accordingly, Washington and London pressed Paris to devise a mutually acceptable solution to the Ruhr problem and to take the initiative in proposing a new Allied policy toward the Federal Republic.

By the end of 1948, therefore, France faced the failure of its restrictive Ruhr policy. The International Ruhr Authority, a body intended to perpetuate French control over the area under the guise of Allied cooperation with the fledgling Federal Republic, had made little headway. French officials gradually grasped the fact that policy toward Germany would have to be revised, not least in order to salvage the all-important and closely related Modernization Plan. Thus, in the months ahead, French officials searched for a strategy that would satisfy their country's overriding concern with security, meet its industrial demands for adequate supplies of coal and markets for steel, and relieve U.S. pressure for a policy compatible with growing German economic capability.[32]

Monnet himself had the most to gain—and the most to lose—from this challenge. After all, the French Modernization Plan, now at risk, was *his* plan. Apart from a vested personal interest in the plan's success, Monnet bore primary responsibility in the French civil service for efforts to overcome exacting economic obstacles. The particular set of problems facing France in 1949 and 1950 offered Monnet a unique opportunity to act. Capitalizing on the growing sentiment in official French circles that policy toward Germany should in future be based on economic association rather than antagonism, he approached Schuman with the imaginative idea of a coal and steel community. Thus, the lifting of Allied restrictions on German steel production and the prospect of a reversal to the status quo ante of Franco-German relations had provided the crisis that, Monnet was certain, would force his government to take a dramatic step on the road to Franco-German reconciliation and European integration.

THE SCHUMAN PLAN

In his memoirs, Monnet describes the melodrama surrounding the Schuman Declaration.[33] Monnet sent his proposal for a supranational coal and steel community to both René Pleven, the French prime minister, and Schuman. Pleven failed to act immediately on the suggestion, thus allowing Schuman to take the initiative that subsequently bore his name. Schuman's background lent particular poignancy to the coal and steel proposal. Coming from the disputed province of Alsace, where he had suffered personally from the incessant conflict between France and Germany, Schuman sought above all else to promote reconciliation between both countries.[34] As a Christian Democrat, Schuman held political principles that reinforced his personal convictions. Constrained by the climate of retribution toward Germany that pervaded postwar France and by a natural reserve and inhibition, Schuman had hitherto refrained from taking any conciliatory steps in the direction of the erstwhile enemy. Now, emboldened by Monnet's suggestion and by the swing in official French opinion toward economic accord with Germany, Schuman floated the fateful proposal with secrecy and speed.

Before the proposal could be made public, Monnet and Schuman needed the approval of three key parties: the French, German, and U.S. governments. On Tuesday, May 9, 1950, Schuman simultaneously placed the proposal before his own cabinet in Paris and brought it to Chancellor Adenauer's attention in Bonn. The German leader responded enthusiastically. Like Schuman, Adenauer had a strong personal yearning for Franco-German reconciliation. Moreover, keenly aware of the depth of French distrust toward the new Federal Republic, Adenauer realized that shared sovereignty pointed the way to Germany's international rehabilitation. Only by integrating closely with neighboring European countries could Germany hope to remove the remaining controls on its domestic and foreign policy. Three months previously, Adenauer had taken the initiative by floating the idea of a full Franco-German union. Although Adenauer's trial balloon had alarmed nervous French officials, it clearly indicated the chancellor's receptiveness to a proposal for integration of any kind.[35]

Monnet had earlier alerted U.S. officials to the French initiative. By chance, U.S. Secretary of State Dean Acheson had arrived in Paris on Sunday, May 7, en route to London for a meeting of British, French, and U.S. foreign ministers to discuss German economic issues. Taking advantage of the secretary of state's unexpected appearance, Monnet and Schuman quickly took him into their confidence. Acheson, they knew, strongly supported not only European integration but also the necessity of French efforts to bring it about. The previous October, Acheson had shared with Schuman his belief that "our policy in Germany, and the development of a German Government which can take its place in Western Europe, depends on the assumption by your country of leadership in Europe on these problems."[36] Unbeknownst to Schuman, at about the same time Acheson had informed U.S. ambassadors in Europe that "France alone can take the decisive leadership in integrating West Germany into Western Europe."[37]

Not surprisingly, Acheson endorsed the Schuman Plan and drafted a statement of support for President Truman to release once the plan became public. Yet Acheson's immediate reaction was cautious and pointed to what would become a persistent source of tension between the United States and the European Community. At first, Acheson feared that the Schuman Plan was a clever cover for "a gigantic European cartel."[38] Although immediately reassured by Monnet, Acheson drafted the presidential statement of support partly to allay his "apprehension that upon receiving partial information, the Antitrust Division in the Department of Justice might stimulate some critical comments, which would have been damaging at that stage."[39] Despite Acheson's acceptance of Monnet's reassurance, U.S. suspicion of the European Community's commitment to international economic competition would deepen in the years ahead, and the Department of Justice would lose none of its hostility.

The unexpectedness of Acheson's arrival in Paris suggests that Monnet and Schuman would not otherwise have advised him in advance of their coal and steel proposal. But U.S. support was too important to have been jeopardized by their waiting to inform Washington until after a public announcement. In the event, Monnet's assiduous and prolonged cultivation of the U.S. establishment now bore fruit as he astutely lined up support by drawing on close friendships with key U.S. policymakers such as John McCloy, high commissioner in Germany. Within a month the United States set up a special Working Group on the Schuman Proposal in its Paris embassy. The working group soon became "a hotbed of Monnet enthusiasts . . . [with] the thinking of Monnet and the young American integrationists . . . often so similar as to be indistinguishable."[40]

Buoyed by Acheson's endorsement and Adenauer's approval, Schuman had little difficulty convincing his cabinet colleagues to support the scheme. A public announcement immediately followed at a hastily convened press conference in the French foreign ministry. The result was "a public relations coup of heroic proportions."[41] Although French officials had been moving in the direction of Franco-German economic association for some time, the Schuman Declaration had all the appearance of a dramatic reversal of policy. Instead of trying to keep the traditional enemy down, France would build a new Europe on the basis of equality with Germany. Coal and steel, the two key sectors of industrial production and war-making potential, would be removed from national control and placed under a single, supranational authority. As Monnet put it, "if . . . the victors and the vanquished agreed to exercise joint sovereignty over part of their joint resources . . . then a solid link would be forged between them, the way would be wide open for further collective action, and a great example would be given to the other nations of Europe."[42]

Schuman's offer to open the proposed coal and steel organization "to the participation of the other countries of Europe" was not as extravagant as it seemed. For one thing, the countries of Eastern Europe were automatically excluded by the onset of the Cold War. For another, the

Scandinavian countries had shown, during the Congress of Europe and subsequently in the Council of Europe, their skepticism about supranationalism. For Schuman and Monnet, European integration meant, essentially, Franco-German integration. Germany was the traditional enemy, the economic powerhouse of Europe, and the country that posed the greatest threat to France. Franco-German reconciliation, by means of "European" integration, apparently offered the only opportunity to avoid a repetition of the disastrous conflict that had characterized the first five decades of the twentieth century. Schuman's image of "the other countries of Europe" meant, in reality, the neighboring countries of Belgium, the Netherlands, and Luxembourg to the north and Italy to the south.

Great Britain was most conspicuous by its absence from the French view of this "new" Europe. After all, as France's traditional twentieth-century ally, Britain was surely the first country to which France would look for support of an international initiative to come to terms with post-war Germany. Indeed, Monnet's first proposal for European integration, the dramatic offer of Anglo-French union, had centered on Britain. Similarly, during the war itself, Robert Marjolin, Monnet's deputy, had stated his "profound conviction" that "the key to any politico-economic reorganization in continental Europe has to be sought in Franco-British relations."[43] Even as late as 1948, "Western European integration without Britain was unacceptable in Washington," where the ultimate decision about Europe's future would be made.[44]

Between 1948 and 1950, however, both France and the United States dropped Britain from their plans for European integration. No single event led to this important development. Instead, Britain's obvious reluctance to involve itself in European integration, despite Churchill's memorable endorsement of a United States of Europe, convinced Washington and Paris that progress would have to be made without British support. Using an architectural metaphor popular in the mid-1980s, when he published his book on the Marshall Plan, Michael Hogan states that the British in the late 1940s "preferred their own room with connecting doors to the U.S. and the Continent and protested when the Americans suggested a suite with the Europeans."[45]

Britain preferred a private room because of a political culture that emphasized national sovereignty and abhorred supranationality; a long history of infrequent direct involvement in continental European affairs and the unique wartime experience of having escaped invasion also contributed. In addition, Britain saw itself as an intermediary between the United States and continental Europe, an aspect of the Anglo-American "special relationship" that London feared would be endangered by participation in European integration, despite Washington's assertions to the contrary. British officials also thought that too close an involvement in the process of European integration would jeopardize London's strong political and economic orientation toward the declining empire and emerging Commonwealth.[46]

Schuman's decision to give the British government no more than a few hours notice of his ground-breaking declaration vividly illustrates French indifference to London's involvement in the future coal and steel community. British foreign minister Ernest Bevin was furious, doubly so when he discovered that Acheson had known all about the impending declaration when he had arrived in London the day before Schuman's press conference.[47] Any French embarrassment at slighting Bevin rapidly dissipated when the British government belittled the plan. The governing Labour Party delayed publication of an important policy document on Europe in order to include an assessment of the French proposal. When it appeared in June 1950, "European Unity: A Statement by the National Executive Committee of the British Labour Party" caused a storm on the Continent. The pamphlet explicitly stated Britain's objections to participation in European integration and barely disguised the government's hostility to the Schuman Plan.

Yet the French government held open the door to British participation in the coal and steel negotiations. Other prospective member states, especially the Benelux countries, hoped that Britain would take the decisive step. But in order to cross the threshold, all participants had to accept the principle of shared sovereignty, whatever that would turn out to mean in practice. Monnet stuck to the position that if the principle of supranationality itself was debatable, the proposed community would soon go the way of the ineffectual OEEC. Following a series of cabinet meetings and diplomatic exchanges with France, the British government reached a predictable but discouraging conclusion. At the definitive cabinet meeting, "there seems to have been a general, resentful agreement to give a negative answer [to France]."[48]

THE ECSC AND THE EDC

With understandable artistic license, Theodore White wrote in retrospect that "Monnet's prestige in French politics was akin to that of George Marshall in American politics. . . . Watching Monnet thread his suggestion [the Schuman Declaration] through the bureaucracies and foreign ministries of Europe was to take delight in his political art."[49] Monnet's standing may indeed have been high, but his proposal for a coal and steel community by no means sailed easily through the relevant government departments of the six negotiating states: France, Germany, Italy, Belgium, the Netherlands, and Luxembourg. John Gillingham, author of an authoritative history of the Schuman Plan, entitled his chapter on the ECSC negotiations "From Summit to Swamp."[50] The summit was the high point of the declaration itself, made in the glare of publicity and self-congratulation; the swamp was the low point of intergovernmental squabbling as each country jockeyed for advantage in pursuit of its own interests. Monnet thought the negotiations, which began in June 1950, would be over by the end of the summer; in the event, they only began in earnest in August 1950 and eventually ended in April 1951. Ratification by the member states' parliaments took nearly another year. The European Coal and Steel Community finally began operating in August 1952.

Monnet negotiated for France and prevailed upon Adenauer to appoint Walter Hallstein, a law professor, state secretary in the foreign office, and later the European Commission's first president, as Germany's representative. The main agenda items were the proposed community's competence, institutions, and decisionmaking procedures. Based on a French discussion document, the negotiators gradually gave substance and shape to the new organization. What emerged was a supranational High Authority, the institutional depository of shared national sovereignty over the coal and steel sectors. The High Authority would be responsible for formulating a common market in coal and steel and for supervising such related issues as pricing, wages, investment, and competition. As Monnet saw it, the purpose of the community was not "to substitute the High Authority for private enterprise, but . . . to make possible real competition throughout a vast market, from which producers, workers and consumers would all gain."[51] Sensitive especially to U.S. concerns, doubly so in view of Acheson's first reaction, Monnet also wove into the treaty a number of antitrust provisions.

Because of the High Authority's small size, national bureaucracies would have to cooperate closely with it to implement community legislation. A separate community institution, the Court of Justice, would adjudicate disputes and ensure member states' compliance with the terms of the treaty. In a move that was to have important repercussions for the future of European integration, the other negotiators forced Monnet to accept a Council of Ministers in the community's institutional framework. Initially intended to be advisory and intermediary, as the embodiment of the member states' interests the Council of Ministers would increasingly act as a brake on supranationalism within the community. Finally, a Common Assembly consisting of delegates of the national parliaments would give the community the appearance of direct democratic accountability.

The contemporaneous controversy over German remilitarization at first imperiled the coal and steel negotiations but ultimately saved them to a great extent. Faced with U.S. demands for German rearmament following the outbreak of the Korean War, French Prime Minister Pleven announced in October 1950 a plan for German remilitarization under the aegis of a European Defense Community (EDC), just as Schuman had earlier proposed German reindustrialization under the aegis of a coal and steel community. Monnet was the architect of both ideas. His advocacy of the EDC grew directly out of his championing of the Schuman Plan. Fierce French hostility to German remilitarization, even in the face of Anglo-American pressure and the seriousness of the Cold War, caused Adenauer to doubt France's commitment to Franco-German reconciliation and European integration. If shared sovereignty was good enough for German industry, Adenauer asked, why was it not also acceptable for German rearmament? Faced with possible German recalcitrance in the coal and steel talks, Monnet pressed Pleven to pursue the parallel idea of a supranational organization for European security.[52]

Negotiations to form the European Defense Community, in which German units would be integrated into a European army, began in February 1951. Five of the six nations negotiating a treaty to establish the coal and steel community simultaneously participated in these discussions (the Netherlands, the odd country out, delayed taking part until October 1951). Although Monnet was not directly involved in the EDC talks, he again used his influence behind the scenes to win powerful U.S. support for the Pleven Plan.[53] True to form, Great Britain resisted U.S. entreaties to enter the EDC talks. Apart from disliking the concept of supranationality, and apart also from their participation in the Brussels Pact of 1948, the British still harbored a deep distrust of their Western European allies' military capability, based on the lessons learned from the collapse of France and the Low Countries in 1940. Despite British remoteness, the Six persevered in their negotiations. After complex and hard bargaining, they signed the EDC treaty on May 27, 1952, in Paris.

The EDC negotiations spawned another initiative that raised federalists' hopes for the future of European integration. Article 38 of the EDC treaty called for the establishment of a supranational political authority to direct the defense community. Deferring to domestic parliamentary opinion, in September 1952 the foreign ministers of the Six acted on a resolution passed by the Council of Europe's Assembly, calling on them to entrust a parliamentary body with the task of implementing Article 38 by drafting the statute for a supranational European Political Community (EPC). Reflecting, perhaps, the six governments' indifference toward the proposed EPC and doubts that it would ever come to anything, the foreign ministers asked a special committee of the newly established ECSC Common Assembly to draft a treaty.[54]

The so-called "constitutional committee" lost little time in drawing up plans for a political community that would not only encompass the EDC and ECSC but also embrace foreign, economic, and monetary policy coordination. The result would have been a community more advanced along the road of European integration than the most optimistic EC member states in the 1991 intergovernmental conferences had thought likely to emerge in the 1992 Maastricht Treaty. Even in the extraordinary climate of the early 1950s, with the Korean War and the attendant acceptance of German rearmament acting as a spur to greater European integration, the Six balked at the consultative committee's extravagant recommendations. At a series of intergovernmental meetings later in 1953 and early in 1954, the Six successfully diluted the more far-reaching institutional and supranational aspects of the draft EPC treaty. Much to the member states' relief, the proposed EPC soon withered away, a casualty of its stillborn sibling, the EDC.

Having survived the penultimate negotiating stage, the EDC foundered on the rock of ratification. Gaullist hostility to sharing sovereignty over sacrosanct national defense policy, coupled with implacable Communist opposition to German rearmament, resulted in August 1954 in defeat of the EDC treaty in the French National Assembly. It was paradoxical that the EDC failed in France, where the original initiative had been taken in 1950 and the treaty had been signed in 1952. In the interim, however, Stalin's death and the end of hostilities in Korea had lessened Cold War tensions and made the issue of German remilitarization far less urgent. Moreover, in the early 1950s Paris had become increasingly preoccupied with a dissipating colonial conflict in Indochina.[55]

Nevertheless, the genie of German rearmament could not be stuffed back in the bottle. With the collapse of the EDC, Anthony Eden, the British prime minister, proposed instead that Germany join the Brussels Pact of 1948 and participate with Britain, France, Italy, and the Benelux countries in the Western European Union (WEU). Eden saw the WEU solely as a vehicle to facilitate German entry into the North Atlantic Treaty Alliance (NATO). As expected, Germany joined NATO via the WEU in May 1955. Thus, in a fitting finale to the EDC debacle, France acquiesced in German membership in NATO, a prospect that five years previously had filled Paris with fright.

The EDC and EPC left an interesting legacy. Having marked the high point of European federalist aspirations, the failed proposals quickly acquired the aura of a great opportunity lost. As the European Community struggled through the political setbacks of the 1960s, the economic difficulties of the 1970s, and a belated revival in the 1980s, supporters of supranationalism harked back to the early 1950s as the European movement's golden age. If only the EDC and EPC had been ratified, the argument goes, European integration would have reached a level now considered unattainable in the 1990s. Yet the collapse of both proposals and the failure of subsequent initiatives along similar lines clearly indicate the limits on European integration in the 1950s and beyond. It was no historical accident that the EDC fell at the final hurdle of French ratification or that the EPC languished in the wings. Only with great reluctance had the

Six confronted the question of a defense community and the equally daunting challenge of a supranational political community. The outcome of both issues allowed them to concentrate instead on the kind of European integration politically possible in the 1950s and for many years thereafter: functional economic integration.

As the epitome of functionalism, the European Coal and Steel Community survived the wreckage of the EDC and EPC. The ECSC treaty outlined the structure and set the rules of the new supranational organization. Together with lofty references to world peace and a "contribution . . . to civilization," the treaty's preamble explicitly stated the ECSC's functionalist, ultimately federalist mission: The community would help to build European unity "through practical achievements which will first of all create real solidarity, and through the establishment of common bases for economic development."[56] By referring to the community's role in rebuilding Europe, the preamble set the seal on Monnet's tendency to blur the distinction between Europe and Western Europe and to confine the geopolitical scope of the ECSC (and later the EC) to a core group of countries centered on the Rhine.

Concerned about the possible consequences of the EDC controversy for the Schuman Plan, Monnet had insisted upon early German ratification of the ECSC treaty. In each prospective member state, the ratification debate proved extremely contentious. Producer associations complained about the High Authority's ability to interfere in their affairs, labor groups fretted about the impact of keener competition, and nationalist politicians railed against the onslaught of supranationalism. In the event, the simultaneous EDC strife channeled the more vehement criticism of shared sovereignty away from the ECSC debate. While the EDC issue raged, the national parliaments of the Six ratified the ECSC treaty. A number of outstanding issues remained to be worked out, however, including the site of the institutions themselves. Despite Monnet's hope that a special area, analogous to the District of Columbia, would be set aside in the community, the member states eventually settled on Luxembourg as the site of the High Authority.[57] It was there, in the capital of the small, sleepy Grand Duchy, that the ECSC began to function in August 1952.

The ECSC disappointed European federalists both in its conceptual framework and in its actual operation. It was an unglamorous organization that inadequately symbolized the high hopes of supranationalism in Europe. Yet the ECSC served a vital purpose in the postwar world in terms of Franco-German reconciliation and the related goal of European integration. To quote John Gillingham at some length, "a supranational authority had been created, a potential nucleus for a European federal system. It would serve in lieu of a peace treaty concluding hostilities between Germany and Western Europe. This was no grand settlement in the manner of Westphalia or Versailles. The agreement to create a heavy industry pool changed no borders, created no new alliances, and reduced only a few commercial and financial barriers. It did not even end the occupation of the Federal Republic. . . . By resolving the coal and steel conflicts that had stood between France and Germany since World War II, it did, however, remove the main obstacle to an economic partnership between the two nations."[58] These were by no means inconsiderable achievements.

THE EEC AND EURATOM

The favorite metaphor of European federalists depicts the European Community as a fragile, delicate craft constantly running aground on the treacherous shoals of national sovereignty and self-interest. With each repair and relaunch the ship is strengthened and streamlined, and navigational hazards are charted and exposed. Eventually, one supposes, the United States of Europe will resemble a supranational supertanker plying stormy economic, political, and security seas, invulnerable to the perils that lurk beneath the surface.

Thus the first relaunch of the community concept (*Relance européenne*) took place immediately after the EDC and EPC foundered in 1954. But there was nothing inevitable or inexorable about the revival of European integration at that time. Certainly the ECSC continued to operate unabated, but it was not a striking success. The High Authority struggled in vain to formulate and implement effective pricing and competition policies and managed only with difficulty to regulate other aspects of the community's industries. Yet the political lessons of functional integration were not lost on the member states. Despite the bitterness engendered by the EDC debate, a willingness persisted at least to maintain, or even extend, functional economic cooperation for the sake of Franco-German reconciliation and European integration.

Moreover, a specific idea for economic integration, floated as part of the moribund European Political Community proposal, survived the defeat of the EDC. This called for the Six to abolish quotas and tariffs on intracommunity trade, establish a joint external tariff, unify trade policy toward the rest of the world, devise common policies for a range of socioeconomic sectors, and organize a single internal market. Monnet thought this idea too ambitious, especially in the aftermath of the EDC debacle. Enamored as always of more definite and practical proposals, he continued to advocate the functional approach of sectoral integration. Even while the ECSC treaty was being negotiated, Monnet knew that coal was rapidly losing its position as the basis of industrial power and, by extension, military might. Atomic energy had already revolutionized strategic doctrine and seemed poised to replace coal and oil as the elixir of the future. Not surprisingly, Monnet now proposed the European Atomic Energy Community, to be structured along the lines of the coal and steel community, in order both to achieve the immediate objectives of the ECSC itself and to promote the distant goal of European federation.

In November 1954, disappointed with the coal and steel community's progress, concerned about the consequences for integration of the EDC's failure, and impatient to play a more active and aggressive role in advocating European unity, Monnet announced his intention to resign from the High Authority. As he explained to the ECSC Common Assembly in Strasbourg, "It is for Parliaments and Governments to decide on the transfer of new powers to the European institutions. The impulse must therefore come from without. [By resigning from the High Authority], I shall be able to join in the efforts of all those who are working to continue and enlarge what has been begun."[59] Monnet's vehicle for influencing "Parliaments and Governments . . . from without" would be the action committee for a United States of Europe, a small, "private supranational organization" of political party and trade union leaders.[60] Monnet envisioned the action committee as a powerful pressure group for his proposed atomic energy community.

Monnet's decision to resign took the member state governments by surprise. At a meeting in Messina in June 1955, ECSC foreign ministers discussed not only Monnet's replacement but also the future of European integration. Paul-Henri Spaak, the Belgian foreign minister, had prepared a memorandum on behalf of the Benelux countries suggesting further integration along the lines of Monnet's idea for an atomic energy community and the rival proposal for a common market. The foreign ministers decided at least to give the question of European integration further thought, asking Spaak to form a committee and write a report on future options. This constituted the first "relaunch of Europe."

Spaak was well suited by temperament and conviction to lead the ensuing intergovernmental discussions. His enthusiasm for integration had already won him the nickname "Mr. Europe." As chairman of the conference that opened in Brussels later in 1955, Spaak steered the work of the various committees and subcommittees that drafted specific parts of the final proposal. Spaak's report, presented to his fellow foreign ministers at a meeting in Venice in May 1956, proposed that the two objectives of sectoral (atomic energy) integration and wider economic integration (a common market) be realized in separate organizations with separate treaties. The Venice foreign ministers' meeting marked the first stage of a protracted process of intergovernmental negotiation that culminated in the establishment of the European Atomic Energy Community (Euratom) and the European Economic Community (EEC).

The October–November 1956 Suez debacle—in which an Anglo-French military intervention ended in political disaster—turned the French government's attention squarely back to the Continent and made the prospect of a wider economic agreement with neighboring countries seem more important than before. As it was, Guy Mollet, the French prime minister, was staunchly in favor of intergrating Europe. Until the Suez crisis cleared the air, however, Mollet refrained from pushing renewed efforts to do so, largely because of the bitter EDC bequest. Yet French political opinion seemed well disposed toward Euratom, which offered an opportunity to share the exorbitant costs of atomic energy research and development while enjoying all the benefits. President Eisenhower's recent "Atoms for Peace" initiative increased Euratom's attraction. Not only was the United States willing to share nuclear technology for peaceful purposes, the State Department also recognized that "the most hopeful avenue for relaunching the movement toward European integration now appears to be the creation of a European common authority, along the lines of the Schuman Plan, to be responsible for the development of atomic energy for peaceful purposes."[61]

By contrast, reaction in France to the possible establishment of a common market was almost uniformly hostile. Robert Marjolin, who advised French Foreign Minister Christian Pinau on European affairs and subsequently participated in the Euratom and EEC treaty negotiations, noted in his memoirs *"the hostility of almost the whole of French opinion to the removal, even gradual, of the protection which French industry enjoyed"* (original emphasis).[62] That hostility led to intense confrontations between Mollet, Pinau, like-minded ministers, and their negotiators in Brussels on the one hand, and recalcitrant ministers and bureaucrats in Paris on the other. In addition to fighting for France in the intergovernmental negotiations in Brussels, Marjolin found himself waging a rearguard action, what he called the "Battle of Paris."[63]

Marjolin and others argued the case for a customs union and common market on its own merits but bolstered their position with the legitimate assertion that France could not have the desirable atomic energy community without the undesirable economic community. With the exception of Britain, which participated in the EEC negotiations until November 1955, France's partners in the intergovernmental conference eagerly sought a common market in Europe. The advantage of a single market in industrial goods was obvious to Germany, although Ludwig Erhard, the finance minister, objected to the proposed community on the grounds that it would be protectionist and therefore would distort world trade. As for Euratom, the other countries in the negotiations did not share France's enthusiasm and doubted the French government would exploit atomic energy only for civil projects.

The decisive French debates on Euratom and the EEC took place not only at the time of the treaties' ratification but also on the occasion of two earlier votes in the National Assembly on whether or not the negotiations should continue. The vote on the Euratom negotiations came first, in July 1956, and resulted in an easy government victory. The later vote on the EEC negotiations, in January 1957, proved far more contentious. A vague desire to improve the country's image after the negative EDC vote of August 1954, a reaction against the Soviet Union and the French Communist Party in the wake of the invasion of Hungary in October 1956, the legacy of Suez, and a concern that France might permanently be left behind its more economically advanced neighbors undoubtedly contributed to the government's success. Yet the outcome was close. Only by guaranteeing clauses in the EEC treaty that favored France's overseas possessions and promising to include agriculture in the proposed common market did the government carry the day.

Having accepted these conditions during the parliamentary debate, the French government had to convince its partners in the Brussels conference to incorporate them into the draft treaties. The other countries agreed to do so in part because of the benefits that would accrue to all from a common agricultural policy and in part because Belgium and the Netherlands would benefit as well from extending community privileges to member states' overseas possessions. But the main reason for the other nations' acquiescence was the importance of including France in the community. A European Community without Britain was possible; a Community without France was impracticable. As Franco-German reconciliation lay at the core of the Community and the Community was the key to Germany's postwar rehabilitation, Adenauer would pay almost any price to placate Paris.

Thus, the intergovernmental negotiations came to an end in a series of high-level meetings in February 1957. The outcome was two treaties, one for Euratom and the other for the EEC. Both were signed at an elaborate ceremony in Rome on March 25. Although officially both are called the Treaties of Rome, in practice only the EEC treaty—the most important of them—is known as the Treaty of Rome.

Only in France was there a serious problem with ratification, posed this time not by concerted Gaullist and Communist opposition but by the fall of Mollet's government during the early summer. Here Monnet's action committee was instrumental, if not decisive, in ensuring swift and successful ratification in the National Assembly. First the committee pressed for early ratification in the German parliament. The committee's influence helped win the support of the Social Democratic Party (SPD), which had previously opposed both the ECSC and the EDC. With German ratification secure, the action committee turned its attention to the French National Assembly, where a comfortable majority endorsed the treaties on July 9, 1957.[64] By the end of the year, the Six had ratified the two treaties, allowing the two new communities to begin operating in January 1958.

In another, far less important respect, however, Monnet's committee failed to prevail. As he had done in the early 1950s, during the launching of the ECSC, Monnet championed the cause of a special "European District" to house the new EC institutions in the late 1950s during the debate about Euratom and the EEC. Following the flood of ECSC officials and associated personnel into the Grand Duchy, the Luxembourg government declined to host the new organizations. Almost by default, Brussels, site of the intergovernmental conference that gave birth to the new communities, became their home.

By the time of the Brussels negotiations, held in the aftermath of the EDC debacle, "supranationality" was a term from which even the most ardent federalists recoiled. As Marjolin noted, "nowhere did it appear in the documents drafted during the negotiations; no one so much as mentioned the word."[65] The preamble of the EEC treaty was far less flamboyant than its ECSC counterpart, referring only to the signatories' determination "to lay the foundations of an ever closer union among the peoples of Europe."[66] The treaty itself outlined the essential principles of the common market: the free movement of goods, persons, services, and capital; a customs union and common external tariffs; and various community policies. Each new community's institutional framework emulated that of the ECSC but included a stronger Council of Ministers and a correspondingly weaker Commission (because of the odium attached to "supranationalism" in the wake of the EDC debacle, the name "Commission" replaced the more pretentious "High Authority" in the Treaty of Rome). In effect, "an institutional system was set up [in the communities] with the aim of doing justice to both the intergovernmental and supranational concepts."[67]

At first sight, the EEC was an even greater disappointment than the ECSC. Neither organization realized the high hopes of advocates of European integration in the postwar period. Despite an apparent curtailment of supranationality in the Treaty of Rome, the EEC's importance was nonetheless profound. In his memoirs, Robert Marjolin, who had fought hard in Brussels and Paris to make the EEC possible, described the EEC's significance in the following way: "I do not believe it is an exaggeration to say that this date [March 25, 1957] represents one of the greatest moments of Europe's history. Who would have thought during the 1930s, and even during the ten years that followed the war, that European states which had been tearing one another apart for so many centuries and some of which, like France and Italy, still had very closed economies, would form a common market intended eventually to become an economic area that could be linked to one great dynamic market?"[68] And who would have thought that the same EEC treaty would be the basis of an extraordinary resurgence of European integration thirty years later, symbolized by the slogan "1992"?

NOTES

1. Pascal Fontaine, *Europe: A Fresh Start: The Schuman Declaration, 1950–90* (Luxembourg: Office for Official Publications of the European Communities, 1990), p. 44.

2. Jean Monnet, *Memoirs* (Garden City, NY: Doubleday, 1978), p. 239.

3. On Monnet's life and career, see Monnet, *Memoirs*; Douglas Brinkley and Clifford Hackett, *Jean Monnet: The Path to European Unity* (New York: St. Martin's Press, 1991); Merry Bromberger and Serge Bromberger, *Jean Monnet and the United States of Europe* (New York: Coward-McCann, 1969); Pierre Uri, "Jean Monnet and the Making of Europe," *Contemporary European Affairs* 2, no. 1 (1989): 135–141.

4. Monnet, *Memoirs,* p. 222.

5. For a comprehensive history of European integration and the European movement, see Walter Lipgens, *History of European Integration*, 2 vols. (London: Oxford University Press, 1981 and 1986); and Raymond Poidevin, ed., *Origins of European Integration: March 1948–May 1950* (Brussels: Bruylant, 1986).

6. On the pan-European idea and the origins of the European movement, see Richard Coudenhove-Kalergi, *Pan-Europa* (Vienna: Pan-Europa-Verlag, 1923); Caroline Webb, "Europeanism and the European Movements," in Martin Kolinsky and William E. Patterson, eds., *Social and Political Movements in Western Europe* (London: Croom Helm, 1976); Arnold Zurcher, *The Struggle to Unite Europe, 1940–1958* (New York: New York University Press, 1958); and Peter Stirk, *European Unity in Context: The Interwar Period* (London: Pinter Publishers, 1989).

7. Altiero Spinelli, "European Union and the Resistance," in Ghita Ionescu, ed., *The New Politics of European Integration* (London: Macmillan, 1972), pp. 5–7.

8. Lipgens, *European Integration*, vol. 1, p. 319.

9. Pierre Gerbert, "The Origins: Early Attempts and the Emergence of the Six (1945–52)," in Roy Pryce, ed., *The Dynamics of European Union* (London: Croom Helm, 1987), pp. 40–44.

10. Roy Jenkins, *A Life at the Centre* (London: Macmillan, 1991), p. 104.

11. Monnet, *Memoirs*, pp. 304–305.

12. Monnet, *Memoirs*, p. 286.

13. Desmond Dinan, *The Politics of Persuasion: British Policy and French African Neutrality, 1940–1942* (Lanham, MD: University Press of America, 1988), p. 5.

14. Significantly, Monnet's *Memoirs* open with a description of the offer of Anglo-French union, pp. 17–35.

15. Monnet, *Memoirs,* p. 225; Robert Marjolin, *Architect of European Unity: Memoirs, 1911–1986* (London: Weidenfeld & Nicolson, 1989), pp. 228–229.

16. For an account of the Marshall Plan and its relationship to European integration, see John Gimbel, *The Origins of the Marshall Plan* (Stanford: Stanford University Press, 1976); Michael Hogan, *The Marshall Plan: America, Britain and the Reconstruction of Western Europe, 1947–1952* (Cambridge: Cambridge University Press, 1987); Charles Maier and Gunter Bischof, *The Marshall Plan and Germany: West German Development Within the Framework of the European Recovery Program* (New York: Berg, 1991); Alan Milward, *The Reconstruction of Western Europe* (London: Methuen, 1984); Henry Pelling, *Britain and the Marshall Plan* (New York: St. Martin's Press, 1988); Forrest Pogue, *George*

C. Marshall, vol. 4, *Statesman, 1945–1959* (New York: Viking Press, 1987); and Imanuel Wexler, *The Marshall Plan Revisited: The European Recovery Program in Economic Perspective* (Westport, CT: Greenwood Press, 1983).

17. Office of the Historian, *Foreign Relations of the United States* (hereafter cited as *FRUS*), 1947, vol. 3 (U.S. Department of State), pp. 230–232.

18. *FRUS*, 1947, vol. 3, pp. 237–239.

19. Zurcher, *Struggle to Unite Europe*, pp. 13–16.

20. Walter Isaacson, *The Wise Men: Six Friends and the World They Made* (New York: Simon and Schuster, 1986), p. 122.

21. Hogan, *Marshall Plan*, p. 52.

22. For contending interpretations of the Cold War, see Charles Maier, ed., *The Cold War in Europe: Era of a Divided Continent* (New York: Weiner, 1991).

23. Milward, *Reconstruction*, pp. 465–466.

24. Hogan, *Marshall Plan*, p. 431.

25. Hogan, *Marshall Plan*, p. 432.

26. Milward, *Reconstruction*, p. 282.

27. Irwin M. Wall, *The United States and the Making of Postwar France* (Cambridge: Cambridge University Press, 1991), pp. 191–192.

28. On the failure of OEEC, see Milward, *Reconstruction*, pp. 466–469.

29. See John W. Young, *France, the Cold War, and the Western Alliance* (New York: St. Martin's Press, 1990).

30. See F. Roy Willis, *France, Germany and the New Europe, 1945–1967* (Stanford: Stanford University Press, 1968), pp. 7–31.

31. Isaacson, *Wise Men*, p. 236.

32. On the change in French thinking that led to the Schuman Plan, see Milward, *Reconstruction*, p. 492, and Raymond Poidevin, *Robert Schuman: Homme d'Etat, 1866–1963* (Paris: Imprimerie Nationale, 1986), pp. 32–58.

33. Monnet, *Memoirs*, pp. 298–306. For an account of the historic declaration, see Roger Bullen and M. E. Pelly, *The Schuman Plan, the Council of Europe and Western European Integration* (London: HMSO, 1986); William Diebold, "Imponderables of the Schuman Plan," in *Foreign Affairs* 29, no. 1 (October 1950): 114–129; and Mark Roseman, *Recasting the Ruhr, 1945–1958: Manpower, Economic Recovery, and Labour Relations* (New York: Berg, 1992).

34. On Schuman's life and career, see Poidevin, *Schuman*.

35. Konrad Adenauer, *Memoirs, 1945–1966* (Chicago: Henry Regnery Co., 1966), pp. 244–248. On Adenauer's commitment to European integration, see Adenauer, *Memoirs*; Dennis Bark and David Gress, *A History of West Germany*, vol. 1, *1945–1963* (Oxford: Blackwell, 1989).

36. *FRUS*, 1949, vol. 3, p. 625.

37. *FRUS*, 1949, vol. 4, pp. 412–415, 419–421, 429, 438–440, 445–447, 456–458.

38. Dean Acheson, *Present at the Creation: My Years in the State Department* (New York: Norton, 1969), p. 383.

39. Acheson, *Creation*, p. 384.

40. John Gillingham, *Coal, Steel and the Rebirth of Europe, 1945–1955: The Germans and French from Ruhr Conflict to Economic Community* (Cambridge: Cambridge University Press, 1991), p. 235.

41. Gillingham, *Coal, Steel*, p. 231.

42. Monnet, *Memoirs*, p. 293.

43. Marjolin, *Memoirs*, p. 126.

44. Milward, *Reconstruction*, p. 255.

45. Hogan, *Marshall Plan*, p. 440.

46. For a discussion of British policy toward postwar Europe, see Alan Bullock, *The Life and Times of Ernest Bevin*, vol. 3, *Ernest Bevin: Foreign Secretary, 1948–1951* (London: Heinemann, 1983); Richard Ovendale, *Foreign Policy of the British Labour Government, 1945–1951* (London: Pinter, 1984); John Young, *Britain, France and the Unity of Europe, 1945–1951* (Leicester: Leicester University Press, 1984).

47. See Bullock, *Bevin*, vol. 3, pp. 731–733 ; and Dean Acheson, *Sketches from Life of Men I Have Known* (New York: H. Hamilton, 1961), pp. 38–41.

48. Milward, *Reconstruction*, p. 404.

49. Theodore White, *In Search of History: A Personal Adventure* (New York: Harper and Row, 1978), pp. 438–439.

50. Gillingham, *Coal, Steel*, p. 229.

51. Monnet, *Memoirs*, p. 329.

52. See Edward Fursdon, *The European Defence Community: A History* (New York: St. Martin's Press, 1980).

53. Monnet, *Memoirs*, p. 358.

54. On the EPC negotiations, see Rita Cardozo, "The Project for Political Union (1952–54)," in Pryce, *Dynamics*, pp. 49–77.

55. See Raymond Aron, *France Defeats EDC* (New York: F. A. Praeger, 1957).

56. Preamble to the Treaty Establishing the ECSC (Treaty of Paris), April 18, 1951.

57. See Monnet, *Memoirs*, pp. 369–370.

58. Gillingham, *Coal, Steel*, pp. 297–298.

59. Monnet, *Memoirs*, p. 400.

60. Walter Yondorf, "Monnet and the Action Committee: The Formative Years of the European Communities," *International Organization* 19 (1965): 909; see also Pascal Fontaine, *Le Comité d'Action pour les Etats Unis d'Europe de Jean Monnet* (Lausanne: Centre de Recherches Européennes, 1974).

61. *FRUS*, 1955–1957, vol. 4, p. 323.

62. Marjolin, *Memoirs*, p. 284.

63. Marjolin, *Memoirs*, p. 284.

64. See Yondorf, "Action Committee," pp. 896–901.

65. Marjolin, *Memoirs*, p. 296.

66. Preamble to the Treaty Establishing the EEC (Treaty of Rome), March 27, 1957.

67. Hanns-Jurgen Küsters, "The Treaties of Rome (1955–57)," in Pryce, *Dynamics*, p. 94.

68. Marjolin, *Memoirs*, p. 306.

2

Constructing the Community:
The Gaullist Challenge, 1958–1969

Three individuals, all French, have contributed most to shaping the European Community. Yet if the Community ever built a pantheon for its heroes, only two of them would be buried there. The first, Jean Monnet, would have pride of place. The second, Jacques Delors, European Commission president since 1985, would repose beside Monnet in almost equal esteem. But the third, Charles de Gaulle, would never be considered for interment in the Community's hallowed ground. On the contrary, de Gaulle would be relegated to the rogues' gallery of Community villains. For in the popular opinion of European integrationists, de Gaulle's anachronistic championing of the nation-state destroyed the Community's development in the 1960s and stunted its institutional growth until the Single European Act of 1986 and the Maastricht Treaty of 1992. In their view, de Gaulle belongs, with Margaret Thatcher, on the scrap heap.

Such an opinion reveals the intolerance of the ideologue. Moreover, it does de Gaulle a disservice, not least by casting him in the same light as Thatcher. De Gaulle and Thatcher can only be compared superficially. Both were ardent nationalists, both shielded sovereignty from the encroachments of supranationality, and both detested European integration. On a personal level, both were often obdurate, arrogant, and overbearing. Despite those similarities, the differences between them are striking. De Gaulle soared above party politics; Thatcher wallowed in them. De Gaulle looked to the future; Thatcher harked to the past. De Gaulle espoused a "European Europe"; Thatcher embraced U.S. hegemony. De Gaulle battled against bipolarity; Thatcher was a creature of the Cold War.

De Gaulle's contribution to the European Community was far from negative. The Common Agricultural Policy (CAP), subsequently denigrated as a drain on Community resources and an impediment to international trade accord, owes its existence to de Gaulle. In the 1960s, the CAP proved a vital instrument of Community solidarity and helped restructure declining Western European agriculture. More important, without the CAP there would not have been a Community of any kind. Just as the French National Assembly had successfully insisted on agricultural provisions in the Treaty of Rome, so, too, had de Gaulle demanded implementation of those provisions as a condition of implementing the Treaty as a whole. The customs union and common external tariff came into being because of, not despite, the CAP.

De Gaulle is best known in the context of the European Community for keeping Britain out and for curtailing the powers of the European Parliament and European Commission. Once again, both seem negative achievements. But allowing Britain to join in the early 1960s would in all likelihood have thwarted the CAP, undermined the Community, and turned the customs union into a broad free trade area. The difficulties of dealing with Britain in the EC, not only under Thatcher in the 1980s but also under previous and succeeding governments, seem to bear out de Gaulle's point. De Gaulle's stand against the Commission in 1965 epitomized his hostility to supranationalism. Yet intergovernmentalism, which de Gaulle so bluntly asserted during the 1965 crisis, laid the basis for the Community's survival in the 1970s and invigoration in the 1980s. Ironically, as Stanley Hoffmann has observed, the Community of the 1990s is "an improbable, yet not ineffectual, blend of de Gaulle and Monnet."[1]

THE DOMESTIC AND COMMUNITY CONTEXTS

De Gaulle's first contribution to the Community was to bring France, then the EC's politically most important and economically most powerful member state, back from the brink of catastrophe.[2] Since the end of World War II, a series of bitter colonial conflicts, first in Indochina and later in North Africa, had progressively undermined the already precarious Fourth Republic. In May 1958, a revolt by French army officers in Algiers, sparked by rumors of impending negotiations between the French government and the Algerian National Liberation Front, proved the last straw. Threatened by a right-wing coup and a left-wing countercoup, the government collapsed. Despite numerous new governments and cabinet reshuffles during the Fourth Republic's brief, unhappy history, the country's hitherto resourceful politicians seemed suddenly incapable of saving the regime.

Twice before at times of national crisis General de Gaulle had come to the rescue. The first occasion was June 1940, when he rejected the armistice with Germany and fled France to carry on the struggle from abroad. Although de Gaulle was reviled in France at the time for his supposed insubordination, Vichy's collaboration with Berlin inevitably transformed his image. By the end of the war, Frenchmen who could agree on little else hailed de Gaulle as their country's savior. Thus acclaimed, de Gaulle delivered France from disaster a second time in August 1944 by overcoming deep political and ideological divisions in the newly liberated country and forming a provisional government.

Fourteen years later, only de Gaulle wielded the moral authority and commanded the national respect necessary once again to save the nation. Exploiting the legend of 1940 and the lessons of 1946, when his provisional government had collapsed in the kind of political strife he had naively hoped to overcome, de Gaulle began negotiations with the political parties (minus the Communists) about forming not only a new government but a new regime. Few argued with the general's demand that the new republic possess a strong presidency, insulated from the factionalism of the National Assembly and having almost exclusive responsibility for foreign policy and defense. In September 1958, a grateful electorate ushered in the Fifth Republic by overwhelmingly endorsing de Gaulle's constitution.

In 1958, as in 1944, de Gaulle claimed to be above partisan politics. But in 1958, unlike in 1944, he encouraged his associates to launch a political party as a means of ensuring a Gaullist majority in the National Assembly. Following the first parliamentary elections of the Fifth Republic, the Gaullists and the conservative Independents formed a government. On December 21, 1958, deputies and local councilors voted for the new republic's first president: de Gaulle won 76 percent of the ballots cast. Four years later, having survived another army revolt and an attempted assassination because of his acquiescence in Algerian independence, de Gaulle held a referendum on direct elections for the presidency. The ensuing endorsement completed the constitutional construction of the Fifth Republic.

Monnet, for one, understood the importance for the Community of a politically stable France. Writing in *Le Monde* in the run-up to the referendum on the new constitution, Monnet declared that "to safeguard our future we must now put an end to the Algerian crisis and ensure governmental stability and authority. These two imperatives are linked."[3] Similarly, Monnet voted "yes" in the referendum on direct elections for the presidency. "I voted in favor of a step," Monnet later wrote, "which would give the executive greater legitimacy and also facilitate the decisions required for the unification of Europe. For sovereignty to be relegated, authority must be well-established."[4] Of course de Gaulle was averse to surrendering any sovereignty whatsoever, as the Community crisis of 1965 would clearly indicate. Thus Monnet voted against de Gaulle in that year's presidential election. But Monnet's point about a strong executive forming the necessary basis for the sharing of sovereignty was prescient, for it was precisely from such a position that President François Mitterrand advanced European integration so effectively in the mid- and late 1980s.

De Gaulle's concomitant financial and monetary reforms proved equally essential for the successful functioning of the European Community. Without de Gaulle's drastic devaluation of the franc in 1958 and related government expenditure cuts and taxation hikes, the fragile French economy could not have survived a sudden plunge into the cold waters of intra-Community tariff reductions.[5] Nor might the first round of tariff cuts, due to be implemented on January 1, 1959, have taken place had the French franc remained so grossly overvalued. There is some truth to de Gaulle's later assertion that when the Community came into being, "it was necessary—in order to achieve something—that we French put in order our economic, financial and monetary affairs. . . . From that moment the Community was in principle viable."[6]

Community membership may have provided a pretext to take financial and monetary measures that would otherwise have proved politically impossible. But the Community meant much more than that to de Gaulle. Despite its threat to French sovereignty, the Community offered de Gaulle an unprecedented opportunity to promote two overriding objectives. The first was French economic advancement; the second was an institutional framework in which to embed Franco-German rapprochement.

During the debate in France on the European Community, in the mid-1950s, de Gaulle, then in the political wilderness, had kept curiously quiet. At the time he reportedly told Michel Debré, who later became his foreign minister, that "we shall tear up [the Treaty of Rome] when we come to power."[7] Whatever de Gaulle said privately or publicly, he supported key aspects of the European Community on pragmatic political and economic grounds. Thus, the Community flourished in its early years not because de Gaulle reluctantly acquiesced in it—either for legal reasons, or because his government depended on the support of the pro-EC Independents in the National Assembly, or because he was preoccupied with Algeria—but because he strongly supported a certain amount of sectoral economic integration. Hence, as David Calleo noted at the time, "of all the national governments, it is de Gaulle's France which has supported most vigorously and constantly . . . the creation of a genuinely integrated European economy."[8]

In his memoirs, Harold Wilson, Britain's prime minister in the mid-1960s and again in the mid-1970s, tells the story of de Gaulle dismissing the discipline of economics as "quartermaster stuff."[9] Despite his fashionable denunciation of the dismal science, de Gaulle appreciated the importance of good quartermasters for the successful functioning of a modern army. Although he had no formal training in economics, de Gaulle took a keen interest in financial and monetary affairs. In 1946 he appointed Monnet to head the new office of economic planning. In 1958, he resolved "to prod the sluggish French economy forward into the industrial age [and] to metamorphose traditional industries through the stimulus of international competition."[10] As de Gaulle remarked in his own memoirs, "International competition . . . offered a lever to stimulate our business sector, to force it to increase productivity . . . hence my decision to promote the Common Market which was still just a collection of paper."[11] De Gaulle's main interest lay in the international arena, but he remained acutely aware that "only if financial stability, economic progress and social well-being are maintained will [my foreign policy] be both endorsed and capable of succeeding."[12] Paradoxically, it was economic weakness, financial instability, and social discord that blighted de Gaulle's foreign policy later in the 1960s and ultimately prompted his resignation in 1969.

Apart from seeking industrial rejuvenation, de Gaulle saw in the EC a unique opportunity to modernize the large and cumbersome French agricultural sector. "How could we maintain on our territory more than two million farms," de Gaulle asked in his memoirs, "three-quarters of which were too small and too poor to be profitable, but on which, nonetheless, nearly one-fifth of the French population live? How, in this day and age, could we leave the agricultural profession to stumble along, without the benefit of technical training, organized markets, and the support of a rational credit system required for it to be competitive?"[13] The solution lay in the proposed Common Agricultural Policy, which would provide a Community-wide outlet for French produce, guarantee high prices for Community farmers regardless of low prices on the world market, and subsidize the export of surplus produce outside the Community itself. In effect, de Gaulle sought to get his Community colleagues, especially the Germans, to prop up French agriculture. His quid pro quo was Germany's expected profit from the lowering and ultimate abandonment of industrial tariffs among the Six. The negotiations ahead would be arduous and acrimonious, but the advantage for France was clear. Hence de Gaulle's admission that "if, on resuming control of our affairs, I indeed embraced the Common Market, it was as much because of our position as an agricultural country as for the progress it would impose on our industry . . . the CAP was a *sine qua non* of [our] participation."[14]

De Gaulle's first battle over the CAP preceded its birth and ensured not only that the policy would come into being but also that the Community would survive. At issue was a British proposal to establish a European free trade area to incorporate and possibly supplant the Community.[15] Having decided not to pursue Community membership, Britain sought instead to enjoy the benefits of free trade in Europe while eschewing a common external tariff, a common agricultural policy, and any form of economic integration. Ludwig Erhard, German economics minister and a future chancellor, supported the British proposal because of his commitment to free trade and fear of Community protectionism. Most member states, however, resented what they saw as Britain's efforts to undermine European integration by diluting the nascent Community in a wider free trade area. Robert Marjolin, a vice president of the new Commission, saw the proposal as "a great danger, that of being more or less sucked into a vast European free trade area in which [the Community] would have lost its individuality, and which might have prevented it from fully establishing itself according to the terms of the Treaty of Rome."[16]

De Gaulle especially took fright at the proposal's implications for agriculture, a sector specifically excluded from the free trade offer. Although talks about a possible free trade area had continued since the second half of 1956, de Gaulle brought them to an abrupt end in November 1958, soon after coming to power. Britain pressed ahead and, in November 1959, formed the European Free Trade Association (EFTA) with Austria, Denmark, Norway, Portugal, Sweden, and Switzerland. EFTA, in turn, sought to link up with the EC, with a view to establishing "a single market embracing some 300 million people."[17] Once again, Community and member state officials feared that an early agreement between the Six and the Seven would thwart proper implementation of the Treaty of Rome. Instead, they resolved to press ahead with closer Community integration, which proved so successful by the early 1960s that Britain applied for EC membership.

De Gaulle's position on the Community complemented his policy toward Germany. On September 14–15, 1958, Chancellor Adenauer paid a highly successful visit to de Gaulle's country residence for the first meeting between both men. Whereas de Gaulle had left the political stage in 1946 advocating a punitive policy toward a weak, divided Germany, he returned in 1958 to a radically altered European scene. With Germany reindustrialized and rearmed, de Gaulle abandoned his earlier position and espoused instead the then-orthodox French policy of reconciliation and rapprochement. The remarkably warm relationship that immediately blossomed between the octogenarian chancellor and septuagenarian president confirmed both leaders in the belief that their countries' future, and the future of Europe, depended above all on close Franco-German accord. At their second meeting, in Bad Kreuznach on November 26, 1958, de Gaulle assured Adenauer of France's commitment to the Treaty of Rome and won German support for his rejection of the EFTA overture. The lesson was clear: "Whatever the cost to Germany's economic interests, the British free trade proposal would not be allowed to interfere with the Franco-German *rapprochement*."[18]

Nor, during the remaining years of Chancellor Adenauer's tenure, would either leader allow other issues to come between France and

Germany. On the contrary, international developments in the late 1950s and early 1960s convinced Adenauer of the wisdom of sticking to the Franco-German course. Coincidentally, during the Bad Kreuznach meeting in November 1958, President Khrushchev of the Soviet Union launched the first in a series of crises over Berlin, the divided former capital of Germany. Khrushchev threatened unspecified action unless the Western powers revised the city's status within six months. De Gaulle immediately offered the chancellor his full support, a position from which France never wavered during the protracted Berlin tension of the coming years. Hans von der Groeben, a commissioner in the 1960s and later a historian of the Community, identified Khrushchev's 1958 ultimatum as being "of crucial importance to further political development and to the establishment of the process of integration."[19] In return for de Gaulle's support in the face of crude Soviet threats, Adenauer reciprocated, often against strong opposition inside his own party and parliament, with support for de Gaulle's controversial positions on the CAP and on Britain's membership application.

Given de Gaulle's antipathy toward Washington, Germany's security dependence on the United States—a fact of life during the Cold War—was the issue most likely to strain the Paris-Bonn accord. In the early 1960s a U.S. proposal to establish the Multilateral Force (MLF), a fully integrated, multinational NATO nuclear contingent, was the number one item on the trans-Atlantic security agenda. The MLF grew out of Washington's wish to placate its European allies, who resented their exclusion from NATO nuclear policymaking, and to bring Germany closer into the NATO fold at a time of growing Gaullist influence in Bonn. Predictably, de Gaulle abhorred the MLF idea, seeing it as both a subtle U.S. attempt to increase hegemony in the Alliance and a not-so-subtle effort to foil France's quest for an independent nuclear deterrent.

Accordingly, de Gaulle not only made every effort to impede the MLF but also made German rejection of it a touchstone of the Paris-Bonn alliance.[20] The MLF proposal posed a dilemma for Adenauer. Would he have to choose between Paris and Washington? Fortunately for Adenauer, the question never arose. Doubts about the MLF's efficacy and wisdom, both within the U.S. administration and among the European allies, convinced Washington to abandon the idea. But the controversy highlighted Germany's security dilemma and eroded Adenauer's political support in Bonn.

In the meantime, the favorable political climate of Franco-German friendship, de Gaulle's benevolence toward certain provisions of the Treaty of Rome, and an extremely buoyant European economy saw the Community off to a strong start when it began operating on January 1, 1958. Robert Marjolin recalled the Community's first four years as "a honeymoon . . . a time of harmony between the governments of the member countries and between [Community] institutions."[21] Walter Hallstein, a former German state secretary for foreign affairs and an early collaborator of Jean Monnet's, presided over the first Commission. With nine members (two each from Germany, France, and Italy, and one each from the other member states), the Commission spent the first few months of its existence settling into temporary quarters in Brussels, allocating responsibilities and portfolios amongst its members, and organizing the necessary staff and services. Commission officials came from the ECSC in Luxembourg, from the member states' civil services, or from academia and the private sector. Setting an important precedent, the first Commission recruited a bureaucracy that struck a national and regional balance "without becoming a slave to proportional representation."[22]

Other institutions similarly set themselves up. The Council of Ministers, the Community's decisionmaking body, began regular meetings in Brussels and located a small secretariat there. The Council also organized a Committee of Permanent Representatives (Coreper), consisting of ambassadors to promote their countries' interests in Brussels on a day-to-day basis. Despite some misgivings about dealing with the ambassadors rather than the ministers themselves, the Commission soon settled down to a harmonious and productive relationship with Coreper. In Luxembourg the Court of Justice quickly found its feet and began to produce an impressive body of Community case law, and the Assembly of the European Community, later to call itself the European Parliament, met for the first time in Strasbourg in January 1958.

The first Commission's nine portfolios, one for each commissioner, are a useful indicator of the Community's early agenda. In addition to one covering administration, there were portfolios for external relations, economic and financial affairs, the internal market, competition, social affairs, agriculture, transport, and overseas countries and territories. In some of these areas the Treaty dictated a specific timetable to implement certain measures; in others, it provided no more than general guidelines and statements of principle. The most immediate and tangible task was to establish the customs union. Thanks to French financial and economic reforms, the first intra-EC tariff reductions took place, on schedule, on January 1, 1959. As other rounds of tariff and quota cuts followed, the Community simultaneously started to erect a common external tariff. So successful were the first steps toward a customs union that the Community soon decided to accelerate its planned implementation. Eventually the customs union came into being on July 1, 1968, eighteen months earlier than stipulated in the Treaty.

The late 1950s and the early 1960s were years of extraordinarily high and sustained rates of economic growth in Western Europe, in large part because of an enormous escalation of international trade. Between 1958 and 1960 alone, trade among the Six grew by 50 percent. Mirrored by a similar development in the 1980s following the launch of the single market program, this dramatic rise was as much a result of "the increased activity of businessmen as [of] the actual reduction of tariffs. As soon as managers were convinced that the common market was going to be established, they started to behave in many ways as if it was already in existence."[23] High growth rates, a healthy balance of payments, and relatively stable prices provided incentives to coordinate the member states' economic policies, a step the Treaty merely hinted at but that the Commission eagerly pursued.

The Community's early economic success facilitated the assertion and general acceptance of its international identity. With the exception of the Soviet Union and its satellites, third countries quickly acknowledged the Commission's responsibility for commercial policy and opened diplomatic missions in Brussels. The Community's early external initiatives pointed in two directions: multilateral trade negotiations and Third World development. Under the former, the Commission assumed responsibility for member state participation in the Dillon and Kennedy rounds of the General Agreement on Tariffs and Trade (GATT). Robert Marjolin's observation on the Community's performance in the Kennedy Round would amuse today's U.S. trade negotiators and illustrates the excitement and naivete that infected Brussels during the EC's infancy: "The active and positive role played by the Community in the Kennedy Round was proof that it was not protectionist-minded and inward-looking, as its opponents charged, and that it was perfectly conscious of its responsibilities on a world scale."[24]

Successful first steps in commercial policy and external relations contrasted with the difficulty of fulfilling other Treaty objectives. Whereas tariff barriers between member states could easily be identified and eliminated, policies in areas such as competition, social affairs, transport, energy, and regional disparities were far harder to formulate. Progress was impeded by a combination of sometimes vague Treaty provisions, member state apathy or outright opposition, and philosophical and ideological differences between and within the Commission and Council of Ministers—factors that are as cogent in the EC today as they were in the early years. The result was a mixed record of policy formulation and implementation. On one important issue, for instance, the Commission took the view that without effective and undistorted competition the common market could not function properly and achieve its full potential. Thus, the Commission laid the groundwork for an ambitious competition policy by conducting numerous investigations and surveys of cartels, monopolies, state aids, preferential treatment, and other possible impediments to competition in the Community.[25] On transport policy, by contrast, the Community fared badly. One of the first academic studies of European integration in the 1960s concluded that "transport . . . is primarily a dismal story of false starts, of politically inept Commission proposals, of persistent Council inaction, of divided government views, and of apparent drift in the direction of more nationally [oriented] policies."[26]

The Community would face its greatest challenge and enjoy its greatest success in agriculture, although arguably at the cost of creating a monster. De Gaulle saw the vagueness of the CAP provisions as evidence of French weakness during the Treaty of Rome negotiations. In his own words, he came to power resolved to "put up a literally desperate fight, sometimes going so far as to threaten to withdraw our membership [in the EC]," until ultimately "France and common sense prevailed."[27] Common sense or no, de Gaulle should have credited the Commission's help. His determination to negotiate a comprehensive agricultural policy made de Gaulle and the Commission unlikely but effective allies. At crucial times, Hallstein's or Agriculture Commissioner Sicco Mansholt's mediation saved the talks from collapse, while the Commission's technical skill and expertise pushed the various proposals forward.

De Gaulle's refusal to acknowledge the Commission's role demonstrated his well-known hatred of the Brussels bureaucracy, a hatred fueled, paradoxically, by the Commission's invaluable assistance in formulating and implementing the CAP. During the course of the CAP negotiations in the early and mid-1960s, the Commission "steadily acquired new tasks, more staff, and enhanced authority and prestige" and simultaneously promoted "its own integrative purposes."[28] In particular, the Commission "saw agricultural negotiations as a golden opportunity to force de Gaulle's hand . . . in order to promote [its] vision of an integrated Europe under a federal executive, responsible to the European Parliament."[29] But the extent to which both sides used each other led to a fatal Commission miscalculation. De Gaulle's eagerness to complete the CAP convinced the Commission that a looming deadline to renegotiate a financial framework for the European Agricultural Guarantee and Guidance Fund (EAGGF) presented an opportunity to advance the integration agenda. As it was, the Commission's growing prominence and political influence infuriated de Gaulle. The Commission's attempt to link a further surrender of sovereignty with a successful conclusion of pending EAGGF negotiations pushed de Gaulle too far and provoked a crisis that paralyzed the Community.

THE 1963 CRISIS

Miriam Camps, a prolific chronicler of the European Community in the 1960s, claims that de Gaulle's rejection of Britain's application in 1963 was "in a very real sense . . . simply the first half of the more serious crisis that began with the French boycott of the Community in July 1965."[30]

Both events are indeed related. At issue was de Gaulle's conception of the Community and his espousal of a "European Europe." For de Gaulle, European integration in the supranational sense would have to be limited to the technical aspects of the Treaty of Rome. The Treaty of Rome could only succeed, however, in the context of a broader political framework of intergovernmental cooperation. Such cooperation was an essential prerequisite for the emergence of an economically strong, politically assertive, and militarily independent Europe. As the UK's worldview differed fundamentally from France's, de Gaulle could not take seriously Britain's candidacy for Community membership. Nor could he allow the Commission's efforts to strengthen supranationalism hinder his goal of intergovernmentalism. Thus the crisis, or crises, of 1963 and 1965 assume an air of inevitability, especially as de Gaulle set about achieving his wide-ranging European objectives in the early 1960s.

The Algerian settlement of 1962 gave de Gaulle security at home, enabling him to pursue a more ambitious policy abroad. At the same time, a warmer Cold War climate in the years following the 1962 Cuban Missile Crisis seemed propitious for de Gaulle's ambitious international initiatives. But de Gaulle did not wait until the mid-1960s to try to implement his European policy. On the contrary, one of his first undertakings upon returning to power in 1958 was to attempt to establish a "Union of States," both as a central plank of his European policy and as a prerequisite for subsequent efforts to challenge the United States and break down global bipolarity.

Having consulted Adenauer, de Gaulle launched his new initiative at a news conference in Paris in September 1960. Because the Community lacked "authority and . . . political effectiveness,"[31] de Gaulle proposed linking European integration with a revision of NATO. Despite the small member states' misgivings, a committee under the chairmanship of Christian Fouchet, French ambassador to Denmark, eventually drafted a design for a confederation of European states. With the goal of a common foreign and defense policy, as well as cooperation on cultural, educational, and scientific matters, the Fouchet Plan outlined an institutional framework that included a ministerial council, a commission of senior foreign ministry officials, and a consultative assembly of delegated national parliamentarians.

The Fouchet Plan was clearly incompatible with European integration as incorporated in the Treaty of Rome. Although Jean Monnet, a number of individual commissioners, and members of the European Parliament had commented favorably on de Gaulle's original idea, Community opposition grew as the plan took shape. Fearing French or Franco-German hegemony in a putative European organization that lacked the safeguards of supranationalism, the other member states followed the Netherlands' lead and fiercely resisted the idea. A series of acrimonious meetings in early 1962 caused the Fouchet Committee to collapse. Later that summer, de Gaulle abandoned his grandiose scheme for a "Union of States."

The failure of the Fouchet Plan had lasting repercussions for the Community and contributed directly to the 1965 crisis. At the height of that imbroglio, Maurice Couve de Murville, de Gaulle's foreign minister, declared that "economic Europe is in [such] a state . . . largely because political agreement did not follow [the Community's initial achievements]."[32] At approximately the same time, during one of his celebrated press conferences, de Gaulle lamented the lack of "an organized cooperation between states evolving . . . towards a confederation."[33] Clearly, de Gaulle's ultimately unsuccessful efforts to organize intergovernmental cooperation in Europe adversely affected the Community's development in the 1960s.

De Gaulle at least salvaged an institutionalized Franco-German alliance from the Fouchet wreckage. By contrast with the indifference and hostility of the smaller European partners, Germany had resolutely backed de Gaulle's scheme. To be more precise, Adenauer had resolutely backed the Fouchet Plan. With Adenauer's political and temporal life obviously drawing to an end (the chancellor was then eighty-seven years old), de Gaulle borrowed the Fouchet Plan's infrastructure to cement Franco-German rapprochement. Thus de Gaulle proposed regular meetings of the French president and the German chancellor, with their relevant ministers, to discuss cultural, economic, educational, and international issues. In the ensuing Franco-German Treaty of Friendship and Reconciliation, signed at the Elysée Palace in January 1963, both sides pledged "to consult each other, prior to any decision, on all questions of foreign policy . . . with a view to reaching an analogous position."[34]

The Elysée treaty was the pinnacle of Adenauer's international career, symbolizing as it did "the reconciliation between France and Germany, [which was] the core of his European policy."[35] But bitter political controversy in Germany came to a head during the ratification debate in May 1963, robbing the treaty of much of its value for de Gaulle. Alarmed by Adenauer's apparent acquiescence in de Gaulle's idiosyncratic European initiatives, a majority within the chancellor's own Christian Democratic Party joined with the parliamentary opposition to attach a crippling codicil to the treaty. A new preamble, inserted at the insistence of a majority in the Bundestag, asserted Germany's primary commitment to existing Alliance obligations. That action by foes of Adenauer's foreign policy "formally crystallized the differences in world view between [France and Germany]. Over the objections of Chancellor Adenauer, the Bundestag solemnly subordinated the Franco-German entente to Germany's multilateral obligations to the Atlantic Alliance, the EEC, and even the GATT. All of the graven images condemned by de Gaulle as obstacles to his European policy were affirmed."[36]

To make matters worse for de Gaulle, Adenauer's humiliation over the Elysée treaty made the chancellor's position untenable. Increasingly enfeebled by old age and dogged by a domestic political scandal, Adenauer resigned in April 1963. His successor, Ludwig Erhard, was a steadfast Atlanticist and an avowed adversary of de Gaulle's. Erhard's tenure as chancellor, from 1963 to 1966, saw a steady deterioration in Franco-German relations. "There is no point deceiving ourselves," de Gaulle remarked after a meeting with Erhard in July 1964, "the Franco-German Treaty of Cooperation has not yet developed as we had hoped. . . . Europe will only be a reality when France and Germany are truly united."[37]

Ironically, the Elysée treaty would achieve its potential and prove its worth not as an engine of European intergovernmental cooperation but as a foundation for closer integration in the Community. Despite his disappointment over the Bundestag's behavior in May 1963, de Gaulle continued to attend regular bilateral meetings under the terms of the treaty. More important, subsequent French presidents and German chancellors, as well as a host of government ministers and officials, similarly stuck to a fixed schedule of bilateral meetings. With the rapid improvement of Franco-German relations in the early 1970s and a growing consensus in both countries about the utility of European integration, these frequent, institutionalized contacts became the motor of Community momentum. As Pierre Pflimlin, a former president of the European Parliament, wrote in 1983: "Today, twenty years later, the [Elysée] Treaty . . . remains the basis for cooperation between the two countries, and is one of the few encouraging signs on the European scene."[38]

Knowledge of the Elysée treaty's subsequent role in strengthening European integration would undoubtedly have further infuriated de Gaulle. At the time, as well as advocating intergovernmentalism as a means of stunting the Community's political growth, de Gaulle sought to prevent the Community's extension geographically. The question of enlargement had formally arisen in 1961, when Britain reversed its policy and applied for Community membership. Harold Macmillan, who became prime minister after the Suez debacle in 1957, led Britain's accession effort. Macmillan advocated British membership for negative rather than positive reasons.[39] By the end of the 1950s it was readily apparent in London that the Commonwealth was an inadequate vehicle through which to promote British influence and prosperity in the world. By contrast, the Community flourished. Earlier attempts to dissolve the Community into a wider free trade area emphasized British fears of economic exclusion from the Continent. The failure of the free trade initiative and the corresponding success of the fledgling customs union convinced Britain's political and business leaders that the country's interests lay in full Community membership.

Yet deep suspicion of European integration and a lingering inclination toward isolationism tempered British enthusiasm. The opposition

Labour Party was deeply divided on the issue. A small group of passionate "pro-marketeers" balanced a corresponding clique of ardent "anti-marketeers," with the bulk of the party either uncertain or moderately hostile to membership. The Conservatives generally favored joining, although Macmillan purged the cabinet of a few "anti-marketeers" and appointed Edward Heath, who ultimately brought Britain into the Community in 1973, to lead the entry negotiations in Brussels.

In Macmillan's view, the decision to apply for Community membership complemented his foreign policy priority: restoring and maintaining the Anglo-American "special relationship." Initially, that meant "repairing the fences between Britain and America that Suez had broken down."[40] No sooner did Macmillan become prime minister than he set off to meet President Eisenhower in Bermuda. The two men had worked together in Algiers in 1943 trying to coordinate Anglo-American policy toward none other than General de Gaulle, then fighting for his political life as leader of the Free French Movement. Memories of the war years helped to put the special relationship back on track. Coincidentally, while Eisenhower and Macmillan reminisced in Bermuda, leaders of the Six signed the Treaty of Rome, which Macmillan did not even mention in his diaries.[41]

President Kennedy's election caused Macmillan to fret again about Anglo-American relations. Kennedy's youth, charisma, and Irish ancestry convinced the older, staid Macmillan that the special relationship was imperiled. At their first meeting, in Key West, Florida, in March 1961, Kennedy put Macmillan's fears to rest. For the remainder of Kennedy's brief administration, a remarkably close personal friendship between the president and prime minister cemented the Anglo-American special relationship.

Kennedy's unequivocal endorsement of British membership in the Community strengthened Macmillan's determination to join but aroused de Gaulle's suspicions. Moreover, Kennedy's "Grand Design" for closer U.S.-EC relations and a stronger Atlantic Alliance, outlined in a famous Independence Day speech in 1962, seemed at variance with de Gaulle's conception of a "European Europe." In de Gaulle's view, an equitable trans-Atlantic relationship was impossible as long as Western Europe was strategically subservient to the United States. Kennedy's espousal of British membership in the Community as part of his Grand Design unsettled de Gaulle further. By linking British accession and U.S. Alliance strategy, Kennedy possibly sealed the fate of Macmillan's application.[42]

Macmillan tried to overcome these profound differences with de Gaulle by appealing to past friendship and pursuing a close personal relationship. On June 30, 1958, soon after de Gaulle returned to power, Macmillan visited Paris. As the prime minister's biographer noted, "it was a momentous occasion for Macmillan, meeting again the man who had first come into his life in the dark days in Algiers fifteen years previously, and for whose cause he had fought so hard then. But for Macmillan's support for de Gaulle against Roosevelt and Churchill, almost certainly de Gaulle would not have been in Paris, at the helm, in 1958."[43] Undoubtedly de Gaulle owed Macmillan a huge political debt, but the latter's efforts to overcome de Gaulle's opposition to Britain's EC membership were pitiful. Macmillan's diary entry for November 26, 1961, written after a private visit from de Gaulle, reveals the prime minister's extreme frustration with, and acute misunderstanding of, the French president's position: "De Gaulle was no more conciliatory over the Common Market . . . the tragedy of it all is that we agree with de Gaulle on almost everything. We like the political Europe that de Gaulle likes. We are anti-federalists; so is he. . . . We agree; but his pride, his inherited hatred of England (since Joan of Arc) . . . above all, his intense 'vanity' for France—she must dominate—make him half welcome, half repel us, with a strange love-hate complex. Sometimes, when I am with him, I feel I have overcome it. But he goes back to his distrust and dislike, like a dog to vomit."[44]

Thus, Britain's entry negotiations took place under ominous circumstances. The talks themselves quickly became mired in a mass of technical detail, mostly over the CAP, the Commonwealth, and EFTA. A British white paper outlined the problems in all three areas. In agriculture, Britain's twin policies of buying low-priced food on the world market and paying farmers direct price support were incompatible with the principles of the CAP. As for the Commonwealth, Britain feared the political and economic impact on its former possessions of a sudden disruption of traditional trade patterns. Finally, "given [Britain's] obligations to our EFTA partners, we should not be able to join the Community until [we agreed upon] . . . ways and means of meeting their legitimate interests."[45]

In the event, developments in Anglo-American relations soon overshadowed the enlargement negotiations. Far from allaying de Gaulle's suspicion of London's subservience to Washington, British behavior throughout the talks convinced him that Britain should not be allowed to join the Community. Matters came to a head in December 1962 at a meeting between Macmillan and Kennedy to negotiate a new Anglo-American missile accord. Under the terms of the Nassau Agreement, Britain would use U.S. Polaris missiles as the delivery system for British nuclear warheads. Moreover, Britain's nuclear force would be integrated into NATO, except when the government "may decide that supreme national interests are at stake."[46]

For de Gaulle, then struggling to develop the French nuclear *force de frappe,* the Nassau Agreement represented a damning surrender of sovereignty. Britain had relinquished to the United States technological and strategic responsibility for a supposedly independent nuclear deterrent. There could have been no more graphic demonstration of Britain's irreconcilability with de Gaulle's "European Europe." Anticipating de Gaulle's negative reaction, Macmillan had gone to France in early December in a vain attempt to reassure the French president. Despite de Gaulle's opposition, Macmillan had then negotiated an agreement with Kennedy that was not only "politically lame and militarily awkward" but "a diplomatic catastrophe on a grand scale."[47] After a year of tough bargaining in Brussels, de Gaulle now had a cogent reason—excuse, really—to break off the enlargement negotiations.

He did so dramatically in a press conference on January 14, 1963. In a long, wide-ranging response to a planted question, de Gaulle catalogued the history of Britain's relationship with the Community. Having attempted to submerge the Community in a broad free trade area, Britain now sought to join, "but on her own conditions." Thus far, the entry negotiations had given little assurance that "Great Britain can place herself . . . inside a tariff which is genuinely common . . . renounce all Commonwealth preferences . . . cease any pretence that her agriculture be privileged, and, more than that . . . treat her engagements with other countries of the Free Trade Area as null and void." More to the point, were Britain to join without fundamentally changing its international orientation, the Community "would not endure for long . . . [but] instead would become a colossal Atlantic community under American domination and direction."[48] De Gaulle's statement amounted to a veto of Britain's EC application.

Paul-Henri Spaak, who chaired the committee that had drafted the Treaty of Rome, wrote melodramatically that January 14, 1963, the date of de Gaulle's press conference, "is fated to go down in history as the 'black Monday' of both European policy and Atlantic policy."[49] But as another observer remarked, the "crisis atmosphere" provoked by de Gaulle's statement "was not of long duration . . . because the concern of France's partners to push the Community forward was stronger than their irritation with French high-mindedness."[50] Though they regretted the way in which the negotiations came to an end, many member states and Community officials agreed that Britain was not yet ready for accession. As Marjolin remarked in his memoirs, de Gaulle's decision to close the door on Britain "offended France's continental partners possibly more through its form than through its content."[51]

The suspension of Britain's application was a serious setback for Macmillan and contrasted starkly with his apparent success in concluding the Nassau Agreement one month before. Nor can Macmillan have failed to notice that "de Gaulle was far from isolated in considering the British as still not yet fully prepared for membership of the Community."[52] There was nothing for Britain to do but await a favorable time in the future at which to reapply for membership and review in the meantime why the negotiations had stalled. Dejected, Macmillan resigned in October 1963 because of a purportedly terminal illness—but he went on to enjoy twenty-three years of robust retirement.

THE 1965 CRISIS

Having seen how decisively de Gaulle dealt with the British challenge to his "European Europe," it is remarkable how soon the Commission, supported by the other member states, set sail on a collision course with him over Community competence and institutional powers. The far more important Empty Chair crisis of 1965 resulted from a combination of Commission opportunism, Community resentment against French unilateralism, and de Gaulle's determination to limit further the Treaty of Rome's already restricted supranational provisions. The immediate result was virtual paralysis of the Community for the latter half of 1965 as French officials boycotted the Council of Ministers. Under the terms of the Luxembourg Compromise of January 1966, France resumed its participation in the Community, but the consequences of the crisis, particularly in terms of the Commission's self-confidence and the Council's decisionmaking procedure, persisted into the early 1980s.

The dispute erupted over the Commission's proposal to fund the CAP for the period between the expiration of the initial financial regulation in July 1965 and the end of the Community's transitional period in 1970. Once fully operational, the CAP was to have been funded by levies on agricultural imports into the Community, supplemented by duties on industrial imports. Together, these sums were to constitute the Community's "own" resources. With the industrial and agricultural common markets due to be completed ahead of schedule in July 1967, the Commission proposed that the Community acquire its own resources at that time. Suggesting that member states give up their import duties early was itself controversial. But emboldened by the successful implementation to date of commercial and agricultural provisions of the Rome treaty and by de Gaulle's obvious interest in securing a new financial regulation for the CAP, the Commission rashly went too far: It proposed a complex budgetary mechanism for the allocation of Community resources, by which the Commission itself and the European Parliament would greatly enhance their powers. The power of the Council of Ministers would correspondingly diminish through the substitution of majority voting for the unanimity requirement in certain cases.

This plan went far beyond what de Gaulle would ever accept and caused the inherently tense Paris-Brussels relationship to explode into open antagonism in the spring of 1965. As it was, de Gaulle despised the Brussels bureaucracy, dismissing Commission officials as stateless and denationalized. He denounced the "tendentious impropriety" of the Commission, a group "of international experts," in calling itself the Community's executive and protested the Commission's practice of accrediting third country diplomats assigned to the Community.[53] De Gaulle especially

detested Commission President Walter Hallstein, who used every opportunity to espouse European union along federal lines and enhance the
Commission's power.

De Gaulle's hatred of Hallstein, repugnance of the Commission,
and suspicion of the Community leap out of a celebrated passage in the
general's memoirs. Although lengthy, it is well worth quoting here:

> Walter Hallstein was Chairman of the Commission. He was
> ardently wedded to the thesis of the super-state, and bent all
> his skillful efforts towards giving the Community the char-
> acter and appearance of one. He had made Brussels, where
> he resided, into a sort of capital. There he sat, surrounded
> with all the trappings of sovereignty, directing his col-
> leagues, allocating jobs among them, controlling several
> thousand officials who were appointed, promoted and re-
> munerated at his discretion, receiving the credentials of for-
> eign ambassadors, laying claim to high honors on the occa-
> sion of his official visits, concerned above all to further the
> amalgamation of the Six, believing that the pressure of
> events would bring about what he envisaged. But after
> meeting him more than once and observing his activities, I
> felt that although Walter Hallstein was in his way a sincere
> European, he was first and foremost a German who was
> ambitious for his own country. For in the Europe that he
> sought lay the framework in which his country could first
> of all regain, free of charge, the respectability and equality
> of rights which the frenzy and defeat of Hitler had cost it,
> then acquire the preponderant influence which its economic
> strength would no doubt earn it.[54]

Marjolin, a member of Hallstein's Commission, warned his colleagues not to persist with the CAP proposals. Apart from their probable
political repercussions, the initiatives violated the Commission's "golden
rule" of not taking any action "likely to encounter an outright veto [by a
member state] that would have left no room for negotiation."[55] Undeterred
by Marjolin's warning, Hallstein pressed ahead and took the additional in-
flammatory step of first announcing the proposals not to the Council of
Ministers in Brussels but to the European Parliament in Strasbourg. Storm
clouds immediately appeared. "Our partners are indulging in wishful
thinking," Couve de Murville declared in the National Assembly on May
20, 1965, "by putting forward proposals which they know France will not
accept."[56]

Antagonized by de Gaulle's conduct in the Community and aware
of his desire to complete the CAP, the other member states prepared to
confront the general and call his bluff. A meeting between de Gaulle and

Erhard on June 11, 1965, failed to avert the crisis. Nor did the other five member states act on a French proposal to continue funding the CAP by national contributions, thereby avoiding the contentious question of Community control of its "own resources." French willingness "to sacrifice the material advantages of full Community support for agriculture in order to avoid the political implications of the Commission's plan" should have alerted the Council to the extent of de Gaulle's opposition.[57] Instead, few in the Five seemed alarmed by the looming deadline of June 30. Negotiations on the CAP, after all, had a reputation for running late.

The crucial Council meeting opened on June 28, with France in the chair. Taking a minimalist position, Couve de Murville pressed for a decision only on funding the CAP after July 1. With the others insisting that the Commission's proposals would have to be considered as a whole, substantive discussions had not even begun by midnight on June 30. Two hours later, the meeting broke up. The French government promptly recalled its permanent representative and announced that French officials would no longer participate in the Council of Ministers or its numerous committees.[58]

Faced with an empty French chair, the Community could do little more than conduct routine business. "By and large, the Five, throughout the summer, seemed anxious to maintain the best possible functioning of Community mechanisms, while at the same time taking care to avoid any actions which would make it more difficult for France to return to the negotiating table."[59] Far from backing down, however, de Gaulle raised the temperature by linking an additional, hitherto unrelated point to the original cause of the conflict. In a typically self-serving press conference on September 9, 1965, full of invective against the Commission and the European Parliament, de Gaulle announced that France would not accept a provision of the Treaty of Rome, due to be implemented on January 1, 1966, introducing qualified majority voting in the Council on a limited range of issues.[60]

De Gaulle attacked qualified majority voting and insisted on unanimity (in which any nation could unilaterally veto Community legislation), greatly exacerbating the crisis. The other member states shared France's concern about being outvoted in the Council but argued that important national interests were unlikely ever to be ignored. At a Council meeting held without France on October 25–26, the Five reaffirmed their commitment to the Community and refusal to renegotiate one of the Treaty's few supranational provisions. At the same time, they expressed willingness to compromise on the Commission's earlier proposals and offered France every opportunity to return to the negotiating table.[61]

The "uniting of the Five into a cohesive body under German leadership"[62] undoubtedly impressed de Gaulle and may have been a factor in his decision to resume talks. French public opinion was arguably a more important consideration. Farmers' organizations and business interests feared the consequences of a protracted Community crisis, and the presidential election of December 1965 gave them a unique opportunity to express their point of view. Although other issues were involved, "for the first time the unity of Europe became the central theme of a national election campaign."[63] François Mitterrand, de Gaulle's main rival, called himself "the candidate of Europe."[64] Deprived of an absolute majority in the first round of balloting, de Gaulle and Mitterrand contested the second round alone. As expected, de Gaulle won, but by the surprisingly narrow margin of 11 percent.

The election result demonstrated the domestic limits on de Gaulle's EC policy. Although notoriously insensitive to French public opinion, as the simmering student unrest of 1967 and 1968 would soon show, de Gaulle undoubtedly got the message. A week after the election, the French foreign minister announced his willingness to attend a meeting of Community counterparts in Luxembourg—without Commission participation. At that meeting, held on January 17–18, 1966, Couve de Murville presented a ten-point memorandum complaining about the Commission's behavior and pressed the case against majority voting in the Council. Both sides seemed eager to compromise.

The crisis finally came to a close at the foreign ministers meeting of January 28–29, 1966. The Six agreed to adopt an interim financial regulation for the CAP, deferring the question of the Community's own resources and, by extension, the European Parliament's budgetary power. Majority voting in the Council of Ministers remained the outstanding issue. After restating their positions, both sides approved a short declaration, the Luxembourg Compromise, which amounted to an agreement to disagree:

1. When issues very important to one or more member countries are at stake, the members of the Council will try, within a reasonable time, to reach solutions which can be adopted by all members of the Council, while respecting their mutual interests, and those of the Community.
2. The French delegation considers that, when very important issues are at stake, discussions must be continued until unanimous agreement is reached.
3. The six delegations note that there is a divergence of views on what should be done in the event of a failure to reach complete agreement.
4. However, they consider that this divergence does not prevent the Community's work being resumed in accordance with the normal procedure.[65]

Ostensibly, the outcome was a draw, perhaps even a victory for the Community: The French presidential election had apparently clipped de Gaulle's wings, the Five had not reneged on majority voting, and the Community soon resumed full operation. In reality, however, the crisis ended in victory for de Gaulle. The Council approved temporary funding for the EAGGF in May 1966, and the CAP continued to function effectively. In the meantime, the Commission's ambitious proposals to revise budgetary procedures had sunk out of sight. From de Gaulle's point of view, the situation in early 1966 was highly satisfactory. Not only was the CAP secure, but "the issue of supranationalism, which the Hallstein Commission had adroitly attempted to tie into the agricultural arrangements, had been dealt a resounding defeat."[66] As a result, the crisis had profoundly undermined both Hallstein's credibility and the Commission's confidence. Thereafter, the Commission refrained from asserting itself in the Community for over a decade.

More important, despite the Five's statement of support for majority voting, the Luxembourg Compromise impeded effective decisionmaking in the Community for a long time to come. De Gaulle's insistence on unanimity heightened the member states' awareness of each other's special interests and increased their reluctance to call a vote in the Council even when no vital interest was at stake. The Luxembourg Compromise did not disrupt established decisionmaking procedures in the Community, because majority voting had never been the norm. Instead, as Joe Weiler has observed, "it symbolized a transformation from a 'Community' spirit to a more selfish and pragmatic 'cost-benefit' attitude of the member states. It was a change of ethos, at first rejected by the Five but later, especially after the first enlargement, eagerly seized upon by all. In this sense the danger to the Community, even if not always tangible, was significant."[67]

To some extent the crisis demonstrated "that the Community is dependent on a political environment over which, in the final analysis, it has little control."[68] But the crisis also helped shape the political climate in which the Community operated during the next decade. Six months of near-paralysis in Brussels, a heavy blow to the Commission's morale, and a substantial setback to majority voting had an invidious effect. In the final analysis, "the Community and the Western European states moved closer to Gaullist confederal notions, while the European federalists lost ground."[69]

THE GAULLIST ILLUSION

The end of the Empty Chair crisis freed de Gaulle to confront the Atlantic Alliance, for him a far more insidious organization than the European

Community. Not that the Community and NATO were unrelated. After all, the United States had supported European integration from the outset, partly for strategic reasons. De Gaulle sensed that a stronger, supranational Community, closely allied to the United States, would enhance U.S. hegemony over the Continent. As it was, the Alliance epitomized and institutionalized U.S. control over Western Europe. De Gaulle was a staunch believer in international alliances but viewed NATO as structurally unsound and strategically unstable. Especially since the Cuban Missile Crisis, when the Soviet Union had implicitly acknowledged its military inferiority, NATO seemed more of a hindrance than a help in enhancing international security.

But attacking NATO was not an end in itself. Instead, it constituted an important part of de Gaulle's plan to "liberate" Europe, East and West. The Warsaw Pact was equally repugnant to de Gaulle, although ostensibly less dangerous than NATO in the post–Cuban Missile Crisis period. In any event, de Gaulle was much better placed to undermine NATO than to undo the Warsaw Pact. As a large, strategically important member of the Alliance, France could diminish from within U.S. ascendancy in Western Europe. At the same time, de Gaulle sought to weaken from outside Soviet control over Eastern Europe. Accordingly, France cultivated close relations with Moscow, simultaneously supporting those Warsaw Pact countries that attempted to pursue an "independent" foreign policy.

The mid-1960s was a crucial time for de Gaulle to assault the superpower system. With the Soviet Union absorbing the lessons of the missile crisis and the United States becoming increasingly embroiled in Vietnam, the two foes seemed to be moving toward a rapprochement with each other. The first stirrings of detente alerted de Gaulle to the danger of superpower condominium in Europe. Far from enhancing Europe's security, the onset of detente threatened to fossilize the Cold War fracture between East and West. Just as the Big Three had met, without France, to carve up the Continent at the end of World War II, now the Big Two would meet, without Europe, to perpetuate bipolarity.

De Gaulle's withdrawal from NATO's integrated military command, his expulsion of Allied troops from France, and his ejection of the Alliance's headquarters are the best-known events in his campaign to weaken the U.S. position in Western Europe. All took place in 1966, "the climactic year of his foreign policy-making," during which de Gaulle also visited Moscow.[70] The Soviet trip produced nothing tangible and hardly compared with theatrical initiatives in NATO. Yet it emphasized de Gaulle's determination to seek an opening in the East commensurate with a lessening of the United States' role in the West.

As a counterpoint to what he saw as U.S. cultural imperialism and Soviet cultural enslavement, de Gaulle championed close cultural and educational links between Western and Eastern Europe. Going beyond such ties, he encouraged efforts by Soviet bloc states to pursue their own foreign policies. Despite its Stalinist domestic practices, Romania seemed ahead of other Eastern European countries in this sphere. Romania's willingness to deviate from the Soviet foreign policy norm reinforced de Gaulle's conviction in the ability of European states, East and West, to weaken and ultimately throw off the superpower yoke. Czechoslovakia's domestic liberalization and agitation inside the Warsaw Pact offered a more striking example.

Britain's second application for EC membership, in May 1967, coincided with the intensive phase of Gaullist internationalism. This time a Labour Party government knocked on the Community's door. Prime Minister Harold Wilson was equivocal about joining the Community but, like Macmillan in the early 1960s, saw no feasible alternative. If anything, Britain's declining political and economic links with the Commonwealth and growing commercial contacts with the Community increased the urgency of accession. Nevertheless, the issue split the Labour Party, pitting a pro-Europe wing on the center and right against the anti-marketeers (with powerful trade union support) on the left. Wilson had to warn his cabinet colleagues, under pain of dismissal, to maintain unity and to adhere to the principle of collective responsibility while the government again explored the option of membership.

Also like Macmillan before him, Wilson based his optimism about overcoming French opposition to British entry partly on personal considerations. Symbolizing a break with the past, Wilson first met de Gaulle at Churchill's funeral in January 1965. In the following months he fostered a warm relationship with de Gaulle, especially during a visit to Paris in April. Apart from offering a fresh personal perspective, Wilson brought with him an ambivalence about the Anglo-American special relationship. As the United States became more involved in Vietnam, he distinguished himself as one of Washington's most severe public critics. Moreover, Wilson shared French concerns about the long-term implication for European industry of U.S. technological superiority. The British prime minister's emphasis on the need for European technological innovation struck a sympathetic chord in Paris.[71]

Despite these seemingly favorable circumstances, Wilson did not take lightly the challenge of a second application. First, he authorized a number of detailed economic studies to bolster the domestic case for membership. Second, he initiated three lengthy parliamentary debates to build political support for another entry attempt. A parliamentary vote overwhelmingly in favor of joining the Community, taken on the eve of the second application, veiled the real extent of division in the House of Commons and in the country. Third, Wilson reassured EFTA representatives about Britain's intentions and sent emissaries to the Commonwealth countries. Fourth, he and his foreign secretary, George Brown, tested the water by visiting Community capitals and exploring with the member states possible problems for both sides should negotiations eventually begin.[72]

Throughout that time, de Gaulle reserved judgment on Britain's intention to reapply for membership. Only when Wilson submitted Britain's second application on May 12, 1967, did the president express an opinion. Four days later, in yet another of his celebrated press conferences, de Gaulle delivered what became known as the "velvet veto." Condescendingly claiming that the British, "so magnificently gifted with ability and courage," had not yet achieved "the profound economic and political transformation which would allow them to join the Six," de Gaulle implied that his objection to Britain's membership of the Community still stood.[73] Six months of confusion followed, during which Britain and the Five attempted to clarify the situation and decide whether negotiations should begin. Following a favorable Commission opinion, talks seemed set to start by the end of 1967. Using the occasion of his biannual press conference, however, de Gaulle clearly spelled out his opposition to Britain's EC entry. Dismissing the application as "the fifth act of a play during which England has taken up very different and apparently inconsistent attitudes towards the Common Market," de Gaulle asserted categorically that Britain's entry "would obviously mean the breaking up of a Community which has been built and which functions according to rules which would not bear such a monumental exception."[74] There was no longer any doubt about the issue. On December 20, 1967, the Foreign Office announced that, in effect, Britain would shelve its application.

De Gaulle had blocked Britain's second application for essentially the same reasons as before. Despite Wilson's frustration with Washington, the Anglo-American special relationship remained fundamentally sound and, in de Gaulle's view, a barrier to British membership in the Community. Nor did de Gaulle wish to tip "the delicate political and economic balance within the [Six] that still favored France's leadership role."[75] Yet de Gaulle was obviously attempting to stem the tide of change inside and outside the EC. Germany, then "an economy in search of a political purpose,"[76] clearly had the potential to displace Paris as the center of gravity in the Community. In the broader international context, whether or not Britain entered the Community would likely have little impact on the configuration of the existing superpower system.

Domestic and international developments in 1968 abruptly ended the Gaullist illusion. At home, social unrest erupted in May 1968 in a series of riots and strikes that threatened to topple not only the government but also the regime. De Gaulle's focus on foreign policy had blinded him to the extent of growing domestic dissatisfaction. Significantly, he was on a visit to Romania when the crisis blew up. Protesting a rigid educational system and declining living standards, millions of students and workers poured onto French city streets. A brutal police response, relayed nightly on television news, exacerbated the problem. After a month of unrest, the Fifth Republic seemed on the brink of collapse. What saved it, perhaps, was the unwillingness or inability of the Communist Party to exploit the situation fully. The government also survived, but not because of de Gaulle. The general fled Paris at the height of the crisis, apparently to assure himself of the support of the French army in Germany, leaving his prime minister, Georges Pompidou, to find a solution. Pompidou did so brilliantly, largely by gambling on time and capitalizing on the inevitable public reaction against incessant instability. Having dissolved parliament and called new elections in June 1968, the Gaullists and their allies won an overall majority.

It proved a pyrrhic victory. The events of May 1968 demolished de Gaulle's personal popularity and fatally compromised his credibility as president. Moreover, the crisis further weakened the country economically and caused serious financial instability. Cumulatively, these factors undermined the domestic basis for de Gaulle's ambitious foreign policy. At the same time, a disastrous development abroad compounded de Gaulle's difficulties at home. The Soviet invasion of Czechoslovakia in August 1968 ruthlessly revealed the limits of "independence" in Eastern Europe and represented a slap in the face for France. The Brezhnev Doctrine, promulgated by the Soviet leader to justify the ouster of a reform government in Prague, put an end to de Gaulle's efforts to free Europe of superpower control.

Although his term of office was not due to expire for another four years, after the domestic and international upheavals of 1968 de Gaulle increasingly looked like a lame-duck president. The Five awaited de Gaulle's departure before taking any new initiatives, and the Community continued to operate and to recover from the disruption of the 1965 crisis. A treaty to merge the institutions of the three communities (ECSC, EEC, and Euratom), signed in April 1965, came into effect on July 1, 1967. Also in 1967, the Kennedy Round of the GATT, in which the Commission negotiated for the member states, came to a successful conclusion. Earlier landmarks in the Community's external relations included association agreements with Greece (1962) and Turkey (1964) and the Yaounde Convention of Association between the Community and seventeen African states and Madagascar (1964).

As the 1960s came to a close, enlargement remained the outstanding external issue for the Community. De Gaulle seemed the sole obstacle to British entry. Yet a curious incident in February 1969 revealed that he might have changed his mind. At a meeting in the Elysée Palace with Christopher Soames, Britain's ambassador in Paris, de Gaulle spoke of possible British membership in a broader and weaker European Community directed by Britain, France, Germany, and Italy, which would form the nucleus of an association of Western European countries independent of the United States. De Gaulle's vague proposal appeared to have been motivated by his recent foreign policy setbacks and by a belated realization of Germany's growing economic and political power within the Community.

According to the British record, de Gaulle suggested to Soames that Britain and France pursue the proposal bilaterally before consulting the other countries concerned.[77] Furious over the two previous vetoes and suspecting a French diplomatic trap, the British Foreign Office released a record of the de Gaulle–Soames conversation to a number of European posts, which in turn informed their host governments. This act incensed de Gaulle, who accused the British of indiscretion and breach of trust.[78] Whether or not de Gaulle had changed his mind about British membership of the Community, the Soames affair ensured that enlargement was not an option as long as he remained in power. For all the international changes of the past six months, Anglo-French relations had reached their lowest ebb since de Gaulle's first veto six years before.

The repercussions of the Soames affair did not last long. To everyone's surprise, de Gaulle was out of office within six weeks. Defeat in two referenda in April 1969, one about the structure of local government and the other about reform of the Senate, prompted de Gaulle's departure. Those relatively inconsequential issues, on the outcome of which he had staked his presidency, brought the decade of de Gaulle abruptly to an end. For France, the immediate question concerned the stability of the regime and the durability of the Gaullist republic without de Gaulle. Presuming that France survived the succession, which it easily did, enlargement would once again become the most pressing point for the Community.

Western European and North American leaders watched de Gaulle go with a mixture of relief and regret—relief because progress within the Community and harmony within the Alliance finally seemed assured; regret because, for all de Gaulle's foibles and illusions, few could doubt his eminence or achievements. De Gaulle had done more than restore French pride and self-esteem. He had saved his country's honor during the occupation and collaboration, ensured its stability during the liberation, and rescued its liberal democratic institutions during the Algerian crisis. In addition to leading France to prominence in the postwar world, de Gaulle gave Europe a greater sense of identity and purpose at a time of subordination to the superpowers. Even the Americans, who suffered most from de Gaulle's assertive foreign policy, readily acknowledged his sagacity and statesmanship.[79] As Stanley Hoffmann observed, whatever one's point of view, "it is impossible not to be impressed by de Gaulle's life and works. . . . One does not often come so clearly in contact with greatness."[80]

NOTES

1. Stanley Hoffmann, review of *De Gaulle: The Rebel, 1890–1944*, by Jean Lacouture, in the *New Republic*, December 17, 1990, p. 34.

2. For an assessment of De Gaulle's extraordinary political career, see Jean Lacouture's two-part biography, *De Gaulle: The Rebel, 1890–1944* (New York: Norton, 1990), and *De Gaulle: The Ruler, 1945–1970* (London: Collins-Harvill, 1991).

3. Quoted in Jean Monnet, *Memoirs* (Garden City, NY: Doubleday, 1978), p. 430.

4. *Ibid.*

5. Edward Kolodziej, *French International Policy Under de Gaulle and Pompidou: The Politics of Grandeur* (Ithaca: Cornell University Press, 1974), pp. 192, 275.

6. *Le Monde,* January 15, 1963.

7. Quoted in Edmond Jouve, *Le Général de Gaulle et la Construction de l'Europe (1940–1966)* (Paris: Librairie Générale de Droit et de Jurisprudence, R. Pichon et R. Durand-Auzias, 1967), p. 253.

8. David Calleo, *Europe's Future: The Grand Alternatives* (New York: Horizon Press, 1965), p. 54.

9. Harold Wilson, *Memoirs: The Making of a Prime Minister, 1916–1986* (London: Weidenfeld & Nicolson, 1986), p. 91.

10. Lois Pattison de Menil, *Who Speaks for Europe?: The Vision of Charles de Gaulle* (London: Weidenfeld & Nicolson, 1977), pp. 132–133.

11. Charles de Gaulle, *Memoirs of Hope: Renewal and Endeavor* (New York: Simon and Schuster, 1971), p. 143.

12. Stanley Hoffmann, "De Gaulle, Europe and the Atlantic Alliance," *International Organization* 18, no. 1 (Winter 1964): 27

13. De Gaulle, *Memoirs,* pp. 165–166.

14. De Gaulle, *Memoirs,* p. 167.

15. See Hans von der Groeben, *The European Community: The Formative Years: The Struggle to Establish the Common Market and the Political Union (1958–66),* European Perspectives Series (Luxembourg: Office for Official Publications of the European Communities, 1985), pp. 51–53.

16. Robert Marjolin, *Architect of European Unity: Memoirs, 1911–1986* (London: Weidenfeld & Nicolson, 1989), p. 318.

17. EFTA Ministerial Communiqué, July 31, 1961, reproduced in Frances Nicholson and Roger East, *From the Six to the Twelve: The Enlargement of the European Communities* (Chicago: St. James, 1987), p. 5.

18. Kolodziej, *French Policy,* pp. 282–283.

19. Von der Groeben, *Formative Years,* p. 32.

20. See Kolodziej, *French Policy,* pp. 118–120.

21. Marjolin, *Memoirs,* p. 310.

22. Von der Groeben, *Formative Years,* p. 45.

23. John Pinder, "Implications for the Operation of the Firm," *Journal of Common Market Studies* 1, no. 1 (1962): 41.

24. Marjolin, *Memoirs,* p. 345.

25. See von der Groeben, *Formative Years,* pp. 59–64.

26. Leon Lindberg, *The Political Dynamics of European Economic Integration* (Stanford: Stanford University Press, 1963), p. 143.

27. De Gaulle, *Memoirs,* pp. 159, 186–187.

28. John Keeler, "De Gaulle and Europe's CAP: The Logic and Legacies of Nationalistic Integration," *Foreign Policy and Security* 8, no. 4, 1966, pp. 66–67.

29. De Menil, *Who Speaks for Europe?* p. 143.

30. Miriam Camps, *European Unification in the Sixties: From the Veto to the Crisis* (New York: McGraw-Hill, for the Council on Foreign Relations, 1966), p. 3. Her other books include *What Kind of Europe?: The Community Since de Gaulle's Veto* (London: Oxford University Press, 1965); *Britain and the European Community, 1955–1963* (Princeton: Princeton University Press, 1964); and *The European Common Market and Free Trade Area* (Princeton: Center for International Studies, 1957).

31. Charles de Gaulle, *Major Addresses, Statements and Press Conferences* (New York: French Embassy, Press and Information, 1964), p. 93.

32. Quoted in Françoise de la Serre, "The EEC and the 1965 Crisis," in F. Roy Willis, ed., *European Integration* (New York: New Viewpoints, 1975), p. 144.

33. *Le Monde,* September 10, 1965.

34. Kolodziej, *French Policy,* p. 316.

35. Wolfram Hanrieder, *Germany, America, Europe: Forty Years of German Foreign Policy* (New Haven: Yale University Press, 1989), p. 261.

36. Kolodziej, *French Policy,* p. 318.

37. Quoted in *Le Monde,* July 7, 1964.

38. Pierre Pflimlin, foreword to von der Groeben, *Formative Years,* p. 9.

39. See Stephen George, *An Awkward Partner: Britain in the European Community* (Oxford: Clarendon Press, 1990), pp. 30–33. For an authoritative account of Britain's first failed attempts to join the Community, see Jock Bruce-Gardyne and Nigel Lawson, *The Power Game: An Examination of Decision-Making in Government* (Hamden, CT: Archon Books, 1976), pp. 38–79.

40. Alastair Horne, *Harold Macmillan,* vol. 2 (New York: Viking, 1989), p. 21.

41. Horne, *Macmillan,* vol. 2, p. 30.

42. See Alfred Grosser, *The Western Alliance: European-American Relations Since 1945* (New York: Vantage, 1982), pp. 199–208.

43. Horne, *Macmillan,* vol. 2, p. 312.

44. Quoted in Horne, *Macmillan,* vol. 2, p. 319.

45. The white paper is reproduced in Nicholson and East, *Enlargement,* pp. 14–21.

46. Nicholson and East, *Enlargement,* pp. 25–26. On the *Skybolt* crisis that precipitated the Nassau Agreement, see Richard Neustadt, *Alliance Politics* (New York: Columbia University Press, 1970), pp. 52–55.

47. Hoffmann, "De Gaulle," pp. 10, 13.

48. Quoted in Nicholson and East, *Enlargement,* pp. 30–32.

49. Paul-Henri Spaak, "Hold Fast," in *Foreign Affairs* 41, no. 4 (1963): 611.

50. De Menil, *Who Speaks for Europe?,* p. 136.

51. Marjolin, *Memoirs,* p. 338.

52. Roy Pryce, "Britain Out of Europe?" *Journal of Common Market Studies* 2, no. 1 (1963): 5.

53. De Gaulle, *Major Addresses,* p. 147.

54. De Gaulle, *Memoirs,* p. 148.

55. Marjolin, *Memoirs,* p. 314.

56. Quoted in de la Serre, "Crisis," p. 134.

57. De Menil, *Who Speaks for Europe?* p. 149.

58. See John Lambert, "The Constitutional Crisis, 1965–66," *Journal of Common Market Studies* 4, no. 3 (May 1966): 205–206.

59. De la Serre, "Crisis," p. 141.

60. *Le Monde,* September 10, 1965.

61. Lambert, "Constitutional Crisis," p. 220.

62. Robert Mowat, *Creating the European Community* (New York: Barnes & Noble, 1973), p. 187.

63. Altiero Spinelli, *The Eurocrats: Conflict and Crisis in the European Community* (Baltimore: Johns Hopkins University Press, 1966), p. 212.

64. Lambert, "Constitutional Crisis," p. 220.

65. Reproduced in Lambert, "Constitutional Crisis," p. 226.

66. De Menil, *Who Speaks for Europe?* p. 154.

67. Joseph Weiler, "The Genscher-Colombo Draft European Act: The Politics of Indecision," *Journal of European Integration* 4, nos. 2 and 3: 134.

68. De la Serre, "Crisis," p. 151.

69. Kolodziej, *French Policy*, p. 337.

70. Anton de Porte, *Europe Between the Superpowers: The Enduring Balance* (New Haven: Yale University Press, 1979), p. 35.

71. Wilson, *Memoirs*, pp. 71 *passim.*

72. Nicholson and East, *Enlargement*, pp. 42–47.

73. Nicholson and East, *Enlargement*, p. 49.

74. Nicholson and East, *Enlargement*, pp. 52–53.

75. Kolodziej, *French Policy*, p. 376.

76. Henry Kissinger, *White House Years* (New York: Little, Brown & Co., 1979), p. 97.

77. Nicholson and East, *Enlargement*, pp. 58–59.

78. In his memoirs, Wilson accused the Foreign Office of exceeding its instructions. See Wilson, *Memoirs*, pp. 607–620.

79. See Kissinger, *White House Years*, pp. 104–111.

80. Hoffmann, review of *De Gaulle: The Rebel*, p. 29.

3

A Community in Flux,
1969–1979

The terms "Eurosclerosis" and "Europessimism" encapsulate the history of the Community in the mid-1970s. After the frustration of the 1960s, the Community seemed set at the start of the 1970s to shake off the shackles of Gaullism and begin an invigorating new phase of its development. "Completion, deepening, enlargement," a slogan popularized by President Pompidou and endorsed by the Six at the Hague summit of 1969, summed up the optimism of the post–de Gaulle era. But the accomplishments of the early 1970s—the accession of three member states, the adoption of a plan for Economic and Monetary Union (EMU), and the launch of a procedure for foreign policy coordination—soon gave way to severe economic and political strains as the Community absorbed the impact of enlargement and reeled under the shock of the oil embargo. For the remainder of the decade, the future of the Community seemed in even greater danger than it had at the height of the Gaullist challenge.

The threat to the Community in the 1970s was of an altogether different kind than that of the 1960s. Whereas the crises of 1963 and 1965 originated in the determination of a single individual to defy and remold the existing international system, the continuous crisis of the mid-1970s had at its heart the Community's struggle with a profound transformation in the international system itself. As Peter Ludlow has pointed out, the development of the Community until 1989 can be divided into two parts. The first, from the early 1950s to the early 1970s, saw a "low policy" Community thrive in the relatively rigid Cold War climate of unquestioned U.S. hegemony, German diplomatic diffidence, generally stable exchange rates, and unprecedented prosperity in the member states. The second, from that time onward, saw the Community gradually acquire a "high policy" profile in the radically changing circumstances of fluctuating superpower relations, marked U.S. decline, growing German assertiveness, oscillating exchange rates, and widely uneven economic performance among the member states.[1] The history of the Community in the 1970s is the history of a Community in flux, attempting to cope with fundamental changes in the international system and fighting for survival in a radically altered political and economic environment.

The emergence of the European Council and the effectiveness of the Paris-Bonn axis, personified for much of the decade by the friendship between President Valéry Giscard d'Estaing and Chancellor Helmut Schmidt, explain to a great extent the Community's durability during that turbulent time. But the formalization of EC summitry and the dynamism of the Franco-German alliance failed in the mid-1970s to invigorate the Community. For all their apparent commitment to European integration, Giscard and Schmidt made little effort to get the Community out of the abyss. Moreover, their highly personalized style accentuated and initially perpetuated one of the Community's gaping weaknesses at the time: the feebleness and impotence of the Commission. Only in the late 1970s, thanks in part to Commission President Roy Jenkins's role in launching the European Monetary System (EMS), did the Commission regain its confidence and sense of purpose.

Thus, the decade after de Gaulle's departure was dispiriting but decisive in the history of the Community. The oil price shocks, economic recession, bloated CAP, and recalcitrant British severely tested the Community's solidarity, especially in view of the optimism generated by the "Spirit of The Hague." Yet the Community survived and ultimately emerged in the early 1980s with a powerful European Council, a directly elected parliament, a proven procedure for foreign policy cooperation, a fledgling monetary system, and an awareness of the need to amend decisionmaking procedures before further enlargement took place. More important, perhaps, the trials and tribulations of the 1970s convinced the Community's leaders in the 1980s—in the Commission, the Parliament, and the member states—of the urgent need for institutional reform and policy innovation. As a result, the years between 1969 and 1978 represent not only a transition in the postwar international system that tested the Community's resilience but also a critical bridge between the Community's early attainments and its later triumphs.

THE SPIRIT OF THE HAGUE

Georges Pompidou, de Gaulle's successor as president of France, held the key to the Community's development in the immediate aftermath of the general's resignation. Having served as prime minister of France for much of the 1960s, Pompidou was steeped in Gaullism. But de Gaulle had dismissed Pompidou in the immediate aftermath of the student unrest in 1968, and relations between them had quickly soured. Pompidou exacted sweet revenge by winning the presidential election in 1969. To what extent would personal bitterness color the new president's European policy?

Pompidou was intelligent, sophisticated, and highly educated. By nature cautious and conservative, he had finely honed political skills and instincts. Pompidou was too clever to let personal pique dictate his policy toward the Community. Instead, he sought to balance Gaullist hostility toward European integration on the one hand with growing resentment throughout the Community against French obduracy on the other. This balancing act inevitably caused Pompidou domestic political difficulty. Was he "a faithful lieutenant merely adapting the General's doctrine to new circumstances, or an ungrateful successor betraying his heritage?"[2] In order to appease the Gaullist right, Pompidou had to emphasize the former; in order to consolidate the support of the Gaullist left and the center of the French political spectrum, he had to encourage a departure from the past.

On one aspect of Community policy, at least, Pompidou was unashamedly Gaullist. Like the general before him, Pompidou rejected supranationalism and espoused intergovernmentalism.[3] Pompidou's election manifesto unequivocally advocated a confederalist rather than a federalist Europe. On other aspects of EC policy, Pompidou was far less dogmatic. Enlargement posed a real dilemma for the new president. For Gaullist diehards, although not necessarily for de Gaulle himself, the veto of Britain's application had become sacrosanct. Yet for a growing portion of the French public and for France's EC partners, revoking the veto was the only means by which France could possibly retain influence and credibility in the Community.

Regardless of Pompidou's personal and political preferences, there was an obvious objective change in France's circumstances in the late 1960s that impelled the president toward accepting enlargement. The events of 1968 had enfeebled France economically. High inflation and a deteriorating balance of trade were a consequence of de Gaulle's generous wage settlement with the unions and his loose monetary policy to boost recovery and stimulate growth. The result was a run on the franc that culminated in Pompidou's decision to devalue by 12.5 percent in August 1969. These persistent economic and monetary problems lowered France's international standing and made continued French participation in the Community more important than ever before. Consequently, Pompidou was in a far weaker position than de Gaulle to veto British membership.

Just as France had declined economically in the late 1960s, Germany had surged ahead. Here was another objective consideration that affected Pompidou's range of EC policy options. Not only was Germany economically resurgent, but under the new chancellor, Willy Brandt, the Federal Republic was also politically assertive. Gone were the days of Adenauer's subservience to, and his successors' awe of, General de Gaulle. Germany's refusal to arrest the declining value of the franc by revaluing the mark emphasized Bonn's determination to assert itself internationally.[4] In addition, the new German government was about to launch an ambitious initiative toward Eastern Europe and the Soviet Union. The combination of Germany's growing economic power and rising political confidence made enlargement a more appealing alternative for Pompidou. Together, Britain and France in the West might counterbalance Germany's increasing weight in the East and establish geopolitical symmetry in the Community.

Germany's *Ostpolitik,* or new policy toward the East, replaced the inflexible Hallstein Doctrine of nonrecognition of any Western state that recognized East Germany diplomatically. As foreign minister in the Grand Coalition government of the mid-1960s, Brandt had taken the first tentative steps in the bold new direction of "normalizing" relations with the East. As chancellor of the Social Democratic–Free Democratic coalition that came to power in September 1969, Brandt elevated *Ostpolitik* to a central tenet of German foreign policy. The Christian Democrats, in opposition for the first time in the history of the Federal Republic, reacted predictably by denouncing *Ostpolitik* as a sellout of German interests in the East and a threat to Germany's Alliance ties in the West.[5]

The domestic controversy over *Ostpolitik* fueled an equally contentious debate in the Atlantic Alliance and the EC. Just as German unification in 1990 caused speculation in the Community that Germany's foreign policy orientation would drift to the East, so too did *Ostpolitik* raise the specter for Germany's allies of a rootless, neutralist Federal Republic loosening its moorings in the West. In its extreme form, this apprehension gave rise to a false dichotomy between the pursuit of an imaginative *Ostpolitik* and a continuing commitment to the EC, which Brandt's domestic opposition eagerly exploited.

Allied and internal Christian Democratic concern about *Ostpolitik* obliged Brandt to emphasize his support for European integration, which in any event he genuinely espoused. Moreover, Brandt stressed the importance of British accession as a means of reassuring those Community member states who feared Germany's resurgence. In the UK, Prime Minister Harold Wilson used *Ostpolitik* to further his goal of EC entry by arguing that British accession would restrain German nationalist ambition. In France, Pompidou similarly cited *Ostpolitik* as a reason to enlarge the Community. Whether or not Pompidou deliberately exploited *Ostpolitik* in order to undermine Gaullist opposition to British entry, undoubtedly he harbored genuine misgivings about the consequences for the Community of Germany's new foreign policy initiative.

From the vantage point of the White House, Henry Kissinger, then President Nixon's national security adviser, watched these developments closely. The United States shared the other Allies' concerns about *Ostpolitik* and welcomed Germany's renewed commitment to the Community as a check against a possible pull to the East. Kissinger noted approvingly that "Brandt's opening to the East had the unintended consequence of spurring West European integration. Of the three most important European leaders, two [Wilson and Pompidou] distrusted the tendencies unleashed by the third [Brandt], and the third needed a gesture by which to assuage these suspicions. British entry into the Common Market provided the mechanism."[6]

In the general atmosphere of inevitability surrounding the enlargement issue in the wake of de Gaulle's departure, therefore, Germany's growing economic power, increasing political assertiveness, and new foreign policy orientation gave added urgency in 1969 to the question of British accession. Faced with incipient Western apprehension about the impact of *Ostpolitik* and domestic pressure for a French initiative in the EC, Pompidou called for a special summit of the Community's heads of government in December 1969. The Hague summit—the Netherlands then held the rotating EC presidency—was the first meeting of Community leaders since the tenth anniversary celebration of the Treaty of Rome in 1967. With de Gaulle gone and enlargement once again at center stage, most member states anticipated a decisive breakthrough. Frustration with the Community's poor political performance in the 1960s even caused an unusual demonstration at the summit: A thousand protesters chanting "United Europe Now" clashed with police outside the hall where the heads of government gathered.[7] This was one of the few instances in the Community's history where people took to the streets to show support for European integration, and it provided a striking contrast with subsequent demonstrations by farmers and other groups obsessed with narrow, sectoral issues.

In the event, the summit spawned the "Spirit of The Hague," a feeling that the Community was once more on the move. Especially in view of what had happened in the mid-1960s and what would happen in the mid-1970s, the Hague summit assumed a retrospective aura of harmony and unprecedented progress. One historian described the summit as marking "a watershed in post-war European history comparable to the Messina conference of 1955."[8] But his appraisal belies the reality of a tense encounter between President Pompidou, trying to square the Gaullist circle, and his Community counterparts, led by an assertive Chancellor Brandt, determined to force the issue of British entry. The summit's concluding sanction of Pompidou's slogan, "completion, deepening, enlargement," disguised the continuing tension between France and the Five but met the disparate demands of the main protagonists—including Britain, hovering in the wings.

It was no accident that "enlargement" came after "completion" and "deepening" in Pompidou's slogan. In an opening address bereft of vision or imagination, Pompidou endorsed enlargement in principle but called first for a strengthening of the existing Community. "Completion" meant finalizing the financing of the CAP, a cherished French objective put in abeyance since the 1965 crisis. Negotiating a financial regulation for the CAP and funding the Community by its own resources would inevitably involve reopening the debate about the European Parliament's budgetary powers, a price Pompidou seemed willing to pay.

"Deepening" meant extending the Community's competence beyond existing policies and activities. Specifically, Pompidou advocated a system of foreign policy cooperation through regular meetings of foreign ministers and, possibly, the establishment of a secretariat in Paris. This smacked to the other Community leaders of a revival of de Gaulle's Fouchet Plan, although they by no means rejected the idea of foreign policy coordination among the Six with a view to reaching common positions. Especially in the context of Germany's *Ostpolitik,* the member states quickly grasped the utility of at least an exchange of information on each other's foreign policies. Accordingly, the leaders appointed Etienne Davignon, a senior Belgian foreign ministry official, to prepare a report during Belgium's forthcoming EC presidency.

The devaluation of August 1969 and the consequent recognition that "the West German currency—and economy—had now become the driving force within the EC" prompted Pompidou also to propose deepening the Community by coordinating the member states' monetary policies.[9] Moreover, Pompidou realized that further monetary instability would endanger the CAP by exposing farm prices to parity fluctuations. Brandt had little time for the CAP; during the Hague summit he repeatedly attacked the rapid accumulation of agricultural surpluses. Nevertheless, he supported the idea of closer monetary policy coordination, not least as a means of demonstrating Germany's commitment to the Community in the face of Allied concern about *Ostpolitik.* But Brandt would not consider monetary cooperation in isolation. An ingrained fear of inflation led him also to urge greater coordination of economic policy in the Community. Pierre Werner, prime minister of Luxembourg, agreed to draft a report on EMU by the middle of the new year.

Thus, enlargement was the one issue on the agenda of the Hague summit still outstanding. Throughout the two-day meeting, Pompidou refused to set a target date for the beginning, let alone the end, of accession negotiations. On the contrary, he insisted that the Community agree to a new system for financing the CAP before opening exploratory talks with the candidate countries. The Dutch countered with the opposite argument—that a financial regulation for the CAP should be concluded only when the Community agreed upon a timetable for enlargement. In this unpromising atmosphere, Brandt made a forceful speech in favor of British entry. For all Pompidou's reluctance, Brandt's arguments were music to French ears: The enlargement issue had held up the Community for too long; it was in the common interest of the Six to extend the Community while trying to improve East-West relations; the Community had to grow beyond its present size in order to compete economically and technologically with the United States; and Britain's accession would reassure member states fearful of Germany's resurgence.[10]

The difference between Pompidou and his Community colleagues led the Dutch prime minister to speculate at the end of the first day's meeting that the summit might soon collapse. Perhaps his statement concentrated French minds. In the event, a bilateral meeting that evening between Pompidou and Brandt provided the basis for a breakthrough. It was a classic Community compromise: In return for a commitment from the Five to resolve the CAP's funding by the end of the year, France assured the others that enlargement negotiations would begin by June 1970. To save face for the French, the summit communiqué omitted any mention of a timetable for the accession talks, but the Dutch prime minister made no secret in his closing press conference of the French climbdown.[11]

Despite Pompidou's posturing, the Hague summit represented an important step forward. Two committees, under the chairmanship of Etienne Davignon and Pierre Werner, were charged with preparing proposals for European political cooperation (EPC) and EMU, respectively. The persistent sore of a financial regulation for the CAP was about to be cured, although the CAP itself loomed larger and larger as a bone of contention in the Community. Enlargement negotiations would resume in the new year, this time with a tacit French understanding that the veto was a thing of the past. Pompidou had disappointed many advocates of European integration with his mixed performance at the summit, whereas Brandt delighted them with his vision and forcefulness. The chancellor had even raised the question of democratic accountability in the Community by advocating direct elections to the European Parliament. Moreover, Brandt's performance and the relative success of the summit strengthened the foundations of *Ostpolitik*. It was no accident that the new German government's first overtures to the East took place a few days after Brandt's return from The Hague.[12]

COMPLETION, DEEPENING, ENLARGEMENT

The Spirit of The Hague soon bore fruit in an agreement to fund the CAP by granting the Community its own resources, consisting of all levies on agricultural products and duties on industrial goods imported into the EC, as well as a small portion (not to exceed 1 percent) of national revenues from value-added tax. By contrast with the original June 1965 proposals that sparked the Empty Chair crisis, the final agreement on Community resources granted the European Parliament modest budgetary powers. Members of Parliament (MEPs) would now have an opportunity to modify the budget but could increase its overall amount only within certain narrow limits. Community foreign ministers approved the new arrangement in an amendment to the Treaty of Rome on April 22, 1970, subject to ratification by the member states.[13] Even in France, ratification proceeded smoothly.

The 1970 budgetary agreement marks an important stage of the Community's development. Undoubtedly the acquisition "of clearly defined financial resources accruing directly to the Community and the expansion of the Parliament's budgetary authority were major steps on the path toward political integration."[14] Yet the 1970 agreement contained a serious flaw. Although it took place after the Hague summit had approved enlargement in principle, the applicant member states were not consulted. The consequence of this omission became apparent almost immediately after Britain's accession. Because it imported far more agricultural produce and industrial goods from outside the Community, Britain, like Germany, would become a net contributor to the Community budget. The Council of Ministers recognized this anomaly but, largely at French insistence, went ahead and concluded the agreement. In so doing, it sowed the seeds of the bitter British budgetary question that dominated the Community in the early 1980s.[15]

Progress on "deepening" the Community was less marked than on completing the financial regulation of the CAP. Efforts to coordinate foreign, economic, and monetary policies encountered not only inevitable differences of interpretation and enthusiasm within the Community but also an increasingly complex and hostile international environment. Under the circumstances, the attempt to coordinate the foreign policies of the Six fared best. Davignon's report, submitted to the Council in May 1970 and eventually adopted the following October, struck the lowest common denominator. Instead of advocating a permanent secretariat in Paris, as Pompidou had proposed, Davignon avoided altogether the issue of a secretariat and therefore of a location; instead, he suggested that EPC consist of biannual meetings of foreign ministers and more frequent meetings of their political directors. The country in the presidency of the Community would also preside over EPC and provide the necessary infrastructural support.[16]

Germany immediately seized upon EPC as a means of building a Community-wide base for *Ostpolitik*. At the first meeting of the six foreign ministers "in EPC"—as distinct from a meeting of the Council of Ministers—in November 1970 during Germany's presidency, the German foreign minister stressed the importance of EPC as a potential contribution to detente in Europe. By that time *Ostpolitik* was well on track, but with only a narrow majority of seats in the German Parliament, Brandt was especially vulnerable to continuing Christian Democratic criticism. EPC helped at least to quell the domestic opposition's clamor by providing an additional forum in which Brandt could explain his Eastern initiative to Germany's Western neighbors.

Of those neighbors, France remained the most skeptical of Germany's new foreign policy orientation. A desire to appease France, and thereby indirectly to appease the domestic opposition, motivated Brandt's approach to EMU as well as to EPC. In October 1970 Pierre Werner presented an ambitious seven-stage plan to achieve EMU in the Community within ten years by means of institutional reform and closer political integration.[17] The plan glossed over the contending French and German emphases on monetary measures and economic policy coordination by proposing parallel progress in both spheres. A related difference between Paris and Bonn soon emerged over the scope and possible implementation of the Werner Plan. Although a firm supporter of monetary policy coordination, Pompidou was loath to take any measure likely to advance supranationalism in the Community. Brandt and the other Community leaders, by contrast, saw the Werner Plan as an ideal opportunity to achieve closer integration.

Discussions in Brussels in the summer of 1970 led the Five to think that France would not object to a rapid move beyond the first stage of the Werner Plan, but the extent of French opposition became fully apparent at a meeting of finance ministers in December 1970. At the Franco-German summit on January 25, 1971, held under the auspices of the 1963 Elysée treaty, Brandt unexpectedly backed down and acquiesced in Pompidou's reluctance to press ahead with closer monetary integration. In return, Brandt won a warm endorsement of his policy toward Eastern Europe. This may have seemed like a "German defeat"[18] on EMU, but it was an important victory on *Ostpolitik*.

Franco-German friction over EMU was not unrelated to the enlargement negotiations then being held. Pompidou surely appreciated that, once in the Community, Britain would support his gradualist position, whereas Brandt similarly sensed that agreement to quicken the pace of EMU would be harder to get after enlargement took place. As Brandt had been willing to sacrifice a bolder position on EMU for the sake of *Ostpolitik* and supported British entry partly for the same reason, the question was moot from Germany's point of view. From the French point of view, Britain's well-known suspicion of supranationalism was a source of comfort. Although as a good Gaullist Pompidou had misgivings about British accession to the Community, he could take some solace from Britain's record of Euroskepticism.

Ironically, Edward Heath, who had replaced Harold Wilson as prime minister in 1970, was the most Europhilic of British politicians.

Heath enthusiastically championed his country's application and deeply regretted the lost opportunity of the early 1960s, when he had negotiated Britain's abortive entry effort. Few of Heath's fellow Conservatives shared the prime minister's ardor for European integration; they saw Community membership largely in negative terms—as Britain's only feasible option. On the other side of the political divide, the issue split the Labour Party. Harold Wilson, the Labour leader, who as prime minister in 1967 had led Britain's second entry effort, now equivocated. As the entry negotiations unfolded, Wilson moved from ambivalence toward open opposition of British accession, bringing the bulk of Labour with him. Roy Jenkins, a future Commission president, led an increasingly isolated pro-EC group on the right wing of the party.[19]

The entry negotiations began on June 30, 1970, in Luxembourg and ended almost a year later in Brussels. Most of the work was done at the permanent representatives' level—with Sir Con O'Neill, a senior diplomat, leading for the United Kingdom—although meetings at ministers' level took place regularly. Familiar issues from Britain's previous applications soon resurfaced. However, the talks were far less contentious and protracted than in the early 1960s. For one thing, Heath was so eager for membership that his approach seemed to be "to gain entry, and then to sort out any differences."[20] For another, Commonwealth and EFTA concerns about British membership in the Community had abated in the intervening decade. The impact on the Commonwealth of Britain's accession to the Community now focused exclusively on specific problems, such as imports of Caribbean sugar and New Zealand dairy products. Nevertheless, the negotiations occasionally stalled, particularly on the controversial questions of Britain's budgetary contribution during the transition phase and the related issue of the dubious benefit to Britain of the CAP.

A meeting between Heath and Pompidou in Paris on May 20–21, 1971, helped resolve the outstanding problems. According to the usually understated London *Times,* relations between the two leaders reached a "dizzy pinnacle of mutual admiration" at the Paris tête-à-tête.[21] The surprisingly close rapport between Pompidou and Heath convinced others in the Community that France had finally jettisoned its lingering opposition to enlargement. Together with the contemporaneous deterioration in relations between Pompidou and Brandt, it also caused speculation that the Paris-London axis would replace the Paris-Bonn axis as the main bilateral motor of Community development, or at least that the Paris-Bonn axis might broaden into a trilateral axis that included Great Britain.[22]

A British government white paper published in July 1971 summarized the results of the accession negotiations and extolled the arguments in favor of entry. "Our country will be more secure," the document declared, "our ability to maintain peace and promote development in the world greater, our economy stronger, and our industries and people more prosperous, if we join the European Communities than if we remain out-side them." On the sensitive question of sovereignty, the white paper blithely asserted that "there is no question of any erosion of essential national sovereignty; what is proposed is a sharing and an enlargement of individual national sovereignties in the general interest."[23] Such patent dissimulation infuriated opponents of entry and left a painful legacy for those in Britain today who advocate greater integration.

The government's proclivity for exaggeration and falsification kindled the highly flammable domestic debate on enlargement. To the government's undisguised joy, the Labour Party suffered most in the ensuing conflagration. Whether motivated by conviction or opportunism, Harold Wilson denounced Heath's entry terms and declared that a Labour government would renegotiate Britain's membership in the Community. At a special Labour Party conference on enlargement on July 17, 1971, a majority of delegates passed a resolution opposing British accession.[24] Nudged by the growing anti-EC sentiment in his party, Wilson moved farther to the left, marooning Roy Jenkins, the deputy leader, on the right. On October 28, 1971, at the end of a six-day parliamentary debate, sixty-nine Labour MPs voted with the government in favor of a motion for entry in "one of the most decisive votes of the century."[25] With ratification looming in 1972, strife within the Labour Party became more and more pronounced.[26]

Pompidou's surprise announcement in March 1972 of a French referendum on enlargement, to be held on April 23, stunned the British government and boosted the anti-marketeers. Despite British government fears of French backsliding on enlargement, though, domestic rather than international political calculations had inspired Pompidou's decision. A snap referendum provided a clever means of splitting the increasingly united opposition by driving a wedge between the Communists, who opposed the mere existence of the Community, and the Socialists, who favored British entry.[27] Moreover, referendums were one of the hallmarks of Gaullist government. It seemed especially appropriate to use a widely recognized Gaullist instrument to undermine an equally well-identifiable Gaullist position on the Community.

The great danger, as de Gaulle's last referendum clearly demonstrated and President Mitterrand's September 1992 referendum on the Maastricht Treaty nearly demonstrated, was that Pompidou could lose. In the event, he easily won, but not as convincingly as expected. Only 60 percent of the French electorate bothered to vote. Of that number, an astonishingly high 7 percent spoiled their ballots, 32 percent voted against, and only 61 percent voted for. The result, like the reason for the referendum, should be seen in domestic political terms. The relatively low number of French voters who endorsed enlargement reflected more on the popularity of Pompidou's presidency than on the merits of Britain's case.[28]

Pompidou had announced the referendum almost as an aside during a press conference in the Elysée, two days before traveling to London for a meeting with Heath. Despite Heath's annoyance with the timing and nature of Pompidou's proclamation, the London meeting, held to discuss the Community's future after enlargement, passed uneventfully. But British opponents of enlargement exploited the French president's initiative to embarrass Heath's government and to advocate a referendum in Britain on the issue. With the three other applicant countries—Denmark, Ireland, and Norway—all holding referendums on enlargement, British anti-marketeers cited the French case as an additional reason to adopt a similar procedure. Earlier, Heath had reminded the House of Commons of the "long-established tradition in this country that decisions on questions of this kind should be taken [only] by the elected representatives of the people in Parliament."[29] Pompidou's decision to consult the electorate directly did nothing to change Heath's mind, but it helped push Wilson into the pro-referendum camp. In April 1972, after yet another Commons debate on the European Communities bill, the Labour leader voted in favor of a referendum on enlargement. Although the motion did not pass, Wilson's support for it provoked Jenkins to resign from the party's front bench.[30] Thus, the referendum issue, which resurfaced and dominated British politics in 1974 and 1975, had already begun to tear Labour apart, just as the Maastricht Treaty would split the Conservative Party twenty years later.

The question of EC membership was even more contentious in Norway, where a narrow majority voted against accession in the referendum of September 24–25, 1972. Although the referendum result did not bind the government, Prime Minister Bratelli had already promised to resign in the event of a "no" vote. Bratelli's Labour government unsuccessfully sought to reassure the electorate about the consequences of membership, especially for fishing and agriculture—even more protected in Norway than in the EC—and the fledgling oil industry. After a bitterly contested campaign that polarized Norwegian opinion, 53.5 percent of the 78 percent who voted opted against accession. True to his word, the prime minister resigned on October 7, 1972. Only in the late 1980s, in response to the pull of the single market, did Norway reopen the domestic debate on Community membership and eventually reapply.

Passions also ran high in Denmark, but the referendum there—held only one week after the Norwegian vote and binding on the government—resulted in an overwhelming endorsement of membership. Like the British, the Danes were, and remain, skeptical about European integration. Once Britain applied for membership, however, Denmark had little option but to follow suit. With the bulk of the country's exports going to the UK and Germany, it would have been economic suicide for Denmark to stay out of the enlarged Community. Despite familiar fears about the erosion of national sovereignty and the possible severance of traditional ties with the Nordic countries, 63 percent of the impressive 90 percent turnout in the referendum voted in favor of accession.

The turnout in the Irish referendum, held on May 10, 1972, was slightly smaller than in Denmark, but it registered stronger support for membership. Far more than Denmark's, Ireland's economic fortunes were tied to those of the UK. It would have been absurd economically for Ireland to stay outside the EC once Britain went in. Added to this sense of economic determinism were complementary elements of opportunism and political calculation. The former had to do with the expected windfall for Irish farmers of participation in the CAP, as well as a host of other benefits, mostly in the form of grants and loans, that would accrue to Ireland in the Community. The latter, by contrast, consisted of the anticipated impact of Community membership on Anglo-Irish relations. Since independence in 1922, Ireland had been relatively isolated from Europe, bound up instead in a suffocatingly close relationship with Britain. EC membership afforded Ireland the chance to place Anglo-Irish relations in a broader, more equitable, multilateral context. It was little wonder that, of the 77 percent who voted in the referendum, a resounding 83 percent endorsed Community membership.[31]

Of the four applicant states who had signed accession treaties on January 22, 1972, only three joined the Community on January 1, 1973. The ratification drama continued in the United Kingdom until almost the last minute. Having survived a series of parliamentary hurdles, the European Communities Act finally passed on October 17, 1972. But that was not the end either of Labour Party posturing or of British recalcitrance about Community affairs. On the contrary, British—and Danish—misgivings about European integration, the inevitable strains of absorbing three new member states, and a hostile international economic environment combined in the mid-1970s to put the European Community sorely to the test.

FROM EUROSUMMIT TO EUROSLUMP

The Paris summit of October 19–20, 1972, which Pompidou convened to set the Community's agenda in the post-enlargement period, marks the high point of Euro-optimism in the 1970s. The summit is famous—or infamous—for the last sentence of a "solemn declaration" that prefixed the concluding communiqué: "The member states of the Community, the driving force of European construction, affirm their intention before the end of the present decade to transform the whole complex of their relations into a European Union."[32] This was an extraordinary statement even by the standard of Community rhetoric. Although nobody knew quite what

"European Union" meant, the commitment to achieve it within eight years put an unnecessary and ultimately embarrassing onus on the member states. As the 1970s passed and nothing remotely resembling European union appeared on the horizon, the Paris declaration served only to highlight the extent of the Community's disarray.

Yet, at the time, the Paris declaration played well politically in the national capitals. The text was sufficiently warm and woolly to escape excessive criticism even in London and Copenhagen. The communiqué also struck a positive chord by expressing the Community's readiness to launch an impressive array of new initiatives. Apart from making inevitable references to EMU and EPC, the communiqué mentioned regional policy, industrial policy, energy, and the environment. Compared with the laundry list produced after the Hague summit, this was a striking catalog of Community "deepening."

Pompidou's apparent retreat from Gaullism should not be exaggerated. A close reading of the communiqué, supplemented by reports of the two-day meeting, suggests that the summit did not represent a radical departure from previous French policy. The proposed European Regional Development Fund, the main mechanism "for correcting . . . in the Community, the strategic and regional imbalances which might affect the realization of economic and monetary union," would benefit France as well as other member states. Pompidou supported the Regional Fund mostly in deference to Heath, who desperately needed to achieve something at the summit from which Britain might profit directly. Coming in the wake of the bitter accession debate, Heath saw the importance of the Paris summit not only in terms of the Community's destiny in the decade ahead but also as a domestic public relations ploy. A promise of financial assistance for depressed industrial and agricultural regions would offset criticism in Britain of the high cost of Community membership.

Pompidou's willingness to help Heath emphasized the rapport between the two leaders and fueled further speculation about the rise of the Anglo-French axis in the Community. Immediately before the summit opened, Pompidou and Heath met privately for an hour to coordinate approaches to the various agenda items. Reciprocating Pompidou's support for the Regional Fund, Heath refrained from backing a Dutch proposal to strengthen the European Parliament. By contrast, the vaunted Franco-German axis seemed moribund. Personally, Pompidou had little time for Brandt since the chancellor stole the show at the Hague summit; politically, Brandt's repeated criticism of the CAP greatly angered the French president. In keeping with his complaints about unwarranted Community expenditure, voiced all the more loudly in the prelude to the approaching federal elections, Brandt distrusted the proposed Regional Fund, which looked too much like "an exercise in old-fashioned, pork-barrel politics rather than a political instrument for the unification of Europe."[33]

The vexed question of economic and monetary policy remained the greatest cause of friction between Paris and Bonn. In the eighteen months before the Paris summit, monetary matters had dominated Community and wider international affairs. Apart from the inherently different French and German approaches to EMU, the collapse of the postwar system of fixed exchange rates had triggered markedly divergent reactions in both countries. In response to the May 1971 monetary crisis, caused by a reduction of interest rates in the United States and the consequent run on the dollar in favor of the more stable German mark, Brandt had advocated either a joint EC or a separate German float. Immediate economic concerns, as well as a desire to appease Washington at a time of growing U.S. annoyance over both *Ostpolitik* and the cost of maintaining troops in Europe, motivated the chancellor. By contrast, Pompidou opposed a joint float because of its likely impact on the competitiveness of European products and because of lack of sympathy with the United States' plight.

Although Pompidou's position softened in the summer of 1971, President Nixon's announcement on August 15 that year of the suspension of dollar convertibility and the imposition of restrictive trade measures reopened a sensitive subject in Franco-German relations. At their meeting on August 20, Community finance ministers failed to agree on a joint response and instead issued a bland communiqué expressing concern about the United States' action. A more harmonious meeting of finance ministers on September 13 led to pointed criticism of the United States and presaged a concerted Community approach to the Smithsonian talks of December 1971 that sought to repair the system. Following the Smithsonian settlement, Pompidou and Brandt reconciled their approaches to economic and monetary policy in the Community at the Franco-German summit of February 1972, much as they had done a little over a year before.

But the crises of May and August 1971 had long-lasting effects and sent the European economies slipping into recession. Corrective measures in early 1972 had the unfortunate but predictable impact of fueling inflation. The circumstances were hardly propitious for the Community's fledgling EMU, although the collapse of the international monetary system inevitably increased calls among the Six for closer coordination of economic and monetary policy. In April 1972 the Six hatched the "snake," a regimen to keep EC currency fluctuations within a 2.5 percent margin inside the "tunnel" established during the Smithsonian talks. Worried especially about the consequences of currency fluctuations for the CAP, Pompidou put EMU high on the agenda of the Paris summit. In response to Pompidou's call for exchange rate stability, Brandt stressed the importance of anti-inflationary measures. The result was a reaffirmation at the Paris summit of the need for parallel progress on economic and monetary measures. Recalling the member states' aspiration to European union by the end of the decade, the summit communiqué reiterated the Community leaders' commitment to EMU, "with a view to its completion not later than December 31, 1980."[34]

Continuing exchange rate fluctuations and divergences of member states' monetary and economic policies almost immediately made nonsense of the 1980 target date. Throughout 1973 soaring inflation, rising unemployment, yawning trade deficits, and a worsening oil crisis began to corrode the Community. The pernicious impact of those developments was blatantly obvious at the Community's next summit, held in Copenhagen on December 14–15, 1973. Once again Pompidou called for the meeting, this time in a vain attempt to instill Community solidarity in the aftermath of the October 1973 Middle East war, the massive hike in oil prices, and the onset of the oil embargo. Coming on top of existing economic and monetary problems, the Middle East crisis put the Community under enormous pressure.

The Copenhagen summit turned into a fiasco. In October 1972, Edward Heath had inserted a paragraph into the Paris summit communiqué asserting the Community's need "to formulate as soon as possible an energy policy guaranteeing certain and lasting supplies under satisfactory economic conditions." At the Copenhagen summit, held in the full knowledge of an impending oil shortage, Heath lost his earlier enthusiasm for an energy initiative, and member states could not agree on a joint strategy, let alone formulate a common policy. Nor did the Commission provide much direction. To make matters worse, by the time of the Copenhagen summit, the energy issue had become inauspiciously linked to other Community problems, notably the fate of the Regional Fund and the far larger question of relations with the United States.

Differences in approaches to economic planning would have made it difficult in any case for the member states to approve a common energy policy in the mid-1970s. The immediate impact of the October 1973 price hike and embargo—approximately 63 percent of the EC's energy needs at the time were met by Middle East oil—shattered any prospect of a joint Community approach. With the port of Rotterdam targeted for total embargo, the Netherlands was worst hit at the beginning of the crisis. Germany supported the Netherlands' call at the Copenhagen summit for a concerted Community response. Britain and France, jealous to preserve what they considered their close relationships with the Arab oil-producing countries, strove to stifle discussion of a common energy policy. At Brandt's insistence, the summit communiqué included a separate, nonbinding declaration on energy policy that included such platitudes as the need for an "orderly functioning of a common market for energy" and "concerted and equitable measures to limit energy consumption."[35]

The arrival of a group of Arab foreign ministers offering to ease the oil embargo in return for EC support in the Middle East peace process threw the summit into greater disarray. But the member states' policy toward the Middle East, as opposed to the possible development of an EC energy policy, came under the rubric of EPC, a process already notorious for its propensity to promote fudging. Germany and the Netherlands succeeded in toning down some of the more blatant pro-Arab points that Britain and France wanted to include in the communiqué's statement on the Middle East. At a meeting of EC foreign ministers on November 6, however, the member states produced a declaration that leaned further toward the Arab position, a development pleasing to the oil producers.[36]

The member states' position on the Middle East greatly exacerbated trans-Atlantic tension. Apart from the declaration's pro-Arab tone, the fact that the Nine adopted a position on such a sensitive international issue without consulting the United States bolstered Washington's negative perception of EPC. Incipient trade disputes, caused largely by the CAP, were a growing irritant in Euro-American relations. Additionally, in 1970 and 1971 the United States bitterly resented Europe's apparent unwillingness to relieve pressure on the dollar and to share more of the expense of keeping U.S. troops overseas. The August 1971 monetary crisis was due in part to Nixon's frustration with his European allies.

Kissinger's response to the deteriorating U.S.-EC relationship was typically extravagant: a call for a "New Atlantic Charter" as part of the United States' "Year of Europe" in 1973.[37] This prompted Michel Jobert, France's foreign minister, to draft a declaration of European identity as a basis for the Nine's international relations. The United States and the Nine toyed with various draft statements on U.S.-European relations in the summer of 1973, before the member states adopted their "Document on the European Identity" on December 14.[38] A visit to Washington by the Danish foreign minister the previous September to present the latest version emphasized the point of Kissinger's legendary question: "Who speaks for Europe?" Denmark, then in the Community presidency, played the part that Kissinger thought should be reserved for a larger country.

Washington's brinkmanship during the Middle East war further strained Euro-American relations, as did Kissinger's call for a coordinated Western response to the subsequent oil crisis. The ensuing effort to formulate a joint consumers' approach exposed deep trans-Atlantic tension, as well as considerable Community disarray. France opposed the initiative, fearing a U.S. attempt to monopolize the West's response and preferring both bilateral consumer-producer contacts on particular supply problems and multilateral negotiations in the UN on general political and economic differences. Nevertheless, France agreed to Community participation at the Washington energy conference, in addition to individual member state representation.

Germany, then in the Community presidency, angered France by supporting the U.S. position and criticizing bilateral consumer-producer deals. Jobert accused his German counterpart of exceeding the presidency's mandate at the conference, a charge the Nine's representatives failed to resolve at a hastily convened caucus.[39] France's refusal to join a U.S.-sponsored oil consumers' group accentuated the Nine's disunity. The result was both a deterioration in Franco-American relations and a setback for Kissinger's efforts to put Euro-American relations on a new footing.

Sharp exchanges at the Washington conference between Jobert and German Foreign Minister Walter Scheel reflected tension at the top between Pompidou and Brandt. Pompidou never overcame his distrust of *Ostpolitik,* which by 1973 had brought about treaties between the Federal Republic and Moscow, Warsaw, and Prague; a Four Power agreement on Berlin; and an accord between the two Germanys. While Bonn took stock of its foreign policy achievements and the Soviet bloc governments similarly assessed the impact of *Ostpolitik,* the pace of Bonn's diplomatic offensive in the East inevitably slowed down. But it was too late to restore harmonious relations between Pompidou and Brandt. Impaired by an illness that would soon prove fatal and fed regular doses of Germanophobia by the egregious Jobert, Pompidou never raised his opinion of Brandt.

Nor were Brandt's relations with Heath much more cordial. British efforts to establish a Regional Fund in 1973 ran into repeated German opposition. With Britain's economy rapidly deteriorating and opposition to EC membership growing, Heath more than ever needed to negotiate a generous Community Regional Fund.[40] Secure in office after the 1972 federal elections and concerned about the nature and extent of Community expenditure, Brandt had no incentive to budge. Conflict came to a head at the Copenhagen summit, when Heath blocked discussion on Community energy policy as long as Germany blocked a resolution on the Regional Fund. German intransigence continued at the joint meeting of Community foreign and finance ministers in Brussels on December 17–18, 1973, but eased at a special meeting of the Council of Ministers to discuss regional policy on January 30, 1974.[41] Yet it proved impossible to reach a satisfactory settlement before Heath left office the following month, deeply disillusioned with Germany's policy in the Community.

The 1973 oil crisis had exacerbated deep divisions in the EC and inflamed relations between the leaders of the Community's three most important member states. Within six months of the Copenhagen summit, however, the leadership of all three countries changed hands. In April 1974 Pompidou died, and on May 19 Giscard d'Estaing won the presidential election. Two weeks before Giscard's victory, Brandt resigned from office following the arrest of his personal assistant on charges of spying for East Germany; Helmut Schmidt, Brandt's finance minister, became the new chancellor. In Britain, Harold Wilson returned to No. 10 Downing Street after Labour's February 1974 election victory. The new constellation of leaders, and the domestic issues they faced, had an obvious impact on the Community. Wilson's indifference to EC membership and demand for a renegotiation of Heath's entry terms inevitably lessened Britain's importance and influence in the Community. At the same time, Giscard and Schmidt grew increasingly close personally and politically, firmly reestablishing the primacy of the Franco-German axis in Community affairs. This was insufficient to pull the EC out of its mid-1970s malaise, but undoubtedly the emergence of the Giscard-Schmidt duopoly helped the Community survive the continuing economic crisis and portended its revival in the early 1980s.

INTO THE ABYSS

An Awkward Partner is the title of Stephen George's book on Britain in the Community. The extent of British awkwardness became fully apparent in 1974, after Wilson's narrow general election victory. Jobert contrasted Heath, "a man of the Rhine," with Wilson, "a man of the Scilly Isles" (a remote resort where Wilson had a holiday cottage).[42] For all his frustration over the Regional Fund, Heath was undoubtedly committed to the Community. Wilson, by contrast, personified Britain's ambivalence toward European integration. Moreover, Wilson led a political party bitterly divided on the question of continued Community membership. The Labour Party manifesto for the February election promised a renegotiation of Britain's accession agreement. Having won the election, Wilson and James Callaghan, his foreign secretary, duly pursued the matter with their Community counterparts.

Jobert's unflattering comparison of Heath and Wilson suggests the degree of difficulty that the French foreign minister and the new British prime minister would have had working together. In the event, Jobert, hardly a man of the Rhine either, exited when Giscard came to power in May 1974. But Giscard strongly opposed Britain's renegotiation of EC membership terms. Although conceding the validity of Britain's budgetary claim, Giscard was unconvinced that a successful renegotiation would end British dissatisfaction with the Community and unsatisfactoriness in the Community. Only Schmidt, a fellow socialist, sympathized with Wilson's predicament. Ultimately, Schmidt brokered the dispute between Giscard and Wilson.

James Callaghan got the renegotiations off to a bad start at a Council of Ministers meeting on April 1, 1974. Callaghan infuriated his fellow foreign ministers by reading them sections of the Labour Party manifesto and won little sympathy for his argument that under the present system Britain's contribution to the Community budget was disproportionately high. Callaghan's other demands included reform of the CAP, retention of British parliamentary sovereignty, freedom to control capital movements, protection of Commonwealth interests, no harmonization of value-added tax, and no tying of the pound to a fixed parity. In the course of the renegotiations, changing circumstances made many of those points either superfluous or counterproductive. For instance, a rise in world food prices in 1974 and 1975 meant that, contrary to previous and subsequent practice, the CAP ensured *lower* food prices in the UK. By the end of 1974, only the budgetary and Commonwealth demands remained active on Britain's agenda. The issue of Commonwealth interests translated into Wilson's personal preference for New Zealand dairy products.

The renegotiations lasted eleven months, dominated two Community summits, and drove Britain's partners to distraction. It is difficult to refute Roy Jenkins's observation that the entire episode "produced the minimum results with the maximum ill-will."[43] At the expense of Britain's prestige in Europe, Wilson seemed to be engaged in a frantic effort to hold the Labour Party together. In the run-up to the October 1974 general election, the second in less than a year, Wilson pledged either another general election or a referendum to validate the renegotiation result. Labour's overall majority in the October 1974 election kept the question of continued Community membership at the top of the political agenda.

Jenkins credits Schmidt not only with successfully concluding the renegotiations but also with convincing a majority of Labour Party members to stay in the Community. Schmidt visited the UK in November 1974 and made a hugely successful speech at the Labour Party conference. At the same time he coached Wilson privately at Chequers on the approach to take with Giscard. Schmidt's most valuable piece of advice was for the prime minister to signal clearly, before the Paris summit on December 9–10, 1974, his personal commitment to British membership in the Community in the event of a satisfactory renegotiation of the original entry terms. This Wilson did in a speech in London a week before the decisive summit. Schmidt also organized a private dinner between Giscard and Wilson on the eve of the summit, from which the British and French leaders emerged with a better understanding of each other's positions.[44]

A formula to break the deadlock over Britain's budgetary contribution emerged at the end of the Paris summit only after protracted Anglo-French wrangling. Under the terms of the compromise, the Commission would design a "correcting mechanism" to prevent Britain, or any other member state, from paying too much into the Community. According to the Commission's proposal, Britain's renegotiation would conclude at a summit in Dublin in March 1975. Wilson told the House of Commons on January 23, 1975, that the government would organize a referendum— an unprecedented constitutional device in the UK—before the end of June to decide whether or not Britain should stay in the Community, based on the Dublin summit result.[45]

Agreement at the Paris summit on the size of the Regional Fund undoubtedly helped Wilson make the case in Britain for continued Community membership. Like Brandt, Schmidt desperately wanted to contain Community spending. But Schmidt also lacked Brandt's personal prejudice against granting Britain—and France—large-scale regional assistance. In the end, the fund was not as large as Heath had originally hoped, but Britain's share would be a sizeable 28 percent. Italy, Ireland, and France would be the other main beneficiaries.[46]

Although dominated by the British budgetary question and notable for the Regional Fund agreement, the Paris summit is now best remembered for two decisions that had a profound impact on the Community's long-term development: to hold direct elections to the European Parliament by 1978 and to hold regular, thrice-yearly Community summits, henceforth known as "European Councils." The move from ad hoc to institutionalized summitry reflected the need for regular meetings of heads of government in order to maintain the Community's political momentum at a time of increasing economic complexity and bureaucratic paralysis. Originally Giscard's idea, the prospect of regular European Councils appealed also to Schmidt. With their unrivaled grasp of economic and monetary issues and their propensity to deal privately with fellow presidents and prime ministers, Giscard and Schmidt saw the European Council (and the annual summits of the major industrialized countries) as an ideal forum in which to direct Community affairs. The simultaneous decision to hold Community-wide elections to the European Parliament, despite British and Danish reservations, was intended both to satisfy an obligation in the Treaty of Rome and to defuse criticism that the European Council would strengthen intergovernmentalism at the expense of supranationalism in the EC.

Two other results of the Paris summit—an agreement in principle to move away from unanimous decisionmaking in the Council of Ministers and a request that Leo Tindemans, prime minister of Belgium, write a report on European union—suggest that the heads of government sought decisively in December 1974 to get the Community going again. Yet neither Giscard nor Schmidt, who emerged from the Paris summit as the Community's undisputed leaders, sought at the time to revive its fortunes. For one thing, nobody (including Tindemans) expected the report on European union to produce tangible results. For another, a promise to forsake the national veto in the Council meant little in practice. Nor would direct elections to Parliament have an immediate impact on the Community's development. The first such elections, scheduled for 1978, were postponed at Britain's request until 1979. In the meantime the European Council provided a useful arena where Community leaders could thrash out thorny problems, but it did not guarantee that those leaders would muster the political will either to find solutions or to launch new initiatives. Few European Councils held in the mid-1970s are memorable today.

The institutionalization of EC summitry could not, in and of itself, revitalize the Community. On the contrary, for the next four years the EC remained in a rut because of its member states' inability or unwillingness to tackle adverse economic and political conditions on a Community-wide basis. The Commission was still ineffectual, with the larger member states declining to give decisive leadership. Germany was strong economically but, for all Brandt's blandishments in the early 1970s, relatively unassertive politically; France was depressed economically and precarious politically, with Giscard under constant threat from left and right; and Britain was seriously ill economically and volatile politically. As Peter Ludlow has pointed out, "the Community was therefore virtually leaderless [in the mid-1970s]. The Germans would not lead, the French could not and the British neither would nor could."[47]

The continuing saga of Britain's "renegotiation" epitomized the Community's malaise. The Commission published its proposals on the budgetary question—in a document quaintly entitled "The Unacceptable Situation and the Correcting Mechanism"—on January 30, 1975. The Council welcomed the Commission document as the basis for an agreement that the heads of government would try to reach at the Dublin summit on March 10–11.[48] Having already conceded that Britain was paying too much into the Community's coffers, the main issue for the European Council in Dublin was the size of Britain's refund. A committee of experts worked frantically through the first night of the summit to come up with an acceptable formula. In the meantime, a successful conclusion seemed to hinge on satisfying Wilson's demand for assurances about New Zealand dairy imports. Finally, out of tedium or despair, the other eight acceded to the New Zealand dairy request, and Wilson and Callaghan determined that the correcting mechanism yielded a reasonable figure on which to base their domestic campaign for Britain to stay in the Community. After "an exceptionally arduous two days," the other heads of government went home "thoroughly bored and resentful of Britain's demands."[49]

On his return from Dublin, Wilson recommended a "yes" vote in the ensuing referendum. But the result of the lengthy renegotiation had failed to reunite the Labour Party. On the other side of the House, the Conservatives had more than their fair share of Euroskeptics, yet the vast majority of members favored staying in the Community. Margaret Thatcher's first major speech as the newly elected Conservative Party leader was on the referendum issue. Though deploring the constitutional precedent of a popular referendum, she strongly advocated a "yes" vote. With the leadership of the two main parties and the small Liberal Party urging a positive result, the outcome of the referendum was hardly in doubt. Jenkins and Heath, the country's most prominent supporters of European integration, led the bipartisan "Britain in Europe" campaign. Both agreed after the event that "it was always the high arguments, the broad discussion of the country's future orientation in both foreign policy and economic terms, which most captured the attention and fired the imagination of audiences."[50] On June 5, of the 64 percent of the electorate who voted, 67 percent cast their ballots for and 33 percent against continued membership in the Community.

Four days after the referendum, Wilson told the House of Commons that "the debate is now over . . . the historic decision has been made. . . . we look forward to continuing to work with [our partners] in promoting the Community's wider interests and in fostering a greater sense of purpose among the member states."[51] By then it was difficult to repair the damage of the renegotiation either inside or outside Britain. At home, according to Roy Jenkins, "the handling of the European question by the leadership throughout the 1970s did more to cause the [Labour] Party's disasters of the 1980s than did any other issue."[52] Abroad, the renegotiation "added to the spirit of irritation and impatience with Britain that had been growing within the Community" since enlargement.[53] Even before Margaret Thatcher came to office in 1979 and promptly reopened the budgetary question, nothing about Britain's behavior after the referendum suggested a willingness to play a positive role in the Community. Callaghan's replacement of Wilson as prime minister in 1976 brought no appreciable change in Britain's approach. Britain's first presidency of the Community, from January to June 1977, was uninspiring, not least because some unreconstructed anti-marketeers in the government had a golden opportunity to chair Council meetings.

Whatever hopes there had been in 1972 for an Anglo-French directorate, or at least a trilateral Anglo-French-German directorate, to replace the Franco-German directorate, by the mid-1970s those hopes were dashed.[54] Partly in response to the challenge of Britain's Community membership, the Franco-German axis, severely strained under Pompidou and Brandt, grew especially intimate under Giscard and Schmidt. The closeness between the new French president and the new German chancellor was not immediate. Both had radically different characters and personalities—Giscard haughty, Olympian, condescending; Schmidt pretentiously unpretentious, moody, and temperamental, "a figure out of Wilhelm Busch, Elbe bargeman's cap and pipe."[55] But both were shrewd, incisive, and highly intelligent. Moreover, before reaching the highest office in their respective countries, both had been unusually knowledgeable and dedicated finance ministers. It was in that capacity, during the disputes over currency fluctuations in the early 1970s, that they got to know, respect, and ultimately like each other. Giscard and Schmidt spoke two common languages: economics and English.

The Privileged Partnership, the title of Haig Simonian's book on Franco-German relations in the 1970s, sums up the unique friendship and affinity between Giscard and Schmidt. To signal his desire for especially harmonious relations with the Federal Republic, Giscard installed Jean Sauvagnargues, a noted Germanist, as French foreign minister. Giscard and Schmidt met for the first time as president and chancellor on May

31–June 1, 1974, and resolved from the outset to set Franco-German relations on a singular plane. Going well beyond the framework of the
Elysée treaty, Giscard and Schmidt got together often for dinner, spoke at
least weekly on the telephone, and caucused regularly on the fringes of
multilateral meetings. The frequency and diversity of their contacts set a
pattern that François Mitterrand and Helmut Kohl followed. Despite the
appearance of an easy Franco-German relationship based on a genuine
friendship between the president and the chancellor, however, both sides
worked hard to resolve occasional disputes and ease inevitable friction. As
William Wallace observed, "the success of the Franco-German relationship [in the 1970s and 1980s] is a record of determination to accommodate divergent interests through positive political action, to explain and
to tolerate differences and to minimize their impact; not a simple record of
convergence in economic, industrial, political or security interests and
outlooks."[56] This was an approach conspicuously absent from Britain's
dealings with other Community member states during the same time.

The Community provided an ideal forum in which to exercise
Franco-German initiative and especially to apply the personal rapport between Giscard and Schmidt. But it would be an exaggeration to say that
Giscard and Schmidt single-handedly revived the Community. Given the
circumstances of the mid-1970s, with the economic recession continuing
unabated, it is more apt to speak of crisis management and damage control
than of rejuvenation. Growing economic divergence between the member
states undermined not only the surviving sense of Community solidarity
but also the prevailing extent of economic integration. Faced with soaring inflation and unemployment, member states applied an array of nontariff barriers and other protectionist measures that conflicted with the
fundamental rationale for the Community.

EMU was an early and inevitable victim of member state unilateralism. The Werner Plan, launched so audaciously in 1972 with a target
date for full implementation of 1980, hardly got off the ground. The Community's currencies wiggled in and out of the "snake": The mark, buoyed
by Germany's low inflation and large trade surplus, pushed through the
top, and the pound, franc, and lire, weakened by their countries' high inflation and large trade deficits, fell through the bottom. By 1975 plans for
EMU were effectively shelved.

The Community's preoccupation in the mid-1970s with such issues
as budgetary contributions, monetary compensation to farmers for the impact of fluctuating exchange rates on the CAP, and Commission representation at the recently launched annual summits of major industrialized
countries illustrated the extent of the malaise. A sense of crisis gripped the
Community, which "seemed set to disintegrate under the stultifying impact of its own petty-mindedness, frivolity and irrelevance."[57] An article
in the *New York Times* in November 1977 pointed to "signs everywhere
. . . that the drive for European unity is running out of steam."[58]

Even in the best of times, however, Giscard's and Schmidt's joint approach to Community affairs would not have been compatible with the kind of all-around renaissance the Community enjoyed in the mid-1980s. Schmidt's reported statement that "Europe can only be brought forward by the will of a few statesmen, and not by thousands of regulations and hundreds of ministerial councils"[59] was only half-right. Schmidt and Giscard's impatience with the Commission and determination to avoid Brussels in favor of Paris and Bonn inhibited the Community's proper functioning. Moreover, "the endless exhibition waltz between Giscard and Schmidt [went on] far too long, and . . . had the Little Five, and indeed Italy as well, as rather bored wallflowers sitting at the edge of the room."[60] A Franco-German initiative was not guaranteed success in the Community, but no initiative could succeed without Franco-German support. However, sometimes "Franco-German collusion became so obvious that it was almost counterproductive."[61]

The inefficiency of the Brussels bureaucracy in the 1970s became a metaphor for the Community's decline. The Commission was dispirited and demoralized. As if to underscore its seeming unimportance, in 1972 the outgoing president, Franco Malfatti, left office early in order to stand for election to the Italian Parliament. At the end of the decade Willy Haferkampf, a vice president, brought the Commission into disrepute over allegations about his extravagant traveling expenses.[62] This scandal was relatively trivial, but it reinforced the Commission's public image as being wasteful and mismanaged. Schmidt's intense dislike of the Commission reinforced Germany's reluctance to send top-rate people to Brussels as either commissioners or permanent representatives ("ambassadors" to the Community). For his part, Giscard inherited de Gaulle's antipathy toward the Commission and lost no opportunity to put its president in his place. Harold Wilson observed that when Giscard floated the proposal for a European Council at a special half-day meeting of Community leaders in the Elysée in September 1974, he asked for a response "from each in turn, until reaching Mr. Francois-Xavier Ortoli, the Commission President . . . he passed [Ortoli] by, and went on to [the next prime minister]."[63] Giscard kept Ortoli out of the inaugural summit of major industrialized countries in November 1975 and lost an epic battle, which "lasted for a month and consumed a good deal of time and even more emotional energy,"[64] to exclude Roy Jenkins, Ortoli's successor as Commission president, from the May 1977 London summit. Giscard told Le Monde that he stayed away from the opening dinner of the London summit, held at Downing Street on May 6, because of Jenkins's presence.[65]

In 1972, well after de Gaulle's departure, the Financial Times commented that "with maddening regularity the French try to cut the Commission down, but the hard reality is that, when the bargaining starts, it plays an absolutely indispensable role. If it did not exist, it would be necessary to invent it."[66] More than the Commission's ineffectualness, the

Council of Ministers' indecisiveness lay at the root of Brussels' institutional immobility. By the early 1970s nearly one thousand Commission proposals were said to be stuck in the decisionmaking pipeline because of the unanimity requirement and the member states' inability to agree.

For all their supposed commitment to the Community, Giscard and Schmidt tinkered with various possible solutions but never injected into the process the political will so desperately lacking. The fate of the Tindemans Report was typical. Having been charged at the 1974 Paris summit with preparing a study on European union, Tindemans toured the Community capitals and interviewed numerous EC and member state officials to collect ideas. Tindemans's report, published in January 1976, focused less on the lofty goal of a federal Europe than on the need to reform existing Community institutions and to strengthen European integration. The report's most controversial element was an exploration, but not specifically an endorsement, of a "two-speed Europe," with differing rates of integration in the Community depending on the will and ability of each member state.[67]

Smaller member states disliked the prospect of first- and second-class Community, and the larger member states—with the exception of Germany and Italy—fretted about a further loss of sovereignty. Giscard took the lead and stifled the report with the kind of bureaucratic asphyxiation that Tindemans had so bitterly complained about. The heads of government asked their foreign ministers to consider the report; the foreign ministers asked their senior officials to do so. The senior officials reported on the report to their foreign ministers; the foreign ministers reported on the report's report to the heads of government at the Hague summit in November 1976. The heads of government thanked Tindemans for his efforts and, as a consolation to him, called for an annual report from the Commission on "Progress Toward European Union."[68]

The notion of a "two-speed Europe," which Tindemans took up in his report, was one of many such concepts floating around in the 1970s. In the absence of real progress in the Community, politicians and political scientists bandied about such pretentious-sounding ideas for the future of European integration as "two-tier Europe," "Europe à la carte," "variable geometry," "differentiation," and "graduated integration."[69] Meanwhile, in the real world, other efforts to revive the Community fell by the wayside. One was an independent review of the Commission, requested by Roy Jenkins and chaired by Dirk Spierenburg, a Dutch diplomat and former ECSC commissioner. Spierenburg presented his report, "Proposals for Reform of the Commission of the European Communities and its Services," to Jenkins in Brussels on September 24, 1979. Despite the Commission president's enthusiasm for some of its suggestions, the Spierenburg Report went the way of the Tindemans Report, into oblivion.

So, too, did yet another report, that of the "Three Wise Men."[70] The report originated in a letter from Giscard to other Community leaders proposing a report on Community reform, without treaty revision, by three eminent Europeans. After the usual haggling over nationality and political orientation, the heads of government settled on Barend Bushevel, a former Dutch prime minister; Edmund Dell, a former British government minister; and Robert Marjolin, a former vice president of the Commission. By now deeply suspicious of Giscard, Jenkins detected in the French president's proposal "a desire . . . to cut down the power of the Commission, to reduce or eliminate our political role, our connection with Parliament, and half to amalgamate us with the Council secretariat and with COREPER, and thus to make us all servants of the European Council."[71]

The Three Wise Men set about their task with enthusiasm. They "quickly realized that [their committee's] own working methods should set a good example. And in many ways the study, analysis, formulation and presentation of its finished product was indeed an enviable model in European policy-making. The Three stuck determinedly to their mandate, their tight timetable, and to their limited budget."[72] To the amazement of the heads of government, the Wise Men presented their report on time, a month before the November 1979 Dublin summit.[73]

At the summit, Giscard noted with pleasure the report's criticism of the Commission and its endorsement of the European Council. Beyond that, he did not delve too deep. After all, the report also criticized successive Community presidencies for lack of direction. France's presidency, in the first half of 1979, had been particularly poor, in part because of Giscard's anger with the outgoing European Parliament for having passed its last budget in a form he thought illegal, and in part because of his concern that the new, directly elected Parliament would be far more assertive. Nor did Giscard like the report's obvious observation that lack of political will was the main obstacle to the Community's development. Thus, after a perfunctory discussion of it at the Dublin summit, the "Report on European Institutions" joined the Tindemans Report and the Spierenburg Report in the Community's archive.

As the decade drew to a close, the Community's fortunes indeed looked bleak. Excessive unemployment and high inflation plagued the member states' economic performance. The political will to revive European integration seemed conspicuously lacking in national capitals. Over the next five years the Community experienced additional shocks and strains, but at the same time it underwent a remarkable metamorphosis that paved the way for its revival and transformation in the mid-1980s. Yet by the end of the 1970s there were few economic, political, and institutional signs that the Community would ever turn the corner.

NOTES

1. Peter Ludlow, *Beyond 1992: Europe and Its World Partners* (Brussels: Center for European Policy Studies, 1989), pp. 1–4.

2. *The Economist,* December 13, 1969, p. 31.

3. Haig Simonian, *The Privileged Partnership: Franco-German Relations in the European Community, 1969–1984* (Oxford: Clarendon Press, 1985), p. 35; Edward Kolodziej, *French International Policy Under de Gaulle and Pompidou: The Politics of Grandeur* (Ithaca: Cornell University Press, 1974), p. 407.

4. See Wolfram Hanrieder, *Germany, America, Europe: Forty Years of German Foreign Policy* (New Haven: Yale University Press, 1989), p. 269.

5. Hanreider, *Germany,* p. 356.

6. Henry Kissinger, *White House Years* (New York: Little, Brown & Co., 1979), p. 422.

7. *The Times* (London), December 2, 1969, p. 1.

8. Simonian, *Partnership,* p. 349.

9. William Wallace, *The Transformation of Western Europe* (New York: Council on Foreign Relations Press, 1990), pp. 24–25.

10. *Le Monde,* December 2, 1969.

11. *Le Monde,* December 3, 1969.

12. Simonian, *Partnership,* pp. 82–83; Hanreider, *Germany,* pp. 284–285.

13. Commission, *1970 General Report*, points 515–518, 544–545.

14. Werner Feld, *West Germany and the European Community: Changing Interests and Competing Policy Objectives* (New York: Praeger, 1981), p. 13.

15. See Stephen George, *An Awkward Partner: Britain in the European Community* (Oxford: Oxford University Press, 1990), pp. 52–53.

16. "First Report of the Foreign Ministers to the Heads of State and Government of the Member States of the European Community (Luxembourg Report)," in Federal Republic of Germany, *European Political Cooperation (EPC),* 4th edition (Wiesbaden: Press and Information Office of the Federal Government, 1982), pp. 28–35.

17. "The Werner Report on Economic and Monetary Union," Bull. EC S/11-1970.

18. Simonian, *Partnership,* p. 92.

19. See Roy Jenkins, *A Life at the Centre* (London: Macmillan, 1991), pp. 310–312.

20. George, *Awkward Partner,* p. 56.

21. *The Times* (London), October 21, 1972, p. 6.

22. Kolodziej, *French Policy,* pp. 412–413; Simonian, *Partnership,* p. 114.

23. British Government "White Paper," *The UK and the European Communities*, Cmnd 4715, July 7, 1971.

24. See Frances Nicholson and Roger East, *From the Six to the Twelve: The Enlargement of the European Communities* (Chicago: St. James Press, 1987), p. 71.

25. Jenkins, *Centre,* p. 329.

26. See Jenkins, *Centre,* pp. 310–330; Anthony Benn, *Diaries, 1968–72* (London: Hutchinson, 1988), pp. 315–316, 353.

27. D. Rudnick, "An Assessment of the Reasons for the Removal of the French Veto to UK Membership of the EEC," *International Relations* 14, no. 6, pp. 658–672.

28. Kolodziej, *French Policy,* p. 432–438; *The Times* (London), March 17, 1972, p. 6; *The Financial Times,* March 18, 1972, p. 14.

29. Quoted in *The Financial Times*, March 17, 1972, p. 1.

30. Jenkins, *Centre,* pp. 327–348.

31. For an account of the 1972 referenda issues and results in Norway, Denmark, and Ireland, see Nicholson and East, *Enlargement,* pp. 97–100, 113–115, and 117–133.

32. Commission, *1972 General Report,* point 5(16).

33. Feld, *West Germany,* p. 67.

34. Commission, *1972 General Report,* point 5(1).

35. Commission, *1973 General Report,* Annex I to Chapter II, pp. 489–491.

36. "Statement of the Nine Foreign Ministers on the Situation in the Middle East," in Federal Republic of Germany, *European Political Cooperation,* pp. 55–56.

37. Kissinger, *White House Years,* p. 1275.

38. "Document on the European Identity," in Federal Republic of Germany, *European Political Cooperation,* pp. 57–63.

39. See Simonian, *Partnership,* pp. 231–240.

40. George, *Awkward Partner,* pp. 65–69.

41. Simonian, *Partnership,* pp. 222–224.

42. Quoted in Roger Morgan, "The Historical Background, 1955–85," in Roger Morgan and Caroline Bray, eds., *Partners and Rivals in Western Europe: Britain, France, and Germany* (Brookfield, VT: Gower, 1986), p. 16.

43. Jenkins, *Centre,* p. 375.

44. Jenkins, *Centre,* pp. 399–40.

45. Nicholson and East, *Enlargement,* pp. 165–180.

46. Commission, *1974 General Report,* Annex to Chapter I, point 24.

47. Peter Ludlow, *The Making of the European Monetary System: A Case Study in the Politics of the European Community* (London: Butterworths Scientific, 1982), p. 33.

48. See Nicholson and East, *Enlargement,* pp. 165–180.

49. *The Times* (London), March 10, 1975, p. 1, and March 11, 1975, p. 1.

50. Jenkins, *Centre,* p. 417.

51. Quoted in Nicholson and East, *Enlargement,* p. 180.

52. Jenkins, *Centre,* p. 342.

53. George, *Awkward Partner,* p. 87.

54. See Simonian, *Partnership,* pp. 139–140; Morgan, "Background," pp. 17–18; William Wallace, introduction to Morgan and Bray, *Partners,* p. 2.

55. James Goldsborough, "The Franco-German Entente," *Foreign Affairs* 54, no. 3 (April 1976): 499.

56. Wallace, introduction to Morgan and Bray, *Partners,* p. 4.

57. Ludlow, *European Monetary System,* p.22.

58. Paul Lewis, "An Unhappy Briton in Brussels," *The New York Times,* November 6, 1977, sec. 3, p. 7.

59. Jonathan Storey, "The Franco-German Alliance Within the European Community," *World Today,* June 1980: 209.

60. Roy Jenkins, *European Diary, 1977–1981* (London: Collins, 1989), pp. 479–480.

61. Goldsborough, "Entente," p. 504.

62. The *Economist* broke the story on January 27, 1979, p. 43.

63. Harold Wilson, "How National Muscle Is Brought to Bear Among the EEC Leaders," *The Times* (London), June 28, 1977, p. 16.

64. Jenkins, *Centre,* p. 459.

65. *Le Monde,* May 7, 1977, p. 1.

66. *The Financial Times,* March 18, 1972, p. 14.

67. Bull. EC S/1-1976.

68. See A. N. Duff, "The Report of the Three Wise Men," *Journal of Common Market Studies* 19, no. 3: 238; and Bull. EC 11-1976, Presidency Conclusions, point 2427.

69. Helen Wallace explains these concepts in *Europe: The Challenge of Diversity* (Boston: Routledge & K. Paul, 1985), pp. 29–49.

70. Commission, *1979 General Report*, point 8.

71. Jenkins, *Diary,* p. 311.

72. Duff, "Wise Men," p. 240.

73. Bull. EC 11-1979, Presidency Conclusions, points 1.5.1–2.

4

Turning the Corner,
1979–1984

At the beginning of the 1980s, there were few outward signs that the Community had survived the challenges of the 1970s. The twenty-fifth anniversary of the Treaty of Rome, observed in March 1982, was a dismal affair. Commenting on the Community's plight, the *Economist* sniped that "a twenty-five year old in a coma is a pitiful sight."[1] Piet Dankert, president of the European Parliament, used a similar analogy. Remarking on a report that the Council of Ministers had canceled the official celebration, he compared the Community to "a feeble cardiac patient whose condition is so poor that he cannot even be disturbed by a birthday party."[2]

Academics were equally alarmed by the patient's precarious health. In *The European Community: Progress or Decline?* five prominent professors from five Community countries expressed their concern. Unusual in an academic publication, the opening paragraph got straight to the point: "This report is born out of a sense of alarm and urgency. The authors, with their different backgrounds as citizens of large or small member states . . . all share the conviction that Western Europe is drifting [and] that the existence of the European Community is under serious threat. . . . If nothing is done, we are faced with the disintegration of the most important European achievement since World War II."[3] As if to prove their thesis, the European Council at Athens in December 1983 ended in ignominy. For the first time in the history of EC summitry, the heads of government could not agree on a concluding communiqué.

The Community's problems were legion: a paralyzed decision-making process, a feeble Commission, a CAP apparently out of control, a new French president (Mitterrand) pursuing a "dash for growth" that further strained Community solidarity, and a new British prime minister (Thatcher) who constantly rebuked her colleagues with incessant demands for a budget rebate. Under the circumstances, Greenland's decision in February 1982 to become the first (and so far only) territory to leave the Community seemed entirely appropriate.

Yet a number of events and developments in the late 1970s and early 1980s presaged the Community's impending revival. A busy 1979 brought an accession treaty with Greece, the first direct elections to the European Parliament, and the launch of the European Monetary System (EMS). Hopes that these events would cure the Community's disorder by prompting institutional reform, deeper integration, and renewed interest in Economic and Monetary Union (EMU) proved justified, but not right away. In the meantime, the Community became embroiled in the debilitating British budgetary question, which dominated the next five years and fifteen summits. Only when the heads of government resolved the budgetary question at Fontainebleau in June 1984 was the Community able to find the time and energy to move ahead.

Once unfettered by acrimonious arguments about Britain's financial contribution, the Community suddenly reveled in the impact of other, less perceptible but no less powerful developments that, over the past four years, had gradually generated momentum for greater integration. These included the trend toward deregulation and liberalization sweeping Europe from the United States; increasing cooperation between the Commission and leading industrialists to boost European competitiveness, especially in the high technology sector; and growing business interest in the realization of a single market. These changes, combined with the European Parliament's determination to revise the Treaty of Rome, member states' worries about Europe's apparent impotence during a sudden drop in Cold War temperatures, and consensus on the need to improve decisionmaking procedures in view of imminent enlargement, helped to set the Community on the road to "1992": i.e., the single market. As Christopher Tugendhat, a commissioner in the early 1980s, remarked at the time, "one has the feeling of ice breaking up and spring approaching."[4]

SECOND ENLARGEMENT, DIRECT ELECTIONS, AND THE EMS

The Commission's 1979 "Progress Toward European Union" report—an annual memento of the Tindemans Report—was unusually upbeat.[5] Three events that year held out the prospect of a modest improvement in the Community's fortunes: the Treaty of Accession with Greece; the first direct elections to the European Parliament; and the inauguration of the EMS. The authors of the Commission report could not have imagined how different the Community would be ten years later. The single market, the European Economic Area (a combined EEC-EFTA market), and revolution in Eastern Europe were beyond their wildest dreams. Little did they realize that Greece's accession—in the broader context of the Community's southern enlargement—direct elections, and the EMS would contribute, indirectly but importantly, to the Community's remarkable revival in the 1980s. Yet, given the Community's miserable record in the recent past, the 1979 progress report's guarded optimism seemed unfounded.

In view of the Community's experience with the first enlargement, Greece's impending accession—and the prospective membership also of Spain and Portugal—were dubious grounds for confidence. Nor did direct elections, delayed for many years and openly unwelcome to a number of member states opposed to a stronger Parliament, seem a likely source of Community resurgence. Even the EMS, an initiative launched with unusual speed to establish a degree of exchange rate stability, appeared to have little potential for the Community's long-term growth. Cumulatively, however, these three developments marked the beginning of the end of the Community's depression. Although major difficulties lay immediately ahead, the Community in 1979 slowly turned the corner toward a dramatic new departure.

Much of the credit should go to Roy Jenkins, Commission president between 1977 and 1981. Having spent his entire career in British politics and with little experience in foreign affairs, Jenkins was a Brussels outsider. He would have preferred to stay in London, but his ardent Europeanism at the time of Britain's accession and during the subsequent "renegotiation" doomed Jenkins's career in the Labour Party. By the end of the Ortoli presidency, most member states agreed that Britain, as a large recent arrival, should provide Ortoli's successor. Jenkins's seniority, pro-Community credentials, and underemployment at home made him the Labour government's obvious choice; the small member states looked forward to a Commission president from a large member state other than France or Germany; Giscard championed Jenkins from the beginning; and Schmidt easily concurred.

Especially because he succeeded the uninspiring Ortoli, Jenkins's arrival in the Berlaymont (the building that houses the Commission) aroused inflated expectations. But Jenkins "got off to a slow and uncertain start. During his first six months or so on the job, he appeared visibly ill at ease and depressed."[6] A bitter dispute with Giscard over Jenkins's participation in the London summit of major industrialized countries in May 1977 took up too much of that time. For all the excitement surrounding his appointment, by mid-1977 it looked as if Jenkins's presidency would be as forgettable as any in the years since Hallstein's resignation.

Yet two of the three developments that later distinguished the Jenkins presidency were already in the works. The first was Greece's accession to the Community. Between 1967 and 1974, during the military regime in Athens, the Community suspended its 1962 association agreement with Greece. Following the restoration of democracy, the Community reactivated the association agreement; soon afterward Greece applied for full membership, which the agreement had in any case envisioned. Assessing the Greek application on its economic merits, in January 1976 the Commission advised against accession. The Council of Ministers, on the other hand, saw the Greek case primarily from a political perspective. As German Foreign Minister Hans-Dietrich Genscher told the Bundestag, "Greece, only recently returned to the democratic fold, would march in future with the Community of European nations."[7] Exploiting such sentiments to the full, Greece began entry negotiations in Brussels on July 27, 1976.

If the Community could have foreseen the problems that Greek membership would pose in the 1980s during the tenure of Andreas Papandreou's anti-EC government, the accession negotiations might not have concluded so swiftly. As it was, the Greek case coincided with the membership applications of Spain and Portugal, which similarly emerged from dictatorship in the mid-1970s. Faced with the prospect of a large southern enlargement, member states soon took the economic implications much more seriously. France especially feared the consequences of competition with another large, agricultural, Mediterranean member state. Skillfully separating his country from the increasingly complex Iberian entry negotiations, Prime Minister Karamanlis successfully reached an accession agreement with the Community in April 1979. Signed in Athens in May 1979 and duly ratified in Greece and the member states, the Treaty of Accession came into effect on January 1, 1981.[8]

Of the three Mediterranean applicants, Jenkins considered Greece "the least qualified for membership."[9] Yet the Commission president appreciated the political arguments in favor of enlargement and hoped that the accession first of Greece, then of Spain and Portugal, would help to propel the Community out of its institutional malaise. If only to prevent greater sluggishness in Community decisionmaking once enlargement took place, Jenkins urged the existing member states to introduce badly needed institutional reforms. Indeed, following Jenkins's departure, the impending accession of Spain and Portugal became an important impetus for change in the Community and was one of a number of factors that gave rise to the Single European Act (SEA). In the meantime, Jenkins had played a modest part in facilitating Greece's accession, launching the Spanish and Portuguese negotiations, and drawing attention to the institutional implications of further enlargement. Yet it was more by accident than design that the southern enlargement had come to the fore during Jenkins's years in Brussels, just as it was beyond Jenkins's control that the Community would enjoy the political benefits of enlargement after his return to London.

By the same token, the first direct elections to the European Parliament had been planned well before the Jenkins presidency, and their role in the Community's subsequent revival only became apparent afterward. The Treaty of Rome provided for a directly elected assembly, but member state recalcitrance had prevented the switch from an appointed to an elected Parliament until the late 1970s. As a gesture to counterbalance the creation of the European Council, the heads of government decided at the 1974 Paris summit to hold direct elections "as soon as possible."[10] Three years later, the European Council was still haggling over the apportionment of seats in the directly elected Parliament. In October 1976 the European Council finally settled on 410 seats, over twice the number in the existing Parliament, distributed among the member states approximately according to population size. Because of Britain's difficulty meeting the summer 1978 deadline for the elections, the European Council decided at the Brussels summit in December 1977 to postpone the elections until 1979.[11]

Among the member states, Britain and France openly disliked direct elections because of concern that a stronger European Parliament would undermine national supremacy in the Community's decisionmaking process. At the other end of the spectrum, Germany, the Netherlands, and Italy traditionally favored a stronger Parliament as a corollary to their inherent support for European integration. Similarly, the Commission saw a stronger Parliament as a natural ally in the inevitable interinstitutional struggle for greater power in the Community. Perhaps because of his years in the British political system, where the government is directly answerable to the House of Commons, Jenkins especially encouraged direct elections and exaggerated their impact on the European Parliament. Thus, he wrote at the time, the first direct elections "produced a potentially formidable new Parliament, twice the size of the old, which [the Commission] approached with a mixture of respect and apprehension."[12]

In the event, the direct elections of June 1979 did not cause a radical redistribution of power in the Community. Only a revision of the Treaty of Rome, as happened in the SEA of 1986 and the Maastricht Treaty of 1992, could enhance the European Parliament's role in Community decisionmaking. However, direct elections brought a new breed of MEP to Strasbourg and noticeably improved the Parliament's morale. The amount of attention paid to it by the Commission and successive Community presidencies also increased Strasbourg's assertiveness. Out of that higher morale, greater confidence, and soaring self-assurance came a "Draft Treaty Establishing the European Union" in February 1984, which played an important part in the Community's subsequent revival. In that sense, the Commission's 1979 "Report on European Union" was prophetic.

The third development in 1979 that helped get the Community out of the doldrums owed a great deal directly to Roy Jenkins. This was the

EMS, an initiative to establish a zone of relative monetary stability in a world of wildly fluctuating exchange rates. The EMS was a striking success and helped participating member states to fight inflation and recover economic growth. According to the Dooge Report of 1985, the EMS "enabled the unity of the Common Market to be preserved, reasonable exchange rates to be maintained, and the foundations of the Community's monetary identity to be laid."[13] Unknown to the Dooge committee at the time, the EMS would also provide a vital underpinning for the spectacularly successful single market program. As Peter Ludlow has observed, "the EMS was a precondition for . . . 1992. Had the EMS not been created and functioned so well, the [1985] White Paper strategy could not have been contemplated, let alone implemented."[14]

Ludlow chronicled the origins of the EMS in a masterly monograph that reads like a novel.[15] Jenkins's extensive *European Diaries* and his later political autobiography verify much of what Ludlow wrote. The story of the EMS has the ingredients of a political thriller: Jenkins's courage and prescience in proposing a monetary initiative after the failure of the Werner Plan and the currency "snake"; Ortoli's initial opposition in the Commission; Schmidt's sudden espousal of a scheme for exchange rate stability and his determination to see it through despite strong domestic opposition; Giscard's less enthusiastic but nonetheless strong support, and his apparent U-turn at the last moment; the efficacy of the Franco-German alliance in convincing the Community to adopt the EMS; Britain's refusal yet again to take the plunge; and the value of the European Council for rapid decisionmaking at the highest level. Altogether, the EMS is a unique but indispensable case study of EC decisionmaking and policy formulation.

Despite the disappointment of his first few months in office, Jenkins yearned for an initiative that would boost the Commission's morale and reinvigorate the Community. Jenkins's knowledge of economics, success as chancellor of the exchequer in the UK, and concern about the impact on the Community of oscillating international exchange rates led him inexorably toward action in the monetary field. Ortoli, he knew, would be skeptical. Renowned for his caution, enjoying considerable prestige as a former Commission president, and holding the senior portfolio of monetary affairs, Ortoli was a formidable potential adversary. Thus, Jenkins had to proceed gingerly in the Commission before broaching the subject publicly.

For someone supposedly inept at handling his Commission colleagues, Jenkins displayed unusual tact and consideration. First he raised the idea of a major monetary initiative with his cabinet during a retreat at his home in England in August 1977. Next he brought up the subject with his Commission colleagues at a retreat in the Ardennes the following month. Ortoli's predictable response presaged an internal Commission struggle that lasted until Schmidt took up the running in early 1978. Jenkins diluted his original proposal in deference to Ortoli so as not to alienate a powerful colleague and jeopardize the entire scheme. At the same time, Jenkins knew that Ortoli's innate sense of loyalty would limit the extent of the former Commission president's opposition.

Jenkins used the occasion of the inaugural Monnet Lecture at the Community-sponsored European University Institute in Florence to fly a trial balloon. Rather than present a precise proposal, Jenkins sought to reopen the debate about monetary union in the context of the Community's political and economic infirmity in the late 1970s. Apart from making predictable points about advancing European integration and helping to realize the common market's full potential, Jenkins argued that monetary union would have the macroeconomic advantages of lowering inflation, increasing investment, and reducing unemployment. Nor, if properly implemented, would monetary union exacerbate regional economic disparities or intensify institutional centralization in Brussels.[16]

Following up his public pronouncement, Jenkins tried to revive the member states' interest in the idea of monetary union. Of his various bilateral meetings that fall, a visit to Chancellor Schmidt in Bonn on November 8 was by far the most important. Given the economic power and increasing political influence of Germany, Bonn's position could make or break Jenkins's initiative. Moreover, Schmidt not only had an unparalleled grasp of international economics but also desired a degree of monetary stability in the Western world that the United States was no longer able to provide. But Jenkins found Schmidt in a characteristically gloomy mood, preoccupied with an extreme-left-wing terrorist campaign and unwilling to take a lead in the Community.

The tension between Jenkins's advocacy of what he called in Florence a bold "leap forward" and Ortoli's step-by-step approach resulted in a surprisingly cautious Commission communication to the Council on the subject of EMU.[17] Nor was there much discussion of EMU at the European Council in Brussels on December 5–6, 1977, where Jenkins noted Schmidt's "benevolent skepticism" and detected "a fair if not tremendously enthusiastic wind behind our monetary union proposals."[18] Despite strong support from the Belgian presidency, which wanted an imaginative Community initiative in the spirit of the Tindemans Report, by the end of 1977 Jenkins's trial balloon seemed to have fallen flat. To compound Jenkins's disappointment, Germany was one of the least interested member states.

Jenkins's attempt to revive EMU would have withered entirely but for Schmidt's sudden conversion to it, or at least to a modified version of what Jenkins wanted, in early 1978. Schmidt told Jenkins about his newfound enthusiasm for an effort to achieve Community-wide exchange rate stability during a meeting in Bonn on February 28, a date that marks the conception of the EMS. Jenkins was at a loss to explain the reason for Schmidt's sudden change of heart. Was it a function of the chancellor's mercurial personality? Was it an antidote to his domestic security problems? Was it anger with the United States over yet another drop in the dollar's value?[19] One or more of those reasons may explain the timing of Schmidt's espousal of a quasi-fixed exchange rate regime. The fundamental cause of his "conversion," however, went much deeper. Persistent depreciation of the dollar and a corresponding appreciation of the mark cut German industrial competitiveness and fed speculation that a U.S. economic recovery was happening at the expense of German prudence and prosperity. "In this situation . . . Schmidt decided to seek a kind of monetary burden-sharing in the EC, i.e. to promote conditions in which dollar weakness would have as its counterpart not a disproportionate appreciation of the DM but a more moderate appreciation of a wider range of European currencies."[20]

Overnight, Schmidt replaced Jenkins as the principal proponent of a monetary policy initiative and championed what subsequently became the EMS. Moreover, Schmidt's crucial collaborator was not the president of the Commission but the president of France. Alone or with Jenkins's sole support, Schmidt might not have been able to bring the monetary initiative rapidly to fruition. But with Giscard's backing the EMS proposal quickly gathered speed. Having survived the March 1978 parliamentary elections, Giscard and Raymond Barre, France's pro-Community prime minister and author of the Commission's first-ever plan for EMU, enthusiastically endorsed Schmidt's scheme. Giscard's support owed more to friendship with Schmidt than to a desire to reduce pressure on the mark. Regardless of Giscard's motivation, however, the birth of the EMS one year later "came from a clear convergence of French and German interests, confirming the two countries' leading roles in the Community."[21]

Regular meetings of the European Council provided Schmidt and Giscard with an opportunity to promote their monetary proposal and a forum in which to approve the EMS at the highest possible decisionmaking level in the Community. In trying to convince the December 1977 Brussels summit to take up his monetary initiative, Jenkins had demonstrated a keen awareness of the European Council's potential. Alone, however, the Commission president proved unable to sway skeptical heads of government. By contrast, Giscard and Schmidt possessed enormous powers of political persuasion. When they unveiled their exchange rate idea in April 1978 at the European Council in Copenhagen, only Callaghan expressed serious concern, as much about apparent Franco-German collusion as about the validity of the proposal itself. Nevertheless, the British prime minister agreed to explore the idea further. Yet resentment of close Franco-German collaboration and doubts about the scheme's validity quickly convinced Callaghan not to allow his personal representative to participate with Giscard's and Schmidt's personal representatives in subsequent planning. Thus, the EMS blueprint put before the next European Council, convened in Bremen in July 1978, bore an exclusive Franco-German imprint.

The Bremen summit marked a decisive stage in the gestation of the EMS. Schmidt's forceful chairmanship contributed to a general acceptance of the Franco-German proposal, although Britain's unwillingness to participate in the future EMS became obvious as the European Council progressed. In his political autobiography, Jenkins vividly described the British delegation's deliberately late arrival: "They marched [into the European Council] in single file like a jungle expedition into hostile territory, first Callaghan, then [Foreign Secretary] Owen, then six or seven senior officials, then about fifteen bearers carrying twice that amount of red despatch boxes, which must . . . have been more for show than use during a twenty-four hour period."[22] Callaghan's sullenness and Owen's aloofness persisted throughout the summit and presaged Britain's eventual self-exclusion from the system. Britain's decision not to take part in the system's Exchange Rate Mechanism was of more than symbolic importance because, as Helen Wallace has pointed out, "for many of those involved the EMS was viewed, rightly or wrongly, as a critical stage in the development of the EC as a whole."[23]

The Franco-German proposal presented at Bremen appeared virtually unchanged in the summit communiqué. It called for an exchange rate mechanism using a parity grid and a divergence indicator based on the European currency unit (ECU).[24] Although still open to amendment, the Bremen proposal became the basis of the future EMS, which the member states hoped to implement as early as January 1979. In the meantime, officials worked diligently in a number of specialized committees to thrash out details of the scheme. At a political level, one of the most contentious last-minute questions concerned compensation for poorer participating countries. Both Ireland and Italy demanded an increase in the Regional Fund and subsidized loans for infrastructural development. The problem of resource redistribution ("concurrent measures" in Eurospeak) became politically charged when France and Britain insisted that their shares of a larger Regional Fund be equal to their shares of the existing fund and Germany balked at paying the bill. Nor would Giscard approve the amount of subsidized loans that Ireland and Italy requested. This bickering did not augur well for the Brussels summit of December 4–5, 1978, the decisive European Council before the expected implementation of the EMS.

At Brussels, Callaghan finally announced Britain's refusal to join, a decision that saddened but hardly surprised the rest of the Community. However, a last-minute compromise by Schmidt broke the "concurrent measures" deadlock and ensured that the remaining member states would participate in the scheme. Yet fears of an aborted EMS seemed warranted when a new problem suddenly arose at the summit involving the impact of the EMS on the CAP.[25] The issue had to do with Giscard's demand for the abolition of monetary compensatory amounts (MCAs), a mechanism introduced in the early 1970s to cushion the CAP from exchange rate fluctuations. This demand proved politically unacceptable to Germany, where MCAs helped to prop up agricultural prices. A meeting of agriculture ministers on December 19, only two weeks before the proposed launch of the EMS, failed to find a solution.

Giscard's last-minute intransigence over MCAs baffled his Community counterparts, not least because of the amount of time and effort he had put into planning the EMS. Annoyance with other developments in the Community, notably over the way in which the European Parliament passed its December 1978 budget, may have accounted for Giscard's action. Moreover, opposing MCAs made sound political sense in France, especially in the prelude to the first direct elections to the European Parliament. In the event, Giscard's abandonment of the MCA issue was as swift as his embracing of it. Following an agreement at a meeting of agriculture ministers in early March 1979 to abolish MCAs without specifying a timetable, Giscard announced his unconditional support for the EMS. On March 13, 1979, the system finally came into operation.

The EMS was substantially different from what Jenkins had originally envisioned. What emerged in 1979 was "a hybrid—not entirely Community, nor entirely outside it."[26] Only EC member states could participate in the EMS, although none was obliged to do so. The EMS was not based on the Treaty of Rome, although closer monetary coordination, and eventually EMU, were cherished Community objectives. Nor did it emerge from a Commission proposal, although Community institutions, notably the Council of Finance Ministers (Ecofin), are central to its successful operation. Thus, for all its peculiarities, the EMS represented an important breakthrough for Brussels. Regardless of its subsequent development, the fact of its existence and the relative speed with which the EMS came into being marked an important milestone in the Community's history.

The launch of the EMS, the accession treaty with Greece, and the first direct elections to the European Parliament ended an otherwise disappointing decade for the Community on a high note. Nevertheless, the long-term beneficial impact of these developments could not have been predicted in 1979. On the contrary, as the 1970s came to a close the Community seemed as desultory as ever before. The French presidency during the first half of the year lacked imagination and direction. Giscard's petulance over the agricultural implications of the EMS set the tone for France's stewardship of the Community. The uneven struggle between the Council and Commission presidencies for power and prestige reopened with a vengeance. For Jenkins, the first six months of 1979 were "a test of nerves such as no other [national] Presidency has provided."[27] Little wonder that, as the year progressed, Jenkins turned his thoughts more and more toward returning to British politics. The unedifying revival of the British budgetary question pushed Jenkins irrevocably in that direction.

THE BRITISH BUDGETARY QUESTION

In May 1979 the Conservative Party won the British general election, and Margaret Thatcher became prime minister. The European Community was no stranger to Thatcher: In 1975 she had stoutly supported Britain's continued membership in the Community in her maiden speech as opposition leader in the House of Commons. Sir Michael Butler, UK permanent representative to the Community between 1979 and 1985, claims that "from the beginning [of her prime ministership] . . . she showed a deep-seated prejudice against the EC."[28] Thatcher also showed ignorance of the Community's institutions and policies and, according to one of her biographers, tended to see the Community as a branch of NATO.[29] But she grasped the potential for British trade of continued Community membership and later became one of the foremost proponents of the single market program. Although the Community was effectively moribund in 1979, she also grasped Brussels's aspiration to promote supranationalism and undermine the nation-state. This she strenuously rejected. In Thatcher's view, European integration should not go beyond the removal of barriers to trade and investment and the coordination of economic and foreign policies exclusively on an intergovernmental basis.

Thatcher grasped another thing about the Community even before she became prime minister: the obvious unfairness of Britain's budgetary contribution. Simply put, Britain paid too much and received too little in return. That anomaly should have been rectified in the mid-1970s at the time of Wilson's "renegotiation" of Britain's membership terms. The 1975 renegotiation, however, had been largely a cosmetic exercise to appease British public opinion and keep the Labour Party together. Moreover, in the intervening years special transitional arrangements for the UK had cushioned the financial burden of membership. Only at the end of the decade did the extent of Britain's injustice become fully apparent. As a substantial importer from outside the Community of food and manufactured goods, Britain paid a huge amount in customs duties and agricultural levies to Brussels; as a country with a small and highly efficient farm sector, Britain got little back from the CAP, which accounted for 70 percent of Community expenditure. The figures were striking: Britain's net payments to the Community averaged 60 million pounds sterling between 1973 and 1976; they amounted to 369 million in 1977, 822 million in 1978, and 947 million in 1979.[30]

Here was a cause dear to Thatcher's heart. Britain's demand for reform was clear-cut, easily comprehensible, fair, and assured of widespread domestic support. The budgetary issue "appealed perfectly to her sense of justice, of economy and of British nationhood."[31] How could her Community colleagues possibly not concede the point? Even the Commission's own figures bolstered Britain's case. Thatcher surely had a natural ally in Helmut Schmidt, whose country also paid too much to the Community (although Germany could afford to do so and was unlikely to complain in any event because of lingering war guilt). Also, righting Britain's wrong would strengthen the Community. Thatcher correctly argued that without budgetary reform, the British public, already equivocal about European integration, would turn solidly against the Community and might even insist on withdrawal. Thus, for Thatcher, the "British budgetary question" became not only a basic question of right and wrong, but also a campaign to save the Community.

Under these circumstances, it seems surprising that the issue nearly wrecked the Community and filled a reservoir of ill feeling toward Britain in Brussels. Admittedly, Britain's Community partners were predisposed not to reopen the budgetary question. Wilson's handling of the original renegotiation five years previously had left a bitter taste in people's mouths. Yet such was the justness of Britain's case that even the most resentful of Eurocrats and member state officials would have had to accept further reform.

What turned a relatively straightforward case into one of the most complex and divisive issues in the Community's history was Thatcher's abrasive personality and truculent approach to the renegotiations. Being the "new kid on the block" at European Council meetings, a woman in a hitherto exclusively male world, may have fired Thatcher's innate aggression. She also suspected the Commission and the other member states of uniformly opposing Britain's position. Thatcher conducted the protracted negotiations over the budgetary question with "the confidence of someone who thought she was on a winning streak and the zeal of a leader who positively relished destroying the shibboleths of quiet diplomacy."[32] Moreover, she soon discovered that an aggressive approach enhanced her reputation at home as a dogged defender of British interests and increased her political standing at a time of otherwise plummeting ratings.

Helmut Schmidt was the first Community leader to visit Thatcher as prime minister. She immediately informed Schmidt of her determination to get a better budgetary deal.[33] That set the stage for her first European Council, held in Strasbourg on June 21–22, 1979. The Strasbourg summit turned into a skirmish, during which Thatcher fired a warning shot. According to Roy Jenkins, who attended as Commission president, Thatcher "spoke shrilly and too frequently, and succeeded in embroiling not only Giscard (which maybe was unavoidable), but also in turn van Agt (the Netherlands), Jorgensen (Denmark) and Lynch (Ireland). Then, worst of all, she got into an altercation with Schmidt, whose support was crucial to her getting the outcome she wanted from the meeting."[34] That summer and fall Thatcher marshaled her forces and prepared for the first pitched battle: the Dublin summit on November 29–30, 1979.

Thatcher's behavior especially upset Jenkins, for whom the initials "BBQ" came to mean not the "British Budgetary Question" but the "Bloody British Question."[35] Jenkins tried before the Dublin summit to narrow the ground between Thatcher and everybody else. His main problem was that the ground had not yet been adequately prepared or defined. Although Thatcher demanded Britain's money back, neither she nor any of her interlocutors had mentioned a precise sum. Not surprisingly, the Dublin summit soon degenerated into open combat. Thatcher's tactics were to grind her enemies down by endlessly repeating her main arguments and keeping everyone up late after dinner. Infuriated, the Danish prime minister hurled insults; bored, the German chancellor feigned sleep; disdainful, the French president ignored her; embarrassed, the Irish prime minister wished it weren't happening.[36] The only positive note at the end of the summit was Thatcher's agreement to approach the next European Council, set for Luxembourg on April 28, 1980, "in a spirit of genuine compromise."[37]

Nevertheless, the Luxembourg summit saw a resumption of hand-to-hand fighting. This time precise figures were mentioned. Indeed, the difference between what Thatcher demanded and what the others offered was relatively small. Helmut Schmidt pointed the way to a solution by suggesting that Britain's budget deficit in the Community in 1980 should not be more than the average for 1978 and 1979. Giscard seconded Schmidt's suggestion and even proposed extending the arrangement for 1981. Thatcher spent lunchtime closeted with her advisers. When she returned, much to everyone's surprise she rejected the offer.[38] Thatcher departed the field of battle bloodied but unbowed; the other combatants left Luxembourg in despair.

Italy, then in the Community presidency, redoubled its efforts to resolve the problem. The decisive encounter took place at the Council of Ministers meeting on May 29, 1980. The Eight refined their earlier offer, which Lord Carrington, Thatcher's foreign secretary and an eminently reasonable person, accepted. Thus, the scene of hostilities switched to the home front, where Carrington had to convince Thatcher to endorse the Council's agreement. Carrington spent a miserable weekend at Chequers, the prime minister's country residence, trying to persuade an obdurate and frequently abusive Thatcher. According to Thatcher's biographer, "the struggle between [them] . . . at Chequers that weekend, as she struggled to deny [Carrington] and herself a considerable success in economic diplomacy, deserves a prominent place in the annals of political perversity."[39]

Thatcher carried on the struggle at the cabinet meeting on Monday morning, but her usually compliant ministers stuck to their guns and recommended acceptance. Reluctantly, Thatcher acquiesced.

Although Thatcher was notoriously averse to compromise, doubtless it was easier for her to concede to her cabinet colleagues than to her Community counterparts. Yet why she wanted to reject Carrington's agreement is unclear. The foreign secretary had brought back from Brussels the best deal possible. Rejecting it would have been tantamount to rejecting the Community, which Thatcher claimed not to want to do. Nor could she have gleaned much more political capital from saying "no" to Brussels. Already, public opinion in Britain was beginning to turn against her European histrionics. It is difficult to avoid the conclusion that Thatcher's fierce determination to settle only on her own terms was part of her political pathology.

Thatcher's antics had caused immense damage to the Community. For nearly a year, while the international economy slid back into recession, Community leaders were preoccupied with the budgetary question. Nor were they able to exploit the potential that Greek accession, direct elections to the European Parliament, and the launch of the EMS held for a renewal of momentum toward greater European integration. Perhaps most damaging of all, Thatcher's behavior robbed Britain of a potential leadership role in Brussels. At home, Thatcher's handling of the budgetary question "implanted the germs which led to the death of the fine legacy of Conservative Europeanism which Macmillan had tentatively revived . . . and Heath had greatly enhanced. It was a heavy price to pay for 400 million ECUs [the difference between both sides at the negotiating table]."[40]

The 1980 agreement was merely a temporary resolution of the British budgetary question. As expected, Thatcher returned to the charge in 1983, the tenth anniversary of Britain's Community membership. This time she sought a permanent solution to the budgetary problem, not merely a series of annual remedies. The Stuttgart summit of June 1983 provided the first opportunity for a showdown. Yet the contrast with 1979 was striking. Then Thatcher had been a newcomer in the exclusive European Council club, long dominated by Giscard and Schmidt, two close friends; now she was a veteran, flanked by François Mitterrand and Helmut Kohl, the relatively new president of France and chancellor of Germany, respectively. With the help of Jacques Delors, his finance minister, Mitterrand in 1983 had jettisoned an early, failed experiment in stimulating employment and economic growth and was in the process of rediscovering the European Community.[41] Kohl was finding his feet domestically and internationally, having replaced Schmidt the previous year. He and Mitterrand had not yet struck up the firm friendship for which they would later become famous. Neither leader could match Thatcher's grasp of detail or passion for the budgetary question; Stuttgart was their baptism of fire.

Two other factors, one domestic and the other European, further strengthened Thatcher's position. First, her popularity at home had soared in the aftermath of the Falklands War. Having taken on the Argentinians, Thatcher was set to take on her Community partners. The British public stood squarely behind her. Even the opposition Labour Party, at that time committed to pulling out of the Community if it ever got back into office, could hardly criticize her efforts to get a better budgetary deal for Britain. Second, the Community was financially strapped. In the early 1980s the CAP had run out of control, with an obscene accumulation of surplus production for which farmers received guaranteed high prices. The Community would have to reform the CAP and/or increase its overall budget. Thatcher favored CAP reform, which she knew the other member states would find politically difficult to agree to, let alone implement. But she was not about to approve a budget increase unless Britain's contribution was once and for all resolved.

If Stuttgart saw the opening clash in a new campaign, the Athens summit of December 1983 provided the first major encounter. Even apart from the looming confrontation over the British budgetary question, the omens for the summit were far from favorable. Countries in the EC presidency generally view the European Council to be held in their country as an opportunity to enhance international prestige and mediate Community disputes. Greece was no exception. Prime Minister Andreas Papandreou took on the role of Community broker with relish and genuinely hoped to find a solution to the vexed issues of the Community budget, the British contribution to it, and CAP reform. But there was little goodwill among the other Community leaders toward Papandreou in particular and Greece in general. Since coming to power in 1981, Papandreou had pursued a virulent anti-U.S. and anti-EC foreign policy. Few were willing to give him the benefit of the doubt at the Athens summit. Under the circumstances, not only did the expected clash with Thatcher dominate the summit, but the heads of government departed without issuing a communiqué.

The situation changed dramatically for the better in January 1984, when France took over the EC presidency. By that time Mitterrand was personally committed to finding a way out of the budgetary impasse and relaunching the Community by reforming its institutions and extending its agenda. The French presidency was due to end with a European Council just outside Paris, in the spectacular setting of the palace at Fontainebleau, which holds a special place in French history as the scene of Napoleon's farewell to his generals. Mitterrand hoped the budgetary questions would be resolved before Fontainebleau so the European Council there could concentrate instead on strategies for the Community's revival. Also, France was far better equipped diplomatically and bureaucratically to resolve the budgetary problem than Ireland, which would take over the presidency in July 1984.

The European Council in Brussels on March 19–20, 1984, afforded an ideal opportunity to thrash out the various budgetary problems three months before the Fontainebleau summit. Mitterrand and Roland Dumas, his European affairs minister, attempted to negotiate an agreement in a series of bilateral meetings with other Community leaders for weeks before the Brussels summit. A decision by agriculture ministers immediately before the European Council to curtail expenditure by limiting milk production augured well for the Brussels summit. Although the summit itself opened badly, with Thatcher in classic inflexible form, French and British negotiators worked throughout the night of March 19 to draft a settlement. They eventually came up with a complicated compensatory mechanism that related Britain's payments to its relative prosperity. Much to their dismay, the proposal collapsed the next morning when Thatcher remained intransigent, Kohl refused to agree, and Garret FitzGerald, the Irish prime minister, walked out because his colleagues on the European Council would not exempt Ireland from the previous week's milk agreement.

Mitterrand and Dumas resumed their quiet diplomacy in preparation for the Fontainebleau summit, despite the president's preoccupation with huge popular protests against his government's recent education reforms. For all Mitterrand's efforts, there was nothing to suggest that a breakthrough on the budget was imminent as the heads of government converged in ceremonial splendor on Fontainebleau on June 25, 1984, covered by an army of thirteen hundred journalists. Talk in previous weeks of a possible "two-speed" Europe, with Britain in the slow lane, had not helped matters; nor had Thatcher's clever definition of what a "two-speed" Europe meant: "Those who pay most are in the top group and those who pay less are not."[42] Continued squabbling over Britain's budgetary contribution was a pitiful prelude not only to the Fontainebleau summit but especially to the second direct elections to the European Parliament.

Mitterrand's strategy at Fontainebleau was to avoid the kind of friction that had marred the opening of the Brussels summit.[43] As the summit progressed, a surprising willingness to compromise gradually became apparent. Thatcher seemed eager to settle the long-standing dispute and move the Community in new directions; the others were equally warweary and desperately wanted to reach a comprehensive budget agreement. That evening, the heads of government asked their foreign ministers to draft a resolution to the British dispute based not on the mechanism proposed at the Brussels summit but on a rebate in the form of a fixed percentage each year of Britain's net contribution. The outstanding issue thus became the precise size of the fixed percentage. Thatcher held out for 66 percent; Kohl demurred. Finally, after some concessions to Germany on the CAP, the chancellor lifted his objections at lunch on June 26. The British budgetary dispute was over.[44]

Had anything good come of it? Undoubtedly Thatcher's conduct antagonized her Community colleagues and protracted the painful negotiations. Yet without her aggressive approach Britain might not have secured such a favorable result: The Fontainebleau agreement saved the UK over 10 billion pounds sterling in the remainder of the 1980s. For all the aggravation and frustration generated during the previous two years, arguably Thatcher needed time to build her case, exhaust the opposition, and secure a satisfactory solution. It also may be argued that resolution of Britain's budgetary dispute helped the Community's long-term development, and not only in the obvious sense of removing a persistent irritant in relations between member states. For Thatcher brought home to the Community the folly of overexpenditure and the need to rein in the CAP. Indeed, the heads of government resolved the British problem in the context of a wider budget reform, involving a decision to curtail CAP spending and increase the Community's own resources, effective in 1986, from 1.0 percent to 1.4 percent of the value-added tax collected in each member state.[45]

In a post-summit press conference Thatcher said she now looked forward to "pressing ahead with the development of the Community."[46] Her Community counterparts could not have agreed more. Mitterrand reveled in the success of "his" European Council not only in ending five years of friction over Britain's contribution to the Community's coffers but also in clearing the way for other improvements and initiatives. At Fontainebleau, Mitterrand had spoken eloquently about the need to revive the Community's policies and institutions and instill a new sense of European identity. Although France would no longer be in the presidency, the Fontainebleau summit created a favorable climate in which to push Mitterrand's pro-Community program.

One Community-wide challenge, which Thatcher identified in her report on the Fontainebleau summit to the British House of Commons, was what she called "the completion of the Common Market in goods and services."[47] Thatcher had not plucked that objective out of thin air. On the contrary, in the early 1980s the idea of implementing a single, Community-wide market had quietly gathered momentum in the shadow of the British budgetary question. More obtrusively, pressure for institutional reform and revision of the Treaty of Rome had also grown. At the Fontainebleau summit, the heads of government decided to convene a committee to consider the Community's future institutional structure and policy agenda. Little did they realize that this "ad hoc" committee would provide the mechanism to fuse the twin goals of a single market and institutional reform and lay the foundation for the 1992 program.

IDEOLOGY, HIGH TECHNOLOGY, AND THE SINGLE MARKET

A number of factors in the early 1980s fueled renewed interest in the Community's long-proclaimed goal of a single market. One was the ideological shift then sweeping Western Europe. Its most obvious manifestation was Thatcher's election victory in 1979. After five years of Labour Party rule, a powerful popular reaction against excessive government intervention in economic and social affairs swept Thatcher to power. The new government immediately launched a program of privatization and deregulation that unleashed pent-up market forces and stimulated individual enterprise.

Across the Channel, by contrast, President Mitterrand pushed a socialist agenda of state intervention and regulation after his election victory in 1981. The consequences were catastrophic. In an effort to reduce unemployment and stimulate economic growth by a policy of national independence, Mitterrand caused inflation to soar and investment to slump. The value of the franc plummeted, forcing devaluation within the EMS and prompting a tough domestic austerity program. By 1983 pragmatism overcame principle when Mitterrand, at the urging of Jacques Delors, his finance minister, abandoned the disastrous doctrinaire approach to economic recovery. Mitterrand began to bend with the prevailing wind of deregulation and neoliberalism blowing from the United States and the UK. The implications for France and the EC were striking, not least because "the French state has been one of the most interventionist among the capitalist nations since the war."[48] Mitterrand's U-turn influenced other socialist leaders, notably Felipe González in Spain and Mário Soares in Portugal, two countries then on their way to Community membership.

The success of Etienne Davignon, the Commission vice president responsible for industrial affairs between 1981 and 1985, in rallying European industry to the cause of cross-border collaboration also contributed to the momentum developing for a single, Community-wide market. As industrial policy commissioner during the Jenkins administration, Davignon got an invaluable insight into Europe's manufacturing problems and made extensive contacts at the highest corporate levels. His profound knowledge of international politics and economics, high social standing, and previous Community experience made him the most formidable member of Gaston Thorn's new Commission. During his second term in the Commission, Davignon decided to make Western Europe's industrial performance and competitiveness a top priority, using the Community as a vehicle to advance transnational collaboration.[49]

Davignon cultivated the CEOs of major European manufacturers in the high technology sector. His so-called Round Table discussion group included leaders of the "Big 12" electronics companies in the Community:

ICL, GEC, and Plessey (UK); AEG, Nixdorf, and Siemens (Germany); Thompson, Bull, and CGE (France); Olivetti and STET (Italy); and Philips (The Netherlands).[50] Davignon gradually succeeded in getting the Community's industrial giants to reconsider the virtues of intra-Community collaboration, something the persistent economic recession in any case predisposed them to do. Commission officials kept discreetly in the background; the last thing Davignon wanted was to scare off the "Big 12" with a display of bureaucratic heavy-handedness.

Davignon's efforts bore fruit in ESPRIT (European Strategic Program for Research and Development in Information Technology), a basic research program involving major manufacturers, smaller firms, and universities throughout the Community. Technological collaboration, in turn, "created an important and vocal constituency . . . impatient for an end to such things as customs delays at borders, conflicting national standards in data processing or arcane rules on property ownership . . . and pressing for the completion of the internal market, for once these firms had lost their national champions status, it was imperative that they maximized the advantages to be gained from the single market."[51] Guy Gyllenhammer, the head of Volvo, catalyzed such thinking in the Community by organizing the European Round Table, a discussion group with a name and purpose similar to Davignon's, although his own firm was located in Sweden, a nonmember state. In the Community itself, Wisse Dekker, the head of Philips, became one of the most vocal and influential advocates of a single market.[52]

Just as the Commission played a prominent role in encouraging technological collaboration in the Community, so too did it champion the cause of the single market. The Commission's increasing agitation for completion of the internal market is chronicled most clearly in the relevant sections of its own annual reports from the early 1980s. The 1980 report merely asserted "the need to continue building the common market" and outlined the advantages to be gained from a fully functioning internal market.[53] However, that year the Commission followed up on a landmark Court of Justice case that was to a have a decisive effect on the interpenetration of member state markets.

In February 1979, in the so-called "Cassis de Dijon" case, the Court struck down a German prohibition on imports from other member states of alcoholic beverages that did not meet minimum alcohol content requirements. Eighteen months later the Commission spelled out the implications for free movement of goods in the Community: "Any product imported from another member state must in principle be admitted . . . if it has been lawfully produced, that is, conforms to rules and processes of manufacture that are customarily and traditionally accepted in the exporting country, and is marketed in the territory of the latter."[54] Thus the Commission developed the principle of mutual recognition and avoided the otherwise impossible process of harmonizing in detail the member states' diverse legal norms.

Based partly on that breakthrough, the 1981 report was far more assertive, opening with the claim that "during the year the Commission set out to restore confidence by stimulating the internal market and developing an industrial strategy for Europe."[55] The report referred to the Commission's communication to the European Council on the pitiful state of the common market, which prompted Community leaders at the June 1981 Luxembourg summit to declare that "a concerted effort must be made to strengthen and develop the free internal market which lies at the very basis of the European Community."[56] Moving from oratory to action, the Commission urged the Council of Ministers that October both to pass a number of proposals that impinged upon the single market and to simplify frontier formalities in the Community involving customs, taxation, and statistics.

In subsequent years the Commission sharpened its strategy of putting forward concrete proposals, notably on standardization, and politicizing the problem by prodding the European Council into action. Based in part on a Commission program to strengthen the internal market, the December 1982 Copenhagen summit reiterated the importance of removing existing barriers to intra-Community commerce.[57] The Commission's prodding bore fruit in 1983 when the Council of Ministers defined a standardization policy for European industry. The next year the Commission prepared a detailed paper for the Fontainebleau summit on a number of internal market issues ranging from the abolition of customs barriers to the free movement of people, capital, and services.[58]

The Commission's approach over the previous four years and its June 1984 pre–European Council paper capitalized on and further fueled businesspeople's interest in completing the single market. The result was to put leading Community politicians, most of whom already embraced newly ascendant neoliberalism, under additional pressure to act. Again Thatcher was at the forefront. She came to Fontainebleau armed with a paper of her own entitled "Europe: The Future." This document contained the classic assertion that "if the problems of growth, outdated industrial structures and unemployment which affect us all are to be tackled effectively, we must create the genuine common market in goods and services which is envisaged in the Treaty of Rome and will be crucial to our ability to meet the U.S. and Japanese technological challenge."[59] In promoting the single market at Fontainebleau, Thatcher sought not only to advance deeply held convictions but also to deflect frustration over the British budgetary question by establishing beyond question her pro-Community credentials.

The Fontainebleau budgetary settlement removed a pretext for Community inaction on a wide range of issues and opened the door to achieving a genuinely single market. During the past few years a consensus had emerged in Brussels and the member states on the need for as much deregulation as possible at the national level, coupled with as little reregulation as necessary at the Community level. Ideological, political, and economic transformations had brought about a reemphasis on the internal market and paved the way for an imminent breakthrough. Other developments, notably tension in the trans-Atlantic relationship, the assertiveness of the first directly elected European Parliament, and the impending accession of Spain and Portugal, caused attention to dwell also on institutional reform and constitutional change in the Community. These objectives—completion of the single market and a revision of the Treaty of Rome—were not unconnected. Each gave added impetus to the other, and both were to combine in the SEA of 1986.

EXTERNAL AND INTERNAL PRESSURES FOR CHANGE

The Community's external relations were every bit as problematical as its internal development in the early 1980s. The onset of the "second Cold War"—the sudden heightening of East-West tension in the late 1970s after a decade of relatively benign relations—tested the Community's ability to act internationally. EPC proved an inadequate instrument for foreign policy coordination, especially in response to sudden crises such as the Soviet invasion of Afghanistan in December 1979 and the imposition of martial law in Poland two years later. At the same time, the unremitting hostility of the United States toward the Soviet Union severely tested Community solidarity and combined with other developments in U.S.-EC relations to put trans-Atlantic ties under enormous strain. The new Reagan administration saw the Soviet Union as the root of all evil and pressured the United States' European allies to cease most economic and trade activities with Eastern Europe. Washington cited Western Europe's more nuanced approach to the question of East-West relations as evidence of weakness and cowardice. Matters came to a head over the Soviet gas pipeline.[60] Since the late 1970s the United States had attempted to end sales by Western European firms of technologically advanced equipment to the Soviet oil and gas industry and purchases by Western European countries of oil and natural gas from the Soviet Union. The dispute centered on a project involving the export of Siberian gas to Western Europe through a pipeline thousands of miles long.

In June 1982 Washington announced sanctions against U.S. subsidiaries and license holders in Western Europe involved in the pipeline project. Such arbitrary action galvanized latent anti-Americanism and alerted many Western European firms and governments to their excessive dependence on the United States It provided a powerful impetus for high technology industries to accelerate collaboration in the Community, thereby asserting a European identity and declaring independence of the United States. To that extent, ESPRIT and other intra-Community high technology research and development programs owe their origin and development to strained U.S.-EC political relations, exacerbated by bitter trans-Atlantic disputes over steel and agricultural exports from the Community.

At the "high policy" level, the United States and the Nine (after January 1981, the Ten) differed over a number of issues beside how best to react to the imposition of martial law in Poland. One was the politically charged question of NATO's deployment in Western Europe of cruise and Pershing II missiles in response to the earlier Soviet deployment in Eastern Europe of SS-20 missiles. What had begun in the late 1970s as a show of Allied solidarity, with NATO adopting the "dual track" approach of missile deployment and arms control negotiations to counter the new Soviet threat, degenerated in the early 1980s into European accusations that the Reagan administration was interested only in deployment and U.S. accusations that the Europeans were giving in to Soviet pressure. The "Euromissile" crisis, played out publicly on the streets of many Western European cities as well as privately in the chancelleries of the Alliance, cast a long shadow over Euro-American relations.

The United States and the Nine also diverged over policy toward the Middle East, an especially sensitive issue for Washington. The United States viewed the Nine's declarations on the Arab-Israeli conflict, which tended to criticize Israel and support the Palestinians, as especially egregious examples of the perniciousness of EPC. The so-called Venice Declaration of June 1980, in which the Nine recognized the special position of Palestine in the Arab-Israeli conflict, greatly irritated the United States, as did the resumption of the "Euro-Arab dialogue" in Luxembourg in November 1980. The United States disliked its European allies' taking an independent and relatively radical position on an issue that was both inherently explosive and part of the wider, all-encompassing Cold War conflict.

Those economic and political disputes with the United States further impelled the Community to undertake fundamental reform. President Mitterrand had already declared his determination to achieve deeper integration, and France was well known for its estrangement from the United States. Even when he pursued a "national" strategy for economic growth between 1981 and 1983, Mitterrand constantly proclaimed his commitment to the Community. Indeed, it was the increasing incompatibility between his domestic economic policy and pro-Community proclivity that led Mitterrand to revise the former in 1983.

In May 1984, during France's Council presidency, Mitterrand made a famous speech to the European Parliament calling for institutional reform in the EC and greater Community competence over internal and external policies. Repeating an earlier call for restricted use of the veto, Mitterrand lamented the Council of Ministers' inability to take decisions on the basis of qualified majority voting, as stipulated in the Treaty of Rome. Nor did he ignore the irony that his own country had brought about the Luxembourg Compromise.[61] The case for curtailing the veto was compelling, not least because of the Community's impending enlargement to include Spain and Portugal. Unanimity was bad enough in a Community of Ten; it would be disastrous in a Community of Twelve.

The Community was already moving toward majority voting, but the Luxembourg Compromise continued to stymie progress. Belgium, in the Community presidency for the first half of 1982, made a concerted effort to curb use of the veto. The Belgians set an important precedent in May 1982 by calling for a vote in the Council on that year's farm prices.[62] Although legally entitled to do so under the terms of the Treaty of Rome, countries in the presidency had previously shied away from majority voting in deference to the Luxembourg Compromise. In May 1982, during the annual farm price haggle, Britain alone blocked agreement. The other member states not only were eager for a settlement but also resented Britain's intransigence on farm prices at precisely the time when the UK exerted tremendous diplomatic pressure on them to impose and maintain sanctions against Argentina during the Falklands War. Despite Britain's objections, Belgium called for a vote, and the other member states obliged. In and of itself, this incident seemed unimportant, but its significance for the demise of unanimity and the future of the Community immediately struck the Commission and the member states.

As for external relations, in his May 1984 speech Mitterrand advocated a permanent secretariat for the conduct of EPC and urged member states to make a common defense effort. His call for a more coherent Community foreign and security policy owed much to the Ten's disillusionment with the United States. No less than other Community countries, Germany shared Western Europe's general resentment toward Washington, although it depended on the United States military much more than other Community countries did. Thus, Bonn had to counterbalance its support for greater Community international assertiveness by assiduously reassuring the United States about Germany's and the Community's intentions. An initiative by Hans-Dietrich Genscher, Germany's foreign minister, sought to strike the right note. Officially launched in November 1981 and rapidly taken up by Emilio Colombo, Italy's foreign minister, the "Draft European Act," popularly known as the "Genscher-Colombo proposals," advocated "more effective decision making structures" as well as greater Community competence in external relations.[63] Thus, Genscher-Colombo sought to change the existing situation whereby, as an unidentified German diplomat described it, "the Community operates in the world arena but acts as if it didn't belong there."[64]

Although Genscher-Colombo soft-pedaled the security implications of a more coherent Community foreign policy–making capacity, the United States expressed concern. Thatcher shared Washington's anxiety. Moreover, for varying reasons a number of smaller Community countries disliked Genscher-Colombo's emphasis on closer security cooperation. Although a NATO member, Denmark resisted efforts to increase the Community's competence in the security domain. Greece, also a NATO member, under Andreas Papandreou's leadership opposed deeper European integration in general and closer security cooperation in particular. Finally, sensitivity to domestic public opinion, which supported nonmembership in NATO and an ill-defined "neutrality," caused an otherwise indifferent Irish government to object to any initiative on security and defense in the Community.

Under the circumstances, Genscher-Colombo did not go far. It gave rise only to the "Solemn Declaration on European Union,"[65] a vague, insubstantial assertion of the Community's international identity. Nevertheless, French, German, and Italian efforts to introduce a security dimension made an important contribution to the Community's efforts in the early 1980s to extend its competence and reform its decisionmaking process. Mitterrand drew on the Genscher-Colombo proposals in his May 1984 speech to the European Parliament, which in turn prepared the ground for the decision at Fontainebleau to establish an ad hoc committee on the future of European integration. The member states' willingness to discuss institutional revision, and especially to consider a possible security and defense community, created a climate conducive to change.

At the same time, an initiative in the first directly elected European Parliament complemented and reinforced the member states' openness to reform. For all the propaganda preceding the June 1979 direct elections, the MEPs who convened in Strasbourg later that summer knew only too well that Parliament lacked power or influence. They also appreciated the extent of the Community's difficulties and hoped both to get the Community out of its present malaise and to revive the process of European integration. Between April 1980 and February 1982, the EP passed no less than eight resolutions advocating institutional reform and progress on political and economic integration in the Community.

Altiero Spinelli, the veteran Eurofederalist, was one of the best-known and most influential MEPs in the newly elected Parliament. In 1970 the Italian government had nominated Spinelli to the European Commission, but he left the Berlaymont unexpectedly in 1976 to join the European Parliament as an independent Communist. Not only was his political affiliation astounding—Spinelli had broken with communism as early as 1937—but his decision to become an MEP in the then relatively powerless Parliament surprised almost everyone. Spinelli was positioning himself to become an instrumental figure in the first directly elected

Parliament, due to convene at the end of the decade. He interpreted the results of the 1979 European elections as nothing less than a mandate to launch a constitutional revision of the Community.

In July 1980 Spinelli gathered together a small number of like-minded MEPs, representing a wide spectrum of political opinion, in the Crocodile Restaurant in Strasbourg. By the end of the year the "Crocodile Club," an otherwise heterogeneous collection of MEPs dedicated to reforming and reviving the Community, had grown from ten to seventy members. Their ideas ranged from a return to the Community's first principles—the need to complete the internal market—to a radical revision of the Treaty of Rome—the need for an improved Community constitution. Gradually a consensus emerged on the urgency of a new treaty to replace the original treaties and for a new European union to replace the original communities.

Too large to meet in their favorite Strasbourg restaurant, the Crocodile Club moved to a committee room at the European Parliament. The group was relatively ineffectual as an unofficial caucus, so in July 1981 Spinelli convinced his parliamentary colleagues to inaugurate a Committee on Institutional Affairs to consider and propose constitutional reform in the Community. The thirty-seven-member committee met for the first time in January 1983, halfway through the Parliament's five-year term of office. Mauro Ferri, the Italian Socialist, was chairman, but Spinelli served in the crucial capacity of *rapporteur,* or report writer.

The institutional affairs committee members appreciated the potential pitfalls surrounding their work. Because Parliament remained relatively powerless and MEPs were correspondingly unimportant in Community affairs, there was a predisposition in Brussels and in member state capitals to dismiss Europarliamentary agitation for reform as the ravings of reckless, overindulged, and underemployed politicians. Spinelli himself had a reputation for being idealistic, unrealistic, and excitable. Moreover, because of Parliament's comparative weakness, national governments expected MEPs to demand a larger Europarliamentary say in Community decisionmaking. The greatest danger facing the institutional affairs committee, therefore, was that its work would not be taken seriously.

Yet the crisis in the Community—prolonged economic recession, declining international competitiveness, institutional inertia, and decisionmaking paralysis—lent credence to the European Parliament's efforts, as did the member states' own initiatives along the same lines, notably the Mitterrand memorandum and the Genscher-Colombo proposals. Fortunately for Parliament, the institutional affairs committee's first six months in operation coincided with the Belgian presidency of the Community. Like the French, Germans, and Italians, the Belgians desperately wanted to get the Community going again and saw Parliament's interest in institutional reform as an asset, not a liability.

For these reasons the institutional affairs committee proceeded cautiously, deliberately, responsibly, and successfully. By the middle of 1982 it had identified the main lines of Community reform and established subgroups to work on them. Issues included the legal personality of a possible new union, its institutional structure, competence, and relationship with the member states. The committee consulted experts throughout the Community in the fall of 1982, notably on two occasions at the European University Institute in Florence. With the invaluable assistance of a group of noted jurists, the proposed reforms painstakingly wound their way procedurally through the committee and the Parliament in 1983, emerging at the end of the year as the "Draft Treaty Establishing the European Union."[66]

The draft treaty sought to substitute the existing treaties establishing the European communities with a single treaty establishing a European Union. The Union would maintain the basic institutional structure and legal competence of the three Communities but revise their decisionmaking procedures and add to them new or expanded authority over certain aspects of economic, social, and political affairs. The purpose of decision-making reform was both to improve efficiency and to close a perceived "democratic deficit." Allowing for the member states' sensitivity to the centralization of power in Brussels, the draft treaty provided for something that received little attention at the time but suddenly became prominent a decade later during the Maastricht Treaty ratification debate: the principle of subsidiarity. In its preamble, the draft treaty stipulated that the Union would be responsible only for tasks that could be undertaken more effectively in common than by the member states acting independently.

In one of the most famous votes ever taken in the European Parliament, on February 14, 1984, the draft treaty passed by a resounding 237 to 31, with 43 abstentions.[67] Most of the preceding debate focused on the future: What impact would the draft treaty have on the course of European integration? The vast majority of MEPs, including the stalwart Crocodile Club members, knew that the draft treaty would never be ratified by the member states. Yet Parliament decided to send it to member state parliaments and governments anyway in an effort to increase the momentum for reform then gathering in the Community. Passage of the draft treaty was especially timely in the run-up to the second direct elections, scheduled for June 1984; it demonstrated Parliament's seriousness and commitment to European integration (although most of the electorate took little interest in Parliament's activities) and constituted a concrete legacy from the first directly elected Parliament to its successors. The timing of the vote on the draft treaty was also auspicious because of France's presidency of the Community during the first six months of 1984, culminating in the Fontainebleau summit. Strasbourg's overwhelming endorsement of the draft treaty provided President Mitterrand, an unquestioned champion of

Community renewal, with additional political ammunition. Resolution of the budgetary crisis at the Fontainebleau summit finally moved debate on the Community's future "to the center of the stage."[68] Synergy between collaborative ventures in high technology, renewed interest in the internal market, concern about the Community's role in the world, and paralysis in the decisionmaking process paved the way for serious consideration of the Community's potential contribution to Western Europe's political and economic development. Similarly, initiatives such as Mitterrand's memorandum and speech, the Genscher-Colombo proposals, the Stuttgart solemn declaration, and the European Parliament's draft treaty were essential precursors of the Community's post-Fontainebleau revival. They provided a climate and a context in which the ad hoc committee on the Community's future, convened after the Fontainebleau summit, could operate successfully. The ad hoc committee, in turn, gave rise to the intergovernmental conference of 1985, the SEA of 1986, and the strikingly successful single market program that symbolized the Community's resurgence in the late 1980s.

NOTES

1. *The Economist,* March 20, 1982, p. 11.

2. Quoted in Steven Lagerfeld, "Europhoria," *Wilson Quarterly* 14 (Winter 1990): 66.

3. Karl Kaiser, et al. (eds.), *The European Community: Progress or Decline* (London: RIIA, 1983), p. 1.

4. Christopher Tugendhat, "How to Get Europe Moving Again," *International Affairs* 61 (Winter 1990): 421.

5. Bull. EC S/1-1979, pp. 12–13.

6. Paul Lewis, "An Unhappy Briton in Brussels," *The New York Times,* November 6, 1977, sec. 3, p. 7.

7. Quoted in Werner Feld, *West Germany and the European Community: Changing Interests and Competing Policy Objectives* (New York: Praeger, 1981), p. 55

8. See Frances Nicholson and Roger East, *From the Six to the Twelve: The Enlargement of the European Community* (Chicago: St. James Press, 1987), pp. 181–206.

9. Roy Jenkins, *European Diary, 1977–1981* (London: Collins, 1989), p. 199.

10. Commission, *1974 General Report,* Annex to Chapter 1, point 18.

11. Bull. EC 12-1977, point 1.12.

12. Jenkins, *European Diary,* p. 375.

13. "Ad Hoc Committee for Institutional Affairs Report to the European Council (Dooge Report), March 1985," Bull. EC 3-1985, point 3.5.1.

14. Peter Ludlow, *Beyond 1992: Europe and Its World Partners* (Brussels: Center for European Policy Studies, 1989), p. 25.

15. Peter Ludlow, *The Making of the European Monetary System: A Case Study in the Politics of the European Community* (London: Butterworths Scientific, 1982).

16. Roy Jenkins, "Europe's Present Challenge and Future Opportunity," speech delivered at the European University Institute (Florence), October 27, 1977.

17. COM(77)620 final, November 16, 1977 (see the bibliography/Official Documents/*COM Documents*).

18. Jenkins, *European Diary*, p. 183.

19. Roy Jenkins, *Life at the Centre* (London: Macmillan, 1991), pp. 470–471.

20. Peter M. Oppenheimer, "Historical Development of the EMS and the UK Decision to Join the Exchange Rate Mechanism," in John Driffill and Massimo Beber, eds., *A Currency for Europe* (London: Lothian Foundation Press, 1991), p. 67.

21. Haig Simonian, *The Privileged Partnership: Franco-German Relations in the European Communities, 1969–1984* (Oxford: Clarendon Press, 1985), p. 277.

22. Jenkins, *Centre*, p. 479.

23. Helen Wallace, "The Conduct of Bilateral Relations by Governments," in Roger Morgan and Caroline Brey, *Partners and Rivals in Western Europe: Britain, France and Germany* (Brookfield, VT: Gower, 1986), p. 154.

24. Bull. EC 6-1978, Presidency Conclusions, point 1.5.2.

25. Bull. EC 12-1978, Presidency Conclusions, point 1.14.

26. William Nicoll and Trevor Salmon, *Understanding the European Communities* (Savage, MD: Barnes & Noble, 1990), p. 197.

27. Jenkins, *European Diary*, p. 372.

28. Sir Michael Butler, "Simply Wrong About Europe," *The Times* (London), November 26, 1991, p. 3.

29. Hugo Young, *One of Us: A Biography of Margaret Thatcher* (London: Macmillan, 1989), p. 388.

30. *The Financial Times*, June 28, 1989, p. 2.

31. Young, *One of Us*, p. 183.

32. *Ibid.,* p. 186.

33. *Ibid.,* p. 184.

34. Jenkins, *Centre*, p. 494.

35. Jenkins, *European Diary*, p. 545.

36. Jenkins, *European Diary*, pp. 529–531.

37. Jenkins, *Centre,* p. 499. Granada Television, a private British television company, produced an entertaining and accurate reenactment of the Dublin summit called "Mrs Thatcher's Billion."

38. Jenkins, *European Diary,* pp. 502–503; Young, *One of Us,* pp. 187–188.

39. Young, *One of Us*, p. 189.

40. Jenkins, *Centre*, pp. 500–501.

41. See François Mitterrand, *Reflexions sur la politique étrangère* (Paris: Fayard, 1986).

42. Quoted in the *Daily Express* (London), June 4, 1984, p. 4.

43. For a lively account of the Fontainebleau summit, see John Newhouse, "One Against Nine," in *The New Yorker*, October 22, 1984, pp. 64–92.

44. See Geoffrey Denton, "Restructuring the EEC Budget: Implications of the Fontainebleau Summit," *Journal of Common Market Studies* 23, no. 2 (December 1984), pp. 117–140.

45. Bull. EC 6-1984, Presidency Conclusions, point 1.1.1. et seq.

46. Quoted in *The Financial Times,* June 28, 1984, p. 14.

47. Quoted in Young, *One of Us*, p. 388.

48. Peter Hall, Jack Hayward, and Howard Machin, *Developments in French Politics* (New York: St. Martin's Press, 1990), p. 28.

49. See Pierre-Henri Laurent, "Forging the European Technology Community," in Michael S. Steinberg, ed., *The Technological Challenges and Opportunities of a United Europe* (Savage, MD: Barnes & Noble, 1990), pp. 59–67.

50. See M. Sharp and C. Shearman, *European Technological Collaboration* (London: Routledge & Keegan Paul, 1987), p. 46.

51. Margaret Sharp, Christopher Freeman, and William Walker, *Technology and the Future of Europe: Global Competition and the Environment in the 1990s* (New York: Pinter, 1991), p. 73.

52. Ludlow, *Beyond 1992*, p. 30.

53. Commission, *1980 General Report*, point 120.

54. OJ C 256, October 3, 1980, pp. 2–3 (see the bibliography/Official Documents/ *Official Journal of the European Communities*).

55. Commission, *1981 General Report*, point 129.

56. Bull. EC 6-1981, Presidency Conclusions, point 1.10.

57. Bull. EC 12-1982, Presidency Conclusions, point 1.12.

58. Commission, *1984 General Report*, point 133.

59. "Europe: the Future," reproduced in the *Journal of Common Market Studies* 23, no. 1 (September 1984), pp. 74–81.

60. See Peter Marsh, "The European Community and East-West Economic Relations," *Journal of Common Market Studies* 23, no. 1 (September 1984), pp. 9–10.

61. François Mitterrand, speech to the European Parliament, May 24, 1984, reprinted in *Vital Speeches of the Day*, August 1, 1984, p. 613.

62. Bull. EC 5-1982, points 2.1.73 to 2.1.97.

63. The Genscher-Colombo proposals are reproduced in European Parliament, Committee on Institutional Affairs, *Selection of Texts Concerning Institutional Matters of the Community from 1950–1982* (Luxembourg: the European Parliament, 1982), pp. 490–499.

64. Quoted in Newhouse, "One Against Nine," p. 68.

65. Bull. EC 6-1983, point 1.6.1.

66. "Draft Treaty Establishing the European Union," Bull. EC 2-1984, point 1.1.2. For a comprehensive assessment of the draft treaty, see Roland Bieber, Jean-Paul Jacque, and Joseph Weiler, eds., *An Ever Closer Union: A Critical Analysis of the Draft Treaty Establishing European Union,* European Perspectives Series (Luxembourg: Office for Official Publications of the European Community, 1985).

67. Bull. EC 2-1984, point 1.1.1.

68. Helen Wallace, *Europe: The Challenge of Diversity* (Boston: Routledge & Keegan Paul, 1985), p. 3.

5

The Transformation of the European Community, 1985–1988

In the mid-1980s the European Community underwent an extraordinary transformation. After years of sluggish growth and institutional immobility, the member states concluded the Single European Act (SEA), a major revision of the Treaty of Rome that underpinned the single market (1992) program and "lifted the Community from its stagnant to its dynamic phase in the late 1980s."[1] Jacques Delors, who became Commission president in January 1985, is generally credited with the Community's metamorphosis. "Delors is as important to the enterprise today," Stanley Hoffmann wrote at the height of the Community's transformation, "as Jean Monnet was in the 1950s."[2]

Yet Delors's importance should not be exaggerated. Undoubtedly he possessed an abundance of ambition, competence, and resourcefulness. The new president sought to infuse the Commission with a renewed sense of purpose and set the Community on the road to European union. But Delors could not possibly have realized those objectives had the economic, political, and international circumstances been unpropitious. It was his good fortune to have become Commission president at precisely the time when internal developments—resolution of the British budgetary question, agitation for institutional reform, and pressure to complete the internal market—and external factors—fundamental changes in the global system—made a dramatic improvement in the Community's fortunes almost inevitable. Without Delors, the single market program and the acceleration of European integration might not have happened exactly as they did, but that is not to say that they would not have happened at all.

One of the most remarkable aspects of the Community's transformation is that it coincided with the potentially disruptive Iberian enlargement.

The accession of relatively impoverished Spain and Portugal threatened to throw European integration further off course. Moreover, without compensating mechanisms, completion of the internal market could have immensely aggravated the social and economic divide between the Community's rich and poor member states. Thus, the SEA was more than a device to launch the single market program. It was a complex bargain to improve decisionmaking, increase efficiency, achieve market liberalization, and at the same time promote cohesion in the Community. The SEA made possible what Pompidou had sought at an earlier stage of the Community's existence: "completion, deepening, enlargement." As Helen Wallace remarked, "the 1992 goal was clearly intended as completion, but new policies had been substantively embraced and institutions had been strengthened, thus deepening was in hand, and widening had occurred for a third time without momentum being lost."[3]

THE THIRD ENLARGEMENT

Formal negotiations to enlarge the Community a third time began with Portugal in October 1978 and Spain in February 1979. Having recently emerged from long periods of authoritarian rule, both countries desperately wanted to join the Community to end their relative international isolation, stabilize their newly established democratic regimes, and help develop their comparatively antiquated economies. As in the contemporaneous case of Greece, the member states encouraged Iberian membership in the Community as a means of reinforcing reform there. As in the case of the newly independent Eastern European countries more than a decade later, however, the likely political and economic challenges of Spanish and Portuguese membership drove a wedge between rhetoric and reality. Spain and Portugal were poor countries that between them had a population almost 20 percent of the existing Community's. Despite Brussels' genuine commitment to consolidating recent political changes on the Iberian Peninsula, the prospect of Spanish and Portuguese membership filled many member states with dread, not least because of the difficulties caused by the Community's first enlargement.[4]

Greece had already succeeded in divorcing its accession negotiations from the Iberian applications. Realizing that the Community feared the economic and social consequences primarily of Spanish membership, Portugal tried also to have its application considered separately and concluded swiftly. Portugal applied to join the Community in March 1977, more than a year before Spain lodged an application with Brussels. Portugal's accession negotiations also began before Spain's, but only four months earlier. Although the Community negotiated separately with each country, the short time between the opening of both sets of talks indicated the degree to which Brussels considered them interrelated.

Portugal ascribed the protracted entry negotiations of the early 1980s to the Community's lumping together of Lisbon's and Madrid's applications and its preoccupation with internal budgetary and institutional issues. Undoubtedly the Community's own difficulties and concerns about Spanish membership affected Lisbon's application, but a number of factors peculiar to Portugal—notably textiles (which represented over 40 percent of the country's industrial output and 33 percent of its exports), migrant workers, and agriculture—accounted as well for the talks' slow progress.[5] Already, in its opinion of May 19, 1978, the Commission had identified a host of economic, structural, and administrative issues that would have to be tackled before Portugal joined the Community.[6] As a result, the Commission refused to recommend a detailed timetable for accession, although Portugal pressed for a Community deadline of January 1, 1983. The fact that substantive negotiations did not get under way until 1980 finally convinced Portugal of the unlikelihood of its gaining entry only three years later.

Meanwhile, both sides signed a supplementary protocol to revise existing bilateral agreements and concluded a generous pre-accession assistance package for Portugal. The aid agreement, which entered into force on January 1, 1981, sought to facilitate Portugal's eventual integration into the Community by providing funds to help modernize the country's economy. In particular, the Community earmarked money for a plethora of projects in the industrial, agricultural, and fisheries sectors, as well as for infrastructural improvement and regional development.[7]

The EC-Portugal aid agreement was welcome evidence of the Community's commitment to eventual enlargement, especially after the political furor triggered by French President Giscard d'Estaing in June 1980. In a speech to French farmers' leaders in Paris, Giscard declared that, especially in view of the British budgetary question, "the Community should give priority to completing the first enlargement" before undertaking another. The president's office later clarified his remarks to apply them to Spain and Portugal, not to Greece. Other member states distanced themselves from Giscard's statement, although German Chancellor Schmidt supported his friend by declaring shortly afterward that "without the indispensable adjustments to its agricultural policy and without a more balanced distribution of burdens the Community cannot finance the tasks which face it in its expansion southwards."[8]

Spain and Portugal reacted with predictable outrage. But the key to Giscard's statement lay in its timing and its audience. With presidential elections less than a year away, Giscard pandered to French farmers, a powerful and vocal constituency. He may also have hoped to spite British Prime Minister Thatcher, who strongly supported Portuguese accession but who had infuriated her Community colleagues during the previous two years by aggressively pursuing Britain's budgetary claims. Thatcher supported Portuguese accession for traditional British foreign policy reasons: the tradition of alliance and friendship with Portugal and the tradition of wanting a wider and weaker Community. Thatcher delighted Portuguese Prime Minister Francisco Pinto Balsemão by declaring, during his visit to London in December 1981, that Spain and Portugal need not accede simultaneously and that Portugal could join by January 1984.[9]

As long as France opposed enlargement, however, there was little hope of early Portuguese accession. Even when François Mitterrand succeeded Giscard in May 1981—and did not have to worry about another presidential election for the next seven years—France refused to endorse the Community's southern enlargement pending an acceptable arrangement for Mediterranean agriculture. In the meantime negotiations progressed on a wide range of thorny issues, including capital movements, regional policy, transport, services, and nuclear cooperation. Yet Commission President Gaston Thorn had to remind his hosts during a visit to Lisbon in April 1982 that, apart from agriculture, such contentious questions as textiles, fisheries, and the free movement of labor remained unresolved between both sides.

The formation of a relatively stable administration in Lisbon by the able and energetic Mário Soares in June 1983 increased Community goodwill toward Portugal, not least because the new government soon reached an agreement with the International Monetary Fund that included measures to reduce the country's substantial foreign debt and further restructure the economy. In the following months, Soares embarked on a frantic round of visits to Community capitals and cultivated a close relationship with Mitterrand, a fellow Socialist. Soares impressed his interlocutors with Portugal's determination to become a model Community member. Rapid agreement on a number of outstanding issues followed, although (much to Soares's annoyance) the fate of the Spanish and Portuguese negotiations became increasingly linked. Without a breakthrough in the Community's talks with Spain, especially concerning agriculture and fisheries, Portugal's prospects for immediate accession looked poor.

French misgivings about southern enlargement focused on Spain far more than on Portugal. Spain's accession would increase the Community's agricultural area by 30 percent and its farm work force by 25 percent. Apart from the financial implications of such a development, especially at a time of budgetary crisis and attempted reform of the CAP, Spain and France would compete directly in the production and sale of fruit, vegetables, and olive oil. Nevertheless, France recognized the political imperative of Spanish membership, especially after an attempted military coup in Madrid in February 1981. The European Council, meeting in Maastricht the following month, expressed "great satisfaction at the reaction of the King, government and people of Spain in the face of the attacks recently made against the democratic system of their country." This reaction, the European Council concluded, "strengthens the political structures which will enable a democratic Spain to accede to the . . . European Communities."[10]

Doubtless the Spanish government appreciated the European Council's concern, but kind words in a European Council communiqué could not compensate for lack of progress in entry negotiations. The fault did not lie entirely with the Community, though. Despite repeated Spanish rhetoric about the country's "European vocation," the government seemed unwilling to embrace all of the obligations of Community membership, especially the need to introduce a value-added tax, curtail subsidies, and end protectionism from the date of accession. Spain's recalcitrance prompted the European Council, meeting in London in November 1981, to chide Madrid by recalling the applicant countries' undertaking to "accede on the basis of the Community treaties and subordinate legislation in force on the date of accession, subject only to such transitional arrangements as may be agreed." Moreover, the European Council urged Spain to "make good use of the period until accession for careful preparations for . . . enlargement by introducing the necessary reforms so that the potential benefits for both sides can be realized."[11]

Thus, apart from some technical arrangements, Spain's entry negotiations made little headway in 1982. Agreement on Spanish agriculture proved particularly elusive, becoming increasingly bound up with the Community's growing budgetary crisis. During a visit to Madrid in June 1982, Mitterrand stated bluntly that Spanish accession "under existing circumstances would mean an unfortunate state of anarchy, adding new pressures to those already facing the Communities."[12] For that reason, impending enlargement provided a catalyst for CAP reform, lest Iberian accession add wine and olive oil to the list of products in which the Community already had a huge surplus.

Earlier, at approximately the same time that Soares became prime minister in Lisbon, Felipe González formed a new government in Madrid. González was a passionate Europhile whose primary political objective was to bring Spain into the Community. Young, personable, and extremely able, González emulated Soares by embarking on a series of visits to Community capitals, using personal charm, political savvy, and, where appropriate, ideological affinity to make the case for Spanish accession. An informal summit of the prime ministers—all Socialists—of the Community's Mediterranean member states and the applicant countries (France, Italy, Greece, Portugal, and Spain) on October 16–17, 1983, may have paved the way for the first breakthrough on agriculture in the enlargement negotiations. At a meeting in Luxembourg only two days later, agriculture ministers approved rules to organize the Community's fruit, vegetable, and olive oil markets.[13]

This was the first stage in the process of settling the contentious agricultural aspect of enlargement. By contrast, fisheries became increasingly disputatious between both sides in 1984. On March 7, French patrol boats fired on two Spanish trawlers in the Bay of Biscay, about 100 miles off the southwest coast of France but well within the Community's 200-mile fisheries limit. At issue was the Community's effort under the common fisheries policy to limit the access of Spain's fishing fleet, which was numerically larger than the combined Community fleet and caught almost 70 percent of the latter's tonnage. The Spanish government lodged an official complaint in Paris, and Spanish fishermen attacked foreign trucks in protest. Community truckers, in turn, blockaded the Spanish border. Such incidents continued throughout the year—thirty-two Spanish trawlers were arrested off the Irish coast alone in 1984.[14]

The fisheries dispute eluded resolution until early 1985, by which time Spanish entry negotiations were well on track. The decisive breakthrough came not in the talks themselves but in the Community's internal affairs. Settlement of the British budgetary question at the Fontainebleau summit in June 1984 removed the biggest obstacle to Iberian accession. The summit communiqué set January 1, 1986, as the date for Spanish and Portuguese membership.[15] As Spain had always suspected France of thwarting further enlargement, Mitterrand's pivotal role in securing a settlement at Fontainebleau greatly improved relations between both countries. In a move calculated to reassure González of French goodwill, Mitterrand flew to Madrid immediately after Fontainebleau to report personally on the summit's outcome.[16]

Yet the summit's call for an end to negotiations by September 30, 1984, proved too ambitious. Agriculture continued to dominate talks for the remainder of the year, and it was not until the Dublin summit in December 1984 that the Community reached an agreement on fish, fruit, vegetables, and wine that was acceptable to the Spanish government.[17] When Delors became Commission president in January 1985, the Dublin agreement still had to be implemented, and a number of outstanding issues remained between Brussels and the applicant countries. Moreover, a new problem had arisen at the Dublin summit when Andreas Papandreou, the Greek prime minister, demanded that the Community finalize the Integrated Mediterranean Programs (IMPs) before concluding accession negotiations. Originating in a 1982 Commission proposal in response to a Greek government demand, IMPs sought to provide financial assistance primarily to Greece but also to Italy and southern France to help develop agriculture, tourism, and small business.[18] The Commission had proposed 6.6 billion ECU for the scheme, a figure Margaret Thatcher dismissed in a "rough but brief confrontation" at the Dublin summit as being "so far out of sight that [it] should never have been mentioned."[19]

Realizing that the final obstacles to accession had to be removed before the Community could advance on other fronts, Delors threw himself into the fray with characteristic energy and resolution, taking personal responsibility for the IMPs. At a meeting in Brussels on February 25–26, 1985, Community agriculture ministers established an effective mechanism to implement the restrictions on wine production agreed to by the heads of government in Dublin. Two weeks later the Community agreed on a five-year enlargement-linked program of structural aid to farmers. The Community hoped to resolve the remaining problems—fisheries, free movement of Spanish and Portuguese workers in the Community, and the applicant countries' budgetary contributions—at a meeting of foreign ministers on March 15–21, 1985. Failure to do so led to another Council meeting on March 28–29, at which the ministers negotiated a settlement acceptable to both sides.[20]

That meeting took place on the eve of a decisive European Council in Brussels. In order to draft and ratify the accession treaty in time for Spanish and Portuguese membership in January 1986, the Community still had to iron out the IMPs. Based on a Commission proposal of February 20, 1985, the member states agreed following heated discussions to a seven-year program of grants and loans to assist the existing Community's Mediterranean regions "to adjust under the best conditions possible to the new situation created by enlargement."[21] Despite Thatcher's earlier outburst, the member states finally accepted the Commission's original figure of 6.6 billion ECU, of which Greece would receive approximately 30 percent. The Greek government had hoped for a larger allocation but obligingly went along with the majority and thus removed the final obstacle to the Community's third enlargement.

The outcome of the Brussels summit was a triumph for the Italian presidency and for Delors, who had staked his political reputation on resolving the IMP issue. Since he had taken personal responsibility for the IMPs, failure to clear the last hurdle on the road to Spanish and Portuguese accession would have seriously undermined the credibility of the new Commission president. After the Brussels summit, a relieved Delors declared that "all the family quarrels have been sorted out. The family is now going to grow and we can think of the future."[22] Indeed, for the first time in nearly twenty years the Community's future looked extremely bright. Developments in the early 1980s—resolution of the British budgetary question, pressure for institutional reform, and renewed efforts to implement the internal market—heralded a rapid acceleration in the pace of European integration. Imminent enlargement provided an additional psychological boost. Under Delors's leadership the new Commission made no secret of its determination to exploit this unique opportunity to improve the Community's fortunes. Following the protracted enlargement negotiations and short but sharp IMP dispute, the decks were cleared for the forthcoming European Council in Milan to consider, as Mitterrand put it, "what Europe will become."[23]

DEVISING A SINGLE MARKET STRATEGY

The Milan summit considered the Community's future on the basis of concrete proposals, not vague aspirations. The Commission's plan—the so-called White Paper[24]—to complete the internal market by the end of 1992 constituted one of two important documents for the European Council's deliberations. Delors and Lord Cockfield, his internal market commissioner, had drafted the White Paper in the spring of 1985. At the same time, Delors made the fateful decision to devote his first presidency principally to promoting the single market program. In retrospect, because of the success of the 1992 strategy, Delors's decision seems inevitable. Yet the Commission president thought carefully before putting most of his eggs in the single market basket. Although he readily grasped the economic importance of a fully functioning internal market, Delors was initially unsure that the single market program alone could generate the popular appeal and political impetus necessary to achieve his overriding objective: a thoroughly revitalized Community.

Apart from completing the internal market, Delors's means toward the greater end of a resurgent European Community included an overhaul of decisionmaking procedures, a new monetary policy initiative, and an extension of Community competence in the field of foreign and defense policy.[25] Delors stressed these themes in his first address as Commission president to the European Parliament on January 14, 1985, and in a number of other speeches during the next few months.[26] As a former finance minister and a committed Eurofederalist, Delors's personal preference was to concentrate primarily on Economic and Monetary Union. Three of the incoming commissioners were also former finance ministers and shared their president's predilection for economic and monetary policy. The relative success of the European Monetary System, then in its seventh year of operation, further encouraged Delors's thoughts in that direction.

Yet Delors's political pragmatism caused him to be wary of the EMU option. Monetary policy lay too close to the core of national sovereignty for an initiative going beyond the EMS to prosper in the mid-1980s. Delors wanted to capitalize on the goodwill generated in the European Council by the successful Fontainebleau summit, not aggravate tension between Community leaders by promoting a politically sensitive proposal. Similarly, an outright assault on unanimity in the Council of Ministers in an effort to improve Community decisionmaking would only have raised member states' hackles. If he was to achieve the goal of a re-vitalized Community, Delors could not afford to risk alienating the heads of government.

By contrast, with institutional reform and EMU, the enormous po-litical advantages of choosing the internal market option soon dawned on Delors. By going back to basics and emphasizing one of the original objec-tives of the Treaty of Rome, Delors could hardly be accused of overween-ing ambition. Moreover, regardless of their political preferences and per-sonal opinions of each other, Community leaders uniformly sang the praises of a single market. Not surprisingly, Margaret Thatcher was especially elo-quent on the virtues of market liberalization. By championing a cause dear to her heart, Delors hoped to reconcile Thatcher to the Community and heal the wounds caused by the protracted British budgetary dispute.

In addition, Delors believed, a single market strategy would indi-rectly but inescapably result in an improvement in decisionmaking proce-dures and renewed interest in EMU. Political will to complete the inter-nal market could never translate into action unless unanimity gave way to qualified majority voting in the Council of Ministers. Without reform of the legislative process, single market proposals would ultimately bog down in disputes between member states. Furthermore, a successful single market strategy would most likely fuel interest in EMU. How could the market be fully integrated without monetary union and a common macro-economic policy? The political, if not the economic, logic of a large, vi-brant internal market pointed inexorably, Delors thought, toward currency union.

The interrelationship between completion of the internal market, decisionmaking reform, and a further monetary initiative intrigued Delors and underlay the entire single market strategy. Yet undue emphasis on the indirect objectives of the single market program threatened to undermine the whole project. Ever watchful for encroachments on national sover-eignty, Thatcher would likely oppose Delors from the outset if he stressed the goal of EMU, let alone majority voting. Nor was Delors sure that Cockfield, Thatcher's senior appointee to the Commission and a former British trade and finance minister, supported more than mere completion of the single market. In the event, Cockfield "went native" in the Com-mission and became a staunch advocate of greater European integration. Predictably, Thatcher did not reappoint him in 1988 for a second term.

Despite their strikingly different political and personal back-grounds, Delors and Cockfield became close colleagues, working tire-lessly in early 1985 to fuel existing interest in the internal market and, eventually, to prepare the White Paper. Both men understood the impor-tance of maintaining private sector support. Thus, Delors kept Etienne Davignon's door to European business leaders ajar and reiterated the Commission's commitment to an active industrial policy. To a great extent the Commission's subsequent proposals for collaborative research and development projects, and its involvement in President Mitterrand's "Eureka" venture—a plan for closer European cooperation in the high technology sector, in response to President Reagan's Strategic Defense ("Star Wars") Initiative—sought to strengthen the Commission-industry alliance in anticipation of the single market program.

European business leaders needed little prompting on the virtues of a single market. In 1984 and 1985 alone, three major manufacturers published pamphlets on the need to complete the internal market as soon as possible.[27] The most striking and influential of these was a tract by Wisse Dekker, the head of Philips and a leading member of Davignon's European Round Table. Dekker's plan for a single market in the Community by 1990 bore a strong resemblance to the Commission's subsequent White Paper. It also reminded Community officials that the biggest challenge confronting them from the private sector was not to generate support for the single market but to allay doubts about the Commission's ability to deliver the goods.

The Commission's pivotal role in planning and implementing a single market strategy was a further reason for Delors's keen interest in the idea. Delors knew the Community's fortunes would never revive without a corresponding increase in the Commission's authority and morale. As incoming president, he wanted to give the Commission new direction and leadership. Conversely, the Commission looked forward to acquiring a fresh sense of mission and importance after the drift of the previous two decades. A strategy to devise and put in place a fully functioning internal market ideally suited both Delors's and the Commission's aspirations. As a political priority involving most of the Commission's directorates-general, a comprehensive single market strategy would invigorate the Berlaymont and return the Commission to center stage in the Community.

By early 1985, as Delors settled into the Commission presidency, there was widespread discussion in political, business, and academic circles about completing the internal market. In his January 1985 speech to the European Parliament, Delors had proposed 1992—the end of two consecutive commissioners' terms of office—as a possible target date. The Commission's program for 1985, presented to the European Parliament on March 12, stressed the importance of the single market and urged the European Council "to pledge itself to completion of a fully unified internal market by 1992 and to approve the necessary program together with a realistic and binding timetable."[28] Delors pressed the point at the Brussels summit later that month. As "the necessary program" and "a realistic and binding timetable" did not yet exist, Delors convinced the heads of government to request the Commission to draw these up before the next European Council, due to take place in Milan at the end of June.

Having helped engineer the European Council's request, Delors accepted the challenge with alacrity. The Commission—fourteen of whose seventeen members were new to the job—threw itself into the task of preparing a detailed plan to complete the internal market with an enthusiasm absent in Brussels since Walter Hallstein's day. Because a successful single market would affect almost every Community activity—from external relations to competition, from information to agriculture—few of the Commission's directorates-general were uninvolved in the ensuing round of meetings and consultations, drafting and redrafting. The result was a "rapid, bold and radical" proposal, presented publicly for the first time on June 15, 1985, two weeks before the Milan summit.[29]

The White Paper—a relatively short document—is often caricatured as a typical Commission product: unintelligible, obtuse, and tedious. Indeed, the highly technical nature of the internal market hardly lends itself to lively prose. Yet the White Paper is a surprisingly lucid piece, containing a ringing defense of market liberalization and a clear exposition of how and why the Community should achieve a single market. If anything, the Commission deliberately downplayed the White Paper's style in order to avoid unfavorable political comment. Only in the final paragraph did its authors put the White Paper in historical perspective, proclaim the venture's political significance, and allow free rein to their hortatory impulses:

> Just as the Customs Union had to precede Economic Integration, so Economic Integration has to precede European Unity. What this White paper proposes therefore is that the Community should now take a further step along the road so clearly delineated in the treaties. To do less would be to fall short of the ambitions of the founders of the Community, incorporated in the Treaties; it would be to betray the trust invested in us; it would be to offer the peoples of Europe a narrower, less rewarding, less secure, less prosperous future than they could otherwise enjoy. That is the measure of the challenge that faces us. Let it never be said that we were incapable of rising to it.[30]

The White Paper is best known for its appendix listing approximately three hundred Commission proposals needing decisions by the Council of Ministers before the internal market could be implemented. Cockfield was able to put such an extensive compilation together in record time because most of the items on it already lay around in draft form, a legacy of the Commission's earlier internal market efforts. Nevertheless, Cockfield's job was much more than simply "one of trawling and of sieving."[31] The indispensable novelty of the White Paper's appendix was not the items listed in it but the way Cockfield organized them according to a timetable ending on December 31, 1992. Thus, the appendix constituted a detailed action plan against which Commission officials, politicians, and businesspeople could measure progress toward a single market.

Yet the White Paper's appendix represented only part of the large legislative agenda likely to be unleashed by the single market program. As mentioned but not spelled out elsewhere in the White Paper, completing the internal market would impinge directly on a wide range of Community policies and activities, notably in the fields of competition, research and development, the environment, consumer protection, social affairs, and EMU. Despite the simplicity of the "single market" slogan and the brevity of the Commission's action plan, the White Paper represented a huge leap forward for the Community. It was up to the heads of government, meeting in Milan only two weeks after the White Paper's publication, to decide whether or not the single market program would get off the ground.

THE DOOGE REPORT AND THE MILAN SUMMIT

The momentum to complete the internal market that had built up in the early 1980s ensured that heads of government, meeting in Milan on June 28–29, 1985, endorsed the Commission's White Paper. Although each country had reservations about specific Commission proposals, the heads of government had long since committed themselves to completing the internal market. But as Delors pointed out in a series of speeches before the Milan summit, the European Council's acceptance of the White Paper would not suffice to ensure the single market program's success. As long as serious procedural problems remained unresolved, the White Paper's detailed proposals likely would languish in the Council of Ministers. The challenge for the Milan summit, therefore, was to tackle the politically charged question of legislative reform in the European Community, a process that resulted in the convening of an intergovernmental conference (IGC) in September 1985 and the conclusion of the SEA in February 1986.

The issue of institutional reform was already on the Milan agenda, not only indirectly in the form of the White Paper but also directly in the form of the Dooge Report. At the end of the Fontainebleau summit almost one year earlier, Mitterrand had urged the establishment of two ad hoc committees to prepare reports on European union. One would consider aspects of European integration having an evident impact on the daily lives of the Community's citizens, such as education, training, and travel. The other would undertake the much more important task of recommending political, economic, and institutional reform in the Community. In the warm afterglow of Fontainebleau, Community leaders appointed personal representatives to both committees, which began deliberating in the fall of 1984. Pietro Adonnino, a former Italian MEP, chaired the Ad Hoc Committee on a People's Europe. James Dooge, an Irish senator and a former foreign minister, chaired the Ad Hoc Committee on Institutional Reform.

The Adonnino Committee's work had little relevance for the Community's immediate development. Neither its composition nor its conclusions were controversial, and few were ever implemented. By contrast, the Dooge Committee's political significance was evident from the outset. Its composition reflected the importance each country's president or prime minister placed on closer European integration and the approach they would probably take in any future negotiation to revise the Treaty of Rome or draft a new constitution for the Community. As a mark of his determination to revive the Community's fortunes, Mitterrand nominated Maurice Faure, a close associate, a lifelong champion of European union, and a signatory of the Treaty of Rome. As a mark of her determination to restrict institutional reform, Thatcher nominated Malcolm Rifkind, a junior foreign and Commonwealth minister, a vigorous advocate of deregulation and market liberalization, and a staunch defender of national sovereignty.

Incessant interest in the Community's revival following the Genscher-Colombo initiative of 1981—fueled by the European Parliament's draft treaty, the inevitability of a third enlargement, and resolution of the British budgetary dispute—at least ensured that the Dooge Committee's report would avoid the fate of the Tindemans Report a decade earlier. "Spaak II," the Dooge Committee's other informal name, heightened expectations about its deliberations by drawing a parallel between the heady days of European integration in the mid-1950s and the Community's possible resurgence in the mid-1980s. Writing in 1984, Pierre Pflimlin, president of the European Parliament, called for "a new Messina . . . to lift Europe out of the rut into which it has sunk."[32] Just as the 1955 Messina conference had given birth to the Spaak Committee, which in turn gave birth to the Treaty of Rome, so EC enthusiasts hoped that the 1984 "Spaak II" committee would similarly stimulate deeper European integration.

Predictably, the committee devoted considerable attention to internal market issues. Malcolm Rifkind identified a "solid consensus" in the committee and in the Community as a whole about completing the single market by 1990, or 1992 at the latest.[33] Partly for that reason, but also because of mounting pressure for institutional reform, the committee examined a host of options for improving the legislative process, strengthening the commission and Parliament, curbing Coreper, and ending decisionmaking deadlock in the Council of Ministers. In addition, the Committee considered formally extending the Community's competence. Of course, a single market strategy immediately suggested new, formal, or additional powers for the Community in such areas as competition, research and development, consumer affairs, and monetary policy. Yet the committee also discussed intensifying European political cooperation and extending it to include security and defense discussions.

In view of the scope of its deliberations, the committee presented a surprisingly short final report to the Brussels summit in March 1985.[34] The report outlined a number of "priority objectives" deemed necessary to realize European union. As expected, they included a "homogeneous internal economic area," restrictions on the use of unanimity in the Council of Ministers, an enhanced legislative role for the European Parliament, greater executive power for the Commission, and new initiatives in selected policy areas. Because of the nature of the committee's mandate and the recognition by committee members of wide differences over the future of European integration, the report was replete with reservations and minority opinions. For instance, as the personal representative of the prime minister of neutral Ireland, Dooge felt obliged to dissociate himself from the report's recommendation that member states attempt to coordinate security as well as foreign policy, although both he and Garret FitzGerald privately endorsed the idea. Much more important, three committee members—the representatives of Britain, Denmark, and Greece—disagreed with the report's central suggestion that the heads of government convene an IGC to negotiate a treaty on European union based on existing Community law, the Stuttgart declaration, and the Dooge Report and "guided by the spirit and method of the [European Parliament's] Draft Treaty."

Preoccupied with critical enlargement negotiations in March 1985, the European Council deferred discussion of the Dooge Report until its Milan meeting. Agreement on enlargement, the vague but far-reaching "Spaak II" Report, and the Commission's recently completed White Paper gave the Milan summit an air of expectation not seen in the Community since the Hague summit of 1969. As at The Hague sixteen years previously, a pro-integration demonstration heightened public awareness of an imminent breakthrough. Moreover, as a vigorous proponent of European union, Italy wanted to end its six-month Community presidency with an historic decision at the Milan summit to launch intergovernmental negotiations for a new treaty, or at least for reform of the existing treaties.

Quick endorsement of the White Paper apparently presaged a smooth summit, but the meeting soon became mired in a difficult procedural discussion. Arguing against a treaty revision, Thatcher instead advocated informal arrangements to quicken decisionmaking in the Council of Ministers. Taking a closely coordinated position, Mitterrand and Kohl urged relatively radical institutional reform but disagreed about the European Parliament's possible new powers. With Delors's strong support, Italian Prime Minister Bettino Craxi finally forced the issue by proposing an IGC to negotiate a treaty on foreign policy and security cooperation, as well as a revision of the Treaty of Rome to improve decisionmaking and extend Community competence. Jealous of their national sovereignty, Britain and Denmark objected, and obstructionist Greece followed suit. Italy again forced the issue by calling for a vote under Article 236, which permits an IGC to be convened if a majority of member states approve. It was unprecedented for the heads of government to vote on anything at a European Council. Yet in the ensuing ballot seven voted in favor of an IGC and three—the British, Danish, and Greek prime ministers—voted against.

It was nothing new for Thatcher, the lone crusader for reform of the Community budget, to be isolated at a European Council. But she found herself in a novel situation at the end of the Milan summit. In the past, Thatcher's intransigence had thwarted the Community's development. Now she was powerless to prevent the Community from holding an IGC that could change its character completely. Thatcher felt especially offended because the single market program, at the root of the Community's metamorphosis, owed much to her inspiration. She also recognized that excessive use of the veto posed a roadblock to efficient decisionmaking and supported closer foreign policy cooperation. Indeed, only days before the Milan summit, Britain had circulated a paper proposing new EPC procedures.

The prospect of an IGC elicited a mixed response from the "progressive" member states. On the one hand, it was gratifying that the Ten, plus the two candidate members, would move forward together into the next stage of the Community's development. On the other, smarting from their isolation at Milan and renowned for their "minimalist" positions on European integration, Britain, Denmark, and Greece might attempt to "sabotage" the IGC from within. Under Papandreou's vindictive leadership, Greece was capable of such an approach, but there was too much for Britain and Denmark to lose by pursuing blatantly negative tactics. In the end, the minority member states defended their interests tenaciously at the IGC but did so in a creditable and constructive manner.

THE SINGLE EUROPEAN ACT

Speaking at the formal opening of the IGC in Luxembourg on September 9, 1985, Delors remarked that "conferences like this one are not convened every five or ten years. There may not be another between now and [the year] 2000."[35] Delors could not have known that the success of the single market program, combined with the revolution that would sweep Eastern Europe only four years later, would bring a commitment in the Community to even greater economic and political integration. As a result, a little over five years after the opening of the IGC in Luxembourg, two new IGCs opened in Rome to negotiate more extensive treaty revisions.

There are striking similarities and dissimilarities between the 1985–1986 IGC that culminated in the Single European Act and the

1990–1991 IGCs that culminated in the Maastricht Treaty. Both took place under the Luxembourg and Netherlands presidencies (although the SEA negotiations spilled over only briefly into the Netherlands presidency and the Maastricht IGCs formally opened under the Italian presidency). It was fortunate for the Community that small countries, ones likely to have fewer vested interests than their large partners, held the Council presidency during the three IGCs. It was especially fortunate that Luxembourg played a pivotal role. Despite its diminutive size, Luxembourg organized the IGCs admirably and presented timely, skillful proposals.

In both sets of IGCs, Britain and Denmark held out against extensive change, whereas France and Germany worked closely together to promote deeper integration, especially in the pre-Maastricht negotiations. A flurry of bilateral meetings, not only between France and Germany but between all conference participants, further characterized the SEA and Maastricht IGCs. The Commission played a strikingly different role in both cases, working at the forefront of the SEA negotiations but surprisingly staying in the background of the Maastricht Treaty negotiations. The SEA and the Maastricht IGCs concerned the European Parliament a great deal, yet in each instance Parliament played only a limited role. The Court of Justice, another EC institutional actor, also hovered in the wings, although it was less prominent in the Maastricht negotiations largely because it had benefited so much from the SEA.

Apart from the global political climate in which they took place, the most obvious difference between the two sets of IGCs was their scope, notably the relative absence of economic and monetary policy issues from the SEA negotiations. Whereas in 1991 negotiations on EMU constituted an entire IGC, economic and monetary policy were hardly featured in the SEA. As Helen Wallace remarked about the Community's revival in the early 1980s, clearly missing "by comparison with previous efforts to relaunch the Community is any compelling proposal for a great leap forward in economic and monetary integration."[36] Delors succeeded only to a limited extent in including what he called a "monetary capacity" in the SEA.

The SEA negotiations were also much shorter than the Maastricht IGC, which lasted an entire year. Although the Luxembourg presidency took up the Milan summit mandate immediately, it was only in early September 1985 that negotiations among the member states began in earnest. The IGC was to have ended less than three months later, at the Luxembourg summit, but unresolved issues caused it to continue until the end of January 1986. Nevertheless, four months was a remarkable record for a constitutional conference of that kind. Nor is there any basis for complaint that a longer conference would have produced better results. On the contrary, the looming deadline of December 1985, extended by only six weeks, resulted in intensive and productive negotiations.

The IGC that brought about the SEA took place formally at the foreign minister level, although the heads of government devoted themselves exclusively to the subject at the Luxembourg summit in December. The foreign ministers opened the IGC in Luxembourg on September 9, 1985, and met for a further six sessions before concluding the conference, again in Luxembourg, on January 27, 1986. In between foreign ministers' meetings, two "working parties" of high-ranking officials thrashed out most of the details. The first, consisting largely of permanent representatives, dealt with treaty revisions. The second, made up of the political directors of the foreign ministries (the "political committee"), tackled EPC and also drafted the act's preamble. In addition to member state ministers and officials, commissioners or Commission officials participated at each level of the conference.[37]

The procedural problem of parliamentary involvement in the negotiations proved almost as contentious as the substantive issue of increasing Strasbourg's political power. MEPs, citing the supposedly pivotal role of the 1984 draft treaty in accelerating European integration and their status as directly elected representatives, claimed a moral right to sit at the conference table. Although Article 236 did not provide for parliamentary participation in the IGC, it required the consent of the Community's institutions before such a conference could take place. The Commission and Council approved without difficulty or delay, but Parliament seized the opportunity to complain about its likely exclusion from the negotiations. Although vainly demanding "full and equal participation in drafting the new treaty," Parliament provided the necessary assent in a resolution on July 9, 1985.[38] This was the first in a series of parliamentary resolutions in 1985 and early 1986 expressing dissatisfaction with the IGC.

At their opening conference session, the member states and the Commission tried to appease Parliament by agreeing to "take account" of the draft treaty and any other parliamentary proposals and to "submit" the results of their deliberations to the European Parliament. The EP pounced on this offer and proposed a mechanism to consider the results of the conference, suggest amendments, and, if necessary, settle differences by a conciliation procedure. Needless to say, the other parties had no intention of adopting such an elaborate system and, after much discussion, explained to the Parliament that "submit" meant no more than "inform." Parliament was welcome to express opinions on whatever the conference submitted to it, but the conference was under no obligation to consider those opinions in turn.

Written submissions from member states and the Commission provided fodder for the IGC. One of the Commission's earliest contributions urged the conference to draft a single concluding document, rather than a treaty on foreign and security cooperation and a separate compilation of Rome treaty revisions. At first the member states were skeptical, but soon they saw the political significance of having a single document emerge from the conference. Yet it was only at their December 16–17, 1985, session that the foreign ministers endorsed the idea of *unicite* and named the eventual outcome of their deliberations the Single European Act.

Other contributions to the conference covered foreign and security policy, the internal market, the environment, research and development, economic and monetary policy, cohesion between rich and poor regions in the Community, culture and education, and institutional affairs. The political committee considered foreign and security policy in a separate working party. Current trends in East-West relations—intensified Cold War rivalry gradually giving way to possible direct U.S.-Soviet bargaining without European involvement—convinced most member states of the need to assert the Community's international political identity. At the same time, they were eager not to risk alienating a sensitive United States by appearing to undermine NATO. In the end, the conference agreed that member states would "coordinate their positions more closely on the political and economic aspects of security" and "endeavor jointly to formulate and implement a European foreign policy." As a sop to the United States and to those member states—notably Britain and the Netherlands—most sensitive about U.S. opinion, the conference declared that greater foreign policy coordination would not "impede closer cooperation in the field of security" between the relevant Community countries "in the framework of the Western European Union or the Atlantic Alliance."

Despite divergent national positions on the conduct and scope of EPC, the political committee's deliberations were far less contentious than those of the working group charged with proposing treaty revisions. The conference had little difficulty endorsing the goal of an internal market, defined as "an area without internal frontiers in which the free movement of goods, persons, services and capital is ensured." But discussion of the procedural steps necessary to implement the internal market was predictably pugnacious. In the end, the conference revised Article 100 to allow majority voting on harmonization, but only for approximately two-thirds of the measures outlined in the White Paper; the remainder—the least tractable ones—still were subject to unanimity. The conference also conceded a number of national derogations for aspects of the single market program. As a result, a despondent Delors wondered whether the Single European Act would suffice to bring about the internal market by 1992.

The conference did not confront head-on the Luxembourg Compromise. In the SEA's commitment to qualified majority voting for most of the single market program, some member states saw the beginning of a concerted effort to undermine the national veto. Others reached the opposite conclusion by citing the use of unanimity for the White Paper's most controversial proposals. Undoubtedly member states would remain sensitive to each other's concerns, thus perpetuating "the very strong in-clination of the Council to seek consensus irrespective of the voting rules."[39] Only time would tell, however, how the formal changes brought about by the SEA in the Council's decisionmaking process would affect ministers' behavior in legislative areas where unanimity had become the norm.

The role of the European Parliament in the Community's decision-making process was an equally sensitive procedural issue. To push the Community more in a federal direction and to increase its democratic le-gitimacy, Germany and Italy urged greater power for the European Par-liament; for ideological reasons Britain took the opposite tack, and for a combination of political and practical purposes France also opposed strengthening Strasbourg's legislative role. The issue dominated a number of conference sessions (and would take up a lot of time at the Luxem-bourg summit on December 2–3, 1985). Eventually the conference agreed to extend "compulsory" consultation between the Council and the Parlia-ment to new policy issues and, more important, to establish a system of "cooperation" to involve Parliament fully in the legislative process, no-tably for most of the single market program. Moreover, the conference gave Parliament the right to approve future accession and association agreements. As these concessions were limited by comparison with those in the draft treaty, the European Parliament, supported by the Italian gov-ernment, expressed serious dissatisfaction.

During the conference, Delors returned repeatedly to his pet proj-ect of including "a certain monetary capacity" in the SEA. This would bring about "an alignment of economic policies" in the Community, "and outside it would enable Europe to make its voice heard more strongly in the world of economic, financial and monetary matters."[40] Community fi-nance ministers considered the question at an informal meeting in Lux-embourg on September 21, 1985—the only sectoral council to discuss IGC issues—after which Delors had submitted a formal proposal, as did the Belgian government on November 21. Britain strongly opposed any move toward EMU; France was broadly in favor; and Germany remained equivocal. Without strong support from a large member state, Delors had succeeded solely in including a new chapter in the Treaty of Rome that recognized the need to converge economic and monetary policies "for the further development of the Community" and mentioned the EMS and the ECU.

The heads of government, meeting in Luxembourg on December 2–3, 1985, failed to resolve the outstanding issues and conclude the SEA even after two full days of discussion. A foreign ministers session on De-cember 16–17 brought agreement closer, but lingering Danish and Italian reservations (the Danes complained that the SEA's institutional provisions went too far, and the Italians complained that they did not go far enough) carried over into the Dutch presidency. The wording of an article on working conditions, buried in a subsection on social policy, also caused last-minute delays. The ultimate ministerial session of the IGC took place in Luxembourg on January 27, 1986, to approve final compromises reached in the working party and the political committee and to sanction the draft SEA put together by the Dutch presidency, the Commission's legal service, and the Council secretariat.

Only nine member states signed the SEA in Luxembourg on February 17, 1986, the date stipulated by the IGC. Denmark, Italy, and Greece were the three recalcitrant countries. The Danish government awaited the outcome of a referendum on ratification called for February 27, following the Folketing's vote against the SEA on January 21; the Italian government needed more time to discuss the SEA in the Italian Parliament; and the Greek government decided to delay signing the SEA until the remaining two states were ready to do so. After the successful outcome of the Danish referendum and the Italian parliamentary debate, the three remaining member states signed the SEA in The Hague on February 28, 1986.

Ratification of the SEA in 1986 was by no means as difficult as ratification of the Maastricht Treaty would be six years later. Despite official British and Danish protestations before and during the IGC, there was little popular concern throughout the Community about an excessive loss of national sovereignty or an exorbitant accumulation of power by the Commission. Most national parliaments held lively debates on the SEA, and almost all voted in favor of ratification. Denmark's Parliament was the exception, but the positive outcome of the subsequent referendum ensured Danish ratification.

One of the act's final provisions stipulated that the SEA would come into force the month after the last country ratified it. The member states and the Commission hoped that the process of ratification would end in December 1986, allowing the SEA to become operational in January 1987. In the event, a last-minute upset in Ireland delayed everything. First, the Irish government delayed ratification proceedings in the national parliament until the year's end. Then a private citizen, concerned about the compatibility of the SEA's political cooperation provisions with Ireland's foreign policy, challenged the act's constitutionality in court. The case went all the way to the Supreme Court and ran into early 1987. When the Supreme Court ruled that the SEA was indeed unconstitutional, an embarrassed Irish government had no option but to call a referendum to change the constitution. Held in May 1987, for practical purposes the referendum became a vote on whether or not Ireland should stay in the Community. The result—70 percent in favor, 30 percent against, with an exceptionally low turnout of less than 45 percent—was far from an overwhelming endorsement of Community membership, but at least it permitted ratification of the SEA. Thus, after an unexpected holdup, the SEA became binding in the Community on July 1, 1987.

Revision of the Treaty of Rome in 1985 and 1986 had proved a messy, protracted, and contentious affair. For that reason Delors especially disliked the stipulation in the act's "monetary capacity" subsection that further steps toward EMU involving institutional change could only be taken in an IGC. Yet his confidence in the likely revival of member states' interest in EMU led Delors to talk presciently at the end of the SEA negotiations about the possibility of a new IGC in a relatively short time.[41] In other respects, too, the SEA disappointed Delors. He felt that member states had been unwilling to take an initiative unless all twelve would agree, thus reducing reform in the Community to the level of the lowest common denominator. In that sense, Franco-German leadership had not been decisive. Far from pushing a radical reform agenda, Mitterrand and Kohl had apparently succumbed to Thatcher's minimalist position.

Simply because the SEA was the first major overhaul of the Treaty of Rome, it is an exaggeration to claim that it constituted "a step of historic dimensions."[42] As the *Common Market Law Review* editorialized at the time, "measured against Parliament's Draft Treaty, the results [of the IGC] are disappointingly meager. They also fall short of the expectations . . . of the Commission and some of the member states. . . . But they reflect the limits of what was possible at the turn of the year [1985–1986]."[43] Thatcher's delight and Delors's disappointment with the SEA aptly indicate its significance in 1986.

Yet the SEA had real potential for the Community's rapid development. First, provision for qualified majority voting could not only expedite the internal market but also encourage the Council of Ministers to be more flexible in areas where unanimity remained the norm. Second, a successful single market program might advance European integration in related economic and social sectors. Third, the SEA's endorsement of the White Paper and formal extension of Community competence could strengthen the Commission's position. Fourth, the introduction of a legislative "cooperation" procedure could help close the Community's supposed "democratic deficit" and boost the European Parliament's institutional importance. Finally, the SEA's incorporation of EPC into the Treaty of Rome and agreement on new procedures to coordinate foreign policy might enhance the Community's international standing. Within a short time, proponents and opponents of greater European integration would know whether and how the SEA's potential would be realized.

MAKING A SUCCESS OF THE SINGLE ACT

In the late 1980s the word "irreversible" crept into the lexicon of the European Community. It came to mean the point at which completing the single market program, both legislatively and economically, became unstoppable and inevitable. A profile of Lord Cockfield in *The Times* of London in November 1987 claimed that the internal market commissioner aimed to create "a feeling of irreversibility" about the 1992 program in case governments failed to agree on vital parts of it.[44] At approximately the same time Lord Young, the British trade and industry secretary, detected "a realization that . . . the internal market is now inevitable. . . . It's going to happen."[45] Young's judgment may have been premature: The following January, in an address to the European Parliament, Delors reported that "progress made to date has lent credibility to the large [single] market but it is not yet irreversible."[46] In the months ahead, Delors declared, "the Commission will concentrate on making the process irreversible." By the end of 1988, in Delors's view, the point of no return had yet to arrive, although the Commission president conceded that "we are almost on the threshold of the irreversible."[47]

Regardless of when, if ever, completion of the single market program became irreversible, undoubtedly it got off to a slow start. In retrospect, the years 1986 and 1987 resemble the eye of the storm, preceded by agitation for reform and succeeded by a rapid acceleration of European integration. Yet the Community hardly needed to catch its breath after the events of the early and mid-1980s that culminated in the Single European Act. On the contrary, few in the Community appreciated at the time the importance of the SEA or what it portended. In June 1986 *The Economist* referred derisively to the "tiny changes that were agreed upon in Luxembourg last December."[48] Quentin Peel, the respected *Financial Times* correspondent, wondered in April 1987 "whether it [the SEA] will change anything in the real world, other than introduce complex new negotiations between the member states and the Parliament."[49]

In the meantime, the Council of Ministers began the legislative task of completing the single market. The UK, in the Council chair during the last half of 1986, predictably made the internal market one of its presidency's priorities. With the SEA still unratified, member states were not obliged to use qualified majority voting, but the political momentum generated by the single market program encouraged rapid decisionmaking in the Council of Ministers. Yet progress remained pitifully slow. By the end of the year, the Council of Ministers had adopted 31 of the White Paper's 300 measures. By March 1987 the Council's record was 56 proposals adopted out of 170 submitted by the Commission. Six months later, the Council had adopted only an additional eight proposals.

Legislative delay did not prevent the single market program from taking off in the real world of business and commerce. "Italian businessmen talk about *it*, the French have visionary dreams about *it*, the West Germans plan quietly for *it*." *It*, the *Economist* informed the unenlightened in February 1988, "is December 31, 1992, the date by which the European Community is supposed to become a true common market."[50] By that time, European entrepreneurs and businesspeople were fully immersed in the single market program. For over two years they had been bombarded by conferences, newsletters, and advertisements, organized and disseminated by the Commission, member state governments, and the private sector, on how to exploit a frontier-free Community. Large enterprises were best able to do so. In 1987 and 1988 "merger mania," part of "a veritable stampede toward big business in Western Europe," swept the Community, as companies attempted to realize economies of scale and improve their transnational distribution networks.[51] Sixty-eight major mergers and acquisitions took place in the Community in 1986; by contrast, three hundred happened the following year.[52]

The Commission based its most extravagant claims about the likely economic benefits of a single market on a report by Paolo Cecchini, a retired Commission official, who in 1986 and 1987 led a group of researchers in a huge, Commission-funded project on the "costs of non-Europe." The purpose of the project was to quantify the cost to the Community of maintaining a fragmented market. Based on data from the four largest member states, Cecchini's team of independent consultants assessed the costs and benefits of maintaining the status quo by analyzing the impact of market barriers and comparing the Community with North America. Cecchini looked at the financial costs to firms of the administrative procedures and delays associated with customs formalities; the opportunity costs of lost trade; and the costs to national governments of customs controls. In early 1988 Cecchini's team produced their optimistic findings in a massive, sixteen-volume publication.[53]

Based in part on the Cecchini Report, the private sector's love affair with 1992 disguised the program's slow legislative progress. The problem lay not only with the complexity and sensitivity of many of the White Paper's proposals—the Council of Ministers dealt swiftly and easily with the least controversial measures—but also with a festering dispute over the Community's budget. Far from bringing about the end of the Community's seemingly interminable budgetary disputes, the Fontainebleau summit had merely put the issue in abeyance. In 1987, the member states quarreled bitterly over that year's budget, with Britain, Spain, and Greece forming a blocking minority. Britain and Spain found themselves on the same side for strikingly different reasons: Britain insisted on limiting expenditure, whereas Spain demanded additional spending on the Community's poorer regions.

The 1987 budget dispute was separate from the contemporaneous controversy over the Commission's proposal to sort out the Community's finances over the next five years, although the member states' positions on the 1987 budget paralleled their positions on the longer-term financial package. The Commission's five-year budgetary plan bore Delors's personal imprint and later became known as "Delors I" to distinguish it from the similar "Delors II" post-Maastricht budgetary proposals. The purpose of the Delors I package was implicit in its official title: "Making a Success of the Single Act."[54] The SEA had committed the Community to achieve a single market by 1992 and to implement a number of related "flanking" policies without which a single market could not come into existence. "Cohesion"—closing the economic gap between the Community's rich and poor states and between rich and poor regions within the member states—was one of those policies.

Cohesion became the largest obstacle blocking implementation of the single market program in 1987, as the southern member states demanded greater spending on regional and social policy in return for market liberalization. During that time, while the private sector embraced the single market program, the Commission, the Council of Ministers, and the European Council became embroiled in a sharp dispute over how much money to spend on cohesion as part of Delors I. Delors himself characterized the package as a "marriage contract between the Twelve"[55] and struggled throughout 1987 to bring Thatcher to the altar. The British prime minister had an instinctive aversion to increasing the size of the Community's coffers and let it be known that, regardless of any budgetary alteration, Britain would retain its current rebate, for which she had fought so hard in the early 1980s. Otherwise, Thatcher applauded Delors's determination to limit spending on agriculture and impose overall budget discipline, two key elements of his financial package.

Thatcher's general dislike of Delors I brought her into conflict with the Commission and the southern member states but apparently aligned her with Helmut Kohl. Like Thatcher, Kohl loathed the idea of increasing the Community's budget, not least because Germany would probably have to pay substantially more. Yet Kohl also deplored Delors I for a reason that put him completely at odds with Thatcher. Far from wanting to curb the CAP, Kohl would happily have sanctioned a rise in agricultural expenditure in order to maintain the electoral support of Germany's small but influential farming community, especially during the 1987 local elections.

The member states fired their first shots in the new budgetary battle at a foreign ministers meeting on May 11, 1987. Deadlock there set the stage for a series of frustrating encounters in two succeeding European Councils. Yet at the first of these, in Brussels the following June, the heads of government made surprising headway toward agreement on Delors I. In an effort to out-Thatcher Thatcher, the other Community leaders approved a communiqué that stressed budgetary discipline and CAP reform but did not adequately tackle the cohesion question. Thatcher remained obdurate, objecting to two points in the long document, one about switching the basis of member state contributions and the other about selecting a base year against which to measure changes in farm spending. For old-timers at the European Council, this was vintage Thatcher; for newcomers such as

Jacques Chirac, the Gaullist prime minister of France who attended the summit alongside the Socialist president, it was unbearable.

In the intervening months before the December 1987 Copenhagen summit, attitudes hardened on all sides. The southern countries, apparently acquiescent at the Brussels summit, grew more assertive in demanding a greater distribution of Community resources. Unofficially led by Felipe González, the Spanish prime minister, the Community's poor countries pressed hard for acceptance of the original Delors package. A series of preparatory meetings in Brussels in late November failed to find common ground between the northern and southern countries and between Thatcher and the rest. At Copenhagen itself, the expected disaster promptly occurred. With Thatcher reverting to her early 1980s negativism, Kohl and Mitterrand reluctant for domestic political reasons to cut the CAP, and González agitating for additional resources, the Copenhagen summit ended in disarray. The European Council's immobility could not have contrasted more sharply with either the vibrancy of the Community's economic development in the entrepreneurial climate of the single market program or the superpowers' ability at their simultaneous Washington summit to make decisions about Western Europe's security over the heads of Western Europe's leaders and people.

Delors was despondent about the failure of the Copenhagen summit. Member states had tossed his budgetary package around for nearly a year without reaching agreement. In the meantime, the single market program had fallen seriously behind schedule. Delors had hoped that Germany, coming into the Community presidency in January 1988, would have been able to devote itself exclusively to pushing the single market program. Instead, it looked as if the German presidency, like the immediately preceding Danish and Belgian presidencies, would remain preoccupied with the budgetary question.

The same concern motivated Kohl to call a special summit to try to resolve the impasse over Delors I. Feeling more secure in office and hoping to turn his presidency to domestic political advantage, Kohl wanted credit for breaking the Community's latest deadlock. As a result he was more willing than he might otherwise have been to pay the cohesion bill. Yet there was no certainty that the extraordinary February 1988 European Council in Brussels would be successful. A month before the event, a concerned Delors warned the European Parliament that "the consequences of failure will be extremely serious. It would mean that we could not put our minds to attaining the objectives of the Single Act."[56]

Even more than Kohl's statesmanship, Thatcher's surprising tractability saved the Brussels summit from becoming yet another flop. Although the summit began badly with Kohl indecisive, Thatcher strident, and Chirac caustic, Community leaders eventually got down to the kind of focused technical negotiations that should properly have been left to subordinates. After intense bargaining, the heads of government agreed by the summit's end to double the structural funds by 1992 and to introduce a new method of budgetary assessment that, to Thatcher's relief, guaranteed Britain's rebate.

As the European Council drew to a close, CAP reform remained the outstanding issue. Whereas the other Community leaders agreed to a price ceiling on cereals if production throughout the Community exceeded 160 tons, Thatcher held out for a lower limit. Suddenly, to everyone's surprise, "the lady turned."[57] By accepting the higher ceiling, Thatcher let Kohl off the hook with Germany's farmers and sealed the success of the Delors I package. Thatcher's change of heart seemed a remarkable climbdown, especially in the context of previous budgetary battles. The prime minister may have been grateful for her colleagues' continuing acceptance of Britain's rebate, but most likely a desire to end the dissipating Delors I struggle and proceed with parts of the single market program that most interested the United Kingdom convinced her to compromise. Whatever the reason, her decision removed a huge obstacle on the road to 1992.

NOTES

1. John Pinder, *The European Community: The Building of a Union* (Oxford: Oxford University Press, 1991), p. 68.

2. Stanley Hoffmann, "The European Community and 1992," *Foreign Affairs* 68, no. 4 (Fall 1989), p. 32.

3. Helen Wallace, "Widening and Deepening: The EC and the New European Agenda," RIIA Discussion Paper Number 23, 1989, p. 6.

4. On the Community's third enlargement, see Frances Nicholson and Roger East, *From the Six to the Twelve: The Enlargement of the European Community* (Chicago: St. James Press, 1987), pp. 213–251.

5. *Ibid.,* pp. 246-248.

6. Bull. EC S/5-78.

7. Bull. EC 10-1980, point 2.2.3.

8. *Le Monde,* June 7, 1980, p. 1; *The Financial Times,* June 10, 1980, p. 42.

9. Nicholson and East, *Enlargement,* p. 246.

10. Bull. EC 3-1981, Presidency Conclusions, point 1.1.5.

11. Bull. EC 11-1981, Presidency Conclusions, point 1.1.5.

12. Quoted in Nicholson and East, *Enlargement,* p. 222.

13. Bull. EC 10-1983, points 1.1.1 to 1.1.20.

14. Nicholson and East, *Enlargement,* pp. 225–226.

15. Bull. EC 6-1984, Presidency Conclusions, point 1.1.5.

16. *Le Monde,* June 30, 1984, p. 2.

17. Bull. EC 12-1984, Presidency Conclusions, point 1.2.15.

18. For the original Commission proposal, see Bull. EC 2-1982, point 1.2.4.

19. *Agence Europe,* February 14, 1985, p. 5.

20. See Bull. EC 2-1985, point 1.1.2; Bull. EC 3-1985, points 1.1.1–1.1.4 and 1.2.2.

21. Bull. EC 2-1985, point 1.2.1.

22. *Le Monde,* April 2, 1986.

23. Both Delors and Mitterrand are quoted in Nicholson and East, *Enlargement,* p. 229.

24. Commission of the European Communities, "Completing the Internal Market: White Paper from the Commission to the European Council," 14 June 1985, COM(85)210 Final.

25. Jacques Delors, et al., *La France par l'Europe* (Paris: Bernard Grasset, 1988), pp. 50–51.

26. See Jacques Delors, address to the European Parliament, January 14, 1985, Bull. EC S/1-1985.

27. Wisse Dekker, *Europe 1990: An Agenda For Action* (Eindhoven, The Netherlands: N. V. Philips Gloeilampenfabrieken, 1984); Fiat, *La Communauté Européenne et l'Industrie* (Turin: Fiat, 1985); and Ford of Europe, *Building a More Competitive Europe* (London: Ford of Europe, 1985).

28. Bull. EC S/4-1985.

29. Helmut Schmitt von Sydow, "The Basic Strategies of the Commission's White Paper," in Roland Bieber, Renaud Dehousse, John Pinder, and Joseph Weiler, eds., *1992: One European Market?* (Baden-Baden: Nomos, 1988), p. 88.

30. Commission, White Paper, p. 55.

31. Nicholas Colchester and David Buchan, *Europower: The Essential Guide to Europe's Economic Transformation in 1992* (New York: Times Books, 1990), pp. 30–31.

32. Hans von der Groeben, *The European Community: The Formative Years: The Struggle to Establish the Common Market and the Political Union (1958–66),* European Perspectives Series (Luxembourg: Office for Official Publications [hereinafter OOP], 1985), p. 7.

33. Quoted in *Agence Europe,* February 1, 1985, p. 1.

34. "Ad hoc Committee for Institutional Affairs Report to the European Council," Bull. EC 3-1985, point 3.5.1.

35. Quoted in Marina Gazzo, ed., *Towards European Union,* vol. 2 (Brussels: Agence Europe, 1986), p. 23.

36. Helen Wallace, *Europe: The Challenge of Diversity* (Boston: Routledge & Keegan Paul, 1985), p. 4.

37. For descriptions and analyses of the IGC and the SEA, see Jean de Ruyt, *L'Acte Unique Européen: Commentaire* (Brussels: Editions de l'Université de Bruxelles, 1987); J. W. De Zwann, "The Single European Act: Conclusion of a Unique Document," *Common Market Law Review* 23 (1986): 747–765; Richard Corbett, "The 1985 Intergovernmental Conference and the Single European Act," in Roy Pryce, ed., *The Dynamics of European Union* (London: Croom Helm, 1987), pp. 238–272; Andrew Moravcsik, "Negotiating the SEA: National Interest and Conventional Statecraft in the European Community," *International Organization* 45 (Winter 1991), pp. 19–56; Von Sydow, "White Paper," pp. 79–106; and David Cameron, "The 1992 Initiative: Causes and Consequences," in Alberta Sbragia, ed., *Europolitics: Institutions and Policymaking in the "New" European Community* (Washington, DC: Brookings Institution, 1992), pp. 23–74. For additional commentary and a comprehensive compilation of documentation, see Marina Gazzo, ed., *Toward European Union,* 2 vols. (Brussels: Agence Europe, 1985 and 1986). For the Single European Act itself, from which many of the quotations in the following pages are taken, see Bull. EC S/2-1986.

38. *OJ* C 229, September 9, 1985, p. 29.

39. Roland Bieber, Jean-Paul Jacques, and Joseph Weiler, eds., *An Ever Closer Union: A Critical Analysis of the Draft Treaty Establishing the European Union* (Luxembourg: OOP, 1985), pp. 372–373.

40. Quoted in Gazzo, *Union,* vol. 2, p. 24.

41. See Gazzo, *Union,* vol. 2, p. 9.

42. Werner Weidenfeld, "The SEA," *Aussenpolitik* 37 (1986), p. 382.

43. *Common Market Law Review* 23 (1986), p. 251.

44. *The Times* (London), November 16, 1987, p. 15.

45. Quoted in *The Times* (London), November 20, 1987, p. 12.

46. Bull. EC, S/1-1988, pp. 8, 26.

47. *The Times* (London), October 27, 1988, p. 6.

48. *The Economist,* June 28, 1986, p. 50.

49. *The Financial Times,* April 11, 1987, p. 2.

50. *The Economist,* February 13, 1988, p. 11.

51. See Donald Puchala, "The Economic and Political Meaning of 1992," in Michael Steinberg, ed., *The Technological Challenges and Opportunities of a United Europe* (Savage, MD: Barnes & Noble, 1990), p. 22.

52. *The Economist,* February 13, 1988, pp. 46–47, and July 9, 1988, p. 30.

53. Commission of the European Communities, *Research on the "Cost of non-Europe": Basic Findings,* 16 vols. (Luxembourg: Office for Official Publications of the European Communities, 1988). For a condensed version of the Cecchini Report, see Paolo Cecchini, *The European Challenge: 1992* (Aldershot: Wildwood House, 1988).

54. Bull. EC S/1-1987.

55. Bull. EC S/1-1988, p. 14.

56. Bull. EC S/1-1988, p. 7.

57. *The Economist,* February 20, 1988, p. 50.

6

A New Europe,
A New Community? 1989–1993

Nineteen-eighty-nine was an *annus mirabilis,* a "miracle year," that ushered in the "New Europe" of the post–Cold War era. It was a year of peaceful revolution that hastened the collapse of communism and led directly to the unification of Germany in 1990 and the disappearance of the Soviet Union in 1991. It was a year in which the Continent's future looked extremely bright, with Western Europe fully immersed in the single market program and about to embark on Economic and Monetary Union (EMU) and Eastern Europe eagerly embracing liberal democracy and discarding central economic planning. More than any other event, the unexpected breach of the Berlin Wall on the night of November 9, 1989, symbolized a renunciation of Europe's Cold War division and an affirmation of the Continent's common destiny.

Yet within a short time the high hopes of 1989 had given way to cynicism and dejection. By 1992, which was to have been the *annus mirabilis* of the single market's completion, economic recession had spread throughout Western Europe, and the former Soviet bloc countries struggled to implement market reforms and consolidate newly established democratic institutions. In the center of the Continent, Germany grappled with the startlingly high social and financial costs of unification. To the southeast, Europe's first post–Cold War conflict engulfed Yugoslavia and threatened to ignite a wider Balkan conflagration.

The Community's fortunes seemed particularly bleak. Responding to the challenge of German unification, in December 1991 the member states had concluded negotiations at the Maastricht summit for a treaty that included commitments to achieve both EMU and EPU. But growing popular concern about further loss of sovereignty and about secretive and undemocratic decisionmaking in Brussels, compounded by the economic recession and intense frustration over the Community's inability to broker a lasting cease-fire in Yugoslavia, almost thwarted the treaty's ratification. The December 1992 Edinburgh summit may have saved Maastricht as a symbol of the member states' commitment to further integration, although the "opt-outs" granted to Denmark from the treaty's most important provisions, together with a continuing crisis in the European Monetary System and the Community's impotence in Yugoslavia, undermined Maastricht's concrete achievements.

At the heart of the Maastricht ratification debacle lay doubts about the Community's relevance in the post–Cold War world. What was the EC's feasibility and utility in such a radically altered international environment? From the outset, the Community had considered itself synonymous with "Europe." With the Cold War over, could the Community foster a sense of pan-European solidarity and genuinely pan-European integration? What impact would German unification ultimately have? Such questions contributed to the climate of uncertainty in which the Maastricht ratification drama unfolded. Resolution of the crisis did not end skepticism about the Community's future, but it did at least ensure that the Community will play a role in Europe beyond merely providing a common agricultural policy or a single market.

THE ACCELERATION OF HISTORY

What Jacques Delors called "the acceleration of History"[1]—the quickening tempo of developments in Eastern Europe that culminated in the revolution of 1989—began the previous summer with a series of leadership changes, strikes, and demonstrations in Hungary, Czechoslovakia, and Poland. The pace of change picked up in May 1989 with the opening of the Iron Curtain between Hungary and Austria, through which thousands of East Germans fled to the West. The Eastern European drama reached a climax in November 1989, when thousands of West Germans tore down the Berlin Wall without resistance from East German guards. In a fitting finale to a remarkable year, on December 29 Vaclav Havel, the internationally known writer and anticommunist dissident, became president of newly independent Czechoslovakia.[2]

The acceleration of history in Eastern Europe in 1988 coincided with a huge boost in the Community's fortunes. Germany's presidency in the earlier part of the year had been unusually productive, notably in resolving the contentious Delors I budgetary dispute and in advancing the single market program. Interest in the internal market, both inside and outside the Community, increased daily. Capitalizing on the single market's success, Delors focused attention on his primary goal—EMU. Pressed by Mitterrand and Delors, and with Kohl's full support, the heads of government decided at the Hanover summit in June 1988 to instruct a group of experts, chaired by Delors and including member state central bankers, to "study and propose concrete changes" that could result in EMU.[3]

In April 1989 the committee produced the Delors Report,[4] which Community leaders considered at their summit in Madrid the following June. The heads of government endorsed the committee's three-stage approach to EMU and decided that Stage I, involving greater coordination of member states' macroeconomic policies, the establishment of free capital movement, and membership of all Community currencies in the EMS, should begin on July 1, 1990. Moreover, the heads of government agreed that an intergovernmental conference to determine the Treaty revisions needed to launch the subsequent stages would meet "once the first stage had begun."[5]

In its first-ever Community presidency during the early part of 1989, Spain contributed considerably to the growing momentum for EMU. Of the other member states, France was the most powerful proponent of the Delors Report. Edouard Balladur, finance minister during the period of right-wing "cohabitation" with Mitterrand's Socialist presidency in 1987 and 1988, had lobbied for a European central bank as a means of ending the Bundesbank's (German central bank's) dominance of Western European monetary policy.[6] Mitterrand fully endorsed the view that only if monetary policy decisions were taken on an EC-wide basis could France hope to regain some of the influence it had lost to Germany in the EMS because of the mark's predominance in the Exchange Rate Mechanism (ERM).[7]

For precisely that reason, Chancellor Kohl was indifferent about EMU, although the Bundesbank seemed surprisingly open to the idea. Karl-Otto Pohl, the Bundesbank president, had played an active part on the Delors Committee. As the Community set out once again on the road to EMU, Pohl resolved that a future European central bank should have as its main goal the Bundesbank's overriding objective of price stability. Better to influence the development of EMU from the outset and from the inside, Pohl apparently thought, than to disregard the idea and subsequently face an unacceptable fait accompli.

Alone among Community leaders, Margaret Thatcher unequivocally opposed EMU, seeing it as an unacceptable abrogation of national sovereignty and an effort to aggrandize power in Brussels.[8] Opposition to EMU had led in part to Thatcher's famous speech at the College of Europe in Bruges, a citadel of Eurofederalism, in October 1988. Thatcher's Bruges speech was a brilliant articulation of her conception of the European

Community and of Britain's role in it.[9] The prime minister listed five "guiding principles" of European integration: intergovernmentalism; efficiency; enterprise; international openness; and maintenance "of a sure defense through NATO." Thatcher peppered her address with barbed attacks against the Commission and against Eurofederalism. The best-remembered part of her speech was music to the ears of British Euroskeptics: "We have not successfully rolled back the frontiers of the state in Britain only to see them reimposed at a European level with a European superstate exercising a new dominance from Brussels."

Yet Thatcher's hostility toward Brussels in general, and EMU in particular, lacked widespread support within both the Conservative Party and the British cabinet. Nigel Lawson, her chancellor of the exchequer, advocated early ERM participation and pursued a policy of "shadowing" the mark by maintaining an unofficial parity. Geoffrey Howe, the foreign secretary, feared the impact on Britain of a wholly negative policy toward the Community. Under intense pressure from Lawson and Howe, at the Madrid summit Thatcher committed Britain to participate eventually in the ERM and reluctantly went along with the decision to launch Stage I of EMU in July 1990. In the words of Britain's former permanent representative to the Community, this was a rare case for the prime minister "of reason triumphing over prejudice."[10]

Reaction to events in Eastern Europe also separated Thatcher from her Community colleagues, although initially not to such an extent as EMU. Community leaders first discussed the rapidly changing Eastern European situation at the Rhodes summit on December 2–3, 1988. Despite Greek Prime Minister Andreas Papandreou's unpopularity in the European Council, the Rhodes summit proved surprisingly serene, perhaps because the Delors Committee was still deliberating and the single market program was largely on target. As for Eastern Europe, the heads of government issued a hortatory statement, titled "International Role of the EC," that called for a closer relationship between the Community and neighboring countries with the aim of overcoming "the division of our continent."[11]

Six months later, the pace of reform in Eastern Europe had quickened appreciably. Preoccupied with the Delors Report on EMU, Community leaders had only a brief discussion at the Madrid summit of the "profound changes" sweeping the Soviet bloc.[12] Madrid proved to be the last summit in 1989 and 1990 at which member states could distinguish rigidly between events in Eastern Europe and other Community developments. Such was the inexorable rate of reform in the Soviet Union and Eastern Europe and the consequent transformation of the international system that several of the assumptions underlying European integration, as well as many of the Community's policies, programs, and procedures, were quickly called into question.

The most immediate issue in late 1989 and early 1990 was the sudden prospect of German unification, which throughout the Community's existence had remained a remote aspiration. It is impossible to exaggerate the shock that probable unification caused the Community and its member states (including Germany). The challenge for the Community was both procedural—how to absorb the underdeveloped German Democratic Republic (GDR)—and political—how to prevent a resurgent, united Germany from tipping the institutional balance and subverting the Community system. The challenge for Germany was to reassure Community partners of its commitment to European integration; the challenge for other member states was to overcome latent fear of Germany's size in the Community (a united Germany would account for 27 percent of the Community's GDP and, with 77 million people, 25 percent of its population). The solution to most of these problems seemed to lie in deeper European integration.

From the fall of the Berlin Wall in early November 1989 until the first free general elections in East Germany in mid-March 1990, unification suddenly seemed probable but not necessarily near at hand. After the East German elections, in which the surprising victory of Kohl's Christian Democratic Party signaled an overwhelming urge for immediate unification, the GDR's incorporation into the Federal Republic appeared inevitable before the end of the year. The pace of political change had already quickened when the East German elections were brought forward by two months. It picked up further when German monetary union, initially scheduled for January 1, 1991, took place instead on July 1, 1990. In a final burst of irredentism, full unification came into effect on October 3.[13]

The period between November 1989 and March 1990, when German unification seemed probable but not imminent, was especially testing for the Community and its member states. This was when Kohl seized the initiative, dealt directly with Gorbachev, and forced the pace of unification. It was also the time when Mitterrand, Council president until the end of 1989, expressed serious reservations about Kohl's haste and unilateralism, thus straining the much-vaunted Franco-German relationship; when Thatcher displayed deep distrust of German motives, thus alienating herself further from the Community; and when Delors enthusiastically endorsed unification and deeper European integration, thus ensuring the Community's centrality in the events that unfolded and cementing his close personal and political connection with Kohl.

Linkage between German unification and deeper political integration and between EMU and European Political Union (EPU) emerged explicitly at the Strasbourg summit in early December 1989. A number of developments in the weeks preceding the summit ensured its unusual importance for the Community. First, Delors's speech on October 20 at the College of Europe in Bruges, where Thatcher had issued her infamous antifederalist manifesto the previous year, pointed the Community squarely in the direction of EPU. Partly to refute Thatcher's earlier Bruges address but largely in response to recent events in Eastern Europe, Delors called for a huge "leap forward" in the Community to meet the challenge of a new international system. Delors specifically advocated greater Community competence, improved decisionmaking, and less centralization of authority in Brussels.[14] Second, intensifying street demonstrations in East German cities and the collapse of the Berlin Wall on November 9 gave added impetus to Delors's remarks by accelerating the process of political change. Third, Community leaders discussed Delors's ideas and the likely consequences for Germany and for Europe of the Berlin Wall's collapse at an extraordinary summit in Paris on November 18. What Dutch Prime Minister Ruud Lubbers called the "gastronomic summit"—a short dinner meeting of Community leaders—afforded participants an opportunity to express informally their initial reactions to the previous week's dramatic developments in Berlin.[15] Delors was delighted; Kohl euphoric; Mitterrand cautious; and Thatcher troubled.

Chancellor Kohl's speech to the Bundestag on November 28, 1989, in which he outlined a ten-point program for German and European unification, was the final prelude to the Strasbourg summit. At the time, Kohl's speech seemed daring, even provocative. He had consulted none of his Community colleagues, let alone Hans-Dietrich Genscher, his foreign minister, who had hitherto directed all aspects of Germany's foreign policy and whose name had become synonymous with the Federal Republic's openness to the East.[16] Thus, apart from its international implications, Kohl's speech signaled the chancellor's determination to take personal charge of Bonn's dynamic *Ostpolitik*.

Kohl's November 28 speech was a political masterpiece that deflected criticism of his supposed lack of vision and rallied support behind an inherently popular cause. Sometimes caricatured for his atheoretical approach, Kohl gleefully conceded that "abstract models are of no assistance" in ending the East German drama. The chancellor also acknowledged that "no one today knows . . . how a united Germany will finally look" but declared his willingness "to develop confederative structures between the two States in Germany, with the object of then creating a federation, that is, a national federal system in Germany." Such a development depended on the emergence of a democratic government in East Germany and on a deepening of European integration. Based on his own conviction and on a need to assuage restive neighboring states, Kohl proclaimed that "the future architecture of Germany must be fitted into the future architecture of Europe as a whole." In particular, the European Community and the Conference on Security and Cooperation in Europe (CSCE) would provide the two essential pillars for a united Germany in post–Cold War Europe.[17]

The relationship between German unification and European integration was a constant theme in subsequent German official pronouncements. Thomas Mann's famous call in 1953 "not for a German Europe, but for a European Germany" became the leitmotif of Bonn's unification policy. Yet Kohl's earliest articulation of it failed to reassure all of his Community colleagues. Thatcher was the most obvious opponent of German unification, and Mitterrand initially followed her lead. Thus, Kohl's unequivocal call for unification on November 28, Thatcher's and Mitterrand's frosty responses, and Delors's earlier appeal for deeper European integration set the scene for the Strasbourg summit of December 8–9, 1989.

Detailed discussion at Strasbourg of probable German unification allowed Kohl to amplify his idea of a "European Germany." Mitterrand, torn between an instinctive antipathy toward German unification (which appeared inevitable in any case), and an equally instinctive affinity for European integration, forged a link between both. Above all, Mitterrand wanted in his second term as president of France to promote "the construction of Europe."[18] Obstructing German unification at the Strasbourg summit, the highlight of France's Community presidency, would have impaired European integration and destroyed the latest initiative for EMU. A key passage in the summit's conclusions outlined the Franco-German bargain, to which other member states subscribed: German unity through free self-determination "should take place peacefully and democratically, in full respect of the relevant agreements and treaties and of all the principles defined by the Helsinki Final Act [of the CSCE], in a context of dialogue and East-West cooperation . . . [and] in the perspective of European integration."[19]

TOWARD THE INTERGOVERNMENTAL CONFERENCES

In concrete terms, the Franco-German bargain manifested itself immediately in a decision at Strasbourg to hold an intergovernmental conference under Article 236 of the Treaty of Rome to work out the changes necessary to move on to Stages II and III of EMU. As Mitterrand announced after the summit, this represented "the sole objective link" in the European Council's deliberations between German and European integration.[20] Unlike at the Milan summit in June 1985, where the European Council president called for a vote to convene the IGC, at Strasbourg the president merely announced that a majority existed to hold a new IGC. Thatcher made no secret of her minority opinion but saw no point in being formally outvoted.

Thatcher's opposition to German unification and EMU persisted. The prime minister's vociferous support for an immediate widening of the Community's membership barely disguised her determination to prevent deepening at all costs. Far from weakening the other member states' resolve to cement the bargain struck at the Strasbourg summit, however,

Thatcher's negativism merely emphasized her isolation in the Community and contributed to her ouster from Downing Street less than a year later. An infamous outburst by Nicholas Ridley, her close confidante and secretary of state for trade and industry, probably reflected Thatcher's private utterances on Germany and Europe. In an interview published in the July 1990 issue of *The Spectator,* Ridley not only decried the emergence of an "uppity" Germany but also denounced deeper EMU as "a German racket."[21] Ridley's prompt resignation failed to dispel a widespread feeling that Thatcher fully agreed with his remarks.

Moves toward EPU were a further concrete manifestation of the Strasbourg summit's agreement on German unification. Yet the rapid pace of events in East Germany continued to discomfit Mitterrand. During a previously scheduled visit to East Berlin and Leipzig on December 20–22, 1989, less than two weeks after the Strasbourg summit, Mitterrand warned against rapid German unification. Mitterrand's misgivings persisted until well into the new year. Four days before the crucial East German elections of March 18, Mitterrand ostentatiously received Oscar Lafontaine, leader of the Social Democratic Party in East Germany and a proponent of long-term rather than immediate unification. Only with Lafontaine's resounding electoral defeat did Mitterrand make a virtue of necessity and throw himself fully behind imminent German unification.

Mitterrand's prevarication undermined the success of the Strasbourg summit, exasperated Kohl, and weakened Franco-German leadership in the Community. Efforts to launch political union were already under way but had little prospect of success without full Franco-German support. In a speech to the European Parliament on January 17, 1990, outlining the Commission's program for the year, Delors called for a stronger executive, a more powerful European Parliament, a more effective procedure for foreign policy cooperation, and implementation of the principle of subsidiarity.[22] On March 20 Belgium became the first member state to submit a formal proposal for EPU, emphasizing institutional reform, reducing the democratic deficit, and developing a common foreign policy. The Belgian document also included a lengthy section on subsidiarity.[23]

In keeping with earlier efforts to revise the treaties, the European Parliament played a prominent part in the renewed initiative to deepen European integration. The second directly elected Parliament, which met for the first time in July 1989, contained a larger number of prominent European politicians than its predecessor. Although not all (for instance, former French President Valéry Giscard d'Estaing) were noted Eurofederalists, at least they concurred on the need to augment the Parliament's powers, increase the Community's democratic legitimacy, and improve its efficiency.

The newly elected Parliament was fully aware of the recently deceased Altiero Spinelli's contribution to European integration and determined to follow Spinelli's lead in the early 1980s by playing an equally constructive part in future negotiations for European union.[24] Accordingly, in the aftermath of the Strasbourg summit various parliamentary committees began to prepare resolutions on ways to deepen European integration. On March 14, 1990, Parliament adopted the first of these, the "Martin Report on Political Union,"[25] which strongly influenced Belgium's March 20 submission.

Gianni de Michelis, Italy's flamboyant and energetic foreign minister, played a key role in pushing the Community toward EPU. Even before Italy's presidency in the last half of 1990, when he occupied center stage, de Michelis strove to win a commitment from the member states to begin negotiations for a radical revision of the treaties. The cause of Community reform combined de Michelis's love of the political limelight with his country's genuine enthusiasm for a federal Europe. Although typically extravagant, de Michelis's remark in early 1990 that "never before have [the member states] been more in tune" revealed a growing consensus in the Community about the need for another intergovernmental conference to negotiate EPU.[26] Only Britain and Denmark remained unconvinced. France was in favor, but Mitterrand's lingering opposition to German unification and the consequent stress in Franco-German relations prevented a clear lead coming from that direction.

The outcome of the East German elections, however, swung Mitterrand fully behind imminent German unification and cleared the way for a Franco-German initiative on EPU. That initiative, representing also an act of Franco-German reconciliation, came in the form of a short letter on April 19, 1990, from Kohl and Mitterrand to Charles Haughey, Ireland's prime minister and president of the European Council.[27] Kohl and Mitterrand linked the need "to accelerate the political construction" of the Community to recent developments in Eastern Europe, as well as to the moves already under way to achieve EMU. The letter also anchored the proposed political changes in the SEA's commitment "to transform relations as a whole among the member states into a European Union."

The Kohl-Mitterrand letter is a landmark in the history of EPU and is rightly credited with getting the negotiations going. It was further testimony to the decisiveness of the Franco-German axis in the Community's development, not least because of Britain's marginalization. Yet the Kohl-Mitterrand letter needs to be understood in the context of a growing momentum in the Community for a revision of the treaties: It gave added impetus to, but did not initiate, the thrust in late 1989 and early 1990 toward EPU.

The Kohl-Mitterrand letter set the agenda for the extraordinary April 28 European Council in Dublin. Instead of discussing German unification and relations with Eastern European countries, the summit would focus on preparations for the IGC on EMU (due to open before the end of the year under Italy's presidency) and the possibility of a parallel inter-governmental conference on EPU. Both EMU and EPU "should enter into force on January 1, 1993 after ratification by the national parliaments." Kohl and Mitterrand did not define EPU but did identify four essential elements of it: stronger democratic legitimacy; more efficient institutions; unity and coherence of economic, monetary, and political action; and a common foreign and security policy.

The Franco-German initiative dominated the Dublin summit ("Dublin I") and won almost unanimous support. Only Thatcher adamantly opposed a parallel IGC, telling her bemused colleagues that the British monarchy and parliament would survive the Community's efforts to force the pace of European integration. In deference to Thatcher, the other Community leaders postponed a formal decision but left no doubt about their determination to proceed sooner rather than later with negotiations on political union.[28]

Two events in mid-May 1990—a Commission-sponsored conference on European integration and an unusually positive Greek memorandum on Community reform (submitted only one month after Constantine Mitsotakis's election victory)—kept up the pressure for a decision to convene a second IGC. At an informal foreign ministers meeting on May 19–20, Douglas Hurd struck a conciliatory note. Thatcher's own position had moderated in the meantime, possibly because of the restraining influence of Hurd and John Major, her chancellor of the exchequer, and a realization that her obduracy in Dublin had proved politically unpopular at home.

Charles Haughey, the Irish prime minister, did not want his end-of-presidency summit ("Dublin II") marred by a row with Thatcher over EPU. Although Haughey and Thatcher reputedly loathed each other, in his pre-summit diplomacy the Irish prime minister urged restraint on the pro- and anti-EPU sides. The Irish presidency prepared a deliberately non-provocative paper that included almost all the suggestions so far made by others on Treaty reform. In the event, the June summit was surprisingly uncontentious. Thatcher went along with the decision, taken under Article 236 of the Treaty of Rome, to convene an IGC "to transform the Community from an entity mainly based on economic integration and political co-operation into a union of a political nature, including a common foreign and security policy." The heads of government agreed that both IGCs (on EMU and EPU) would begin at the Rome summit in December 1990.[29]

By the time the member states decided to hold an IGC on political union, the Community was well on its way to absorbing the German Democratic Republic. Even during the Cold War, East Germany had enjoyed a unique relationship with the Community involving an exemption of intra-German trade from the Common Customs Tariff. Yet German unification presented enormous administrative challenges for the Community.

A special group of commissioners chaired by Martin Bangemann (Germany's senior commissioner) met weekly to provide overall direction. On April 19, 1990, the Commission produced a paper on the legal, financial, institutional, and external implications of German unification.[30] A temporary committee of the European Parliament convened for the first time in March 1990 to consider the implications of German unification. It produced a comprehensive and generally positive report (the Donnelly Report) four months later.[31] Both the Commission and Parliament took care to involve East German officials in their deliberations. The European Council followed suit, inviting East German Prime Minister Lothar de Maiziere to attend lunch at the June 1990 Dublin summit, the first outsider ever accorded such an honor.[32]

As agreed at the June 1990 Dublin summit, the two IGCs on European union did not begin until the Rome summit six months later. The intervening period, which covered most of Italy's presidency, saw the member states' understanding of EMU come into sharper focus and their understanding of EPU become more blurred. This reflected the concrete nature of EMU, especially after the European Council's acceptance of the Delors Report, and the inherently imprecise nature of EPU. The ultimate goal of EMU was obvious, whereas the definitive objective of EPU was far from certain. Most member states agreed on what EPU could or should include—closing the democratic deficit, strengthening subsidiarity, improving decisionmaking, increasing Community competence, reforming EPC, and devising a common foreign and security policy (CFSP)—but disagreed on the extent of those changes and how to bring them about. With the approach of the IGCs, a consensus on EPU seemed more remote than ever.

Moves toward EMU received a further boost at the extraordinary European Council in Rome on October 27–28, 1990, when eleven member states agreed to launch Stage II on January 1, 1994. The summit's conclusions identified Britain as the odd man out in discussions of both EMU and EPU.[33] Thatcher's recalcitrance had an unexpected side effect: It precipitated her ouster as Conservative Party leader and prime minister. Ever since their poor performance in the June 1989 European Parliament elections, British Conservatives saw Thatcher's implacable opposition to European integration as a serious liability. By itself, Thatcher's detestation of EMU and EPU would not have lost a general election; combined with a hugely unpopular tax reform, it threatened to tip the scales in favor of Labour. Thatcher's strident remarks on her return from Rome sparked a leadership struggle the following month, which John Major surprisingly won. This was the first time in the EC's history that "Community affairs" had impinged so dramatically and so directly on domestic politics.

While Britain's domestic political drama unfolded, the worsening Gulf crisis focused Community attention on the need to develop a CFSP.

The Community responded swiftly to Iraq's aggression: Two days after the August 2 invasion, the EC embargoed oil from Iraq and occupied Kuwait.[34] But member states failed thereafter to develop a coherent and effective response to the crisis. To some extent the Community was a victim of its own success: Rampant Europhoria in the summer of 1990, including pervasive talk about a CFSP, had raised false expectations about the Community's ability to take joint military action.

The Gulf crisis, hurtling toward a climax in mid-January, cast a shadow over the impending IGCs and added to the Community's deepening gloom. Whereas in the summer of 1990 Europhoria apparently knew no bounds, less than six months later attitudes had changed perceptibly. Exhilaration over the revolution in Eastern Europe and its apparent spread to the Soviet Union gradually gave way to concern about economic, political, and military instability in the East. Guarded optimism about German unification conflicted with latent fear of the country's resurgence and more realistic anxiety about the unexpectedly high cost of assimilating East Germany into the Federal Republic. At the same time, U.S.-EC relations seemed set to collide at the Brussels ministerial meeting of the Uruguay Round, scheduled for mid-December 1990.

Thus, at the December Rome summit, Community leaders inaugurated the IGCs with trepidation rather than elation. John Major's replacement of the irascible Margaret Thatcher alleviated some of the gloom. Although, as the *Economist* facetiously remarked, Thatcher's departure had robbed the Community of "the grit around which the other eleven formed their Euro-pearl,"[35] her erstwhile colleagues were glad to see her go. It was impossible at that stage to judge whether Major's ascendancy represented more than a welcome stylistic change in Britain's dealings with Brussels. Nevertheless, Community leaders happily gave Major the benefit of the doubt.

Apart from the neophyte British prime minister, Helmut Kohl was one of the few heads of government in a buoyant mood at the summit. Having easily won the first all-German general elections only the previous week, Kohl was understandably elated. Otherwise, despite the inevitable excitement surrounding the IGCs' launch, few Community leaders seemed to share the Italian prime minister's conviction that "we are moving toward a progressive and irreversible growth of the supranational momentum, from which will emerge European Union."[36]

NEGOTIATING THE MAASTRICHT TREATY

The two IGCs that opened in Rome in December 1990 resumed in Brussels early in the new year. Some member states hoped that the IGCs might conclude as early as the Luxembourg summit in June 1991 or at a special summit during the Dutch presidency in the second half of the year. In the event, negotiations continued until December 1991, culminating in an intensive bargaining session at the Netherlands' regular end-of-presidency summit, held in the southern city of Maastricht.

Procedure

At their October 1990 summit in Rome, the heads of government charged the General Affairs Council with maintaining "parallelism" between both conferences. Regular contacts between the presidents of the Commission and the Council of Ministers would also help to ensure consistency, as would summit meetings. In addition to the regular end-of-presidency European Councils, there was one extraordinary summit in 1991. It took place in Luxembourg on April 8 but concentrated almost exclusively on the political aftermath of the Gulf War and touched only briefly on the IGCs.

What did parallelism really mean? After all, the precise objectives of the conferences were not closely related. Despite rhetoric to the contrary, the member states could have devised EMU without EPU and vice versa. Indeed, they had already decided to launch a new monetary initiative before events in Eastern Europe and the prospect of German unification impelled them also toward EPU. If the purpose of EPU was to establish a single European government to which a European central bank, responsible for monetary policy, would be answerable, then the negotiations would indeed have had to be congruent. But a single European government was far from what the member states had in mind in the IGC on political union. Conversely, apart from the Council of Ministers, existing Community institutions would not be centrally involved in the achievement of EMU.

Because the conferences on EMU and EPU would contribute to the ultimate attainment of European union and because the Commission wanted to maximize its involvement in all aspects of European integration, the Brussels bureaucracy had a keen interest in linking the two sets of negotiations as closely as possible. But few member states did. Only Germany advocated a close linkage between EMU and EPU, to the point of threatening to veto EMU without a far-reaching agreement on EPU. The reason, quite simply, was that Germany had the most to lose from EMU and the most to gain from EPU. By agreeing to a single European currency, Germany would be giving up the mark and surrendering control over European monetary policy, which it currently enjoyed in the EMS. In return, Germany wanted a Community with a familiar federal system of government in which controversial domestic issues (such as asylum policy and defense) might be resolved and in which a more powerful European

Parliament (with a large German contingent) would play a greater legislative role.

Negotiations took place at the heads-of-government level (during European Councils), at the ministerial level (monthly meetings of finance ministers to discuss EMU and foreign ministers to discuss EPU), and at the official level (bimonthly meetings of finance ministry and central bank officials to discuss EMU and weekly meetings of the foreign ministers' personal representatives—mostly the permanent representatives in Brussels—to discuss EPU). Although the negotiations were intergovernmental, the Commission participated at all levels, but it lacked the authority to veto a final agreement.

Member State Perspectives

Each delegation brought to the table a particular set of expectations and objectives.[37] Of the larger member states, Germany was most committed to EMU and EPU. On EMU the Bundesbank, rather than the government, seemed to determine Germany's position. Even before the IGC opened, Karl-Otto Pohl, the Bundesbank president, outlined Germany's objectives in a number of forceful speeches and lectures. His main point was the indivisibility of monetary policy. Responsibility for it at the European level would have to reside in a single, independent institution with the unambiguous, statutory mandate of maintaining price stability. In other words, the proposed European central bank should replicate the Bundesbank. Pohl also urged a gradual approach to EMU, stressing the need for economic convergence between potential participants. Because of the disparity in economic performance between Community countries, Pohl raised the unpopular prospect of a two- or multispeed move to EMU.

Pohl's blunt statements about EMU and about the excessive cost of German economic and monetary union did not endear him to Chancellor Kohl. Nevertheless, Pohl's resignation in mid-1991, four years before the end of his second term as Bundesbank president, was unexpected. Far from letting up on the government, however, Pohl's successor continued the offensive, focusing especially on the danger of establishing a European central bank (ECB) at the beginning of Stage II, before the Community was ready to launch a single currency. The Bundesbank's stridency caused a rift in the German government, with Theo Waigel, the finance minister, echoing Frankfurt's position and Kohl and Genscher, the foreign minister, taking a more flexible line.

France wanted EMU at almost any cost and did not have an independent central bank counseling caution. Mitterrand was not eager to have an independent ECB but conceded the point early in the negotiations. However, France strongly urged the inauguration of an ECB at the beginning of Stage II rather than Stage III. According to the French, a functioning ECB and a strict timetable for a single currency would spur member states to prepare their economies for EMU.

Although overeager for EMU, France had reservations about many aspects of EPU. While advocating EPU as a means of tying united Germany closer to the Community, France pursued traditional institutional objectives at the IGC. In particular, France opposed giving the European Parliament any more power and sought a stronger European Council at the expense of both Parliament and the Commission.[38]

Britain was profoundly skeptical of both EMU and EPU. Only late in the negotiations did the British government subscribe to the prevailing conception of a single currency and abandon its alternative "hard ECU" proposal. John Major, then chancellor of the exchequer, had made the proposal in June 1990, six months before the IGCs opened. Major's complicated and clever idea was to turn a hardened ECU (an ECU that could not be devalued against its component currencies) into another, parallel currency that could circulate alongside existing national currencies. A new institution, to be called the Hard ECU Bank or the European Monetary Fund, would issue the hard ECU. In time, the hard ECU could develop into a dominant common currency, even into a single currency if the Community so decided. According to the Bank of England, "the pace of the Hard ECU's development would be determined by the interaction between judicious supply of hard ECUs by the authorities and market demand for a strong common currency, in contrast to other schemes [i.e., the Delors Plan] that foresee the transition to a single currency being determined purely by administrative fiat. . . . It would be a genuinely evolutionary, market-based approach."[39]

The hard ECU proposal showed that, unlike Thatcher, at least Major took EMU seriously. But his idea was too idiosyncratic and came too late to influence the debate. Nevertheless, the prime minister continued to advocate the hard ECU until almost the end of the IGC. By the time Major quietly dropped the idea, Britain's main concern was to stay in the fast track of a de facto two-speed Community but keep the option of not participating in a single currency. In a House of Commons debate on November 20, 1991, Major described the opt-out provision of the proposed EMU treaty as "a clause that we have secured enabling us to opt-in. *If* we wish, *when* we wish, and in the conditions that *we* judge to be right."[40]

In a series of speeches in early 1991, Major had promised to put the UK "at the very heart of the Community." The new prime minister's message sounded strikingly similar to Thatcher's statement in November 1990 that "Britain's future lies in the EC: not on the fringes of it, but in the mainstream."[41] Such was the aversion toward Thatcher in the Community, however, that Major's declaration seemed a radical reversal of British policy. In fact, an arcane attachment to national sovereignty, in an age of increasing economic and political interdependence, continued to fuel British opposition to a single currency and to a Community organized on federal lines. Britain's performance in both IGCs demonstrated the philosophical and ideological distance between London and other Community capitals. On a range of issues—from legislative reform to CFSP decisionmaking to extending the Community's competence—Britain took a minimalist position.

A prolonged controversy over the "F-word" demonstrated the difference between Britain and its Community partners. A revised draft treaty presented by the Luxembourg presidency in June 1991 described European integration as "a process leading to a Union with a federal goal." Douglas Hurd, the British foreign secretary, immediately announced that his country did "not intend to be committed to the implications which, in the English language, the phrase 'federal goal' carries."[42] The issue was not simply linguistic. After all, Americans understood "federalism" to mean something positive and worthwhile. Lord O'Hagan, a British MEP, explained the problem differently: "On the Continent, [federalism] is a harmless label, neither exciting nor controversial. In Britain, it carries connotations of unspeakable disloyalty and unmentionable perversity."[43]

O'Hagan should have been more specific: On the Conservative back-benches in the House of Commons, rather than elsewhere in the country, federalism had extremely negative connotations. Conservative Euroskeptics equated federalism with the excessive centralization of power in Brussels. Margaret Thatcher, the leading Conservative back-bench Euroskeptic after her ouster as party leader, warned shortly after leaving Downing Street that "coming together in Europe" must not mean "more centralization. That would be a most undesirable constraint on liberty. Much of the rest of the world is finding liberty in devolution of power away from the center; it would be ironic if the Community were to move in the opposite direction."[44] Thatcher later developed the "liberty" theme before a sympathetic U.S. audience, contrasting the Community's supposed centralization with the Soviet bloc's disintegration.[45]

Thatcher was right to caution against an unreasonable concentration of power in Brussels. But by 1991 the Commission was fully committed to subsidiarity—a federal principle—thanks partly to Thatcher's earlier warnings. Indeed, a desire to enshrine subsidiarity in the new treaty was one of the few issues in the political union negotiations on which every delegation agreed. The irony was not that the Community was going the way of the former Soviet bloc but that Thatcher subscribed to a federal remedy (subsidiarity) for a supposed federal affliction (centralization) and that during her eleven years as Britain's prime minister she had further centralized power in an already overcentralized state.

With Thatcher hovering in the wings and a general election looming, it was not surprising that the British government protested about the

"F-word." It was an easy battle to fight because there was nothing of substance at stake. At the Luxembourg summit in June 1991, Major denounced the draft treaty's reference to a "federal goal." To his annoyance, the new Dutch presidency merely changed this phrase to "federal vocation." As the IGCs intensified, Major escalated his campaign to excise the "F-word." Eventually, shortly before the Maastricht summit, his colleagues gave in. "What does the word matter, as long as we have the actual thing?" asked Delors.[46] The word mattered, of course, because Major needed to claim a political victory.

By contrast with the UK, Italy was a wholehearted champion of supranationalism in the Community. As a weak and highly decentralized state with strong regional rather than national allegiances, Italy welcomed the emergence of a federal Europe. There were few proposals on political union to which Italy objected. However, because of its excessive budget deficit, Italy feared being relegated to the second division of EMU. Spain shared Italy's concern about a two-speed EMU and advocated a lengthy transition from Stages II to III. In addition, as part of an EMU package, Spain demanded compensatory finance for poorer Community countries. Spain bolstered its case by claiming that the country was about to become a net contributor to the Community's budget. Prime Minister González's threat to block agreement at Maastricht unless his colleagues approved a "cohesion fund" nearly undid the IGCs.

Smaller Community countries shared many of the larger member states' objectives but lacked the political clout to influence the negotiations' outcome. Ireland and Portugal contributed creditably to the debate on economic and social cohesion, whereas Greece, hitherto kept out of the Western European Union (WEU) because of its feud with fellow NATO member Turkey, spent most of its time at the IGC demanding WEU membership. Luxembourg—the smallest member state—had unusual leverage by virtue of being in the presidency during the first half of 1991. But as in the pre-SEA negotiations, which coincidentally it also chaired, Luxembourg scrupulously played the role of honest broker.

Drafting the Treaty

Based on extensive bilateral meetings and on shrewd observations made during negotiating sessions, in mid-April Luxembourg produced a lengthy draft treaty on political union. The most striking feature of the Luxembourg "nonpaper" was its unusual architectural design for the putative European Union. Instead of a single structure, the Union would consist of three "pillars": the Treaty of Rome (including provisions for EMU and other new competences agreed in the negotiations on political union); the CFSP; and cooperation on judicial and home affairs (such as immigration and internal security). The European Council would form the entablature, or capstone, spanning these pillars. By keeping the CFSP and cooperation on home affairs on an intergovernmental basis outside the Rome treaty, Luxembourg hoped to reconcile the two extremes of Community opinion epitomized by Germany, Italy, and the Netherlands on the profederalist side and Britain and Denmark on the antifederalist side.

Predictable profederalist criticism of the Luxembourg "nonpaper," especially at a foreign ministers meeting in Dresden on June 3, led to a revised version on June 18. Mark Eyskens, the Belgian foreign minister, argued at Dresden for a "tree with branches" rather than a "temple with pillars"; in other words, for a unitary treaty structure.[47] The new Luxembourg draft did not abandon the three pillars approach but stressed the institutional links between them and, in a concession to the "maximalist" member states, included a reference to the Union's federal goal.

During its presidency, Luxembourg also tabled a draft treaty on EMU. The extremely complex negotiations on EMU had made little progress in early 1991, not for want of proposals from member states but because government officials stuck to rigid positions at the IGC. The length and purpose of Stage II posed a major point of dispute. For practical and symbolic reasons, France and the Commission wanted to establish the ECB at the beginning of a relatively short Stage II. Although a single currency would not be introduced until Stage III, the prior existence of the ECB, together with a deadline for the end of Stage II, would encourage member states to expedite preparations for a single currency. In the meantime, the ECB would reinforce monetary cooperation among national central banks and supervise development of the ECU.

Germany (specifically, the Bundesbank) saw great danger in establishing the ECB during Stage II. The ECB would be unable to perform its main function until the launch of a single currency in Stage III, and in the meantime it could lose sight of its primary objective: price stability. Moreover, an underemployed ECB would forfeit morale and prestige. The Luxembourg draft treaty, presented at a finance ministers meeting on May 11, proposed a relatively insubstantial Stage II in which a Committee of Central Bank Governors would try to coordinate national monetary positions. The ECB would be established in 1996, toward the end of Stage II. Although Germany successfully held out for the contemporaneous launch of an ECB and a single currency, at least the Luxembourg draft broke the EMU stalemate.

The Luxembourg draft treaty on EMU sparked the first serious discussion of convergence criteria and of possible opt-outs from a single currency. At the May 11 finance ministers meeting, a general consensus emerged that no country should be allowed for political or economic reasons to prevent others from moving to Stage III. Nor would any country (i.e., the UK) be forced to adopt a single currency. That informal agreement proved decisive for the IGC's success. As Luxembourg's finance minister remarked after the May 11 meeting, "the prospect of a two-speed monetary union was raised, and no one was shocked."[48]

Luxembourg's Community presidency and stewardship of the IGCs culminated in the June 25–26 European Council. The heads of government were not yet ready to conclude the IGCs, although, paradoxically, the agreement eventually reached at Maastricht bore a striking resemblance to the draft treaties on EMU and EPU prepared by the Luxembourg presidency. On his return to London, Major told the House of Commons that the Luxembourg summit had been "a stock-taking exercise," with each delegation explaining its positions on EMU and EPU.[49] The opportunity for serious negotiations had diminished in any case with the outbreak of war in Yugoslavia. The Troika of foreign ministers—Gianni de Michelis (Italy), Jacques Poos (Luxembourg), and Hans van den Broek (the Netherlands)—hurried to Yugoslavia on June 25 to mediate a settlement between the federal government and secessionist Slovenia, returning to Luxembourg the following morning. Like the Gulf War six months earlier, the Yugoslav war emphasized the need for a comprehensive CFSP. Yet also like the Gulf War, the protracted and—for the Community— much more serious Yugoslav war would make an effective CFSP far harder to achieve.[50]

The Netherlands presidency of the Community and chairmanship of the IGCs in the second half of 1991 was controversial and, at the outset, ineffectual. For one thing, the Christian Democratic–Labour coalition government was deeply divided and became embroiled in late 1991 in a domestic political dispute over social welfare payments. For another, it took on too many international responsibilities. Foreign Minister Hans van den Broek spent most of his time trying to mediate the war in Yugoslavia. Prime Minister Ruud Lubbers became preoccupied with an initiative to help the Soviet Union by developing its oil and natural gas industries (his proposed "Energy Charter" involved a large international conference in The Hague and continuous negotiations in Brussels). Other pressing international issues during the Dutch presidency included the final stages of the EC-EFTA negotiations and the ubiquitous Uruguay Round.

Lubbers's and van den Broek's other commitments meant that Piet Dankert, the junior foreign minister and a former president of the European Parliament, had an unusually influential role in formulating Dutch policy toward the IGCs. A committed federalist, Dankert was unhappy with certain aspects of the Luxembourg draft treaties. He particularly disliked Luxembourg's proposal for a "temple," which he sought to replace with a "tree." Despite an understanding at the June summit that the revised Luxembourg "nonpaper" would form the basis for future negotiations, Dankert resolved to introduce a radically different draft on political union.

As word of Dankert's intentions spread, other member states warned the Netherlands not to take drastic action. Trading on the historically close relationship between Britain and the Netherlands, Major traveled to The Hague for discussions with Lubbers on September 18 and argued strongly against changing the treaty structure proposed by Luxembourg.[51] At an IGC session on September 27, a majority of foreign ministers' representatives cautioned their Dutch colleague to stick to the pillars approach. By that time the Dutch had drafted a treaty with a unitary structure to which, according to a government spokesman, "we are ready to make some changes in specific areas, but there is no question of us throwing our draft away and going back to the proposals of the Luxembourg presidency earlier this year."[52]

Predictably, the Dutch draft triggered an angry reaction when presented at a foreign ministers meeting on "Black Monday," September 30. Only Belgium supported the text, which Lubbers had earlier proclaimed "acceptable to all our partners."[53] The near-unanimous rejection of the new draft represented a serious setback for the Dutch presidency. A combination of characteristic haughtiness and uncharacteristic political miscalculation—based largely on supposed German support—accounted for the Dutch disaster, which had a profound impact on the negotiations themselves. By inadvertently putting the Luxembourg "nonpaper" on a pedestal, "Black Monday" ensured that the final treaty would include the three-pillars structure.

Earlier in September, Wim Kok, the Dutch finance minister, had suffered a similar rebuke in the negotiations on EMU. At a stormy meeting of finance ministers in Brussels on September 9, Kok had presented an unofficial Dutch draft treaty on EMU that included a proposal for an explicit two-speed system. According to the new draft, any six Community countries that met specific economic criteria concerning inflation rates, low budgetary deficits, stable interest rates, and stable exchange rates by 1996 could establish their own central bank and single currency. The laggardly member states would be excluded not only from the single currency but also from decisionmaking about Stage III. Although the draft treaty did not mention any country by name, there was a general feeling that France, Germany, the Netherlands, Belgium, Luxembourg, and Denmark were the top six.

The member states had already discussed and effectively endorsed an *implicit* two-speed EMU, but only Germany supported the Dutch draft for an *explicit* two-speed system. The other member states, regardless of economic performance, resented a proposal that would have created a permanent underclass of Community countries. Faced with such opposition, Kok backed down, disavowing responsibility for the draft. In the ensuing discussion, a consensus emerged that the Community should decide collectively when to move to Stage III and establish a single currency, although not every country would be economically able, and no country would be politically forced, to join the currency union at the outset.[54]

Bargaining and Coalition Building

No two countries had identical positions on EMU and EPU, and no single country—not even the UK—was completely isolated. Regardless of the reason for a country's position—whether principle, pragmatism, tradition, or size—enormous scope existed for ad hoc coalition building, which took place at a series of formal and informal meetings between member states. For instance, in late November 1991 leaders of the six Community countries with Christian Democratic governments—Germany, Italy, Belgium, the Netherlands, Luxembourg, and Greece—met to preview the Maastricht summit. Despite differences over many details of EMU and EPU, the Christian Democratic leaders shared a commitment to deeper European integration, especially along federal lines. The meeting was a useful opportunity to gauge their willingness to compromise at Maastricht. Thus, knowing how much Major disliked the "F-word," they proposed dropping it from the text of the draft treaty in return for a British concession on CFSP and home affairs.

Major's visit to Dublin on December 4, less than a week before Maastricht, is a good example of the kind of coalition building that took place as the negotiations reached a climax. Major was a right-winger, Haughey a centrist. Britain generally opposed EMU and EPU; Ireland generally favored deeper integration. Yet both countries opposed a stronger European Parliament (Britain wanted to protect national sovereignty; Ireland felt underrepresented in Strasbourg), opposed the social chapter, a package of policy provisions (Britain on principle, Ireland for financial reasons), favored unanimity in CFSP decisionmaking (Britain wanted to protect national sovereignty; Ireland was sensitive about neutrality), and opposed an EC-WEU merger (Britain because of its Atlanticism; Ireland again because of its neutrality).

Occasionally bilateral contacts resulted in formal initiatives at the IGCs. Various Franco-German proposals are obvious examples. An Anglo-Italian initiative on defense policy was a more unusual and therefore a more striking instance. The joint declaration, issued on October 7, 1991, called for "a stronger European defense identity with the longer-term perspective of a common defense policy compatible with the common defense policy we already have with all our Allies in NATO" and advocated developing the WEU as the defense component of the European Union.[55] The initiative reconciled Britain's Atlanticist and Italy's Europeanist positions, contributed to the IGC debate on defense policy, and dispelled the impression that the negotiations pitted Britain against the other eleven on every issue.

Despite the frequent and close contacts at all levels between France and Germany during the IGCs, the two countries disagreed sharply on many points. On EMU, France took a less rigorous approach than Germany, notably on the convergence criteria and on the independence of the ECB, which it wanted established at the beginning of Stage II. On EPU, France wanted a stronger European Council and a weaker European Parliament and pushed hard for an aggressive Community industrial policy. Germany disputed all of those demands and differed from France in supporting a unitary treaty structure.

Major's assiduous cultivation of Chancellor Kohl in early 1991, particularly during the annual Anglo-German summit in Bonn on March 11, fueled predictable speculation about an emerging Anglo-German or Anglo-Franco-German alliance in the Community to rival the Franco-German axis. The British media made much of the warm relationship between Major, the young prime minister, and Kohl, the avuncular elder statesman.[56] Yet a marked improvement in Britain's relations with Germany could hardly diminish, let alone supplant, the Franco-German axis that lay at the heart of the Community's development. Moreover, it became obvious in the run-up to the Maastricht summit that Major was as unyielding in his defense of British interests as Thatcher had ever been. Nevertheless, Major's friendship with Kohl may have paid dividends during the summit itself, especially when Kohl helped Lubbers and Major to reach a last-minute agreement on the social chapter.

Public and Parliamentary Interest

Despite the difficult and highly publicized Maastricht Treaty ratification process, there was little public or national parliamentary interest throughout the Community in the negotiations themselves. Britain was a notable exception. There, an opportunist opposition, a sizeable minority of Euroskeptic MPs on the government's back benches, and a general election due to take place by mid-1992 ensured that the IGCs became a contentious political issue. Many commentators thought Major would hold the election before December in an effort to win an undisputed mandate for the Maastricht summit. Instead the prime minister called a two-day Commons debate on the IGCs in late November in which he delineated for the country and the Community the limits of Britain's tolerance on EMU and EPU. By postponing the election until 1992 and pointing out to his Community colleagues the unreliability of a Labour government, Major hoped to strengthen his position at Maastricht.

The Bundestag, the lower house of Germany's Parliament, took little interest in the IGCs. By contrast, the Bundesrat, the upper house, pressed the case for subsidiarity from the outset. As the representative of the federal states, the Bundesrat opposed excessive centralization of power in either Brussels or Bonn. The Bundesrat retained a keen interest after the Maastricht summit, threatening in 1992 to block ratification of the treaty unless the government gave it a greater say in Community affairs. Only on the eve of Maastricht did the IGCs become a lively public issue in Germany, and then not because of subsidiarity but because of the single currency. Before and during the negotiations themselves, Bundesbank president Pohl and his successor tried to alert public opinion to the dangers, as they saw them, of EMU. Pohl repeatedly pointed out that Germany would lose the mark, that the Bundesbank would no longer formulate monetary policy but instead would become a regional member of a federal central banking system, that the rest of Europe lacked Germany's historical fear of inflation, and that the ECB might not be as rigorously independent of political control as the Bundesbank was. These harangues stiffened the government's resolve in the IGC on EMU but otherwise, until the last moment, fell on deaf ears. Then, days before the Maastricht summit, a series of articles in the mass-circulation *Bild* newspaper launched a populist campaign against EMU. On December 11, a banner headline characterized the summit's contribution to Europe's future as "The End of the D-Mark." Growing popular concern in Germany about the implications of EMU, fueled by the rising costs of unification, happened too late to affect the Maastricht summit itself but became a powerful factor in the treaty ratification crisis.

The IGCs sparked little public discussion or political controversy in France. Most major parties supported the government's objective of a strong franc and, eventually, a single European currency. In any event, opposition parties could hardly challenge the president's extremely powerful position in foreign policy formulation. Undoubtedly the Socialist government's popularity declined during the IGCs, but not because of the negotiations themselves. Conversely, a change of leadership in June 1991, when Edith Cresson replaced Michel Rocard as prime minister, emphasized the government's commitment to an interventionist industrial policy at national and Community levels but hardly affected the negotiations in Brussels.

Surprisingly, in view of what happened in 1992, there was little public discussion of the IGCs in Denmark. The Danish Parliament's EC committee monitored the negotiations and insisted that Denmark have the right to decide by referendum later in the century whether or not to participate in Stage III of EMU. Despite Denmark's traditional distrust of deeper European integration, the government played a constructive part in the negotiations on EPU. Nothing in Denmark's performance at the IGCs or in the public's reaction to the treaty presaged the protracted ratification crisis of 1992 and 1993.

Institutional Input

Despite the explicitly intergovernmental nature of the IGCs, the Commission participated fully in both sets of negotiations. Delors, given his long-standing interest in the subject and the impact of his committee's report, took a particularly keen interest in EMU. Delors lost the battle to establish the ECB at the beginning of Stage II rather than at the beginning of Stage III, with the launch of the single currency, but won the more important arguments—in favor of a timetable for the final stages of EMU and against a formal "two-tier" structure. Yet Delors had been one of the first to raise the possibility of an informal two-tier system when he proposed, in November 1990, letting Stage III begin with less than a full complement of Community member states.[57] Based on a suggestion by Commission vice president Leon Brittan, Delors also proposed an "opt-out" for any member state not wishing to join the currency union until a later date. Thus the Commission generally favored the treaty's final provisions on EMU.

Preoccupied with EMU and with a host of other issues in 1991—CAP reform, the Uruguay Round, relations with Eastern Europe and the disintegrating Soviet Union, and negotiations with the EFTA countries for a European Economic Area—the Commission fared poorly in the EPU conference. Early in the year, the Commission suggested several treaty reforms with which a majority of member states strongly disagreed. These included a radical increase in the Commission's responsibility for international economic relations and greater powers of implementation for Brussels. In addition, Delors made a famous speech in London in March 1991 on security and defense policy. Only weeks after the end of the Gulf War and in the midst of a contentious debate between member states on a possible CFSP, Delors called for the Community to subsume the WEU and advocated greater independence of the United States.[58]

Delors's speech and some of the Commission's formal proposals on EPU caused a backlash in certain member states. Thereafter, the Commission was on the defensive in the IGC, fighting a rear-guard action to defend its existing prerogatives. In particular, Delors had to fend off a strong attack on the Commission's exclusive right to initiate legislation and a move to permit the Council of Ministers to amend Commission proposals by qualified majority voting instead of unanimity. Had the latter happened, Delors told the European Parliament on April 18, the Commission would have been reduced to "a sort of Secretariat General" for the Council.[59]

Delors blamed the Luxembourg presidency and the close cooperation between it and the Council secretariat for many of the Commission's difficulties in the early stages of the EPU negotiations. In particular, Delors took exception to the apparent ascendancy in the IGC of Neils Ersbøll, the Council's pragmatic and highly political secretary-general. Even before the IGC began, Ersbøll had helped draft the discussion document on EPU for the December 1990 Rome summit; the document eventually became the basis for the negotiations themselves. Subsequently, Ersbøll contributed extensively to Luxembourg's lengthy draft treaty of April 1991. Ersbøll had no intention of upsetting the Community's delicate institutional balance, but he had little sympathy for Delors's desire for a stronger Commission and even less for the Commission's efforts to strengthen the European Parliament.

From Delors's perspective, the structure of the Luxembourg draft treaty was its most egregious aspect and the most obvious example of Ersbøll's influence. Delors wanted a unitary structure, in which everything came under the Rome treaty, rather than a structure placing the treaty as only one of three "pillars" alongside CFSP and cooperation in the field of justice and home affairs. The humiliating fate on Black Monday of the first Dutch draft treaty, which revised the Luxembourg draft structurally, was as much of a setback for Delors as for the Dutch presidency. Despite an apparent consensus at the Luxembourg summit in June to negotiate a final treaty on the basis of a "temple" rather than a "tree," Delors fully supported the Dutch revision. Inevitably, the other member states' near-unanimous rejection of it weakened Delors's position in the conference. With typical sullenness, Delors later described the temple approach as "organized schizophrenia" and threatened to denounce the final version.[60] Yet a day after the Maastricht summit, Delors commended the Treaty on European Union to the Parliament in Strasbourg.[61] One of the many ironies of the subsequent ratification crisis was that, by default, Delors defended a treaty that benefited the Commission little but that the public perceived as having greatly enhanced the Commission's power.

Unlike the Commission, the European Parliament was not a participant in the IGCs. Mindful of Parliament's assertiveness during the IGC that preceded the SEA, the heads of government decided at the October 1990 Rome summit to involve Parliament in the forthcoming negotiations by establishing regular contacts between the presidents of the Council, the Commission, and the Parliament and by allowing the president of the Parliament to address ministerial sessions of the conference. Of course, Parliament considered those measures inadequate. Its president, Enrique Baron Crespo, visited all twelve Community capitals during the IGCs, a more productive procedure than interinstitutional meetings.[62] Parliament itself could not veto the IGCs, but two countries, Belgium and Italy, threatened not to ratify the final treaty unless Parliament approved it.

Parliament had outlined its objectives for the IGCs in a series of reports named after David Martin, *rapporteur* of the Committee on Institutional Affairs.[63] On July 11, 1990, the same day that it adopted the Martin II Report, Parliament also adopted the Colombo Report on a new draft treaty (a possible sequel to the Spinelli Report), the Giscard d'Estaing

Report on subsidiarity, and the Duverger Report on relations with national parliaments.[64] With reference to the IGCs, the reports called for a radical extension of Community competence, more supranational decisionmaking, and, not surprisingly, greater power for the European Parliament, including legislative co-decision with the Council and a right to initiate legislation.

As the negotiations proceeded and Parliament's exorbitant demands came nowhere near being met, a torrent of speeches and resolutions condemning the IGCs flowed out of Strasbourg. Speaking in Athens on the 2,500th anniversary of democracy, Baron Crespo could not forgo an opportunity to deplore the IGCs' stinginess toward the European Parliament.[65] Although a number of member states—notably Germany, Italy, and Belgium—sought greater parliamentary power, it was obvious in the approach to Maastricht that legislative co-decision would, at most, give the EP the ability to block decisions in the Council. As expected, the results of the Maastricht summit disappointed Parliament in that respect and in a number of other ways. Yet despite its dissatisfaction, Parliament was markedly less angry than it had been six years previously, at the end of the SEA negotiations; it had learned that seemingly small gains could be turned to large political advantage. In 1986, after all, the newly agreed-upon cooperation procedure seemed to be a paltry parliamentary advance, yet within a short time it had immeasurably enhanced Strasbourg's previously limited legislative power.

The Maastricht Summit

The Maastricht summit of December 9–10, 1991, crowned a year-long series of negotiations in which the lowest common denominator often prevailed but which nonetheless marked a decisive shift in the Community's development. The IGCs had been a process of intensive bargaining between member states, with the Commission as a formal participant, the Council secretariat playing a crucial behind-the-scenes role, and the European Parliament practically marginalized. Although government officials and ministers had discussed numerous controversial issues at great length during the intervening months, key aspects of the final treaty remained in doubt as the heads of government convened in Maastricht.

Despite the Netherlands' poor presidential performance, the success of the Maastricht Summit owed much to Prime Minister Lubbers's negotiating skills. Late in the evening of the second day, it seemed that the IGCs were about to collapse because of Britain's rejection of greater Community involvement in social policy. Lubbers first proposed weakening the provisions on social policy; when Major refused to budge, Lubbers proposed removing the social chapter entirely from the treaty. This set a dangerous precedent for European integration, and reinforced the emergence of a "multispeed" Europe already inherent in the provisions for EMU. In a prophetic comment on British opposition to the Social Chapter, Helen Wallace had written in 1989 that a decision by the other eleven member states to go ahead without Britain "would be an example of deepening and narrowing."[66] Such a development was hardly in the Community's interest, but removing the chapter may have prevented a British walkout and thereby saved the Maastricht Treaty.

Under the terms of the Maastricht Treaty, the third stage of EMU, involving the introduction of a common currency, would take place by 1999 at the latest. On EPU, the member states approved new cooperative arrangements for foreign and security policy and for judicial and home affairs. The European Parliament acquired an enhanced role in Community affairs—including a right of enquiry, a more formal right of petition, and the appointment of an ombudsman—and greater legislative power through extensive use of the co-decision procedure. The treaty redefined or extended Community competence in a number of areas, notably education, training, cohesion, research and development, environment, trans-European networks, industry, health, culture, consumer protection, and development cooperation, although with only limited moves toward qualified majority voting.

Some member states had scored more negotiating points than others during the IGCs and at the Maastricht summit, but none was an absolute winner or loser. For the Community's institutions, by contrast, the IGCs' outcome was more clear-cut: The Council of Ministers and the Parliament gained most, and the Commission gained least. As well as being an intensive bargaining session, the Maastricht summit was an essential political exercise to permit each participant, including the Commission, to claim victory on a variety of issues. By December 9–10, 1991, widespread public indifference about the IGCs had given way to intensive media coverage. Almost fifteen hundred journalists descended on Maastricht for the European Council. At the end of the two-day event, they eagerly reported the government heads' reactions to the final agreement. Clearly, there was something in it for everyone. Even John Major, whose country conceded so much during the IGCs, was able to claim "game, set, and match" for Britain.[67]

THE RATIFICATION CRISIS

In 1986 a majority of Danes endorsed the SEA after the Danish Parliament's rejection of it. At the end of 1986 the Irish Supreme Court judged the SEA unconstitutional, thereby obliging the government to hold a referendum. The Supreme Court's ruling and the subsequent referendum delayed implementation of the SEA until July 1987. Yet at no time after the Danish Parliament's rejection of the SEA or the Irish Supreme Court's ruling on it did anyone talk about a crisis in the Community. In June 1992, by contrast, the Danish electorate's narrow rejection of the Maastricht Treaty jeopardized the future of European integration and shook the Community to its core.

The impact of the Danish result was all the more striking because ratification was proceeding smoothly in every other member state. As early as April 1992, two months before the Danish referendum, the European Parliament called by a resounding vote of 226 to 62 (with 31 abstentions) for member states to ratify the treaty as quickly as possible. Even after the Danish referendum, ratification continued relatively smoothly except in France, where François Mitterrand called for a referendum, and in Britain, where a combination of bad luck and poor judgment impeded the government's efforts. Indeed, with the exception of Denmark, Britain, and Germany, where a legal challenge to the treaty's constitutionality held up proceedings, every member state ratified the treaty by the target date of December 1992.

The Danish Referendum

Like the SEA, the Maastricht Treaty had to be ratified by each member state in order to come into force. The ratification process differed from country to country. In Denmark's case, it was up to the electorate to decide, in a referendum, whether or not to approve the treaty. Consequently, the negative result of the June 2 referendum—by a remarkably narrow margin of 50.7 percent against to 49.3 percent in favor—tied the government's hands and thwarted implementation of the treaty.

Danish opinion seemed evenly divided immediately before the referendum. Nevertheless, the result came as a complete shock to the Commission and to national governments. Denmark was known for its ambivalence toward European integration, but the positive results of the 1972 accession referendum and the 1986 SEA referendum suggested that, on polling day, a majority would support the Maastricht Treaty. The Commission, the Danish government, and other governments were extraordinarily complacent. Having spent a year negotiating the treaty, they never considered that a majority of Danes, or of any other nationality, would vote against it.

Although oblivious to the possibility of a "no" vote, Community leaders immediately grasped the seriousness of the Danish result. There was no question of renegotiating the treaty. Member states had already rejected an Irish request to change a protocol dealing exclusively with a

clause in the country's constitution. Most governments feared that renegotiation of any treaty provision or protocol, however specific or technical, would open a Pandora's box. Clearly groping for a solution, the General Affairs Council announced on June 4 that other member states would
press ahead with ratification in the hope that Denmark would reconsider
before the end of 1992.[68]

Fewer than 30,000 votes had determined the outcome of the Danish referendum. Exhaustive analyses indicated a host of reasons for the result. Some were peculiarly Danish, others were common to the Community; some were reasonable, others irrational; some were consistent, others
contradictory. They included concerns about EMU, about losing national
identity, about the role of small states in the Community, about the Commission's overweening ambition, about the European Parliament's increasing power, about the Common Fisheries Policy, about acquiring a
common currency, about the economic and political impact of German
unification, about the possible emergence of a European army, about Germans' ability to buy Danish holiday homes, and about a diminution of environmental and social welfare standards.

Whatever the reasons, the result showed how oblivious the Danish
and other governments were to growing public resentment of how the
Community operated. The Council of Ministers seemed secretive and self-
serving, the Commission remote and technocratic, and the Parliament expensive and irrelevant. There had been little public interest in the IGCs
themselves, but Maastricht soon became a topic of popular discourse.
Without even having read the treaty, people fretted about its contents.
Worries ranged from the desirability of EMU, to the rigors of convergence,
to voting rights for non-nationals, to the prospect of mass migration, to the
likelihood of bureaucratic intrusion from Brussels. In most cases, a perusal
of the treaty's unintelligible text merely reinforced popular antipathy
toward it.

The Irish and French Referendums

Ireland was the only other member state constitutionally obliged to ratify
the treaty by referendum. Coming two weeks after the Danish result, the
Irish referendum assumed special significance. Given Ireland's traditional
support for European integration, a positive result seemed inevitable and
would do little to revive the Community's fortunes. A negative result,
however, would have worsened the Community's predicament. The government's referendum campaign concentrated on crude calculations of economic self-interest. Without any basis in fact, Prime Minister Albert
Reynolds warned the electorate that Ireland would lose $10 billion in Com-
munity assistance in the event of a "no" vote. Despite the government's

threats, the result was by no means an unequivocal endorsement of the Maastricht Treaty. Of the 57 percent who voted (low by Irish standards), 69 percent were in favor and 31 percent against. Undaunted, the prime minister called the outcome "a tribute to the maturity of the Irish people" and proclaimed that "Eurosceptics do not have much of a following here."[69]

A much more important test for the treaty came on September 20, when the French electorate went to the polls. Although France could have ratified the treaty by an easily obtainable three-fifths majority of both houses of Parliament meeting in joint session, Mitterrand announced immediately after the Danish result that France would also ratify by referendum. Mitterrand's motives were mixed. He had speculated about holding a referendum in the fall of 1992 as a means of regaining lost political ground. Taking a leaf from President Pompidou's book in 1972, he decided to use the Maastricht Treaty to drive a wedge into the conservative opposition, which was already divided on the issue of closer European integration. The danger, of course, was that a combination of Mitterrand's and the Maastricht Treaty's unpopularity would produce a negative result. If that happened, Mitterrand would possibly resign, the French franc would come under unbearable pressure, and the treaty would be unsalvageable. The stakes for Mitterrand, for France, and for the Community were extraordinarily high.

The timing and manner of Mitterrand's announcement suggest that he acted impetuously and unwisely. Mitterrand was a master politician, yet risking so much on a highly unpredictable referendum result seemed out of character. Then in the middle of his second seven-year term, Mitterrand was deeply committed to European integration. By winning a resounding referendum victory, he hoped both to breathe new life into the Maastricht Treaty and to give his presidency an indelible "European" imprint. Clearly Mitterrand believed that France's historical contribution to the Community and the electorate's appreciation of the Maastricht Treaty's importance for the future of European integration would produce a comfortable majority and dispel the gloom caused by the Danish result.[70]

August is usually quiet in France, and the government did not throw itself into the referendum campaign until early September. By contrast, the anti-Maastricht side seized the initiative and turned the usual summer lull to its advantage. Developments in France and elsewhere favored the treaty's opponents. In June 1992 Mitterrand reluctantly replaced Edith Cresson, his hugely unpopular prime minister. The president's own popularity continued to slump as the economic situation worsened and unemployment rose. The deteriorating situation in Bosnia reflected poorly on Mitterrand, who had shown his solidarity with the besieged citizens of Sarajevo by flying there in June 1992, and especially on the European Community, whose London peace conference did nothing to stop the fighting. Opinion polls in late August showed that the treaty's opponents were inching ahead and that frustration over the Community's inability to broker a Bosnian cease-fire was a powerful impetus to vote "no."

The concurrent EMS crisis further eroded confidence in the Community. If anything, the currency turmoil in late 1992 should have strengthened support for EMU and by default for the Maastricht Treaty. The high cost of unification and the Bundesbank's correspondingly high interest rates had exacerbated the Community's economic situation and fueled resentment of Germany. People instinctively recoiled from what they saw as a German-designed EMU. In fact, though, EMU offered the best chance to curb German unilateralism and end currency instability.

The French government went on the offensive late in the campaign, cajoling the electorate to vote "yes." Mitterrand assigned Jack Lang, his former culture minister, to coordinate the government's efforts and appointed the photogenic Elizabeth Guigou, minister for European affairs, as leading spokesperson. In keeping with the earlier Danish and Irish campaigns, Lang used an unlikely array of arguments to bolster support for Maastricht. "A 'no' vote would be unimaginable," he declared. "It would destroy the collective work of Charles de Gaulle, Georges Pompidou, Valéry Giscard d'Estaing, and François Mitterrand . . . it would mean that Washington and Tokyo would rub their hands, that the yen and the dollar would triumph, and that the mark would become Europe's definitive currency . . . [it would cause] a bourse crisis, a crisis of confidence, a depression that would hit the whole of Europe."[71] The normally unexcitable Le Monde editorialized on the eve of the referendum that "a 'no' vote would be for France and for Europe the greatest catastrophe since Hitler's coming to power."[72]

Lang's histrionics may have alienated as many people as they attracted. In the event, Mitterrand's gamble narrowly paid off. In a 70 percent turnout, 51.05 percent voted in favor and 48.95 percent voted against. The result was too close to justify the political and emotional effort invested in it. Far from boosting Mitterrand or Maastricht, it accelerated the president's political decline—his Socialist government lost heavily in the March 1993 general election—and further shook the Community's confidence.

Subsidiarity

Jacques Delors was quick to respond to the Danish referendum result. Alert to the extent of popular alienation from Community policies and institutions, Delors resolved to break the bureaucratic barrier surrounding Brussels, make the legislative process more transparent, and emphasize subsidiarity as the best way to insure the Community's compatibility with the political aspirations of its citizens. In search of a federal doctrine that would allow the Community to become involved in certain "high political" issues traditionally at the core of national sovereignty without encroaching on policy areas that ought to remain in the national or regional domain, Delors had begun to explore subsidiarity from the time that he became Commission president in 1985.[73] As he told *Le Figaro* in June 1992, subsidiarity was the essence of federalism because "the federal approach is to define clearly who does what."[74] Thus, subsidiarity would provide guidelines as to where Brussels could or could not act, just as similar constitutional provisions determine the proper functioning of U.S. or German federalism.

Unlike the Tenth Amendment to the U.S. Constitution, which reserves for the states all powers not delegated to the federal government, or Germany's Basic Law, which vests all powers in the Lander except those prescribed in Article 30, subsidiarity was notoriously difficult to define. According to Commission vice president Leon Brittan, "subsidiarity must be treated as a guiding political principle as well as a legal restraint." Brittan claimed that Article 3b of the Maastricht Treaty, which formalized the principle of subsidiarity, "places a legally-binding limitation on the scope of action of the Community; it applies without caveat, limitation or exception. . . . Once the Treaty has come into effect, every single new legislative act of the Community can be held up and judged under this standard."[75] Yet Article 3b was imprecise and open to many interpretations. In the prevailing climate of resentment against Brussels, the Community needed a far firmer definition of subsidiarity and explanation of its possible use.

Even before the ratification crisis erupted, the Commission started to drop proposed legislation that seemingly belonged at the national level. For instance, in April 1992 it abruptly shelved two draft proposals for directives to monitor energy use in buildings, an essential part of the Community's plans to curb "greenhouse gases." After the Danish result, the Commission redoubled its efforts to concentrate on key policy areas and divest itself of issues best dealt with at other levels of government. With public opinion swinging sharply against Brussels, subsidiarity assumed added political importance.

Member states eagerly jumped on the subsidiarity bandwagon, advocating the idea as a means of allaying popular concern about excessive centralization in Brussels and possibly hoping to use it to roll back intrusive but generally beneficial policies such as the aggressive enforcement of competition law. In Britain, where opposition to Maastricht flourished as a result of the Danish referendum, subsidiarity became a political panacea for the Community's manifest ills. Inevitably, the British government and the Commission understood the term to mean completely different things. For London, subsidiarity was a vital safeguard of national sovereignty and a way to prevent the Community from involving itself unduly in member states' affairs; for Brussels, subsidiarity was a central tenet of Eurofederalism.

The Lisbon summit on June 26–27, 1992, gave Community leaders their first opportunity to assess the Danish debacle. Predictably but unrealistically, the heads of government reaffirmed their determination to press ahead with the treaty's ratification "with no renegotiation and no modification, to ensure [its] entry into force on January 1, 1993." As if to emphasize "business as usual," the European Council extended Delors's term as Commission president. After hearing a report on subsidiarity from Delors and discussing the issue in depth, the European Council "stressed the need for this principle to be strictly applied, both in existing and in future legislation, and called on the Commission and the Council to look at the procedural and practical steps needed to implement it and to report back to the [December 1992] European Council in Edinburgh." The Commission undertook to justify future proposals on the basis of subsidiarity, and the heads of government instructed the Council of Ministers to do the same if it decided to amend an original Commission proposal.[76]

After the extraordinary Birmingham summit on October 16, 1992, the heads of government issued a folksy explanation of subsidiarity: "We reaffirm that decisions must be taken as closely as possible to the citizen. Greater unity can be achieved without excessive centralization. It is for each Member State to decide how its powers should be exercised domestically. The Community can only act where Member States have given it the power to do so in the treaties. Action at the Community level should happen only when proper and necessary . . . 'subsidiarity' or 'nearness' is essential if the Community is to develop with the support of its citizens."[77]

Less than two weeks after the Birmingham summit, the Commission submitted to the Council and Parliament a lengthy political, technical, and legal analysis of subsidiarity. The Commission developed the "two dimensions" of subsidiarity—the need for action and the intensity (proportionality) of action—and asserted that the burden of proof in both cases lay with the Community's institutions. Because of its exclusive right of initiative, the Commission accepted special responsibility in that regard. But the Commission also argued that subsidiarity could not become an excuse for member states either to blame Brussels for unpopular actions or to curb the Commission's legitimate legislative and executive authority.[78]

The Commission's communication, together with a foreign ministers' report, set the stage for the Edinburgh summit's discussions on subsidiarity. The summit conclusions included a lengthy section outlining the basic principles of subsidiarity, guidelines for their application, and institutional procedures and practices, as well as concrete examples of pending proposals and existing legislation in light of the "need for action" and "proportionality" criteria. The European Council also called for an inter-institutional agreement on the effective application of subsidiarity.[79]

The Community's elucidation of subsidiarity in late 1992 was the culmination of a process accelerated by the ratification crisis but begun at least a decade before, when the European Parliament's draft treaty on European union first developed the principle in the context of European integration. Although subsidiarity remains ambiguous and misunderstood, at least the ratification crisis forced the Community to come to terms with it and to flesh out the features and meaning of Eurofederalism. An interinstitutional agreement would give more substance to subsidiarity, as would an inevitable body of case law on the subject. Thus, the practical implications of subsidiarity may have to await a number of landmark rulings from the Court of Justice, which hardly relishes the prospect of adjudicating such politically charged cases.

Transparency and Openness

The development of subsidiarity in late 1992 went hand in hand with efforts to make the Community's legislative process more transparent. The heads of government acknowledged the need for greater openness at the Lisbon summit in June and fleshed out some ideas in the Birmingham summit declaration four months later.[80] These included wider use of pre-legislative consultation documents (green papers), greater public access to the work of the Council of Ministers and the Commission, and clearer and simpler legislation. At the December 1992 Edinburgh summit, Community leaders adopted a number of specific measures to promote transparency. Foremost among them was a decision to televise the opening sessions of General Affairs and Ecofin councils and to publish the record of formal votes taken in the Council of Ministers.[81] Given the Council's history of secretiveness, these were truly remarkable measures. Even more so than the debate on subsidiarity, the European Council's frenzied efforts at the Birmingham and Edinburgh summits to make the Community more comprehensible to its citizens demonstrated the profound impact on member state governments of the Maastricht Treaty ratification crisis.

The Danish Opt-Outs

The European Council promoted subsidiarity, transparency, and openness to placate irate and alienated citizens throughout the Community but especially in Denmark. Indeed, the Community's response to the ratification crisis was primarily to make the treaty more palatable to Danish voters. Despite the Community's earlier statements that the treaty would not be modified, the Commission and national governments realized that unless

Denmark won opt-outs from specific provisions and protocols, the electorate was unlikely to ratify it in a second referendum. The challenge for
the Community, therefore, was to give Denmark certain opt-outs in order
to appease the electorate without undermining the treaty's validity or relevance for the Community as a whole.

In early October, the Danish government produced a lengthy white
paper outlining eight options for a solution to the Community's dilemma.
Two of these involved negotiating special concessions that would free
Denmark from certain treaty obligations. At the end of the month, Denmark submitted a memorandum to its Community partners identifying a
number of sticking points, including the treaty's defense policy dimension, the third stage of EMU, Union citizenship, and cooperation in the
fields of justice and home affairs. Based on the Danish memorandum and
on the member states' desperateness for a solution, the Twelve hammered
out an agreement at the Edinburgh summit. The most important points
were that Denmark would not participate in the single currency or be
bound by rules concerning economic policy applicable to Stage III of
EMU and would not participate in CFSP discussions, decisions, or actions
with defense implications. The European Council affirmed that the opt-
outs agreed upon at Edinburgh "are fully compatible with the Treaty, are
designed to meet Danish concerns, and therefore apply exclusively to
Denmark and not to other existing or acceding Member States."[82]

The new Danish government, which came into office in January
1993, maintained its predecessor's support for the Maastricht Treaty. Denmark's main political parties, in or out of government, rightly believed
that the Edinburgh opt-outs would sway undecided voters and produce a
positive result in the May 18 referendum. Because the mainstream political parties and the opinion pollsters were so wrong about the original
Maastricht referendum and because the stakes were so high for the Community, there was no complacency in the run-up to the second referendum. In the event, the result was a comfortable 56.8 percent in favor of
ratification.

A second Danish rejection would have spelled the end of the treaty,
although the success of the Edinburgh summit suggested that the Community
had already passed the psychological milestone that Maastricht represented.
The opt-outs agreed to at Edinburgh were politically expedient and probably rescued the treaty, but they reinforced the tendency toward an à la carte
Community in which, depending on their leverage and negotiating power,
member states may pick and choose whatever policies suit them. Of course,
the European Council pointed to the unique nature of the Edinburgh agreement and stressed that other member states (and especially future member
states) could not expect a similar arrangement. Yet the combined effect of
the treaty's provisions on EMU, the social chapter, and the Edinburgh agreement with Denmark was to emphasize the emergence of variable geometry.

The British Problem

A combination of weak political leadership, unfortunate timing, and arcane parliamentary procedures produced a potentially disastrous ratification debacle in the UK. Given Major's supposed triumph at Maastricht and his election victory in April 1992, Britain should have ratified the treaty without undue delay. Although about thirty government MPs (the diehard Euroskeptics) vehemently opposed Maastricht, a majority of opposition MPs supported it. As a result, in a free vote (unencumbered by the obligations of party allegiance), around two-thirds of Britain's 650 MPs would have supported the treaty.

The first hint of trouble came immediately after the Danish referendum, when the government announced a postponement of the Commons debate pending legal clarification. But Major insisted that Britain would ratify the treaty as planned, before the end of 1992, and nothing seemed seriously amiss when Britain took over the Council presidency in July 1992. Within a short time, however, the ERM crisis turned Britain's presidency into one of the worst in the Community's history, a point ruthlessly exploited by the opposition Labour Party. It was difficult for Major to put Britain "at the heart of Europe" after his country left the ERM so suddenly and disastrously in September. Recrimination over the currency crisis exacerbated tension between London and Bonn, and Major lost political support in the Community capital that mattered most.

After the French narrowly voted "yes" on September 20, the British government pressed ahead with ratification. By that time, however, the prime minister was a hostage of the Euroskeptics in his own party, who capitalized on the treaty's growing unpopularity and on the opposition's determination to discomfit the government. Seriously mauled at the Conservative Party conference in early October, Major looked for salvation to the specially convened European Council in Birmingham.

The Birmingham summit was one of the least purposeful in the Community's history. Ostensibly called to discuss the ERM and Maastricht ratification crises, its real objective was to prop up Major's languishing domestic leadership and help get the treaty through the Commons. But a government announcement two days before the European Council, of plans to close more than thirty coal mines, provoked a popular outcry that completely overshadowed the summit. Major's Community colleagues left Birmingham despairing of the British government's ability to focus on the Community at a critical time in the ratification process. Their despondency seemed justified when the treaty barely survived a Commons vote on November 4, and Major promptly announced that Britain would delay ratification until after the second Danish referendum in May 1993.

The British government redeemed its otherwise uninspiring presidential performance by successfully chairing the Edinburgh summit.

Moreover, Major grew increasingly assertive in early 1993 when the Labour Party tried to link British acceptance of the social chapter with ratification of the treaty. Considering Major's rejection of the social chapter at the Maastricht summit, he was not about to embrace it during the ratification debate because of domestic political circumstances. Nevertheless, peculiar parliamentary procedures gave opponents of the treaty enormous scope to filibuster and influence the legislative timetable and almost bring the government down in July 1993. But even the staunchest Euroskeptics admitted the unlikelihood of being able to prevent ratification, which, after the successful outcome of the second Danish referendum, seemed inevitable.

NOTES

1. Jacques Delors, speech at the College of Europe, Bruges, October 20, 1989.
2. See Roger East, *Revolutions in Eastern Europe* (London: Pinter, 1992).
3. Bull. EC 6-1988, 1.1.14. For an examination of the origins and development of EMU in the 1980s, see David Andrews, "The Global Origins of the Maastricht Treaty on EMU: Closing the Window of Opportunity," in Alan Cafruny and Glenda Rosenthal, eds., *The State of the European Community: The Maastricht Debates and Beyond* (Boulder, CO: Lynne Rienner, 1993), pp. 107–123.
4. *Report of the Committee for the Study of Economic and Monetary Union* (Luxembourg: Office of Official Publications, 1989).
5. Bull. EC 6-1989, Presidency Conclusions, 1.1.11.
6. See *Le Monde,* January 8 and January 15, 1988.
7. Ronald Tiersky, "Mitterrand, France and Europe," *French Politics and Society,* 9, no. 1 (Winter 1991), p. 16.
8. See Hugo Young, *One Of Us: A Biography of Margaret Thatcher* (London: Macmillan, 1989), pp. 551–560.
9. Margaret Thatcher, *Britain in the European Community* (London: Conservative Political Centre, 1988).
10. Sir Michael Butler, "Simply Wrong About Europe," *The Times* (London), November 26, 1991, p. 10.
11. Bull. EC 12-1988, Presidency Conclusions, 1.1.10.
12. Bull. EC 6-1989, Presidency Conclusions, 1.1.16.
13. See Adam Daniel Rothfeld and Walther Stutzle, eds., *Germany and Europe in Transition* (Oxford: Oxford University Press, 1991); and Renata Fritsch-Bournazel, *Europe and German Unification* (New York: Berg, 1992).
14. Jacques Delors, speech at the College of Europe, Bruges, October 20, 1989.
15. Quoted in Jan Werts, *The European Council* (Amsterdam: North-Holland, 1992), p. 288.
16. See Emil Kirchner, "Genscher and What Lies Behind Genscherism," *West European Politics,* 13, no. 2 (April 1990), pp. 159–177.
17. Chancellor's Press Release, 134/1989, p. 1141, ff.

18. See Franz-Olivier Giesbert, *Le Président* (Paris: Seuil, 1990), p. 363.

19. Bull. EC 12-1989, Presidency Conclusions, 1.1.20.

20. Quoted in *Le Monde,* December 9, 1989. p. 1.

21. Nicholas Ridley, Interview by Dominic Lawson in *The Spectator,* July 14, 1990.

22. Bull. EC S/1-90, *Commission's Program for 1990.*

23. The Belgian proposal is reproduced in Finn Laursen and Sophie Vanhoonacker, eds., *The Intergovernmental Conference on Political Union* (Maastricht: EIPA, 1992), pp. 269–275.

24. See Sophie Vanhoonacker, "The Role of the Parliament," in Laursen and Vanhoonacker, *The Intergovernmental Conference,* p. 216.

25. OJ C96, April 17, 1990.

26. Quoted in *The Financial Times,* March 30, 1990, p. 2.

27. Reproduced in Laursen and Vanhoonacker, *Intergovernmental Conference,* p. 276.

28. Bull. EC 4-1990, Presidency Conclusions, 1.1–12; *Agence Europe,* April 30 and May 1, 1990.

29. Bull. EC 6-1990, p. 7.

30. Reproduced in Bull. EC S/4–90, *The European Community and German Unification,* pp. 9–16.

31. European Parliament Session Documents, Doc. A3-183/90, July 9, 1990.

32. See Lily Gardner Feldman, "The EC and German Unification," in Leon Hurwitz and Christian Lequesne, *The State of the European Community: Policies, Institutions and Debates in the Transition Years* (Boulder, CO: Lynne Rienner, 1991), p. 319.

33. Bull. EC 10-1990, Presidency Conclusions, 1.2-6.

34. Bull. EC 7/8-1990, 1.5.11.

35. *The Economist,* March 23, 1991, p. 15.

36. Speech to the European Parliament, November 21, 1990, *Debates of the European Parliament,* OJ 3–396, November 1990, p. 138.

37. On the EMU negotiations, see Wayne Sandholtz, "Monetary Bargains: The Treaty on EMU," in Cafruny and Rosenthal, *Maastricht and Beyond,* pp. 125–141.

38. See *Le Monde,* April 12, 1990, p. 1.

39. Bank of England statement on the Hard ECU, reproduced in The *Financial Times,* June 23, 1990.

40. Major's speech is reproduced in Laursen and Vanhoonacker, *Intergovernmental Conference,* pp. 419–428.

41. Margaret Thatcher, "My Vision," *The Financial Times,* November 19, 1990, p. 10.

42. Quoted in *The Financial Times,* June 18, 1991, p. 1.

43. Lord O'Hagan, "Federalism," in the *Manchester Guardian Weekly,* July 7, 1991, p. 12.

44. Thatcher, "My Vision."

45. *The New York Times,* June 24, 1991, p. A1.

46. Quoted in *Agence Europe,* December 6, 1991, p. 4.

47. *Agence Europe,* June 4, 1991, p. 1.

48. Quoted in *The Financial Times,* May 13, 1991, p. 3.

49. Quoted in Reuters, July 1, 1991.

50. See Pia Christina Wood, "EPC: Lessons from the Gulf War and Yugoslavia," in Cafruny and Rosenthal, *Maastricht and Beyond,* pp. 227–244.

51. See *The Financial Times,* September 19, 1991, p. 1.

52. Quoted in *The Guardian,* September 28, 1991, p. 2.

53. Quoted in *The Financial Times,* September 21–22, 1991, p. 3.

54. *Agence Europe,* September 15, 1991.

55. AE Documents, 1735, October 7–8, 1991.

56. See, for instance, the *Manchester Guardian Weekly,* July 14, 1991, p. 7.

57. *Agence Europe,* November 10, 1990.

58. Jacques Delors, speech at the Royal Institute for International Affairs, London, March 20, 1991.

59. *Agence Europe,* April 18, 1991.

60. Speech to the European Parliament, November 20, 1991, *Debates of the European Parliament,* OJ 3 411, November 1991, p. 126.

61. *Debates of the European Parliament,* OJ 3 412, December 1991, pp. 232–236.

62. See Vanhoonacker, "The Role of Parliament," p. 219.

63. Martin I, PE A3-47-90; Martin II, PE A3-166-90.

64. Colombo Report, PE A3–165–90; Giscard d'Estaing Report, A3–163–90; Duverger Report, A3-162-90.

65. *Agence Europe,* September 27, 1991, p. 3.

66. Helen Wallace, "Widening and Deepening: The EC and the New European Agenda," RIIA Discussion Paper no. 23, 1989, p. 8.

67. Quoted in *The Financial Times,* December 12, 1991, p. 3.

68. Bull. EC 6-96, point 1.1.3.

69. Quoted in *The Cork Examiner,* June 20, 1992, p. 1.

70. For a discussion of the French referendum's importance for the Community, see Andrew Moravcsik, "Idealism and Interest in the European Community: The Case of the French Referendum," *French Politics and Society* 11, no. 1 (Winter 1993), pp. 45–56, and Sophie Meunier-Aitsahalia and George Ross, "Democratic Deficit or Democratic Surplus: A Reply to Andrew Moravcsik's Comments on the French Referendum," *French Politics and Society* 11, no. 1 (Winter 1993), pp. 57–69.

71. See *Le Monde,* "L'Europe de Maastricht," Special Supplement, August–September 1992, p. 2.

72. *Le Monde,* September 20–21, 1992, p. 1.

73. See Jacques Delors, *Le Nouveau Concert Européen* (Paris: Editions Odile Jacob, 1992), and his speech to the European Parliament in January 1985, Bull. EC S/1–1985.

74. *Le Figaro,* June 8, 1992, p. 1.

75. Leon Brittan, speech delivered at the European University Institute, June 11, 1992, IP/92 1477, 92/06/11.

76. Bull. EC 6-1992, Presidency Conclusions, point 1.1.

77. Bull. EC 10-1992, Presidency Conclusions, point 1.8.

78. Commission, "The Principle of Subsidiarity," SEC(92)1990 final, October 27, 1992.

79. Bull. EC 12-1992, Presidency Conclusions, point. 1.4.

80. Bull. EC 6-1992, Presidency Conclusions, point 1.6; and Bull. EC 10-1992, Presidency Conclusions, point 1.8.

81. Bull. EC 12-1992, Presidency Conclusions, point 1.24.

82. Bull. EC 12-1992, Presidency Conclusions, points 1.33.-1.44.

PART II

Institutions

7

The European Commission

The European Community has a singular governmental structure. Superficially, it resembles that of a familiar national system: The Community has a Council of Ministers, a Parliament, and a Court of Justice, apparently replicating a national government's executive, legislature, and judiciary. Yet the similarity is seriously misleading. The Council of Ministers, made up of member states' cabinet members, is the Community's decisionmaking body; and the Parliament, directly elected every five years, has little legislative authority. Only the Court of Justice, consisting of judges appointed by the Community's member states, closely resembles its national counterpart.

In addition, the Community has a number of unusual ancillary institutions and bodies. The Court of Justice includes a lower court, the Court of First Instance. A Court of Auditors examines the Community's financial affairs and officially has the same status of the Council of Ministers, Parliament, or Court of Justice. The Economic and Social Committee formally represents vocational interests in the decisionmaking process, and a new Committee of the Regions similarly represents subnational interests. The European Investment Bank is an independent financial body within the Community. Hundreds of committees, ranging from the powerful Committee of Permanent Representatives (member states' ambassadors to the EC), or Coreper, to obscure committees on arcane aspects of Community legislation, buttress the EC's institutional structure.

Last but by no means least, the Community has another institution—the European Commission—with no analogue in national governmental systems. With its seventeen members appointed by national governments but pledged to act in the Community's interests, its multinational civil service, its exclusive right to initiate legislation, and its quasi-executive authority, the Commission epitomizes supranationalism and lies at the center of the Community system. Not surprisingly, the Commission and the Berlaymont, its headquarters building in Brussels, are popularly synonymous with the Community itself.

Yet the Berlaymont—a large, star-shaped glass and concrete structure—has become a potent symbol of the Commission's ubiquitous unpopularity. Like the name "Commission," the building seems remote, technocratic, and uninviting. The Berlaymont's fate also symbolizes the institution's apparent decline in 1992 and 1993: In 1991 the Commission evacuated it "on the grounds that health and safety conditions had become altogether unsatisfactory."[1] Pending a thorough renovation, the Berlaymont stands empty, directly across the street from the Council of Ministers' huge new office complex. Nothing could illustrate more graphically the Commission's institutional retreat in the face of a more assertive Council.

Paradoxically, the Berlaymont's emptiness and the Commission's relative weakness conflict with a widespread misunderstanding, throughout the Community and abroad, that the Commission is greedy for power and eager to acquire as many of the prerogatives of a national government as possible. The Commission's efforts over the years to harmonize standards were undoubtedly heavy-handed, intrusive, and sometimes offensive, and its poor press increased dramatically during the Maastricht ratification crisis in 1992. Ironically, the Commission neither played a prominent role in negotiating the Maastricht Treaty nor benefited greatly from its provisions. Yet politicians and the press generally blamed the Commission for the treaty's defects. During the ratification crisis, the Commission found itself in the unenviable position of advocating a treaty it privately disliked, knowing that such advocacy would deepen popular paranoia about the Brussels bureaucracy.

Revulsion of the Commission is especially widespread in Britain. Margaret Thatcher launched a furious attack against "Brussels"—a code word for the Commission—in her September 1988 Bruges speech. Using typically pugnacious prose, the prime minister denounced the supposed attempt to establish a "European conglomerate . . . [a] superstate exercising a new dominance" over the sacrosanct nation-state.[2] British mistrust of the Commission did not diminish after Thatcher's departure. In an equally celebrated assault in January 1992, Douglas Hurd, Britain's foreign secretary, castigated the Commission for intruding into "every nook and cranny of daily life."[3]

Jacques Delors, Commission president since 1985, is a lightning rod for much of the criticism directed against his institution. For those who dislike the Commission, Delors personifies all that is wrong: He is overambitious, aloof, and arrogant. For those who admire the Commission despite its faults, Delors is a hero: He cut the Gordian knot of Iberian enlargement, launched the single market program, negotiated the 1988 budget agreement, and initiated the 1991 intergovernmental conferences on Economic and Monetary Union (EMU) and European Political Union (EPU). In the words of Stanley Hoffmann, one of Delors's greatest admirers: "While the Community's progress has depended on a series of bargains among its main members, Delors has skillfully prodded them and enlarged the opportunities for further integration."[4] As Hoffmann and others point out, Delors's leadership of the Commission has been atypical. But the extent to which that leadership has altered the nature of the Commission and its presidency is a difficult question to answer.

TOWARD AN IMPERIAL PRESIDENCY?

The Commission—in the sense of the seventeen commissioners—is supposed to be collegiate. As "first among equals," the Commission president sets the tone for the Commission's term in office. Not surprisingly, Commissions are generally known by the president's name. Since 1985, people have routinely spoken of "the Delors Commission."

Delors has had a profound impact on the office he has held longer than any of his predecessors and for nearly a quarter of the Community's history. When he became Commission president, Delors fit the profile of previous incumbents. All were male, late middle-aged, and thoroughly immersed in their own country's political processes.

A Commission president's term lasts two years, although renewal for another two years—to coincide with his commissioners' four-year terms—is usually automatic. In June 1992 the European Council reappointed Delors for an unprecedented fifth two-year term, allowing him to head an interim Commission until, under the terms of the Maastricht Treaty, the new five-year Commission would begin its term of office in January 1995.

Delors's original selection was unexceptional; indeed, it serves as a useful guide to the abstruse politics of choosing a Commission president. In 1984 Gaston Thorn, Delors's immediate predecessor, lacked enthusiasm and sufficient support to remain in office. According to the unofficial rota, Germany's turn was next. After all, Germany had not had a Commission president since Walter Hallstein in the 1960s. But domestic political circumstances prevented Chancellor Kohl from coming up with a candidate. That gave Belgium an opportunity to promote Etienne Davignon, a vice president in Jenkins's Commission and a longtime Brussels insider. Belgium would have preferred a Flemish-speaking candidate— Jean Rey, Belgium's previous commissioner, was a Walloon—but knew that Davignon's case rested on his stature rather than his country's claim

Table 7.1 Commission Presidents

Name (Years Served)	Member State	Highest Position Held in National Government[a]	Type of Leadership
Walter Hallstein (1958–1967)	Germany	State Secretary, German Foreign Office	active
Jean Rey (1967–1970)	Belgium	Minister of Economic Affairs	passive
Franco Malfatti (1970–1972)	Italy	Minister for Posts and Telecommunications	passive
Sicco Mansholt (1972)	The Netherlands	Minister of Agriculture	passive
François-Xavier Ortoli (1973–1977)	France	Minister of Finance	passive
Roy Jenkins (1977–1981)	United Kingdom	Chancellor of the Exchequer	active
Gaston Thorn (1981–1985)	Luxembourg	Prime Minister	passive
Jacques Delors (1985–)	France	Minister for the Economy, Finance, and Budget	active

a. Before assuming the Commission presidency

to the presidency. Germany was not keen on Davignon because of the way he had restructured the Community's steel industry in the early 1980s, but it would probably have accepted him as president. Only France stood seriously in the way of Davignon's nomination.

Having held the Commission presidency in the mid-1970s, France ordinarily would not have had a turn again until the 1990s. But when Germany bowed out, Mitterrand seized the initiative. Claude Cheysson, the French foreign minister and a former commissioner, was Mitterrand's presumed candidate. Instead Mitterrand nominated Delors, his finance minister. Despite a relative lack of Brussels experience (although he had briefly been an MEP), Delors's stature and reputation, not to mention solid German support, easily secured the position.

Similar bargaining characterized the choice of Delors's predecessors as Commission president. It was the length of his tenure and the forcefulness of his leadership that distinguished his presidency. Delors brought unique attributes and skills to the job. He was an experienced and able administrator, had shrewd political judgment and a firm grasp of economics, and was an inspiring speaker. Moreover, Delors had a vision to communicate; the vision of a strong, politically and economically united Community, organized on federal lines, comprising a cohesive "social space," asserting itself internationally vis-à-vis the superpowers. When the Cold War came to a sudden end, Delors's vision soared: The European Community would anchor the New Europe and form the inner of a series of concentric circles radiating outward geographically, economically, and strategically. Delors believed strongly in his and the Community's destiny and their collective place in history.

Delors had other advantages that he exploited to the full, notably a formidable reputation as a powerful politician with a future in French national politics and close friendships with a number of key Community leaders, especially Helmut Kohl. The prospect of an important career in national politics distinguished Delors from other Commission presidents. With the exception of Franco Malfatti, who resigned from the Commission in order to contest Italian parliamentary elections, previous Commission presidents were political has-beens, which weakened their credibility when dealing with forceful, egomaniacal leaders in the member states. Whereas Malfatti—an inconsequential president in any case—returned to political life in Italy, Delors had the prospect of returning to political life in France, one of the two most important Community countries. Moreover, Delors was tipped to return either as prime minister or as a candidate for the French presidency, which he had a good chance of winning until the Maastricht setback. The perception of Delors as a potential president of France, not merely as president of the European Commission, enhanced his stature immeasurably.

Building on such a solid foundation, Delors contributed enormously to the Commission's and the Community's transformation in the late 1980s. Delors viewed the Commission as the indispensable "engineer of European integration"; without a revitalized Commission, the Community would remain moribund.[5] Thus the Community's achievements at that time—the breakthrough on Iberian enlargement, negotiation of the Single European Act, resolution of the Delors I budgetary crisis, success of the single market program, and the launch of EMU—owed much to Delors's personal and the Commission's political leadership.

Delors's prominence and forcefulness in the late 1980s became particularly apparent at meetings of the European Council. Roy Jenkins had won for the Commission a right to participate fully in European Community summits. Gaston Thorn, Commission president between Jenkins and Delors, dutifully attended European Councils but never made much of an impression. Delors, by contrast, reveled in the limelight. Some of his and the Commission's greatest triumphs came at European Council meetings.

Similarly, Delors capitalized on his reputation as architect of the single market program and his unrivaled grasp of complex economic questions to assert the Commission's identity on the broader international stage. Once again, Jenkins had fought hard to win Commission participation at the annual economic summits of the seven most industrialized countries (G7). It was appropriate that the Commission received its greatest international recognition at the Paris economic summit in July 1989, when U.S. President George Bush requested it to lead the Western aid effort for Hungary and Poland. The Transatlantic Declaration of November 1990, which institutionalized meetings between the U.S. president, the president of the Council, and the Commission president, was a further tribute to Delors's and the Commission's growing international stature.

The president's *cabinet* (private office) plays a crucial role in asserting his authority in the Commission and throughout the Community. Inevitably, Delors's *cabinet* consists of extremely capable and dynamic people. Pascal Lamy, Delors's *chef de cabinet* (private office director), is "arguably the single most powerful individual in the Commission after Delors himself."[6]

Delors's achievements prove the point that a Commission president's performance depends not as much on the attributes of the office itself as on his personality, country of origin, national political experience and prospects, the economic and political circumstances in the Community, and the caliber of his closest advisers. The experiences of Walter Hallstein and Roy Jenkins are similarly revealing. Hallstein, a forceful character from a large member state (although Germany was then economically underdeveloped and politically meek), had considerable political experience as a senior government official but not much prospect of a future career in politics. Like Delors, Hallstein served as Commission president during a period of sustained economic growth. Also like Delors, he pushed hard to increase the Commission's power and promote supra-nationalism. But unlike Delors, Hallstein had to contend with a leader of the Community's most important country who abhorred political integration. (Because of Britain's relative weakness within the Community, Delors's confrontation with Thatcher cannot fairly be compared to Hallstein's confrontation with de Gaulle.) Jenkins was the only other incumbent on a par with Hallstein and Delors, although he presided over the Commission at a time of economic recession and political gloom in the Community. Moreover, Jenkins tried too hard to appease both his Commission colleagues and the powerful partnership of French President Giscard d'Estaing and German Chancellor Helmut Schmidt.

Despite his unquestioned achievements, Delors's contribution to the Commission and the Community may not have been entirely constructive. Three controversies stand out. One is Delors's responsibility for the Commission's inability to assert itself in the IGC on political union. By 1991, the Commission's workload included completing the single market program, extending the single market into a European Economic Area encompassing the EFTA countries, preparing opinions on prospective members' applications, coordinating Western aid to Hungary, Poland, and Czechoslovakia, preparing for the negotiations on EMU and EPU, reforming the CAP, and trying to conclude the Uruguay Round of the GATT. Preoccupied with so many issues in early 1991, Delors failed to assert the Commission's position at the IGCs and overplayed his hand by supporting the doomed Dutch draft treaty in September 1991. Jealous of their sovereignty and authority, national governments effectively curbed the Commission's involvement in important aspects of the putative EPU.

Another controversy about Delors's leadership concerns his role in provoking the Maastricht Treaty ratification crisis. Asked by the European Council to prepare a paper on the institutional implications of enlargement for the June 1992 Lisbon summit, Delors spoke indiscreetly in the European Parliament and on French television about the need for a drastic revision of the Community's institutions, including a far more formidable Commission. His remarks engendered considerable hostility in a Community increasingly worried about excessive centralization in Brussels and may even have contributed to the "no" vote in the Danish referendum.

The third controversial aspect of Delors's presidency is the extent to which his overbearing style upset the Commission's supposed collegiality. During his first years as president, the Commission operated along collegial lines. The only serious criticism was that Delors and his close advisers—all French—were too responsive to political pressure at home. However, in late 1988 Delors negotiated deftly with Community leaders to juggle around portfolios so that, by the time his second Commission took office in January 1989, he had unrivaled control of key policy areas.

Delors assumed direct responsibility for monetary affairs and divided Lord Cockfield's internal market portfolio among three new commissioners.

As a result, Delors became increasingly powerful within the Commission, no longer merely "first among equals." With a few notable exceptions, the new commissioners were easily intimidated. Many of them, not to mention their senior officials, grew to fear Pascal Lamy, Delors's *chef de cabinet.* Lamy often dealt directly with Delors's Commission colleagues, dominated the regular Monday morning meeting of *chefs de cabinet,* and jealously guarded access to the president.

Perhaps because of Delors's domineering presidency, member states generally nominated (or renominated) forceful commissioners in 1993. Martin Bangemann and Leon Brittan—two political heavyweights in Delors's second Commission—were reappointed, and Hans van den Broek and Joao de Deus Pinhero—two senior government ministers during Delors's second Commission—were appointed for the first time. Although the new Commission still contains a few political featherweights, it has a far more formidable "core group" than any other Commission in history.

Despite the Maastricht crisis and the possible drawbacks of Delors's leadership, the lessons of his presidency are clear: An activist with a stellar political past, and ideally with a powerful political future in a leading member state, is best suited to advance the Commission's interests and "engineer" deeper European integration. Perhaps it is time for the heads of government to acknowledge that an effective Commission president cannot be, and should not be, merely "first among equals." In the rough-and-tumble world of intra-Community bargaining, a Commission president needs to be forceful, authoritative, and direct. It is difficult for a Commission president to act decisively in the European Council and on the broader international stage without being equally decisive in the Commission itself. Thus, Delors's success points to another lesson: As currently constituted, the Commission is unable to sustain the achievements of a dynamic president. Even with the changes envisioned in the Maastricht Treaty, commissioners will still be appointed arbitrarily, the civil service will remain understaffed, and the Commission's ability to execute policy will not improve substantially. Delors exacerbated those faults by sometimes riding roughshod over his fellow commissioners and over the civil service, occasionally engendering deep resentment throughout the bureaucracy. Had he not done so, however, the Commission would hardly have enjoyed the resurgence it did in the late 1980s.

THE UNCOLLEGIATE COMMISSION

Platitudes about the Commission's collegiality notwithstanding, in reality commissioners are far from equal. The way commissioners are popularly known emphasizes the point. Rather than using names, commentators frequently refer to nationality: the "Portuguese commissioner," the "Dutch commissioner," the "senior German commissioner." Because Germany is a far more powerful country than either Portugal or the Netherlands, the senior German commissioner generally has far more power and influence than his Portuguese and Dutch counterparts. Governments decide the Commission's composition and bargain among themselves and with the Commission president to allocate portfolios among the other commissioners. Not surprisingly, larger countries fare best.

Member states generally announce their choice of commissioner(s) (France, Germany, Britain, Italy, and Spain have two each; the other countries have one each) in the months before the current Commission's four-year term expires. Governments have complete discretion in choosing commissioners "on the grounds of their general competence."[7] Personal and political considerations, rather than ability or merit, determine who gets the prestigious and powerful Commission appointments. In countries that appoint two commissioners, there is generally an understanding that one commissioner will come from the governing party and one from the opposition, or that each commissioner will come from a particular party or group of parties in a coalition government. In countries that appoint a single commissioner, nominees rarely come from outside the governing party or coalition.

A famous exception illustrates the extent to which national leaders dominate the Commission appointment process. In 1982 Charles Haughey, the Irish prime minister, nominated an opposition member of the Irish Parliament to replace Ireland's commissioner, who had resigned to return to national politics. Haughey's decision infuriated his own party faithful, both because it squandered a plum assignment on a member of another party and because Richard Burke, the nominee in question, had previously served without distinction as a commissioner in Brussels. Yet by nominating Burke, who promptly accepted the offer, Haughey precipitated a by-election in Burke's constituency, which the prime minister hoped to win in order to strengthen his party's precarious hold on government. In the event, Haughey's party lost the by-election, but his ploy demonstrated the complete discretion national leaders have over Commission appointments and the cynicism with which they sometimes use it.

In contrast to early commissioners, most are now career politicians whose standing at home enhances their status and performance in the Commission. Yet hailing from a large country and having a formidable political reputation are not preconditions for success in the Commission. Etienne Davignon, a Belgian public servant, dominated the Thorn Commission (1981–1985). Commissioners may be reappointed any number of times. Hans von der Groeben, a German commissioner, served for fourteen years. It is not unusual for commissioners to serve two four-year terms. Commissioners may resign from office but cannot be recalled by

Table 7.2 Commissioners per Member State

Dates	Number of Member States	Member States (Number of Commissioners)	Total Number of Commissioners
1967[a]–1972	6	France, Germany, and Italy (2 each); Belgium, The Netherlands, and Luxembourg (1 each)	9
1973–1980	9	France, Germany, Italy, and the **United Kingdom** (2 each); Belgium, The Netherlands, Luxembourg, **Denmark**, and **Ireland** (1 each)	13
1981–1985	10	France, Germany, Italy, and the United Kingdom (2 each); Belgium, The Netherlands, Luxembourg, Denmark, Ireland, and **Greece** (1 each)	14
1986–	12	France, Germany, Italy, the United Kingdom, and **Spain** (2 each); Belgium, The Netherlands, Luxembourg, Denmark, Ireland, Greece, and **Portugal** (1 each)	17

a. Under the terms of the Merger Treaty, which came into effect on July 1, 1967, the ECSC High Authority combined with the Commission of the EEC and Euratom to form the Commission of the European Communities. Subsequent changes were the result of the accession of new member states, which in the table appear in **boldface**.

their member states. Nor must they step down if their political patrons at home resign from government or lose an election.

By a two-thirds majority, the European Parliament may sack the entire Commission—one of the least likely things ever to happen in the Community—but the Parliament may not dismiss individual commissioners. Under the terms of the Maastricht Treaty, the Commission's term of office will increase to five years beginning in January 1995, bringing it into line with the European Parliament's five-year term. The Maastricht Treaty also stipulates that a new Commission "shall be subject as a body to a vote of approval by the European Parliament. After approval by the European Parliament, the President and the other members of the Commission shall be appointed by common accord of the governments of the member states."

That provision formalizes a practice begun by Delors whereby his two Commissions received votes of confidence from the Parliament before taking their oaths of office at the Court of Justice. Delors's deference to Parliament helped to consolidate the bond between Brussels and

Strasbourg, natural institutional allies in an embryonic federal system. In Delors's words, the European Parliament's vote of confidence in January 1985 marked "a period in which our two institutions have learned to work more and more closely together." Delors also extolled the annual presentation to Parliament of the Commission's program as "the high point of our working relationship."[8]

Parliament has no authority to decide which commissioner gets what portfolio. Those important decisions remain with the Commission president and the heads of government. The distribution of portfolios among the current Commissioners is instructive. Delors knew that the large countries' senior commissioners would have to get important portfolios, although France traditionally does not claim agriculture. After a lot of consultation, Britain got external economic affairs, commercial policy, and regional policy; France got customs, taxation, and consumer policy (as well as the Commission presidency); Germany got industrial affairs, information and telecommunications technology, budgets, and cohesion; and Italy got the internal market, institutional affairs, R&D, and education. In something of a coup for a small country heavily dependent on the primary sector, Ireland got agriculture in Delors's second Commission.

The fierceness with which governments fight for important portfolios suggests that the Commission is not "completely independent in the performance of [its] duties," as the Treaty of Rome claims that it should be and as commissioners swear in their oath of office that they will be. The refusal of large member states to appoint only one commissioner reinforces the point. As early as 1977, only four years after the Community's first enlargement, British Prime Minister Harold Wilson remarked on "the excessive number of Commissioners" and their "continuing search for work."[9] The 1979 Spierenburg Report recommended that member states appoint only one commissioner each, but to no avail. Thus, as Roy Jenkins, who authorized the report, bitterly remarked, "the position of too many Commissioners chasing too few jobs, with which I was confronted [as Commission President] in 1977, was exacerbated by the Greek entry of 1981 and the Spanish and Portuguese entry of 1986."[10] The Dooge Report also recommended only one commissioner per member state, but neither the SEA nor the Maastricht Treaty addressed the issue.

The perception that too many commissioners are chasing too few important portfolios feeds the related allegation that commissioners are in their national governments' pockets. Indeed, commissioners who aspire to high political office after their time in Brussels are especially susceptible to domestic concerns, not least because political advancement at home may depend on exceptional performance in the Commission. Journalists and politicians frequently accused Jacques Delors of undue sensitivity to French national interests. Especially in the field of competition and industrial policy, a notoriously touchy issue in France, Delors seemed inordinately

Table 7.3   Delors's Second Commission (1989–1993) and Portfolios

Jacques Delors *France*	President; secretariat-general; monetary affairs; Forward Studies Unit; Joint Interpreting and Conference Service; Security Office; Spokesman's Service
Frans Andriessen *The Netherlands*	Vice president; external relations; commercial policy; cooperation with other European countries
Henning Christopherson *Denmark*	Vice president; economic and financial affairs; coordination of structural policies; Statistical Office
Manuel Marín *Spain*	Vice president; cooperation and development; fisheries
Filippo Maria Pandolfi *Italy*	Vice president; science, research, and development; telecommunications, industries, and innovation; Joint Research Center
Martin Bangemann *Germany*	Vice president; internal market and industrial affairs; relations with the European Parliament
Sir Leon Brittan *United Kingdom*	Vice president; competition; financial institutions and company law
Carlo Ripa di Meana[a] *Italy*	Environment and nuclear safety; civil protection
Antonio Cardoso E Cunha *Portugal*	Personnel and administration; energy; enterprise policy, trade, tourism, and social economy
Abel Matutes *Spain*	Mediterranean policy; relations with Latin America and Asia; north-south relations
Peter Schmidhuber *Germany*	Budgets; financial control
Christiane Scrivener *France*	Customs union and indirect taxation
Bruce Millan *United Kingdom*	Regional policy
Jean Dondelinger *Luxembourg*	Information, communication, and culture
Ray MacSharry *Ireland*	Agriculture; rural development
Karel Van Miert *Belgium*	Transport; credit and investments; consumer policy
Vasso Papandreou *Greece*	Employment, industrial relations, and social affairs; relations with the Economic and Social Committee; human resources, education, and training

a. Left the Commission in June 1992 to join the Italian government
Source: The Commission of the European Communities

Table 7.4   Delors's Third Commission (1993–1995) and Portfolios

Jacques Delors *France*	President; secretariat-general; monetary matters; inspectorate-general; Forward Studies Unit; Legal Service; Joint Interpreting and Conference Service; Security Office; Spokesman's Service
Henning Christopherson *Denmark*	Vice president; economic and financial affairs; monetary matters (in agreement with President Delors); credits and investments; Statistical Office
Manuel Marín *Spain*	Vice president; cooperation and development; European Community Humanitarian Aid Office
Martin Bangemann *Germany*	Vice president; industrial affairs; information and telecommunications technology
Sir Leon Brittan *United Kingdom*	Vice president; external economic affairs; commercial policy
Karel van Miert *Belgium*	Vice president; competition; personnel and administration policy, translation, and informantics
Antonio Ruberti *Italy*	Vice president; science, research, and development; Joint Research Center; human resources, education, training, and youth
Abel Matutes *Spain*	Energy and Euratom Supply Agency; transport
Peter Schmidhuber *Germany*	Budgets; financial control; fraud prevention; Cohesion Fund: coordination and management
Christiane Scrivener *France*	Customs and indirect taxation; direct taxation; consumer policy
Bruce Millan *United Kingdom*	Regional policy; relations with the Committee of the Regions
Hans van den Broek *The Netherlands*	External political relations; Common Foreign and Security Policy; enlargement negotiations (task force)
Joao de Deus Pinheiro *Portugal*	Relations with the European Parliament; internal relations with member states with regard to openness, communication, and information; culture and audio-visual; Office for Official Publications
Pádraig Flynn *Ireland*	Social affairs and employment; relations with the Economic and Social Committee; questions linked to immigration, internal, and judicial affairs
René Steichen *Luxembourg*	Agriculture and rural development
Iannis Paleokrassas *Greece*	Environment, nuclear safety, and civil protection; fisheries
Raniero Vanni d'Archirafi *Italy*	Institutional questions; internal market; financial institutions; enterprise policy

Source: The Commission of the European Communities

partisan. But there is an important distinction between recognizing and upholding a national interest and taking instructions from a national government. The commission functions best when commissioners thrash out proposals from their own ideological, political, and national perspectives as well as on the abstract basis of what is best for the Community. It is not to the Community's discredit or disadvantage that "Commissioners . . . are national champions who defend their national positions in the Commission."[11]

Walter Hallstein denied "most emphatically that the relative strengths or weaknesses of the individual Commissioners brought the slightest advantage or disadvantage to the member countries whose nationals they were."[12] That may have been the case during the Community's first decade, when Hallstein was Commission president. But the scramble for portfolios at the beginning of each new Commission since the late 1970s suggests a widespread perception by governments that commissioners generally serve the national interest. Ray MacSharry was the commissioner charged with reforming the CAP; his reforms proved unpopular in Ireland, but under another agriculture commissioner Irish farmers would probably have fared worse.

Commissioners often use their *cabinets* to absorb excessive national pressure and conduct a public relations campaign for domestic consumption. The *cabinet* system reflects a strong French influence on the Community's administrative apparatus. Over the years, *cabinets* have grown larger and more powerful. Most Commissioners have a seven-member *cabinet* that includes career Eurocrats and appointees who came to Brussels with the commissioner. A good *cabinet* can boost the standing of an otherwise poor commissioner, and a poor *cabinet* can pull down an otherwise good commissioner. It is no coincidence that the most effective commissioners in the current commission have the best-staffed and best-organized *cabinets*.

The Commission has six vice presidents, five more than it needs. A vice president occasionally stands in for the Commission president, as happened in July 1993, when Delors was too ill to travel to the Tokyo G7 summit. On that occasion the six vice presidents competed for the honor and visibility of representing the Community, and Henning Christopherson emerged as the compromise candidate.

By tacit agreement, governments distribute vice presidencies between the five larger member states (France, Germany, the UK, Italy, and Spain—excluding any large member state that happens to have the presidency), with the remaining one or two positions given to a smaller country. The Italian government's inability to choose between the country's two commissioners delayed vice presidential appointments in Delors's third Commission until July 1993.[13] The Maastricht Treaty reduces the number of vice presidents to two, thus raising the prospect of further fights between member states for the prestigious but otherwise unimportant positions.

Commissioners meet every Wednesday in Brussels, or in Strasbourg if the European Parliament is in plenary session, to discuss and resolve various initiatives and proposals to go before the Council of Ministers. The Commission met forty-seven times in 1992.[14] Usually Delors has his way, although Commission meetings sometimes become bruising battles that he does not always win. The most notable struggles have been over competition policy and agriculture. A simple majority vote may finally decide an issue. The increasing uncollegiality of the Commission does not always work to the president's advantage. Just as a strong president has a lot of discretionary power, a strong commissioner may also act independently. Commissioners frequently make speeches or release statements that are intended to annoy the president or score domestic political points rather than elucidate Commission policy.

THE SUBDUED CIVIL SERVICE

The Commission's civil service is surprisingly small. Despite the picture Margaret Thatcher likes to paint of a vast bureaucracy spreading its tentacles throughout the Community, the Commission has a staff of less than 17,000, including 3,200 personnel at the Joint Research Center's institutes (a legacy of Euratom) and 3,000 interpreters and translators (the Community works in nine official languages).[15] Apart from the research institutes, the bureaucracy is organized into more than twenty directorates-general (DGs) corresponding to the Commission's activities and responsibilities.

Neither the number nor the responsibilities of the DGs corresponds to the number or the portfolios of the commissioners. Thus, a commissioner may have more than one DG in his portfolio, and the responsibilities of a DG may be spread over the portfolios of more than one commissioner. Conversely, a commissioner may not have a directorate-general at all. The Commission includes a number of other services alongside the DGs, such as the legal service and spokesman's service, and various task forces. The Commission's secretariat-general is a separate unit.

The Commission is also surprisingly spread out. A majority of its officials work in Brussels, but some are based in Luxembourg. In Brussels itself, the Commission is dispersed in scores of buildings rented from or through the Belgian government. The seventeen commissioners, their *cabinets,* and the secretariat-general are lodged in the Breydel building, a short walk from the empty Berlaymont.

The Commission recruits civil servants for its administrative grades through a highly competitive, Community-wide selection process

**Table 7.5   The Commission's Directorates-General (DGs)
During Reorganization in 1993**

I.	External Economic Relations
IA.	Foreign Policy and Security, Enlargement
II.	Economic and Financial Affairs
III.	Industrial Affairs, Information Industries
IV.	Competition
V.	Employment, Industrial Relations and Social Affairs
VI.	Agriculture
VII.	Transport
VIII.	Development
IX.	Personnel and Administration
X.	Information, Communication and Culture
XI.	Environment, Nuclear Safety and Civil Protection
XII.	Science, Research and Education
XIII.	Telecommunications
XIV.	Fisheries
XV.	Internal Market, Financial Institutions, Company Law, Direct Taxation
XVI.	Regional Policy
XVII.	Energy Policy
XVIII.	Credit and Investments
XIX.	Budgets
XX.	Financial Control
XXI.	Customs Union and Indirect Taxation
XXII.	Coordination of Structural Policy
XXIII.	Enterprise Policy, Trade, Tourism, and Social Economy

(the *concours*) for university graduates. The small number of successful candidates who pass the *concours*'s aptitude tests, written examinations, interviews, and language proficiency tests begin work mostly at the A7 level. Some may already have gained experience in the Commission as *stagiaires,* or paid student interns. Based on previous experience or personal predilection, a new recruit may ask to work in a particular DG or service but is unlikely to get the assignment of his or her choice.

From the beginning of their careers, Commission civil servants enter a world of unstated but finely balanced national quotas. Because the Eurocracy needs to reflect the population distribution and size of the Community's member states, the intake of new recruits and their promotion through the ranks is subject to an unofficial allocation of positions among each member state's nationals at each rung of the ladder. Enlargement causes these quotas to be recalculated, as nationals of new member states need to be accommodated at all levels of the correspondingly expanded civil service.

It is difficult to say precisely what motivates people to join the Eurocracy. Money is probably the deciding factor. Commission civil servants are extremely well paid and enjoy many fringe benefits unavailable to their national counterparts. Idealism may also play a part, although rampant cynicism in the Commission would soon cause even the most idealistic new arrival to rethink the importance of European integration. A desire to live and work abroad may prompt some candidates (excluding Belgians) to take the *concours,* although Brussels is by no means Europe's most interesting or appealing city. High regard for public service could also point toward a Commission career. Yet there are greater opportunities for advancement and for assorted assignments in national bureaucracies, and some countries with strong bureaucratic traditions, such as Britain and France, encourage their young people to eschew the Commission in favor of the national civil service.

Promotion through the junior and mid-career grades is generally predictable and uncontroversial and is based largely on seniority. However, entry into the senior grades—A3 and above—is highly politicized and extremely difficult. Not only is there a smaller number of jobs available than at lower levels, but national civil servants and others who "parachute" into the senior ranks of the Commission—for instance, as part of a commissioner's *cabinet*—reduce the availability of senior jobs for career Eurocrats. Despite a Court of Justice ruling in March 1993 that the Commission was breaking EC rules by using national quotas rather than merit to recruit high-ranking officials, an unofficial national quota system still applies at the higher levels. Thus, promotion to grades A3 and above tends to be granted as part of a package involving a number of people and negotiated by the commissioners, their *chefs de cabinet,* and the directors-general (heads of the directorates-general). No wonder that, in Roy Jenkins's experience as Commission president, director-generalships (grade A1) had to be "balanced almost as carefully as Commission portfolios."[16]

The difficulty of progressing beyond A4 engenders a lot of frustration and resentment in the mid-career level of the Commission. The politicized nature of promotion and an obsession with national quotas at the senior level mean that competence and merit become less and less relevant at the top. In an address to the Commission's twenty-three directors-general in March 1991, Delors reportedly warned that some were doing a bad job, that he knew who they were, and that he would, if he could, fire them.[17] But the president's inability to get rid of poor performers and the stranglehold that national governments have on certain senior positions expose some of the Commission's serious administrative weaknesses. The Spierenburg Report pointed those problems out as early as 1979, but most of its recommendations were never implemented.

The preoccupation with national prerogatives that stymies promotion also prevents mobility in the Commission. Commissioners and directors-general clung to existing staff levels even as the Commission's priorities shifted dramatically in the late 1980s. Thus, the Commission itself is far from overstaffed, but certain parts of it have become bloated while others, notably DG I (External Relations) and DG IV (Competition) have remained seriously undermanned. Nor will the member states sanction a sizeable increase in the civil service, especially in the aftermath of the Maastricht crisis.

Delors's appointment as president in 1985 raised the Commission's morale, as did the SEA and the launch of the single market program. Yet by the end of the decade Eurocrats identified Delors himself as part of the Commission's problem. Delors's disregard for fellow commissioners, disdain for many directors-general, and aggrandizement of power in his *cabinet* fueled so much resentment and backbiting that, according to a recently retired A1, "internally the Commission has come to resemble Tammany Hall with a French accent."[18] With the unexpected rise in the Commission's responsibilities in 1989 and 1990 and no commensurate increase in its size or efficiency, many officials felt the institution would soon self-destruct. During the Maastricht crisis, when the Commission unfairly came under widespread attack, the Eurocracy's morale reached rock bottom.

Despite his dismay at the turn of events in the summer of 1992, Delors seized the opportunity presented by the ratification crisis to streamline the Commission. Popular resentment of the Brussels bureaucracy gave Delors ammunition to overcome the member states' reluctance to restructure the organization. Delors sought to cut down the number of directorates-general (and consequently directors-general) and combine responsibility for certain central issues currently spread among a number of DGs, such as external relations and social affairs, into larger, better-structured DGs. The much-maligned Directorate-General for Information (DGX), which bore the brunt of criticism inside the Commission for the Maastricht public relations disaster, was a prime candidate for restructuring.

Any reorganization of the Commission would probably involve strengthening the secretariat-general and increasing the powers of the secretary-general. The secretariat-general is, first and foremost, the commissioners' own secretariat. For that reason, the secretary-general is the only noncommissioner allowed to participate in the Commission's formal meetings (other than a *chef de cabinet* standing in for a commissioner unable to attend). The secretary-general also presides over the regular Monday morning meeting of *chefs de cabinet* and the regular Thursday morning meeting of directors-general and attends European Councils with the Commission president.

The Commission has had only two secretaries-general in its history: Emile Noel and David Williamson. Noel, secretary-general from 1958 to 1987, was a brilliant administrator and a close confidant of several Commission presidents. Discreet and understated, he often provided an insight or an idea that allowed the Commission to resolve a divisive problem or broker an agreement between member states.

Williamson became secretary-general during the final stages of the Delors I budgetary dispute. Based on his previous position in the Cabinet Office in London, he helped persuade Margaret Thatcher to accept a settlement at the February 1988 Brussels summit. Williamson soon grew politically close to Delors, helping to provide "the administrative base of the Presidential regime."[19] Also using his London experience, Williamson set up better lines of communication not only between the Commission's notoriously territorial directorates-general, but also between the Commission and the Parliament and between the Commission and the Council of Ministers' secretariat. Williamson himself presided over the most important of the interdepartmental committees established in the late 1980s. Without Williamson's crisis management, the Commission might not have been able to cope with the explosion of its responsibilities in 1989 and 1990.

THE COMMISSION'S CHANGING POWERS AND RESPONSIBILITIES

The Commission is often described as the Community's executive body, yet it has only limited authority and ability to execute Community policy. The Commission is more accurately and informally called the "motor" of European integration, not only because of its right to initiate policy but also because of its history, composition, culture, and "Community" (rather than national) outlook. Moreover, the Commission protects treaties from infringement or violation and traditionally defends the interests of small member states both inside and outside the Community. As stipulated in the treaties and developed over time, the Commission's primary responsibilities include:

- Proposing legislation
- Implementing Community policy
- Managing the Community budget
- Conducting external relations
- Policing Community law
- Pointing the way forward

Power to Propose Legislation

It is an old axiom that "the Commission proposes and the Council disposes." Article 155 of the Treaty of Rome authorizes the Commission to flesh out the Treaty's skeletal framework by formulating recommendations or delivering opinions. Most of the Commission's proposals have a clear legal base in the three treaties or in amendments to the treaties. Others may flow from legislation already adopted under the treaties or from a judgment of the Court. Member states sometimes dispute the legal base of a Commission proposal, either because of a genuine difference of interpretation or for political reasons: They may not want the Community to involve itself in certain matters or may not want a legal base that involves qualified majority voting in the Council of Ministers or the cooperation and co-decision procedures in the European Parliament. In the post-Maastricht climate of suspicion toward the Community's legislative agenda, some member states are likely to invoke subsidiarity both to prevent action at the Community level and to delay implementation of Community legislation at the national level.

In the area of environmental policy, a member state could invoke subsidiarity on the basis of Article 130r(4) of the SEA: "The Community shall take action relating to the environment to the extent to which the objectives of [environmental policy] . . . can be attained better at Community level than at the level of the individual Member States." More generally, member states could invoke subsidiarity on the basis of Article 3b of the Maastricht Treaty: "In areas that do not fall within its exclusive competence, the Community shall take action, in accordance with the principle of subsidiarity, only if and in so far as the objectives of the proposed action cannot be sufficiently achieved by the member states and can therefore, by reason of the scale or effects of the proposed action, be better achieved by the Community."

Regardless of what the Commission proposes, it has an almost exclusive and jealously guarded right to make proposals. Since the introduction of direct elections, the increasingly assertive European Parliament has attempted to win for itself a similar right of initiative. Demands for "prior consultation" before the Commission makes a formal proposal, "the adoption of Parliamentary own-initiative resolutions intended to encourage the Commission to make proposals in a particular area, and the exercise of an indirect right of proposal in connection with the budget "[20] are evidence of Parliament's pushiness in the legislative arena. The Commission has successfully resisted Parliament's efforts to acquire a formal right of initiative, although under the Maastricht Treaty the EP may request the Commission to submit a proposal, just as the Council of Ministers can do so under Article 152 of the EEC treaty. And under the Maastricht Treaty, the Commission won a shared right of initiative in the Community's proposed foreign and security policy, which is an intergovernmental rather than a supranational undertaking.

Having successfully fended off efforts during the 1991 IGC to dilute its right to initiate legislation, the Commission faced a renewed threat in October 1992, this time from the German government. Again in the name of subsidiarity, Germany reportedly circulated a paper to the other member states suggesting a "screening process" for Commission proposals in each national capital. In that way, Germany argued, governments could satisfy themselves that subsidiarity was being applied. Bonn claimed this mechanism would not amount to a veto over Commission proposals, but the smaller member states thought otherwise. Aware that the Commission traditionally acts as a defender of small countries' interests, the Irish government complained that the German proposal would "upset the institutional balance of the EC."[21]

Apart from the formal right of the Council and Parliament to ask the Commission to initiate legislation, proposals may originate in any number of ways. A zealous Commission president, commissioner, director-general, or section director might ask his subordinates to prepare legislation, or an ambitious and energetic junior or mid-level Commission official could bombard his superiors with ideas for draft proposals. Similarly, a proposal could come as a result of a widely perceived need to develop Community policy, as a response to the suggestion of a member state or an interest group, or "following a study or a piece of research or [Commission] participation in a program run by an outside body."[22]

After the launch of the single market program and implementation of the SEA, the Commission set out to develop an annual legislative program with the European Parliament. In early 1988, the Commission sent Parliament a list of the main proposals it intended to submit during the year. The Commission wanted to identify priority objectives and help ensure the success of the new legislative cooperation procedure between Parliament and the Council, introduced in the SEA. In 1991 a representative of the Council presidency attended for the first time the Commission-Parliament discussions to agree on a legislative program. Both institutions now firmly contend that "legislative programming is indispensable if the Community's decision-making procedure is to operate effectively."[23]

However they originate and whether or not they are part of the Commission-Parliament legislative program, proposals must work their way through the Commission bureaucracy. A network of internal and external committees assists the Commission's work. Internal committees are mostly ad hoc and are convened to ensure coordination between various parts of the Commission if a proposal cuts across departmental boundaries. The secretariat-general plays a key coordinating role, as do the commissioners' *cabinets*. Of course, there is frequent informal coordination between commissioners, members of their *cabinets,* and other senior Commission officials, which may take place casually in a corridor, at lunch, or over coffee.

External committees, most of which are chaired and serviced by the Commission, are of two kinds: expert committees and consultative committees. Expert committees consist of specialists from inside and outside the government appointed by the member states. These committees are especially important, not only because they provide useful technical advice but also because some of the national civil servants who sit on them may also sit on the Council committees that will evaluate the proposal when the Commission formally submits it. The consultative committees are larger and more diverse and consist entirely of Commission nominees drawn mostly from interest groups and professional associations. Consultative committees are also valued for their technical advice and help the Commission keep in tune with the real world of business and commerce.[24]

Ideally, the seventeen commissioners would discuss and approve proposals before formally submitting them to the Council of Ministers. But the sheer volume of proposals prepared annually makes that impossible. To expedite the process and cut down on the commissioners' workloads, draft proposals that seem uncomplicated and uncontroversial are circulated among the commissioners and, if not objected to within one week, are adopted by default. Alternatively, a subgroup of commissioners may agree to deal with routine proposals on behalf of their colleagues. Either way, the commissioners' *cabinets* play a decisive role.

The advisory committees' input, as well as the political astuteness of most of the commissioners and their *cabinets,* usually assures that the Commission never submits a proposal that the Council of Ministers would attempt to reject outright. The Commission does not want to alienate the Council and risk paralyzing the Community's legislative process. But the Commission is not servile or afraid to introduce controversial proposals. It rarely wants to isolate or embarrass member states, yet it knows that certain states are likely to oppose particular proposals. However, the Council must be unanimous in any decision to change a Commission proposal. The Commission objected strongly to a suggestion during the 1991 IGC on political union that the Council be allowed to change Commission proposals by qualified majority voting instead of unanimity. As Delors told the European Parliament in April 1991, such a reform would turn the Commission into an organ of the Council and the Parliament for the preparation of their legislative work.[25]

Despite an inherent tension in the Commission-Council relationship, close cooperation between both institutions is a vital ingredient for efficient and timely Community decisionmaking. At the beginning of each Council presidency, virtually the entire seventeen-member Commission and the entire *cabinet* of the presidency country meet for a full day's discussion. The purpose of the meeting is to try to reconcile each side's legislative agenda so that the forthcoming presidency can be as productive as possible. During the presidency itself, officials from the Commission and the presidency country meet regularly to iron out policymaking problems.

Close coordination between the presidency and the Commission is especially important for the success of General Affairs Council meetings. Before each General Affairs Council, the presiding foreign minister usually meets with the Commission president and/or the relevant commissioner. This meeting is essential "because of the Commission's special powers and its unique role in introducing legislation, but, more to the point, because it is able to modify its proposals as the discussion goes on in the Council."[26] Little wonder that "efficient Presidencies, as a general rule, are those that have maintained a close and confident working relationship with the Commission."[27]

Powers of Implementation

Despite being the Community's law making body, the Council of Ministers has neither the time nor the resources to pass every law and make every rule necessary to implement Community legislation. Accordingly, as the Council began to flesh out the framework of the EEC treaty with a program of "secondary legislation," it also conferred considerable legislative powers on the Commission. As a result, the Commission now issues approximately 5,000 directives, regulations, and decisions annually. These deal with highly technical aspects of the CAP and other Community activities, although in a few cases the Commission's implementing powers touch on "policy" rather than simply "administrative" law.[28]

The increasing encroachment of Commission regulations, directives, and decisions into everyday life in the Community is a major reason for growing public hostility toward the Brussels bureaucracy. The Commission is too easily caricatured and reviled for its real or supposed rules on such arcane issues as the length of a British sausage, the local environmental impact of a public works project, or the size and shape of potted plants. Most people do not realize that the Commission lacks a free hand in implementing Community policy. Jealous of their national prerogatives, member states from the outset devised a complicated procedure to constrain the Commission's powers of execution.

Since the early 1960s, the Commission has had to implement Community legislation mostly through three types of committees—advisory, management, and regulatory—all chaired by Commission officials but made up of national civil servants. As the name suggests, advisory committees merely counsel the Commission on rule making. Management and regulatory committees, by contrast, are able to send proposed legislative measures to the Council for review. Management committees were first set up in 1962 to help implement the CAP, whereas regulatory committees came about to help manage the Common Customs Tariff and are now concerned with a wide range of harmonization issues.

With the launch of the single market program in the mid-1980s and an anticipated increase in the Community's legislative agenda, member states began an obscure debate about "comitology," or delegated legislative powers. The SEA amended Article 145 of the EEC treaty, making it a general rule that powers of implementation be conferred on the Commission, but member states could not agree during the IGC on a set of principles and rules to define the exercise of those powers. In March 1986 the Commission proposed to the Council that the three "tried and tested procedures" (the advisory committee, the management committee, and the regulatory committee) remain in use but urged the Council to give the advisory committee predominance in matters concerning the single market.[29] The European Parliament delivered a nonbinding opinion in October 1986 expressing concern that comitology might tie the Commission's hands and make implementation of certain single market directives impossible.

It took the Council of Ministers until July 1987 to decide on new procedures.[30] The Council stipulated that the Commission would exercise powers of implementation either alone or by one of the three committee procedures. However, the Council added two variants on the regulatory committee and inserted a safeguard clause, to which the Commission strongly objected. In a speech to the European Parliament on January 20, 1988, Delors complained that "the Council has not hesitated to resort to institutional guerrilla tactics . . . to impose [procedural changes] which are incompatible with efficient administration and fly in the face of the SEA."[31] The Council's reluctance to allow the Commission to use the advisory committees in implementing harmonization legislation in the single market program especially angered Delors. Between 1987 and 1991, the Council used the advisory committee procedure only thirteen times out of the fifty-seven proposed by the Commission.[32]

The Commission is particularly protective of its rule-making authority because it so conspicuously lacks the ability to implement Community policy "on the ground." There is no Community customs service, immigration service, veterinary service, or any of the myriad other services that are necessary to give real effect to Community legislation. Instead, the Commission depends heavily on the member states' civil services. Without assistance from the member states' agriculture departments, for instance, the Commission could not possibly make the CAP work. Thus, at the level where Community legislation should matter most—on farms, in factories, at airports and docks—the Commission depends entirely on national officials. Yet national officials can be notoriously recalcitrant when it comes to implementing Community legislation, either because they do not want to lose their jobs (as in the case of customs services), because they resent interference from Brussels, or because they genuinely misunderstand the latest Commission regulation.

Budgetary Responsibilities

Each year, the Commission submits a preliminary draft budget to the two arms of the Community's budgetary authority: the Council and the Parliament. The Commission's preliminary draft is the first step necessary to translate into material terms the Community's political, economic, and social objectives. Following the Delors I budgetary agreement of February 1988, the Commission submitted its annual draft budget in the context of a five-year forecast for 1988–1992. The Commission submits current draft budgets in the context of a new framework for 1993–1997.

The Commission has some obligations on the revenue side—namely, overseeing the collection of Community income—but its responsibilities lie primarily on the expenditure side. These include administering appropriations for:

- the Guarantee Section of the European Agricultural Guidance and Guarantee Fund (the main mechanism for financing the CAP), which still accounts for approximately 50 percent of total Community expenditure; and
- structural funds—made up of the European Social Fund, the Guidance Section of the European Agricultural Guidance and Guarantee Fund, and the European Regional Development Fund—which now account for approximately 25 percent of total Community expenditure.

Since 1990 the Commission has had to manage large-scale financial appropriations made as a result of the Community's increasing external policy responsibilities. Thus the Commission administers Community funds to assist the countries most directly affected by the Gulf War, the emerging democracies in Central and Eastern Europe, and the former Soviet republics. At the same time, the Commission took on the burden of managing emergency aid to the Kurds in Iraq and a special program of food aid for Africa.

External Relations Responsibilities

The Commission is an international actor whose stature has increased dramatically since the revolution in Eastern Europe in 1989. In July of that year the Commission assumed responsibility for coordinating Western aid to Hungary and Poland. Since then, the Commission has become the main interlocutor for the Community in its dealings with the new democracies in Central and Eastern Europe and with the former Soviet republics. The Transatlantic Declaration of November 1990 strengthened the Commission's role in U.S.-EC relations, and the protracted Uruguay Round of the GATT highlighted the Commission's importance as an international trade negotiator.

Most third countries and international organizations have diplomatic relations with the Community, and the Commission maintains nearly one hundred delegations and offices throughout the world. For instance, in the United States the Commission has a delegation (headed by an ambassador) in Washington, a mission at the UN in New York, and information offices in New York and San Francisco. Yet the Commission does not have a foreign ministry or a foreign service. Directorate general IA (external political relations), under former Dutch foreign minister Hans van den Broek, comes closest to performing those functions, but Commission officials abroad are drawn from other directorates-general also.

Because the Community lacks competence over "traditional" foreign policy and defense—European political cooperation and the proposed Common Foreign and Security Policy are intergovernmental procedures with which the Commission is associated but not centrally involved—the Commission's external relations activities focus mostly on trade and technical issues. For that reason the Commission often lacks balance and perspective, being either unable or unwilling to see the overall foreign policy implications of a trade or technology issue. Nevertheless, the establishment in 1992 of a new Commission portfolio for external political relations and the assignment of it to van den Broek strengthened the Commission's capacity to act internationally.

Article 113 of the EEC treaty authorizes the Commission to conduct the Community's international trade negotiations, but the Council of Ministers is closely involved in the process. The Council approves the Commission's negotiating mandate and must endorse the final agreement, officially by qualified majority vote but in practice by unanimity. This is especially the case in the Uruguay Round, where the French government even threatened not to attend the October 1992 extraordinary Birmingham summit in protest of a possible breakthrough in the GATT talks that would supposedly sell out French farmers.

As well as endorsing the final agreement, member states exert considerable influence over the Commission's conduct of international trade negotiations themselves. The so-called 113 Committee (named after Article 113 of the EEC treaty) of member state civil servants meets regularly with Commission officials to approve the Commission's negotiating strategy and proposals. During the Uruguay Round negotiations, for instance, the committee met Commission officials weekly in Brussels and sent observers along to the negotiating sessions in Geneva. Although members of the 113 Committee could not participate in the negotiations, their presence at the sessions ensured that the Commission negotiators stuck to the agreed-upon Council position. Commission negotiators often turned such oversight to the Community's advantage by pointing out to other GATT negotiators the impossibility of accepting a proposal without first getting member states' approval.

In addition to liaising internationally for the Community and negotiating trade agreements, the Commission negotiates association agreements with third countries and plays an important part in the process of Community enlargement. Association agreements are more than trade agreements but less than accession agreements. They are sometimes a prelude to Community membership, as in the case of the Greek association agreement and possibly in the case of the "Europe Agreements" signed in December 1991 with Hungary, Poland, and Czechoslovakia and later with Romania and Bulgaria. The Commission's role in the enlargement process involves delivering opinions on applicant countries' membership requests and negotiating the terms of accession. The Council need not heed the Commission's advice about accession; after all, the Commission recommended in 1976 that Greece not become a full Community member.

Policing Community Law

The Commission is sometimes grandiloquently called the "guardian" of the three treaties. This means that, under Article 169 of the EEC treaty, the Commission may bring a member state before the Court of Justice for alleged nonfulfillment of treaty obligations. Member states frequently fail to live up to their Community commitments, and the Commission occasionally institutes judicial proceedings. But member states generally respect the treaties; otherwise the Community would collapse. Most member state violations result from genuine misunderstandings or misinterpretations or from delays in transposing Community legislation into national law. Deliberate noncompliance nonetheless exists, notably in the area of competition policy and the internal market. For political and public relations reasons, the member states and the Commission are generally reluctant to pursue cases all the way to the Court of Justice, and most disputes are resolved at an early stage.

The Commission may become aware of a possible infringement for any number of reasons. An individual, an enterprise, or another member state may complain, or an investigation by Commission officials could uncover possible violations. If the Commission decides to take action, it first sends a "letter of formal notice" asking the member state concerned to explain the alleged breach. The state then has about two months to reply. If it fails to reply or does not provide a satisfactory explanation, the Commission issues a "reasoned opinion" outlining why it considers the member state to be in violation of the Treaty. Again, the Commission usually gives the member state two months to comply. Most cases end with a letter of notice or a reasoned opinion. The Commission generates approximately one thousand letters of notice annually.

Compliance with Community law is a sensitive political issue both for member states and for the Commission. Member states resent being taken to court, and the Commission is reluctant to risk alienating opinion in a Community capital. However, the Commission realizes that noncompliance by one member state is unfair to the others and that the Community's credibility may be at stake. Yet examples of political deals between the Commission and the member states abound. To save the British government possible embarrassment and to help establish good relations with London during the UK presidency in the second half of 1992, for instance, the Commission reputedly requested the Court of Justice to postpone a number of highly publicized environmental law cases against Britain.

With the launch of the single market program, the Commission won some important new powers with which to enforce Community law, notably in the area of competition policy. A vigorous competition policy was a logical corollary of the single market program. As Peter Sutherland, competition commissioner in Delors's first Commission, pointed out in 1988, "there is an inherent contradiction in working for the creation of an internal market by 1992 and denying the independent role and obligation of [the Commission] to enforce Community [competition] law fairly even when this is contrary to the wishes of a national government."[33] Sutherland and Leon Brittan, his successor as competition commissioner, fought tenaciously to win for the Commission sole authority to approve or block large EC mergers and acquisitions. Under the terms of the December 1989 Community regulation on merger control, the Commission has one month after notification to begin an inquiry into a proposed merger and another four months to issue a legal decision.

The Commission now has a fifty-member merger task force, predictably called the "Trust Busters." The task force's handling of approximately 120 cases to date has generally won the respect of European companies and national competition watchdogs. The task force sends its recommendations to the full Commission, which so far, despite enormous political pressure from national governments in particular cases, has accepted all of them. The Commission's responsibility for merger control generally escaped criticism during the 1992 Maastricht ratification crisis, although member states were tempted to exploit the fashion for subsidiarity to try to clip the competition directorate-general's wings.

Pointing the Way Forward

During a celebration in Rome in March 1987 to mark the Community's thirtieth anniversary, Delors described the Commission as a "strategic authority" established by the founding fathers to "guarantee the continuity of the [integration] project despite the political or geopolitical hazards." Acting as a "custodian of European interests . . . [and] as a repository of past achievements," Delors declared that the Commission has a unique obligation to point "the way to the goal ahead."[34] Speaking to the European Parliament the following January, Delors explained that "the Commission itself cannot achieve much but it can generate ideas. Its main weapon is its conviction."[35]

The history of the Community is replete with examples of the Commission pointing the way ahead, notably during the Hallstein, Jenkins, and Delors presidencies. The single market program is a classic case. Capitalizing on the member states' eagerness to complete the internal market, the Commission put the necessary package of proposals together and mapped out a strategy to succeed. The Commission provided the encouragement, explication, and enthusiasm to push the program forward from its inception in 1985 until its completion in 1993. By contrast, the Community usually stagnates when the Commission is either unable or unwilling to lead.

The Maastricht Treaty ratification crisis fueled speculation that "the motor [of European integration] has all but stalled."[36] Undoubtedly developments in 1992 shattered the Commission's self-confidence. At a time of serious economic recession and political uncertainty, it was difficult for the Commission, even under Delors's leadership, to regain the initiative and forge ahead. Invidious comparisons were made between the setback to the Commission's fortunes under Hallstein in 1966 and that under Delors in 1992. But the Community has progressed too far and the world has changed too much for the Commission to lie dormant for the next fifteen years. The Commission faced an unexpected challenge in 1993 to restore to itself and to the Community a strong commitment to European integration. Only by successfully meeting that challenge can the Commission hope to reaffirm and ultimately achieve the Community's fundamental strategic objective of deeper economic and political integration.

NOTES

1. Commission, *1991 General Report*, point 1196.
2. Margaret Thatcher, *Britain and the European Community* (London: Conservative Political Centre, 1988).
3. *The Financial Times,* January 10, 1992, p. 1.
4. Stanley Hoffmann, "The Case for Leadership," *Foreign Policy* 81 (Winter 1990–1991), p. 24.
5. Jacques Delors, address to the European Parliament, January 20, 1988, Bull. EC S/1-88, p. 8; Delors, *Le Nouveau Concert Européen* (Paris: Editions Odile Jacob, 1992).

6. George Ross, "Sliding Into Industrial Policy: Inside the European Commission," *French Politics and Society* 11, no. 1 (Winter 1993), p. 26. (Ross was in a unique position to judge; in 1991 he was an academic observer inside the Delors *cabinet.*)

7. Maastricht Treaty, Article 157.1.

8. Delors, address to the EP, January 20, 1988, Bull. EC S/1–88, p. 1.

9. Harold Wilson, *The Times* (London), June 28, 1977, p. 16.

10. Roy Jenkins, *A Life at the Centre* (London: Macmillan, 1991), p. 376.

11. Peter Ludlow, "The European Commission," in Robert Keohane and Stanley Hoffmann, eds., *The European Community: Decisionmaking and Institutional Change* (Boulder, CO: Westview Press, 1991), p. 91.

12. Walter Hallstein, *Europe in the Making* (London: Allen and Unwin, 1972), pp. 60–61.

13. *Agence Europe,* July 2, 1993.

14. *1992 General Report,* point 1106.

15. *1992 General Report,* point 1107.

16. Roy Jenkins, *European Diary, 1977–1981* (London: Collins, 1989), p. 30.

17. See Ross, "Sliding Into Industrial Policy," p. 32.

18. Roy Denman, letter to the editor, *The Times* (London), January 27, 1992, p. 10.

19. Ludlow, "Commission," p. 120.

20. Francesco Capotorti, *The European Union Treaty: Commentary on the Draft Adopted by the European Parliament on 14 February 1984* (Oxford: Clarendon Press, 1986), pp. 146–147.

21. See *The Financial Times,* October 6, 1992, p. 3.

22. William Nicoll and Trevor Salmon, *Understanding the European Communities* (Savage, MD: Barnes & Noble, 1990), p. 53.

23. Commission, *1991 General Report,* point 1145.

24. See Michael Georges, "Interest Intermediation in the EC After Maastricht," in Alan Cafruny and Glenda Rosenthal, *The State of the European Community: The Maastricht Years and Beyond* (Boulder, CO: Lynne Rienner, 1993), pp. 79–80.

25. *Debates of the European Parliament,* OJ 3-404, April 17, 1991, pp. 113–114.

26. Guy de Bassompierre, *Changing the Guard in Brussels: An Insider's View of the EC Presidency* (New York: Praeger, 1988), p. 25.

27. *Ibid.,* p. 25.

28. For those exceptions, see N. Nugent, *The Government and Politics of the European Community* (Durham, NC: Duke University Press, 1992), pp. 78–79.

29. *OJ* C 70, 25 March 1986; Bull. EC 2-1986, point 2.4.14 (see the bibliography/Official Documents).

30. *OJ* L 197, 18 July 1987.

31. Jacques Delors, address to the European Parliament, Bull. EC S/1-88, p. 10.

32. Commission, *1991 General Report,* point 1150.

33. *The Times* (London), October 22, 1988, p. 10.

34. Jacques Delors, speech on the occasion of the thirtieth anniversary of the signing of the Treaty of Rome, March 25, 1987, Bull. EC S/2-1987, p. 10.

35. Delors, address to the European Parliament, January 20, 1988, Bull. EC S/1–88, p. 9.

36. See *The Economist,* October 10, 1992, p. 66.

8

The European Council
and the Council of Ministers

The European Council and the Council of Ministers are related but separate entities. Strictly speaking, only the Council of Ministers is a Community institution. Known as "the Council," it consists of government
ministers and a European commissioner who meet frequently to reconcile
national interests and enact EC legislation. By contrast, the European
Council consists of each country's top political leader and the Commission president, assisted by their foreign ministers and a Commission vice
president. Members of the European Council may also constitute the
Council of Ministers—after all, they are "representatives of each member
state at ministerial level authorized to commit the government of that
member state"[1]—but invariably they meet not to adopt formal legal texts
but to resolve otherwise intractable problems and to lead the Community
at the highest political level.

Many meetings of the European Council stand out as definitive
turning points in the Community's history: Bremen in 1978 (decision to
launch the EMS); Fontainebleau in 1984 (resolution of the British budgetary question); Milan in 1985 (go-ahead for the intergovernmental conference that led to the Single European Act); Brussels in 1988 (negotiation of the Delors I package); Maastricht in 1991 (agreement on the
European union treaty); and Edinburgh in 1992 (acceptance of the Danish opt-outs). Some of the most prominent and portentous summits took
place even before the European Council formally came into existence in
1975: the 1969 Hague summit that endorsed "completion, deepening, enlargement"; and the 1972 Paris summit that called for EMU by the end of
the decade.

That partial list of historical landmarks indicates the political importance of the European Council. Without regular working sessions of government leaders, the Community would not have survived Eurosclerosis in the 1970s or successfully launched the single market program in the mid-1980s. Nor could the Community have adjusted, however hesitatingly and inadequately, to a radically altered international environment in the early 1990s. Thus the European Council is far more than a glorified meeting of the Council of Ministers, although it sometimes runs the risk of doing the Council's job.

The Council of Ministers combines elements of intergovernmentalism and supranationalism (it consists of member states' representatives, who agree under certain circumstances to be outvoted in the decision-making process). By contrast, the European Council is "the epitome of intergovernmentalism in institutionalized Europe."[2] Ardent Eurofederalists therefore lament the European Council's ascendancy. Yet the European Council's emergence in the 1970s coincided with a gradual strengthening, rather than weakening, of supranationalism in the Community. Aware of the threat to supranationalism that regular summitry could pose, when launching the European Council in 1974 the heads of government deliberately called for direct elections to the European Parliament as a counterweight to more intergovernmentalism in the Community. Member states took other steps to strengthen supranationalism—modest expansion of the EP's powers and increasing use of majority voting in the Council of Ministers—at subsequent Community summits. Thus, the European Council's appearance in the 1970s generated a dynamic interrelationship between intergovernmentalism and supranationalism that contributed to the Community's transformation in the mid-1980s.

THE ROTATING PRESIDENCY

The rotating presidency of the European Council and the Council of Ministers is one of the Community's most distinctive features. Every six months, on the first of January and the first of July, a different country assumes the presidency of both bodies. The rotation is based on an alphabetical listing of the name of each country (in its own official language). However, in January 1993 the alphabetical sequence switched in order to distribute the presidency's workload evenly between member states. Because Community decisionmaking virtually ceases during the holidays in August and accelerates rapidly at other times of the year according to a fixed legislative calendar, it would be unfair for the same countries always to be in the presidency either in the first or the second half of the year.

Switching the alphabetical sequence suggests that the presidency's work is preordained, and to a certain extent it is. Particular Community

Table 8.1 The Council Presidency Rota, 1987–1994

Belgium	January–June, 1987
Denmark	July–December, 1987
Germany (Deutschland)	January–June, 1988
Greece (Ellas)	July–December, 1988
Spain (España)	January–June, 1989
France	July–December, 1989
Ireland	January–June, 1990
Italy	July–December, 1990
Luxembourg	January–June, 1991
The Netherlands	July–December, 1991
Portugal	January–June, 1992
United Kingdom	July–December, 1992
Denmark[a]	January–June, 1993
Belgium	July–December, 1993
Greece	January–June, 1994
Germany	July–December, 1994

a. Beginning of a new rota in which the alphabetical sequence is reversed each calendar year

business must be transacted at definite times of the year—for instance, farm price negotiations (each spring) and a budget agreement (each fall). Also, specific Community programs (such as the dismantling of tariff barriers in the 1960s or completion of the single market in the late 1980s and early 1990s) have relatively rigid timetables regardless of the country in the Council presidency.

Nevertheless, for three main reasons it matters a great deal which country holds the presidency at any particular time. First, each country's approach to even the most routine and uncontroversial Community business is bound to be slightly idiosyncratic. Second, countries inevitably have preferences for certain Community policies, programs, or activities. Third, changing circumstances inside and outside the Community frequently confront a presidency with unexpected challenges that call for imaginative responses. Accordingly, the variables most likely to determine a country's presidential performance are size and resources, diplomatic experience and tradition, familiarity with the Community system, degree of commitment to European integration, and domestic political circumstances.

The presidency's importance has grown steadily throughout the Community's history because of a number of related developments: the progressive deepening of European integration; the Council of Ministers' enhanced institutional status; the profusion of technical or sectoral councils; the corresponding expansion of the Committee of Permanent Representatives' (Coreper's) influence and authority; the proliferation of Council working groups; the emergence and growing prominence of the European Council; and the impact of European political cooperation

(EPC). As a result, the presidency's functions and responsibilities have expanded over the years and now include:

- Preparing and chairing meetings of the European Council
- Preparing and chairing meetings of the Council of Ministers, Coreper, special committees (such as the 113 Committee, the Standing Committee on Employment, and the Budget Committee), and a large number of standing or ad hoc working parties
- Achieving consensus and brokering deals in the Council of Ministers in order to enact legislation
- Launching strategic policy initiatives
- Acting as a Community spokesman
- Representing the Community internationally
- Managing EPC/CFSP and meetings of ministers responsible for immigration
- Coordinating member states' positions at international conferences and negotiations in which the Community participates

In Eurospeak, the terms "presidency" and "chair" are often synonymous, because the foremost responsibility of a country in the presidency is to chair the European Council, the Council of Ministers and its attendant committees, and meetings of member state representatives in EPC. The Council's rules of procedure for the presidency include such routine functions as planning the Council's six-month calendar, convening meetings, preparing the agenda and minutes, and drafting conclusions. Member states still judge presidential performance primarily by how a country manages European Council, Council of Ministers, and EPC meetings during its six months in the chair.

Running a good meeting is not purely procedural; an essential asset concerns the chair's ability to negotiate a compromise and steer participants toward a decision. A country may organize meetings well, but unless it knows the issues adequately, understands other countries' points of view, appreciates how a discussion is developing, and properly perceives when to call for breaks, adjournments, or decisions, the best-prepared meetings can end inconclusively or disastrously. Brokering not just a single agreement but a whole package of agreements is therefore an indispensable task of the presidency.

Countries in the presidency play a dual role in Council and EPC meetings and have a split personality. They seek both to advance their own positions and to act as impartial arbiters. That dichotomy is formally recognized in Council and EPC meetings, where the country in the presidency not only sits at the head of the table but also maintains a separate national representation immediately perpendicular to it, on the right-hand side of the table. Yet the difference between a country's national and presidential roles should not be exaggerated. Of the two representatives present, the most senior minister or official always wears the presidency hat, and countries generally see presidential service as being in their national interest. But it is not rare for countries in the presidency to vote in their own national interest in order to produce unanimity or the required majority.

Responsibility for organizing, chairing, and running hundreds of meetings during a Council presidency puts enormous pressure materially and politically on the member state in question. Large countries have an obvious advantage: Their big bureaucracies provide solid infrastructural support. By contrast, it is sometimes difficult for small countries to find enough qualified people to chair all the meetings that take place during a six-month period, especially when unforeseen circumstances increase the presidency's workload. Most small countries—Ireland in early 1990, Portugal in early 1992—radically reorganize their bureaucracies in order to absorb the shock of the presidency, often at the cost of a marked diminution in domestic government service.

Appointing chairpersons is a classic way in which a president can influence the conduct of Community business. When the presidency opposes a particular legislative proposal, appointing an ineffectual chairperson to the relevant working group is too obvious a way to impede progress; the presidency has a better chance of procrastinating by appointing a clever chairperson. Similarly, organizing the Council's agenda and chairing Council meetings affords the presidency considerable control over the pace of Community legislation. If the presidency wants progress on a certain issue, "it will secure determined support from the Commission, as well as from some other member states. And it will put into place an active and capable working group chairman."[3]

The presidency is also responsible for maintaining good relations with other Community institutions. Because of inherent political tension between the Council and the Commission and the latter's institutional decline from the mid-1960s to the mid-1980s, relations between the Council and the Commission are potentially awkward. Yet harmonious relations between the institutions are essential for effective decisionmaking. Clearly, a successful presidency involves continuous contact with officials at all levels in the Commission and requires especially close cooperation between the Council secretariat and the Commission's secretariat-general.

Because of the European Parliament's increasing legislative importance, it is especially critical for the Council to liaise closely with Strasbourg. However, the Council-Parliament relationship is far touchier than the Council-Commission relationship. Parliament tends to see the Council as a jealous guardian of intergovernmentalism, and the Council tends to see Parliament as greedy in its demands for greater power and ineffectual in its exercise of existing power. The country in the presidency thus has the politically sensitive task of liaising with parliamentary committees, reporting to Parliament after each European summit and at the beginning and end of each term in office, and answering a series of written and oral questions from MEPs.

Foreign ministers outline their countries' presidential agendas during an inaugural address to the European Parliament. These speeches contain predictable rhetoric about European integration and emphasize what a country hopes to achieve during its six months in office. Of course, there is no guarantee that the presidency's legislative objectives will ever be realized. Much depends on the prevailing political and economic climate and on the prestige, popularity, and skill of the country in the presidency.

Whether in speeches to the European Parliament or elsewhere, the Council president may also launch strategic policy initiatives, a prerogative shared with the Commission president. Just as some Commission presidents are more active than others, some countries are more likely to launch strategic initiatives than others, and prominent politicians in a particular country inevitably differ in their degrees of Euro-activism. The conjunction of a conspicuously dynamic Commission president, a country in the Council presidency with a reputation for promoting European integration, and imaginative leaders in that country can benefit the Community enormously. Such was the case in the second half of 1991, when Delors was Commission president, Italy was in the Council presidency, and Foreign Minister Gianni de Michelis advocated a number of important initiatives at a time of profound international transformation. As a result, the Italian presidency laid a solid foundation for the intergovernmental conferences on EMU and EPU that opened in Rome in December 1990 and culminated in the Maastricht Treaty a year later.

Along with the Commission president, the Council president speaks on behalf of the Community. Having two prominent institution presidents acting as official spokesmen makes the Community even more confusing to outsiders. However, each president supposedly deals only with specific subjects, depending on whether they come under Community competence or mixed (member state and Community) competence. The Commission and Council presidents customarily give a joint press conference at the end of each European summit and sometimes give noticeably different accounts and interpretations of the same negotiations from their respective institutional perspectives.

Dual representation is particularly prominent in the Community's external relations. Nowhere is it more evident than in dealings with the United States. Under the terms of the 1990 Transatlantic Declaration, the president of the United States meets every six months with the presidents of the Commission and of the Council. Similarly, at the annual G7 economic summits, the Council and Commission presidents represent the Community. As long as one of the four EC countries in the G7—Britain,

France, Germany, and Italy—happens to be in the Council presidency, such dual representation hardly matters. But when one of the smaller Community countries is in the Council chair during a G7 summit, the Community's dual representation seems especially anomalous.

When representing the Twelve in EPC, the Council president is unencumbered by joint Commission representation. The 1974 Paris summit communiqué stipulated that "the President-in-office will be the spokesman for the [member states] and will set out their views in international diplomacy. He will insure that the necessary consultations always take place in good time."[4] The SEA established a legal basis for the presidency's role in EPC and codified existing practices whereby the Council president managed the process of political cooperation. Furthermore, the SEA established a small EPC secretariat, housed in the Council building, that carries out "its duties under the authority of the Presidency."[5]

The presidency's prominent role in EPC and in the nascent Common Foreign and Security Policy (CFSP) puts particular pressure on small countries and highlights some disadvantages of the current system. The large number of EPC working groups calls for a sizeable pool of competent chairpersons, which small member states have great difficulty providing. In addition, the presidency's responsibility to represent the Twelve in EPC may be detrimental to the Community's status and influence when a small country is in the chair. For instance, having Luxembourg in the presidency during the 1991 Gulf War reinforced the international image of a weak and indecisive Community response to the conflict.

Small countries in the presidency depend heavily for logistical support on the Council secretariat. With a staff of approximately 2,000 people, including about 200 "A" grade officials, the Council secretariat assists the Council by helping to draft the six-month legislative program, providing legal advice, briefing government ministers on current Community issues, preparing the agenda for Council meetings, and drafting the meetings' minutes. Nearly two-thirds of the Council staff are translators and interpreters. Like the Commission secretariat, the Council secretariat is divided into directorates-general, although along far different lines. At present, the Council secretariat-general consists of the secretary-general's private office, a legal service, and seven directorates-general. The legal service represents the Council before the Court of Justice, ensures that all texts adopted are compatible, and advises the Council at all levels. The Council's legal service played a pivotal role in drafting the Danish opt-outs agreed to at the December 1992 Edinburgh summit.

The Council secretariat describes itself as "entirely at the service of the Presidency, supporting it in its efforts to find compromise solutions, coordinate work or arrive at an overall view."[6] Indeed, the presidency *is* the presidency plus the Council secretariat. What is involved is much more than close cooperation; it is a form of common action or symbiosis

Table 8.2 The Council Secretariat

Secretary-General	Financial control; general information, publications, documentation; press and topical information; inter-governmental cooperation
Legal Service	
Directorate-General A	Administration and personnel; protocol, organization, security, infrastructures; translation and document production
Directorate-General B	Agriculture; fisheries
Directorate-General C	Internal market; customs union, industrial policy, approximation of laws, right of establishment, and freedom to provide services; company law; intellectual property
Directorate-General D	Research; energy; transport; environment; consumer protection
Directorate-General E	External relations and development cooperation
Directorate-General F	Relations with the European Parliament and the Economic and Social Committee; institutional affairs; budget and staff regulations
Directorate-General G	Economic, financial, and social affairs

in regard to preparing and carrying out the presidency program. A member of the secretariat, at the ministerial, senior official, or third secretary level always accompanies the presidency unless a particular bilateral issue is being discussed.

The Council secretariat has acquired a higher public and political profile since Neils Ersbøll's appointment as secretary-general in 1980. Ersbøll paid particular attention to developing and promoting the presidency's legislative agenda.[7] The Council secretariat, Ersbøll in particular, successfully took on new tasks in the 1985 and 1991 IGCs, acting in support of successive presidencies. Insofar as heads of government and foreign ministers treat their secretary-general as a preferred adviser, the Commission president and his colleagues often charge that he is exercising undue influence, not least when the European Council and the Council of Ministers decide not to follow the Commission's advice.

Despite the onerous responsibilities of the Council presidency—even with the Council secretariat's expert assistance—member states jealously guard their right to take a turn at the Community's helm. Small countries especially welcome the opportunity to play a more prominent part in shaping the Community's agenda and understandably enjoy being in the international limelight. The presidency can easily be turned to domestic political advantage, either by distracting attention from pressing problems or by enhancing the government's prestige and popularity. Charles Haughey, the Irish prime minister, never lost sight of the presidency's political potential during his country's tenure in early 1990. Following the June 1990 Dublin summit, Haughey hoped to reap the electoral reward of the image he had tried to project during his presidency of Ireland "as a modern nation with a contribution to make in world affairs."[8] By the same token, the presidency can hold a crumbling coalition together. The Dutch coalition government survived a political crisis in August 1991 over social welfare partly because all parties agreed that the cabinet's collapse would have further impaired the country's Community presidency.[9] The Danish government was not so lucky in January 1992, when holding the Council presidency did not prevent it from falling as a result of a domestic political scandal.

The presidency hosts numerous events during a six-month term, ranging from at least one European Council to informal meetings of Community ministers to cultural and academic conferences. By distributing these spoils throughout the country, the government can score valuable political points. Of the eighty events hosted in the UK during Britain's presidency in July–December 1992, no fewer that twenty-five, including the end-of-term summit, took place in Scotland. The government distributed the rest throughout England and Wales and held an extra summit in Birmingham, in the economically depressed midlands.

In their eagerness to trumpet presidential achievements, member states take credit for agreements reached during their term in office, even if the necessary preparatory work took place during a previous presidency. Countries about to assume the presidency may be tempted to obstruct decisionmaking during the dying days of their predecessors' presidencies in order to delay agreement until they themselves are sitting in the Council chair. However, the risks are great that such behavior would rebound on the incoming presidency. As a result, member states almost always play by the rules.

Also for domestic political reasons, the president-in-office is more likely than other member states to make concessions in an effort to increase its presidency's productivity and prestige. Resolution of the Delors I budgetary dispute is a classic example. The dispute should have ended at the Copenhagen summit in December 1987, but Germany blocked a settlement. Yet three months later, at the special Brussels summit held early in its presidency, Germany offered a generous concession and successfully brokered an agreement. In 1992 the prospects for acceptance of the Delors II package looked poor in part because impoverished Portugal and bankrupt Britain held the presidency, although agreement was eventually reached at the December Edinburgh summit.

The rotating presidency is a powerful symbol of equality between member states. It also brings home to each government "the full responsibilities of Community membership."[10] Yet the system is inherently inefficient: Small countries have great difficulty managing a successful presidency; six months is arguably too short a term to pursue a particular legislative program; and frequent rotation impedes the continuity of Community and EPC activities. Member states have tackled the problem of continuity by establishing the "Troika": the foreign ministers of the current, immediately preceding, and immediately succeeding presidencies, plus the external affairs commissioner. Because of the presidential rota, the Troika has the additional advantage of usually including a large member state.

The Community has frequently addressed but never resolved the problems of the rotating presidency. The 1975 Tindemans Report advocated extending the presidency to twelve months, but without effect.[11] However, a twelve-month presidency would mean that countries would have to wait twice as long for their turn in the limelight, a prospect uncongenial to politicians and national civil servants alike. Alternative proposals include allowing only the larger countries to assume the presidency alone, with other member states sharing the office on a regional basis. Suggestions to that effect by Jacques Delors in early 1992 triggered a strong reaction in Denmark and may have caused some voters there to reject the Maastricht Treaty in the fateful June referendum.

Roy Jenkins observed in his *European Diary* that "the authority of Council presidencies varies substantially. A new member country can be overawed, a small country over-strained and even a big old member country like Germany can suffer from a lack of coordination within its government. France was neither new nor small and its government, whatever else could be said about it, did not suffer from a lack of coordination. The tradition and the expectations therefore were that France provided the most authoritative Presidency."[12] Jenkins experienced a particularly bumpy French presidency in early 1979, when Giscard was at his most ambivalent about European integration. Yet subsequent French presidencies proved extremely productive. Under Mitterrand's strong pro-Community guidance, France provided excellent leadership in early 1984 during the final stages of the British budgetary question and in late 1989 during the revolution in Eastern Europe.

Portugal held its first-ever presidency in the first half of 1992. Despite intense preparation in Lisbon, few Community countries believed that Portugal had the experience or resources to do an adequate job. Partly for that reason, member states resolved to wrap up the IGCs at Maastricht in December 1991 and not, as happened during the 1985 IGC, delay important decisions until the new year. In the event, the Portuguese presidency conducted routine Community business competently and skillfully, made impressive progress on the single market program, and negotiated the final stage of the CAP reform. It was unfortunate for Portugal that the Danish referendum and the outbreak of war in Bosnia took place during its watch.

Britain has a mixed record as Council president but has a well-deserved reputation at least for running good meetings. The EMS and Maastricht ratification crises turned Britain's 1992 presidency into one of the worst in the Community's history. By the end of the year, the ratification crisis was more acute than ever, the Delors II package was no nearer agreement, Britain and Germany were at loggerheads, and Prime Minister Major lacked the necessary political weight to help save the endangered Uruguay Round. Britain's domestic preoccupations meant that even routine Community business began to suffer. Yet, having hosted a disastrous special summit in October, the British pulled off a successful end-of-presidency summit in December.

The Community's experience in late 1992 and early 1993—Denmark, the country that sparked the Maastricht ratification crisis, followed the UK as Council president—highlighted the increasing impracticability of a rotating presidency. As the Commission acknowledged in a report to the European Council at Lisbon in June 1992, matters are bound to get worse in the post-Maastricht period of Community enlargement.[13] In a Community of fifteen, twenty, or twenty-five member states, it would be absurd to "change the guard" in Brussels every six months, as happens at present. It can be awkward explaining why small countries like Ireland, Luxembourg, or Portugal sometimes represent the Community internationally; imagine the difficulty of explaining Malta's or Cyprus's Community presidency.

EUROPE'S MOST EXCLUSIVE CLUB

In a press conference at the end of the December 1974 Paris summit, French President Giscard d'Estaing declared with a rhetorical flourish that "the European Summit is dead, long live the European Council."[14] The Community's leaders had just decided to replace their ad hoc meetings with regular triannual get-togethers. The Paris summit communiqué can therefore be called "the constitution of the European Council";[15] but the European Council never became a formal Community institution. Article 4 of the Treaty of Rome lists the Community's institutions and stipulates that new ones can only be created by amending the Treaty under Article 236. In the two sets of amendments—the SEA and the Maastricht Treaty —subsequently enacted under Article 236, the European Council never received the status of an official institution. The SEA merely recognized the European Council's existence and importance, whereas the Maastricht Treaty codified its composition and number of annual meetings. The Maastricht Treaty nevertheless specified that "the European Council shall provide the Union with the necessary impetus for its development and shall define the general guidelines thereof."[16]

It seems paradoxical that the Maastricht Treaty enhanced the European Council's political importance but failed to formalize its institutional status. From the outset, however, informality and spontaneity have characterized the European Council and assured its effectiveness. Undoubtedly, meetings of the European Council have become more methodical, structured, and stylized over the years, yet their relative freedom from legal rules and regulations remains a key ingredient of their success. Nor do the member states want to tip the Community's constitutional balance in favor of intergovernmentalism by formally institutionalizing the European Council. Although the emergence of the European Council did not weaken supranationalism, by elevating it to the status of an institution the member states would implicitly reinforce intergovernmentalism in the Community system.

Giscard d'Estaing was primarily responsible for the European Council's emergence, but most of his Community colleagues agreed by 1974 that top-level meetings would have to take place more often. The decisive contribution of the 1969 Hague summit and the 1972 Paris summit to the Community's revitalization after the "decade of de Gaulle" convinced most government leaders of the need for regular meetings. Giscard, who had a penchant for intimate gatherings of powerful people, invited his fellow Community leaders to meet without foreign ministers or civil servants at the Elysée Palace in September 1974 to discuss the Community's future. British Prime Minister Harold Wilson, who had replaced Heath earlier that year, recalled sitting uncomfortably "in high-backed chairs [without tables] in a horse-shoe formation" while Giscard proposed holding regular summit meetings.[17] Wilson and Chancellor Schmidt suggested that foreign ministers attend also, and all agreed to defer a decision until later in the year.

Fundamental changes in the international system, rather than simply de Gaulle's departure, had made regular summit meetings more important than ever before. The early 1970s were years of rapid political, economic, and monetary transformation. The zenith of detente, the launch of *Ostpolitik,* the unveiling of EPC, international currency turmoil, and the onset of Eurosclerosis broke down barriers between domestic and foreign policy and called for closer coordination between member states. The Community's institutional framework was ill-equipped to provide the kind of direction and leadership needed in a distinct new phase of the postwar period. Only the heads of government had the authority and perspective required to steer the Community through the shoals ahead.

In his final contribution to European integration, Jean Monnet, then in his nineties but still intellectually alert, advocated a "provisional European government" to cope with the changing circumstances of the early 1970s.[18] Giscard and others never saw the European Council in that light, but their desire for regular summitry squared with Monnet's call for stronger political leadership in the Community. Monnet's valedictory blessing enhanced the European Council's legitimacy and helped protect it from charges that it unduly strengthened intergovernmentalism in the Community system.

The first European Council took place in Dublin in March 1975 and brought the renegotiation of Britain's Community membership to a successful conclusion. However, for the remainder of the 1970s the European Council dealt less with emergency matters than with prevailing economic and political problems. With decisionmaking in the Council of Ministers thrown into low gear by the Luxembourg Compromise and member states reeling from the impact of the oil crisis and the ensuing recession, the European Council played a pivotal role in keeping the Community together. These were the years of undisguised Franco-German predominance, personified by the Giscard-Schmidt duopoly of Community leadership. The French and German leaders dominated European Council proceedings with masterful, impromptu presentations on international affairs. They barely tolerated the Commission president's attendance, although Roy Jenkins eventually won their respect. In his diary, Jenkins recalls a summit at which Schmidt took Jenkins aside while Giscard was speaking. "Giscard allowed this to go by without comment or sign of umbrage. If one is so foolish as to believe in the equality of the [European] Council," Jenkins remarked, "one has only to think how differently he would have reacted if it had been, say, [Irish Prime Minister] Lynch or [Luxembourg Prime Minister] Thorn who had come round the table and taken me away."[19]

In the early 1980s, the European Council's composition, rationale, and internal dynamics changed dramatically. Over a three-year period Mitterrand and Kohl replaced Giscard and Schmidt. The Franco-German alliance continued to predominate, but Mitterrand and Kohl lacked their predecessors' intellectual sharpness and personal closeness. For five years, while the European Council was bogged down in the British budgetary question, the heads of government found themselves debating the minutiae of agricultural prices and member states' financial contributions. Resolution of the budgetary dispute at Fontainebleau in June 1984 finally allowed the European Council to revert to its original role as a forum for discussion of the Community's long-term political and economic direction.

Nevertheless, the European Council remained directly involved in the Community's immediate development and became "the decisive actor, the final arbiter, in the development of the internal market."[20] The heads of government immersed themselves in detailed bargaining during the intergovernmental conference that led to the SEA, spending twenty hours at the December 1985 Luxembourg summit locked in technical negotiations. Undoubtedly the European Council had proved its usefulness, although three meetings annually seemed unnecessary. Accordingly, the

SEA stipulated that the European Council "shall meet at least twice a year."[21] Shortly before taking over the Council presidency in January 1986, the Dutch government decided that two meetings a year would suffice, thus setting the trend for an end-of-term summit during each country's presidency.

If the European Council appeared to be lapsing into lethargy after the decisive deliberations leading up to the SEA, developments in the late 1980s and early 1990s—the success of the single market program, the challenge of the Eastern European revolution, and the Maastricht Treaty ratification crisis—emphasized the significance of summitry for the Community's future. Having opted for biannual meetings, Community leaders found themselves convening special sessions of the European Council to resolve such fundamental issues and discuss such critical questions as the Delors I budgetary package (Brussels, February 1988), the fall of the Berlin Wall (Paris, November 1989), imminent German unification (Dublin, April 1990), and the impending IGCs (Rome, October 1990).

Table 8.3 European Councils (Summits), 1987–1993

Brussels	June 29–30, 1987
Copenhagen	December 4–5, 1987
Brussels[a]	February 11–13, 1988
Hanover	June 27–28, 1988
Rhodes	December 2–3, 1988
Madrid	June 26–27, 1989
Paris[a]	November 19, 1989
Strasbourg	December 8–9, 1989
Dublin[a]	April 28, 1990
Dublin	June 25–26, 1990
Rome[a]	October 27–28, 1990
Rome	December 13–15, 1990
Luxembourg[a]	April 8, 1991
Luxembourg	June 28–29, 1991
Maastricht	December 9–10, 1991
Lisbon	June 26–27, 1992
Birmingham[a]	October 16, 1992
Edinburgh	December 11–12, 1992
Copenhagen	June 21–22, 1993
Brussels[a]	October 29, 1993
Brussels	December 10–11, 1993

a. Extraordinary European Councils

Just as changes in the international system had precipitated the European Council's inauguration in the mid-1970s, a sudden transformation to an entirely new international system enhanced the European Council's importance in the early 1990s. Community leaders became as involved in negotiating the Treaty on European Union at the Maastricht summit of December 1991 as they had been in thrashing out details of the SEA at the Luxembourg summit of December 1985. Moreover, only the heads of government were in a position to meet the challenges confronting the Community in the post–Cold War period.

Today, more than ever before, the European Council's primary purpose is to provide strategic direction by considering the Community's and the member states' policies and priorities as an organic whole rather than as separate and competing ingredients. Other functions that have either existed from the outset or developed during the last two decades include acquainting the heads of government with each other and with each other's views on economic, social, and political issues; discussing recent international developments and issuing important foreign policy statements and declarations; reconciling divergences between the Community's external economic relations and the member states' foreign policies; resolving extraordinary budgetary disputes and deciding the Community's five-year budgetary framework; setting the agenda for further integration; negotiating key treaty revisions during intergovernmental conferences; and appointing the Commission president.

Those functions are peculiar to the European Council and could not be performed by another Community body. But the European Council serves another purpose that possibly weakens the Community system. By acting as a "court of appeal" for the Council of Ministers, the European Council undermines its own and the Council of Ministers' efficiency. Although the European Council must take ultimate responsibility, too often it becomes involved in deciding issues that should have been settled at a lower level.

The "Three Wise Men" advised in 1979 that the European Council should not allow regular Community decisionmaking to dominate its agenda lest it become merely "an extension of the Council of Ministers."[22] Six years later, the Dooge Report warned emphatically that "the trend toward the European Council becoming simply another body dealing with the day-to-day business of the Community must be reversed."[23] The increasing use of qualified majority voting since the early 1980s has reduced some of the pressure on the European Council to replicate the Council of Ministers' work, but a continuing need for unanimity on certain issues ensures that, to some extent, the European Council will always be the final decisionmaking authority.

Whatever its functions, the European Council's format has not changed much over time. Most summits are two-day affairs, usually beginning with lunch on day one and ending on the afternoon of day two. Extraordinary summits tend to be shorter, lasting no more than a day or, as happened on two occasions (Brussels in February 1988 and Luxembourg in

April 1991), a single evening. The heads of government, their foreign
ministers, the Commission president, and a Commission vice president
participate in almost all of the sessions, and the Council and Commission
secretary-generals are present throughout. Since 1987, the president of the
European Parliament has made a statement before each European Council
formally begins but does not attend the summit. In the European Council's
nearly twenty-year history, few Community leaders have ever missed a
meeting.[24]

Although the principals meet in a relatively small group, an army
of advisers and handlers is always on hand. Permanent representatives, the
EPC political committee, and other high-level officials cluster in groups
of twelve in adjoining rooms, furiously drafting bits of the communiqué
that, piece by piece, comes before the heads of government for adoption.
The Danish presidency set a precedent at the Copenhagen summit in April
1978 by asking the Council secretariat to provide note-takers at the main
sessions. However, the note-takers' main function is unofficial: After their
twenty-minute spells with the heads of government, they immediately tell
accompanying officials what transpired in the meeting. Including interpreters, a relatively small number of people—usually about thirty-five—
are privy to the European Council's deliberations.

Dinner at the end of day one is restricted to the heads of government and the Commission president. Depending on the length of the preceding session, dinner can begin late and end in the early hours of the
morning. (The extraordinary summits in Brussels in February 1988 and
Luxembourg in April 1991 consisted entirely of a dinner for the heads of
government.) Dinner is usually followed by the traditional "fireside chat,"
when the Community leaders are supposedly at their most relaxed and informal. The halcyon days of the fireside chat were in the 1970s, during the
Giscard-Schmidt duopoly. Since then, Community leaders have often canceled the European Council's most intimate session in order to resume ordinary business.

Most summits end with the Council and Commission presidents'
press conference after the morning session on day two. Occasionally
summits run late into the afternoon or evening of day two. Such was the
case at Maastricht in December 1991, where agreement on the social
chapter proved elusive. In addition to making various political and intellectual arguments, Ruud Lubbers, the Dutch prime minister, used hunger,
fatigue, and exasperation to coax a settlement and save the treaty. The relatively youthful Lubbers and Major had considerably more stamina that
their older colleagues, notably the septuagenarian François Mitterrand.

Heads of government meet often and get to know each other well.
In addition to convening at European Councils, they meet at other international events and in an intricate network of bilateral visits. Despite

ideological and personal differences, the heads of government have a powerful common denominator: All were elected to their country's highest office. Knowing the perils and pitfalls of political life and enjoying membership in Europe's most exclusive club, they are careful never to do or say anything that could weaken their colleagues' domestic positions. Even Margaret Thatcher, who infuriated her Community counterparts, enjoyed their respect as a superb politician. Only Greek Prime Minister Andreas Papandreou, a vituperative critic of the Community, was despised in the European Council to the point that other leaders longed for his political downfall, and regretted his return to power in October 1993.

The European Council agenda is prepared by member state civil servants involved in either Community business or foreign policy cooperation and Community officials from either the Commission or the Council secretariat. An informal agenda begins to take shape at meetings of Coreper and the EPC's political committee and is discussed at length at a foreign ministers meeting held about two weeks before each summit. In keeping with the European Council's supposed informality, participants decide the final agenda themselves at the opening session. Apart from good preparatory work and a competent presidency, material considerations such as the summit's location can affect the outcome. Roy Jenkins believed that the ancient setting and cozy conference room in which the 1978 Bremen summit took place greatly facilitated agreement on the EMS.[25]

Being astute politicians, Community leaders appreciate the European Council's publicity value. "All summit meetings are to a greater or lesser degree public relations exercises,"[26] and recent European Councils have turned into huge media events. Over fifteen hundred journalists covered the Maastricht summit. Procedural rules drawn up at the 1977 London summit emphasize that meetings of the European Council should take place "in greatest privacy."[27] Although intimate, summit deliberations are far from confidential. Even as discussions continue, the note-takers' reports to officials quickly make their way to waiting journalists and into news bulletins. During session breaks and immediately after the summit, ministers and officials brief journalists—especially journalists from their own countries—on what has transpired.

Responding during the Maastricht Treaty ratification crisis to public criticism of the Community's opaque decisionmaking process, John Major proposed holding a one-hour opening session of the special Birmingham summit in public. His Community colleagues were horrified. Allowing television cameras into the summit, even for a short session, would encourage posturing and grandstanding and wreck the European Council's intimacy. In any event, summits are relatively transparent; as Roy Jenkins remarked, the European Council is "a restricted meeting with full subsequent publicity, which is perhaps not a bad formula."[28]

THE COUNCIL OF MINISTERS

By contrast with the European Council, the Council of Ministers' deliberations were rarely disclosed to the public until the Maastricht Treaty ratification crisis. Indeed, because of excessive secretiveness, "[political] behavior inside the Council of Ministers is the least well studied or understood part of the activities of the European Community."[29] This is especially unsatisfactory because the Council is the Community's real legislature and the only one in the world that severely curtails public access. The Council's opaqueness is a major cause of the Community's democratic deficit, and it inflamed the Maastricht ratification crisis. In a bid to regain public confidence, Community leaders pledged themselves at the Birmingham summit in October 1992 to open up the work of Community institutions, "including the possibility of some open Council discussions."[30]

Government ministers have never been shy about publicizing their achievements in the Council, but they usually do so in a way that increases the perception of democratic unaccountability and heightens institutional tension. In the run-up to Birmingham, an unidentified Commission spokesman deplored the way that ministers manipulated the media and vilified the Commission after Council meetings. "Ministers who hold their own press conferences for journalists from their countries in rooms reserved for national representatives at the top of the Council building," the Commission official complained, "have a disgraceful habit of presenting the outcome as a victory of their national delegation against the Commission. That's not the best attitude to adopt if you want to create a European spirit."[31]

Pressure from the public and from other institutions for transparency in Community decisionmaking appalled Coreper, the Council secretariat, and the ministers themselves. As far as national and Council civil servants are concerned, public involvement would distract decisionmakers and impair the Council's efficiency. As for the ministers themselves, the confidentiality of Council deliberations is a welcome corrective to the intrusiveness that generally pervades domestic political decisionmaking. Given that neither body wanted to open its doors, it is ironic that the Council charged Coreper with finding ways to implement the Birmingham summit's promise of greater transparency and that the opening sessions of Council meetings were televised during the Danish presidency in early 1993.

There are several councils, organized along sectoral lines (agriculture, internal market, transport, etc.) and all technically equal. The number of these councils has grown steadily over the years to keep pace with the Community's expanding competence (in 1992 there were over twenty). The multiplication of councils not only increases efficiency by allowing government ministers to decide issues in their particular areas of expertise but also distributes responsibility for Community decision-making among a wider circle of cabinet colleagues.

The number of council meetings held annually depends on the scope and intensity of Community legislation. Some councils meet monthly; others meet every six months. Regardless of which sector it represents, a council has supreme decisionmaking authority. Nor must it make decisions only in a particular area of expertise. A council automatically approves the "A points" on its agenda, which Coreper has carefully vetted. That explains, for example, why the Fisheries Council adopted a directive on the protection of pregnant workers in October 1992.[32]

Despite the official pretense of equality, there is a strict hierarchy of sectoral councils based on economic significance and political importance. The Council of Foreign Ministers—the so-called General Affairs Council—is at the top. This placement harks back to the early days of European integration, when countries saw Community membership as a fundamental foreign policy concern. As integration intruded into the nooks and crannies of everyday life, however, it became impossible to distinguish between the foreign and domestic implications of Community membership. Accordingly, finance and economics ministers demanded a greater say in Community affairs; in many member states they challenged their foreign affairs colleagues for preeminence in Community decision-making. National bureaucratic rivalry over policymaking toward Brussels, and over decisionmaking in Brussels itself, remains endemic. Yet foreign ministers and foreign ministries have retained their predominant bureaucratic positions largely because they possess a broad political and economic perspective on European integration that other ministers and ministries lack.

Responsibility for EPC and CFSP further enhances the status of the General Affairs Council's members. Originally, foreign ministers had to distinguish rigidly between Community business and foreign policy cooperation. But as member states grew less sensitive about EPC and more concerned about reconciling the Community's external economic relations with their own foreign policies, the distinction became blurred. Finally, member states agreed in the SEA that as well as meeting specifically to discuss international issues, foreign ministers could "discuss foreign policy matters within the framework of Political Cooperation on the occasion of meetings of the Council of the European Communities."[33]

The General Affairs Council meets every month except August, either in Brussels (September, November–March, May, and July) or Luxembourg (April, June, and October). Meetings usually last from the morning or lunchtime of day one until the afternoon of day two. The agenda includes "high political issues" that cut across sectoral lines, as well as issues that the sectoral councils could not decide. Here the General Affairs

Council runs the same risk as the European Council: that issues that should be settled at a lower level are pushed up to a higher level. The General Affairs Council's tendency to become a glorified sectoral council or even a glorified Coreper can increase absenteeism. When that happens, junior ministers or permanent representatives take their ministers' places, thus diminishing the likelihood of reaching agreement.

Foreign ministers' extraordinary travel schedules also explain why they occasionally miss regular General Affairs Councils. In addition to attending numerous bilateral and multilateral meetings in the Community and EPC contexts, foreign ministers participate in a host of other meetings—for instance, meetings of the United Nations, the Conference on Security and Cooperation in Europe, the Western European Union, the European Economic Area, the G7 and G24 groups of countries, and NATO. At these gatherings, they have additional opportunities to conduct Community business—they convened a General Affairs Council on the fringes of the UN General Assembly in New York in September 1992 to discuss the favorable outcome of the French referendum on Maastricht—and to get to know each other better.

Personal considerations and political empathy are as important in the General Affairs Council as in the European Council. By chance, most of the larger member states' foreign ministers served for long periods in the 1980s and early 1990s. Hans-Dietrich Genscher, foreign minister of Germany for eighteen years until his retirement in May 1992, was the doyen of the General Affairs Council. He and French foreign minister Roland Dumas, another longtime General Affairs Council member, got on famously and personified the Franco-German axis at the level immediately below that of Kohl and Mitterrand. Conversely, Klaus Kinkel, Genscher's replacement, rocked the General Affairs Council boat in late 1992 when he irritated Douglas Hurd by criticizing Britain's economic policy and failure to ratify the Maastricht Treaty.

Although they see each other often, foreign ministers have far less intimate meetings in the General Affairs Council than their bosses have in the European Council. Whereas attendance at the European Council is strictly limited, General Affairs Councils include large numbers of officials. Offended by the "football pitch atmosphere," British Foreign Secretary David Owen tried to reduce the attendance at General Affairs Councils during Britain's presidency in 1977.[34] Using the same metaphor, Roy Jenkins described the General Affairs Council as having "up to 300 people present in a huge room, talking from one end of the table to the other as though across an empty football pitch."[35]

In fact, each delegation has three seats at the General Affairs Council table and six seats behind. Foreign ministers, their most senior foreign ministry advisers, and their permanent representatives occupy the seats at the table, along with the Commission president and vice president.

In Luxembourg, where the Council meeting room is larger than in Brussels, as many as ten additional advisers accompany each delegation's top three. The Council president can cut down on the number present by calling for a restricted session—usually "inner table only," rarely ministers and Commissioner only. Lunch affords an opportunity for an intimate gathering of the meeting's main participants. The presidency circulates a list of items to be discussed at lunch, where important decisions are often made informally.

Once during each presidency, the foreign ministers and the Commission president or vice president escape with their spouses and a few aides for an informal discussion of foreign and security policy. The first such event was at Schloss Gymnich, during Germany's presidency in early 1974. These biannual retreats are now known as "Gymnich-type" meetings and always take place in lavish settings and surroundings. Most are memorable for their cuisine and conviviality rather than for serious work. The British presidency's "Gymnich-type" retreat took place at Brocket Hall in Hertfordshire on September 12–13, 1992, but was marred by anxiety about the outcome of the impending French referendum on Maastricht.

The Council of Finance Ministers (Ecofin) occupies a prominent position one rung immediately below its foreign ministry counterpart. Like the General Affairs Council, Ecofin meets monthly and holds a biannual retreat. The advent of the EMS in 1979 greatly increased Ecofin's importance, as did the emergence of EMU a decade later. Rivalry between foreign and finance ministers over the conduct of Community affairs permeates Ecofin's work. It emerged publicly during the early days of the 1992 British presidency, when the chancellor of the exchequer reportedly pushed for greater Ecofin involvement in negotiating the Delors II package.[36] At their meeting on July 20, 1992, foreign ministers agreed that Ecofin "has an important part to play in the process, [but] without prejudice to the central role that the General Affairs Council traditionally plays in that domain and in [making] final preparations for the European Council."[37]

The Agriculture Council comes next in the informal council hierarchy (some would place it on a par with Ecofin). Despite the steady decline in Community spending on agriculture, it would be wrong to think that the Agriculture Council's importance is decreasing. Protracted debate in the early 1990s about CAP reform, especially about farm subsidies during the Uruguay Round negotiations, maintained the Agriculture Council's political prominence. Of the other councils, the Internal Market Council is especially important. Founded in 1983 to help remove nontariff barriers in the Community, the Internal Market Council was instrumental in launching and sustaining the 1992 program.

Regardless of which council is in session and how many officials attend, the protocol is identical. Ministers and a few officials sit at a rectangular table, with the Council presidency at one end and the Commission representatives at the other. His permanent representative and national officials sit to the right of the Council president; Council secretariat officials sit to the left. Other national delegations sit on either side of the table according to the Community's alphabetical rota.

Coreper—the Committee of Permanent Representatives (national ambassadors to the Community)—plays a vital part in preparing council meetings. Article 4 of the 1965 merger treaty recognized Coreper's existence and responsibilities. A separate development early the following year further enhanced Coreper's standing: The Luxembourg Compromise of January 1966 boosted the institutional position of the Council of Ministers vis-à-vis the Commission and in the process strengthened Coreper's role. At the Paris summit in December 1974, the heads of government decided to give Coreper additional power "so that only the most important problems need to be discussed in the Council."[38]

The Commission has always looked askance at Coreper, a highly influential committee of the member states' most senior civil servants. As the Commission's own position strengthened under Delors, however, relations with Coreper improved. Indeed, the harmonious Coreper-Commission relationship—specifically, the relationship between Coreper and the Commission's secretariat-general—was a key ingredient of the Community's transformation in the late 1980s and early 1990s.

The member states' permanent representations (embassies) to the European Community include national bureaucrats from a range of government departments on assignment in Brussels. Member states rank the permanent representation among their most important diplomatic missions. The caliber and effectiveness of permanent representative officials determines to a great extent how countries fare in the Community. As for the officials themselves, it may be more prestigious to serve in Washington, DC, or in the capital of another member state (notably London, Paris, or Bonn), but a posting to the permanent representation in Brussels is a sound career move.

The heads of the permanent representations sit on Coreper, although the committee's huge workload has resulted in Coreper I, consisting of the deputy permanent representatives, and Coreper II, consisting of the permanent representatives. Coreper I has an especially heavy workload, covering agriculture, fisheries, the internal market, industry, the budget, research, transport, the environment, social affairs, energy, education, cultural affairs, health, and consumer protection. Coreper II deals with "high policy issues" that come before the General Affairs and Ecofin councils. Once a subject is given to Coreper I, Coreper II has nothing more to do with it. The division between one list of subjects and another is strict.

Coreper's job is to prepare the Councils' agendas, to decide which issues go to which council, and to set up and monitor legislative working groups of permanent representatives or other national officials (at least ten such groups meet on a given workday in Brussels). Each part of Coreper meets at least once a week. The permanent representatives also brief visiting ministers and other dignitaries and report regularly to their national capitals on developments in the Community. Like their ministerial bosses, permanent representatives become well acquainted with each other. Also like their senior ministers, they enjoy biannual retreats at the expense of the Council presidency.

A special agriculture committee substitutes for Coreper by preparing meetings of the Agriculture Council, although Coreper continues to deal with the political implications of agricultural issues (such as CAP reform or international trade agreements) on behalf of the General Affairs Council. Ecofin also has a committee that sidesteps Coreper on certain matters. Whereas Coreper prepares most of Ecofin's meetings, a separate monetary committee made up of officials from national finance ministries advises Ecofin on EMS affairs without reference to Coreper.

Coreper escaped criticism during the Maastricht ratification crisis because its existence and functions are little known outside Brussels. Yet Coreper is extremely powerful and even more secretive than the Council of Ministers. Coreper's ability to shape the Council's agenda and influence decisionmaking by categorizing items as either ready for automatic approval ("A items") or for discussion and decision ("B items") illustrates its importance. Coreper's unaccountability to the electorate and inaccessibility to the public are key contributors to the Community's democratic deficit. Despite general unawareness of Coreper throughout the Community, its role will surely come more to light during the debate on institutional reform triggered by the Maastricht ratification crisis.

DECISIONMAKING

Speaking at the opening session of the intergovernmental conference that preceded the SEA, Jacques Delors denounced "the ball and chain of unanimity that bedevils the whole Community system."[39] Under the terms of the Treaty of Rome, a number of issues became subject to majority voting in the Council of Ministers on January 1, 1966. Politically, however, the Luxembourg Compromise at the end of the month meant that "the Community did not move to majority voting, as the Treaty provided."[40] Instead, decisionmaking in the Council slowed to a snail's pace as member states refrained from calling for a vote in deference to each other's real or supposed "vital national interests." Legislative paralysis became chronic in the mid-1970s following the first enlargement (Britain and Denmark strongly opposed majority voting) and during the decade's economic recession (most countries sought national rather than Community solutions to Eurosclerosis).

The legislative situation improved gradually in the early 1980s as political pressure mounted to complete the single market and revive European integration. A plethora of Community reports and proposals—from Tindemans (1975) to the Three Wise Men (1979) to Genscher-Colombo (1981)—called on member states to expedite decisionmaking by voting rather than vetoing in the Council of Ministers. In a famous speech to the European Parliament in May 1984, President Mitterrand renounced the Luxembourg Compromise, which de Gaulle had been instrumental in bringing about, and advocated a "return to the Treaty" through "the more frequent practice of voting on important issues."[41]

The Community's imminent enlargement and the member states' increasing interest in completing an internal market focused attention in the mid-1980s squarely on reform of the Council's decisionmaking procedure. In the SEA, national governments not only committed themselves to achieving a single market by the end of 1992 but also agreed to do so largely through majority voting in the Council. By implication, this was the end of the Luxembourg Compromise. Subsequent practice confirmed that countries were indeed willing to play by new rules and risk being outvoted on a wide range of issues.

Paradoxically, the post-SEA demise of the Luxembourg Compromise generally means majority voting in *principle* rather than in *practice*. In other words, member states agree to abide by majority decisions, but because of deference to national sensitivities and a deep-rooted culture of consensus, issues rarely come to a vote in the Council. The presidency may *call* for a vote, but voting does not always follow. Instead, the country or countries in the minority may simply accept the inevitable and acquiesce in the passage of legislation.

Another paradox of majority voting, whether in principle or in practice, is that it deepens the democratic deficit. Although majority voting in the Council is inherently democratic, it weakens the already tenuous ties between governments and national parliaments on Community issues. By renouncing the national veto, governments reduce their parliaments' already weak leverage over Community legislation. After all, a national parliament could try to punish its government for not vetoing controversial legislation if the government was *able* to impose a veto. But a national parliament can hardly hold its government accountable for being outvoted.

Although some issues may be decided by a simple majority, voting in the Council is mostly on the basis of a qualified majority. Votes are weighted crudely according to each country's size. Article 148 of the EEC treaty, amended by successive accession agreements but not by the Maastricht Treaty, stipulates the member states' votes:

Belgium	5
Denmark	3
Germany	10
Greece	5
Spain	8
France	10
Ireland	3
Italy	10
Luxembourg	2
The Netherlands	5
Portugal	5
United Kingdom	10

A qualified majority equals fifty-four votes and a blocking minority twenty-three votes. The post-Maastricht round of Community enlargement will change these sums considerably.[42]

In the meantime, the arithmetic of qualified majority voting means that no single country can block legislation, and even two of the largest countries acting together lack enough votes to constitute a blocking minority. Thus, on any particular proposal, both sides (for and against) need to muster coalitions in order to prevail. Such is the nature of Community affairs, however, that coalitions change dramatically according to the item under discussion. Only on budgetary issues, in particular on the question of cohesion, is there an identifiable north-south divide.

Depending on its legal base in the Treaty and its stage in the legislative process, a proposal before the Council may be subject to a simple majority vote, a qualified majority vote, or unanimity. At Council meetings, ministers automatically approve the "A" items. The Council may also approve without a vote some of the "B" items on its agenda, usually after considerable discussion. Occasionally the president will call for an "indicative vote" on contentious "B" items to see where each country stands. Depending on the outcome, he may resume discussion and try to reach consensus, call for a definitive vote, or postpone the issue until another meeting.

Contentious items often become part of a "package deal" that accumulates during a number of Council meetings. Shortly after becoming Commission president in 1985, Delors deplored what he called "linkage diplomacy": the member states' tendency to link issues in an effort to negotiate the best deal possible.[43] Despite Delors's denunciation of it, linkage diplomacy flourished during the single market program. Indeed, the inherent give and take of legislative package dealing made it possible to make rapid progress toward the 1992 target date.

After each meeting, the Council issues a press release that lists the legislation just enacted (if any). Since the Maastricht ratification crisis, the Council has also revealed how member states voted (*if* a formal vote took place). Journalists reconstruct what happened by piecing together information from the national delegations, the Commission's spokesman, and the Council press office. The Council president and the relevant commissioner usually give a press conference. Based on such evidence, it seems that voting is relatively infrequent and that consensus remains the preferred path for the enactment of EC legislation.[44]

NOTES

1. Treaty on European Union (Maastricht Treaty), Article 165.

2. Joseph Weiler, "The Genscher-Colombo Draft European Act: The Politics of Indecision," *Journal of European Integration* 4, nos. 2 and 3 (1983), p. 140. David Cameron called the European Council "an extra-treaty manifestation of *institutionalized intergovernmentalism*" in his article, "The 1992 Initiative: Causes and Consequences," in Alberta Sbragia, ed., *Euro-Politics: Institutions and Policymaking in the "New" European Community* (Washington, DC: Brookings Institution, 1992), p. 63 (emphasis in the original).

3. Guy de Bassompierre, *Changing the Guard in Brussels: An Insider's View of the EC Presidency* (New York: Praeger, 1988), p. 12.

4. Commission, *1984 General Report*, p. 297.

5. SEA, Title III, Article 10 (g).

6. Council of the European Communities General Secretariat, *The Council of the European Community: An Introduction to Its Services and Activities* (Luxembourg: OOP, 1991), p. 29.

7. See Helen Wallace, "The Presidency: Tasks and Evolution," in Colm O'Nuallain, ed., *The Presidency of the European Council of Ministers: Impacts and Implications for National Governments* (London: Croom Helm, 1985), p. 12.

8. Quoted in *The Irish Times*, July 4, 1990, p. 1.

9. See Alfred Pijpers, "Between the Gulf War and a European Political Union," in Alfred Pijpers, ed., *The European Community at the Crossroads* (Dordrecht, The Netherlands: Martinus Nijhoff, 1992), p. 274.

10. Helen Wallace and Geoffrey Edwards, *The Council of Ministers of the European Community and the President-in-Office* (London: The Federal Trust, 1977), p. 550.

11. Tindemans Report, Bull. EC S/1–76, p. 31.

12. Roy Jenkins, *European Diary, 1977–1981* (London: Collins, 1989), p. 371.

13. "Europe and the Challenge of Enlargement," Bull. EC, S/3–92.

14. *Agence Europe,* December 17, 1974, p. 4.

15. Council of the European Communities, *Report on European Institutions Presented by the Committee of Three to the European Council* (Luxembourg, OOP, 1981).

16. Maastricht Treaty, Article III.

17. *The Times* (London), June 28, 1977, p. 10.

18. Jean Monnet, *Memoirs* (Garden City, NY: Doubleday, 1977), pp. 598–599.

19. Jenkins, *European Diary*, pp. 248–249.

20. Cameron, "The 1992 Initiative," in Sbragia, *Euro-Politics,* p. 63.

21. SEA, Title I, Article 2.

22. Report of the Three Wise Men, pp. 16–17.

23. Ad Hoc Committee for Institutional Affairs Report to the European Council (Dooge Report), March 1985, Bull. EC 3–1985, point 3.5.1.

24. See Jan Werts, *The European Council* (Amsterdam: North-Holland, 1992), pp. 159–160.

25. Jenkins, *European Diary,* p. 289.

26. Annette Morgan, *From Summit to Council: Evolution in the EEC* (London: Chatham House, 1976), p. 56.

27. Bull. EC, 6-1977, point 2.3.1.

28. Jenkins, *European Diary,* p. 75.

29. Helen Wallace, "The Council and the Commission After the Single European Act," in Leon Hurwitz and Christian Lequesne, eds., *The State of the European Community: Policies, Institutions, and Debates in the Transition Years* (Boulder, CO: Lynne Rienner Publishers, 1991), p. 20.

30. Bull. EC 10-1992, Presidency Conclusions, point 1.8.

31. Quoted in *Le Monde*, October 13, 1992. p. 2.

32. 1608th Council Meeting, Fisheries, Luxembourg, October 19, 1992, Press Release 9041/92.

33. SEA, Title III.

34. *The Times* (London), June 28, 1977, p. 16.

35. Jenkins, *European Diary,* p. 74.

36. Reuters, July 13, 1992.

37. Council Press Release 7676/92, p. 4.

38. Commission, *1974 General Report,* Annex to Chapter I, point 8.

39. Quoted in Marina Gazzo, ed., *Towards European Union*, vol. 1 (Brussels: Agence Europe, 1985), p. 26.

40. William Nicoll, "The Luxembourg Compromise," *Journal of Common Market Studies* 23, no. 1 (September 1984), p. 38.

41. François Mitterrand, speech to the European Parliament, May 24, 1984, reprinted in *Vital Speeches of the Day*, August 1, 1984, p. 613.

42. See Commission report on enlargement, Bull. EC S/3-1992, p. 15.

43. Jacques Delors, speech to the European Parliament, March 12, 1985, Bull. EC S/4-1985, p. 6.

44. See Wallace, "After the SEA," in Hurwitz and Lequesne, *Policies, Institutions,* p. 26.

9

The European Parliament

Just as the Commission has no analogue in national political systems, the European Parliament is easily misperceived as the Community equivalent of a national legislature. Most members of the European Parliament (MEPs) think the EP *should* be the Community's legislature, or at least its colegislature alongside the Council of Ministers. They argue that Parliament's relative lack of legislative power undermines the Community's democratic legitimacy and find it "unacceptable that a union of democratic states should not itself be democratic."[1] Directly elected every five years in Community-wide elections, MEPs are understandably aggrieved that the European Parliament lacks the political clout of the Council and Commission.

The history of the European Parliament is a history of relentless attempts by MEPs to increase their institution's power. Using the argument of democratic unaccountability in the Community—the so-called "democratic deficit"—as a potent weapon, MEPs have sought, especially since the advent of direct elections in 1979, to redress the institutional imbalance between the Commission, Council, and Parliament. With the indispensable assistance of genuinely sympathetic or guilt-ridden governments, Parliament managed in the 1980s and early 1990s to obtain substantially more legislative and supervisory authority.

By introducing a "cooperation" procedure (the right to a second reading for certain legislation, notably concerning the single market), the Single European Act (SEA) was a turning point in Parliament's procurement of legislative power. So was the Maastricht Treaty, which extended cooperation to other important areas and gave Parliament a limited form of legislative "co-decision." In the 1970s, the member states had given Parliament significant budgetary authority. The combination of budgetary

257

and limited legislative power, the assent procedure for ratification of association and accession agreements, and the ability to scrutinize the activities of other institutions greatly enhanced Parliament's political position.

Using the democratic deficit like a battering ram to break down national governments' reluctance to cede more power to Parliament, some MEPs seized on the Maastricht Treaty ratification crisis and growing public concern about Community affairs to press for additional authority. Before the 1992 crisis, MEPs waged a war for more parliamentary power not only at occasional intergovernmental conferences but also on a daily basis in dealings with national politicians, Commission officials, and the Council secretariat. Institutional relations between the Council and Parliament are inherently tense, and personal relations between Council officials and MEPs are frequently acrimonious. Parliamentary committee meetings and plenary sessions provide ample and highly visible opportunities for MEPs to attack government ministers and Council officials for not being more accountable to the Community's electorate.

MEPs claim the high moral ground in the interinstitutional and intergovernmental struggle concerning Parliament's role and authority. Yet MEPs' management of parliamentary affairs weakens their case considerably. The monthly trek between Brussels and Strasbourg, five hours apart by road or rail, is an obvious but important example. MEPs spend three weeks each month in Brussels attending committee and political group meetings and the other week in Strasbourg attending plenary sessions. A large part of the Parliament's secretariat is located in Luxembourg, approximately halfway between Brussels and Strasbourg. The expense of constantly transporting MEPs, officials, and innumerable boxes of papers in a six-hundred-mile circuit amounts to approximately $50 million a year.[2] The cost and inconvenience of moving every month and of maintaining three separate office sites have seriously and possibly irreparably eroded public confidence in the European Parliament.[3]

In their defense, MEPs point out that the Parliament would like to move to Brussels, that it already took the initiative to hold committee and political group meetings there, but that national governments are responsible for the practice of holding plenary sessions in Strasbourg and for keeping the secretariat in Luxembourg. Over the years the governments of France and Luxembourg went to great lengths, including taking legal action and blocking decisions about where to locate new Community institutions and agencies, to prevent Parliament's plenary sessions and secretariat from moving permanently to Brussels. At the December 1992 Edinburgh summit, the heads of government decided that Parliament's secretariat would forever stay in Luxembourg and that Parliament would always hold its monthly plenaries in Strasbourg but that additional plenaries could take place in Brussels.[4]

Although MEPs can legitimately claim that the decision to stay in Strasbourg was beyond their control, they continue to bear the political brunt of Parliament's monthly migration. MEPs could counter the negative consequences of their itinerant existence by moving unilaterally to Brussels, where the Parliament recently constructed a huge complex of offices and assembly halls. Such a move would provoke a legal and political crisis in the Community, but it is perhaps the only way for MEPs to win the popular support they now conspicuously lack. However, not only would the vast majority of MEPs *not* countenance a constitutional crisis over the apparently trivial question of Parliament's location, but most seem to enjoy too much their monthly stays in Strasbourg, a city far prettier than Brussels and livelier than Luxembourg.

MEPs' generous allowances and seemingly lavish lifestyles, as well as Parliament's peculiar procedures, linguistic muddle (the Community's nine official languages are constantly used), and poorly attended plenaries, contribute to the EP's low public esteem. They also generate an endless supply of silly stories, even in the sympathetic press, causing the institution enormous political damage. Undoubtedly a majority of MEPs are hardworking, dedicated, and sensitive to popular cynicism about parliamentarians in general and Europarliamentarians in particular. But until the European Parliament ends its monthly road show, simplifies its procedures, and makes it easier for the public to attend committee meetings in Brussels and plenaries in Strasbourg (one of Western Europe's least accessible cities), redressing the institutional imbalance by giving Parliament more legislative power will not resolve the democratic deficit. For the democratic deficit is based on popular perception as well as political reality, and most Europeans tend to see the European Parliament as part of the problem rather than part of the solution.

DIRECT ELECTIONS, POLITICAL PARTIES, AND POLITICAL GROUPS

The adjective "direct" distinguishes the current system for MEP selection from the "indirect" system in operation before 1979. Originally, national parliaments nominated a number of members to sit also as MEPs in Strasbourg. The size of each national delegation was vaguely proportional to a country's population, and the composition of each delegation depended on the distribution of seats between political parties in the national parliaments.

Article 138(3) of the Treaty of Rome calls on Parliament to "draw up proposals for elections by direct universal suffrage in accordance with a uniform procedure in all Member States." Parliament drew up the required proposals in 1961 (and again in 1963 and 1969), but the Council never proceeded under the terms of Article 138(3) "to lay down [unanimously] the appropriate provisions, which it shall recommend to Member States for adoption in accordance with their respective constitutional requirements." Efforts to move from "indirect" to "direct" elections fell victim to the ubiquitous struggle between supranationalism and intergovernmentalism. Supranationalists hoped, and intergovernmentalists feared, that direct elections would strengthen Parliament's legitimacy and power and thereby weaken the Council's authority. De Gaulle's guardianship of intergovernmentalism and disdain for the Strasbourg assembly ensured that direct elections did not come about in the 1960s.

The Community's "relaunch" after de Gaulle's departure revived the question of direct elections. A decision at the 1974 Paris summit to offset the nascent European Council (an institutionalization of intergovernmentalism) with direct elections to the European Parliament (a sop to supranationalism) prompted Parliament to conclude the revision of its electoral proposals begun in 1973. Parliament adopted new proposals in January 1975, and the European Council reached a compromise agreement at its July 1976 Brussels summit.[5] Apart from the lingering reluctance of some old (notably France) and new (notably Britain) member states to give Parliament additional authority by moving from indirect to direct elections, governments differed widely on a myriad of organizational and procedural points. As a result, in September 1976 the Council of Ministers finally authorized direct elections to be held every five years, but not "in accordance with a uniform procedure in all Member States."[6]

Procedural differences between member states, which persist to this day, include the way in which candidates are nominated, the order of names on voting lists (in cases where such an electoral system is used), campaign rules, the validation of election results, the filling of vacant seats, and the choice of election day (within a three- or four-day period in mid-June). Other, more important, differences include:

• *Eligibility to vote and stand for elections.* Apart from the same minimum voting age (eighteen) in all member states, voting rights differ markedly throughout the Community. Some member states restrict the right to vote to their own nationals; others extend it to residents from any Community country. Some member states allow absentee voting without restrictions; others extend it only to their nationals resident elsewhere in the Community. The minimum age to stand as a candidate varies throughout the Community, as do nationality and residency requirements. However, under Article 8b of the Maastricht Treaty the Council must approve arrangements by December 31, 1993, to allow "Union citizens" to vote and stand as candidates in European elections in the member states where they live—even if they are nationals of another Community country —under the same conditions as nationals of that state. Aware of the sensitivity of voting rights in the Community, and acknowledging the un-likelihood of uniform voting rights by the end of 1993, the treaty permits derogations "where warranted by problems specific to a Member State."

• *The electoral system.* Eleven member states use various systems of proportional representation, and one (the UK) uses a "first-past-the-post system" (except in Northern Ireland). The British system, used also in domestic elections, is notorious for causing overrepresentation or un-derrepresentation of political parties in the Commons and in Strasbourg. Thus, a small swing in electoral support for a British political party could result in a large gain or loss of seats for that party in Strasbourg and could thereby determine which political group (coalition of national political parties) forms a majority in the European Parliament.

• *Constituency boundaries.* In eight member states (Denmark, France, Germany, Greece, Luxembourg, the Netherlands, Spain, and Por-tugal), the whole country forms a single constituency. Four member states (Belgium, Ireland, Italy, and the UK) have divided their countries into a number of "Euroconstituencies." Only in Britain do those constituencies correspond to the constituencies used in national elections; in Germany, parties may submit lists of candidates either for each state or for the entire country. Consequently, it is difficult to develop close constituent-MEP re-lations in a majority of member states. Because British and Irish con-stituencies are relatively small, voters may have a particular affinity with their MEP. In a large country that forms a single constituency, by contrast, constituents may never get to know or identify with a particular MEP.

The distribution of seats between countries accentuates that prob-lem and is one of the most striking anomalies in the European parliamen-tary system. Following the sudden addition in October 1990 of 17 million East Germans to the Federal Republic's population, Germany asked for extra representation in Strasbourg, kindling fears that Germany's delega-tion would dominate Parliament. The heads of government decided at the December 1992 Edinburgh summit to redistribute and increase the total number of seats in Strasbourg.

Regardless of the "German question," the dispute in 1991 and 1992 about the redistribution of seats in Parliament was the latest in a se-ries of battles between member states over the size of their delegations in Strasbourg. Especially since the 1976 decision to hold direct elections, de-termining the size of parliamentary delegations has involved intense in-tergovernmental bargaining. Even the governments that liked Parliament least and resisted supranationalism most fought tenaciously for larger na-tional representation. Clearly, the size of a parliamentary delegation is as much a matter of national pride as of political advantage.

So far, there have been three direct elections to the European Par-liament (1979, 1984, and 1989). At the time of the third election, in the

Table 9.1 Current EP Seat Distribution and Population/Seat Ratio

	Present Number of Seats	Population (million)	Population/Seat Ratio (thousand)
Germany	81	79.7	984
Italy	81	57.7	712
United Kingdom	81	57.5	710
France	81	56.9	702
Spain	60	39.0	650
Netherlands	25	15.0	600
Portugal	24	9.9	413
Greece	24	10.2	425
Belgium	24	9.9	413
Denmark	16	5.1	319
Ireland	15	3.5	233
Luxembourg	6	0.4	66
EC 12	518	344.8	

Source: Eurostat

Table 9.2 Revised EP Seat Distribution and Population/Seat Ratio[a]

	Revised Number of Seats		Population (million)	Population/Seat Ratio (thousand)
Germany	99	(+18)	79.7	805
Italy	87	(+6)	57.7	663
United Kingdom	87	(+6)	57.5	660
France	87	(+6)	56.9	654
Spain	64	(+4)	39.0	609
Netherlands	31	(+6)	15.0	484
Portugal	25	(+1)	9.9	396
Greece	25	(+1)	10.2	408
Belgium	25	(+1)	9.9	396
Denmark	16		5.1	319
Ireland	15		3.5	233
Luxembourg	6		0.4	66
EC 12	567	(+49)	344.8	

a. Based on an agreement reached at the Edinburgh European Council, December 1992, subject to implementation by the member states.
Source: Edinburgh Summit Conclusions, Eurostat

aftermath of the SEA, Parliament had considerably more power than before and the single market program was in full swing. Yet in terms of political party behavior and voter turnout, all three elections were disappointing. Turnout varied greatly from country to country but declined steadily over the eleven-year period, from 62.5 percent in 1979 to 59 percent in 1984 to 57.2 percent in 1989.[7] With the exception of farmers, whose livelihoods depended on the CAP, voters generally appeared unaware of or uninterested in the European Parliament's existence and function.

Although most candidates campaigned to some extent on Community issues and proclaimed their political group affiliation, national political parties and issues predominated. In some countries (for instance, Greece, Ireland, and Luxembourg in 1989), general elections coincided with and completely overshadowed European elections. In other countries, European elections invariably became a referendum on the government.

Just as they dominated the election campaigns, political parties also dominated the selection of candidates. Eurocandidates (and consequently MEPs) tended to fall into one of the following categories:

- Aspiring politicians who failed to win selection as candidates for national elections
- Aspiring politicians who won selection as candidates for national elections but subsequently lost the election
- Established politicians temporarily out of national office because of resignation or a government reshuffle
- Successful local politicians
- People with or without a background in local or national politics who wanted to make a career as MEPs
- Prominent trade unionists and farmers leaders

A handful of well-known MEPs are either former commissioners (e.g., Willy de Clerq) or elder statesmen (e.g., Valéry Giscard d'Estaing).

A few MEPs still hold the "dual mandate": They are members of both their national parliaments and the European Parliament. The European Parliament disapproves of the dual mandate,[8] and a number of countries and political parties have prohibited it. The dual mandate has the advantage of personifying a close relationship between national parliaments and the European Parliament, but the demands of being an MP and MEP make it difficult for someone to hold both positions simultaneously. Because holders of the dual mandate tend to devote more time to national politics, they unwittingly reinforce a negative stereotype of the European Parliament as a publicly supported leisure center.

National political parties dominate Euro-elections, and coalitions of national political parties dominate the European Parliament. Called political groups, these coalitions are based on ideological affinity, sectoral interest, and convenience. The European Parliament respects the individuality of its members but encourages them to form groups across national lines. Where three nationalities are involved, as few as twelve members may form a group, whereas a minimum of eighteen members are required from only two member states and twenty-three from a single member state.[9]

Currently, there are eight political groups in the Parliament, representing more than ninety political parties. In addition, twenty-one MEPs sit as independents. The relatively small number of unattached MEPs testifies to the procedural advantages of belonging to a political group. After the first direct election in 1979, a number of otherwise unattached MEPs launched the Group for the Technical Coordination and Defense of Independents (TCDI) in order to enjoy the benefits of group affiliation. The TCDI, an odd assortment of mavericks, eccentrics, and extremists, dissolved in 1984, after the second direct election. Some of its members lost their seats, some joined existing or new groups, and others relished the more congenial but less convenient status of complete independence.

From the beginning of the party group system in the mid-1950s, three generic groupings—Socialist, Christian Democratic, and Liberal—have eclipsed all others in the European Parliament. Since the third direct election in 1989, the Socialist and Christian Democratic "families" have predominated. Political group nomenclature can be confusing. At least the Socialist Group has had the same, simple name since its inception; the Christian Democrats renamed their group the European People's Party (EPP) in 1976. Both are the only groups to include political parties or individual politicians from all twelve member states, and both have provided the bulk of European Parliament presidents.

The Socialist Group benefited more than the Christian Democrats from successive enlargements, although the sizeable British Labour contingent only took its seats in Parliament after the successful outcome of the 1975 referendum. The Socialists also benefited most from Spanish and Portuguese accession. The impact of Iberian enlargement and social democracy's strong appeal in the late 1980s made the Socialists the largest group in the third directly elected Parliament. In an interesting postscript to the end of the Cold War, in January 1993 twenty Communists (mostly Italians) crossed over and joined the Socialist Group.

After the first enlargement, the Christian Democrats did not enjoy an influx of British and Danish Conservatives, who instead set up their own group, the European Conservatives, which later changed its name to the European Democratic Group (EDG). However, immediately after the 1989 direct elections the EDG requested membership in the EPP "because of its special Christian Democratic and European federalistic identity, with which they . . . wish to identify."[10] The EPP rejected the Conservatives' request in July 1989, asking them to apply again in 1991. In the meantime, John Major's replacement of Margaret Thatcher as British Conservative Party leader in November 1990, and his "resolute, systematic effort to give the party both europolitically [sic] and, in particular, economically and sociopolitically a new profile which tends towards that of the EPP," increased the prospects for a successful reconsideration of the EDG's request.[11] In 1991 the groups established a consultative committee to prepare for the EPP's incorporation of the EDG's members, which eventually took place the following year.

The Liberals—gathered since the second direct election into the Liberal, Democratic, and Reformist Group—experienced a relative decline as a result of successive enlargements. Moreover, in 1965 the Gaullists broke away to form the European Democratic Union (EDU). After the first enlargement, Ireland's Fianna Fail MEPs joined the Gaullists, who first renamed their group the European Progressive Democrats, later the European Democratic Alliance.

Other political developments since the 1970s spawned new political groups. The Eurocommunist movement led in 1973 to the establishment of the Communist Group. Fissiparous tendencies on the far left, especially after the collapse of communism in Eastern Europe, caused the Communists to split after the 1989 direct election into two separate groups, the United European Left and Left Unity. Despite the declaration of solidarity implicit in each group's title, United European Left consisted mostly of Italian and Spanish Communists, whereas the small, more doctrinaire Left Unity consisted mostly of French, Greek, and Portuguese Communists. The decision by twenty Italian Communists to join the Socialist Group in January 1993 brought the United European Left's existence to an end.

The reemergence of the extreme right in Europe in the mid-1980s manifested itself in the appearance in the European Parliament of the Technical Group of the European Right. The prefix "Technical Group" indicates a marriage of convenience. The French National Front had too few seats to form its own group, and coalesced uneasily with the German Republican Party, with which it at least agreed on the supposed evils of immigration. The handful of Italian Social Movement MEPs would ordinarily have joined the European Right group, but the Italian and German rightists fell out over an historical dispute concerning the South Tyrol. Accordingly, the Italian Social Movement MEPs are unattached in Parliament. Regardless of where far-right MEPs sit, they are despised and treated as "outsiders" by the vast majority of other MEPs.[12]

In 1984, newly elected Green and alternative MEPS joined with a few independents to form the Rainbow Group. Five years later, after the third direct election, a larger Green contingent formed its own group, and the Rainbow Group became a heterogeneous collection of regional parties, disaffected members of other parties, and a few Danes dedicated to taking their country out of the Community.

Parliament's groups cover the wide spectrum of European politics—a much broader spectrum than exists in the United States—from the far left to the far right. It is easy to place the Communists (Left Unity) and

Table 9.3 EP Political Groups: Number of Parties and Individual Members[a]

	Number of Parties	Belgium	Denmark	Germany	Greece	Spain	France	Ireland	Italy	Luxembourg	Netherlands	Portugal	UK	EC12
SOC	19	8	3	31	8	27	22	1	34	2	8	8	46	198
EPP	18	7	4	32	10	17	12	4	27	3	10	3	33	162
LIB	17	4	3	5	0	5	10	2	3	1	4	9	0	46
Greens	11	3	1	6	0	1	8	0	7	0	2	0	0	28
EDA	4	0	0	0	1	2	11	6	0	0	0	0	0	20
ER	3	1	0	3	0	0	10	0	0	0	0	0	0	14
LU	4	0	0	0	3	0	7	0	0	0	0	3	0	13
RBW	10	1	4	1	0	3	1	1	3	0	0	1	1	16
NA	7	0	1	3	2	5	0	1	7	0	1	0	1	21
Total	93	24	16	81	24	60	81	15	81	6	25	24	81	518

Key: SOC: Socialist Group; EPP: European People's Party; LIB: Liberal, Democratic, and Reformist Group; Greens: The Greens Group in the European Parliament; EDA: Group of the European Democratic Alliance; ER: Technical Group of the European Right; LU: Left Unity; RBW: Rainbow Group in the European Parliament; NA: Non-attached

a. As of January 1993

Source: European Parliament

the neo-Fascists (European Right) at opposite extremes. The Socialist Group is squarely on the left; the Liberals and the Christian Democrats are right of center; and the European Democratic Alliance (mostly Gaullists) are squarely on the right. Because these are "catch-all" groups, some include political parties that could be placed elsewhere, although not far away, on the political spectrum.

It is difficult to place the Rainbow Group and the Greens on the political spectrum. Fulvio Attina, an Italian political scientist who specializes in European party politics, excludes them from the political spectrum because most parties in both groups defy conventional ideological categorization. Whereas some of the Greens' parties are definitely on the left, most are not, and almost all the Rainbow Group's parties are organized on regional lines and lack a particular ideological orientation.[13]

With six political groups spanning the political spectrum and two organized along regional and ecological lines, the political group system in the European Parliament resembles the political party system in national parliaments. Moreover, two of the European Parliament's political groups (the Socialists and Christian Democrats) are substantially larger than the others and are on opposite sides of the left-right divide, although the political group system is by no means rigidly bipolar. More often than not, both groups collaborate in order to form majorities for or against specific legislative proposals. Unlike in most national legislatures, however, the purpose of political groups in the European Parliament is not to form or support a government. Not only do political groups lack that competitive rationale, they also have a mutual interest in collaborating with each other to promote the EP's institutional agenda.

A "tacit agreement"[14] between the Socialists and the EPP to alternate the presidency of the Parliament during the 1989–1994 session demonstrates the extent of their collaboration. MEPs elect a new president every two and a half years, immediately after direct elections and halfway through the EP's five-year term. In July 1989 the EPP supported the candidacy of Enrique Baron Crespo, a Spanish Socialist, who easily won. Although larger than the EPP, the Socialists reciprocated in January 1992 and supported the candidacy of Egon Klepsch, a German Christian Democrat. The Socialist-EPP alliance demonstrates the dissimilarity between the European Parliament and national parliaments, despite MEPs' emulation of the latter.

The role of "intergroups" also illustrates the inherent weakness of the political group system, in marked contrast to the political party system at the national level. As the name implies, intergroups consist of MEPs from a variety of political groups who share a common interest. Intergroups range in subject matter from specific issues (such as apartheid in South Africa) to broad themes (such as disarmament). Altiero Spinelli's Crocodile Club, an informal association of federalist MEPs that led to the founding of the Committee on Institutional Affairs and subsequently to the 1984 "Draft Treaty on European Union," is Parliament's best-known intergroup. In 1986 the Crocodile Club formally became the Federalist Intergroup for European Union. Francis Jacobs and Richard Corbett estimate that there are about fifty intergroups in the third directly elected Parliament.[15]

Intergroups serve a useful social and political purpose. By linking members of different political groups, they help to build broad support for important initiatives and proposals. Yet their existence, or at least the existence of the overtly political intergroups, highlights a relative lack of party group discipline and emphasizes the difference between the national parliamentary and the European Parliament systems.

If the European Parliament becomes more powerful and influential, political groups may form the basis of Community-wide parties at the European level. Since its formation before the first direct elections, the EPP has seen itself as a political party, not simply a group of parties. The Socialist and the Liberal groups—the Confederation of Socialist Parties of the European Community, and the Federation of Liberal, Democratic and Reformist Parties, respectively—serve as umbrella organizations for their constituent political parties. Neither aspires to become a transnational party, but each provides an infrastructure for increasing cooperation between national political parties whose MEPs sit in the same group.

In keeping with its federalist thrust, the Maastricht Treaty (Article 138a) recognized that "political parties at the European level are important as a factor for integration within the Union. They contribute to forming a European awareness and to expressing the political will of the citizens of the Union." Thus, Community-wide party organizations would reflect the federal structure of the emerging European Union. Moreover, the treaty's implicit encouragement of transnational political parties is linked to its concept of Union citizenship and extension of voting rights in local and European elections to Union citizens resident in a Community country other than their own. Party activity at the European level would make it easier for Union citizens throughout the Community, regardless of their national origin, to participate in European elections.

The next round of Community enlargement will increase the number of seats in the European Parliament and alter the composition of political groups. Both of the main political groups are likely to benefit most from an influx of new MEPs from Austria and the Scandinavian countries. The impact of Scandinavian enlargement will affect more than simply the size of political groups, however. Like their Danish counterparts, Scandinavian parliamentarians are known for their assertion of legislative authority. The accession of countries with strong national legislatures and the addition of aggressive MEPs could change the dynamic of national parliament–European Parliament relations and of interinstitutional relations in the Community.

THE EP IN THE COMMUNITY SYSTEM

Whatever else may be said of it, the European Parliament cannot be dismissed as a "windy debating chamber." MEPs spend only one week—in effect, three days—each month in full plenary sessions. Plenary sessions include agenda setting, voting, question time with or without debate, speeches by commissioners or the Council presidency, discussions of emergency issues, and debates on general topics. Speaking time is carefully parceled out to political groups and independent MEPs and strictly controlled—usually by the simple stratagem of turning off the microphone. MEPs rarely have an opportunity to prattle on. Moreover, some continental political cultures discourage intense parliamentary exchanges. British MEPs, whose domestic political system thrives on fierce debate, find Europarliamentary discussions disappointingly tame.

Apart from procedural problems and cultural differences, language is another obstacle to purposeful debate. Few MEPs are fluent in a second Community language. Thus, the Community's nine official languages (providing seventy-two linguistic combinations for simultaneous interpretation) are always used in Strasbourg. An anthropologist who observed the European Parliament in action was struck most by "the amputation that political speech undergoes during interpretation. . . . To make oneself understood through the interpreter, one must be brief and simplify one's language to the maximum—there is room neither for rhetoric, nor for wit. And despite all this, the message sometimes doesn't get through." The costs of interpreting and translating are exorbitant, accounting for nearly one-third of Parliament's total staff and about 30 percent of its annual budget.[16] In the anthropologist's opinion, "the inability to choose a single headquarters for the European Parliament is echoed by the impossibility of finding a common language."[17]

Despite those constraints, debates are an important part of the legislative process in Parliament and an opportunity for it to try to raise awareness and consciousness throughout the Community of certain important issues. For instance, the European Parliament prides itself on its advocacy of human rights, always one of the five areas selected each month for urgent debate in plenary. Parliament's new Committee on Foreign Affairs and Security (successor to the influential Political Affairs Committee) monitors human rights in third countries with the assistance of a special human rights unit. The committee's annual report on human rights forms the basis of a major parliamentary debate.

The formation of a foreign affairs and security committee indicates the Community's increasing competence in external relations and Parliament's determination to become fully involved in that field. Parliament's role in the post-Maastricht CFSP builds on its involvement in EPC. When they signed the SEA in 1986, foreign ministers set out details of the EP's role in EPC. As a result, the old Political Affairs Committee regularly discussed foreign policy issues, held a special colloquy four times a year with the Council president on EPC, and organized meetings between its leadership and the political directors of national foreign ministries. In addition, plenary sessions included a short period for EPC-related questions to the Council president and Community foreign ministers.[18]

Article J.7 of the Maastricht Treaty stipulates that "the Presidency shall consult the European Parliament on the main aspects and the basic choices of the common foreign and security policy and shall ensure that the views of the European Parliament are duly taken into consideration." The Committee on Foreign Affairs and Security will play a key intermediary role between the Council presidency and Commission on the one hand and Parliament on the other. Parliament will continue to quiz the Council presidency on foreign policy issues and, under the terms of the Maastricht Treaty, "will hold an annual debate on progress in implementing the common foreign and security policy."

Parliament is coequal with the Council in an important foreign policy sphere: Community enlargement and association with third countries. Under the assent procedure introduced by the SEA, an absolute majority of MEPs must approve accession and association agreements. Initially, this seemed a small concession to Parliament: In 1986, after the third enlargement, the Community's boundaries looked set for several years to come. Nor did a new series of association agreements appear imminent. Yet the single market's success and the Cold War's sudden end gave rise to a new round of accession negotiations and association agreements. Moreover, the assent procedure covers revisions or additions to existing association agreements, such as financial protocols. In the late 1980s, Parliament twice used the assent procedure to promote human rights by blocking protocols to the Turkish and Israeli association agreements. In January 1992, Parliament blocked 468 million ECU worth of aid to Morocco and 140 million ECU worth of aid to Syria on human rights grounds.[19]

The Maastricht Treaty extended the assent procedure to all international agreements that set up institutions, have major financial implications, or require legislation under co-decision. The treaty also introduced the assent procedure into a number of internal Community affairs such as creation of a uniform electoral procedure, adoption of provisions for Union citizenship residency rights, and the use of structural funds.

On other internal matters, Parliament has a variety of powers and responsibilities. Members may submit written and oral questions as a limited means of parliamentary supervision over the Council and Commission. Additional supervisory powers conferred on Parliament by the EEC treaty range from the innocuous (discussion of the Commission's *Annual*

General Report) to the vigorous (ability to force the Commission to resign as a body by a two-thirds majority). Fearful of provoking a major political crisis beyond its control, Parliament has never adopted a motion of censure against the Commission.

Although the EEC treaty did not give Parliament a role in appointing the Commission, since 1981 Parliament has voted on the investiture of the newly appointed Commission. The Maastricht Treaty obliges the member states to consult Parliament before nominating the Commission president and requires a vote of approval by Parliament of the full Commission.

Apart from limited supervisory powers, Parliament has extensive budgetary and legislative authority.

Budgetary Powers

Parliaments have the "power of the purse" in liberal democratic regimes. Inspired by that analogy but reluctant to cede too much authority, in the early 1970s the member states gave Parliament considerable budgetary power when the Community acquired its own resources and became independent of national financial contributions. As a result of amendments to the Treaty of Rome in April 1970 and July 1975, Parliament and the Council constituted the Community's "budgetary authority," sharing responsibility for Community spending but not for raising revenue. Inevitably, the relationship between the two branches of the budgetary authority was far from harmonious: Parliament rejected the budget in 1979 and 1984 and continually tried to increase the size of "noncompulsory expenditure" (spending over which the Community has some discretion—for instance, the Regional Fund and social fund—and for which Parliament has the power to make budgetary amendments).

Because of the likelihood of budgetary disputes between them, Parliament and the Council established a conciliation procedure as early as 1971. The procedure involves biannual Council-Parliament meetings, first when the Council prepares to adopt the draft budget, and later when the Council is about to decide on Parliament's proposed amendments. In addition, the Council president, the budget committee chair, and the budget commissioner hold "budgetary cooperation meetings" in December, during the plenary session at which Parliament adopts the budget.

In 1975 Parliament and the Council extended such cooperation to incorporate legislation with financial implications. The procedure involves a joint Parliament-Council "conciliation committee," in which the Commission participates and tries to broker a settlement. Conciliation committees are increasingly common, but because they are interinstitutional rather than constitutional devices, Parliament loses political leverage. The Council, after all, has ultimate legislative responsibility. Perhaps because of the conciliation procedure's failings, the member states did not include it in the extension of Parliament's legislative power under the SEA. Yet six years later they provided for a conciliation committee in the Maastricht Treaty's new co-decision procedure to give Parliament greater legislative authority. According to the 1993 Prag Report, Parliament strongly supports using conciliation in the legislative process and would like to have it extended to the cooperation procedure.

The budgetary cooperation procedure did not prevent the Council and Parliament from clashing repeatedly in the 1970s and 1980s. Parliament's main concerns were to curb agricultural expenditure and increase spending on other policy areas, notably structural funds and development assistance. Only in 1988, as a result of the Delors I package and ensuing interinstitutional agreement, did the Council-Parliament budgetary relationship improve. The 1988 reform curbed spending on agriculture and substantially increased expenditure to promote "economic and social cohesion" through the structural funds. It also set a high annual ceiling (expressed in terms of Community GNP) for the Community's budget for 1988–1992 and held appropriations for expenditure over the five-year period below those ceilings.[20]

The new financial framework removed much of the rancor from the annual budgetary procedure. Significantly, Parliament and the Council completed the 1989 budget on time, without a major dispute. The Community never ran over budget during the lifetime of the 1988 interinstitutional agreement, despite the financial consequences of the revolution in Eastern Europe and the Gulf War. The positive impact of Delors I generated momentum for Delors II, although the adverse economic climate of the early 1990s strengthened opposition in the Community's northern countries to a large cohesion fund for the southern member states. In the event, acceptance of the Delors II package at the December 1992 Edinburgh summit owed as much to the success of the 1988 budgetary reform as to the inherent importance of the additional expenditures needed to move "from the Single Act to Maastricht and beyond."[21]

Based on a 1975 agreement that became operational in 1977, Parliament has exclusive authority to grant a "discharge" of the general budget. This is the only budgetary power vested solely in the EP. The purpose of granting a discharge is to verify the accuracy of the Commission's budgetary management and to determine precise revenue and expenditure for a given year. The discharge procedure is time consuming and demanding and involves close cooperation with the Court of Auditors. Parliament usually votes on the issue two years after the budget in question. For instance, in November 1992 Parliament granted a discharge to the Commission with respect to the 1990 budget.[22]

The political implications of Parliament's exclusive power to grant a discharge are considerable. Since 1977, Parliament has used that power to improve its institutional position and to pressure the Commission.

According to a leading expert on the Community's public finances, "the political nature of Parliament's action in the exercise of its power to grant discharge has increased each year to the detriment of the budgetary and accounting aspects, which have become increasingly subordinate."[23] Indeed, Parliament sees the discharge procedure as a potential means of censuring the Commission. At a plenary session of Parliament in July 1979, the budget commissioner opined that refusal to grant a discharge would be "a political sanction . . . an event of exceptional seriousness . . . [that] would have to lead to the dismissal of the existing [Commission] team. I venture to think that we shall never reach that point."[24] Yet five years later, in November 1984, Parliament refused a discharge of the 1982 budget as a means of censuring the Thorn Commission. A political crisis was averted only by the imminent departure of the Thorn Commission and its replacement by the first Delors Commission. Parliament finally granted a discharge for the 1982 budget in March 1985.

Since the early 1970s, especially since direct elections in 1979, Parliament has successfully used its budgetary powers of establishment and implementation to enhance its institutional standing. But Parliament's political maneuvering should be put in perspective by keeping in mind the small size of the Community's budget. Devoid of responsibility for such big-ticket items as health, social security, defense, and education, the Community's public finances are puny in comparison with those of a nation-state. It may be argued that this is a major factor preventing the emergence of a strong European Parliament. The EP may have acquired some budgetary authority, but as long as the budget remains relatively insignificant and Parliament cannot raise any revenue its power will remain correspondingly weak. As David Coombes has observed, "the history of representative government in Europe and elsewhere suggests that the Community's weakness in public finance" is an important reason for "its failure to develop [strong] parliamentary institutions."[25]

Legislative Powers

Parliament's relatively limited legislative authority testifies to its institutional weakness vis-à-vis the Commission and especially vis-à-vis the Council. Nevertheless, in the legislative field, as in the budgetary field, Parliament has successfully struggled to acquire greater powers. Parliament does not have the right to initiate legislation, although the Maastricht Treaty formally gave it the same authority the Council has to request that the Commission submit legislative proposals. Instead, Parliament has considerable ability to shape legislation once the Commission submits a proposal. Parliament exercises those powers through three legislative procedures: consultation, cooperation, and co-decision.

Consultation Procedure

This procedure gives Parliament the right to submit a nonbinding opinion before the Council adopts a Commission proposal. The EEC treaty designated twenty-two articles under which the Council could not enact legislation without first consulting Parliament. Article 149 of the EEC treaty outlines the consultation procedure:

- Step 1 The Commission submits a proposal to the Council, which asks the EP for its opinion.
- Step 2 Parliament gives its opinion (no time limit).
- Step 3 The Commission may amend its proposal on the basis of Parliament's opinion but is not obliged to do so.
- Step 4 On the basis of unanimity or qualified majority voting, the Council may adopt the (amended) proposal or may by unanimity amend the (amended) proposal. If it fails to reach agreement, the proposal stays on the table, sometimes indefinitely.

Initially, the consultation procedure appeared to give Parliament no more of a legislative role than that of the advisory Economic and Social Committee. However, the Treaty did not place a time limit on Parliament's obligation to submit an opinion. In a landmark decision in 1980 (the Isoglucose case), the Court of Justice annulled a legislative act because Parliament had not yet given its opinion in an area covered by the Treaty's consultation procedure. The Council had violated the Treaty by acting without a parliamentary opinion, which, the Court claimed, represented "a fundamental principle that the people should take part in the exercise of power through the intermediary of a representative assembly."[26]

Earlier, in the 1960s and 1970s, the Council and Commission had developed the practice of "nonmandatory consultation." The Commission agreed to adopt EP amendments whenever possible and submit them to the Council, just as it would under the mandatory consultation procedure stipulated in the Treaty of Rome. The Council and Commission also agreed to explain in detail to Parliament their reasons for not adopting amendments proposed by Parliament.

The development of nonmandatory consultation suggested a harmonious legislative relationship between the Council, Commission, and Parliament. If such harmony ever existed, the Isoglucose case soon brought it to an end. The Council of Ministers argued in the Isoglucose case that it had waited for a parliamentary opinion but that Parliament had procrastinated. Parliament counterargued that the Council had proceeded peremptorily. Regardless of what happened, the Court's ruling gave Parliament de facto delaying power over legislation subject to the consultation procedure.

The first directly elected Parliament quickly changed its rules to make the most of the Court's decision. Since then, Parliament's strategy has been to vote on amendments to a proposal and then, before preparing a formal opinion by voting on the resolution as a whole, to try to get the Commission to accept the amendments. Even if the Commission agrees, there is no guarantee that the Council will approve the amended proposal. Clearly, the degree of parliamentary leverage over the Council depends on how badly the Council wants a particular piece of legislation.

For its part, the Council rarely explained adequately why it rejected parliamentary amendments, and in cases where legislative action was not pressing, it resorted to taking decisions "subject to Parliament's opinion." By taking decisions "in principle," before Parliament had delivered an opinion, the Council signaled its intention to ignore Parliament's point of view.[27] This resulted not only in legislative stalemate but also in a serious deterioration of Council-Parliament relations.

By radically revising the Community's decisionmaking procedures, the SEA and Maastricht Treaty have changed the legislative applicability of consultation. Under the Maastricht Treaty, the consultation procedure applies in the following areas:

- New or strengthened rights in the area of citizenship (Article 8a, 8b, 8d, 8e)
- Certain aspects of transport policy (Article 75.3)
- Application of rules on state aid (Article 94)
- Fiscal harmonization (Article 99)
- Approximation of laws (Article 100)
- Uniform format for visas (Article 100c.3)
- Certain aspects of economic and monetary policy (Articles 104c14; 106.6; 109.1; 109a.2b; 109f.1; 109f.7; 109j.2; 109j.4, and 109k.2)
- Industry (Article 130)
- Economic and social cohesion: the adoption of specific actions outside the Structural Funds (Article 130b)
- Community budget (Articles 201; 209)
- Common Foreign and Security Policy (Article J.7)
- Justice and home affairs: principal activities in the areas covered in this title (Article J.7);
- Amendment of the treaties (Article N).

The consultation procedure will operate differently for the CFSP and for cooperation in the sphere of justice and internal affairs. The Council president will consult Parliament on the main aspects and basic choices of policy and will "ensure" that Parliament's opinions are taken into account. The Council presidency and the Commission will be responsible for keeping Parliament informed of developments in CFSP and of discussions on justice and home affairs issues. In both areas, Parliament will have the right to put questions or make recommendations to the Council and hold annual debates on progress in implementing policy in both spheres.

Cooperation Procedure

The SEA sought to increase Parliament's legislative power and to improve the efficiency of Community decisionmaking. It did so by giving Parliament the right to have a second reading of certain draft legislation and by extending the use of qualified majority voting in the Council of Ministers. The cooperation procedure incorporated both measures and formed "the institutional core of the SEA."[28] Originally the new procedure applied to ten Treaty of Rome articles, most dealing with the single market program; the Maastricht Treaty extended its use to fourteen policy areas.

The bewildering array of options in the cooperation procedure revolutionized Parliament's legislative role and introduced a new dimension into Community decisionmaking. Although unhappy with the new procedure's limited scope, Parliament resolved from the outset to realize the SEA's political and institutional potential. In December 1986 Parliament radically revised its rules to make the most of the cooperation procedure. It especially appreciated the importance of the first reading, using it to apprise the Council of its intentions and to begin to build the coalition required to amend, or possibly reject, a common position. For its part, the Council sought to avoid major parliamentary amendments and, especially, outright rejection of its common position, which it could only counter by an often unobtainable unanimous vote. Finally, the cooperation procedure cast the Commission in the role of arbitrator between the Council and Parliament.

The cooperation procedure had a profound impact on political group behavior in the European Parliament. Parliament could only amend or reject a common position by a vote of 260 or more (an absolute majority of MEPs), and only political groups could organize MEPs and muster the required number of votes. On ideological issues, either the Socialists or the Christian Democrats form the core of a parliamentary majority, vying for the support of groups in the center. Whereas the Socialists can usually depend on support from the far left, the Christian Democrats dislike having to depend on support from the far right. When issues are not contested along ideological lines, the two major political groups often collaborate in amending or rejecting a common position, not only to improve draft legislation but also to promote Parliament's institutional position.

The increasing importance of majority voting has instilled in political groups a greater sense of identity and cohesion and enhanced consensus and coalition building between them. Nevertheless, political group discipline is extremely lax by the standards of national parliaments, where

Table 9.4 The Cooperation Procedure

Article 149 of the EEC treaty, amended by Article 7 of the SEA, outlines the cooperation procedure:

Step 1 The Commission submits a proposal to the Council, which asks the EP for its opinion.

Step 2 Parliament gives its opinion (no time limit).

Step 3 The Commission may amend its proposal on the basis of Parliament's opinion but is not obliged to do so.

Step 4 On the basis of unanimity or qualified majority voting, the Council may adopt the (amended) proposal or may by unanimity amend the (amended) proposal. The Council's decision becomes its "common position."

Step 5 Parliament has three months (may be extended to four months) to consider the common position, during which it may

(A) accept the common position (by an absolute majority of votes cast, not an absolute majority of MEPs) or fail to act. In either case, the Council adopts the act in accordance with the common position.

(B) reject the common position (by an absolute majority of MEPs, not an absolute majority of votes cast), in which case the Council has three months to overrule the rejection unanimously.

(C) Propose amendments to the common position (by an absolute majority of MEPs, not an absolute majority of votes cast), in which case

(C1) if the Commission supports Parliament's amendment, the Council has three months to overrule the amended proposal unanimously, to accept it by qualified majority voting, or to take no action and let the proposed legislation lapse.

(C2) if the Commission does not support Parliament's amendment, the Council may adopt the proposal unanimously or adopt the act in accordance with its common position.

a government's survival may depend on fierce party loyalty. In addition, the heterogeneity and cultural diversity of political groups militates against strict control of members' behavior. Most important, "one must never underestimate the fact that [MEPs] always consider themselves as representatives of national interests."[29] Consequently, when pressed, MEPs will vote along regional or national rather than ideological or political group lines.

The cooperation procedure also resulted in a profusion of lobbying at the European Parliament. Before the SEA, lobbyists had little reason to cultivate the favor of MEPs. Afterward, when Parliament acquired more power and MEPs became proficient at using the cooperation procedure, lobbyists seized the opportunity to shape legislation through amendments. In many cases, lobbyists alerted MEPs to the cooperation procedure's potential and provided them with information about impending legislation that their small staffs were often otherwise unable to obtain. Given the strength of MEPs' commitments to their own countries, industries and interest groups frequently organize lobbies along national lines, at least for the larger delegations.

Lobbyists cover committee meetings in Brussels and flock to Strasbourg for plenary sessions of Parliament. *Euroconfidentiel Annuaire 1992,* a private publication providing information on the European Community, lists 289 Community lobbyists; a widely held estimate puts the number closer to 2,000. The exact figure is unknown because, until recently, the Community made no effort to regulate lobbying. The situation began to change in 1991, when the Commission and Parliament grew increasingly concerned about the profusion of lobbyists in Brussels and Strasbourg. The Commission's *Program for 1992* declared that "relations between the Community's institutions and interest groups, useful though they may be, must be more clearly defined"[30] and referred to efforts in the European Parliament to develop both a register and a code of conduct for Eurolobbyists. Those efforts culminated in a report by Marc Galle, a French MEP, which the Parliament's Procedural Committee adopted on October 2, 1992.[31] The Commission is likely to emulate Parliament's action by taking similar steps to control consultants in Brussels.

At least the escalation of lobbying in the European Parliament attests to the cooperation procedure's apparent success. Of the 259 acts adopted under the cooperation procedure between implementation of the SEA and the end of September 1992, the Council accepted 44 percent of Parliament's first-reading amendments and 26 percent of its second-reading amendments.[32] Although those figures suggest that Parliament is having a considerable impact on Community decisionmaking, it is impossible to judge from them an amendment's political importance.

Parliament and the Commission are generally pleased with the cooperation procedure. According to the January 1993 Prag Report, it "transformed the role of Parliament in . . . limited though vital fields, and introduced a degree of democratic control over the establishment of a single market by the end of 1992." Nevertheless, the report identified three major defects in the procedure: its limited scope (despite the Maastricht Treaty changes), the Council's ability to "kill legislation by default," and the Council's "right to adopt legislation in face of Parliament's rejection of all or parts of it."[33] The Commission also sees the procedure's shortcomings but appreciates the progress made in Community decisionmaking since 1987. Joao de Deus Pinhero, the commissioner responsible for relations with Parliament, remarked in January 1993 that the cooperation procedure "had worked during a period of intense legislative activity," proving that "democracy and efficiency are compatible."[34]

The Council of Ministers is least enamored of the cooperation procedure, seeing it as an opportunity for Parliament to promote its institutional agenda at the expense of effective decisionmaking. Although the procedure requires close interinstitutional collaboration to work properly, the Council tends to remain aloof. For instance, Parliament persistently complains that the Council refuses to explain fully its reasons for rejecting parliamentary amendments. The Prag Report called on the Council to reveal "the results of the votes [on common positions] in the Council and the views of each Member State, enabling the peoples and parliaments of the Community to form a view of their governments' position."

Disputes between the Council and Parliament over the cooperation procedure focus mostly on the choice of "legal base," the relevant Treaty article on which the Community bases its legislative action. If the legal base is ambiguous, Parliament invariably opts for an article that stipulates the cooperation procedure, whereas the Council chooses the consultation procedure in order to avoid a second reading. Until the Maastricht Treaty, environmental issues lent themselves to great ambiguity because the SEA extended Community competence to environmental policy (Article 130s) subject to the *consultation* procedure but also introduced a new article for the harmonization of national standards (Article 100a) subject to the *cooperation* procedure. Thus, for certain environmental legislation, the Council favored Article 130s as a legal base, whereas Parliament preferred Article 100a. Although the Maastricht Treaty made environmental policy subject to the cooperation procedure, there is plenty of scope elsewhere for disagreement between the Council and Parliament over the choice of legal base, not least because of the post-Maastricht co-decision option.

As well as introducing a new legislative procedure, the Maastricht Treaty incorporated the cooperation procedure into a new article (189c), unchanged from its SEA formulation. Although Maastricht switched some policy areas from cooperation to the new co-decision procedure, it also switched a number of others from consultation to cooperation. As a result, the cooperation procedure will cover fourteen policy areas, making it the most important legislative procedure used in Community decisionmaking.

The cooperation procedure (described in the text of the treaty as "the procedure referred to in Article 189c") applies to the following areas:

- Discrimination on nationality grounds (Article 6.2)
- Transport policy (Article 75.1)
- Certain aspects of economic and monetary policy (Articles 103.5; 104a.2; 104b.2; 105a.2)
- European Social Fund (Article 125)
- Vocational training (Article 127.4)
- Trans-European networks (Article 129d)
- Economic and social cohesion—i.e., implementation of decisions relating to the European Regional Development Fund (Article 130e);

- Aspects of environment policy (Article 130s.1)
- Development cooperation (Article 130w.1)

Co-decision Procedure

The European Parliament regards the cooperation procedure as "part of a preparatory stage in the introduction of genuine co-decision."[35] "Genuine co-decision" means endowing Parliament with legislative power equal to that of the Council. However, the form of co-decision introduced by the Maastricht Treaty disappointed Parliament, which received only a limited right of rejection rather than a positive right of approval.

The new co-decision procedure is extremely complicated (see Table 9.5). It gives Parliament the right to a third reading and establishes a conciliation committee in which the Council and Parliament, with the Commission's assistance, attempt to reach agreement on draft legislation.

Described in the Maastricht Treaty as "the procedure referred to in Article 189b," co-decision will apply in the following areas:

- Free movement of persons (Article 49)
- Right of establishment (Articles 54.2; 56.2; 57)
- Internal market (Article 100a)
- Education (Article 126)
- Culture (Article 128)
- Public health (Article 129)
- Consumer protection (Article 129a)
- Trans-European networks (Article 129d)
- Research and technological development (Article 130i)
- Environmental action programs (Article 130s)

Co-decision could be a protracted as well as a complicated process. However, Parliament's experience with the cooperation procedure suggests that it will also master co-decision. As with the cooperation procedure in the post-SEA period, Parliament's ability to exploit co-decision after Maastricht will depend on how it organizes its time and rewrites its rules. Accordingly, the role of committees and plenary sessions will become more important than ever before.

INTERNAL ORGANIZATION

Parliament carries out its supervisory, budgetary, legislative, and other responsibilities through an elaborate leadership structure, a strong committee system, and frenzied plenary sessions.

Table 9.5 The Co-decision Procedure

Step 1   The Commission submits a proposal to the Council, which asks the EP for its opinion.

Step 2   Parliament gives its opinion (no time limit).

Step 3   The Commission may amend its proposal on the basis of Parliament's opinion but is not obliged to do so.

Step 4   On the basis of unanimity or qualified majority voting, the Council may adopt the (amended) proposal. The Council's decision becomes its "common position."

Step 5   Parliament has three months (may be extended to four months) to consider the common position, during which it may

         (A) accept the common position (by an absolute majority of votes cast, not an absolute majority of MEPs) or fail to act. In either case, the Council adopts the act in accordance with its common position.

         (B) indicate (by an absolute majority of MEPs, not by an absolute majority of votes cast) that it intends to reject the common position, in which case the Council may convene a meeting of the conciliation committee (see Step 7). By an absolute majority of MEPs, Parliament may confirm its rejection, in which case the act is not adopted.

         (C) propose amendments to the common position (by an absolute majority of MEPs, not an absolute majority of votes cast).

Step 6   The Council has three months (may be extended to four months) to consider Parliament's amendments and may

         (A) accept the amendments by qualified majority, amend its common position accordingly, and adopt the act.

         (B) accept the amendments unanimously if the Commission did not endorse them.

         (C) if the Commission did not endorse the amendments proposed by Parliament, confirm its common position and adopt it by qualified majority.

         If the Council cannot muster the necessary majority to adopt the act, the Council president may, in agreement with the EP president, convene a meeting of the conciliation committee.

Step 7   An equal number of Council members (or their representatives) and MEPs will make up the conciliation committee and try to reach agreement on a joint text. In the case of the Council, decisions in the conciliation committee will be taken by a majority vote, and in the case of Parliament by a majority of its members. The Commission will help to reconcile the positions of the Council and the Parliament.

         The conciliation committee has six weeks (may be extended by two weeks) to examine a text. If both sides reach agreement, the joint text is forwarded to Parliament and the Council.

Step 8   Parliament has a further six weeks (may be extended by two weeks) to adopt the text by an absolute majority of votes cast; the Council also has six weeks (may be extended by two weeks) to adopt the text by qualified majority. If one of the two institutions fails to approve the text, it cannot be adopted, and the legislation falls.

Step 9   If the conciliation committee does not approve a joint text, the proposal cannot be adopted. However, within six weeks (may be extended by two weeks) of the expiration of the period within which the conciliation committee meets, the Council may go back to the common position it agreed upon before the beginning of the conciliation procedure and adopt the act by qualified majority. In so doing it may decide to accept some of the amendments suggested by Parliament in the conciliation committee.

Step 10   Within six weeks (may be extended by two weeks) of this decision, Parliament may overturn it by an absolute majority of MEPs. In that case, the legislation falls.

Leadership Structure

Parliament's leadership consists of a president and fourteen vice presidents (who form the "Bureau"), the political group bosses (who together with the president and vice presidents form the "Enlarged Bureau"), and five "quaestors." All are elected positions. As with the presidency, elections for the other offices take place every two and a half years, at the beginning and in the middle of Parliament's five-year term.

The most recent elections took place in January 1992, in the immediate aftermath of the Maastricht summit. Because of a pact between the Socialists and Christian Democrats, Egon Klepsch, the Christian Democrats' leader, easily won the presidential election. Klepsch replaced Enrique Baron Crespo, a Spanish Socialist whose presidency was undistinguished. Unlike Crespo, Klepsch is a serious politician interested primarily in internal parliamentary reform. Nevertheless, Klepsch has a mixed reputation—he did not excel as a deputy in the German Parliament before deciding to become a full-time MEP in 1979, and in 1981 he reportedly voted in the European Parliament for an absent party colleague (since then, in Eurospeak the verb "to Klepsch" has meant to vote early and often). However, Klepsch knows Parliament and its procedures exceedingly well (having been an MEP for nearly fifteen years), is a consummate deal maker (an important attribute in a Parliament that needs at least 260 votes to amend or reject proposals under the co-decision procedure), and is close to Chancellor Kohl (a potential advantage during interinstitutional bargaining).

The outcome of the presidential election determines the outcome of the elections for other leadership positions (except for political group leaders, who are elected by political group members)—although such elections are supposedly open, the political groups decide between them who gets what. The leadership's composition generally reflects the distribution of seats in Parliament by political group and nationality. The results of the January 1992 elections are given in Table 9.6.

The responsibilities of the president and vice presidents—individually, in the Bureau, and (together with the political group leaders) in the Enlarged Bureau—are as follows:

- The *president* presides over plenary sessions, chairs meetings of the Bureau and Enlarged Bureau, represents Parliament at interinstitutional meetings, represents Parliament at the European Council, and signs the budget into law.
- *Vice presidents* preside over plenary sessions when the president is absent and participate in the Bureau and Enlarged Bureau.
- The *Bureau* makes important personnel decisions and budgetary proposals.

Table 9.6 EP Leadership

	Name	Political Group	Member State
President	Egon Klepsch	EPP	Germany
Vice Presidents	Nicole Pery	SOC	France
	Nicole Fontaine	EPP	France
	Roberto Barzanti	SOC	Italy
	Hans Peters	SOC	Germany
	Joao Cravinho	SOC	Portugal
	Georgios Anastassopoulos	EPP	Greece
	Georgios Romeos	SOC	Greece
	Antonio Capucho	LIB	Portugal
	Nicolas Estgen	EPP	Luxembourg
	Maria Magnani Noya	SOC	Italy
	Josep Verde Aldea	SOC	Spain
	Anne Marie Isler-Beguin	Greens	France
	David Martin	SOC	UK
	Jack Stewart-Clark	EPP	UK
Quaestors	Anthony Simpson	EPP	UK
	Mel Read	SOC	UK
	Domenec Romera I Alcazar	EPP	Spain
	Manuel Porto	LIB	Portugal
	Andrea Raggio	SOC	Italy

Key: EPP: European People's Party; LIB: Liberal, Democratic, and Reformist Group; SOC: Socialist Group

- The *Enlarged Bureau* decides the agenda for plenary sessions; discusses the annual legislative program, interinstitutional relations, and relations with non-Community institutions; and manages the committee system.
- *Quaestors* make administrative and financial decisions that directly affect MEPs.

The Bureau, Enlarged Bureau, and quaestors meet approximately twice a month in Strasbourg during the plenary session and in Brussels during committee or political group meetings.

Committee System

The European Parliament could not manage its burgeoning budgetary, legislative, and nonlegislative agenda without an adequate committee system. Parliament's committee system evolved along with the Community, changing over the years to reflect the Community's increasing competence and

Parliament's growing assertiveness and responsibility. Parliament currently has nineteen committees covering every facet of Community activity. The most recent changes took place in January 1992 to coincide with the election of a new parliamentary leadership and with the conclusion of the intergovernmental conferences on EMU and EPU. As a result, Parliament has a renamed Political Affairs Committee (now the Committee on Foreign Affairs and Security) and a new Committee on Civil Liberties and Internal Affairs to deal with issues arising from the second and third pillars of the Maastricht Treaty.

Objectively, some committees are more important than others. For instance, the Environment Committee and the Committee on Budgetary Control are influential because Parliament exercises considerable power in those areas. The importance of the Budgets Committee (as distinct from the Committee on Budgetary Control) is undiminished despite the new interinstitutional arrangement for medium-term financial planning. Other committees, such as the Committee on Transport and Tourism, have always been unimportant.

A committee's popularity in Parliament is not necessarily related to its inherent importance, although popularity can enhance a committee's influence. The Environment Committee is popular with MEPs (it has fifty-one members) not only because Parliament has legislative authority in that area but also because environmental issues are in vogue. By contrast, the Committee on Budgetary Control, one of the most powerful in Parliament, deals with a complicated and colorless issue and thus has only twenty-five members. Foreign policy is as fashionable as environmental policy. Consequently, the new Committee on Foreign Affairs and Security has fifty-six members and a prominent chairman (Enrique Baron Crespo, Klepsch's immediate predecessor as president) but has only limited power. The Committee on Institutional Affairs has no real power either, yet it attracts MEPs (it has thirty-seven members) because of Altiero Spinelli's legacy and the committee's contribution to the 1984 "Draft Treaty on European Union."

Because there are more committee seats than there are MEPs, in a few cases MEPs sit on more than one committee. The leadership divides committee seats among political groups according to their strength in Parliament, and the groups in turn allocate committee seats to their members based on seniority, personal preference, and nationality. Certain political groups and nationalities have strong preferences for particular committee assignments. Obvious examples are the Greens (Environment, Energy) and the Irish (Agriculture, Regional Policy). Committee assignments are reallocated every two and a half years, and there is no time limit on an MEP's committee service.

Parliament designates two weeks each month for committee meetings. The frequency of each committee's meetings depends on the business

Table 9.7 EP Committees and Their Chairs

Committee (Number of Members)	Chair	Political Group	Member State
Foreign Affairs and Security (56)	Enrique Baron Crespo	SOC	Spain
Agriculture, Fisheries, and Rural Development (47)	Franco Borgo	EPP	Italy
Budgets (32)	Thomas von der Vring	SOC	Germany
Economic and Monetary Affairs and Industrial Policy (52)	Bourke Beumer	EPP	Netherlands
Energy, Research, and Technology (35)	Claude Desama	SOC	Belgium
External Economic Relations (29)	Willy de Clerq	LIB	Belgium
Legal Affairs and Citizens' Rights (34)	Franz Stauffenberg	EPP	Germany
Social Affairs, Employment, and the Working Environment (41)	Willem van Velzen	SOC	Netherlands
Regional Policy and Regional Planning (35)	Antoni Gutierrez Diaz	SOC	Spain
Transport and Tourism (30)	Nel van Dijk	Greens	Netherlands
Environment, Public Health, and Consumer Protection (51)	Ken Collins	SOC	UK
Culture, Education, Youth, and the Media (30)	Antonio la Pergola	SOC	Italy
Development and Cooperation (43)	Henri Saby	SOC	France
Civil Liberties and Internal Affairs (30)	Amedee Turner	EPP	UK
Budgetary Control (25)	Alan Lamassoure	EPP	France
Institutional Affairs (37)	Marcelino Oreja Aguirre	EPP	Spain
Rules of Procedure, the Verification of Credentials, and Immunities (25)	Florus Wijsenbeek	LIB	Netherlands
Women's Rights (30)	Christine Crawley	SOC	UK
Petitions (25)	Rosaria Bindi	EPP	Italy

Key: EPP: European People's Party; LIB: Liberal, Democratic, and Reformist Group; SOC: Socialist Group before it; most meet at least monthly. Committee meetings take place in Parliament's Brussels building, a complex of offices and conference rooms near Schuman Circle. Most meetings last the equivalent of one full day. Committee sizes range from twenty-five to fifty-six MEPs, although attendance at meetings can be sporadic. Meetings may be attended by officials of the Parliament, Council, and Commission, and occasionally by commissioners and council presidents, in addition to the MEPs themselves.

Given the smaller size and less formal nature of committee meetings, the language problem is not as formidable during committee meetings in Brussels as during plenary sessions in Strasbourg. Nevertheless, interpreters not only provide the essential service of making people mutually intelligible but also, because of the costs involved, ensure that meetings do not run overtime. Apart from paying for simultaneous interpretation, committees run up extra costs by producing documents in nine languages. Each step of the legislative process necessitates translation into each official language. The most striking sight on entering a committee meeting, regardless of the committee's size, is a mountain of documents immediately inside the door.

The committee leadership structure replicates Parliament's leadership structure: Each committee has a chair and three vice chairs, who form the Bureau. Each committee also has a coordinator, who marshals its members for key votes, and several *rapporteurs,* who draft its reports. Parliamentary reports are commonly known by the names of their *rapporteurs* (the Spinelli Report, the Martin Report, the Prag Report, etc.).

In the case of legislative proposals, committees do the preliminary work on which Parliament as a whole bases its decisions during plenary sessions. Before examining proposals in detail, committees verify the legal base in consultation with the Legal Affairs Committee. If proposals are subject to the cooperation procedure, *rapporteurs* follow the draft legislation's progress through the Council. Committee preparation of draft amendments gives interested parties an opportunity to influence legislation. Predictably, certain committees are a target of intense lobbying.

Despite Parliament's admonition of the Council for excessive secrecy, a number of committees routinely met in private as recently as 1992. In January of that year, when the committee system was last reorganized, Parliament decided to oblige all committees to vote on whether or not to hold unrestricted meetings. Even when committee meetings are open, however, it is difficult for the public to attend, because non-EC officials can only enter the building with special passes.

As well as maintaining standing committees, Parliament occasionally forms "committees of inquiry" and "temporary committees." Committees of inquiry investigate alleged breaches of Community law or instances of maladministration. The Maastricht Treaty confirmed Parliament's right to set up such committees (Article 138c). Parliament has established more formidable "temporary committees" to explore specific topical issues that could profoundly affect the Community. For instance, in 1990 it formed the twenty-five-member Temporary Committee on German Unification. Finally, standing committees sometimes organize "working parties" to examine specific issues within the committee's remit.

Plenary Sessions

Plenaries are the most visible and least flattering part of Parliament's existence. For a week each month (in reality, from 3:00 p.m. on Monday until 2:00 p.m. on Friday, although most MEPs leave on Thursday evening), parliamentarians participate in a full session of the entire assembly. Plenaries include debates, speeches by commissioners and the Council presidency, question time, and, most important, votes on legislative amendments and other resolutions. Outside the chamber itself (in Eurospeak, the "hemicycle") but within the cavernous Palace of Europe, in which plenaries take place, MEPs hold political group, intergroup, and occasional committee meetings; entertain constituents; and parry lobbyists (a corner of the concourse near the entrance to the hemicycle is appropriately called the "lobbyists' bench").[36]

    At plenaries, too much takes place in too short a time. Voting alone can occupy eight hours, despite a change of rules in January 1992 reducing the number of amendments (previously about one thousand per session) reaching the hemicycle. Such is the pressure of voting and the impossibility of knowing what each vote means that many MEPs simply stay away. Because amendments require at least 260 votes to pass, rampant absenteeism frequently causes important amendments to fail. No wonder President Klepsch has urged his fellow MEPs to "deal with technicalities in committee, and keep the plenaries for debating the big issues that people care about."[37]

    Even with a change of rules to cut down on voting during plenaries, the new co-decision procedure will increase Parliament's legislative workload. Additional plenary sessions are undoubtedly necessary, although in January 1993 Parliament rejected a proposal by Derek Prag, vice chairman of the Committee on Institutional Affairs, to hold additional sessions regularly, preferring instead to hold them only as needed.[38] However, the European Council's December 1992 decision to keep the Parliament in Strasbourg did include a provision permitting additional plenaries to take place in Brussels, where the EP has a brand-new hemicycle. The first Brussels plenary took place in September 1993.

Staff

MEPs have an allowance to hire staff, generally administrative assistants (often their own spouses). MEPs rely for policy and legislative assistance on their political group's staff. Staff size depends on the number of MEPs in each group. The Socialist Group has a staff of about fifty "A" grade officials and eighty-five assistants.[39] Committees have small staffs of their own to help *rapporteurs* draft and write reports, and large national delegations also have separate staffs funded by the political groups of the national political parties. Finally, Parliament has a secretariat, similar to the Council secretariat and Commission civil service, to provide support services ranging from research to public relations to translation and interpretation. As in other branches of the Community's civil service, promotion in the upper echelons of Parliament's secretariat is highly political and depends on ideological affinity as well as nationality.

Table 9.8 The EP Secretariat

Secretary-General	
Legal Service	
Directorate-General I	Sessional services
Directorate-General II	Committee and delegations
Directorate-General III	Information and public relations
Directorate-General IV	Research
Directorate-General V	Personnel, budget, and finance
Directorate-General VI	Administration
Directorate-General VII	Translation and general services

CLOSING THE DEMOCRATIC DEFICIT

David Martin, a vice president of the European Parliament, likes to point out that if the European Community was a state and it applied to join the EC, it would be turned down on the grounds that it was not a democracy.[40] Martin's comment highlights the "democratic deficit," which is not new in the Community's history but which has become increasingly noticeable since the mid-1980s.[41] In a narrow sense, the democratic deficit is the gap between the power of the Commission, Council of Ministers, and European Council on the one hand, and that of national parliaments and the European Parliament on the other. It results in part from the transfer of powers from member states to the European Community. Before the transfer, national parliaments held power to pass laws in the areas concerned, but at the Community level the same powers are often held by institutions other than the European Parliament. As the Community acquired greater competence, national parliaments relinquished power not to the European Parliament but to the Council of Ministers, European Commission, and European Council, all of which have considerable legislative *and* executive authority.

National parliaments lost legislative authority not only because the Community acquired new competences but also because in the early 1980s the Council of Ministers gradually abandoned unanimity in favor of qualified majority voting. The SEA incorporated qualified majority voting into much of the single market program, but the decline of unanimity meant the decline also of national parliaments' control over their governments. As long as a government could veto Community legislation, its national parliament could hold it accountable for exercising (or not exercising) that veto. Once governments subscribed to qualified majority voting, however, national parliaments could not reasonably hold them responsible for being outvoted and accepting the majority decision.

Before the SEA, few national parliaments ever paid much attention to Community decisionmaking. Denmark's was an exception. The Folketing's powerful Committee for Relations with the Common Market held government ministers strictly accountable for their behavior in the Council of Ministers and European Council. Denmark's parliament disliked the antidemocratic implications of qualified majority voting and voted down the SEA in 1986.

It was cold comfort for the Danish and other national parliaments that the European Parliament, which had always enjoyed limited legislative authority (the consultation procedure), gained additional power (the cooperation procedure) under the SEA to offset the extension of qualified majority voting. The European Parliament itself was unhappy with the cooperation procedure's relatively narrow scope, especially with the existence after the SEA of a number of policy areas subject to qualified majority voting but not subject to the cooperation procedure. As the Council of Ministers successfully implemented the single market program in the late 1980s, using qualified majority rule to great effect, the national parliaments and the European Parliament became increasingly alarmed by the widening democratic deficit.

MEPs have consistently proposed a predictable solution for the democratic deficit: giving the European Parliament more legislative, budgetary, and supervisory powers. But the member states' extension of the cooperation procedure and introduction of the co-decision procedure under the Maastricht Treaty did not go far enough to meet MEPs' demands. Moreover, Maastricht's expansion of the European Parliament's legislative authority increased national parliaments' estrangement from the Community's decisionmaking apparatus. Anticipating such a reaction and concerned about the democratic deficit, governments issued a call in the Maastricht Treaty for closer cooperation between the European Parliament and national parliaments.

Before direct elections, MEPs were also members of their national parliaments. Since then, the vast majority of MEPs have had little formal involvement with their national parliaments (the handful of MEPs still holding the dual mandate are an obvious exception). National MPs generally resent their European counterparts' lifestyles and posturing, and MEPs resent not being taken seriously by their national counterparts. Restoring the dual mandate is neither practical nor desirable, but closer contacts between MPs and MEPs are urgently needed.

Informal contact between MPs and MEPs usually takes place through the political groups and will become customary if European political parties emerge later in the 1990s. Formal institutional contacts between national parliaments and the European Parliament currently include:

- Conferences of presidents of parliamentary assemblies of the Community member states and the European Parliament
- Meetings between representatives of national parliamentary committees dealing with EC affairs and representatives of the European Parliament
- Conferences of MPs and MEPs (the so-called "assizes")

The first assize took place in Rome in November 1990, on the eve of the IGCs. Ratification of the Maastricht Treaty will lead to an increase in the frequency of interparliamentary assizes.

Regardless of institutionalized links with the European Parliament, national parliaments are likely to become more involved in Community affairs in the post-Maastricht period, despite their loss of legislative responsibility since the SEA. For instance, the German Parliament pressed the government successfully during the Maastricht ratification debate for the right to evaluate draft Community legislation. Also, the next round of enlargement will bring into the Community countries whose parliaments have strong traditions of involvement in foreign affairs and are unlikely to cede oversight of Community legislation. This change could have profound implications for the mechanics and the legitimacy of Community decisionmaking. Indeed, "the inclusion of national legislatures into the Community's policymaking process may prove to be absolutely necessary if the Community is to gain the support needed to create institutions capable of effective policymaking in the next century."[42]

Apart from the European Parliament's comparative weakness and the failure to date of national parliaments to become more involved in Community affairs, the democratic deficit means "the absence of a genuine European political culture and discussion of key policy matters outside of elite circles."[43] Writing in 1991 during the IGCs, two British academics commented presciently that "the shortcomings of the Community lie in the feelings of remoteness and lack of influence and involvement on the part of many of its citizens."[44] Indeed, public disquiet over the elitism and obscurity of Community decisionmaking, rather than over the relative impotence of the European Parliament and national parliaments in Community affairs, burst into the open in 1992 during the Maastricht Treaty ratification crisis. The Danish referendum may have been lost by less than fifty thousand votes and for a variety of trivial and substantial reasons, but it brought home the extent of popular alienation from Brussels. The margin of victory in the French referendum was almost as slender as the margin of defeat in the Danish referendum. Governments learned a costly lesson: As the Community encroaches more and more on people's daily lives and the distinction between domestic affairs and Community affairs disappears, the public wants greater openness and involvement in Community decisionmaking.

The Maastricht Treaty included a number of provisions to promote a "people's Europe." The concept of Union citizenship and the extension of voting rights for local and Euro-elections were the most important. In addition, the treaty attempted to increase the European Parliament's involvement in everyday life by confirming the public's right to petition Parliament on matters of Community competence (a practice that has existed since the 1970s), formalizing Parliament's right to set up temporary committees of inquiry to investigate miscellaneous issues (a practice that has existed since direct elections), and authorizing Parliament to appoint an ombudsman to whom any citizen may complain about "maladministration in the activities of the Community institutions" (Article 138).

Those provisions will hardly make a dent in the democratic deficit. Few people outside the European Parliament consider it capable of providing a solution to the Community's crisis of democratic legitimacy. MEPs are marginal figures at the national level, regardless of their political power. The public did not clamor in 1992 for national governments to give more authority to the European Parliament, and nobody objected when the European Council condemned the Parliament to relative institutional insignificance by deciding to keep it permanently in Strasbourg. Not only is Strasbourg a difficult place for people to get to, but the Maastricht Treaty further muddles Parliament's already complicated legislative procedures. Paradoxically, at a time when the Community is trying to become more open, "the existence of multiple decision-making procedures, in which the role of the European Parliament varies from case to case, will be detrimental to the transparency of the EC legislative process and will only increase the already considerable confusion existing among European citizens over the role played by the European Parliament."[45]

Will the democratic deficit ever be rectified? Certainly not simply by giving more power to the European Parliament, regardless of its failings and foibles. David Martin's analogy notwithstanding, the Community is *not* a state, and its institutional framework and political system will never correspond to that of a classic liberal democracy. Similarly, the Commission will never acquire the characteristics of a national executive. The Community is a unique system with unique institutions; the solution to the democratic deficit will be equally novel and unconventional.

Perhaps the growth of regionalism in the 1990s—reflected in the Maastricht Treaty's provision to establish an advisory Committee of the Regions—will have a positive impact on political representation, legitimacy, and decisionmaking in the European Community. As it is, conventional views of the democratic deficit and conventional proposals for its resolution are obsolete. Undoubtedly the European Parliament will remain an essential ingredient of political accountability in the European Community. But in an evolving Community of traditional or transformed nation-states, the democratic deficit will have to be resolved by an imaginative blend of public representation and involvement at the regional, national, and Community levels.

NOTES

1. Prag Report on the Cooperation Procedure, as reproduced in *Agence Europe Documents*, 1820/21, January 30, 1993, pp. 10–12.

2. See *EP News*, September 14–18, 1992, p. 2.

3. See Shirley Williams, "Sovereignty and Accountability in the European Community," in Keohane and Hoffmann, *The New Community*, p. 172.

4. Bull. EC 12–1992, Presidency Conclusions, point 1.14.

5. Bull. EC 7/8–1976, points 1101–1109.

6. Bull. EC 9–76, points 5201–5207.

7. See Francis Jacobs, Richard Corbett, and M. Shackleton, *The European Parliament* (Boulder, CO: Westview Press, 1990), p. 25.

8. Hoon Report, 1988, DOC A2-0065/88.

9. Jacobs, Corbett, and Shackleton, *The European Parliament*, p. 54.

10. *EPP Bulletin* 2 (June 1991), p. 1.

11. *Ibid.*, p. 2.

12. Jacobs, Corbett, and Shackleton, *The European Parliament*, pp. 83, 98.

13. Fulvio Attina, "Parties, Party Systems and Democracy in the European Union," in *The International Spectator* 27, no. 3 (July–September 1992), p. 79.

14. Jacobs, Corbett, and Shackleton, *The European Parliament*, p. 88.

15. *Ibid.*, p. 147.

16. *EP News*, September 14–18, 1992, p. 2.

17. Marc Abeles, "Political Anthropology of a Transnational Institution: The European Parliament," *French Politics and Society* 11, no. 1 (Winter 1993), pp. 16–17.

18. See James Ellis, "The Foreign Policy Role of the European Parliament," *The Washington Quarterly* (Fall 1990), pp. 69–77.

19. Debates of the European Parliament, OJ 3-413, January 15, 1992, p. 15.

20. Commission, *1988 General Report*, points 80–84.

21. See Commission of the European Communities, *From the Single Act to Maastricht and Beyond: The Means to Match our Ambitions*, COM (92) 2000 final, Brussels, February 11, 1992.

22. Commission, *1992 General Report*, point 1166.

23. Daniel Strasser, *The Finances of Europe*, 7th edition (Luxembourg: OOP, 1991), p. 290.

24. Quoted in Strasser, *Finances of Europe*, p. 408.

25. David Coombes, "Public Provision in an Economic and Monetary Union: New Functions for the Budget of the European Community," paper presented at the Second Biennial Conference of the European Community Studies Association, George Mason University, May 1991, p. 1.

26. Cases 138 and 139/79 of October 29, 1980.

27. Jacobs, Corbett, and Shackleton, *The European Parliament*, p. 166.

28. John Fitzmaurice, "An Analysis of the European Community's Cooperation Procedure," *Journal of Common Market Studies* 26, no. 4 (June 1988), p. 390.

29. Abeles, "Political Anthropology of a Transnational Institution," p. 12.

30. The Commission's Program for 1992, Bull. EC S 1/92, p. 45.

31. *The Financial Times,* October 5, 1992, p. 1.

32. Prag Report.

33. Prag Report.

34. *Agence Europe,* January 22, 1992, p. 1.

35. Prag Report.

36. See Abeles, "Political Anthropology," p. 5.

37. Quoted in *The Financial Times*, January 22, 1992, p. 10.

38. *Agence Europe,* 5903, January 22, 1993, p. 1.

39. Jacobs, Corbett, and Shackleton, *The European Parliament*, p. 76.

40. See, for instance, David Martin, remarks at the European Community Studies Association's Second International Conference, George Mason University, May 27, 1991.

41. See Williams, "Sovereignty and Accountability," pp. 155, 162.

42. See Alberta Sbragia, "Maastricht, Enlargement, and the Future of Institutional Change," paper delivered at the conference on The European Community: Moving Toward Union or Falling Back?, U.S. Department of State, February 1, 1993, p. 7.

43. Sophie Meunier-Aitsahalia and George Ross, "Democratic Deficit or Democratic Surplus: A Reply to Andrew Moravcsik's Comments About the French Referendum," *French Politics and Society* 11, no. 1 (Winter 1993), p. 63.

44. Vernon Bogdanor and Geoffrey Woodcock, "The European Community and Sovereignty," *Parliamentary Affairs* 44, no. 1 (October 1991), p. 492.

45. Sophie Vanhoonacker, "The European Parliament," in Finn Laursen and Sophie Vanhoonacker, eds., *The Intergovernmental Conference on Political Union* (Maastricht: EIPA, 1992).

10

The Court of Justice and Other Institutions and Bodies

Article 4 of the Maastricht Treaty identifies five Community institutions—the European Parliament, the Council of Ministers, the European Commission, the Court of Justice, and the Court of Auditors—and two advisory bodies—the Economic and Social Committee and the Committee of the Regions. The Community system also includes a Court of First Instance (attached to the Court of Justice) and an autonomous lending institution, the European Investment Bank.

THE COURT OF JUSTICE

For much of its existence, the European Court of Justice (ECJ) was the Community's least-known institution. Located in Luxembourg, far from the political fray in Brussels and Strasbourg, the Court initially received little outside attention as it waded through a growing number of seemingly arcane and unimportant cases. Only gradually did the significance of the Court's rulings become apparent to the nonlegal world. In the dark days of the late 1960s and the 1970s, while the Community stagnated politically, economically, and institutionally, the ECJ persevered and produced an impressive amount of case law that maintained the momentum for deeper integration. In so doing, the Court not only defined and shaped a new legal order but also contributed to the Community's revival and transformation in the 1980s.

Opponents of European integration have accused the Court of judicial activism, a testimony to its enormous impact on the Community's development.[1] Despite a few striking instances of judicial activism in the late 1980s and early 1990s, the Court arguably has grown less adventurous in recent years, not least because other institutions have become more involved in constructing the Community and expediting European integration. Yet the Court is unlikely to regain the solitude and anonymity it once enjoyed. If anything, the Community's struggle with such issues as subsidiarity and the Maastricht Treaty's social chapter will thrust the Court into the unfamiliar and uncomfortable political limelight.

Community Law

The Court's principal purpose is "to ensure that in the interpretation and application of [the treaties] the law is observed."[2] The original treaties (the ECSC, the EEC, and Euratom treaties), the treaties of accession, and the various treaty amendments constitute the Community's "primary legislation," whereas the laws made by Community institutions in accordance with the treaties constitute the Community's "secondary legislation." Primary and secondary legislation are the main sources of Community law, a "self-sufficient body of law that is binding on [the member states] and on their subjects."[3]

From the outset, the ECJ has seen the original treaties not simply as narrow international agreements but, because of the member states' unique decision to share sovereignty, as the basis of a constitutional framework for the Community. "If one were asked to synthesize the direction in which the case law produced in Luxembourg has moved since 1957," Federico Mancini, a member of the Court of Justice, recently wrote, "one would have to say that it coincides with the making of a constitution for Europe."[4] Moreover, in a compelling series of cases the Court showed that the Community's "constitution" is based on custom and on shared values as well as on treaties and secondary legislation.

Although the original treaties made no mention of fundamental human rights—an essential ingredient of any constitutional democracy—the preamble of the SEA acknowledged the Court's repeated emphasis on the issue by declaring the member states' determination "to work together to promote democracy on the basis of the fundamental rights recognized in the constitutions and laws of the Member States, in the Convention for the Protection of Human Rights and Fundamental Freedoms and the European Social Charter, notably freedom, equality and social justice." The Maastricht Treaty did not institute a charter of fundamental rights and freedoms, as the European Parliament wanted it to,[5] but it did include a new article explicitly stating that "the Union shall respect fundamental rights, as guaranteed by the European Convention for the Protection of Human Rights and Fundamental Freedoms signed in Rome on November

4, 1950, and as they result from the constitutional traditions common to the Member States, as general principles of Community law." As it did with human rights, the ECJ developed the concept of European citizenship before the member states gave substance to it in the Maastricht Treaty.[6]

Apart from identifying the sources of Community law and endowing the treaties with the attributes of a constitution, the Court also developed two key principles on which the new legal order rests: direct effect and supremacy. These twin pillars emerged in a series of cases early in the Community's history and clarified the working relationship between the national and Community legal orders.

Direct Effect

The Court first ruled on the direct effect of primary legislation in a case that, though technical and tedious, raised a fundamental principle of Community law. In *Van Gend & Loos* (1963), a Dutch transport firm brought a complaint against Dutch customs for increasing the duty on a product imported from Germany. The firm argued that the Dutch authorities had breached Article 12 of the EEC treaty, which prohibits member states from introducing new duties or increasing existing duties in the common market. Thus, the Dutch firm claimed protection, citing the "direct effect" of Community law.

The Court agreed. In a landmark judgment it ruled that Article 12 had direct effect because it contained a "clear and unconditional prohibition." Seizing the opportunity to make its mark, the Court declared that any unconditionally worded treaty provision, being "self-sufficient and legally complete," did not require further intervention at the national or Community levels and therefore applied directly to individuals. Not mincing its words, the Court stated that "the Community constitutes a new legal order . . . the subjects of which comprise not only the member states but also their nationals. Independently of the legislation of member states, Community law not only imposes obligations on individuals but . . . also confers rights upon them. These rights arise not only where they are expressly granted by the Treaty, but also by reason of obligations which the Treaty of Rome imposes in a clearly defined way upon individuals as well as upon member states and upon the institutions of the Community."[7]

The Court continued to push the principle of direct effect in cases involving directives (addressed to member states) as well as regulations (addressed to individuals) and treaty provisions. In 1970 the Court delivered a landmark judgment in *Grad v. Finanzamt Traunstein* by ruling that a Council decision in conjunction with a directive had direct effect. In *Grad* and related cases, the Court ruled that, to have direct effect, a directive must contain a clear and unconditional obligation on a member state and must not have been implemented by that state within the period prescribed in the directive. The reasoning was that "a Member State should not be able to take advantage of the fact that it had infringed the Treaties by failing to implement the directive or by failing to implement it properly. The individual citizen must be able to rely on his legal position under Community law before the national courts."[8]

Supremacy of Community Law

The principle of direct effect would have had little impact if Community law did not supersede national law. Otherwise member states would simply ignore Community rules that conflicted with national rules. Although the Treaty of Rome is equivocal on that issue, the ECJ had no hesitation in asserting the supremacy of Community law over national law. The Court's first chance to do so came in *Costa v. ENEL* (1964), only a year after *Van Gend & Loos*. Mr. Costa was a shareholder in an electricity company nationalized by the Italian government. As a protest, he refused to pay his electricity bill and claimed in the ensuing Italian court case that nationalization of the electricity company had infringed Community law. When asked for a ruling, the ECJ did not question the legality of nationalization, but it developed the supremacy of Community law over national law by pointing out that member states had definitively transferred sovereign rights to the Community and that Community law could not be overridden by domestic legal provisions without the legal basis of the Community itself being called into question.[9]

Coming within a year of each other, the *Costa* and *Van Gend & Loos* cases established the twin principles of direct effect and primacy of Community law, taking the national courts by surprise. Some national courts reacted strongly against what they saw as the encroachment of a new legal order. The greatest threat came in the late 1960s, when the constitutional courts of Italy and Germany hinted that because Community law apparently guaranteed a lower standard of fundamental rights than national law, the validity of Community law could be called into question at the national level. In a move that developed the Community's human rights case law and warded off a potentially serious threat from the national courts, the ECJ held in *Nold v. Commission* (1974) that "fundamental rights form an integral part of the general principles of [Community] law." In its ruling, the ECJ identified international treaties and "constitutional traditions common to the member states" as the source of its judgment.[10]

It is perhaps surprising not that the ECJ has repeatedly upheld the supremacy of Community law over national law but that national courts have generally and relatively easily accepted Community law and become an integral part of the new legal order. Although the pervasiveness of Community law no longer astonishes national courts, it can still shock politicians and the public. Such was the case in 1991, when the ECJ for the first time overruled a British act of Parliament, which had banned Spanish trawlers from operating in UK waters. In *The Queen v. Secretary of State for Transport, ex parte Factortame* (1991), the Court ruled that the 1988 Merchant Shipping Act, which states that 75 percent of directors and shareholders in companies operating fishing vessels in UK waters must be British, contravened Community law. Basing their ruling on the freedom of establishment and freedom to provide services, the Court said that the UK could not demand strict residence and nationality requirements from owners and crew before granting their vessels British registration.[11]

The 1988 Merchant Shipping Act was an attempt to stop "quota-hopping" by Spanish vessels taking advantage of British registration to avail of the UK's quotas under the Community's fisheries policy. The Court's ruling outraged British fishermen and was grist for the mill of the country's anti-EC lobby. The *Factortame* ruling prompted William Cash, chairman of the Europhobic Bruges Group, to doubt "whether the competence of the Commons will continue as it has in the past."[12]

Preliminary Rulings

The general complicity of national courts in consolidating Community law is all the more striking because, in most cases, landmark ECJ judgments have come in response to requests from national courts for preliminary rulings on points of Community law. Under Article 177 of the EEC treaty, lower national courts *may* seek "authoritative guidance" from the ECJ in cases involving Community law, but the highest national courts *must* do so. The original intent of Article 177 was to ensure uniform interpretation and application of Community law in each member state. Almost immediately, however, Article 177 became a powerful tool with which the ECJ could strengthen Community law and the Court's own role within the Community system. It also became a device citizens could use to ascertain the compatibility of national and Community law. As a result, "the preliminary rulings procedure is of fundamental importance to the proper functioning of the legal and economic system established by the EEC Treaty. It is in the framework of that procedure that basic principles of the Community legal order, such as direct effect and primacy, have been developed."[13]

Preliminary rulings are applicable to the Community's treaty provisions and secondary legislation. Under Article 177, a national court does not generally interpret Community law and then ask the ECJ if its interpretation is correct. Instead, it asks Luxembourg for guidance on an aspect of Community law raised by a particular case. Based on the ECJ's advice, the national court resumes the case and decides whether the national rule is compatible with the Community's. Increasingly, the ECJ has reformulated national courts' questions in order to elucidate what it considers to be the most important points at issue. By the same token, national courts tend to ask the ECJ unequivocally whether a national rule is in violation of Community law, and the ECJ tends to respond directly, paying due homage to the treaty's language by referring to the national rule only in abstract terms.

Clearly, the success of Community law depends on the willingness of national courts to seek preliminary rulings and abide by them. Requests for preliminary rulings came slowly at first but accelerated in the 1970s and 1980s. There were 182 requests for preliminary rulings in 1991, 162 in 1992.[14] The increasing rate of preliminary ruling requests from lower courts has enhanced the stature of the ECJ, effectively giving it the power to review national law and thereby turning it into a supreme court. Correspondingly, Article 177 has undermined the authority of the highest national courts. Why do so many lower national court judges apply for preliminary rulings, "given that such judges must attend to their career prospects within hierarchically organized national judicial systems?"[15] According to Donal Barrington, a member of the Court of First Instance, the answer may be simply that "the concept of a Community governed by law is naturally attractive to all Judges." Whatever the reason, Article 177 has brought about a special relationship, indeed a close partnership, between national courts and the ECJ. As a result, "the National Judge . . . in his capacity as Community Judge, becomes the upholder of Community Law in his own member state."[16]

In late 1992 the ECJ came under sharp criticism from the German government for some preliminary rulings protecting the rights of Italian and non-Community migrants. The Germans' criticism focused on the very right of lower national courts to ask the ECJ for preliminary rulings and on the ECJ itself for giving preliminary rulings supposedly hostile to national governments' interests. According to Federico Mancini, the German government's displeasure could lead to a far-reaching proposal at the 1996 IGC to abrogate the paragraph in Article 177 that allows lower courts to refer questions of Community law to the Court of Justice.[17] If so, the ECJ will be in danger of losing one of its most effective vehicles for enunciating Community law.

Direct Actions

References for preliminary rulings constitute one branch of ECJ case law; direct actions—in which a member state, institution, natural or legal person brings a case straight to the Court—make up the other. Direct actions usually take one of the following forms:

• Cases brought by the Commission or, rarely, by a member state against another member state for failing to fulfill a legal obligation

(Articles 169 and 170). If the Court agrees that the case is well founded, it declares that an obligation has not been fulfilled. The number of such cases has increased steadily over the years and now averages about a hundred annually.

• Cases against the Commission or Council concerning the legality of a particular directive, regulation, or decision (Articles 184 and 197). These are called "proceedings for annulment," because the Court may annul a particular act. Grounds for annulment include lack of competence, infringement of an essential procedural requirement, infringement of the treaties or of any rules relating to their application, and misuse of powers. The Court's famous *Isoglucose* (1980) ruling—in which it annulled a regulation because the Council acted before Parliament had delivered its opinion, thereby infringing one of the essential Treaty provisions concerning allocation of powers—falls into this category.

• Cases brought by member states or other institutions against the Commission or Council for failure to act (Article 175). The most famous case of that kind was *Parliament v. Council* (1985), in which Parliament brought the Council to court for failing to lay the foundation of a common transport policy. Parliament was only partially successful.

• Cases for damages against the Communities (actions to establish liability) for the wrongful act of a Community institution or a Community servant (Articles 178 and 215.2).

• Cases brought by Community servants (staff cases) for unfair dismissal, unlawful failure to promote, etc.

Under Article 228 of the EEC treaty, the Council, the Commission, or a member state may ask the Court's opinion on the compatibility of an international agreement with Community law, even if the Community is not a party to the agreement. In a reflection of the Court's growing importance, the Commission availed of that previously little-used procedure in 1991 to ask the Court's opinion of the European Economic Area (EEA) Agreement, which the Community had just negotiated with the European Free Trade Association. To the Commission's and the Council's dismay, the Court ruled that the EEA's judicial review arrangements were indeed incompatible with the Treaty of Rome, thus obliging the Commission to reopen negotiations. Six months later the Commission submitted the revised EEA agreement, including amended judicial review provisions, which the Court approved.[18]

Impact of Community Case Law

Apart from establishing the principles of direct effect and supremacy, Community case law has profoundly advanced the Treaty of Rome's objectives. Indeed, some of the landmark rulings in the elaboration of direct effect and supremacy have also proved decisive in helping to achieve the Community's economic and social goals. Some of the most important examples are:

• Free movement of people: In *Van Duyn v. Home Office* (1974) and *Reyners* (1974), the Court upheld an individual's right to take up employment in another member state under the same conditions as a national of that state.

• Free movement of goods: In the famous *Cassis de Dijon* (1979) case, the Court gave the Commission an opportunity to develop the principle of mutual recognition, which underpinned the single market program.

• Freedom to provide services: The Court's ruling in *Vereniging Bond van Adverteerders v. The Netherlands State* (1988), a case involving cross-border telecommunications services, opened the way to the removal of barriers against the provision of services throughout the Community.

• Competition policy: A number of Court rulings have furthered the Community's competition policy, notably by confirming the Commission's powers to order repayment of illegal government aid to industry and by interpreting the Treaty's provisions on public enterprises and enterprises granted special or exclusive rights.

• Social policy: The Court's activism in this area is especially marked in the realm of women's rights. The Court's *Defrenne* rulings on equal pay emboldened the Commission to implement a series of directives on women's issues that forced member states to end systematic and blatant discrimination. A subsequent stream of cases dealt with pensions, training, promotions, part-time work, and so forth.

Relations with Other Institutions

Because the other institutions are often litigants in court cases, the ECJ has a unique relationship with the Council, Commission, and Parliament. Although the Court has often ruled against the Commission, the Commission is nonetheless an obvious ally. After all, the Commission sees itself as the "guardian of the treaties." As Jacques Delors remarked in September 1992, "the European Community is a Community governed by law, where the Court of Justice plays an essential role and where one of the Commission's duties is to see that the rules are observed by all."[19] Moreover, the Commission and the Court work together closely in the pursuit of economic integration, including the use of competition policy to achieve it.

Conversely, the Court's relations with the Council are inherently tense. Whereas the Council generally upholds national interests in the

Community system, the ECJ has made an undisguised effort to interpret the treaties liberally by promoting closer economic and political integration. In other words, the Council represents intergovernmentalism and the Court upholds supranationalism.

The Court's relationship with Parliament is more complicated than with the other two institutions. As institutions that support a more supranational Community, Parliament and the Court have an obvious affinity. Indeed, the Court has generally promoted Parliament's institutional interests, most notably in the *Isoglucose* case. The Court also corrected the anomaly whereby, under Article 173, the Parliament could not bring proceedings for judicial review of Community acts, a provision that seemed especially incongruous in view of Parliament's enhanced legislative power under the SEA.

When Parliament first tried to institute proceedings under Article 173, in the *Comitology* (1988) case, the Court reluctantly ruled against it. Yet only two years later, in the *Chernobyl* case, the Court reversed its earlier decision and ruled that in order to ensure the institutional equilibrium in the Treaty as amended by the SEA, Parliament should have the right to take action against Council and Commission acts in cases involving parliamentary prerogatives. Despite inevitable criticism of the Court's judicial activism after the *Chernobyl* ruling, "the authors of the Maastricht Treaty incorporated almost *verbatim* the operative part of the judgment into their new version of Article 173."[20]

Enforcement

Although national courts and member state governments accept the principles of direct effect and supremacy of Community law, the problem of enforcement remains acute. The Court is well aware that inability or refusal to implement Community rules uniformly in each member state will erode public confidence in Community law. In *Johnson v. RUC*, the Court declared that the right to a judicial remedy is a general principle of EC law[21] and continued its assault on the enforcement problem in a series of cases in the early 1990s. The most important of these was *Francovich and Bonifaci v. Italy* (1991), in which the Court held that, in certain circumstances, individuals are entitled to sue governments for damages sustained as a result of the government's failure to implement a directive within the prescribed period. Although its full implications have yet to be understood, the *Francovich* ruling could give enormous backing to the Community's efforts to end late or shoddy implementation of EC law by member states. The worst areas of noncompliance are environmental policy, the single market, and agriculture; the worst offenders are Italy, Greece, Spain, and Portugal.

Aware of their responsibility in that regard, the member states agreed during the 1991 intergovernmental conference on political union to give the Court some enforcement power. One of the Maastricht Treaty's least-publicized provisions—with which the Court was not entirely happy—allows the Court to impose a fine on a member state for refusing to act upon a Court ruling that "it failed to fulfill its obligations under the Treaty" (Article 171). As with recent case law on member state noncompliance, the impact of ECJ fines on recalcitrant member states will only become apparent later in the decade.

Organization and Procedure

Articles 164–188 of the EEC treaty stipulate the role, composition, location, procedure, jurisdiction, and powers of the Court. The Court's size has increased over time to reflect the Community's enlargement. It currently has thirteen judges and six advocates-general.

Although the treaty does not declare that each member state should appoint a judge, in practice that is what happens. An extra, thirteenth judge is necessary to provide an uneven number. Under a formula agreed upon before Greek accession in 1981, when an eleventh judge became necessary, the Council agreed to award the additional judgeship to the four largest member states, in rotation. That formula broke down after the Community's third enlargement, when Spain insisted on joining the rota for the extra seat on the Court. A year-long dispute broke out in 1988 when Spain demanded the thirteenth seat, due to become vacant at the end of the year, and Italy made a counterclaim based on the original rota. After an unseemly squabble that caused Lord Mackenzie Stuart, the ECJ president, to complain publicly about the Council's behavior, Italy gave in and Spain carried the day.

The dispute over the thirteenth seat suggests that member states enjoy an advantage by holding it. In fact, they derive only additional prestige. The treaty stipulates that judges must act independently, and generally they do. Moreover, the president of the Court never asks one of the judges to be the *rapporteur* for a case involving that judge's member state (the *rapporteur* is responsible for writing the "report for the hearing"—a summary setting out the facts, procedural history, and arguments of the case—for use by the judges). Nevertheless, the principle of one judge per member state is an important factor in the evolution of Community law and in the acceptance of the Court's rulings by the member states.

As the Court's impact on the Community's development becomes even more conspicuous, the judiciary's independence will need to be safeguarded. Sooner rather than later, the Court will have to decide what the principle of subsidiarity means in a particular case.[22] When the Court begins to adjudicate such politically charged cases under media scrutiny, member states will be tempted to pressure or influence "their" judges. A government's most evident leverage is renewal of a judge's six-year term. At the same time, the European Parliament wants a say in judicial appointments, supposedly as a way of strengthening the judiciary's independence. The solution could be to lengthen the judges' terms to twelve years, a suggestion Mackenzie Stuart made in the late 1970s on the grounds that judges need a long time to familiarize themselves with Community law and build essential camaraderie and rapport.[23]

Judges come from the upper levels of national judiciaries, from the legal profession, and from academia. The six advocates-general, who have similar backgrounds, complete the Court's membership. Advocates-general are also appointed according to an unofficial national quota: four from the larger member states and two others from smaller member states, selected by rota. Advocates-general consider cases and give opinions for the Court's guidance at the end of the oral procedure. The judges are free to accept or reject an advocate-general's opinion but usually accept them. The landmark *Van Gend & Loos* case was a rare instance in which the judges rejected the advocate-general's advice.

By majority vote, after consulting the advocates-general the judges elect a registrar (*greffier*) for a renewable six-year term. The registrar is responsible for conducting proceedings before the Court, maintaining records, publishing the Court's judgments, and administering the Court. The registrar meets regularly with members of the Court to schedule cases and decide procedural aspects.

The Court meets either in plenary session (with a quorum of seven members) or in chambers. There are four chambers of three judges and two chambers of five judges. The Court's rules of procedure determine where cases are heard (for instance, cases brought by member states or institutions must be heard before the full Court), although the Maastricht Treaty made greater allowance for cases to be dealt with by chambers of judges. The Court hears cases two days a week and has an administrative session every two weeks.

Because national courts must await a result before proceeding with the case in question, the ECJ gives requests for preliminary rulings a higher priority than direct actions. Direct action cases involve written proceedings, an investigation or preparatory enquiry, oral proceedings, and the judgment. Requests for preliminary rulings are not contentious and have a less cumbersome procedure than direct actions, although the original parties may submit written observations to the Court and may attend the oral hearing. Cases are heard in the Community's official languages, but French is the Court's working language.

Each judge has a small *cabinet* of legal secretaries, although most judges draft without assistance after internal deliberations limited exclusively to the judiciary. The judges neither prepare nor issue minority opinions, nor do they indicate how many of them supported a decision, which the Court always announces as unanimous. Understandably, legal scholars complain that this makes it "difficult to track the influence of individual judges' policy preferences and political philosophies on the institutional output of the court,"[24] although judges occasionally make speeches, publish articles, and give interviews.

The Court has a relatively small staff of Eurocrats (approximately six hundred), who provide research, language, and administrative support.

THE COURT OF FIRST INSTANCE

For more than thirty-five years the Community had only one court, responsible for hearing cases involving everything from important issues of Community law and constitutional interpretation to trivial matters of staff promotion and dismissal. Apart from its wide jurisdiction, the Court's rapidly increasing caseload threatened to become unmanageable. The Court and the Commission appreciated the problem by the early 1970s and asked the Council to help, suggesting it establish a tribunal to hear staff cases. In 1978 the Court formally complained to the Council, but to no avail. Some member states thought the only way to ease the Court's burden was to amend the Treaty, which would require an intergovernmental conference (IGC). Given the state of European integration in the late 1970s and early 1980s, though, an IGC was out of the question.[25]

When the Community's fortunes revived, however, and the member states convened an IGC in 1985, the Court rekindled the issue of judicial reform. By that time the Court's problems were pressing: As the caseload increased, the time taken to hear cases also increased. The Court's caseload had jumped from 79 in 1970 to 433 in 1985; the average length of proceedings for a preliminary ruling rose from six months in 1975 to fourteen months in 1985; and the average length of a direct action increased from nine months in 1975 to twenty months in 1985. As a result, the Court's accumulated backlog went from 100 cases in 1970 to 527 cases in 1985.[26]

In October 1985, shortly after the IGC began, Lord Mackenzie Stuart raised the prospect of a subsidiary court in a letter to the Luxembourg presidency. Member states responded by delegating the issue to a group of experts, who proposed amending Article 168 of the Treaty "to attach to the Court of Justice a court with jurisdiction to hear and determine at first instance" certain cases. Article 168a of the SEA duly empowered the Council, acting unanimously on a proposal from the Court and after

consulting the Commission and Parliament, to attach a Court of First Instance to the ECJ.[27] The SEA thereby gave rise to "a hierarchy of judicial
institutions at the Community level."[28]

After implementation of the SEA, the Court of Justice duly presented a proposal to the Commission to establish the Court of First Instance (CFI). Following lengthy deliberations by an ad hoc committee
drawn from the permanent representations, the Council decided in October 1988 on the CFI's composition and jurisdiction.[29] The new Court
began operating in October 1989, delivered its first judgment in January
1990, and adopted its own rules of procedure in May 1991,[30] which became effective the following July.

Jurisdiction

Given the pressure under which the Court of Justice operated, the new
Court's jurisdiction was surprisingly narrow. It encompassed:

- Competition cases (generally actions by firms contesting fines
  imposed by the Commission under the Community's competition policy)
- ECSC cases (most stemming from the system of production
  quotas imposed on the steel industry in an effort to deal with recession and overcapacity)
- Staff cases
- Claims for damages brought by natural or legal persons where
  the damage allegedly arises from an action or failure to act
  which falls into one of the three categories outlined above.[31]

In June 1993 the Council decided to expand the CFI's competence
by transferring from the ECJ all proceedings brought by individuals and
companies, with the exception of proceedings against Community trade
defense measures (antidumping, etc.).[32]

The CFI's initially narrow jurisdiction reflected the member states'
difficulty in deciding what to hive off from the ECJ's caseload. Member
states were unsure what to entrust to the CFI, apart from staff cases. Their
uncertainty was already evident in Article 168a of the SEA, which denied
the CFI any jurisdiction over cases brought by member states or Community institutions or over questions referred for preliminary ruling under
Article 177. Thus the CFI could only hear "certain classes of action or
proceedings brought by natural or legal persons." In the event, the Council's October 1988 decision gave the CFI even narrower jurisdiction than
that contemplated in the SEA.

Prestige, politics, and familiarity with the Court of Justice seem to account for the member states' decision that only the ECJ could hear cases brought by the member states and by institutions. After all, such cases do not always raise constitutionally important issues. Moreover, "it is surprising . . . that the Member States and the Institutions . . . should have deprived themselves of the protection of a right to appeal by providing that in cases where they were plaintiffs the existing Court of Justice was to be a court of first instance from which there was no appeal."[33]

According to the Council, the purpose of the new court is to hear cases that require "an examination of complex facts."[34] For instance, ECSC and competition cases usually involve intricate technical legislation and detailed questions of fact. Thus, "for the most effective functioning of Community law, the Court of First Instance is the judge of factual matters, while the Court of Justice is in principle the judge of points of law."[35]

Composition and Procedure

The CFI consists of twelve judges (one per member state) appointed for renewable six-year terms. It has no advocates-general, but any judge may be asked to perform the task of advocate-general for a particular case. As with their counterparts on the ECJ, judges on the Court of First Instance must be independent of national governments. In view of the highly technical work they sometimes perform, CFI judges need not come from the legal profession, although in practice almost all of them do. To maintain continuity between the new and the existing courts, a number of the CFI's first judges were closely connected with the ECJ. For instance, Jose Luis da Cruz Vilaca, the CFI's first president, was a former ECJ advocate-general.

The CFI has five chambers: two chambers of five judges each and three chambers of three judges each. According to a legal scholar, "the five-judge chamber is widely regarded as being a particularly effective formation for judging cases: small enough to be flexible and responsive but large enough to be able to develop new case law with authority."[36] The court occasionally meets in plenary session for important cases. The judges elect one of their members to serve as president for a renewable three-year term and elect a registrar, who serves in a capacity similar to that of the ECJ's registrar.

In providing for a court of first instance, the SEA included a right of appeal to the Court of Justice. However, litigants may appeal to the ECJ on a point of law only, such as the CFI's lack of competence to hear the original case, breach of procedure, or infringement of Community law. An appeal must be lodged within two months of notification of the decision being appealed against.

Performance and Future Prospects

The ECJ referred a total of 153 cases (mostly competition and staff cases) to the new court upon its creation. The CFI dealt with virtually all of these by 1992. In the meantime, of course, it acquired new cases of its own: 55 in 1990; 93 in 1991; and 115 in 1992. Nevertheless, the CFI has the capacity and the experience to take on more work.

Meanwhile, the ECJ remains overburdened. But that does not reflect poorly on the CFI. If the CFI did not exist, the ECJ would have to hear all the cases that currently come before the CFI (as it is, the ECJ hears about 20 percent of them on appeal). Based on these figures and on his experience, Bo Vesterdorf, a judge on the CFI, concluded that the new court has performed effectively and has saved the ECJ a considerable amount of additional work.[37]

President da Cruz Vilaca remarked at the CFI's official launch in September 1989 that "this moment does not mark the end of an era in European judicial history, but rather a stage along the road towards the ultimate maturity of the judicial system of the Communities."[38] Only a year later, the CFI published a paper urging an increase in its jurisdiction.[39] Under renewed pressure from the Court of Justice, at the 1991 IGC on political union the member states rewrote Article 168a to permit an extension of CFI jurisdiction. However, the Maastricht Treaty reiterated the prohibition against the CFI's hearing requests for preliminary rulings.

With the CFI underutilized and the ECJ overburdened, it makes sense to redistribute more of the ECJ's caseload to the CFI. Despite the CFI's establishment, the ECJ continues to deal with mundane issues. What Donal Barrington, a CFI judge, wrote in 1991 is still applicable today: "It is absurd that a Court which is the final Court of Appeal in a Community of 300 million people should have to apply itself to routine questions concerning the rate of VAT or Customs Duties which raise no issue of principle. Such routine matters should be delegated to the CFI and there should be a system of filtration to ensure that only those cases which raise some fundamental principle of Community Law reach the ultimate Court of Appeal."[40]

The IGC scheduled for 1996 will give member states another opportunity to reform the judicial system. In the meantime, the ECJ's and the CFI's membership will increase if more countries join the Community. But the 1996 IGC may not be entirely beneficial for the courts. With growing concern about supposed judicial activism, the uses (and perceived abuses) of Article 177, and the applicability of subsidiarity, the courts could suffer a serious setback at the forthcoming IGC. More immediate problems include the Court's exclusion from the Maastricht Treaty's provisions for a CFSP and for cooperation on judicial and home affairs, as well as the confusion surrounding implementation of the treaty's social policy protocol.

THE COURT OF AUDITORS

Article 4 of the Maastricht Treaty elevated the Court of Auditors to the institutional status of the Parliament, Council, Commission, and Court of Justice. Moreover, a declaration appended to the Maastricht Treaty emphasizes the Court of Auditors' "special importance" and calls on "other Community institutions to consider . . . ways of enhancing the effectiveness of its work."[41]

The Court of Auditors' enhanced stature and significance reflects not only a substantial increase in the Community's revenue and expenditure since the late 1980s but also growing public and political concern about fraud, waste, and mismanagement of Community resources.[42] The Court of Auditors is not a judicial court; its responsibility lies solely in examining the Community's financial affairs. By exposing financial irregularities in the Community, however, it can exert enormous moral pressure for reform.

Indeed, the court's scrutiny of Community spending has afforded telling evidence to substantiate anecdotal accounts of financial squandering and incompetence. By boosting the court's status, member states tacitly warned the Community to put its financial house in order. The exposure in 1993 of massive Italian corruption, possibly involving also the European Community, will further enhance the Court of Auditors' institutional and public profile.

The problem of inadequate control over Community resources is as old as the Community itself. In an effort to rectify the situation, the 1975 budget treaty replaced the old Auditor Board with the new Court of Auditors, which began functioning in October 1977. The 1975 treaty extended the court's authority to cover all bodies created by the Community and all payments made before the year's accounts are closed.[43] In a financial regulation of December 1977, revised in March 1990, member states gave the court complete administrative and budgetary autonomy.

The court consists of twelve members having experience with the financial control of public funds in their own countries. In practice, each Community country nominates a member of the court. The Council then appoints the members unanimously, after consulting Parliament. Here, as elsewhere, Parliament has attempted to extend its authority by insisting on a right of approval. Parliament's objection to two court appointees in 1989 caused a political furor, and as a result one member state changed its nominee.[44] In November 1992 Parliament decided on the procedure it will follow when next consulted on the appointment of members of the court.[45]

An auditor's renewable term of office lasts six years. Because four of the court's first auditors were appointed for only four years, the court's membership does not change completely every six years. The auditors elect one of their members as president to serve a renewable three-year term. Located in Luxembourg and assisted by approximately four hundred officials, the Court of Auditors is supposed to be completely independent of national governments.

The court's work consists of a "financial audit" (an examination of accounts, together with an examination of whether all revenues were received and all expenditures made in a lawful and regular manner) and an assessment of "financial management."[46] Assessing financial management involves comparing the general goals and specific targets of Community policies and programs with the results obtained. The court usually applies the criteria of "effectiveness, economy, and efficiency." Such assessments can be politically sensitive and often irritate the Commission, which objects to what it sees as the court's tendency to make critical political judgments.[47]

Despite an inherently adversarial relationship, the court works closely and harmoniously with the Commission. On a day-to-day basis, the court deals mostly with the Commission's financial controller and with the directorate-general for budgets. Notwithstanding the problem of how auditors are appointed, the court also enjoys good relations with Parliament. The court has helped to increase Parliament's budgetary authority, especially in the area of discharge, and Parliament has helped to boost the court's institutional status.

Other Community institutions, as well as national audit bodies and government departments, must provide the court with documents on request. If necessary, the court may examine these "on the spot in the other institutions . . . and in the Member States."[48] The court works closely with its national counterparts when carrying out investigations in member states. Special liaison officers ensure that the court and the national audit bodies collaborate successfully. The liaison officers meet in Luxembourg at least once a year, and the presidents of the court and the twelve national bodies meet annually either in Luxembourg or in a national capital.

Each year the court adopts, by a majority vote of its members, regular reports, special reports, and opinions. The annual report on the Community's institutions, including responses from them to the court's observations, appears in the *Official Journal*. The court divides the annual report into a financial audit and a much larger financial management assessment. Other annual reports cover the European Center for the Development of Vocational Training in Berlin, the European Foundation for the Improvement of Living and Working Conditions in Dublin, the European Schools, the Atomic Energy Community's supply agency, and the Joint European Torus (JET).

The court "may also, at any time, submit observations, particularly in the form of special reports, on specific questions and deliver opinions at the request of one of the other institutions."[49] Special reports allow the court more flexibility than do annual reports, and their highly critical assessments of Community policies and programs often attract media attention. For instance, in 1992 the court adopted a scathing report on the environment.[50] The court sends its special reports to the Council and Parliament, which may or may not act on them. Some of the court's special reports have been so incriminating, however, that the other institutions have had little choice but to try to rectify matters. The court's opinions are fewer than its special reports, but not necessarily less spirited.

THE ECONOMIC AND SOCIAL COMMITTEE

The Economic and Social Committee (ESC) is an obscure, relatively unimportant body. It consists of 189 workers, employers, professionals, and consumers who meet in plenary session about ten times a year, more frequently in smaller sections. The committee's purpose is to advise the Commission and the Council on social and economic issues, but neither institution is obligated to heed the advice. More often than not the committee's reports sit, unread, in Council meetings; thus the Council fulfills its responsibility to solicit the committee's views on certain kinds of legislative proposals.

The ESC is modeled on national systems for institutionalizing interest group participation in policy formulation and implementation. The committee's raison d'être is to increase democratic accountability, make Community decisionmaking more transparent, and familiarize the economic and social sectors with the Council's legislative output. Originally the ESC had almost the same institutional stature as the European Parliament, but since the adoption of direct elections the Parliament has become far more powerful and prominent. Similarly, the proliferation of lobbyists and interest groups in Brussels is an indicator of the ESC's ineffectiveness, further undermining the committee's position.

Member states fill the following number of ESC seats: Germany, France, Italy, and the UK, twenty-four each; Spain, twenty-one; Belgium, Greece, the Netherlands, and Portugal, twelve each; Denmark and Ireland, nine each; Luxembourg, six.

Members represent a wide variety of social and economic interests in the Community and form three distinct groups of approximately equal size: employers (from industry and the service sector), workers (mostly from national trade unions), and other interest groups (farmers, environmentalists, consumers, professionals, etc.).

Committee members are unpaid but receive expenses. Although the committee has little clout, its members enjoy occasional trips to Brussels and the prestige of being involved in Community affairs. National governments look upon the committee as a means of dispensing patronage. The committee's permanent staff is about five hundred strong.

Despite the committee's relative insignificance, it generally produces readable and relevant reports, either in response to a Commission request or on its own initiative. Article 198 of the EEC treaty specifies certain policy areas, such as agriculture, transport, and social policy, where the Council and Commission *must* consult the ESC. The SEA extended the area of mandatory consultations to areas such as the environment, the single market, cohesion, and research and technology. In addition, the Council and Commission *may* consult the committee "in all cases in which they consider it appropriate." Finally, since the Paris summit of 1972, the ESC has had the authority to submit opinions on its own initiative.

The ESC elects a president to represent it in relations with Community institutions, member states, nonmember states, and interest groups. The president and the elected bureau assign members to one of nine sections, each comprising a mix of nationalities and groups. The sections cover: agriculture; industry, commerce, crafts, and services; economic, financial, and monetary questions; social, family, educational, and cultural affairs; transport and communications; external relations; energy, nuclear questions, and research; regional development; and environment, public health, and consumer affairs.

Sections draft opinions and reports on their respective policy areas and may solicit expert advice on technical matters. Opinions are adopted in the plenary sessions. Needless to say, consensus is almost impossible to achieve in such a diverse committee, and opinions often include dissenting points of view.

The ESC held nine plenary sessions in 1992 (a tenth session was canceled for budgetary reasons). During that time it adopted 171 documents—156 relating to Commission proposals and recommendations, 12 self-initiated opinions, and 3 information reports. The most important of these—in the sense of possible influence on EC legislation—were on CAP reform, premiums for tobacco producers, farm prices, and the protection of young people at work.[51]

The ESC looks to the Commission for political support. Relations between the ESC and the Commission are especially close because of Delors's affection for the committee. As a former trade unionist with a strong interest in social policy, he has an affinity with many of its members and an appreciation of its potential importance. Delors briefly brought the committee to prominence in 1988 when he asked for its advice on the proposed Social Charter, a listing of fundamental workers' rights. Delors presents the Commission's annual program at an ESC plenary session early each year and insists that commissioners with relevant portfolios attend at least one ESC plenary session annually. ESC opinions almost always support the Commission's position, at least as regards general objectives.

The Council generally ignores the ESC, although a representative of the Council presidency—usually a junior minister—outlines the presidency's six-month program at an ESC plenary. For its part, Parliament no longer sees the ESC as any kind of threat.

At the 1991 IGC on political union, the ESC asked the member states to take it more seriously and give it more responsibility. First, the committee wanted a guarantee that the Council would at least read, discuss, and respond to its opinions. Second, the ESC requested more procedural and administrative autonomy. Third, it asked for more money to cover its members' modest expenses.[52] By attempting to raise its role at the IGC, the ESC risked being disbanded by indifferent member states. In the event, however, the member states decided that it would be more trouble to abolish than to maintain the committee. Indeed, they agreed in the Maastricht Treaty to give the ESC more independence, especially over its rules of procedure.

Despite its marginal role, the committee serves some useful functions. It brings to Brussels representatives of influential social and economic interests and provides a forum where they can hold regular and systematic exchanges of views on important issues. The ESC also acts as a conduit for information from Brussels to the member states and alerts people to the implications of social and economic policy. Nevertheless, the committee aspires to a greater role and undoubtedly has the talent and expertise to make an important contribution. Unfortunately, however, the combination of a stronger, more effective European Parliament and a highly organized lobby of interest groups in Brussels leaves little room for the ESC.

Even after the establishment of the ESC in 1958, the ECSC's equivalent body—the Consultative Committee—continued to function. The ECSC Consultative Committee now has ninety-six members, divided into equal groups of producers, workers, consumers, and retailers. The ECSC Consultative Committee held seven meetings in 1992 and produced reports on such issues as the application of state aid rules to the steel industry and the provisions relating to coal and steel in the EEA Agreement.[53]

THE COMMITTEE OF THE REGIONS

"Europe of the Regions" is a popular catchphrase in the Community. It describes a Community made more inclusive and democratically accountable by the involvement of local and regional representatives in its decision-making process. In 1985, on their own initiative, individual regions came together and formed the Assembly of European Regions (AER), a pan-European body looking for a formal Community role.

Partly for reasons of democratic legitimacy and partly because it sees regionalism as integral to federalism, the Commission supported the AER's efforts to give regions and localities a greater sense of involvement in the Community system. But the AER itself was too large and unwieldy to play such a role, and some of its members were not even in the Community. Accordingly, in October 1991 the Commission submitted a paper to the IGC on political union proposing the establishment of a Committee of the Regions to advise the Council and Commission on relevant issues.[54] The member states concurred and included in the Maastricht Treaty a provision to that effect. According to Article 198 of the treaty, the committee will consist of "representatives of regional and local bodies." It will elect its chairman and officers from among its members for a two-year term and submit its rules of procedure to the Council for unanimous approval. The chairman will convene the committee either at the request of the Council or the Commission or on his or her own initiative.

The committee will not have any legislative authority. However, the Council and Commission will consult it where the Maastricht Treaty so provides and in all other cases where either of the two institutions considers it appropriate. The committee may also meet and issue opinions on its own initiative if it deems specific regional interests to be involved. The Council or the Commission can set a one-month time limit for submission of an opinion.

With a total membership of 189, the new committee's composition will be identical to that of the ESC: Germany, France, Italy, and the UK, twenty-four each; Spain, twenty-one; Belgium, Greece, the Netherlands, and Portugal, twelve each; Denmark and Ireland, nine each; and Luxembourg, six. As usual in the Community, the distribution of seats between member states relates only vaguely to population size. In this case, the anomaly of giving six seats to Luxembourg, a country smaller than most other member states' regions, is striking.

Acting unanimously on proposals from the member states, the Council will appoint members and alternate members for a renewable four-year term. The Commission clearly stated in its June 1991 submission to the IGC that the new committee's members should hold *elective office* at the regional or local level, but Article 198a does not include that condition. Moreover, the Council decided in June 1992 that it was up to each government, using its own criteria, to nominate people to represent regional and local communities.

The new committee became a vexed political question in Britain. As a highly centralized state that opposes a Community organized on federal lines, Britain instinctively opposed the Commission's proposal to establish a Committee of the Regions but reluctantly went along with the idea at Maastricht. Because the Maastricht Treaty gives governments complete discretion to nominate members of the new committee and because the UK lacks an institutionalized regional structure, Scotland, Wales, and Northern Ireland were left with no right to send representatives to the new committee. In the event, the government apparently discriminated against England—the most populous part of the UK—by giving Scotland and Wales almost half of Britain's seats on the committee. Glyn Ford, a British MEP, accused the government of having "sacrificed the best interests of regions all over England by striking a squalid deal with nationalist parties [in Scotland and Wales]."[55] The government's criteria for selecting Britain's representatives to the Committee of the Regions also proved contentious during the Maastricht Treaty ratification debate in the House of Commons.[56]

In a series of written questions in 1992, MEPs expressed concern about the new committee's relationship with the European Parliament and with the Economic and Social Committee. In reply, the Council pointed out that apart from sharing facilities and administrative support, the Economic and Social Committee and the Committee of the Regions will be independent of each other. The Council also asserted that the Committee of the Regions "will have no direct dealings with the EP" and will not duplicate Parliament's role in any way.[57]

Another MEP asked the Commission in June 1992 whether the Committee of the Regions was already in danger "of becoming an incoherent and largely unrepresentative body." Predictably, Commissioner Milan replied that "the Commission continues to attach great importance to the establishment of the Committee of Regions . . . the Commission considers the consultation of local and regional authorities through the Committee a significant achievement of the Maastricht Treaty."[58] As if to allay concerns about the committee's future, at the October 1992 Birmingham summit the heads of government underlined "the importance they attach to the . . . Committee of the Regions."[59] Nevertheless, the history of the Economic and Social Committee, the Community's only other advisory committee, does not bode well for the Committee of the Regions.

THE EUROPEAN INVESTMENT BANK

The European Investment Bank (EIB) is an autonomous public financial body within the Community. Established in 1958 under Articles 129 and 130 of the Treaty of Rome, the EIB seeks to assist the Community's economic development. It does so by offering loans to the public and private sectors, guaranteeing loans from other financial institutions, and putting financial packages together. The Commission and the recipient country's government must confirm that an EIB loan will help to meet national and Community objectives. Initially, most of the bank's loans went to southern Italy; indeed, Italy remains the bank's largest borrower, followed by the UK, Spain, and France. The EIB lent a total of 15.3 billion ECU in 1992, up from 7.03 billion ECU in 1991.[60]

The twelve member states are the EIB's shareholders, and the size of their subscriptions depends on their economic weight. Thus Germany, France, Italy, and the UK each subscribe 19 percent of the EIB's capital, whereas Luxembourg subscribes only 0.1 percent. The bank almost doubled its capital base to 57.6 billion ECU in January 1991, partly by raising new subscriptions from the member states. This is guarantee capital; only 7.5 percent is actually paid in. The bank's statute stipulates that aggregate loans and guarantees may not exceed 250 percent of subscribed capital.

The EIB raises almost all funds necessary to finance its lending operations by borrowing on capital markets, mainly through public bond issues quoted on the world's major stock exchanges. The bank's enviable record and reputable shareholders give it a top (AAA) credit rating. This good credit allows it to mobilize extensive resources without burdening the budgets of the member states and to channel resources in an economically efficient way to regions and sectors in need of support. The EIB borrows more than any other international financing institution, including the World Bank. It borrows and lends in about fifteen currencies, the most important of which is the ECU.

The EIB makes long- and medium-term loans in keeping with strict banking management. But the EIB is not a "normal" bank: It waits for projects to be brought to it and expects them to be largely financed commercially first. The bank can contribute up to 50 percent of a project's cost but typically lends only about 25 percent. Also, the bank's lending rates are highly competitive because of its excellent credit rating and non-profit status. As well as offering loans, the bank finds co-financiers and increasingly issues guarantees to commercial banks to encourage them to lend rather than lending directly itself.

The bank is located in Luxembourg and has a staff of about 750. It has its own legal personality and a unique administrative structure:

• *Board of Governors:* Twelve government ministers (usually finance); chairmanship rotates in the same order as in the Council of Ministers, but for a full year (June–June). Lays down general directives on credit policy; approves the balance sheet and annual report; decides on capital increases; appoints members of the Board of Directors, Management Committee, and Audit Committee.

• *Board of Directors:* Twenty-two members (twenty-one nominated by the Board of Governors and one by the Commission); five-year terms. Decides on loans and guarantees, fund-raising, and lending rates; decisions may be taken by majority, but majority must represent at least 45 percent of subscribed capital; meets on average ten times a year under the chairmanship of the bank's president.

• *Management Committee:* Seven members (the bank's president and six vice presidents); six-year terms. Controls all current operations; recommends decisions to the directors and then carries them out.

• *Audit Committee:* Three members; three-year terms. Verifies that the bank has carried out its operations and kept its books in order.

A number of developments in the late 1980s greatly enhanced the EIB's stature and importance. First, the single market program increased demand for EIB loans to improve the Community's infrastructure and increase industrial competitiveness. Second, the SEA's emphasis on economic and social cohesion, and the subsequent reform of the Community's structural funds, led to massive EIB financing for projects located in regional development areas. Third, German unification further fueled demand for EIB financing, notably for environmental programs and automobile industry restructuring. Fourth, the Commission's leadership of the Eastern European assistance effort extended the bank's financing activities in that direction.

The Maastricht Treaty confirmed the EIB's centrality to the Community system and essential role in financing European integration.[61] As with the articles concerning the Court of Auditors, the articles concerning the EIB were moved to the section on institutions. The treaty reaffirmed that the bank's main task is to provide funding for investment in underdeveloped regions and included a new paragraph instructing the bank to "facilitate the financing of investment programs in conjunction with assistance from the structural funds and other Community financial instruments." The treaty also called for a common policy in areas in which the bank is already heavily committed: trans-European transport, telecommunications, and energy supply networks; industrial competitiveness; environmental protection; and Community development cooperation with third countries.[62]

Regional development remains the EIB's top priority and accounts for most EIB lending. In 1992, loans for investment contributing to regional development accounted for almost 70 percent of EIB lending, the bulk of it in areas covered by activities under the structural funds.[63] Most EIB lending goes to projects in the Community's less privileged rural regions (in Ireland, Portugal, Greece, Spain, and Italy) and in declining industrial areas (in the UK, France, and the Netherlands).

The bank's activities within the Community can be broken down into the following major categories:

• Improving the transport and telecommunications infrastructure, including highways, airports, railways (for instance, the TGV high-speed train), and communications networks. The Channel tunnel is the EIB's largest single project. According to the EIB's president, "financing the tunnel fits the EIB's task of furthering the development and integration of the EC. It forms a key element in the development of the transport infrastructure necessary to meet the challenges of the single market."[64] Infrastructural projects account for about 45 percent of the bank's lending activity in the Community.

• Protecting the environment. Even before the Maastricht Treaty emphasized the need for environmental protection, the bank had identified this as a priority area. The EIB assesses the environmental impact of all projects under consideration.

• Strengthening the international competitive position of EC industry and promoting cross-border collaboration. The bank assists industry's adjustment to structural change and promotes growth of enterprise and innovation.

• Supporting the activities of small- and medium-sized enterprises (SMEs). The bank channels money to SMEs mostly through "European" global loans concluded with intermediary institutions.

Over 90 percent of the EIB's lending activity takes place inside the Community (including the Community's overseas countries and territories). Outside the Community, the bank provides assistance under various financial agreements, mainly with three groups of countries. The Mediterranean Environmental Technical Assistance Program, the bank's showcase activity in the Mediterranean region, is a collaborative venture involving the World Bank and the UN Development Programme. Under the Lomé convention, the EIB offers subsidized loans and risk capital assistance to African, Caribbean, and Pacific countries for industrial, agricultural, tourism, telecommunications, and transportation programs. Finally, the EIB has assisted economic development in Central and Eastern Europe since 1990. The EIB helped the European Bank for Reconstruction and Development (EBRD) get started in the early 1990s, subscribed 3 percent of the new bank's capital, and cofinances projects with the EBRD.

In 1992, the Council of Ministers asked the EIB to extend its lending activities to those Latin American and Asian countries with which the Community has cooperation agreements, subject to a low ceiling of 250 million ECU a year over a three-year period.

In addition to upholding its existing obligations inside and outside the Community, the EIB received a new responsibility at the Edinburgh summit in December 1992. As part of its emergency growth package to stimulate economic recovery in the Community, the European Council asked the EIB to manage a new, temporary lending facility of 5 billion

ECU. This would help fill the huge, recession-induced gap in EC investment and accelerate the financing of capital infrastructure projects. The heads of government asked the EIB to provide a maximum of 75 percent of planned financing.[65]

The European Council also called on the EIB, the Commission, and other financial institutions to establish as quickly as possible a European Investment Fund (EIF). The EIB will subscribe 40 percent of the new fund's 2 billion ECU capital, with the Commission and other institutions subscribing 30 percent each. The EIF's capital base will allow it to give guarantees worth between 5 and 10 billion ECU for various infrastructural projects.

NOTES

1. See, for instance, G. Smith, *The ECJ: Judges or Policy Makers?* (London: Bruges Group, 1990).

2. Article 164 EEC Treaty, Article 316 Euratom Treaty, and Article 31 ECSC Treaty (the language is identical in all three treaties).

3. Klaus-Dieter Borchardt, *ABC of Community Law,* 3rd edition (Luxembourg: OOP, 1991), p. 38.

4. G. Federico Mancini, "The Making of a Constitution for Europe," in Keohane and Hoffmann, *The New European Community,* p. 177.

5. See the Parliament's resolution of April 12, 1989 in OJ C120, May 16, 1989, p. 51, and the Martin Report on the results of the IGC, European Parliament Session Documents, DOC A3–123/92, March 26, 1992 (PE 155.444 Fin).

6. See especially Case 186/87, *Cowan v. Tresor Public.*

7. Borchardt, *ABC,* p. 40.

8. Carl Otto Lenz, "The Court of Justice of the European Communities," in *European Law Review* 14, no. 3 (June 1989), p. 133.

9. Case 6/64, *Costa v. ENEL* (1964), ECR 585.

10. Case 4/73, *Nold v. Commission* (1974) ECR 491; see also Mancini, "Constitution," pp. 188–189.

11. Case C-221/89, *The Queen v. Secretary of State for Transport, ex parte Factortame* (1991) not yet reported.

12. Quoted in *The Financial Times,* July 26, 1991, p. 14.

13. Anthony Arnull, "Reference to the European Court," in *European Law Review* 15 (October 1990), p. 391.

14. Commission, *1991 General Report,* point 1174, and *1992 General Report,* point 1111.

15. Martin Shapiro, "The European Court of Justice," in Alberta Sbragia, *Euro-Politics: Institutions and Policymaking in the "New" European Community* (Washington, DC: Brookings Institution, 1992), p. 127.

16. Donal Barrington, "Progress Toward European Union: EC Institutional Perspectives on the Inter-Governmental Conferences," paper presented at the European Community Studies Association's second international conference, George Mason University, May 23, 1991, pp. 7–8.

17. G. Federico Mancini, remarks at Whose Community? a conference organized by the Center for European Studies, Harvard University, January 30, 1993.

18. Commission, *1991 General Report,* point 1248, and *1992 General Report,* point 1212.

19. Quoted in *Agence Europe,* 1795, September 10, 1992.

20. G. Federico Mancini, "Whose Community?" conference remarks.

21. Case 222/84, *Johnston v. RUC* (1984).

22. Bull. EC 12–1992, Presidency Conclusions, point 1.15.

23. Lord Mackenzie Stuart, "The European Communities and the Court of Law," Hamlyn Lectures, 29th series (London: Stevens, 1977).

24. Shapiro, "Court of Justice," p. 124, n1.

25. See Tom Kennedy, "The Essential Minimum: The Establishment of the Court of First Instance," *European Law Review* 14 (1989), pp. 7–12.

26. See Spiros A. Pappas, *The Court of First Instance of the European Communities,* EIPA Professional Papers (Maastricht: EIPA, 1990), p. xi.

27. Kennedy, "Essential Minimum," p. 13.

28. Phil Fennell, "The Court of First Instance," *European Access* 1 (February 1990), p. 11.

29. Council Decision 88/591, (OJ L 319, November 25, 1988, p. 1).

30. OJ L 136, May 30, 1991, Rules of Procedure of the Court of First Instance of the European Communities of May 2, 1991.

31. See Fennell, "Court of First Instance," p. 12.

32. OJ L 144, June 16, 1993.

33. Barrington, "Toward European Union," p. 3.

34. OJ L 319, November 25, 1988.

35. Pappas, *Court of First Instance,* p. xii

36. Timothy Millet, "The New European Court of First Instance," *International and Comparative Law Quarterly* 38, no. 4 (1989), pp. 812–813.

37. Bo Vesterdorf, "The Court of First Instance of the European Communities After Two Full Years in Operation," *Common Market Law Review* 29, no. 5 (1992), pp. 897–915.

38. Jose Luis da Cruz Vilaca, speech at the official launch of the CFI, September 25, 1989, reproduced in Pappas, *Court of First Instance,* p. 10.

39. CFI, "Reflections on the Future Development of the Community Judicial System," December 3, 1990, reproduced in the *European Law Review* 16, no. 3 (June 1991), pp. 175–189.

40. Barrington, "Toward European Union," pp. 3–4.

41. "Declaration on the Court of Auditors," Treaty on European Union, p. 233.

42. See *European Council in Copenhagen: Presidency Conclusions,* June 21–22, 1993, SN 190/93, point 16.

43. See Daniel Strasser, *The Finances of Europe,* 7th edition (Luxembourg: OOP, 1991), p. 272.

44. Debates of the European Parliament, OJ 3–383, November 1989, pp. 7–8.

45. Bull. EC 11-1992, 1.7.24.

46. See Article 188c.2, Treaty on European Union.

47. See Strasser, *Finances of Europe,* p. 279.

48. Treaty on European Union, Article 188c.3.

49. Treaty on European Union, Article 188c.4.

50. Bull. EC 6-1992, 1.7.33.

51. Commission, *1992 General Report,* point 1118.

52. Commission, *1991 General Report,* points 1179-1182.

53. Commission, *1992 General Report,* points 1126-1129.

54. Bull. EC S/2–1991, pp. 178–179.

55. Quoted in *Agence Europe,* 5954, April 3, 1993, p. 4.

56. See Anthony Bevins, "EC Regions Committee Could Deflect Demands for Devolution," the *Independent* (London), January 20, 1993, p. 7.

57. Written question #1250/92, OJ C 247, Vol. 35, September 24, 1992, p. 53, and written question #1206/92, OJ C 6, Vol. 36, January 11, 1993, pp. 10–11.

58. Written question #1623/92, OJ C 658, Vol. 36, March 1, 1993, p. 27.

59. Bull. EC 10–1992, point 1.8.

60. Commission, *1992 General Report,* point 53.

61. Articles 198d and 198e, Treaty on European Union.

62. See European Investment Bank, *European Investment Bank: The European Community's Financial Institution,* 1992 edition (Leuven: Ceuterick, 1992), p. 1.

63. Commission, *1992 General Report,* point 53.

64. Hans-Gunther Broder, interview in *Europe* magazine (November 1991), p. 20.

65. Bull. EC 12–1992, Presidency Conclusions, point 1.30.

PART III

Policies and Programs

11

The Common
Agricultural Policy

The Common Agricultural Policy (CAP) is the oldest and most controversial Community policy. Even before the Community came into existence, agriculture was a politically sensitive sector for a number of reasons. Near-famine conditions in much of postwar Europe made food security a national priority. At the same time, the importance of peasant proprietorship in Western European political culture, the romantic lure of the land, and the emergence of a disproportionately influential farmers' lobby alerted governments to the potential pitfalls of agricultural issues. A decline in the economic importance of the primary sector and a corresponding drop in income for Europe's farmers raised the political stakes. Not surprisingly, by the mid-1950s agriculture had become a heavily protected and subsidized sector.

Notwithstanding their interest in European integration, governments were loath to forsake the option of sealing borders or limiting entry to their country's markets as a means of protecting domestic price levels and buttressing farmers' earnings. Thus, agriculture became an extremely touchy subject during the intergovernmental negotiations that resulted in the Treaty of Rome. Governments could agree on the CAP's main goals but not on how to achieve them. "The generality and vagueness of the Treaty provisions on the proposed CAP [were] testimony to the difficulties the government negotiators . . . encountered trying to reconcile their divergent interests. There had been agreement that there should be a collective effort to solve the problem of agriculture, but none on the form such joint policies should take."[1]

Article 39 outlined the CAP's general objectives:

- Increase agricultural productivity
- Ensure a fair standard of living for farmers
- Stabilize agricultural markets
- Guarantee regular supplies of food
- Ensure reasonable prices for consumers

Given agriculture's controversial nature and the Treaty's vague provisions, it is hardly surprising that "during the [Community's] first five years the question that dominated all others, by far, was the progressive construction of the CAP."[2] In July 1958, Sicco Mansholt, vice president of the Commission with responsibility for agriculture, convened a conference of Commission officials, member state delegates, and farmers group representatives in Stresa to devise the CAP's basic operational principles. In order to win political approval, the CAP had to replace individual member states' systems of customs duties, import quotas, and minimum prices with a harmonized Community-wide market, free intra-Community trade in agricultural products, and common protection vis-à-vis third countries. Thus, the CAP's guiding principles were (and are):

- A single market—agricultural produce should be able to move freely throughout the Community
- Community preference—priority should be given to EC produce over that of other countries
- Financial solidarity—the cost of the policy should be borne by the Community rather than by the individual member states

Although officially unstated, another principle subsequently emerged: Farmers should receive an income "equivalent" to that received by other sectors of society.[3]

Detailed discussions to formulate a mutually agreeable set of market rules culminated in a series of legendary marathon meetings of the Council of Ministers in late December 1961 and early January 1962. By the simple stratagem of "stopping the clock" at midnight on December 31, the ministers ostensibly reached agreement by the statutory deadline, although talks continued until January 14.[4] The result was a package that included a common system of price supports covering 85 percent of total EC production, a framework to raise levies on imports into the Community, and the establishment of the European Agricultural Guarantee and Guidance Fund (EAGGF) to underwrite the entire operation. "At this point, the EEC members relinquished a traditional sovereign right—to restrict access to the domestic market so as to control domestic price levels—and empowered the Commission to administer the EAGGF, the key agency of the new CAP."[5] The Council agreed to finance the EAGGF by member state contributions only for the first three years, after which a new arrangement would have to apply. Commission proposals to fund the EAGGF from July 1965 onward sparked the infamous Empty Chair crisis. It was only in 1970 that member states agreed to fund the CAP through the Community's own resources.

In the meantime, arduous talks took place to set common prices for a variety of crops. Setting a common price for wheat, politically and economically the most important commodity in the Community, dominated EC discussions in the mid-1960s and caused serious tension in Franco-German relations. Although far higher than France's wheat prices, the proposed Community rate was substantially lower than Germany's. Not only would Germany be contributing disproportionately to French agriculture through the EAGGF, but German farmers would also experience a drop in income. Charles de Gaulle used his considerable powers of persuasion to win German agreement and vindicate his faith in Germany's commitment to the Community.

The German government obliged but had to appease the politically powerful farmers union with a generous compensation package. Following another round of apparently endless meetings, the Council eventually established a fixed price for wheat and feed grains throughout the Community for the farm year beginning July 1, 1967, the date set for frontier-free trade in most agricultural products. However, because "the cut in nominal prices and the corresponding increase in competition from the other member countries was felt to cause considerable hardship," most German farmers and many officials in the German Ministry of Agriculture regarded the CAP as "a national disaster."[6]

From its implementation in the late 1960s, the CAP operated through instruments and mechanisms that vary from commodity to commodity but generally include: guaranteed prices, with the Community purchasing surplus produce; quotas, levies, and tariffs on imports to prevent external supplies from undercutting Community produce; and support for Community exports, mainly by refunds, to allow them to compete on world markets. The CAP's problems, inside and outside the Community, are inherent in those arrangements. As a result:

- Guaranteed prices bear no relation to demand and encourage over-production.
- Surplus produce has to be stored in "intervention," at additional cost to Community taxpayers.
- Big farmers produce more and thereby earn more money, whereas small farmers, who most need assistance, earn less.
- In order to produce more on their already overworked land, farmers use more herbicides, pesticides, and artificial fertilizers, thus accentuating the Community's acute environmental problems.

- Quotas, levies, and tariffs are protectionist measures that inhibit global market liberalization.
- Export price supports distort world prices and undercut other exporters, leading to trade disputes.

All of these problems or potential problems became apparent early in the CAP's existence. At the end of the 1960s Sicco Mansholt tried to rectify some of the CAP's most obvious excesses. The Mansholt Plan was the first, ill-fated effort to avoid surpluses yet still provide an adequate income to those who stayed on the land.[7] The Community's first enlargement made matters worse, but by that time vested agribusiness and rural interests had a firm grip on the CAP and successfully resisted reform.

Farmers succeeded in maximizing political support for the CAP by organizing effectively and by portraying themselves as a disadvantaged and beleaguered group that provides a vital service to society. The non-farming sector had relatively little information about or interest in the CAP and failed to appreciate the program's pernicious economic impact. Thus, politicians could win farmers' votes without alienating the support of other social groups and political constituencies.[8] As a result, foreign ministers and heads of government aggressively advocated their farmers' interests, often invoking the national veto to do so.

The idiosyncratic nature of the Agriculture Council compounded the problem. The Agriculture Council is unique in a number of respects: It convenes more often than most other councils; the Special Committee on Agriculture, rather than Coreper, prepares its meetings; the annual fixing of CAP prices is the highlight of the Agriculture Council's year and brings ministers together for intensive, late-night sessions; and agriculture ministers tend to be ex-farmers with strong ties in the rural community and a strong personal and political awareness of the CAP's importance.[9] Harold Wilson, Britain's prime minister in the mid-1970s, often "heard the most powerful heads of government aver that the agricultural cabal in the EEC—their own ministers—have so powerful a leverage that they have become a power center transcending the authority of national cabinets and prime ministers."[10]

Despite the popular notion that France, the EC's agricultural superpower, is the CAP's most tenacious defender, Germany has proved more obdurate than other member states in perpetuating price-driven support and blocking meaningful reform. Bitter experience with the CAP's implementation, as well as the farm lobby's added influence in a fragile national political system, toughened the German government's position on agricultural issues. Not surprisingly, it was a German initiative that led to the introduction of "green money" for the CAP. This agrimonetary system, and the related monetary compensatory amounts (border taxes and subsidies that have compensated for price differences within the Community caused by fluctuating exchange rates since the late 1960s), allowed Germany to keep its support prices substantially higher than other member states'.[11]

Obscene levels of overproduction in the late 1970s triggered a renewed discussion of CAP reform. In 1979 the Council introduced a modest change in the system of price guarantees and imposed a "co-responsibility" levy on dairy farmers to help meet the cost of intervention storage and subsidized sales of surplus produce. When the co-responsibility levy failed to curb excess output, the Commission proposed a production quota.[12] To his Community colleagues' surprise, Ignaz Kiechle, the powerful German agriculture minister, supported the Commission's proposal. Although a former Bavarian dairy farmer, Kiechle saw milk quotas as the only alternative to price cuts. After an intensive series of negotiations at the highest level, which at one point saw Garrett FitzGerald, the Irish prime minister, walk out of a European Council, the Community agreed in March 1984 on a quota system for milk production.[13]

The milk quota was an inadequate response to the problem of overproduction and hardly slowed down the rate at which the CAP consumed Community resources (by 1984 the CAP accounted for over 70 percent of Community spending). The possibility of bankruptcy, impending enlargement, and Margaret Thatcher's insistence on budgetary reform should have forced Community leaders to take radical action. Indeed, as part of the budgetary package agreed to at the June 1984 Fontainebleau summit, the heads of government resolved to curtail the growth of CAP expenditure.[14] At the same time, however, they agreed to increase the Community's own resources, thereby eliminating the most compelling reason for far-reaching CAP reform. As the *Economist* put it, "by agreeing to raise the EEC's income, the Ten have removed the most direct pressure for reforming a runaway farm policy, namely the threat of running out of money."[15]

Budgetary pressure brought the question of CAP reform to the top of the Community's agenda in 1987 and 1988. As part of the Delors I budgetary package, the Commission proposed a mix of measures to prevent overproduction, limit expenditure, diversify support for farmers, and promote rural development.[16] Proposals to strengthen budget discipline included land set-aside arrangements and production ceilings. Called "stabilizers," the proposed limits on output sought to control Community spending by establishing for each major product (with the exception of milk and sugar, already subject to quotas) a maximum guaranteed quantity (MGQ), beyond which support payments to farmers would be automatically reduced. The ensuing cut in payments would apply to *all* production, not just the portion above the MGQ.

Far from wanting to curb the CAP, Chancellor Kohl would happily have sanctioned a rise in agricultural expenditure. During most of 1987,

Kohl's fragile coalition government faced crucial local elections. Curtailing the CAP was an unpopular option with Germany's small but influential farm sector and could have cost the government valuable votes. The Delors I negotiations therefore made little progress until the extraordinary Brussels summit in February 1988. With a generous financial transfer to the "poor" southern countries having been approved, CAP reform was the outstanding issue as the summit came to an end. Whereas the other Community leaders proposed an MGQ of 160 tons for cereals, Thatcher held out for 155 tons. Suddenly, to everyone's surprise, Thatcher acquiesced. By accepting the higher ceiling, Thatcher let Kohl off the hook with Germany's farmers and ensured the success of the Delors I package.[17] The extra five tons would cost the Community 400 million ECU a year, a small sum by the CAP's bloated standards.

Like previous reform efforts, the 1988 package proved only moderately successful. Pressure for effective reform continued to build, not only because of the CAP's exorbitant cost but also because of two new developments. First, the CAP encouraged unfavorable international comment on the recently launched single market program. Although the single market program was immensely popular within the Community, it raised fears abroad about the possible emergence of a "Fortress Europe." Undoubtedly, the CAP's abominable international image fueled concern in third countries about the single market's consequences. If the protectionist and trade-distorting CAP was an example of a common policy in action, the single market would hardly help the rest of the world. Thus, the Community's vigorous efforts to combat pessimistic prognoses about the single market's external impact intensified internal pressure for CAP reform.

Second, poor progress in the Uruguay Round negotiations of the General Agreement on Tariffs and Trade (GATT), due largely to disagreements over agricultural export subsidies, heightened international revulsion of the CAP and concern about the single market program. More important, the Uruguay Round's midterm review in December 1988 and concluding ministerial meeting in December 1990 broke down largely because the Community refused to offer adequate cuts in farm subsidies. A German agricultural economist had urged in 1988 that "a very sensible approach [for the Community] would be to view the Uruguay Round negotiations as a helpful process, rather than thinking of them as an external threat to the CAP. The binding of farm support levels in the GATT and their agreed multilateral reduction make much more economic sense than any domestic criteria for price policy. At the same time, an international agreement is a much better basis for unpopular policy decisions at home."[18] Indeed, pressure from the Community's trading partners for reductions in agricultural price supports provided a powerful impetus to undertake serious CAP reform. Not wanting to be seen as acting under duress, the Community initially denied that any linkage existed.

Thus the single market program, the Uruguay Round, continued overproduction, and spiraling costs set the scene for a renewed reform effort. Moreover, the 1990–1991 embargo against Iraq, German unification, and developments in Central and Eastern Europe caused a sharp drop in export prices and aggravated the CAP's imbalances. This was the context in which the Commission reopened the reform debate with a February 1991 "Reflection Paper on the Development and Future of the CAP."[19] As well as offering the usual mix of corrective mechanisms, the Commission for the first time recommended a proposal to break the automatic link between price support and volume of food production. To balance the deepest price cuts ever contemplated by the Community, the Commission proposed full compensation for small farmers and scaled compensation for big farmers, subject to big farmers' removal of large tracts of land from production.

Agriculture Commissioner Ray MacSharry was the plan's architect and prime political mover. As Ireland's first-ever agriculture commissioner, MacSharry seemed more suited to maintaining the status quo, but the extent of the CAP's inefficiency genuinely appalled him. During a heated debate in the European Parliament in July 1991, MacSharry pleaded with MEPs "to look at the background of these proposals and the situation that exists in European agriculture today . . . we have 20 million tonnes of cereals in intervention [which] is going to rise to 30 million tonnes. . . . There are almost 1 million tonnes of dairy produce in intervention and that cannot be given away throughout the world. . . . There are 750,000 tonnes of beef in intervention and rising at the rate of 15,000 to 20,000 *per week*."[20]

MacSharry was just as passionate about the inequitable distribution of price supports between big and small farmers, not least because his political roots lay in the poor west of Ireland. The most effective method of CAP reform would have been to replace the system of guaranteed payments entirely with a fair program of income support for farmers. But the visible cost of such a program was politically unacceptable. Farmers liked to pretend that they operated in a free market system; direct aid would have revealed the truth. Moreover, massive public assistance would be "a prime target for economies in the budgetary process."[21] Nor would it have been easy to target assistance to those farmers who needed it most. Accordingly, although the MacSharry Plan included some direct income support, it did not propose to abolish guaranteed prices.

Predictably, agriculture ministers and farmers organizations almost uniformly opposed the MacSharry Plan. The leader of the Irish Farmers Association compared MacSharry to Oliver Cromwell, the seventeenth-century English general who destroyed Irish towns and slaughtered their inhabitants, and accused the agriculture commissioner of attempting "to destroy the CAP."[22] Representatives of other farmers organizations were less excitable but equally irresponsible, claiming that the plan would bankrupt small farmers and unfairly penalize big, efficient producers.

Given the unfavorable reaction engendered by the reflection paper, it seems remarkable that the Agriculture Council approved the plan, albeit in a modified form, over a year later. At first MacSharry appeared to lack even the Commission's support. Fearful of alienating French political opinion, Commission President Delors never backed MacSharry completely. Because of the CAP reform's likely beneficial impact on the Uruguay Round, External Relations Commissioner Frans Andriessen should have supported MacSharry enthusiastically. But as a former Dutch agriculture minister and a former agriculture commissioner, Andriessen equivocated. Only after intensive discussion did the Commission eventually approve the plan in July 1991 and forward it to the Council.[23]

Discussion of the MacSharry Plan in the Council of Ministers proved far more contentious than in the Commission, lasting until May 1992. British, Dutch, and Danish ministers complained that the plan discriminated against large producers; Spanish, Greek, Portuguese, and Irish ministers complained that it did not compensate small farmers adequately; and the French government opposed reform of any kind. Unusually, Ignaz Kiechle, Germany's veteran agriculture minister, stood up to the farmers union and rallied to the MacSharry Plan. Eager to reach a GATT agreement before the G7 economic summit in Munich in July 1992 and apprehensive about the impact of German unification on farm policy, the German government abandoned its unconditional defense of the CAP.

The agreement finally reached by the Agriculture Council on May 21, 1992, after a classic fifty-hour meeting, was a triumph for the Commission and for the Portuguese presidency, which got the package through by qualified majority vote.[24] Although smaller than the cuts in MacSharry's original proposal, the price reductions approved by the Council were nonetheless substantial and included a 29 percent drop in cereals prices over four years. The package succeeded in shifting the basis of agricultural assistance from price supports to direct income supplements paid to large farmers in return for land set-asides of 15 percent. As a concession to the French and British governments, the compensation offered to large producers was substantially higher than MacSharry's original offer.

Paradoxically, the generous compensation package agreed to by the Agriculture Council made the reformed CAP more expensive than the unreformed CAP. But by cutting guaranteed prices and taking land out of production, the reform should substantially reduce the Community's ruinous agricultural surpluses and eventually translate into lower food prices for consumers. Because price cuts could also eliminate export subsidies within four or five years, the reform gave a badly needed boost to the moribund Uruguay Round.

The 1992 reform was especially important in view of the Community's prospective enlargement. The four EFTA countries that began entry negotiations in 1993 have small, highly protected farm sectors. It will be much more difficult for applicant states to accommodate themselves to the CAP than for the CAP to accommodate itself to new Nordic and alpine member states. More than these states, however, prospective member states in Central and Eastern Europe pose a challenge to the Community's agricultural regime. The Community could hardly afford to extend the CAP, even in its reformed state, to large, inefficient Central European producers, especially in Poland. As a result, further radical CAP reform seems likely before the Community contemplates accession negotiations with the Central and Eastern European countries. Conversely, political resistance to further CAP reform could prevent the Community from beginning accession negotiations with those countries.

Despite the 1992 reform, the agriculture lobby's residual influence should not be underestimated. French farmers, angry over CAP reform, the November 1992 U.S.-EC oilseeds agreement, and a possible Uruguay Round accord, helped to crush the government in the March 1993 general elections. Similarly, European farmers' political clout resulted in a package of measures, approved by the Council of Ministers in December 1992, that included retention for two years of a "switchover" mechanism to compensate farmers for the abolition of monetary compensatory amounts with the advent of the single market on January 1, 1993.[25] The total package, which had something for almost every Community country, is likely to cost 2.5 billion ECU.

NOTES

1. Leon Lindberg, *The Political Dynamics of Economic Integration* (Stanford: Stanford University Press, 1963), p. 145.

2. Robert Marjolin, *Architect of European Union: Memoirs, 1911–1986* (London: Weidenfeld & Nicolson, 1989), p. 312.

3. See Graham Avery, "New Options for Agricultural Policy," *European Affairs* 1, no. 87, p. 64.

4. For an account of the CAP's origin and development, see Hans von der Groeben, *The European Community: The Formative Years: The Struggle to Establish the Common Market and the Political Union (1958–1966)* (Luxembourg: OOP, 1987), pp. 70–78. See also Lindberg, *Dynamics,* pp. 145–151.

5. John Keeler, "De Gaulle and Europe's Common Agricultural Policy: The Logic and Legacies of Nationalistic Integration," *Foreign Policy and Security* 8, no. 4, pp. 66–67.

6. Stefan Tangermann and David Kelch, "Agricultural Policymaking in Germany," International Agricultural Trade Research Consortium Working Paper # 91–8, October 1991, p. 13.

7. Com (68)1000, December 21, 1968.

8. See G. Schmitt, "Warum die Agrarpolitik ist, wie sie ist, und nicht, wie sie sein sollte," *Agrarwirtschaft* 33 (1984), pp. 129–136.

9. See Alan Swinbank, "The CAP and the Politics of European Decision Making," *Journal of Common Market Studies* 27, no. 4 (June 1989), pp. 304–307.

10. Quoted in *The Times* (London), June 28, 1977, p. 16.

11. See Tangermann and Kelch, "Agricultural Policymaking in Germany," pp. 29–30.

12. Bull. EC S/4-1983, point. 4.14.

13. See Michael Petit, et al., *Agricultural Policy Formation in the European Community* (Amsterdam: Elsevier, 1987).

14. Bull. EC 6-1984, point 1.1.7.

15. *The Economist,* June 3, 1984, p. 38.

16. COM(87)100.

17. See *The Financial Times,* February 20, 1988.

18. Stefan Tangermann, "Evaluation of the Current CAP Reform Package," *The World Economy* 12, no. 2 (June 1989), p. 187.

19. COM(91)100, February 1, 1991.

20. Debates of the European Parliament, OJ 3-407, July 11, 1991, p. 282.

21. Avery, "New Options," pp. 66–67.

22. Quoted in the *Irish Times,* July 10, 1991, p. 1.

23. COM(91)258, July 22, 1991.

24. 1579th Council Meeting (Agriculture), Press Release, 6539/92, May 18–21, 1992.

25. 1631st Council Meeting (Agriculture), Press Release 10793/92, December 14–17, 1992.

12

The Single Market Program

By identifying the steps necessary to complete the internal market, the Commission's 1985 White Paper[1] underpinned the 1992 program. Despite its comprehensiveness and seemingly microscopic specificity (it included, for instance, proposals on lawn mower noise and the taxation of fuel in truck tanks), the White Paper represented an educated estimate of the measures needed to bring about a single market rather than a revealed truth. It also served to give new momentum to old proposals by repackaging them as part of an exciting new initiative. A few, notably in the area of company law, had languished before the Council for years, whereas others had been withdrawn for lack of interest. Moreover, the White Paper was far from sacrosanct: The number of proposals to complete the single market hovered around 282, but they were not always the same 282. Some were discreetly deemed unnecessary when they failed to win support; others spawned additional measures. Given the complexity of the EC market, it is not surprising that the lines between the Commission's three categories of barriers to integration—physical, technical, and fiscal—were neither neat nor self-evident. Thus, the White Paper classified value-added tax harmonization as a fiscal barrier but put rules on company taxation in the technical barrier category.

PHYSICAL BARRIERS

Physical barriers—customs and immigration posts at border crossings between member states—were the most tangible obstacles to a single market. Accordingly, the Commission sought unequivocally "to eliminate in their entirety . . . internal frontier barriers and controls . . . by 1992."

335

Physical barriers included impediments to the movement of people (covering passport controls and residence restrictions) and goods. The latter proved far easier to remove than the former.

Movement of Goods

Customs formalities, paperwork, and inspections are common at border posts. The Commission took a two-step approach toward virtually eliminating paperwork at Community frontiers. First, member states consolidated all paperwork into a standard format called the Single Administrative Document (SAD), phased in at the beginning of 1985. Second, they largely abolished the SAD on January 1, 1993, causing the elimination of 60 million documents a year. (Documentation requirements remained for some categories of goods, such as dual-use civilian-military products). Accompanying measures to abolish customs formalities and inspections included miscellaneous provisions, such as duty-free admission for the fuel in the tanks of goods lorries, an end to routine checks of passenger car documentation, and a new statistical system for tracking trade among member states once border posts disappeared.

Ending onerous and costly border delays proved politically uncontentious. Indeed, by the end of 1991 the Council had adopted all the necessary provisions. In October 1992 the Commission published the Common Customs Code, supplementing it with a long-overdue digest of customs practices relating to issues such as entry, valuation, and bonded warehouses.[2]

Yet the vast bulk of the work to be done in the area of physical barriers involved the less visible sphere of agriculture. Border checks ensured compliance with a wide array of plant and animal health requirements and attempted to control the spread of diseases and the shipment of vegetables and fruit containing pesticide residues. Under the byzantine CAP rules, farmers were compensated at internal borders, and border checks enforced quota arrangements granted to Spain and Portugal at the time of their accession. Sixty-three of the White Paper's proposals covered disease control and livestock trade generally, as well as trade in meat, poultry, fish, and similar food products. Another eighteen covered phytosanitary (plant health) measures, the control of pests common to plants, pesticide residue limits, and the gene pool of ornamental plants. Of the eighty-one measures in these two categories, only three remained outstanding at the end of 1992.

Movement of People

Barriers to the movement of people have proved the most intractable part of the 1992 program and the most frustrating for the Commission. Key elements, such as passport controls and visa requirements, remain the exclusive province of member states. In order to permit the free movement of people as stipulated in Article 8a of the SEA, member states vowed to develop common rules for political asylum, immigration, and visas for foreign nationals, as well as to improve police networks and replace border measures directed against terrorism, drug smuggling, and other criminal activity. Their efforts resulted in three major agreements: the Dublin Convention on asylum rules; the convention on external borders; and the Schengen Agreement to eliminate all border formalities. Earlier, member states concluded the *Terrorisme, Radicalisme, Extremisme, Violence, Information* (TREVI) agreement on police cooperation, partly to compensate for the disappearance of criminal enforcement at intra-Community borders.

Of the three, only Schengen came close to becoming a reality. Starting with France, Germany, and the Benelux in 1985, the Schengen Agreement (named after a small town in Luxembourg) had expanded by the end of 1992 to include Italy, Spain, Portugal, and Greece and was finally due to come into force at the end of 1993. Three member states (the UK, Ireland, and Denmark) remain outside Schengen and are unlikely ever to remove controls on the movement of people, citing security and other concerns. The Dublin Convention has yet to be fully ratified, and the convention on external borders remains blocked by a disagreement between the UK and Spain over Gibraltar.

The Commission failed to break the impasse between member states over the free movement of people. In May 1992 it issued a communication describing the situation as "worrying at all political levels" and reminded member states of their commitment under Article 8a to abolish all controls at frontiers, without exception, by December 31, 1992.[3] Despite successive European Council statements about the need for free movement of people, the Commission's efforts merely elicited a suggestion that recalcitrant member states might allow EC nationals to show, but not hand over, their passports at the border—a maneuver derisively known as the "Bangemann wave."

Although the May 1992 communication hinted that the Commission would haul disobedient member states before the Court of Justice, Brussels brought no formal challenges by the summer of 1993. Instead, the Commission shifted to a lame emphasis on the need for "confidence building" to occur before passport checks can be eliminated throughout the Community and once again urged the European Council, at the June 1993 Copenhagen summit, "to ensure that the goals of Article 8A in the area of the free movement of persons are realized."[4] An earlier announcement that France would continue border checks on non-EC nationals (which, by implication, means some border control of all individuals entering the country until member state visa policies are fully harmonized) gives little cause for optimism. Some consumer organizations, less reticent and politically constrained than the Commission, have announced their search for suitable test cases with which to embarrass member states before the Court of Justice.

TECHNICAL BARRIERS

The White Paper used the term "technical barriers" almost as a catch-all: Proposals under this heading cover product standards, testing and certification, movement of capital, public procurement, free movement of labor and the professions, free movement of services, transport, new technologies, company law, intellectual property, and company taxation. Not surprisingly, it is by far the largest category of White Paper measures.

Standards, Testing, and Certification

The use of different standards in each member state for particular products can form technical barriers to trade. Despite a general prohibition on technical barriers in Article 30 of the EEC treaty, member states frequently abused the escape clause in Article 36, which allowed them to impose their own product standards for reasons of health and safety. Article 100 provides for "approximation" (harmonization) of standards in the event of differences between member states under Article 36. However, the arduous and politically sensitive process of harmonization led to a huge backlog of cases before the Council of Ministers by the mid-1980s.

To end the backlog and remove an enormous obstacle to the free movement of goods, the Commission developed the principle of mutual recognition of national regulations and standards. Instead of trying to harmonize a potentially limitless number of product standards throughout the Community, member states would recognize and accept each other's standards, as long as those standards satisfied certain health and safety concerns. The principle of mutual recognition rested squarely on a 1979 Court of Justice decision in a dispute over the importation of Cassis de Dijon, a French liqueur, into Germany. German authorities, supported by their national courts, had forbidden the sale of Cassis as a liqueur because it failed to meet the country's alcohol-content standards. But in a case brought by the aggrieved German importer, the Court of Justice ruled that because Cassis met French standards, it could not be kept out of the German market.[5]

Building on the Cassis de Dijon judgment, the White Paper proclaimed that "subject to certain important constraints . . . if a product is lawfully manufactured and marketed in one member state, there is no reason why it should not be sold freely throughout the Community." By emphasizing mutual recognition on the basis of Treaty obligations and Community case law, the Commission expected to trigger "the withdrawal of numerous harmonization proposals pending before the Council and . . . the abandonment of even more drafts envisaged by the Commission's staff."[6] Moreover, the Commission hoped that a combination of self-interest, common sense, goodwill, and peer pressure would reduce member states' recourse to Article 36. Yet there could be no question of member states' forsaking legitimate health and safety concerns about specific products manufactured elsewhere in the Community. The White Paper sought to maximize mutual recognition, not to abolish harmonization. Where harmonization remained essential, the White Paper proposed a two-track strategy. The first followed the traditional route of sectoral harmonization, and the second involved a path-breaking new approach.

On May 7, 1985, while the White Paper was still being drafted, the Council of Ministers approved "A New Approach to Technical Harmonization and Standards."[7] The new approach limited legislative harmonization by means of Article 100 to the establishment of essential health and safety requirements with which products had to conform. Member states would transpose those fundamental requirements into national regulations but could not impose further regulatory requirements on the products in question.[8] The White Paper included "New Approach" directives on a wide range of products, such as toys, machinery, and implantable medical devices. The "New Approach" dossier of eleven measures also included two horizontal directives: rules to prevent electrical appliances from causing electromagnetic disturbances, such as radio interference, or from being excessively sensitive to the electromagnetic fields of other appliances; and a directive expanding member states' obligations under existing legislation (Directive 83/189) both to report technical regulations and mandatory standards to the Commission and to delay implementation of those regulations on request. The directive broadened the list of regulations subject to notification to include those affecting agricultural products, foodstuffs, medicinal products, and cosmetics. Adopted in 1988, the revised directive already appeared obsolete by the end of 1992, when the Commission proposed a further broadening of it to include environmental, social, and other measures affected by the circulation of goods.

Because manufacturers would have some problems legally establishing that their products met fundamental requirements without the aid of further technical specification, the second part of the new approach required the Commission to contract with European standards organizations—CEN (European Standardization Committee), CENELEC (European Electrotechnical Standardization Committee), and ETSI (European Telecom Standards Institute)—to develop voluntary European standards (European norms, or EN). According to the 1985 Council decision, manufacturers adhering to those standards would be presumed to comply with the essential require-ments set in the directive, and their products would therefore be assured free circulation throughout the twelve member states. Manufacturers would also have the option of complying with national standards or, per-haps with less promise of success, of trying to demonstrate compliance with the essential requirements without the assistance of any standard.

In order to make the system work, member states would have to reach agreement not only on the essential requirements themselves but also on the level of proof needed to demonstrate compliance (i.e., reach a consensus on testing and certification requirements). The Council filled the gap in December 1989 by adopting a decision based on the Commis-sion's proposed "global approach."[9] The global approach described a set of standard "modules" for testing and certification of products, in most cases offering manufacturers some degree of choice. The options ranged from the least burdensome—in which a manufacturer could simply de-clare that a product met essential requirements—to the most burdensome, where, for instance, a third party (such as a nationally approved labora-tory) would test and evaluate the product.

Another option involved a "quality systems" approach, in which a manufacturer's consistent application of quality control measures from de-sign through production (in accordance with existing European standards for quality control) would be certified by an outside body. The rigor of the testing and certification requirements specified in the "New Approach" di-rectives—the module(s) that manufactures are required to follow—varies according to the perceived risk attached to the product. Thus, a manufac-turer of stuffed animals may declare his products in compliance without further certification, whereas a maker of cardiac pacemakers would need to seek third-party certification of the product or of his quality systems. Where required, "notified bodies"—laboratories or other institutions nom-inated by national governments—would perform third-party tests or cer-tification. In a further application of the principle of mutual recognition, member states are required to allow free circulation of goods certified by the notified bodies of other member states.

The CE mark, to be applied to products to show that they meet the essential requirements of all the applicable directives, plays a key part. The mark would either be applied by the manufacturer or by the notified body certifying the product. CE marks are intended primarily to show cus-toms and regulatory authorities that products comply with essential re-quirements; they should not be confused with quality marks, such as those awarded by other national bodies.

The "New Approach" directives, covering a wide range of prod-ucts, were largely completed by the end of 1992. However, the European standards bodies, highly bureaucratic and accustomed to a slow pace, soon lagged behind in developing the EN necessary to allow manufacturers to comply with the directives. As a result of inadequate coordination and long-range planning within the Commission, requirements for application of the CE mark turned out to be inconsistent and in some cases incompatible—that is, a product subject to more than one directive (e.g., the machinery directive and the electromagnetic compatibility directive) might not be able to comply with both sets of marking requirements. A directive on the CE mark retroactively harmonizing existing directives and laying down a single set of rules reached political agreement in April 1993.

The continuing lag in development of standards was a more serious problem. A 1989 Commission green paper, suggesting ways to remove bottlenecks, met with a frosty response from the leadership of CEN and CENELEC and raised concerns outside the Community that hasty setting of standards could lead to divergences between European and international standards. In the end there were few fundamental changes, but at least the standards bodies agreed to streamline procedures as much as possible. Nevertheless, by early 1993 a substantial backlog of unwritten European standards remained. To some extent, transition periods in the directive compensated for this problem; however, for manufacturers with long design cycles, such as makers of medical devices, such uncertainty had the potential to disrupt product development. Likewise, the slow pace at which member states notified testing bodies created another possible bottleneck in the system, especially because the bodies so notified would face an initial surge in demand as manufacturers rushed to certify their existing product lines.

Recognizing that the New Approach could not be applied to all sectors, the Commission took the old approach of working toward total sectoral harmonization—developing a single, detailed set of technical specifications for a given product that all member states would have to accept—in a number of key areas traditionally subject to intensive member state regulation because of safety risks and/or public concern. In the White Paper, the Commission advocated the old approach for motor vehicles and tractors, food, pharmaceuticals, chemicals, construction, and a number of other items.

The White Paper included eleven proposals on technical requirements for *motor vehicles*. The Community now harmonizes all technical regulations applying to motor vehicles in a voluminous package of forty-four directives covering a multitude of aspects, from weights and dimensions to exhaust emissions to protection from side crashes. Included in the program was a proposal for "EC-type approval," which would require member states to approve for sale any vehicle meeting the EC standards set forth in the sectoral harmonization directives. Other member states would be obligated to recognize this approval, thereby saving manufacturers the enormous cost of seeking multiple approvals, often with slightly varying specifications, for a single vehicle model. Three additional directives set up a similar system for tractors.

The seemingly dull *food* dossier became one of the most contentious in the single market program. Inevitably, the question of food content and preparation stirred up more passions than, for instance, the proper specifications for tractor tires. Food has therefore been a source of continuing public controversy as well as some critical Community jurisprudence (e.g., the Cassis de Dijon decision, German beer rules, and Italian prohibition of German pasta).

Because member states may continue to bar the free movement of goods on the basis of public health or consumer interest (member states routinely do so with regard to food products), a "New Approach" framework would not have succeeded in guaranteeing free circulation. The Commission therefore embarked on a detailed sectoral harmonization program that eventually included eighteen directives. Framework directives lay down general requirements—protection of public health, consumers, and the environment, as well as transparency and fairness of commercial transactions (e.g., truth in labeling)—to be supplemented by additional standards developed by the Commission and the Standing Committee on Foodstuffs, a scientific and technical advisory body. Directives addressed numerous issues, including: additives; labeling; inspection and tracking of food products; and hygiene.

The listing of permitted and prohibited additives caught public attention early on, especially in the UK, where the media complained that Commission recommendations on certain additives would undermine such treasured institutions as the prawn-flavored potato crisp. Consumer groups and MEPs took a highly restrictive approach to the use of additives, whereas producers sought to maintain their freedom of action and also to protect locally beloved staples. This highly politicized debate resulted in some anomalies, such as derogations permitting the use of certain additives in some traditional local products. One MEP complained during a debate on colorants that the British public had no idea what a pea really looked like; another suggested that products subject to derogations be labeled only in their native languages so that consumers in other countries would be discouraged from buying them.[10]

Nevertheless, by the end of 1992 the Commission had succeeded in getting eighteen of its nineteen proposals adopted, although work continued on the lists themselves. The remaining directive concerns rules for marketing food preserved by irradiation and remains on the table. Combining as it does two major public bogeymen—food safety and nuclear radiation—it probably has little hope of passage.

The *pharmaceutical* market in Europe is highly fragmented. Manufacturers must still go to national authorities for approval even to market drugs already on the shelf elsewhere in the Community. The powerful role of public health authorities in the purchasing area, reinforced by formal price controls in some member states, further complicates the issue.

The White Paper proposed fifteen directives addressing such questions as common testing rules, price transparency, patient information, advertising, and, above all, centralized approval of new drugs. The Commission envisioned a Community-level agency that would eventually take responsibility for all new drug approvals, backed by a host of new harmonizing directives laying down common procedures for testing and approval and ensuring free movement for human and veterinary medicines.

Although the bulk of the work on common testing rules, residue limits, and the like had been completed by the end of 1990, debate continued over the status and function of the proposed new agency. On the basis of the catch-all Article 235 of the Treaty of Rome, member states finally decided in 1992 to establish a European Agency for the Evaluation of Medicinal Products, but it had a far more limited function (at least initially) than originally planned. Composed of a secretariat and two existing committees of member state representatives (the Committee for Proprietary Medicinal Products and the Committee for Veterinary Medicinal Products), the new agency would be responsible for approving all medicines based on biotechnology and all veterinary medicines likely to improve the productivity of farm animals. This peculiar list resulted from a previous debate over the safety of biotechnology generally and over the possible approval of BST, a controversial new drug that improves milk yields of dairy cows. A number of EC member states allied themselves with the Commission and opposed approval of BST, ostensibly because its health effects were still unclear but undoubtedly also because it threatened to bankrupt the CAP.

Manufacturers of "innovative" medicines would have the option of applying to the European medicinal agency for centralized approval, which would be valid in all twelve member states. Manufacturers of other types of drugs must submit them for member state approval, subject to mutual recognition and with binding arbitration at the agency in the case of disputes. Because committees of member state representatives will direct the agency, national governments will retain considerable control over its decisions, leading some manufacturers to fear that political considerations will remain an essential part of the process.

EC-wide rules on classification, packaging, and labeling of dangerous *chemicals* date back to 1973. The White Paper continued the process, amending existing directives on classification, packaging, and labeling of chemicals and on marketing and use of certain dangerous substances and preparations (adding PCBs, PCTs, asbestos, cadmium, and other undesirables to the list of restricted substances and consolidating existing legislation in the area). Other relevant directives addressed the biodegradability of detergents and the marketing of fertilizers.

The White Paper included a short and far from comprehensive list of measures in the *construction* area covering noise levels of tower cranes, minimum standards for fire safety in hotels (a Council recommendation), and a "New Approach" directive setting out essential health and safety requirements for construction products. Finally, the White Paper included a *miscellaneous* set of directives touching on other sectors: noise levels of household appliances and lawn mowers, noise levels of construction equipment such as excavators and bulldozers, good laboratory practice for chemical product testing. The most eccentric of all was a directive on products "appearing to be other than what they are," such as toys that look like food.

Despite the daunting complexity of the system for standards, testing, and certification, and despite the system's continuing gaps, the net result should be to reduce costs and delays resulting from inconsistent member state regulation and the need for multiple approvals in some product areas. In the case of both the "New Approach" directives and the sectoral harmonization directives, the Commission's strategy was to develop centralized rules in order to reduce regulation at the member state level. Regardless of the standards finally chosen in each area, it is incontestable that compliance with one regulatory regime is bound to be less costly for manufacturers than compliance with twelve. Aside from small producers who never sold outside their own member states, manufacturers will undoubtedly benefit from the White Paper's reforms once they become fully operational. However, implementation delays, transition periods, and the pace of standards development mean that this essential aspect of the single market will mature gradually in the post-1992 period.

Movement of Capital

Three proposals addressed the problem of capital movement in the Community. Beginning in the 1960s, a steadily growing body of Community law had achieved considerable liberalization of the initially tight postwar restrictions on capital flows. As member states became richer and more confident of their own stability, many lifted restrictions unilaterally. Three White Paper directives aimed to complete the process with a sequence of measures intended to phase out controls, gradually leading to complete liberalization by the end of 1992.

The first directive, adopted in 1985, liberalized rules governing cross-border securities transactions. The second, adopted in 1986, liberalized rules on long-term commercial loans, securities transactions, and admission of corporate securities to capital markets in other member states (e.g., stock exchanges). And the third, adopted in 1988, superseded the first two. It obliged member states to lift all restrictions on capital movements except measures intended to ensure the continuing liquidity of local banks or temporary restrictions in response to major disruptions in foreign exchange markets. It also included derogations for Spain, Greece, Portugal, and Ireland.

The Commission saw enactment of these measures (the third of which came into force in 1990) as a final step on the road to "an effective and stable Community financial system"—a prerequisite for Economic and Monetary Union. The Commission's hopes may have been dashed by the 1992 exchange rate mechanism crisis, which forced Spain, Portugal, and Ireland hastily to invoke their derogations (until the end of 1992) and reimpose some exchange controls. The derogation for Greece is still in effect.

Corollary initiatives in this area included a 1991 directive on money laundering and a proposal, which is languishing before the Council, freeing pension funds for investment throughout the Community.

Public Procurement

The Community made initial moves toward opening procurement in the 1970s with two directives intended to increase transparency in Europe's traditionally protected public markets, which account for as much as 15 percent of Community GDP. However, transparency alone did little to improve the success of cross-border bids on public tenders. For a variety of reasons, ranging from active obstruction by local authorities to the inadequacy of the directives themselves, public procurement remained overwhelmingly the preserve of national suppliers. In 1992, the Commission estimated that only 2 percent of the 600 billion ECU public market had been won by firms from outside the home country.

The Commission correctly characterized such a distortion of competition as "anachronistic" and contrary to the spirit of a free market. Moreover, the Commission had a particular concern about the telecommunications sector, fearing that closed public markets and a cozy relationship between public authorities and cosseted but internationally weak "national champions" would hinder the development of a European telecommunications industry capable of competing in the harsher world market. The need to open public procurement and encourage competition generally became a recurring theme of the Commission's putative industrial policy.

The White Paper proposed seven directives to eliminate distortions caused by local procurement bias. Proposals covered essential elements of an open bidding system, such as transparency (effective public notice), review procedures to penalize violations, use of common standards (national or European), and procedures for award of public contracts. The directives also extended the scope of those rules to cover nearly all public procurement above certain thresholds (which vary by sector and by type of contract—i.e., supply, work, or service contracts).

A directive extending Community public procurement rules to *all* enterprises (not necessarily publicly owned) offering public services in the water, energy, transport, and telecommunications sectors formed the core of the Commission's liberalization program in procurement. Known as the Utilities Directive or the Excluded Sectors Directive, the draft regulation has the potential to open an enormous market to all European firms and applies to entities benefiting from public monopoly status. As with the other directives, this measure sets out minimum thresholds for application of its rules; requires use of common standards in most cases; sets out procedures to ensure transparency (such as a notice of tender in the *Official Journal* or the use of a published list of qualified suppliers, minimum periods for responses, and the obligation to publish results); and requires public authorities to evaluate bids on objective and nondiscriminatory criteria—e.g., lowest price or most economically advantageous package. (An exception to this rule later caused trouble with the United States: Article 29 allows member states to discard bids with less than 50 percent EC content and provides a 3 percent price preference for EC bids.)

The other six directives applied similar principles to supply of services and public works (i.e., construction and similar projects) and developed legal remedies for violations. All but one were adopted by the end of 1992; the remaining proposal, on procurement of services in the excluded sectors, was adopted in the spring of 1993.

Free Movement of Labor and the Professions

The White Paper included proposals for putting into consistent practice the right, enshrined in the Treaty of Rome, of EC citizens to live and work in other member states. Directives extending residency rights throughout the Community to students, retired persons, and other members of the nonworking population came into force on June 30, 1992. Those relating to workers and their families built on a 1968 directive guaranteeing nondiscrimination in employment and a right of establishment. White Paper proposals sought to extend nondiscrimination to various employment-related subsidies and social benefits, as well as granting residence and social and educational rights to non-EC nationals in the extended family of EC national workers. These proposals proved to be a tough sell, touching on rising fears among member state publics of uncontrolled immigration. They remained blocked in the Council as of 1993.

In order to facilitate the movement of workers among countries, the Commission also took on the task of establishing equivalencies between the various types of professional and vocational training available in each member state and of removing traditional restrictions that prevented members of regulated professions (e.g., doctors and lawyers) from freely offering their services in other member states. The Council adopted two directives on the recognition of diplomas (one on training of less than three years, the other on training of three years or more). In addition, the Commission has undertaken extensive studies and published comparative lists of member state qualifications and credentials covering over 200 vocations, enabling employers to evaluate qualifications in nonregulated areas.

Freedom of Movement for Services, by Sector

The White Paper proposed eight directives intended to allow banks incorporated in one member state to operate across national borders without having to seek authorization from up to eleven national regulatory authorities. The Commission based its efforts on three basic principles: harmonization of basic regulatory structures and requirements across member states; "home-country control"—i.e., making a bank's branches the responsibility of the member state in which the bank's head office is located; and mutual recognition among regulatory authorities.

Clearly, member states would have to agree to common rules and criteria for judging the soundness of banks in order to develop the necessary mutual confidence to allow the home-country control system to work. Harmonizing directives addressed the following regulatory issues:

- Supervision of financial groups (e.g., financial or diversified holding companies)
- Harmonized formats for annual accounts and balance sheets
- Consolidation of accounts of foreign institutions (so that they do not have to file separate statements in each member state)
- "Own funds" (i.e., which items may be included in judging the capital position of banks)
- Minimum requirements for deposit guarantee schemes
- Common rules and standards for limiting large exposures (e.g., loans to a single client or group)
- Freedom of establishment for mortgage credit institutions
- Solvency ratios for credit institutions (banks are obligated to adhere to a minimum ratio of assets and liabilities)
- Rules to prevent money laundering

The system of common rules for regulating banks supports the rules laid down in the Second Banking Directive, which guarantees free establishment of credit institutions throughout the Community and mutual recognition of member state authorizations for financial institutions. The Second Banking Directive establishes a single banking license, valid throughout the Community, allowing banks to open branches anywhere without additional authorizations. Issuance of such a license by a member state is subject to certain basic rules on initial capital and allowable investments. Overall supervision of a bank with multiple branches is to be a cooperative venture: The home country monitors solvency, and the country in which a branch is located may monitor the liquidity of the branch and impose other local conduct operations. The Second Banking Directive also contains provisions on foreign banks designed to give the Commission leverage in negotiating conditions for EC banks in foreign markets.

Adopted in 1989, the Second Banking Directive entered into force January 1, 1993. All but one of the remaining directives were adopted before the end of 1992.

The Commission based its approach to creating a single market for *insurance services* on the principles used in the banking sector: agreement on standards of supervision, mutual recognition of the supervisory powers of other member states, and home-country supervision of the activities of insurance firms operating across borders, supplemented by consultation among member state authorities. White Paper directives built on an existing body of Community legislation in the insurance area, beginning with a 1973 directive harmonizing criteria for the formation and activities of non–life insurance firms. The nine White Paper directives in this area involve the following:

- Harmonizing accounting practices for insurance firms
- Harmonizing procedures for compulsory winding-up (liquidation) of insurance companies
- Harmonizing information requirements, obligations of policyholders and insurers, and other aspects of insurance contracts
- Harmonizing laws on insurance coverage for legal expenses
- Broadening the 1973 directive to allow cross-border sales of motor vehicle insurance
- Providing common rules for cross-border sales of life insurance
- Establishing a "single license" system for supervision of life insurance companies operating across borders
- Establishing common rules and a single license system for supervision of non–life insurance companies operating across borders
- Establishing an insurance committee of member state representatives to consult with the Commission on the exercise of the supervisory authorities conferred on it by the preceding directives.

The *securities transactions* dossier followed the same three basic principles as the first two financial services dossiers: harmonization of essential standards, mutual recognition among supervisory authorities, and home-country supervision. The essential standards to be harmonized in the securities area included the following:

- Rules for mutual recognition of listing particulars (information required for the admission of securities to listing on stock exchanges)
- Requirements for prospectus for public offerings of securities
- Requirements for information to be provided on major holdings
- Regulation of insider trading
- Common rules for operation of unit trusts (known as mutual funds in the United States)

Building on these common standards, the Investment Services Directive set out the system for a single market in investment services and a single authorization procedure, reciprocity with third countries, common prudential rules, cooperation among supervisory authorities, and other necessary elements. The Commission proposed a directive harmonizing member state capital requirements (capital adequacy) to supplement the Investment Services Directive. Both the Investment Services Directive and the supplementary directive had reached the common position stage in the Council but had not been formally adopted when the single market supposedly became operational on January 1, 1993.

Transport

Opening up the Community's highly regulated transport markets required twelve directives covering six discrete and dissimilar sectors including air, road haulage (goods), and maritime transport.

Most *international air transport* markets are regulated by government agreements that usually inhibit competition. The situation in Europe was a particularly egregious example, combining a number of relatively small markets with "national champions" (frequently government-owned) protected through market-sharing arrangements, fixed fares, and occasional massive subsidies—all governed by two hundred bilateral agreements covering twenty-two countries. Not surprisingly, the result was high consumer costs. The Commission tackled the ensuing morass in three stages, and the Council adopted aviation packages in 1987, 1990, and 1992, gradually liberalizing the market in areas such as competition on fares, sharing of passenger capacity, access to routes for all operators, application of EC competition rules, and a right to carry passengers between two cities inside another member state (cabotage) for European airlines starting in January 1997.

Before the White Paper, *road haulage* between member states was generally subject to quotas that restricted rights to carry cargo on the return leg of any journey. As a result, large numbers of empty trucks traveled Community roads, adding to congestion and pollution and raising transport costs. Truckers were also prohibited from making runs between two points in any member state other than their own (cabotage). In addition, trucks were subject to different and often incompatible work rules or technical specifications (e.g., weight and size limits). The Commission approached the problem with three initiatives: harmonization to the extent possible of technical specifications and work rules; abolition by January 1, 1993, of all quotas on road haulage between member states; and the gradual introduction (via quotas) of cabotage (which can be reversed if effects on local haulers are too disruptive). Full cabotage rights—the final step in establishing a single transport market—were finally granted in June 1993, when member states agreed on a fair way to assess road taxes on foreign operators (a point particularly important to Germany).

In the area of *water transport,* the Council adopted directives allowing cabotage by EC-national operators on inland waterways and introducing cabotage, over a transition period, to ocean transport by member state nationals.

New Technologies

The White Paper included five directives on "new technologies," focusing on opening the markets for such technologies as cable and satellite broadcasting. The most important were

- a directive on mutual recognition of member state approvals for telecommunications terminal equipment (telephones, faxes, modems, etc).
- a framework directive on open network provisions (ONP) in the telecommunications area to ensure open access for equipment and service providers to the public telecommunications infrastructure. The directive prohibits public telecommunications networks from restricting access except on grounds of security, data protection, or the need to preserve interoperability. It also provides for a gradual development of mutual recognition of authorizations for service providers.
- a follow-up directive on open competition in the market for non-voice telecommunications services.
- the "Television Without Frontiers" directive, which liberalized member state television markets by prohibiting discrimination against works from other member states (with the exception of some remaining language quotas). The directive also harmonized

advertising standards (e.g., prohibiting advertising of tobacco) and obliged broadcasters to encourage local talent by showing a majority of EC-origin programming where practicable.

Other related directives covered mobile telephones, a European code of conduct for electronic payments systems, radio frequencies, data protection, and high-definition television standards. Also included was a Council decision calling on the Commission to develop an action plan to develop a European market for information services.

Company Law

Article 58 of the Treaty of Rome empowers Community institutions to take action in this field "to coordinate . . . safeguards . . . required by member states of companies or firms . . . with a view to making such safeguards equivalent throughout the Community." In 1968 the Council adopted the first in a long and often arcane series of directives in this area; like those that initially followed, its purpose was to approximate member state law to allow maximum freedom of movement for enterprises. The White Paper directives went beyond that goal by aiming to create a Community framework regulating cross-border corporate activity. As in the case of the procurement directives, one of the Commission's objectives was to increase the competitiveness of European firms by allowing them to become larger and more efficient.

The White Paper proposed a number of directives in this area—the fifth, tenth, eleventh, twelfth, and thirteenth company law directives. (The fifth directive, the odd man out in this series, was first proposed in 1972; its inclusion in the White Paper was an effort to improve its apparently dim prospects of success). Also proposed were the European Company Statute and a regulation defining the European Economic Interest Grouping (EEIG), a legal entity created to accommodate firms or other entities wanting to pool their resources for a common goal, but not wanting to merge. Perhaps the best-known example is Airbus Industrie. Some trade associations have also applied for recognition as an EEIG.

The EEIG measure was adopted by the end of 1992, as were the eleventh company law directive (disclosure requirements for branch operations), the twelfth directive (single-member companies), and a directive covering transparency in major holdings in company capital. The Commission had far less success with the remainder of the program. After years of blockage, it eventually made a virtue of necessity and declared the fifth, tenth, and thirteenth directives (dealing respectively with corporate structure and voting rights, cross-border mergers, and harmonization of rules on takeover bids) "nonpriority" for the creation of the single market. In a triumph of hope over experience, however, the Commission declared that the European Company Statute remained a top priority for the spring of 1993.

Despite the symbolic resonance of its name, the European Company Statute remains the Cinderella of company law. It sets out rules allowing enterprises to declare themselves "European Companies" subject primarily to EC law, rather than nationals of a member state subject to member state law. Originally proposed in 1970, the statute was inserted into the program in the hope that the momentum of 1992 would carry it through. In the event, it foundered once again on fundamental conflicts among member states over the issues of worker rights and provision for a European Works Council of union representatives in multinational firms operating under the statute. By early 1993, after years of unavailing discussion (including sixteen separate Council debates), some member states began again to question the necessity for such a statute.

Intellectual Property

Also under the general heading of removing technical barriers, the Commission proposed nine directives dealing with various aspects of intellectual property rights. They included the following:

- A regulation, and directives for its implementation, to create a Community trademark valid in all twelve member states
- A directive on legal protection of the topographies of semiconductors
- Legal protection of computer programs (the Software Directive)
- A proposal on copyright and related rights connected to cable and satellite transmissions
- A directive on rental and lending of copyright works
- Legal protection of biotechnological inventions
- A proposal for a Council decision obliging member states to join the international Berne Convention on copyright

Despite a brisk battle over the degree of protection for software products, the Commission succeeded in getting the Council to adopt four of these nine directives by the end of 1992. The issues of legal protection for biotechnological inventions and cable and satellite transmissions proved harder to resolve and remained on the table in 1993. But the major failure in this area was the legislation establishing the Community Trademark Office, which was thoroughly derailed by nonsubstantive but intractable disputes over the location of the office itself and the working languages to be used.

Company Taxation

To address the question of differing rates of tax on corporations in different member states, the Council finally adopted three proposals in 1990 that had been on the table for nearly twenty years. One covered taxes on capital gains resulting from mergers, share exchanges, and other forms of company restructuring; the other two concerned the problem of double taxation on intracompany dividend transfers and on profits of affiliated companies. Other proposals still under consideration include the offsetting of losses by a company affiliate in one member state against profits of the parent company in another and abolition of withholding taxes on intracompany interest and royalty payments.

FISCAL BARRIERS

The White Paper included an ambitious set of initiatives for harmonizing taxation—a prerequisite not only for eliminating borders (where many taxes were assessed) but also for reducing distortion and segmentation of the EC market through disparate tax practices. To take one of the more extreme examples, consumers groups calculate that the cost of a car varies as much as 100 percent across Europe because of excise, value-added, and other tax differentials.

Value-Added Tax

Of the wide variety of indirect taxes assessed on European goods, value-added tax (VAT) is the most visible and probably the most important. Before 1992, standard VAT rates varied up to 11 percent among member states. Some states charged luxury rates on certain categories of goods or charged no VAT at all on others. The White Paper called on member states to harmonize VAT rates and to develop a system for charging VAT on cross-border sales once border posts had been eliminated.

The road to VAT harmonization proved especially arduous. Because VAT revenues were in many cases the mainstay of member state social welfare systems, high-VAT countries could be relied upon to resist harmonization downward, even into the broad bands proposed by the Commission. Governments feared having to explain to voters why they were cutting back on prized social security regimes for the sake of the single market. There was speculation in 1992 that popular anxiety in that regard contributed to Denmark's narrow rejection of the Maastricht Treaty. Elimination of such local exceptions to VAT as food or children's clothing was equally certain to create political fallout. The alternative, proposed by some member states such as the UK, was to leave VAT unharmonized and let the market force member states align their VAT rates with those of their neighbors, if need be. This was a prospect only an island nation could face with equanimity; others feared that hordes of consumers, streaming across borders to get the best tax deal, would bankrupt local retailers and cut into the revenues of high-tax states.

Member states eventually reached agreement in June 1991 on a general framework for harmonization, which they formally adopted in October 1992. The main element was agreement on a standard rate of 15 percent or above in each country as of January 1993. Luxury rates were to be abolished, but member states could apply lower rates, or zero rates, to an agreed list of items during a transition period. Itself a result of political horse trading, the list yielded a few anomalies: In deference to the UK, for example, member states may apply lower rates to food but must apply the standard rate to "snacks" (needless to say, consumers would not be allowed to make the distinction between food and snacks). Some loose ends remain, such as decisions on rates for gold, passenger transport, and secondhand goods.

As well as harmonizing rates, member states agreed on rules for who should pay VAT and where. In 1987 the Commission proposed a straightforward system: VAT was to be paid in the country of sale. To address the problem of revenues lost by member states whose citizens shopped across borders, the Commission proposed a clearinghouse mechanism for redistributing VAT revenues to reimburse the countries running deficits in cross-border purchases. However, member states insisted on adopting a more ungainly "transitional" system (at least through 1997) in which VAT on cross-border trade must be paid in the country of destination. To make the system work, sellers and buyers are required to declare their cross-border transactions regularly to tax authorities, including such information as the VAT registration number of the buyer, and pay the VAT applicable in their own country on imports from other member states. (Firms whose cross-border transactions fall below a threshold are exempt from regular reporting.) Private consumers shopping in other member states, by contrast, will pay VAT in the country of sale—except on mail-order purchases and on cars, for which VAT is payable at registration.

The Commission set up a computerized VAT information exchange system to supply firms with necessary information, such as VAT numbers of firms in other member states, and to allow computer-literate businessmen to report and pay online. Whether this is really an improvement over paying VAT at the border remains an open question for many businessmen; some smaller enterprises found the new system so intimidating that they announced their intention either to end foreign purchases or to cut them down in order to remain below the thresholds—the exact opposite of the Commission's intended effect. Nevertheless, the Commission remains confident that once the bugs are worked out, firms will find it more convenient than the previous system of paying VAT at the border, with its attendant paperwork and delays.

Excise Tax

The second aspect of the indirect taxation dossier concerned excise taxes—internal taxes levied mainly on fuels, liquor, and tobacco. Member states reached agreement on a harmonized structure and rates for excise duties in July 1992, and legal texts were formally adopted in October of that year. Earlier, in March 1991, the Council decided to eliminate restrictions on cross-border purchases of those items by ordinary consumers. When harmonizing rates, the Council set "indicative levels" to help enforcement officers distinguish between ordinary citizens and commercial traders. As a result, citizens may now carry up to 800 cigarettes, 90 liters of wine, 110 liters of beer, 20 liters of aperitif, and 10 liters of spirits across borders for their own use.

     The logical consequence of removing fiscal frontiers should have been an end to duty-free shops in airports and on ferries. However, economics overcame logic in this case: Many airports and ferry operators gather a large chunk of their operating revenues from highly profitable duty-free operations. Accordingly, the Council decided to put off the demise of duty-free shopping until 1999.

BEYOND THE WHITE PAPER

In order to eliminate internal borders, the Commission also had to address the problem of quotas and other restraints imposed by individual member states under Article 115 of the Treaty of Rome. Nearly a thousand such measures, including over a hundred restrictive quotas, were in place at the beginning of the single market program. Using its power to deny quotas under Article 115, the Commission managed to phase out all but six of them by July 1992. This led the Commission to proclaim that its track record "dispels in concrete terms the too widespread notion that a Fortress Europe is being constructed."[11]

     For exporters to the Community of certain products—notably textiles, bananas, and Japanese cars—the Commission's exultation was premature. For instance, member state quotas on textiles phased out by the Commission had been codified under the long-standing Multifiber Arrangement (MFA), a web of import quotas imposed mainly on developing countries by developed ones. Although the Community continued to negotiate in the GATT for an eventual phaseout of the MFA, elimination of those quotas was not politically feasible. As a result, they were replaced by a set of bilateral quotas negotiated by the Commission on behalf of the EC as a whole, effective January 1, 1993. To assuage lingering member state discomfort, particularly in Spain and Portugal, over the possibility of market disruption resulting from the elimination of country-specific quotas, the Commission appropriated a substantial chunk of new EC funding to restructure the textile industry.

Nor were Japanese car manufacturers fated to enjoy the benefits of an open Community market. Responding to French and Italian consternation at the prospect of losing their harsh import restrictions and at the potentially disastrous consequences for their sluggish national champions, the Commission negotiated a voluntary restraint agreement with Japan. Coyly entitled "Elements of Consensus," the EC-Japan auto agreement restricts the growth of Japanese imports until the end of the century. The crux of the agreement was that Japanese car imports would be allowed a steadily increasing market share, reaching a ceiling of 15.2 percent of the European auto market by 1999, after which the Community would lift all restrictions. Import ceilings would also apply to markets that had previously had quotas or other restrictive arrangements (mainly France, Italy, Spain, and Portugal). At least in theory, production of Japanese-brand cars in Europe, so-called "transplants," will not be counted as part of the overall ceiling. Nevertheless, the agreement represents a considerable obstacle to highly competitive imports; in its first year of operation, the Commission, citing the comatose state of the European market, forced the Japanese to cut imports further.

One of the bitterest rows to emerge from the internal market program erupted over banana quotas. Seeking to protect the market position of high-cost bananas from former colonies (as well as some even more inefficient growers in the Canary Islands), France, Britain, Spain, and Portugal imposed upon an indignant Germany and Holland a restrictive tariff quota limiting imports of so-called "dollar bananas" from Latin America. Outvoted in the Council, Germany, whose per-capita banana consumption had hitherto been highest in Europe, threatened to bring the decision to the Court of Justice, and the Latin Americans initiated a GATT challenge to the Community. To compound matters, the Community allowed France and the UK to retain their individual quotas for an additional six months; only in the summer of 1993 did the single banana market become a reality.

Other member state practices also had the potential to block the full abolition of borders. In June 1992, a Commission communication claimed to have identified over five hundred different controls normally carried out at the border.[12] Some were scheduled to disappear at the end of 1992; others, such as Italian controls on currency exports, did not seem to justify retention of border measures. The Commission included some of the remaining controls in its 1992 internal market work program. The most difficult to resolve were those in which member states were suspicious of the ability or will of other member states to enforce existing obligations or where the disappearance of border controls required member states to develop a framework to carry out each other's decisions.

Some outstanding issues include:

• Controls on export of dual-use goods (those with military applications). Here, because of lack of Community competence (member states, not the Commission, were members of COCOM, the ad hoc group setting standards for dual-use export controls), the Commission was confined to proposing procedural measures for carrying out controls at external Community borders. Actual implementation of Community-wide controls would have to await completion of a common list of controlled items and destinations by member states, a process far from complete by the end of 1992.

• Controls on trade in endangered species under the Convention on Trade in Endangered Species (CITES). Until early 1993, Greece had not acceded to this convention. Some member states distrusted the quality of enforcement of the convention in other member states (e.g., Italy). The Commission therefore proposed a regulation laying down uniform enforcement of CITES rules, a measure that also remained on the table at the beginning of 1993.

• Controls on the movement of waste, both regular and radioactive. Disappearance of border authorities meant that member states had to find new ways to control the shipment of waste. After an extended controversy, the Council adopted a regulation on transfrontier movement of waste, a measure that, whatever its environmental merits, hardly contributed to the single market: It allowed member states to refuse shipments of waste from other member states in most circumstances.

• Procedures for controlling the export of cultural treasures. A number of southern member states feared that loss of border controls would lead to wholesale looting of national antiquities. In response, the Commission proposed two measures, one obligating member states to cooperate in controlling exports of certain types of artifacts from other member states, the other setting out legal procedures for restitution of cultural treasures illegally exported from other member states. A dispute over the time limit after which the losing state could not apply for restitution of illegally exported treasures delayed both measures. Northern states, with an eye on their museums, suggested a couple of decades; southerners, possibly recalling such offenses as the theft of the Elgin Marbles, initially wanted no time limit at all.

• Finding a way to abolish member state inspections of gold at the border.

Finally, a seemingly minor but politically explosive issue remains far from resolved: "accompanying animals." A directive on that innocent-sounding subject would require the UK and Ireland to lift their rabies quarantine requirements in the case of animals with proof of vaccination. Although justifiable on both veterinary and internal market grounds, such a proposal would undoubtedly provoke a visceral public reaction. Originally scheduled for release just before the 1992 Irish referendum on Maastricht, the draft directive inexplicably failed to appear and has not been seen since.

THE SUTHERLAND REPORT

In April 1992, the Commission charged an ad hoc committee, chaired by former commissioner Peter Sutherland, with developing a strategy to ensure the proper functioning of the internal market after January 1, 1993. Released in October 1992, the Sutherland Report advocated a number of broad initiatives that could apply not only to the internal market but also to general Community legislation. It paid ritual homage to the politically correct principle of subsidiarity, noting the need for balance between maximizing the role of national and local authorities and avoiding fragmentation of the single market.

The Sutherland Report stressed two areas in which Community practice needed improvement: transparency and enforcement. The Commission and member states should develop a "communication strategy" to inform consumers and firms of their rights and should publicize draft legislation, or intent to draft legislation, at a much earlier stage. The report also called for codification of Community law to help people wade through long strings of directives intended to amend other directives and suggested that all directives be systematically succeeded by regulations on the same topic to ensure consistent interpretation. Finally, the report proposed a Commission legislative unit that would reduce the distressing rate of inconsistencies among directives.

Although laudable, many of the report's recommendations were somewhat hortatory. For instance, the report called on the Commission to make "a wide-ranging analysis of the political, social and economic impact" of draft legislation. An alarming aspect of that particular recommendation was the implication that at present the Commission pays little or no attention to the wider implications of its draft legislation.

On enforcement, the report called for a greater role for national courts, possibly including efforts to train lawyers and judges in Community law. In addition, the report suggested developing enforcement networks among member states to compare notes on the transposition into national law of EC directives. Under the system suggested, prime responsibility for enforcing product regulations would lie with the "home authority" in the place where the product was made or imported, with Commission oversight.

In December 1992, the commission responded with a communication promising to follow many of the report's guidelines and adjuring member states to improve their administrative infrastructures in order to do likewise. Specifically, the Commission promised to publish an annual report on the internal market, establish a legislative unit, make more systematic use of green papers to publicize contemplated legislation, consult with interested parties, and, of course, conduct "a wide-ranging analysis" of proposed directives.[13]

IS 1992 A SUCCESS?

The official unveiling of the single market on January 1, 1993, happened at an inauspicious time. The Community was in the doldrums, with parts of it, such as the UK, in a disastrous recession. The brisk growth of the late 1980s, which lent credence to the Cecchini Report's extravagant claims for the single market, had suddenly dissipated. It seemed unlikely that merely announcing the official existence of the single market would get the economy going again.

Sensing public skepticism and even hostility during the Maastricht Treaty ratification crisis, the Commission kept the celebrations low-key. Aside from sponsoring a chain of bonfires across Europe and a fireworks display in Brussels, the Commission's main response was to issue reams of information keyed to perceived citizen concerns about such issues as conditions for transporting horses or the fate of unemployed customs agents.

Under the circumstances, the long-awaited advent of the single market came almost as an anticlimax. As the bonfires smoldered, the griping began. Businessmen complained vociferously about the computerized VAT reporting system, with smaller firms threatening to stop shipping across European borders. MEPs were irate when asked for their passports in the Strasbourg airport, and journalists tried to provoke border guards by walking through border posts carrying armloads of bananas. The only conspicuously happy constituency was the horde of Britons reboarding ferries at Calais with trunks full of cheap French wine.

Amid all the bluster, there were some real grounds for criticism: Transition periods and derogations stretching toward the end of the century meant that the single market program was far from being entirely in place on January 1, 1993. The highly visible failure to abolish border checks on people was bound to tarnish the image of the single market, already under fire from environmental and social groups characterizing it as a heartless sellout to business interests. There were smaller failures as well. Important flanking measures, such as rules on export of dual-use goods or trade in endangered species, were unfinished. Manufacturers of products covered by "New Approach" directives faced uncertainty and disruption over the pace at which European standards could be developed and introduced. Taxation policies and exemptions from competition rules that prevent cross-border price shopping meant that customers would benefit little from lowered manufacturers' costs brought about by harmonization. Consumer banking charges, especially in the foreign exchange area, remained opaque and disparate. The double-barreled VAT system may become a fertile source of confusion. All in all, the internal market today is a patchwork full of derogations, exceptions, missing links, transitions, and anomalies.

When comparing the single market's shortcomings with the original aim of the White Paper, however, a much brighter picture emerges. Despite the lack of perfection and logic—inevitable in any political process—the White Paper functioned as intended. In tying so many elements to a politically coherent and attractive vision, the Commission managed to push the Council into adopting proposals that would not otherwise have engendered much political enthusiasm. Obviously the White Paper package had its limits; in late 1992 the Commission tacitly abandoned some proposals by hastily demoting them to "nonpriority" status. There was also a risk that the Commission would become a victim of its own publicity success, that failure to "complete" the single market precisely on time would deal a crushing political blow to the Commission's credibility. In the event, public reaction was measured, and the Council has continued to adopt the remaining proposals at a respectable pace. Now that 1992 has arrived, it may also be possible for the Commission quietly to drop some of its hopelessly blocked proposals, such as the European Company Statute and the Community Trademark Office.

The main achievement of the 1992 initiative may well have been psychological. It created a climate in which individuals as well as firms could begin to identify themselves as European and look for opportunities beyond their own borders. It also created an atmosphere in which national governments could contemplate surrendering further sovereignty. Those attitudinal and psychological changes are likely to prove lasting, despite lingering citizen anxieties about cultural identity and economic competition. The single market program, and the drive and energy displayed by the Commission in pushing it through, restored the image of the EC as a vital and modern entity and paved the way for the broader initiatives, such as EMU and EPU, that followed. Relative to them, moreover, it stands out as a practical measure with real benefits to the European economy.

In the long run, the success of the single market will depend on two factors: the level and quality of member state implementation and the Commission's ability to resist the proliferation of new trade barriers. Implementation quickly became part of the Commission's countdown to 1992; league tables ranked member states on their level of implementation of directives in force, and the press mulled over the occasional dramatic leaps registered by Italy or the irony that politically recalcitrant Denmark consistently topped the charts. Yet such tables yielded little real information on the state of the single market. They reflected neither the quality of implementing legislation nor the likelihood that directives would be enforced by member state authorities or courts. Since the advent of the single market, the Commission has publicly adopted a circumspect tone on member state implementation, with the new internal market commissioner even suggesting that gentle encouragement was the best means of moving forward.[14] In private the Commission has reportedly taken a tougher line, backed up with legal action; in 1993 the Commission had over two hundred infringement actions pending with regard to nonimplementation of White Paper measures (amounting to about 10 percent of member states' total obligations).

New trade barriers that could render the White Paper's liberalizations irrelevant or ineffective are a serious concern. High on the list are certain types of environmental measures, such as restrictions on packaging, that could hinder the free circulation of goods and be extremely difficult to challenge. Member states have demonstrated a tendency to resist limiting their own freedom to enact environmental restrictions affecting products; environmental activists are especially resistant to arguments favoring trade benefits over environmental ones. Other markets, such as the pharmaceutical market, remain fragmented by restrictions such as pricing provisions.

A proposal for revision of Directive 83-189 (which currently requires member states to notify "technical regulations" and gives the Commission the right to impose a standstill) is one weapon available to the Commission to combat deterioration of the internal market. The revised directive would broaden the scope of such legislation to include environmental and other measures having an effect on the market and prevent member states from claiming that a certain market-closing measure was not a "technical regulation." That should at least increase transparency. However, without a commitment by member states to preserve the achievements of the internal market program, the Commission will forever fight a losing battle.

NOTES

1. COM 85(310) final, June 14, 1985.

2. Council Regulation 2913/92, Bull. EC 10-1992, 1.3.18.

3. Bull. EC 5-192, point 1.1.7.

4. European Council in Copenhagen 21–22 June, 1993, Presidency Conclusions, SN 180/93, June 22, 1993.

5. See "Rowe-Zentral AG vs. Bundesmonopolverwaltung fur Branntwein," Case 128/78, *Reports of Cases Before the Court* (1979): 649–675.

6. Helmut Schmitt Von Sydow, "The Basic Strategies of the Commission's White Paper," in Roland Bieber, Renaud Dehousse, John Pinder, and Joseph Weiler, eds., *1992: One European Market? A Critical Analysis of the Community's Internal Market Strategy* (Baden-Baden: Nomos Verlagsgesellschaft, 1988), p. 93.

7. Council Resolution, May 7, 1985, OJ C 136, p. 1.

8. See Jacques Pelkmans, "The New Approach to Technical Harmonization and Standardization," *Journal of Common Market Studies* 25, no. 3, March 1987.

9. Council Resolution, OJ C 10, January 16, 1990.

10. European Parliament, Committee Meeting on Health and the Environment, Brussels, February 1993.

11. Commission press release IP(92)546, July 3, 1992.

12. Bull. EC 6-92, point 1.3.15.

13. SEC(92)2277, December 2, 1992.

14. See *The Financial Times,* January 22, 1993, pp. 1, 2.

13

A Level Playing Field

The Treaty of Rome identified certain policy areas and legislative activities in which the Community would have to become involved in order to buttress the projected common market and create a level playing field. Competition is an obvious example: Without rigorous antitrust rules, control of state subsidies, and liberalization of restricted industries, the common market would be seriously undermined. As the Community's fortunes fluctuated in the 1960s and 1970s, however, there was little progress in completing the internal market, let alone in developing related policies. Consequently, when efforts to complete the internal market gathered momentum in the early 1980s, inevitably attention focused also on such closely related issues as industrial policy and competition policy. The SEA marked a turning point not only by putting the 1992 program firmly on track but also by strengthening the Community's ability to act in those legislative areas.

INDUSTRIAL POLICY

In its narrowest, traditional sense, industrial policy implies government intervention to underwrite specific enterprises or sectors, whose survival the government deems essential for socioeconomic or strategic reasons. The instruments of such a policy could include "soft" loans, grants, tax concessions, guaranteed procurement contracts, export assistance, and trade barriers. Left-wing governments are usually cited as zealous proponents of government intervention in industrial affairs, as is 1960s France. Of course, France in the 1960s had right-wing governments, thereby demonstrating that nationalism as much as ideology underpins the pursuit of an interventionist industrial policy.[1]

A laissez faire approach is the opposite form of industrial policy and is often associated with right-wing governments. Even if they deliberately eschew direct intervention, however, governments have an enormous influence on industrial planning and production. Public contracts and defense-related procurement are obvious ways in which all governments, regardless of political persuasion, intentionally or unintentionally assist national manufacturers.

The EC inherited a strong interventionist ethos. Indeed, the CAP is a classic example of an intrusive industrial policy in the agricultural sector. But member states agreed to share responsibility for agriculture for peculiar political reasons and because the agricultural sector was in serious social and economic decline. Member states retained as much power as possible over other sectors, including the right to support "national champions." Thus, although it dealt with certain aspects of regional policy and social policy, the Treaty of Rome included few provisions for an interventionist, Community-level industrial policy.

Yet the Treaty of Rome embodied an industrial policy in the broadest sense of mapping out a strategy for industrial development. The projected internal market and related competition law would create an economic framework conducive to industrial growth. In the prosperous 1960s, however, governments had little incentive to go beyond a rudimentary common market, and in the recessionary 1970s they resorted to restrictive practices to protect national champions. Following the agriculture precedent, governments allowed Brussels to intervene directly only in those industries in serious economic trouble: steel, shipbuilding, and textiles.

Restructuring Declining Industries

Given the history of the Schuman Plan, the steel industry occupies a special place in the Community. Following steady economic growth in the 1950s and 1960s, declining demand and poor economic planning caused a crisis in the steel industry beginning in the 1970s. Production declined and then stagnated, resulting in a massive underutilization of capacity, no new investment, and substantial unemployment. Citing the Treaty's provisions for dealing with a "manifest crisis," in 1980 the Community responded by intervening directly to restructure the industry. With a view to ensuring the steel industry's "return to competitiveness and financial health under normal market conditions," the Commission established a virtual cartel, imposing price controls, import restrictions, and mandatory curbs on production.[2]

Textiles faced an equally bleak future. The Commission helped in two ways: first, by negotiating bilateral agreements under Article 4 of the

Multifiber Arrangement to restrict imports of textiles from East Asia and Latin America; and second, by proposing specific measures to assist restructuring of the industry and retraining of its work force.[3] With a view to helping the badly battered shipbuilding industry, the Community authorized high levels of state subsidies, stipulating piously that "the granting of such aid should be linked to the achievement of restructuring objectives."[4]

The High Technology Sector

Steel, textiles, and shipbuilding were old, declining industries. The Community's high technology sector (including computers, consumer electronics, and telecommunications) was new yet apparently also in trouble. *The American Challenge,* the title of a popular book on Europe's declining competitiveness, seemed to sum up the problem. Throughout the 1960s, Europeans had fretted about a supposed "technology gap" between themselves and the United States. *The American Challenge* confirmed their fears by portraying the United States as a powerful predator encroaching on Europe's weak and fragmented market in the increasingly lucrative and strategically important high technology sector.[5] Compared to U.S. industry's enterprise, advantage of scale, and international ambition, European firms seemed severely handicapped.

For the next decade European governments responded to the U.S. challenge largely by supporting national champions—huge firms that enjoyed a virtual monopoly in their country's sizeable public sector markets. France, with a well-deserved reputation for *dirigisme,* was not the only culprit. Despite its supposed inclination toward market liberalism, Germany also promoted national champions, as did the UK, under Labour leadership for much of the 1970s. Yet by the early 1980s the trans-Atlantic technology gap had apparently widened, and a new chasm was opening between Western Europe and Japan. Poor economic performance during the previous decade exacerbated Europe's predicament. With little economic growth, industries had no incentive to invest heavily in research and development. Nor did the limited and relatively small size of their domestic markets encourage new initiatives.

At the same time, European companies had undertaken a number of collaborative ventures, notably in aircraft manufacturing and marketing. Concorde, the joint Anglo-French effort to produce a supersonic passenger plane, is the most obvious and expensive example. In the early 1960s France and Britain also began to collaborate on Airbus, a project to produce short- to medium-range, wide-bodied passenger aircraft. Germany joined the consortium in 1966, and Britain departed in 1968. Despite its success in the 1980s, Airbus began badly, with numerous cost and time overruns. Whereas Concorde was already in service by the late 1960s, the first Airbus still remained on the drawing board. Only in the mid-1970s, when Airbus broadened its base to include Dutch and Spanish participation and received its first non-European orders, did the venture really take off.

The Community did not participate in those collaborative projects, although in 1967 the Commission established the Directorate-General for Industrial Affairs (DG III) to encourage cross-border cooperation. DG III's birth reflected a growing awareness in the Community of the need to concentrate resources and promote intra-EC mergers. Early Community efforts to increase European competitiveness were not confined to the member states, however. In 1971 the Community joined with neighboring Western European countries to launch COST (European Cooperation in the Field of Scientific and Technical Research), an institutional framework and source of funds for joint research projects in such areas as informatics and telecommunications.

Despite collaborative and Community efforts, by the end of the 1970s Europe's high technology sector seemed as badly off as before. Political and ideological problems beset both endeavors. Governments disputed the wisdom and practicability of cross-border industrial cooperation; within the Commission itself, the Directorate-General for Competition (DG IV) kept a close eye on DG III's potentially interventionist activities. Yet the Community's acute industrial difficulties, the soaring cost of research and development, the increasing importance of new technologies—especially in microelectronics and semiconductors—and the continuing U.S. and Japanese threat convinced many European manufacturers, politicians, and government officials that closer collaboration under the Community's auspices held the key to European industry's survival and success. By contrast, the notion of national champions became increasingly outmoded.

Etienne Davignon, Commission vice president with responsibility for industrial affairs between 1981 and 1985, took the lead in promoting Community-wide technological collaboration. By cultivating the CEOs of major European manufacturers in the high technology sector, Davignon developed a powerful industrial support group for cross-border collaboration. European industrialists were especially receptive to Davignon's ideas because of renewed economic recession and the evident failure of the national champion approach.

In May 1982 the Commission unveiled a proposal, "Toward a European Strategic Program for Research and Development in Information Technology" (ESPRIT), which the Council of Ministers, already lobbied by Davignon's group of European manufacturers, approved the following June.[6] The ensuing ESPRIT program called for major European manufacturers, smaller firms, universities, and institutes throughout the Community to collaborate on "pre-competitive," or basic, research. That distinction helped to reduce friction between the industrial participants and satisfy the concerns of the Commission's competition watchdog. A pilot scheme of thirty-eight projects, funded by the Community and the private sector, got under way in 1983 and constituted "the first step toward the development of a genuine, long-term European industrial policy."[7]

Within a short time the Community launched not only a full-fledged ESPRIT but also related research initiatives with catchy names such as RACE (advanced communications technologies), BRITE/EURAM (industrial technologies and advanced materials), and BAP (biotechnology). Later in the 1980s the Community launched BRIDGE (biotechnology), ECLAIR (linkage of agriculture and industry), FLAIR (agroindustry), and COMETT (education and training for technology). In 1985 the Community became a founding member of EUREKA, a highly successful French-led effort to develop European technology as a response to the U.S. Strategic Defense Initiative.[8]

Building on the earliest R&D initiatives, the SEA recognized that one of the Community's objectives is "to strengthen the scientific and technological base of European industry and to encourage it to become more competitive at an international level."[9] Accordingly, the SEA stipulated that the Council should unanimously adopt multiannual "framework programs" delineating the main scientific and technological objectives and defining priorities. The program itself would be implemented by a series of specific subprograms, most involving Community-industry cost sharing.

The Single Market Program

The SEA's main objective—to implement the single market program—owed much to ESPRIT's early success and constituted a major tenet of EC industrial policy. Whatever its impact on European industrial competitiveness, the ESPRIT pilot scheme—run by a joint public-private task force—at least satisfied European industrialists that the Commission was a constructive and competent partner. That partnership, in turn, led to awareness on both sides of the Community's potential for economic revival in Europe. If the Commission could bring industrialists together to improve Europe's competitiveness, why could it not help end the fragmentation of Europe's own market by breaking down the plethora of nontariff barriers that impeded intra-Community business and trade? Why not use the Commission's authority to promote liberalization, harmonization, and standardization? Instead of limiting industrial policy to trying to help Europe's global competitiveness, why not broaden its scope to prize open public procurement in Europe? Thus Davignon's endeavors to promote industrial competitiveness in the Community contributed to a growing momentum in the early 1980s for completion of the internal market.

Indeed, by giving European industry "a political program on which it could finally base concrete action plans for restructuring operations, for increasing economies of scale, and for improving the efficient use of vital resources,"[10] completion of the single market became an integral part of the Community's industrial strategy. According to Martin Bangemann, Commission vice president with responsibility for industrial affairs, the competitive discipline imposed by the single market provided the best medicine possible for European manufacturers.[11] In the sense that it opened up enormous opportunities for European industry, not least by forcing many national champions to restructure radically, the single market program became the most important instrument of Community industrial policy in the late 1980s.

The single market program also represented a triumph for economic liberalism and a temporary setback for interventionism. But the Commissions's aggressive pursuit of competition policy as a means of opening up the marketplace—and therefore as an integral part of the Community's industrial strategy—appeared to thwart the emergence of "Eurochampions": European multinationals that could compete and win globally. The problem seemed especially acute in the electronics industry, which encountered serious difficulties in the early 1990s despite market liberalization and a series of framework programs. European electronics manufacturers' pressure on Brussels for old-fashioned industrial assistance became especially intense, not least because the French government owned two of them (Bull and Thomson).

Jacques Delors sympathized with the electronics industry's pleas for protection. Apart from his political aspirations in France, Delors had a strong interventionist streak. His advocacy of an "organized European space" included Community assistance for industry that might otherwise succumb to competition from the United States or Japan. That put Delors at odds with Leon Brittan, the fiercely anti-interventionist competition commissioner. It also distinguished Delors from Bangemann, another free marketeer. But Bangemann took a far more flexible approach than Brittan, believing that different solutions were appropriate for different industries in different circumstances.[12]

Toward a Post-1992 Industrial Policy

In an effort to lay the ground rules for a post–single market industrial strategy, in November 1990 the Commission produced a paper entitled "Industrial Policy in an Open and Competitive Environment: Guidelines for a Community Approach."[13] The Commission offered the paper as a response to a "growing consensus" that the EC needed an industrial policy, but declined to offer any industrial policy measures in the traditional (i.e., *dirigiste*) sense of the term. Instead, it rejected sectoral policies as ineffective and stressed that the Community's role should be to maintain a competitive environment. In elaborating on this position, the paper accomplished two important Commission objectives: It established a coherent philosophical framework to justify the policies the Commission was already pursuing, and it firmly dashed expectations that the Community would act to support and protect a given sector, no matter how strategic.

In the Commission's analysis, the role of government (hence that of the EC, with due regard for subsidiarity) should be limited to providing, first, a competitive business climate and, second, "catalysts to encourage firms to adjust rapidly to changing circumstances." The need for a competitive environment as an industrial policy objective implied vigorous competition policy—including strict control of state aids—in addition to macroeconomic stability. Moreover, it suggested a relatively open trade policy to allow European firms to become seasoned international competitors. Other prerequisites for competitive industry included a tough environmental policy, greater economic and social cohesion, and a higher educational level among workers.

The paper found a convenient niche in this framework for the single market as the Community's chief catalyst for structural adjustment. It noted the benefits, inter alia, of common standards, mutual recognition, open procurement, abolition of Article 115 quotas, and the development of trans-European networks for encouraging rapid structural adjustment and offering greater economies of scale. On the R&D side, the paper suggested that the Community should aim not only to develop but also to diffuse generic technologies—encouraging greater use of information technology, an area where Europeans lag behind both as producers and as consumers.

Emphasizing the importance of a competitive business climate in which firms make key decisions, the paper stressed that Community assistance would be "horizontal" rather than industry-specific and would consist largely of policing the marketplace to guard against protectionism and private market power. The Commission also reiterated the current conception of industrial policy as a combination of environmental, social, regional, and competition policies contributing together to a "level playing field" for European manufacturers, as well as an aggressive trade policy to ensure that the international economic environment was as fair as possible.

The Commission proposed to follow up this broad conceptual framework with a series of papers applying its principles to various troubled sectors (notably electronics, autos, textiles, and aerospace), together with an analytical paper on industrial competitiveness and environmental regulation. The first testing ground for the Commission's noninterventionist stance was the European electronics industry, battered by foreign competition and holding onto less than half of its own domestic market. After a spirited tussle between Bangemann's DG III and the largely French-influenced DG XIII (Technology), the Commission produced a relatively non-*dirigiste* paper.[14] The Commission's paper described the state of the electronics sector in Europe relative to the United States and Japan and blamed the feeble state of Europe's electronics industry on market fragmentation and high capital costs. It also advocated trans-European networks, training, more market-oriented EC R&D, and completion of the Uruguay Round as Community approaches to resolving the industry's problems. Predictably, the Commission's paper infuriated the French and many in the private sector who wanted outright financial assistance and protection.

Following publication of the Commission's paper, the CEOs of Europe's major electronics firms had a "mini-summit" with Delors, Bangemann, and Filippo Pandolfi, the research commissioner.[15] Delors may have wanted to meet their *dirigiste* demands, but in light of the Commission's broadly defined industrial policy—to say nothing of the Community's GATT obligations—it was politically impossible for him to do so. Instead he urged closer intra-industry cooperation, with a view to strategic alliances that would bolster the European firms' global competitiveness. Few of the industrialists present heeded his advice, choosing instead to pursue strategic alliances with U.S. or Japanese firms.

The Commission's position against demands by the French and others for a more interventionist approach was strengthened by a coalition of member states with no national champions to protect. Transcending north-south differences, Britain, Ireland, Spain, and Portugal feared that protection of European industry would hamper foreign investment in their countries, harm consumers, and divert scarce Community resources to giant firms in France, Germany, and the Benelux. In the event, it was far from clear where new sectoral subsidies could come from, either in Community or member state budgets. France suggested redeploying existing Community funds; Bangemann cleverly countered that the Commission should start with the CAP. Eventually, in a clear victory for Bangemann (and Brittan), the Council adopted a resolution along the lines of the Commission's paper.[16]

Subsequent papers met a much less stormy reception; perhaps all sides had learned the pitfalls of trying to push a *dirigiste* policy in the Community context. The debate over electronics clearly demonstrated that conflicting member state interests made it impossible to support sectoral initiatives at the Community level, to say nothing of the substantial new funding that such policies would require. Despite auto producers' panic at the thought of fully opening markets to the Japanese in 1999 (the long grace period is itself a concession to the need for structural adjustment among overprotected national champions), they were unable to wring

much more from the Commission than some modest worker-training proposals for firms in poorer regions. The Commission applied the Bangemann principles to other sectors with increasing confidence and decreasing backlash from firms and member states.

Reflecting the ongoing debate on industrial policy, the Maastricht
Treaty contained a new Title (Article 130) on the subject. Like the language in the Commission's 1990 paper, the treaty's provisions on industrial policy are vague, calling on the Community and its member states "to
ensure that the conditions needed to make Community industry competitive are met in a system of open and competitive markets." In order to
achieve the objectives of structural change, a favorable business environment, and better exploitation of innovation and research, the treaty stipulates that the Council "may adopt specific measures in support of action
taken by member states." However, the Council may only act *unanimously,* thereby denying the Community more authority in the area of industrial policy.

Despite the Commission's recent communications on general and
sector-specific support, and despite the Maastricht Treaty's new title on
the subject, industrial policy remains a pressing issue in the Community.
Not least because of Europe's increasing economic openness, expanding
global corporate alliances, and faster technological obsolescence, national
governments and the Commission are likely to revisit the issue later in the
1990s.[17] Moreover, political and economic trends would seem to point in
the direction of a more interventionist industrial policy in the Community
and elsewhere. At a time of renewed recession, a widening trade deficit
with Japan, and growing economic nationalism on both sides of the Atlantic, inevitably interventionists are making their voices heard.[18]

Yet the emasculation in April 1993 of DG XIII (in charge of high
technology and research) suggests that, despite the Commission's failed
effort to shore up Philips and other EC firms through a mandated—and
obsolescent—HDTV standard, free market forces are still alive inside the
Commission. Known for its close association with the electronics industry
and its advocacy of sector-specific support, DG XIII was a bastion of old-
fashioned *dirigisme.* Although the redoubtable Leon Brittan no longer has
responsibility for competition, he remains extremely influential in the
Commission. Karel van Miert, a Belgian Socialist and Brittan's successor,
has taken a surprisingly strong free market stand, and Bangemann, who
retains industrial affairs, firmly adheres to free market principles. Nobody
knows what Raniero Vanni d'Archirafi, the new internal market commissioner and a former Italian diplomat, thinks about the issue. In any event,
the difficulty of designing a sectoral policy that will give real benefits to
the affected sector without distorting competition, retarding cohesion, and
drawing fire from member states whose industries would be disadvantaged (or who are competing for the same benefits) may be the most

effective brake on efforts within the Commission to depart from a horizontal approach, especially in view of the highly restrictive Maastricht language.

In the post-Maastricht period, the Community will continue to pursue an active R&D policy, based on ESPRIT and other programs. Yet the crisis confronting Europe's electronics industry in the early 1990s suggests that ESPRIT has had only limited success. Although ESPRIT was never intended as a panacea for Europe's high technology sector or as a substitute for industrywide restructuring, the Community's R&D programs appear increasingly inadequate. Perhaps because of an emphasis on precompetitive research, they have so far produced little commercially useful technology.

Finally, Community spending is only a small part of total Community-wide spending on R&D—hence the need for greater coordination between national- and Community-sponsored R&D to ensure consistency and value for money. The Maastricht Treaty calls for such collaboration, which the Commission elaborated upon in a paper entitled "Research After Maastricht: An Assessment, A Strategy."[19] Thus, R&D remains an essential element of Community industrial policy in the broader context of the EC's single market strategy.

COMPETITION POLICY

Competition policy comprises two main branches, one with regard to the activities of private enterprise, the other with regard to the activities of member states and state-sponsored bodies. The first covers what is generally referred to in the United States as "antitrust": prevention of practices by private entities (such as restrictive agreements or abuse of dominant position) that could inhibit competition and distort the marketplace. The second relates to the control of "state aids" (all forms of public subsidies to firms) and the liberalization of "regulated industries" (companies either owned by, or having a special relationship with, national governments).

The Community's antitrust efforts draw heavily on the U.S. experience. U.S. Secretary of State Dean Acheson's first reaction to the Schuman Plan—that it might bring into being "a gigantic European cartel"— strengthened Monnet's determination to include robust antitrust measures in the ECSC treaty, both to assuage U.S. concern and to ensure fair play for European producers.[20] U.S. antitrust lawyers helped Monnet to set up the ECSC. Later, U.S. antitrust doctrine exerted considerable influence over officials in the Commission's competition directorate-general (DG IV), many of whom studied U.S. law.[21] Paradoxically, by the mid-1980s, after a protracted Commission investigation of IBM, "the prevalent American conception of the EC's antitrust policy is that it invariably protects Community industries which are important for the achievement of social and economic goals and . . . promotes anti-competitive business agreements."[22]

Unlike competition policy in the United States, however, competition policy in the Community deals not only with private sector abuses in the marketplace but also with massive government financial assistance to national enterprises and with utility services—such as electricity, water, and telecommunications—which European governments have traditionally controlled. By including efforts to curb state subsidies to industry and confront government monopolies, therefore, Community competition policy involves much more than antitrust.

Moreover, competition policy has a political purpose in the Community that goes far beyond its economic objective in the United States. As well as policing the marketplace, Community competition policy seeks to break down barriers between national markets, thereby promoting European integration. Speaking at the University of Chicago—famous for its scholarship on antitrust law and economics—Sir Leon Brittan, the former competition commissioner, jocosely described the "Brussels School" of competition policy: "It includes rules on state aids and on firms granted special or exclusive rights, and has special concerns to promote market [and European] integration."[23]

Competition policy's relevance for market integration became readily apparent in the mid-1980s with the launch of the 1992 program. Enforcement of competition law was an obvious corollary to the development of a single market. Without the vigorous application of competition rules, the benefits of market liberalization could easily have been nullified by price fixing and market sharing between firms, as well as by rampant government intervention.

Antitrust

Articles 85 and 86 of the EEC treaty form the legal basis of the Community's antitrust policy. Article 85 prohibits agreements and concerted practices between undertakings that restrict competition at the Community level, subject to individual or block exemptions under certain circumstances. Article 86 prohibits any abuse by one or more undertakings of a dominant position that distorts trade between member states. Such abuse could consist of setting unfair prices, limiting production or markets, applying dissimilar conditions, and making the conclusion of contracts subject to acceptance of supplementary obligations.

Clearly, Community antitrust law would have had little effect without practical means of implementation. Accordingly, in 1962 the Council adopted a regulation giving the Commission extensive powers of investigation, adjudication, and enforcement.[24] The Commission's ability to counter infringements depends to a great extent on the information at DG IV's disposal. Most companies cooperate with the Commission, however grudgingly. In the event that some would not, the 1962 regulation authorized Commission officials to arrive unannounced at businesses throughout the Community and conduct immediate on-site investigations. After a flurry of activity in the late 1970s, the Commission shied away from doing anything of the sort. Only after the launch of the single market program did DG IV's "trust-busters" once again go on the offensive, under the energetic leadership of competition commissioners Sutherland (1985–1989) and Brittan (1989–1991).

Nevertheless, it is misleading to imagine Commission officials conducting dramatic dawn raids. Unannounced on-site inspections take place during normal working hours and are the exception, not the rule. However, the unexpected arrival of Commission officials usually yields otherwise unobtainable evidence of wrongdoing. In 1980, the Court of Justice upheld the Commission's power to order and carry out investigations without warning the companies in advance; since then it has upheld the Commission's right, once inside a company, to carry out an active examination of its files and records without hindrance or restriction.[25]

The Commission resolves about 90 percent of these cases informally, before ever carrying out exhaustive investigations. If the Commission decides to take formal action, it sends the firm in question a detailed statement of objections. Firms are entitled to respond in writing and to present their case (including witnesses) at a hearing. Not least because of the political sensitivity of some cases and the possibility that firms will appeal to the Court of Justice, the Commission deliberates extremely carefully before reaching a decision.

If it concludes that there is an infringement, the Commission may impose a fine—not exceeding 10 percent of the firm's total turnover. Substantial though that amount seems—the Commission routinely imposes 10 million ECU fines—it is often insufficient to deter large firms from conducting other abusive practices. As Leon Brittan has remarked, "some firms seem to regard [Commission] fines as just another overhead."[26]

The *Tetra Pak* case is a striking example of Commission action against abuse of a dominant position. Tetra Pak, a Swedish company based in Switzerland, is the largest supplier of packaging (cartons) for milk and fruit juices. In some cases the company enjoyed a virtual monopoly (95 percent of the market) for machinery and for packaging of "long-life" liquids. A lengthy Commission investigation, based on a competitor's complaint, revealed that Tetra Pak's marketing policy, customer contracts policy, and pricing policy had deliberately infringed Article 86. The Commission ordered Tetra Pak to end its anticompetitive behavior and imposed a fine of 75 million ECU on the firm.[27]

Merger Policy

The Treaty of Rome said nothing about mergers and acquisitions. However, an extensive body of case law, based on the Continental Can doctrine (called after a celebrated court case[28]), extended the scope of Article 86 to include structural changes through mergers and acquisitions. Accordingly, a firm contravened Article 86 if it held a dominant position and strengthened it by means of a takeover or merger. Yet the Community's limited merger control was retrospective; it applied to cases where a dominant market position had already been established. Merger control reform had been on the Community's agenda since 1973, but little progress was made until a plethora of mergers and acquisitions took place in the mid-1980s, at the outset of the single market program.

The number, size, and speed of 1992-induced mergers gave Competition Commissioner Peter Sutherland a legitimate pretext upon which to press national governments to cede more regulatory authority to Brussels. Member states appreciated the threat that uncontrolled Community-wide mergers posed to the emerging single market but disagreed on the criteria for Commission vetting and approval. Germany and Britain, member states with the strongest national competition authorities, were the most reluctant to cede merger control to Brussels. As a result, it was not until December 1989 that the Council adopted a regulation making provision for the prior authorization of mergers, thus enabling the Commission to control the build-up of dominant firms.[29] The 1989 merger regulation constitutes a cornerstone of the Community's competition policy and single market program.

Based on a number of key principles and provisos, the regulation makes a clear distinction between mergers with a "Community dimension," where the Commission has the power to intervene, and those that have their main impact on a particular member state. A Community dimension exists when all of the following are true:

- The firms involved have an aggregate worldwide turnover of more than 5 billion ECU
- Each of at least two of the firms involved has an aggregate Community-wide turnover of more than 250 million ECU
- At least one of the firms involved has less than two-thirds of its aggregate Community-wide turnover within one particular member state (i.e., requirement of transnationality)

For mergers coming under the Commission's scrutiny, the crucial test is that of "dominant position," taking into account such factors as the structure of the markets concerned, actual or potential competition, the market position of the firms involved, the opportunities open to third parties, barriers to entry, the interests of consumers, and technical and economic progress. The regulation also includes compulsory prior notification by the firms concerned and a strict timetable for Commission decisionmaking.[30]

The Commission established a merger task force to implement the new regulation, which came into force in September 1990. The task force, and the regulation itself, were a striking success. In its first two years the task force dealt with nearly 150 notifications, clearing the vast majority within a month. Only a handful went to a full-scale, four-month, phase-two investigation. Firms seem pleased to have a single Community-level procedure to deal with instead of a number of procedures at the national level, and they have complied fully with the notification requirement.[31] However, the regulation's jurisdictional division between mergers having a Community and a national dimension is sometimes confusing.[32]

The Commission blocked only one merger under the new regime—the 1991 bid by France's Aerospatiale and Italy's Aliena for Canadian aircraft manufacturer De Havilland. The issue split the Commission, with one side (including Delors and Bangemann) arguing that the merger would boost European competitiveness by giving manufacturers a bridgehead in the North American market and the other side, led by Brittan, claiming that the merger would give Aerospatiale and Aliena a near-monopoly in the EC marketplace for turboprop commuter aircraft.

The controversy over the De Havilland decision was partly a result of national and international politics—the French, Italian, and Canadian governments lobbied hard on behalf of their firms, in favor of the merger—and partly to industrial policy considerations. By contrast, Brittan interpreted the 1989 merger regulation strictly as an instrument of competition policy. In 1991 Brittan's view narrowly prevailed: "The Commission believes that a rigorous competition policy is an essential element in the Community's industrial policy. Maintaining effective competition is one of the key factors in ensuring that Community industry is successful."[33]

A subsequent case, involving the Swiss food group Nestle's takeover of Perrier, France's largest mineral water supplier, represented another advance for the Community's rapidly developing merger control policy. The merger task force challenged the deal on the grounds that it would give two companies, Nestle and BSN, a duopoly of the lucrative French mineral water market. After four months of hard bargaining, the Commission approved the merger in July 1992, when Nestle agreed to give up control of about 20 percent of the French market.[34] Although the deal left Nestle and BSN with more than 65 percent of the mineral water market, it set a precedent by allowing the Commission to challenge duopolies as well as monopolies.

State Aid

Control of state aid is an even more politically sensitive subject than merger policy. Although member states agreed in Article 92 of the EEC treaty that state aid should be prohibited in most circumstances, in practice they have allowed themselves broad latitude under the exceptions included in the treaty—notably for aid to poorer regions—especially during economic recession and when facing political and social fallout from the precipitous decline of industries. Nor have they always informed the Commission in advance of plans to grant or alter aid. Moreover, the mixed character of the European economy, where government ownership of industry is considered an acceptable instrument of economic development, means that the precise level of state support is often difficult to determine.

Like the lack of a Community-level merger policy, state aid was a chronic problem that became a major issue in the mid-1980s with the launch of the 1992 program. Article 93 of the EEC treaty authorized the Commission, in cooperation with member states, to monitor state aid closely, and Article 94 allowed the Council, acting by a qualified majority on a proposal from the Commission, to adopt appropriate regulations to prohibit market-distorting public assistance. A weak Commission and a deep recession combined in the 1970s virtually to end Community-level efforts to control state aid. With Community solidarity almost nonexistent and governments vying with each other to prop up infirm industries, state aid was rampant. From 1981 to 1986 member states reported between 92 and 200 cases of state aid each year; the Council acted against fewer than 10 percent.[35]

An enormous increase in state aid in the early 1980s, along with national rivalry in the provision of public support, strengthened the Commission's hand. In 1983 the Commission sent a communication to member state governments announcing that it would require them to refund any aid granted without prior notification of the Commission or a prior ruling by the Commission on the aid's compatibility with Article 92.[36] The onset of the single market program further boosted the Commission's position.

Strict control of state aid became as vital as the vigorous application of antitrust law for the success of the single market. By subsidizing companies in their own countries, national governments distorted competition throughout the whole Community and put nonsubsidized companies at an obvious disadvantage. Yet governments were loath to surrender such a powerful political, economic, and social instrument. Peter Sutherland led the Commission's offensive to tackle the state aid scandal, pointing out to member states the "inherent contradiction in working for the creation of an internal market by 1992 and denying the independent role and obligation of Community institutions to enforce Community [competition] law fairly, even when this is contrary to the wishes of a national government."[37]

Soon after taking over from Sutherland, Brittan began a comprehensive review of state aid policy, with a view to ascertaining the real level of aid being granted, taking strong measures against the most anticompetitive and wasteful subsidies, and rolling back the general level of aid. The Commission lacked an implementing regulation for state aid comparable to the 1962 antitrust regulation. However, based on case law, a more favorable political climate, and a number of specific actions, the Commission began to make an impression.

Brittan also launched a procedure to tackle the problem of aid being granted without prior notification to the Commission. Under his plan, the Commission would require the member state to supply full details of the aid in question within thirty days, sooner in urgent cases. If the member state failed to reply or gave an unsatisfactory response, the Commission would make a provisional decision requiring the state to suspend application of the aid within fifteen days and initiate the procedure under Article 93(2) to make the member state provide the necessary data. If the member state still failed to comply, the Commission could adopt a final decision of incompatibility and require repayment of the amount of state aid allocated. Should the member state refuse to abide by the Commission's decision, the Commission would refer the matter to the Court of Justice.[38]

The Commission's communication on public undertakings, adopted in July 1991, was to have been an important step toward curtailing state aid.[39] It required member states to submit annual reports for all publicly owned companies with a turnover of more than 250 million ECU in the manufacturing sector. Apart from promoting transparency, the measure helped the Commission ascertain the degree of state aid involved in the financial relationship (for instance, what is the return on government capital?). Accordingly, the procedure served to ensure that public and private companies were treated equally and that there was no distortion of competition arising from the capital structure of publicly owned companies.[40] However, in June 1993 the Court of Justice upheld a French complaint that it was unreasonable for the Commission to expect an annual report on financial links between governments and publicly owned enterprises, thus obliging the Commission to amend the relevant directive.[41]

The most striking measure taken by the Commission in the area of state aid also involves transparency. In an effort to publicize the extent of the problem, Brittan launched a series of surveys on state aid. The third, released in July 1992, showed that public assistance had fallen slightly from an annual average of 93 billion ECU in 1986–1988 to 89 billion ECU in 1988–1990. The four biggest economies—Germany, France, Italy, and Britain—account for a growing share of state aid, most of which goes to the Community's better-off regions.[42]

Regulated Industries

Governments have sheltered certain industries from competition because of those industries' fundamental economic importance. Thus, telecommunications, energy (electricity and natural gas), banking, insurance, and transport have traditionally been highly regulated. Moreover, in many cases they are wholly or partly government-owned. In close association with the single market program, the Commission has begun to apply competition law to liberalize those sectors, often in the teeth of fierce member state opposition.

Article 90 of the EEC treaty provides for the full application of treaty rules, including those on competition and free movement of goods and services, to companies owned by, or in a special relationship with, member states—except where the application of such rules would prevent the companies from carrying out their public service obligations. The Commission ensures the application of Article 90 by adopting appropriate directives or decisions, thereby attempting to reconcile "the provision of goods and services of general interest with the objective of avoiding unnecessary restrictions of competition."[43]

The Commission has used Article 90 frequently in the telecommunications sector, requiring member states to open up the provision of terminals and services to competition.[44] The Court of Justice upheld the Commission's right to do so and in a number of important cases explained the extent to which member states may grant statutory monopolies or special rights.[45] As a result, there is much less uncertainty now about the proper application of Article 90.

Much remains to be done in the telecommunications field, notably in the area of voice communication. Government monopolies ensure that calls between member states often cost twice as much as calls of equivalent distance within member states. As Claus-Dieter Ehlermann, the director-general for competition, pointed out, "this constitutes a surcharge on trade and a block to the internal market process."[46]

The Commission is pursuing an equally forceful approach toward energy monopolies, within two fundamental constraints: the need to provide security of supply and the related public service obligation of universal, uninterrupted provision. By moving to a Community security-of-supply system, the Commission seeks to cut down on the amount of energy that national governments protect on such grounds. Similarly, the Commission expects that a competitive regime, accompanied by the necessary regulation imposing certain indispensable constraints, will satisfy the requirement for safe, uninterrupted supply to all parts of the Community.[47]

As an opening gambit, the Commission decided in 1991 that an agreement concluded between a number of electricity companies constituted an infringement of Article 85(1) of the EEC treaty, insofar as it had the effect of impeding imports and exports by private industrial consumers. Generally, however, the Commission is taking a flexible and gradual approach to energy market liberalization, hoping to some extent that the 1992 momentum will push the electricity and gas monopolies into a more competitive environment.

The Politics of Competition Policy

Competition policy is an extremely sensitive subject for the Commission. It must balance concern for preventing market distortion with the need to avoid overreaching its own political (as distinct from legal) authority with member states. Although striving for integrity, the Commission cannot divorce from politics the process of implementing antitrust law, merger policy, control of state aid, and liberalization of regulated industries. Decisions are taken by the full Commission, which must consider such things as political timing and the need to maintain the appearance of regional impartiality. Member states are quick to accuse the Commission of favoritism. Inevitably, commissioners come under intense pressure from their governments and from firms in their countries during contentious competition cases.

Sir Leon Brittan ruffled his colleagues' feathers by taking a hardline approach to competition policy. Although also a free trader, Martin Bangemann despaired of Brittan's single-mindedness, lashing out on one celebrated occasion against the Commission's competition "ayatollahs," who assumed that more competitors necessarily meant more competition and that more competition necessarily meant that European firms would become competitive.[48] Jacques Calvet, the chairman of Peugeot, took up Bangemann's theme in a blistering attack against Sutherland, Brittan, and DG IV.[49] Given Calvet's craving for state aid and his penchant for protectionism, however, his criticism should really be construed as a tribute to the Commission's effectiveness in improving competition in the Community, for the benefit of consumers and producers alike.

NOTES

1. See Sherill Brown Wells, *French Industrial Policy: A History, 1945–81* (Washington, DC: Office of the Historian, U.S. Department of State, 1991), pp. 61–80.

2. Commission, *The European Community's Industrial Strategy* (Luxembourg: OOP, 1983), p. 47.

3. See Geoffrey Shepherd, ed., *Europe's Industries: Public and Private Strategies for Change* (Ithaca, NY: Cornell University Press, 1983).

4. OJL 137, April 28, 1981, 81/363/EEC.

5. Jean-Jacques Servan-Schreiber, *Le Défi Américain* (Paris: Denoel, 1967).

6. See Bull. EC 5-1982, point 2.1.152; Bull. EC 6–1983, points 2.1.268-269.

7. Walter Grunsteidl, "An Industrial Policy for Europe," *European Affairs* 3, no. 90 (Fall 1990), p. 17.

8. See Margaret Sharp, "The Single Market and European Policies for Advanced Technologies," in Colin Crouch and David Marquand, eds., *The Politics of 1992: Beyond the Single European Market* (Oxford: Basil Blackwell, 1990), pp. 100–120.

9. SEA, Article 130f.

10. Grunsteidl, "Industrial Policy," p. 19

11. See Martin Bangemann, *Meeting the Global Challenge: Establishing a Successful European Industrial Policy* (London: Kogan, Page, Pounds, 1992), p. 8.

12. See George Ross, "Sliding Into Industrial Policy: Inside the European Commission," *French Politics and Society* 11, no. 1 (Winter 1993), pp. 20–44.

13. "Industrial Policy in an Open and Competitive Environment: Guidelines for a Community Approach," COM(90)556 Final, November 16, 1990.

14. SEC(91)565, April 3, 1991.

15. Ross, "Sliding Into Industrial Policy," pp. 37–38.

16. EC Council Resolution, November 18, 1991.

17. For an assessment of some of the Commission's options, see Peter Montagnon, ed., *European Competition Policy* (London: RIIA, 1990); and Phedon Nicolaides, ed., *Industrial Policy in the European Community: A Necessary Response to Economic Integration?* (Maastricht: EIPA, 1992).

18. See Walter Goldstein, "The EC as a Capitalist or Dirigiste Regime?" in Alan Cafruny and Glenda Rosenthal, *The State of the European Community: The Maastricht Years and Beyond* (Boulder, CO: Lynne Rienner, 1993), pp. 303–319.

19. SEC(92)682 final.

20. Dean Acheson, *Present at the Creation: My Years in the State Department* (New York: Norton, 1969), p. 383.

21. See Nicholas Green, review of D. G. Goyder, *EEC Competition Law* (Oxford: Clarendon, 1988), in the *Journal of Common Market Studies* 28, no. 1 (September 1989), p. 86.

22. J. Patrick Raines, "Common Market Competition Policy: The EC-IBM Settlement," *Journal of Common Market Studies* 24, no. 2 (December 1985), p. 137.

23. Sir Leon Brittan, "Competition Law: Its Importance to the European Community and to International Trade," speech at the University of Chicago Law School, Chicago, April 24, 1992, p. 8.

24. Council Regulation Number 17/62, OJ Sp Ed 1959-62 87.

25. See Richard Plender, *Plender and Usher's Cases and Materials on the Law of the European Communities*, 2nd edition (London: Butterworths, 1989), pp. 459–473.

26. Sir Leon Brittan, *European Competition Policy: Keeping the Playing Field Level* (Brussels: CEPS, 1992), p. 18.

27. OJ L 72, March 18, 1992, p. 1.

28. *Europemballage Corp. and Continental Can Co. v. Commission,* Case 6/72 (1973), ECR 215.

29. Regulation number 4064/89, December 21, 1989, OJ L 395, December 30, 1989, p. 1.

30. See Bull. EC 12–1989, point 2.1.78.

31. See Commission, *21st Report on Competition Policy* (Luxembourg: OOP, 1992), pp. 18–19.

32. Donald Partan, "Merger Control in the EC: Federalism With a European Flavor," in Cafruny and Rosenthal, *Beyond Maastricht,* p. 286.

33. Commission, *21st Report on Competition Policy,* p. 22.

34. Bull. EC 7-1992, point 1.3.47.

35. See European Parliament, *Fact Sheets on the European Parliament and the Activities of the European Community* (Luxembourg: OOP, 1991), p. 1.

36. OJ C 319/1983.

37. Peter Sutherland, "The European Community: Unity Without Tears," in *The Times* (London), October 22, 1988, p. 10.

38. See Brittan, *Competition Policy,* pp. 48–50.

39. OJ C 273, October 18, 1991.

40. Commission, *21st Report on Competition Policy,* pp. 21–22.

41. See *Agence Europe,* June 24, 1993.

42. Bull EC 7/8-1992, point 1.3.59.

43. Commission, *21st Competition Report,* p. 27.

44. See Wilson Dizard, "Europe Calling Europe: Creating an Integrated Telecommunications Network," in Cafruny and Rosenthal, *Maastricht and Beyond,* pp. 321–336.

45. Commission, *21st Competition Report,* pp. 27, 117.

46. Quoted in *The Financial Times,* May 14, 1992, p. 3.

47. See Sir Leon Brittan, "Competition in the Electricity and Gas Markets," *Target 92,* no. 6 (June 1991), p. 1.

48. See *The Financial Times,* April 30, 1992, p. 16.

49. Jacques Calvet, "The New Utopias That Threaten Europe," in *The Financial Times*, April 30, 1992, p. 15.

14

Beyond the Marketplace

Like the Single European Act (SEA), the Maastricht Treaty included provisions on a wide range of policies and programs relating to the Community marketplace. Moreover, Article 235 of the Treaty of Rome contains an "implied powers" provision, which lets the Community attain objectives mentioned in the Treaty but not spelled out in any detail. Accordingly, in the late 1980s and early 1990s the Community acquired and rediscovered a wide range of instruments with which to strengthen the single market by promoting closely related policies, notably concerning the environment, working conditions, and cohesion.

Although closely associated with the 1992 program, those policy areas promote important objectives in their own right. Regardless of the single market, it is important for Europeans to breathe cleaner air, to enjoy equality in the workplace, and to reduce regional disparities. An additional, intangible benefit is the sense of solidarity and "community" that the successful implementation of such policies imparts, thereby contributing significantly to the process of European integration.

ENVIRONMENTAL POLICY

Although not originally mentioned in the Treaty of Rome, environmental policy is now one of the most important and highly regulated areas of Community competence. Growing popular distress about environmental degradation, the impact of a number of heavily publicized environmental disasters, and the politicization of the environmental movement in the 1960s and 1970s account for the Community's increasing involvement in the issue. Moreover, fearing that national environmental measures would distort the single market, governments strengthened the Community's environmental policy-making power as a corollary to the 1992 program. Apart from internal developments, a number of global concerns—climate change, depletion of the ozone layer, dwindling natural resources, and excessive pollution—increased the Community's involvement in international environmental affairs. As a result, environmental policy is at the top of the Community's political and economic agenda in the early 1990s.[1]

From the Paris Summit to the Maastricht Treaty

Early EC environmental legislation tended to be narrow and technical, justified either as an internal market measure or on the basis of a vague Treaty commitment to improve "the living and working conditions" of people in the Community.[2] Examples include a 1967 directive on the classification, packaging, and labeling of dangerous substances and 1970 directives on noise levels. As the environmental movement gathered momentum throughout Western Europe, however, national governments and the Commission developed a keen interest in environmental issues. At the 1972 Paris summit, Community leaders took the unprecedented step of calling for an EC environmental policy.

Within a year the Commission proposed and the Council adopted the first of five Environmental Action Programs (EAPs). The first two programs (1973 and 1977) listed various measures that were essentially corrective in nature, whereas subsequent EAPs emphasized preventive measures. Reflecting the economic malaise of the early 1980s, the third EAP (1982) specifically called for environmental action that would contribute to economic growth and job creation through the development of less-polluting industries. It also advocated a Community-level environmental impact assessment procedure and, for the first time, offered some Community financing for environmental projects.

The 1985 intergovernmental conference gave Community leaders an opportunity to incorporate environmental policy into the Treaty. Accordingly, the SEA devoted an entire section (Title VII, Article 130r–130t) to environmental policy and included a new environmental provision relating specifically to the internal market (Article 130r[4]). Whereas Article 130r(1) gave the Community wide scope for environmental action, Article 100a(4) seemed to limit that scope by invoking, for the first time in the EEC treaty, the principle of subsidiarity.

Moreover, Articles 100a and 130t used different decisionmaking procedures to achieve the same result. The former (using qualified majority voting) allowed member states to continue to apply stricter national standards after passage of a single market measure if those standards concerned "protection of the environment" and if the Commission confirmed that they were not a disguised trade restriction; the latter (using unanimity) stated that Community environmental legislation "shall not prevent any member state from maintaining or introducing more stringent protective measures compatible with the Treaty."

Little wonder that the SEA's environmental provisions seemed "confusing, ambiguous, and contradictory."[3] Yet to a great extent they worked. Based on the SEA and on the designation of 1987 as the "European Year of the Environment," the Community developed new environmental principles and measures in its fourth EAP (1987). References to environmental policy in successive European Council communiqués testified to growing public concern about the issue. At a macro level, the Commission pursued a new approach, making environmental policy an integral part of all other policies—notably economic, industrial, transport, energy, agricultural, and social—whether at the national or Community level. At a micro level, the Commission worked on priority areas such as atmospheric and marine pollution, waste management, biotechnology, and enforcement of environmental legislation.

The Maastricht Treaty reiterated the importance of taking environmental policy into account when formulating and implementing other Community policies. In addition, the treaty assuaged poorer countries' concerns by allowing temporary derogations and/or financial support from the Cohesion Fund to compensate poorer member states for environmental measures involving disproportionately high costs. However, the Maastricht Treaty's most important environmental provisions relate to the decisionmaking process. Article 130s specified three legislative methods: the cooperation procedure (for most environmental measures); unanimity in the Council (for specified measures); and the co-decision procedure (for general action programs).

Written with the Maastricht Treaty in mind, the Community's fifth EAP (1993) noted a "slow but relentless deterioration . . . of the environment" despite two decades of Community action. The report advocated "sustainable development," defined in general terms as that which "meets the needs of the present without compromising the ability of future generations to meet their own needs." More specifically, the report called for waste reduction through reuse and recycling, lower energy use, a change of general consumption patterns, integrated pollution control measures, environmentally friendly transport, and industrial risk assessment. It identified five target sectors: industry, energy, transport, agriculture, and tourism. (The choice of tourism may seem surprising, but recent data shows that, by the year 2000, solid and liquid wastes attributable to tourism will have more than doubled, as will the amount of land devoted to tourism and leisure activities.)[4] One of the report's most striking aspects is a shift in the Community's general approach from purely regulatory measures (e.g., emissions limits) to an emphasis on economic and fiscal measures (including taxes, incentives, and subsidies through the structural funds).

The Community's Role in International Environmental Affairs

The Maastricht Treaty also strengthened the international dimension of Community environmental policy. Realizing that pollution knew no bounds and that environmental degradation was a global problem, in 1973 member states undertook (as part of a "gentleman's agreement" on environmental issues) to coordinate their international positions. On that basis, the Community became increasingly involved in worldwide environmental affairs.

The SEA authorized the Community to enter into international agreements on environmental issues "with third countries and with . . . relevant international organizations," and the fourth EAP called on member states and the Community to participate actively on the international stage to protect the environment. As a result, the Community is now party to a number of international and regional conventions on the environment. The Community also participates in environmental activities with the OECD, the UN Environment Programme, and the Economic Commission for Europe. In addition, environmental criteria are integral to the Community's Third World development policy (for instance, the Lomé Convention provides for general environmental cooperation and includes a specific ban on exports of hazardous waste to African, Caribbean, and Pacific countries) and its efforts to assist the countries of Central and Eastern Europe.

Along with the Twelve, the Community participated in the June 1992 UN Conference on the Environment and Development (the Rio Conference), which adopted three basic texts: the Rio Declaration on the Environment and Development (general principles relating to the environmental implications of economic development); Agenda 21 (a comprehensive work program covering virtually every aspect of environment and development); and a nonbinding statement on forest principles. Moreover, the Community and the Twelve signed the UN Framework Convention on Climate Change and the Convention on Biodiversity, both of which emerged from negotiations begun well before the Rio Conference. Efforts to meet political and financial commitments made at Rio are likely to play a large role in the Community's international activities in the years ahead.

Key General Legislation

• *Seveso Directive:* Following the 1976 industrial disaster in Seveso, Italy, the EC adopted a directive (82/501/EEC) requiring manufacturers to notify authorities of the details of use in their operations (storage, handling, quantities used, etc.) of 180 dangerous substances and to consult with affected members of the public on emergency planning measures. The directive seeks to ensure that manufacturers using dangerous materials, as well as local authorities, have adequate contingency plans to limit the environmental impact of accidents.

• *Environmental Impact Assessment:* In 1985 the EC adopted a directive requiring member states to demand environmental impact assessments (EIAs) before giving consent to projects that by virtue of size, nature, or location are likely to have a significant impact on the environment. The directive sets out procedural requirements for conducting EIAs, although it does not include substantive standards for judging impact. Assessments are mandatory for certain types of installations, such as oil refineries, large power stations (including nuclear), steel mills, chemical plants, highways, waterways, and hazardous waste plants. Twelve other types of activity, including agriculture, mining, metal processing, glass manufacturing, food processing, and infrastructure projects, may be subject to EIAs at the discretion of member states.

• *European Environment Agency:* A 1990 regulation (210/90/EEC) created a European Environment Agency to collect and disseminate facts on the environment, thereby partially filling the information gap that has plagued EC efforts to formulate and enforce environmental policy. A dispute over the siting of European agencies delayed formal establishment of the environment agency until late 1993.

• *Ecolabeling:* In 1992 the Council adopted a regulation laying out rules for a Community scheme to award "ecolabels" to environmentally friendly products. Under the scheme, authorized bodies in the member states would award ecolabels to particular products based on uniform, Community-wide criteria for general product groups. A committee of member state representatives must approve the Commission's criteria. Work is currently under way on criteria for a number of product groups, ranging from detergent to refrigerators.

• *Ecoauditing:* In March 1993 the Council adopted a regulation setting out the rules for a Community Eco-Management and Audit Scheme. Under the voluntary regulation, participating companies improve and periodically assess their environmental performance, provide adequate public information, and submit their systems and public statements to a review by a panel of independent experts. In return, companies are allowed to use a logo indicating their participation in the scheme. However, they are not allowed to publicize participation in the scheme in their product advertising.

• *Integrated Pollution Prevention and Control (IPPC):* The Commission is working on a draft directive to oblige member states to adopt regulatory systems that would issue a single permit to enterprises covering all types of emissions (air, water, and soil). Hence, regulatory authorities would have to evaluate the overall effect of a given operation on the environment, not only by using criteria based on environmental quality standards but also by comparing emissions levels to those possible with the "best available technology."

Key Legislation on Habitats, Ecosystems, and Wildlife

• *CITES:* A 1982 directive instituted a system of licensing to implement the 1973 international Convention on Trade in Endangered Species (CITES). In response to the impending elimination of border controls, in 1992 the Commission proposed further measures to improve internal implementation of CITES rules.

• *Wild Birds Directive:* This directive is designed to protect wild birds and their habitats through protection and management of existing habitats, creation of new ones, and prohibitions against deliberate killing or capture, sale, disturbance of nests, or disruption of breeding of over a hundred "particularly vulnerable" species. The directive also restricts hunting of additional species, but this provision is widely disregarded in certain member states because of the strength of hunting lobbies.

• *Habitats Directive:* In May 1992 the Council adopted a directive (9243/EEC) establishing a general program for the protection of natural habitats and the species inhabiting them. The purpose of the directive is to consolidate areas designated under the wild birds directive and other special protection areas into a "coherent European ecological network," to be called "Natura 2000." The Community may designate sites as special conservation areas even if they have not been proposed by member states and provide Community cofinancing to maintain those sites. The directive includes a general list of types of habitats that should be designated as special areas of conservation and lists of species for which special protection applies.

Key Legislation on Air

• *Motor Vehicle Emissions:* Responding to steadily increasing volumes of motor vehicle traffic and to public concern, Community standards have become stricter over time. The Commission estimates that stricter standards have reduced emissions by an astounding 80–90 percent per car since 1980.

A 1970 directive (70/220/EEC) began the process by setting technical standards for emissions of CO_2 and unburnt hydrocarbons for most gasoline-powered vehicles (except tractors and public works vehicles). The 1970 directive was based on "optional harmonization": Member states were not obligated to implement the standards set forth in the directive but had to approve vehicles from other member states that met those standards. Related directives covered diesel engines. In a series of directives designed to ensure that lead-free gasoline was available throughout Europe at competitive prices, the Community also took action to lower emissions of lead by motor vehicles.

The Council amended its landmark 1970 motor vehicle emissions directive several times during the 1980s. However, the standards set by the amendments lagged behind those set in other large markets, notably the United States. The Commission and Council entered into an extended debate over updating EC emission standards in 1988 and 1989, with member states split over whether or not to introduce stricter standards for small cars (there was strong opposition from France and Italy, whose producers would be most affected). Eventually, bowing to pressure from the European Parliament and the Dutch government, the Community adopted a directive (89/458/EEC) requiring cars marketed in the EC after January 1, 1993, to meet standards equivalent to those prevailing in the United States (in other words, all new cars must be equipped with catalytic converters).

A subsequent directive (91/441/EEC) further tightened standards and called on the Commission to propose even stricter guidelines by 1996. In December 1992 the Commission adopted a draft directive lowering emissions limits for gasoline-powered cars by a further 20 percent for CO_2 and 50 percent for other gases from 1996 onward. However, the Commission has also concluded that further improvements in vehicle emissions will have to come from sources other than cars themselves (e.g., new fuel mixes, better mandatory maintenance and inspection, and reduction in the use of cars).

• *Other Air Quality Directives:* Other legislation covering air pollution can be divided roughly into two categories: air quality standards and emissions limits. Following serious damage caused by acid rain to many European forests and the resulting public outcry, in the late 1970s the Community took action to limit emissions of sulfur dioxide (SO_2) and nitrous oxide (NO_2). Emissions of lead are also restricted. Other pollutants, such as carbon monoxide and ozone, are not limited but are monitored nationally. In addition, five directives limit emissions into the atmosphere by industrial plants, incinerators, and other installations of SO_2, hydrochloric acid, dust, heavy metals, and other pollutants, together with a requirement that plants use best available technology "not entailing excessive costs."

• *Protection of the Ozone Layer:* As concern grew over the effect of widely used chlorofluorocarbons (CFCs) on the earth's protective ozone layer, the EC took steps to limit use of CFCs in the early 1980s. The Commission and member states participated in the negotiation of the 1985 Vienna Convention for the Protection of the Ozone Layer, the 1987

Montreal Protocol (which created a mechanism for limiting use of CFCs and other ozone-damaging chemicals), and subsequent protocols in 1991 and 1992 tightening these restrictions and accelerating the phaseout of some substances. A 1991 regulation (594-91) implemented the Montreal Protocol; further implementing proposals are before the Council.

• *Climate Change and CO_2 Emissions:* Amid rising public concern about the prospect of global warming and scientific findings that it could cause rising sea levels and other disasters, a joint Energy-Environment Council agreed in 1990 to commit the Community to stabilizing emissions of carbon dioxide at a 1990 benchmark level by the year 2000.

In a communication outlining a strategy for fulfilling that goal, the Commission proposed a combined Community tax on energy and CO_2 emissions to be imposed by member state governments. The proposed measure would raise energy prices by the equivalent of $10 per barrel of oil over a ten-year period. Despite an offer of exemptions for energy-intensive industries, the proposal inevitably engendered strong opposition in many quarters. Environment ministers cautiously endorsed it, but industry and finance ministers showed less enthusiasm. Lack of progress so incensed the flamboyant Carlo Ripa di Meana, commissioner for the environment, that he boycotted the Rio Conference. Outstanding problems concerning the proposal include the technical task of designing the tax itself and the political issue of exemptions for poorer member states.

Key Legislation on Water

The Commission divides legislation on water into three categories: quality objectives or other requirements; industry or sector regulations; and limits on the discharge of dangerous substances.

Building on a 1976 framework directive (76/464/EEC), the Community enacted most of its legislation on water quality in the 1970s and early 1980s. The framework directive identified substances deemed to pose a threat to the environment, dividing them into a "blacklist"—carcinogens and other dangerous substances, such as mercury or cadmium, for which discharges *are* prohibited—and a "graylist"—certain other metals and substances that affect the taste or smell of water, for which discharges *should be* restricted. Follow-up directives dealt with specific substances, industries, and sectors. Despite a subsequent (1986) framework directive to streamline the procedure, progress remains slow. (For instance, the Community has taken action on only a small fraction of the hundred-plus substances originally identified on the graylist.) For the remaining substances, member states are required to set limits that satisfy the water quality objectives set in the framework directive.

In addition, major horizontal directives cover quality of drinking water (80/778/EEC), bathing water (71/160/EEC), discharges to groundwater (80/68/EEC), quality of waters containing freshwater fish (78/659/EEC) and shellfish (79/923/EEC), surface water for drinking (75/440/EEC), and treatment of urban wastewater (91/271/EEC). In the Commission's view, the urban wastewater directive represents a departure from the traditional emphasis on quality standards and discharge limits and embodies a more general approach to confronting water pollution. It requires member states to provide for treatment of all urban wastewaters within a specific time frame (tailored to individual states and regions). The goal is to have primary and secondary treatment of all wastewaters from cities and towns of over 15,000 residents by the end of the decade.

Key Legislation on Waste

The Community began regulating waste disposal in 1975 with adoption of a framework directive (75/442/EEC, amended in 1991) that defined waste in general terms ("any substance disposed of by the holder") and required member states to designate competent authorities and set up permit systems for waste disposal. A series of directives dealing with specific areas of waste disposal, relating mainly to hazardous wastes, followed the original framework directive:

• *Toxic and dangerous waste (1978):* required member states, producers, holders, and disposers of toxic wastes to keep close track of the movement and disposal of those wastes through the use of permits and extensive documentation. A subsequent directive (91/689/EEC) defines hazardous waste, establishes general requirements for facilities that deal with it, tightens documentation requirements to include registration of all wastes discharged at waste sites, establishes a consignment note system for transfer of such wastes, and restricts mixing of hazardous wastes with each other or with nonhazardous wastes.
• *Transfrontier shipment of hazardous waste (1984):* created a system of compulsory prior notification and authorization for transport of hazardous wastes across national borders, including uniform documentation requirements.
• *Specific wastes:* a series of directives since the mid-1970s regulate treatment and disposal of specific types of waste, including polychlorinated biphenyls (PCBs) and polychlorinated terphenyls (PCTs), waste oils, asbestos, batteries and accumulators, and waste arising from the manufacture of titanium dioxide.

The Commission made its first foray into reduction of nonhazardous waste with a directive (85/339/EEC) requiring member states to draw up a four-year program to reduce the contribution of beverage containers to the waste stream. In 1989, with the release of its communication on Community strategy for waste management, the Commission took a broader approach, promising to make a series of proposals covering multiple aspects of waste management, including:

- Stricter controls on the movement of all waste and ratification of the Basel Convention and OECD decision on transboundary movement of waste
- A directive on civil liability for damage caused by waste
- Directives on uniform site design for landfills and standards for incineration of hazardous waste
- A proposal on recycling waste packaging

Among these, the directive on shipments of waste (93/93/259) is probably the most important. Numerous disputes over Community competence and national sovereignty (including whether or not shipments within member states should be covered and whether or not a member state could ban imports of waste from another member state) delayed adoption for well over a year. In its final version, the regulation covers shipments *between* states only, although it obliges governments to establish "an appropriate system" for control of shipments within their own borders and to notify the Commission of that system. In keeping with the "proximity" principle (wastes should be disposed of as near as possible to where they were generated), the Commission conceded that member states should be allowed to ban waste imports systematically, except in cases that involve specialized wastes coming from small member states.

Other elements of the Commission's strategy were even harder to enact. The draft directive on civil liability for damage caused by waste made little progress in the Council and was eventually subsumed into a green paper on remedying environmental damage, released by the Commission in March 1993. The directives on landfills and incineration remain on the Council table.

The Commission's proposal for a directive on packaging and packaging waste took on added urgency after Germany adopted legislation requiring producers to take back, or guarantee recycling of, all packaging waste from consumer products. Released in the summer of 1992, the Commission's proposal calls for recycling of 60 percent of each type of packaging waste and energy recovery (incineration) of a further 30 percent within ten years. It also requires extensive tracking of waste generation and disposal trends in the packaging area, leaving precise methods of implementing the targets to individual member states. The proposal has sparked its share of controversy, with some member states complaining that the directive is too lax and industry objecting that the targets are technologically unreachable for certain types of materials. Not surprisingly, it remains before the Council.

Key Legislation on Chemicals

The Community began regulating chemicals as early as 1967, with its first directive on packaging, classification, and labeling of dangerous substances. However, the directive addressed the need of users and consumers for information on how to handle dangerous chemicals, rather than focusing on specifically environmental concerns. As the directive was successively amended to include testing regimes and a pre-market notification requirement, many more substances were brought under the Community's formal danger classification. In 1990 the Council agreed on a definition of "environmentally dangerous" substances, covering 40–50 percent of chemicals currently on the market. Under a recently adopted regulation, existing chemicals, grandfathered when the pre-market notification system was adopted in 1979, will be systematically reevaluated for health and environmental effects. The Community also requires exporters of hazardous chemicals to obtain in advance the consent of the country of destination and to ship only to countries capable of disposing of those chemicals safely.

Problems of Enforcement

Enforcement is a critical problem in the search for an effective EC environmental policy. Differing legal regimes, economic concerns, degrees of public concern, and levels of political interest among member states have contributed to uneven implementation of environmental directives throughout the Community. A dearth of reliable data on the state of the environment in Europe, compounded by the Commission's reliance on national governments for the information needed to pursue infringement actions, makes matters worse.

The Commission has painted a gloomy picture of enforcement of Community environmental rules by the member states, with only Denmark escaping criticism. Problems range from egregiously late transposal of EC measures to failure to conform to standards established in Community legislation to nonsubmission of required reports.

The environmental impact assessment (EIA) directive is often disregarded. It has also been a fruitful source of conflict between the Commission and the member states, not least because it allows environmental organizations to appeal to another, highly visible authority the action (or inaction) of their own governments regarding local development issues. By the end of 1992 the Commission had begun proceedings against eleven member states (all but Denmark) for failure to implement the EIA in full. The Commission complained that "even where the procedure laid down by the directive is formally complied with, impact studies are often of a mediocre quality and almost always underestimate the harm to the environment."[5]

The politically contentious EIAs erupted into a public row in October 1991, when the British government reacted vehemently to a letter of infringement from the Commission concerning the siting of a new road. The incident elicited British Foreign Secretary Douglas Hurd's famous charge that the Commission was intruding into "every nook and cranny" of daily life.[6] The ensuing controversy added fuel to the debate on subsidiarity, especially during the Maastricht Treaty ratification crisis.

In areas covered by substantive legislation (air, water, waste, etc.), the Commission observed that "the situation is at its least satisfactory where Community legislation lays down obligations to plan ahead."[7] Water quality is a prime example: Many member states simply have not undertaken the massive public investment programs necessary to meet the standards to which they agreed in the Council of Ministers. This failure is especially evident with respect to the drinking and bathing water directives, where concentrations of certain pollutants routinely exceed Community norms, sometimes with the explicit permission of national authorities. There are a number of flagrant abuses in the area of air quality (Athens comes immediately to mind), although the problem here is often lack of information on the real situation in member states.

In addition to the usual plethora of disputes over conformity of implementing legislation, a key problem in the area of waste is violation of control and documentation rules by waste shippers and an increase in uncontrolled or illegal tips or landfills. It was "by no means certain," the Commission concluded in 1992, that member states were disposing of waste in accordance with EC law.[8] In the area of nature protection, the Commission cites continual problems with member states over their failure to designate adequate numbers of special preserves, as well as the persistence of hunting regulations that violate the directives on wild birds and other wildlife protection measures.

SOCIAL POLICY

The Community's social policy builds on a long history and a strong tradition of social legislation in the member states. Only the UK, during nearly fifteen years of Conservative government, disputed the philosophical underpinnings of Western Europe's social policy agenda. Thus, Brussels became the battleground for ideological, political, and economic disputes over such issues as women's rights, workers' rights, and, especially, "industrial democracy"—employee participation in company decisionmaking. More than simply trying to improve working and living conditions in the Community, however, the Commission has aggressively advocated social policy as a means of promoting a "people's Europe." Because legislation on social issues potentially affects the everyday existence of almost everybody in the Community, a progressive social policy is an invaluable means by which Brussels can stress the relevance of European integration and, in the broadest sense, attempt to close the democratic deficit.

From the Treaty of Rome to the Social Charter

The Treaty of Rome contains a number of social policy provisions. Articles 48–52 relate to labor mobility, one of the prerequisites for a fully functioning internal market. Article 100, pertaining specifically to the internal market, empowers the Council to act when divergent social policies endanger competition in the Community. Article 119 contains a binding obligation on member states to offer equal pay for equal work performed by men and women, and Articles 123–127 set up a European Social Fund to help achieve the Community's social policy objectives, most of which (apart from the Treaty's specific provisions) are mentioned in the preamble, Article 2, Article 117 (improved working conditions and an improved standard of living), and Article 118 (close cooperation between member states on labor issues).

The Community built the first phase of its social policy in the 1960s almost entirely on Articles 48–52. However, movement of labor and the professions remained restricted for another twenty years, until the momentum of the single market program finally made it possible to resolve outstanding issues. In the meantime, broader aspects of social policy got off to a good start in the early 1970s. Thanks to the enthusiasm generated by the 1969 Hague summit, "it seemed . . . for the first time . . . that there was a genuine political acceptance among [member states] of the pursuit of social goals on a Community level."[9] Capitalizing on the "Spirit of The Hague" and pushed by Willy Brandt, Germany's Social Democratic chancellor, the heads of government reiterated their commitment to a comprehensive and effective social policy at the 1972 Paris summit.

Given the economic setbacks about to beset the Community, the Paris summit was a false dawn. Like other Community activities, social policy suffered from the political retrenchment that followed. Yet the initial impression was misleading. Buoyed by the heads of governments' endorsement of an active social policy, in 1974 the Commission proposed and the Council accepted the Community's first Social Action Program.[10] The program included wide-ranging measures to achieve full employment, better living and working conditions, worker participation in industrial decisionmaking, and equal treatment of men and women in the workplace.

A flurry of activity followed, but the legislative output was disappointing. Successful measures included directives on workers' information and consultation rights and on equal pay and equal treatment for women. The fifth company law directive and the European Company Statute—company law measures that included provisions for worker participation—became bogged down in disputes between member states and European trade unions over which model of industrial democracy to use. Apart from its legislative agenda, the Community established two institutions—the European Foundation for the Improvement of Living and Working Conditions and the European Center for the Development of Vocational Training—to conduct research on social issues. Nevertheless, the Community's performance paled in comparison with the promise of the Paris summit and the first Social Action Program. It was a sad commentary on what followed that a leading scholar on the subject described the mid-1970s as "probably the high-tide of European social policy."[11]

The infamous Vredeling draft directive of 1980 showed how politically out of touch the Commission had become, not only on the issue of worker participation but on social policy in general. Popularly known by the name of the then-commissioner for social affairs, the directive proposed to expand workers' information and consultation rights in multinational companies. Whereas previous proposals relating to information and consultation in the workplace had largely followed current member state practices, the Vredeling directive went well beyond existing provisions at the national level by requiring multinationals to give employees details of the company's entire operations, including those outside the Community.

Lingering Eurosclerosis fueled a powerful political backlash against the Vredeling directive. Fresh ideological winds also boded ill for social policy in the Community. Margaret Thatcher, who came to power in 1979, embodied prevailing political opinion about government intervention in economic and social affairs. Although other Community leaders were by no means as doctrinaire, few supported as active a social agenda as the Commission proposed. Thus, a combination of renewed economic recession and emerging market forces pushed social policy onto the back burner in the early 1980s.

That helps to explain why the single market program initially lacked a social dimension. The 1985 White Paper touched on social policy only in relation to the free movement of people (workers and professions). The SEA went farther, affirming in its preamble the need to "improve the [Community's] economic and social situation by extending common policies and pursuing new objectives" and by including a new title on economic and social cohesion. Moreover, the SEA introduced qualified majority voting for legislation on "the health and safety of workers" (Article 118a). Not only did the health and safety area produce the largest and most important body of social policy legislation in the late 1980s and early 1990s, but also the majority voting provision for health and safety legislation opened a loophole through which the Commission tried to enact other social measures.

In an effort to ameliorate the possible adverse effects of economic liberalization and to counter criticism that 1992 was for the benefit of businesspeople only, in 1988 Delors began a "careful consideration of [the single market's] social consequences." Delors explored the social dimension of 1992, calling it one of the SEA's priorities and a "key to the success of the large market."[12] With the obvious exception of Thatcher, most heads of government enthusiastically supported Delors. Some sympathized with the ideological underpinnings of a social dimension and saw an EC-level initiative as a way to improve social policy at home without losing competitiveness abroad. They also feared "social dumping," the possibility that Community countries with higher labor costs would lose market share to Community countries with lower labor costs or, worse, that firms would relocate from the former to the latter.

With the single market well on track, political support for an active social policy quickly gathered speed. Meeting in Hanover in June 1988, the heads of government stressed the social dimension's relevance for the 1992 program. The presidency conclusions noted that, as the internal market had to be conceived "in such a manner as to benefit all our people," it was necessary to improve working conditions, living standards, protection of health and safety, access to vocational training, and dialogue between the two sides of industry.[13]

Buoyed by the European Council's support, the Commission released a working paper in September 1988 on the social dimension of the single market.[14] Using a format similar to the White Paper's, the Commission outlined the social dimension's intellectual and economic rationale and listed eighty possible measures (but without a timetable for implementation). Proposals covered the familiar and the new, with an emphasis on creating conditions necessary to bring about worker mobility, an essential attribute of a free market. By giving substance to the social dimension, the Commission successfully built a "second pillar" for the single market program.

Inspired by similar declarations from the Council of Europe, the International Labour Organisation, and the OECD and eager to dramatize the single market's social dimension, Delors proposed a Community charter of basic social rights, asking the Economic and Social Committee (ESC) for its opinion. Although less concerned about making a symbolic declaration than about taking concrete measures to protect social rights in the Community, the committee's report contributed to the political momentum behind Delors's initiative. So, too, did the French government's determination to push social policy during its 1989 Council presidency. In October of that year the Commission produced a final draft, "Community Charter of the Fundamental Social Rights of Workers." Despite other pressing issues, such as EMU and the events in Eastern Europe, eleven of the twelve heads of government adopted the Social Charter at the December 1989 Strasbourg summit (Thatcher was the lone dissenter).[15]

Following a preamble that outlined the development of social policy at the Community level, the Charter listed twelve categories of workers' fundamental social rights:

- Freedom of movement
- Employment and remuneration
- Improvement of living and working conditions
- Social protection
- Freedom of association and collective bargaining
- Vocational training
- Equal treatment for men and women
- Information, consultation, and participation for workers
- Health protection and safety at the workplace
- Protection of children and adolescents
- Elderly persons
- Disabled persons

According to Social Affairs Commissioner Vasso Papandreou, the Charter formed "a keystone of the social dimension in the construction of Europe, in the spirit of the Treaty of Rome supplemented by the Single European Act."[16] Being entirely hortatory and declaratory, however, it lacked binding legal force. Nevertheless, the Charter's importance should not be underestimated: In addition to identifying the Community's social agenda during and beyond the single market program, the Social Charter received political approval at the highest possible level.

Yet the Charter never had much popular appeal. Despite its potential to improve the lives of millions of Community citizens, from the outset it seemed too lofty and remote. Persistently high unemployment contrasted with the Charter's rhetoric and threatened to erode popular support for the single market program itself. Potential popular disaffection offered a powerful impetus for member states to focus on the nuts and bolts of social policy in the late 1980s. Thus, although it endorsed the Social Charter at the Strasbourg summit, the European Council stressed that "integration of unemployed young persons into working life and the fight against long-term unemployment . . . and those relating to vocational training . . . constitute decisive aspects of the Community social dimension."[17]

Hence the political imperative to put legislative flesh on the Charter's rhetorical bones as soon as possible. Indeed, the Charter's brief concluding section called on the Commission to submit proposals to implement those rights for which the Community had competence. Sensitive to the subsidiarity issue, the Commission did not want to encroach upon aspects of social policy that could best be dealt with at the national level. Nor did it want governments to use subsidiarity as a way to avoid legislation, either in national capitals or in Brussels. Accordingly, the Commission's "action program" sought to strike a balance between what was desirable, what was appropriate, and what was feasible at the Community level.

Of the action program's forty-seven measures, only seventeen were new.[18] The predominance of preexisting measures testified to the Community's poor record of social policy legislation. Inevitably, familiar proposals dealing with industrial democracy, women's issues, and vocational training resurfaced in the action program, with their proponents hoping that the momentum generated by the Social Charter would somehow carry them through. Aware of the huge stumbling block posed by the unanimity required for most social legislation, the Commission resorted in many cases to Community instruments other than legally binding directives or recommendations.

The Social Charter also called on the Commission to prepare an annual report "on the application of the Charter by the Member States and by the Community." Those reports—the first of which appeared in December 1991—are an indispensable guide to the state of social policy in the post–single market period. The most recent report shows that, by the end of 1992, the Commission had prepared proposals on virtually all of the measures listed in the action program.[19] However, in keeping with the principle of subsidiarity, only twenty-eight of the Commission's proposals required action at the Community level.

The Council's treatment of those twenty-eight measures demonstrates the continuing controversy surrounding social policy. By the end of 1992 the Council had adopted only fifteen of the Commission's proposals, resulting in eight directives (including two based on unanimity) concerned primarily with the less contentious question of health and safety at work. According to the Commission, "discussions on most of the proposals for directives on important matters have not made sufficient progress to enable a final text to be adopted." In other words, at least one member state—usually but not always the UK—has prevented the Council from reaching unanimity on key draft directives covering such issues as the organization of working time, atypical work, European works councils, and transport for the disabled.

Not surprisingly, the Commission promised in its general program for 1993–1994 to "endeavor to mobilize the support it needs to improve the results to date" on implementation of the social action program. Concerned about rising unemployment, the Commission also pledged "to add [in 1993] a new dimension to Community action to promote employment and combat marginalization."[20] By extending majority voting to more aspects of social policy, the Maastricht Treaty offers some hope for achieving the Commission's objective. Britain's exclusion from the treaty's social policy protocol, however, raises serious jurisdictional and legislative problems.

The Maastricht Treaty

The Maastricht summit almost foundered on the "social chapter," a package of social policy provisions negotiated during the IGC on political union for incorporation into the new treaty. The social chapter included:

- Revised policy objectives, such as the promotion of employment
- An extension of qualified majority voting procedures to cover proposals on working conditions, consultation of workers, and equality between men and women with regard to labor market opportunities and treatment at work
- Unanimous decisionmaking in areas such as social security, termination of employment, and third-country worker protection
- A greater role for the "social partners" (employers' and employees' representatives)

For ideological and political reasons, and because of the supposed cost in jobs and competitiveness, John Major refused to accept the social chapter at the Maastricht summit. Realizing the extent of Major's intransigence, late in the evening of the second day the others agreed to remove the social chapter entirely from the treaty. All twelve member states subsequently signed a protocol on social policy, which authorized eleven member states (Britain being the exception) to proceed along the lines laid down in the Social Charter and to use the Community's institutions and decisionmaking procedures for that purpose. Thus, the UK would not take part in relevant Council deliberations or decisionmaking; in such cases, the Council would decide by a qualified majority of forty-four votes. Needless to say, any legislation adopted in that way would not apply to Britain.

Britain did not opt out of the treaty's social chapter; instead, the other eleven decided to take the social chapter out of the treaty and to form their own "Social Community." Britain is still subject to the original treaty's social policy provisions as revised by the SEA. But the new arrangement's institutional implications are, to say the least, "anomalous and uncertain."[21] For instance, it is unclear what role British MEPs will play during parliamentary deliberations of social chapter provisions or how the British presidency will handle such dossiers in the Council of Ministers.[22]

The social protocol's broader implications for the Community system and for European integration are even more dubious, and profoundly disturbing. The protocol sets a dangerous precedent for a two-tier Community, a development reinforced by the treaty's provisions on EMU. Britain's exclusion from certain labor legislation will distort competition and adversely affect the internal market. Other member states' fears of social dumping as a result of the social protocol appeared to be realized even before ratification of the treaty when Hoover announced its decision to relocate a manufacturing plant from Burgundy to Scotland. The ensuing controversy revived discussion of the single market's social dimension, especially of a draft directive on European works councils.[23]

The Social Dialogue

The SEA charged the Commission with developing a dialogue between employers' and employees' representatives "which could, if the two sides consider it desirable, lead to relations based on agreement." This put an additional stamp of approval on the "Val Duchesse process," begun in 1985 when the Commission convened a meeting to encourage the "social partners" to develop a working relationship at the Community level. The dialogue also served to strengthen the participants' input into the Community's legislative process. The intensity of the social dialogue has varied since 1985, as have the composition and the subject matter of working parties (consisting of representatives of the Commission, employers, and employees) set up under the auspices of the Val Duchesse process. The social partners include:

- The European Union of Employers' Confederations (UNICE)
- The European Trades Union Confederation (ETUC)
- The European Center of Public Enterprises (CEEP)

Without a social dialogue, the Commission would have made even less progress on implementing its social action plan. The social partners helped by adopting six nonbinding opinions on education, training, and labor market issues.[24] In recognition of the social dialogue's contribution, member states included a provision in the social policy protocol of the Maastricht Treaty allowing the social partners to implement Council directives.

The Commission, the European Parliament, and the ESC

Although the Commission and the European Parliament are involved in almost every Community activity, their role in social policy deserves special mention. Far from being an impartial civil service, the Commission has consistently acted as a lobbyist and pursued a progressive social policy. In her book on the social dimension, Beverly Springer notes repeatedly that the Commission in general, and DG V (social affairs) in particular, had cogent political and bureaucratic reasons to advance the Community's social agenda. Yet the social affairs portfolio is rarely allocated to a senior commissioner. Vasso Papandreou, social affairs commissioner from 1989 to 1993, stood out solely because she was one of only two women ever to be a commissioner. Pádraig Flynn, her successor, is perhaps one of the weakest commissioners in Delors's current administration. Ironically for someone with responsibility for women's affairs, he is notorious in his native Ireland for a reputed antipathy toward women's rights.

The European Parliament has traditionally taken a strong stand in support of women's rights, industrial democracy, and other staples of Community social policy. In recent years, the main thrust of Parliament's work in the social sphere has been the fight to curb unemployment and create jobs. Parliament has produced numerous reports on social issues and focused especially on improving the conditions of the most vulnerable groups in society: the disabled, migrant workers, and the poor.

As its name implies, the Economic and Social Committee was established to institutionalize discussions between workers' and employers' representatives on all social and economic issues. Apart from its involvement in early deliberations on the Social Charter, however, the ESC has been conspicuous by its absence from the high-level social dialogue launched in 1985 and by its marginal impact on the Community's social legislation.

The Social Fund

Since the 1988 structural funds reform, the European Social Fund has helped to combat long-term unemployment and to facilitate the occupational integration of young people. That generally involves vocational training and subsidies for recruitment in newly created jobs and for the creation of self-employment opportunities. The Social Fund's role in promoting social and economic cohesion is discussed in the next section.

Education and Youth

The Maastricht Treaty formally introduced education and youth programs as a new area of Community activity. Under Article 126, the Community is to support and supplement action taken by member states in areas such as cooperation between educational establishments, student and teacher mobility, youth exchanges, and language teaching. To that end, the Council will adopt "incentive measures" using the co-decision procedure and make recommendations via qualified majority voting on proposals from the Commission. Those provisions follow up a number of extremely successful educational and exchange programs organized by the Community since the late 1980s, including:

- *Erasmus*—a program to encourage student and faculty exchange throughout the Community. Since its inception in 1987, the Erasmus program has involved over 50,000 students and 1,500 higher education institutions. The program offers grants to facilitate exchanges, curriculum development, and a badly needed course credit transfer system.
- *Lingua*—to a great extent an Erasmus companion program, Lingua provides financial support to encourage second- and third-language acquisition.
- *Tempus*—a program to link universities in Eastern and Western Europe and the United States. Tempus funds joint research projects in a wide variety of disciplines.

STRUCTURAL POLICY

Structural policy is the means by which the Community promotes cohesion (i.e., reduction of economic and social disparities between richer and poorer regions). It is a generic term encompassing regional policy (reduce spatial disparities, regenerate old industrial areas, assist rural development), aspects of social policy (combat long-term unemployment, foster vocational education and training), and a small part of the CAP (assist rural development). Similarly, the Community's structural funds (the main instruments of structural policy) are the regional policy's European Regional Development Fund (ERDF), the social policy's European Social Fund (ESF), and the guidance section of the CAP's European Agricultural Guarantee and Guidance Fund (EAGGF). The European Investment Bank (EIB) and the ECSC are additional instruments with structural policy objectives.

Structural policy developed late in the Community's history. The preamble of the Treaty of Rome mentioned the need to reduce regional disparities, but the Treaty itself included few redistributive mechanisms. The ESF and the EIB, both established by the Treaty, were not intended primarily to promote cohesion but rather were expected to help the Community's poorer regions. Similarly, Article 92(3) declared that state aids were compatible with the common market if they promoted "the economic development of areas where the standard of living is abnormally low or where there is serious underemployment."

Apart from those concessions, the prevailing attitude in 1957—enunciated in Article 2 of the Treaty—was that the common market would, of its own accord, "promote throughout the Community a harmonious development of economic activities" and thereby lessen disparities between regions. After all, the Treaty was a package deal to distribute losses and gains between member states, not to redistribute resources between rich and poor regions. In any case, with the notable exception of the south of Italy, regional disparities in the Community of Six were not as striking as in the Community of Nine, Ten, or Twelve.

Impact of Enlargement

Successive enlargements increased regional disparities with regard to income, employment, education and training, productivity, and infrastructure. In a word, the contrast in *competitiveness* between the Community's regions became more and more marked. The Community's growing regional differences manifested themselves in a north-south divide, with Ireland included in the southern camp. The spatial characteristics of the Community's regional imbalance conformed to the core-periphery concept used extensively by economists and social scientists to analyze inequalities between or among regions. As a result, the Community built its structural policy largely on the assumption of a poor periphery (Scotland, Ireland, Portugal, central and southern Spain, Corsica, southern Italy, Greece, and eastern Germany) and a rich core (southern England, northeastern France, the low countries, northwestern Germany, and northern Italy).[25]

Protocol 30 of Ireland's 1972 act of accession emphasized the need to end regional disparities in the Community, but the European Regional Development Fund was established only in 1975, largely to compensate the UK for its poor return from the CAP. The Community began to coordinate member states' regional aid schemes in the late 1970s, although its own regional aid policy remained rudimentary.[26] According to a 1980 academic assessment, "Community regional policy is still in the developing stage; the very first steps have just been taken to arrive at a comprehensive approach to the problems . . . [of] regional disparities. . . . The means to implement such a policy are still extremely modest but the foundations have been laid which will allow the Community to remedy one of its most dramatic shortcomings."[27]

The extent of the common market's or the Community's failure to redress regional imbalances became more apparent after Greek accession and in the run-up to Spanish and Portuguese accession. Concern that the

Community's existing disadvantaged regions in southern Italy and Greece would suffer as a result of Iberian enlargement precipitated a row in early 1985 over Integrated Mediterranean Programs (IMPs). By taking personal responsibility for resolving the IMP issue, Delors signaled the enhanced importance of structural policy during his administration.

Economic, political, and moral arguments underpinned the Commission's efforts to promote cohesion in the aftermath of the Community's second and third enlargements. Delors had long been aware of a growing rich-poor divide in the Community, which the accession of Spain and Portugal would greatly exacerbate. The Commission's program for 1985 cautioned that regional disparities "could become a permanent source of political confrontation" and urged that the south be given "a fairer share of the benefits of economic development."[28] The new Commission president warned the European Parliament in March 1985 that enlargement negotiations with Greece, Spain, and Portugal had "revealed a tension in Europe which is, let's face it, a tension between north and south. It stems not only from financial problems but from a lack of understanding, from a clash of culture, which seems to be promoting certain countries to turn their backs on the solidarity pact that should be one of the cornerstones of the Community, solidarity being conceived not in terms of assistance, but rather as an expression of the common-weal, contributing to the vigor of the European entity."[29]

The Single Market and Single European Act

The single market program greatly boosted the Commission's and the poorer countries' arguments in favor of a vigorous structural policy. The gradual worsening of regional disparities since the 1960s suggested that market liberalization would broaden rather than narrow the Community's rich-poor divide. Advocates of a stronger structural policy exploited uncertainty about the distributional consequences of the single market program to press their claims for cohesion. Fear that the single market would make rich regions richer and poor regions poorer, that the dynamic of market liberalization would intensify existing disparities, led to an explicit linkage between structural policy and the 1992 program. In the Commission's words, "the reduction of disparities and the strengthening of economic and social cohesion should go hand in hand with the implementation of the large internal market."[30]

Apart from the "solidarity principle," the likely economic and political impact of greater regional disequilibrium strengthened the case for cohesion. The Community would not prosper, let alone survive, if excessive disparities caused poorer member states to block legislation and impede implementation of the single market program. Accordingly, during the 1985 IGC the Commission advocated a substantial redistribution of resources to the Community's less prosperous regions. Although one of the attractions of the single market program for a financially strapped Community was its relative lack of cost, the Commission's emphasis on cohesion raised the prospect of a sizeable budgetary hike. The conference deferred until later a decision about increasing the amount of structural funds, EIB loans, and other forms of Community assistance for poorer regions but committed member states to promoting economic cohesion and reducing regional diversity.

As a result, Article 23 of the SEA added a new title, on "Economic and Social Cohesion," to the Treaty of Rome. This amendment committed the Community to "reducing disparities between the various regions and the backwardness of the least favored nations," called for coordination between other Community policies and cohesion, and obliged the Council to reform the structural funds within a year of the SEA's implementation on the basis of a Commission proposal. Delors subsequently described the revised Treaty's provisions on structural policy as one of the SEA's "fundamental objectives."[31]

Delors I and Reform of the Structural Funds

In February 1987 the Commission introduced a five-year budgetary package to control agricultural spending, increase the Community's own resources, and impose budgetary discipline. The Delors I package also proposed reform of the structural funds, a doubling in real terms of the resources available through them (making a total of 60 billion ECU available from 1989 to 1993), and a particular focus on regions with a per capita income below 75 percent of the Community average.[32] Just as Delors had used the voluminous Cecchini Report to bolster his arguments in support of the single market, he now cited the Padoa-Schioppa Report to make a compelling case for reform of the structural funds. Published in April 1987, the report assessed the "implications for the economic system of the Community of . . . [the] adoption of the internal market program and the latest enlargement." One of its major conclusions pointed out "the serious risks of aggravated regional imbalances in the course of market liberalization" and, in a memorable phrase, warned that "any easy extrapolation of 'invisible hand' ideas into the real world of regional economics in the process of market opening would be unwarranted in the light of economic history and theory."[33]

This was grist to Delors's mill and strengthened the southern countries' determination to win a sizeable redistribution of resources. As a staunch conservative, however, Margaret Thatcher instinctively rejected Padoa-Schioppa's advocacy of guiding the "invisible hand." In her view, market liberalization throughout the Community would foster rather than hinder economic development in the southern member states. Helmut Kohl sympathized with the southern states but knew that Germany would have to contribute most of the proposed budgetary increase. Thus, the battle lines were drawn for a protracted dispute, which, thanks to Kohl's largess, the European Council eventually resolved at the special Brussels summit in February 1988. A delighted Delors called the European Council's decision to double the structural funds by 1993 "a second Marshall Plan."[34] Despite Thatcher's misgivings, the northern countries' endorsement of the Delors I package demonstrated their acceptance of redistributional solidarity as part of market integration.

Having agreed to double the combined size of the ERDF, ESF, and the EAGGF's guidance section, the Council adopted regulations in June and December 1988 reforming the Community's structural policy. Substantially increasing the structural funds was not enough to redress regional imbalances. As Delors told the European Parliament in January 1988, "Cohesion is not simply a matter of throwing money at problems . . . it implies rather a willingness to act at Community level to redress the disparities between regions and between different social groups."[35] Accordingly, the 1988 reform sought to turn the structural funds—hitherto "a rather expensive mechanism for the transfer of resources between member states, where the criteria governing the share out [were] essentially political"[36]—into effective instruments of economic development. That transformation involved welding the Community's regional policy and aspects of its social and agricultural policies into a powerful mechanism to narrow the north-south divide.

The 1988 reform radically revised the Community's structural policy by introducing a number of new principles and procedures and strengthening existing ones. They include:

• *Additionality:* Structural funds must add to, not substitute for, member state public expenditure.

• *Partnership:* The partnership principle is the key to involving regions, not just national governments, in formulating and implementing structural policy. Because Community operations complement corresponding national measures, there must be close consultation and cooperation between the Commission, member states, and regional or local bodies at all stages of a structural program. Eligible member state plans for regional assistance are incorporated into community support frameworks (CSFs), contractual agreements between the Commission, national governments, and regional authorities. CSFs set out the program's priorities, type of aid, methods of financing, and so forth. Moreover, the Commission can take the initiative and propose that member states and regions participate in operations of particular interest to it. Programs usually last five years.

• *Programming:* The structural funds reform involves a major switch from project-related assistance to program assistance and decentralized management. This puts the emphasis on planning and continuity rather than on ad hoc activities. Under the old system, the Commission dealt with thousands of separate projects; now the Commission oversees a much smaller number of CSFs.

• *Concentration:* Instead of spreading the Community's financial resources widely and ineffectively, structural funds now concentrate on a few major objectives. Functional and geographic concentration restricts Community assistance to five priorities:

> *Objective 1:* Assist "regions whose development is lagging behind" (regions with a per capita GDP of less than 75 percent of the Community average). Includes all of Greece, Portugal, and the island of Ireland; large parts of Spain; southern Italy; Corsica; and the French overseas departments. Accounts for about 20 percent of the Community's population. Funding source: ERDF, ESF, EAGGF guidance section, EIB, and ECSC. The ERDF is the largest structural fund, and the Community spends almost 80 percent of it on Objective 1.
>
> *Objective 2:* Promote economic conversion and modernization in declining industrial areas. Includes about sixty sites in nine member states, notably the UK, Spain, France, and Germany. The Community primarily helps small and medium-size enterprises in new economic sectors and supports vocational training. Funding source: ERDF, ESF, EIB, and ECSC.
>
> *Objective 3:* Combat long-term unemployment by assisting workers over twenty-five, anywhere in the Community, who have been unemployed for more than one year. Funding source: ESF, EIB, and ECSC.
>
> *Objective 4:* Integrate young people, anywhere in the Community, into the work force. Funding source: ESF, EIB, and ECSC.
>
> *Objective 5:* Develop rural areas (about fifty-six Community regions, 17 percent of Community land, and 5 percent of Community population).
>
>> *Objective 5a:* With a view to CAP reform, aim to adjust production, processing, and marketing structures in agriculture and forestry. Funding source: EAGGF Guidance Fund.
>>
>> *Objective 5b:* Promote small industry and services, mainly. Funding sources: ERDF, EAGGF Guidance Fund, ESF, and EIB.

Objectives 1, 2, and 5b have a specific regional dimension, whereas Objectives 3, 4, and 5a are horizontal in nature. The allocation of structural funds since the reform came into effect in 1989 corresponds to the priorities set by the Commission and the Council:

- Objective 1: 38.3 billion ECU (63.5 percent)
- Objective 2: 7.2 billion ECU (12 percent)
- Objectives 3 and 4: 7.5 billion ECU (12.4 percent)
- Objective 5a: 3.4 billion ECU (5.7 percent)
- Objective 5b: 2.8 billion ECU (4.6 percent)
- Transitional measures: 1.2 billion ECU (2 percent)[37]

EMU and the Maastricht Treaty

Moves toward EMU in the late 1980s raised concerns in the Community's poorer countries similar to those raised by efforts to complete the internal market earlier in the decade. For Delors, the architect of structural policy reform, EMU was inconceivable without a sizeable increase in Community assistance for disadvantaged regions. The 1989 Delors Report pointed out that because EMU would deprive member states of their ability to devalue, it could worsen the balance of payments difficulties of poorer countries. Indeed, the need for member states to harmonize their budgetary policies, coupled with a loss of exchange rate flexibility, portended serious problems for less developed regions.

During the IGC on political union, Ireland, Spain, and Portugal attached the highest priority to strengthening structural policy and called for a new framework to enable the Community to promote cohesion in the context of closer political and economic integration. Predictably, the three countries asserted that, in the absence of mechanisms to redistribute the benefits of EMU, the more central and prosperous regions would gain disproportionately. Using moral, political, and economic arguments honed during the Delors I debate, the poorer countries claimed that failure to meet their demands could undermine the union's foundations. Felipe González, the Spanish prime minister and the poor countries' standard-bearer, fought tenaciously in the run-up to the Maastricht summit to win a greater Community commitment to cohesion.

From the poorer countries' point of view, the Maastricht Treaty was highly satisfactory. Articles 2 and 3, which enumerated the Community's tasks and activities, specifically mentioned cohesion. Amendments to Article 130 listed rural development as an objective of structural policy; stipulated that the Commission must report every three years on progress made toward achieving cohesion; conceded that new mechanisms, outside existing funds, could be introduced; and provided a framework for extending and deepening Community policies and actions to promote cohesion proportionate to the degree of political, economic, and monetary integration in the EC.

Article 130d stipulated that the Council, acting unanimously on a proposal from the Commission and with the assent of Parliament, would set up a Cohesion Fund by the end of December 1993 to contribute to projects on the environment and transport infrastructure. The purpose of the Cohesion Fund was to reconcile the apparent contradiction in the treaty between the budgetary rigor necessary for convergence and the budgetary lenience inherent in cohesion.

At Spain's insistence, a special protocol supplemented the treaty's cohesion provisions. Apart from allowing for review of the size of the structural funds and greater flexibility to meet new needs, the protocol specified that the Cohesion Fund would benefit member states with a per capita GDP less than 90 percent of the Community average and a program designed to achieve convergence. In effect, that meant Spain, Portugal, Ireland, and Greece. Without mentioning a figure, the protocol earmarked 85–90 percent of the fund to support environmental and transport projects.

Delors II

In a repeat of its 1987 performance, in February 1992 the Commission sent the Council a five-year (1993–1997) budgetary package. Entitled "The Means to Match Our Ambitions," the Commission's financial perspective covered the costs of implementing the Maastricht Treaty.[38] In addition to the cost of cohesion, these included expenditures for economic convergence, promotion of Community competitiveness, and "amplification of external action." The Commission proposed increasing the Community's budgetary ceiling from 1.2 percent to 1.37 percent of GDP by 1997 (an annual budgetary growth rate of 5 percent), and allocating 11 billion ECU for cohesion.

The Commission also proposed improving structural fund operations. Together with the Cohesion Fund, a projected 66 percent increase in Objective 1 funding would boost Community financial support for Spain, Portugal, Ireland, and Greece by 100 percent. Some of the new spending on Objective 1 would go to the five new German Lander, which had received a special structural funds appropriation for 1991–1993. Other objectives would receive a 50 percent increase in funding, and assistance for "regions dependent on fishing" would become Objective 6.

Circumstances in 1992 were hardly propitious for such an ambitious proposal. In its first-ever Community presidency, Portugal made little headway on Delors II. At the June 1992 Lisbon summit, the heads of government agreed only to postpone a decision on it until the Edinburgh summit six months later.[39] Britain, in the Community presidency for the second half of 1992, had little sympathy for Delors II and fretted about the security of its budget rebate. A deepening economic recession and Germany's effort to meet the costs of unification put the future of Delors II further in doubt.

Ironically, the Maastricht ratification crisis—another gloomy development—may have saved Delors II. Battered by a year of economic and political setbacks, Community leaders wanted to establish at Edinburgh their ability to act decisively in the Community's interest. As Michael Shackleton has pointed out, it was imperative for the Community "to avoid the high costs of a failure whose repercussions would have extended well beyond the budgetary arena."[40] The Delors II package was also an ideal opportunity to demonstrate that redistributional solidarity had survived the year's setbacks. Once again, Felipe González represented the southern countries' interests, and, after intense bargaining at the Edinburgh summit, Helmut Kohl conceded most. The new financial perspective agreed to at the summit more than doubled Community assistance for the least prosperous countries (to 30 billion ECU in 1999).[41] As the southern member states must have known, with the Central and Eastern European countries knocking on the Community's door, Delors II was probably their last chance to get a big share of the Community budget.

Progress to Date

A 1990 Commission report, the fourth in a series of reports on the social and economic situation in the regions, painted a grim picture. The report acknowledged that, despite economic growth in the late 1980s, structural policy had not managed to reduce regional disparities. The regional situation at the beginning of the 1990s was far from encouraging: On a scale of 100, Greece had a GDP of 53, whereas Luxembourg had a GDP of 129; using the same scale, the Community's poorest region (Vorio Egeo, in Greece) had a GDP of 40, and the Community's richest region (Groningen, in the Netherlands) had a GDP of 183. The level of income in the ten regions at the top of the scale was more than three times higher than that in the ten regions at the bottom end. Although differences in unemployment levels had decreased at the national level, they had increased at the regional level.[42]

The report was not merely descriptive. It looked at the competitive advantage of regions and assessed the likely impact of deeper integration and efforts to strengthen cohesion. The Commission concluded that the structural funds address the underlying causes of lack of competitiveness but that "reducing regional disparities must be seen as a long-term challenge. Past experience shows that the weaker regions are unlikely to be able to sustain a rate of growth far enough above the Community average to reduce income disparities significantly in under two decades."

The Commission's findings bear out the long-term nature of the problem. If a region with a per capita gross national product of 50 percent of the Community average wished to increase its relative income level to 70 percent, it would need to sustain a growth rate 1.25 percent *higher* than the Community average for 20 years, or 1.75 percent higher for fifteen years. The same applies to employment disparities. In order to reduce the unemployment rate by 5 percent, a region would need an annual employment growth rate of 2.25 percent for five years, 1.5 percent for ten years, or 1.25 percent for fifteen years.[43]

Another Commission report on implementation of the structural funds, published two years later, struck a more optimistic note. Although it called for additional administrative and procedural reform, the report concluded that "the overall result is positive."[44] Despite a huge increase in structural funds since 1988, both reports admit, neither Community nor national regional policies have been as successful as hoped. The solution would appear to be an unlikely combination of high and sustained economic growth, a considerably larger allocation of resources, and closer coordination in the formulation and implementation of Community and national structural policies.[45]

Political Implications of Structural Policy

Community structural policy has a number of striking political as well as economic implications. One, arguably, is to blunt initiative and increase dependency in recipient states. In 1986 Community assistance accounted for 2–3 percent of the GDP of Greece, Ireland, and Portugal. In 1992 the figure for Ireland and Greece was 6 percent. The political consequences of such largess are especially striking in Ireland. According to a leading Irish historian, it has reinforced the "begging bowl" mentality that pervades Irish public life.[46] This was embarrassingly evident during the 1992 Maastricht referendum campaign, when the government urged a "yes" vote almost entirely on the basis of Ireland's expected windfall from the Delors II package.

By the same token, structural policy reinforces the political marginalization of some member states. Because an assumption of core-peripheral dependence underpins structural policy, recipient regions may think of themselves as politically peripheral as well as geographically and economically peripheral. Indeed, they are more likely to exaggerate their marginalization in order to increase their share of Community funding. Moreover, instead of contributing to the development of European integration in the broadest sense, poorer countries are inclined to focus unduly on structural policy.

At a macro level, recent structural policy reform could contribute to a profound change in the Community system. The principles of concentration and partnership mean that the Commission works closely with regional authorities, often bypassing national governments. The Commission is using its contacts with local representatives "to act as a lever for regions that are not yet traditionally recognized"[47] and actively promoting the emergence of new "Euroregions" that straddle national frontiers. Most regions have offices in Brussels and are active in the Assembly of European Regions (a Brussels-based interest group). The Maastricht Treaty reinforced the trend toward regionalism in the Community by establishing a new consultative body, the Committee of the Regions. Increasingly, therefore, the process of European integration complements and strengthens the process of European regionalization and contributes to the development of Eurofederalism.[48]

Profound changes in the international political system since the end of the Cold War are accelerating the emergence of a "Europe of the Regions." Regional political parties are increasingly influential at the national level and in the European Parliament. At the same time, uncertainty about the emerging international system, and even about the future of the nation-state, have strengthened regional identity and self-confidence. The trend in most Community countries is toward greater regional autonomy, with Belgium, Spain, and Italy providing the best examples. But the most dramatic demonstration of regional assertiveness in the early 1990s happened in Germany and Belgium during the Maastricht ratification debate. Exploiting the opportunity provided by the ratification process and the implications of deeper European integration, the German Lander won the right to become directly involved in policymaking on relevant issues in Bonn, Berlin, and Brussels. Similarly, the parliaments of Flanders, Wallonia, and the Brussels region voted to ratify the Maastricht Treaty separately from the Belgian parliament. Doubtless the Lander and the Belgian regions will also exploit the Committee of the Regions and the Community's changing structural policy to promote regionalism and integration in the years ahead.

NOTES

1. See Alberta Sbragia, "EC Environmental Policy: Atypical Ambitions and Typical Problems?" in Alan Cafruny and Glenda Rosenthal, *The State of the European Community: The Maastrict Years and Beyond* (Boulder, CO: Lynne Rienner, 1993), pp. 337–352.

2. EEC treaty, preamble.

3. Ida Johanne Koppen, *The European Community's Environment Policy: From the Summit in Paris, 1972, to the Single European Act, 1986*, EUI Working Paper # 88/328 (Florence: EUI, 1988), p. 62.

4. See Nicolo D'Aquino, "The New Green Europe," *Europe Magazine* (June 1992), p. 10.

5. EP Written Question 1337/92, OJ C 40/26, February 15, 1992.

6. Quoted in *The Financial Times,* January 10, 1992, p. 2.

7. Commission, *9th Annual Report on Implementation of EC Legislation,* OJ C 150, 1992.

8. *Ibid.*

9. Harriet Warner, "EC Social Policy in Practice," *Journal of Common Market Studies* 23, no. 2, p. 147.

10. OJ C 13, January 21, 1974.

11. Beverly Springer, *The Social Dimension of 1992* (New York: Praeger, 1992), p. 39.

12. Jacques Delors, speech to the European Parliament outlining the Commission's program for 1988, January 20, 1988. Bull EC S1/88, p. 12.

13. Bull EC 6-1988, Presidency Conclusions, point 1.1.1.

14. Bull EC 9-1988, points 1.1.1-6.

15. Bull EC 12-1989, Presidency Conclusions, 1.1.10.

16. Commission, *Social Europe: First Report on Application of the Social Charter of Fundamental Social Rights for Workers* (Luxembourg: OOP, 1992), p. 5.

17. Bull 12-1989, Presidency Conclusions, point 1.1.10.

18. COM(89)568 final, November 29, 1989.

19. COM(92)562 final, December 23, 1992.

20. "The Commission's Program for 1992," Bull EC S/1-1992, p. 8.

21. Antonio Lo Faro, "EC Social Policy and 1993: The Dark Side of European Integration?" *Comparative Labor Law Journal* 14, no. 1 (Fall 1992), p. 28.

22. See Alan Butt Philip, "European Social Policy After Maastricht," *Journal of European Social Policy* 2, no. 2 (1992), pp. 121–124.

23. See *The Financial Times,* February 5, 1993, p. 1.

24. See *Social Europe: Second Report on Application of the Social Charter of Fundamental Social Rights for Workers,* COM(92)562 final, December 23, 1992, p. 4.

25. See Roger Stough, "Restructuring and Change in the Space Economy of the European Common Market," in Antoni Kuklinski, ed., *Globality Versus Locality* (Warsaw: University of Warsaw, 1990), p. 210.

26. See N. Vanhove and L. H. Klaassen, *Regional Policy: A European Perspective,* 2nd edition (London: Gower, 1987).

27. P.S.R.F. Mathijsen, *A Guide to European Community Law,* 3rd edition (London: Sweet and Maxwell, 1980), pp. 185–186.

28. Commission's Program for 1985, Bull. EC S/1-1985, p. 15.

29. Bull. EC S/4-1985, p. 6.

30. Commission, *Reform of the Structural Funds: A Tool to Promote Economic and Social Cohesion* (Luxembourg: OOP, 1992), p. 9.

31. Jacques Delors, address to the European Parliament, January 20, 1988, Bull. EC S/1-1988, p. 11.

32. *Making a Success of the Single Act,* COM(87)100.

33. Tommaso Padoa-Schioppa, et al., *Efficiency, Stability and Equity: A Strategy for the Evolution of the Economic System of the European Community* (Oxford: Oxford University Press, 1987), pp. 3, 4, 10.

34. Quoted in *The Economist,* February 27, 1988, p. 41

35. Jacques Delors, address to the European Parliament, January 20, 1988, Bull. EC S/1-1988, p. 11.

36. Michael Shackleton, "The EC's Budget Under a Single Market: Magnitude, Significance, and Obstacles," paper presented at the American Political Science Association annual meeting, Atlanta, August 31, 1989, p. 19.

37. From Egon Schonweg, "EC Regional Policy and the Outlook for 1992," *Target 92* (January 1992), p. 1.

38. Commission, "From the Single Act to Maastricht and Beyond: The Means to Match Our Ambitions," Bull. EC S/1-1992.

39. Bull. EC 6-1992, Presidency Conclusions, point 1.5.

40. Michael Shackleton, "The Community Budget After Maastricht," in Cafruny and Rosenthal, *The State of the EC*, p. 387.

41. Bull. EC 12-1992, Presidency Conclusions, points 1.45-72.

42. Commission, *Fourth Periodic Report on the Social and Economic Situation and Development of the Regions of the Community,* COM(90)609.

43. *Fourth Periodic Report,* p. 47.

44. Commission, *Reform of the Structural Funds: A Tool to Promote Economic and Social Cohesion* (Luxembourg: OOP, 1992), p. 41.

45. See A. J. Marques Mendes, "Economic Cohesion in Europe: The Impact of the Delors Plan," *Journal of Common Market Studies* 29 (September 1990), pp. 17–36, for a similar assessment.

46. See Joseph Lee, *Ireland: 1922–85* (Cambridge: Cambridge University Press, 1991), pp. 462–463.

47. Commission, *Reform of the Structural Funds,* p. 18.

48. See David Coombes, "Public Provision in an Economic and Monetary Union: New Functions for the Budget of the European Community," paper presented at the European Community Studies Association's second international conference, George Mason University, May 27, 1991; Gary Marks, "Structural Policy in the EC," in Alberta Sbagria, ed., *Euro-Politics: Institutions and Policymaking in the "New" European Community* (Washington, DC: Brookings Institution, 1992), pp. 212–224; and Gary Marks, "Structural Policy and Multilevel Governance in the EC," in Cafruny and Rosenthal, pp. 391–410.

15

Economic and Monetary Union

There have been three major monetary initiatives in the history of the European Community: the 1971 Werner Plan and subsequent currency "snake"; the 1979 European Monetary System (EMS); and the 1989 Delors Report and ensuing intergovernmental conference on Economic and Monetary Union (EMU). All three were motivated, in part, by deliberate decisions to "relaunch" European integration. Unlike the Delors Report, the two earlier efforts were also a response to international currency crises or challenges. In the case of the Werner Plan and currency snake, international exchange rate fluctuations, culminating in the Bretton Woods system's collapse, impelled the Community to act; in the case of the EMS, the destabilizing impact of foreign currency movements, notably the dollar, had the same effect.

By comparison, the Delors Plan came about at a time of stable exchange rates between member states, thanks to the relative success of the EMS. Moreover, in marked contrast to the 1970s, the late 1980s was a period of economic buoyancy in the Community. The single market program boosted business confidence enormously and set the stage for deeper European integration. The circumstances seemed particularly propitious not only for a new monetary initiative but also for the achievement of economic union.

The "E" had been conspicuously weak in the Community's first attempt to achieve EMU in the 1970s. Economic union means, essentially, the existence of a single market plus close coordination of member states' economic policies. In the 1970s the common market was incomplete, and Community solidarity collapsed under the weight of economic recession. Building on economic union, the "MU" in EMU involves fixed exchange rates and a common monetary policy, possibly—but not necessarily—with a single currency. The absence of a single market and close economic co-ordination in the 1970s had made 1980 an unattainable target date for EMU.

THE NEW IMPETUS TOWARD EMU

Following the October 1990 Rome summit, at which the heads of government decided to launch Stage II of EMU in January 1994, Jacques Delors declared emphatically that "we need a single currency before the year 2000."[1] The necessity of EMU was debatable on economic grounds, but Delors's remark demonstrated his personal drive and political ambition. As finance minister in 1983, he had reversed Mitterrand's economic policy by committing France uncompromisingly to the ERM, arguably saving both the French government and the EMS in the process. As a strong supporter of European monetary integration, Delors wanted to make EMU the primary objective of his first Commission presidency but opted instead for completion of the single market.

The SEA and the successful launch of the single market program greatly enhanced Delors's standing. By the end of his first presidency in 1988, Delors was in an enviable political position. His personal stature and continuing preoccupation with monetary policy provided a powerful new impetus for EMU. It was no coincidence that Delors chaired the committee charged by the June 1988 Hanover summit to plot a path to EMU or that the committee's report unofficially bore his name. As an anonymous German official commented in 1991, Delors "is too emotionally involved in the subject."[2]

By advocating EMU, Delors championed a long-standing objective of European integration. The Treaty of Rome's goal of market integration and espousal of "ever closer union" implicitly endorsed EMU. Yet the Treaty had few provisions for economic and monetary coordination (Articles 103–109), partly because of the political constraints on European integration in the late 1950s in the aftermath of the failed European Defense Community initiative. In addition, the fully functioning fixed exchange rates of the Bretton Woods system, to which the six Community countries belonged, made monetary union redundant.

Predictably, the Community's first overt espousal of EMU came in the wake of the painful French devaluation and German revaluation of 1969, amid fears of the consequences of further exchange rate fluctuations for the Common Agricultural Policy. The Community leaders' call in 1972 for EMU by the end of the decade was premature and unrealistic, but it constituted an important political assertion of EMU's significance for European integration. The SEA reinforced that point, specifically renewing the 1972 Paris summit's commitment to "the objective of the progressive realization of economic and monetary union."[3] The SEA's modest provisions for the Community's "monetary capacity" and pointed reference to "the experience acquired in cooperation within the framework of the European Monetary System . . . and in developing the ECU" constituted an additional political push toward EMU. The Hanover summit, in authorizing the Delors Committee to examine EMU, took its cue from the SEA.

The single market program, which also took off with the SEA, greatly advanced the goal of EMU. The maintenance of exchange rates seemed inconsistent with and contradictory to the objectives of the single market. In the early 1980s, before the launch of the single market program, academics argued that "a common market with common policies can be viable in the long run only within a coherent framework of macroeconomic and monetary policies."[4] With the single market program off to a strong start in 1987 and 1988, the symbiotic relationship between 1992 and EMU became a new Community orthodoxy. In his influential 1987 report on the single market program's implications for the Community's economic system, Tomaso Padoa-Schioppa strongly endorsed the link between completing the single market and embarking on EMU.[5]

By the end of the 1980s, the single market rationale for EMU was almost unquestioned. A communication by the Commission in August 1990 developed the linkage: "A single currency is the natural complement of a single market. The full potential of the latter will not be achieved without the former. Going further, there is a need for economic and monetary union in part to consolidate the potential gains from completing the internal market, without which there would be risks of weakening the present momentum of the 1992 process. Economic and monetary union therefore offers the prospect of consolidating the single market as well as bringing its own value-added to the performance of the Community economy."[6]

The Commission's much-quoted cost-benefit analysis of EMU, *One Market, One Money,* appeared two months later. Its title reinforced the 1992-EMU linkage and became a mantra for advocates of a single currency. The Commission's message was unequivocal: "One market needs one money."[7] Although the Delors Report had shied away from recommending a single currency as a corollary of EMU, subsequent Commission pronouncements implied that EMU was inconceivable without it. Thus a Commission publication, prepared by the information directorate-general for mass dissemination, maintains that "the creation of a single currency is a natural and necessary attribute of a smoothly functioning single market."[8]

The EMS, which had made the single market possible, was another impetus toward EMU in the late 1980s. Padoa-Schioppa had pointed out that with complete capital mobility (a feature of the single market program), the ERM and the existing degree of monetary policy coordination would be insufficient to promote price stability and ensure orderly trade relations within the Community. "In a quite fundamental way," Padoa-Schioppa concluded, "capital mobility [1992] and exchange rate fixity [the EMS] together leave no room for independent monetary policies."[9] Quite simply, a unified market with a free flow of capital could put the EMS under enormous pressure.

The Community would discover the extent of that pressure during the currency crisis of 1992. In the meantime, the success of the EMS in the late 1980s increased the momentum for EMU. Given the stability of the ERM since early 1987, when the last general alignment had occurred, the EMS tended to be seen as a forerunner of EMU. Further economic convergence, it seemed, would reinforce exchange rate stability and turn the EMS into a quasi-monetary union. Therefore, moving from the EMS to EMU seemed logical and relatively effortless. As Commission Vice President Leon Brittan remarked in October 1990, "The ERM is the kernel of the future single European currency."[10]

Brittan's audience of businesspeople was predisposed to the idea of monetary union, thanks to the success of both the EMS and the single market program. In 1990, management consultants Ernst and Young conducted a survey for the Commission that showed widespread optimism in business circles about the economic impact of monetary union combined with completion of the single market.[11] The experience of working together in the ERM also reconciled many government officials and politicians to the prospect of EMU. Twenty years earlier Leo Tindemans had reported regretfully that there was not enough trust between member states to transfer responsibility for EMU to a central authority.[12] Without doubt, the EMS helped to overcome such distrust.

The decisive Delors Report did not take an explicit stand on whether monetary union was necessary to ensure the success of the single market program. Nor did it develop a cost-benefit analysis of EMU. Instead, the committee of twelve central bank governors, two commissioners, and three independent experts outlined what EMU would look like and devised specific steps that could result in its achievement. Taking a lead from the Werner Report, the Delors Committee defined monetary union as "the assurance of total and irreversible convertibility of currencies; the complete liberalization of capital transactions and full integration of banking and other financial markets; and the elimination of margins of fluctuation and the irrevocable locking of exchange rate parities."[13] Although the committee did not explicitly endorse a single currency, its definition of monetary union necessarily involved a centralized monetary policy for the Community.

The Delors Report identified four basic elements of economic union:

- The single market, within which persons, goods, services, and capital can move freely
- Competition policy and other measures aimed at strengthening market mechanisms
- Common policies aimed at structural change and regional development
- Macroeconomic policy coordination, including binding rules for budgetary policies

The importance of an effective competition policy to create a "level playing field" in the single market was obvious. Similarly, the Community had agreed in February 1988 that a huge increase in regional development assistance was integral to "making a success of the single market."[14] Moreover, in 1979 the Community had offered financial assistance to poorer countries participating in the ERM and for the same reason would establish a sizeable cohesion fund in 1992 for disadvantaged member states hoping to embark on EMU.

Only macroeconomic coordination, the last of the four elements of EMU identified in the Delors Report, would represent a radical new departure for the Community. Yet, unlike monetary union, economic union would not necessitate a single economic policy. Nevertheless, the Delors Report's insistence on binding budgetary rules proved controversial. Although the Community's own budget would remain small (approximately 2 percent of total government expenditure in the member states), the Delors Report stressed the need for Community control over national fiscal policies in order to operate EMU successfully. Therefore, it advocated effective upper limits on the budget deficits of individual member states, no recourse to direct central bank credit and other forms of monetary financing, and limited recourse to borrowing in non-Community currencies.[15]

The Delors Report proposed a European System of Central Banks (ESCB), organized along federal lines and made up of a central institution and constituent national central banks, to formulate and implement the Community's monetary policy. Reflecting both the influence of Karl-Otto Pohl, the Bundesbank president and a member of the committee, and a high degree of satisfaction with the existing EMS, the report emphatically identified price stability as the ESCB's primary objective. Like the Bundesbank's directorate, the ESCB's council would be rigidly independent of government influence or control.

The Delors Report is best known for proposing a three-stage approach to EMU. A phased approach was inevitable, and the contents of each stage were not surprising. Mindful of the embarrassment caused by the Paris summit's commitment in 1972 to achieve EMU by the end of the decade, the Delors Report declined to develop a timetable for the Community's renewed effort to realize that goal. The report merely recommended that Stage I start no later than July 1, 1990, when capital movements were due to be liberalized as part of the single market program.

Table 15.1   The Delors Report's Three Stages of EMU

Stage One	Establishment of free capital movement in the Community and closer monetary and macroeconomic cooperation between the member states and their central banks.
Stage Two	New treaty comes into force. Establishment of a European system of central banks to monitor and coordinate national monetary policies. Stronger supervisory powers are granted to EC institutions, most notably the European Parliament and the Council of Ministers. Circumstances permitting, margins of fluctuation within the exchange rate mechanism are progressively narrowed.
Stage Three	Creation of "irrevocably fixed" exchange rate parities. Full authority for establishing economic and monetary policy is transferred to EC institutions.

Source: Committee for the Study of Economic and Monetary Union, *Report on Economic and Monetary Union in the European Community,* April 1989, pp. 34–40

Although the report's phased approach to EMU was not unexpected, the committee's stricture that the *"creation of an economic and monetary union must be viewed as a single process"* and that "the decision to enter upon the first stage should be a decision to embark on the entire process," seemed unnecessarily forceful (original emphasis).[16] According to Niels Thygesen, one of the three independent experts on the committee, the intention was to develop momentum, which, in his view, the heads of government maintained when they approved the Delors Report at the Madrid summit in June 1989 and agreed that an intergovernmental conference to decide the Treaty revisions necessary to move to Stages II and III would begin after Stage I was launched.[17]

The Delors Report sparked a lively debate. The most explosive political point, inherent in any discussion of EMU, centered on the question of national sovereignty. Most ERM participants had already lost control over their national monetary policies. By the late 1980s their currencies were pegged to the mark, the system's unofficial anchor. The Bundesbank formulated monetary policy in the EMS, and member states reaped the political and economic rewards of low inflation and stable exchange rates. In effect, Germany's partners in the EMS gave up using interest rates and nominal exchange rates as instruments of national policy. In any case, prevailing opinion in the 1980s held that using devaluations to tackle such problems as declining demand for a country's products was both ineffective and likely to fuel inflation.

As far as monetary union was concerned, most EMS members stood to gain sovereignty rather than lose it. As participants in a federal monetary system, they would wrest some power back from the Bundesbank in Frankfurt. By that calculation, Germany should have been the least happy about monetary union. Indeed, the Bundesbank had serious concerns about surrendering its virtual monopoly of decisionmaking, at least until it could be sure that an alternative arrangement offered as good a prospect of price stability and economic growth as did the existing mechanism. But the German government, which in any event supported monetary union for political reasons, could hardly argue in favor of maintaining a monopoly over monetary policy formulation in the Community.

Economic union would involve less centralization of power than would monetary union, because a single economic policy did not seem essential. Sensitive to the political climate of the late 1980s, the Commission claimed that "the Community's involvement in economic decisionmaking should be based on a balance between subsidiarity and parallelism [between the economic and monetary parts of EMU]."[18] Whereas economic policy could be formulated at different levels of government, responsibility for monetary policy would rest squarely with a new Community institution, the "Eurofed."

The debate over national sovereignty was loudest in Britain, where the economic benefits of EMU were also least apparent. In a speech to the House of Commons in January 1991, the chancellor of the exchequer explained that safeguarding the "sovereign right of Parliament" would be one of his four priorities in the forthcoming intergovernmental conference on EMU.[19] Even before the IGC began, Margaret Thatcher complained in July 1991 that the ERM, into which she had reluctantly brought Britain the previous October, was "tearing the heart out of parliamentary sovereignty." As for EMU, handing over responsibility for monetary policy to the putative European Central Bank would reduce "national finance ministers to the status of innocent bystanders at the scene of an accident."[20]

The question of sovereignty also hinged on powerful political symbols. Money was both a means of transacting business and a badge of national identity or, in the event of a single currency, a symbol of European unity. As a compromise, Leon Brittan suggested keeping existing coins and bank notes and simply denominating their ECU value on one side.[21] A number of countries designed new currency along those lines. But as the Maastricht ratification crisis would show, attachment to the national symbolism of money ran deep throughout the Community, especially in Germany, where the mark epitomized postwar prosperity and stability.

The Commission did not try to calculate the political costs or benefits of EMU, apart from an oblique reference to possible "psychological" problems.[22] Member states would have to reach their own conclusions, but for most it was clear that the anticipated benefits of EMU outweighed the intangible political costs. Not only had most countries already sacrificed national sovereignty by participating in the ERM but some—notably Italy—saw future Community curbs on national fiscal policy as the only way to cut their exorbitant budget deficits.

Instead, the Commission focused on economic losses and gains, and it identified the elimination of transaction costs and exchange rate vulnerability, resulting in greater trade and investment, as a major advantage. The Commission estimated that Community-wide savings on transaction costs could amount to as much as 0.3 percent to 0.4 percent of GDP.[23] Yet the Commission conceded that the Community was not an "optimum currency area" in which labor would move freely in order to offset country-specific shocks, nor would Brussels have a fiscal system capable of making income-stabilizing transfers. Given that economic shocks would continue to affect each member state differently, that labor would remain relatively immobile because of cultural and linguistic barriers, and that the Community would not acquire a sizeable fiscal system, the advantages of EMU seemed far from obvious. Based on additional analysis applied to the Community's actual structure and situation, however, the Commission not surprisingly concluded that "the case [for EMU] can stand powerfully on economic criteria alone."[24]

The Commission's arguments failed to satisfy some influential economists on both sides of the EMU debate. Peter Kenen, professor of economics and international finance at Princeton University and a supporter of monetary integration, regretted that *One Market, One Money* did not prove conclusively "that the benefits would exceed the costs," its title being "as close as the study came to making a case for EMU."[25] Martin Feldstein, professor of economics at Harvard University and an opponent of EMU, refuted the assertion that a single market needs a single currency, let alone monetary union. Feldstein argued that monetary union would not necessarily increase trade and that the success of the EMS weakened the anti-inflationary argument for EMU.[26] Perhaps the Commission should have produced an aggregate estimate of the impact of EMU, along the lines of the Cecchini Report on the single market. The Commission explained in August 1990, however, that the nature of EMU, conditional as it was on "the responses of governments as well as private economic agents," made such an approach unfeasible.[27]

In the event, as Feldstein noted disapprovingly, the main push for EMU was political, not economic. Indeed, the conclusions of successive European summits chronicled the seemingly unstoppable political pressure that had developed for EMU in the late 1980s. It was striking that the Hanover summit had charged the Delors Committee not with exploring the rationale for EMU but with suggesting concrete steps for achieving it.[28] Twelve months later, at the Madrid summit, the heads of government reiterated their "determination progressively to achieve economic and

Table 15.2 The Costs and Benefits of EMU

(i) **Efficiency and growth.** Elimination of exchange rate uncertainty and transaction costs, and further refinements to the single market, are sure to yield gains in efficiency. Through improving the risk-adjusted rate of return on capital and the business climate more generally there are good chances that a credible commitment to achieving EMU in the not-too-distant future will help further strengthen the trend of investment and growth.

(ii) **Price stability.** This is a generally accepted objective, and beneficial economically in its own right. The problem is that of attaining price stability at least cost, and then maintaining it. The Community has the opportunity of being able to build its monetary union on the basis of reputation for monetary stability of its least inflationary Member States. Given the paramount importance of credibility and expectations in winning the continuous fight against inflation at least cost, this is a great advantage.

(iii) **Public finance.** A new framework of incentives and constraints will condition national budgetary policies, for which the key words will be autonomy (to respond to country-specific problems), discipline (to avoid excessive deficits) and coordination (to assure an appropriate over-all policy mix in the Community). EMU will also bring valuable gains for many countries', national budgets through reductions in interest rates, as inflation and exchange risk premiums are eliminated. These benefits will very probably outweigh the loss of seigniorage revenue to be experienced by some countries.

(iv) **Adjusting to economic shocks.** The main potential cost of EMU is that represented by the loss of monetary and exchange rate policy as an instrument of economic adjustment at the national level. This loss should not be exaggerated since exchange rate changes by the Community in relation to the rest of the world will remain possible, whereas within the EMS the nominal exchange rate instrument is already largely abandoned, and EMU will reduce the incidence of country-specific shocks. Relative real labor costs will still be able to change; budgetary policies at national and Community levels will also absorb shocks and aid adjustment, and the external current account constraint will disappear.

Moreover, model simulations suggest that with EMU, compared to other regimes, the Community would have been able to absorb the major economic shocks of the last two decades with less disturbance in terms of the rate of inflation and, to some extent also, the level of real activity. This is of renewed relevance, given that the Gulf crisis of the summer of 1990 once again subjects the Community to a potentially damaging economic shock.

(v) **The international system.** With the ECU becoming a major international currency, there will be advantages for the Community as banks and enterprises conduct more of their international business in their own currency; moreover the monetary authorities will be able to economize in external reserves and achieve some international seigniorage gains. EMU will also mean that the Community will be better placed, through its unity, to secure its interests in international coordination processes and negotiate for a balanced multipolar system.

Source: Commission of the European Communities, *One Market, One Money*, October 1992, p. 11

monetary union as provided for in the Single Act and confirmed at the European Council meeting in Hanover" and approved the Delors Report.[29] At the Strasbourg summit in December 1989, Mitterrand noted that the necessary majority existed to convene an intergovernmental conference on EMU under Article 236 of the Treaty.[30] The European Council decided in Dublin in June 1990 to begin the IGC six months later in Rome, with a view to concluding and ratifying a treaty before the end of 1992.[31]

WHAT MAASTRICHT MEANS

The Maastricht Treaty adopted the three-stage process toward EMU but differed from the Delors Report in a number of important respects. Stage I had already begun on July 1, 1990, and Stage II would begin automatically on January 1, 1994. In a departure from the Delors Report, the Maastricht Treaty stipulated that the European Monetary Institute (EMI), a forerunner of the European Central Bank, would be constituted at the outset of Stage II. The EMI, in turn, would succeed and supplant the Committee of Central Bank Governors, which met monthly in Basel, Switzerland (the only Community organ to meet regularly in a nonmember state). The central bank governors played a prominent part in the intergovernmental conference on EMU and, by helping to coordinate member states' monetary policies, would help to pave the way for Stage II. The governors of the national central banks would form the council of the EMI, and one of them would be its vice president. But the EMI council president would be "selected from among persons of recognized standing and professional experience in monetary or banking matters" from outside the circle of central bank governors.

The EMI has responsibility for enhancing cooperation between national central banks; strengthening the coordination of member states' monetary policies to ensure price stability; monitoring the EMS; holding consultations on national central bank issues that affect the stability of financial institutions and markets; taking over the tasks of the EMS's European Monetary Cooperation Fund; and facilitating the use of the ECU. To prepare for Stage III, the EMI will perform a number of procedural and technical tasks, including compiling and distributing of statistics and preparing ECU bank notes. By December 31, 1996, at the latest, the EMI will specify the regulatory, organizational, and logistical framework necessary for the ESCB to operate successfully on the first day of Stage III. Finally, by acting on a two-thirds majority vote of the Council of Ministers, the EMI may make recommendations to national central banks on the conduct of their monetary policies.

Stage II also includes provisions for member states to coordinate their economic policies. From the beginning of Stage II, all restrictions on capital movement will be prohibited (except in Portugal and Greece for another two years); central bank credits to public authorities and privileged access to financial institutions will be banned; and there will be no automatic financial assistance for member states in trouble because of excessive budget deficits (the "no bailout" rule). The Council will decide whether an excessive deficit exists and, if so, make recommendations to the member state in question. During Stage II member states will, as appropriate, free their central banks from political control in order to bring national legislation into line with the statute of the ESCB.

Stage III will begin by January 1, 1999, at the latest. But before the end of 1996 the Council of Ministers, meeting at the level of heads of government, will assess the degree of economic convergence between member states. If the European Council decides, by qualified majority vote, that a majority of member states meet the criteria, it will set a date in 1997 or 1998 for the launch of EMU. If Britain decides to opt out of EMU by that time, neither Britain nor Denmark (which already decided to opt out of EMU) will be included among the member states when the European Council decides whether a majority exists. If a majority exists, member states that do not participate from the outset will receive a derogation from EMU's provisions on monetary policy and on sanctions against excessive deficits.

The European Council will base its decision about an early launch of EMU on four criteria:

- Price stability: an average inflation rate not exceeding by more than 1.5 percent that of the three best-performing member states
- Budgetary discipline: a budget deficit of less than 3 percent of GDP and a public debt ratio not exceeding 60 percent of GDP
- Currency stability: respect for normal fluctuation margins (2.5 percent) of the ERM "without severe tensions" for at least two years with no devaluations
- Interest rate convergence: an average nominal long-term interest rate not exceeding by more than 2 percent that of the three best-performing member states

Although the convergence criteria appear to be "absurdly stringent,"[32] the Maastricht Treaty gives the European Council some discretion in selecting member states for participation in Stage III. For instance, the exchange rate criterion does not preclude realignments, and the budget criterion is hedged with qualifications. The deficit may exceed 3 percent of GDP either if "the ratio has declined substantially and continuously and reached a level that comes close" to the reference value or if "the excess over the reference value is only exceptional and temporary." Similarly, government debt may exceed 60 percent of GDP if "the ratio is sufficiently diminishing and approaching the reference value at a satisfactory pace." As well as looking at the convergence criteria, the European Council will consider other indicators of economic performance, such as the balance of payments and unit labor costs.

If the European Council fails by the end of 1997 to set a date for Stage III, it must decide before July 1, 1998, which countries meet the convergence criteria. Regardless of whether or not they constitute a majority, the select group will launch Stage III on January 1, 1999.

From the beginning of Stage III (in 1997, 1998, or 1999), exchange rates between participating countries will be irrevocably fixed and a single currency (the ECU) will be introduced. The ESCB, consisting of the European Central Bank (ECB) and the national central banks, will replace the EMI on the eve of Stage III and formulate the participating states' single monetary policy. National central banks will become branches of the ECB and will carry out operations necessary to implement a single monetary policy. The ECB's Governing Council, consisting of a six-member executive board and governors of the national central banks, will be the ESCB's highest decisionmaking body, responsible for monetary policy, foreign exchange operations, management of the official foreign reserves of member states, and smooth operation of a payments system. The executive board will manage monetary policy on a day-to-day basis in accordance with the decisions and guidelines laid down by the Governing Council.

The primary objective of the ESCB is to maintain price stability (i.e., to combat inflation). In addition, it will promote the Community's general economic policies without prejudice to that goal. The ESCB will be independent of member state governments and other Community institutions (Articles 107 and 108). The European Council will appoint members of the executive board on recommendations made by the Council of Ministers after it has consulted the European Parliament and the Governing Council. To help ensure their independence, executive board members will have nonrenewable eight-year terms, whereas national central bank governors will have five-year minimum terms.

The issue of exchange rate policy relates closely to the ESCB's independence. The Maastricht Treaty makes a distinction between formal agreements on an exchange rate system for the ECU vis-à-vis non-Community currencies (for instance, a new Bretton Woods system), on the one hand, and day-to-day interventions on foreign exchange markets, on the other. In both cases the Council of Ministers will have ultimate political responsibility. Although this provision appears to compromise the ESCB's independence, the treaty's persistent emphasis on the overriding objective of price stability should greatly strengthen the ECB's autonomy in the management of exchange rate policy.

Member states will retain responsibility for economic policy, subject to multilateral surveillance in order to ensure a high degree of coordination within the Community. The Council of Ministers will adopt broad economic policy guidelines and, based on Commission reports, assess the consistency of member state policies. If a member state diverges from the Community's guidelines, the Council may address a specific recommendation to it and, if necessary, make the recommendation public.

The treaty includes strict rules about budget deficits. In addition to applying the budgetary provisions of Stage II (which apply also to Stage III), the Council may act on a recommendation of the Commission if a member state continues to run an "excessive" deficit. The Commission will base its judgment in part on the budget criterion initially used for entry into EMU. If the Council acts on a Commission recommendation and decides that an excessive deficit exists, it may take a number of steps to bring the errant member state back into line. Failing that, the Council may prescribe measures for deficit reduction. In the event of additional noncompliance, the Council may enact a series of sanctions, culminating in the imposition of fines.

Clearly, the treaty's provisions for EMU are comprehensive and complicated. But will they work? In a reply to Martin Feldstein's criticism of EMU, a number of eminent European economists described the endeavor as "full of calculated risk . . . [but] a risk worth taking."[33] The authors of the treaty tried to minimize the risk by elaborating what they considered to be sound institutional and procedural prerequisites. Given the politics of the IGC and the unpredictability of international economics, the treaty's provisions for EMU could hardly have been flawless. Inevitably, the 1992–1993 ratification and currency crises magnified the treaty's imperfections and cast the whole venture in doubt.

PROSPECTS FOR EMU

On April 6, 1992, Portugal became the last member state, apart from Greece, to join the ERM. Marking a first in the ERM's history, Portugal requested the Community's finance ministers to set the benchmark central rate for its escudo against the ECU rather than against the mark. According to Portugal's prime minister, "the decision . . . to chose the ECU as the reference for the escudo's entry . . . underlines [the ECU's] growing importance"[34]

The timing and manner of Portugal's ERM entry appeared to augur well for both the EMS and EMU. Additionally, in response to Sweden's request for participation in the narrow band of the ERM, finance ministers asked their central bank governors in April 1992 to study the possibility of opening the EMS to non-EC currencies. Two months later, Cyprus became the fourth non-Community country to link its currency unofficially to the ECU and to align its future exchange rate policy with that of the Community member states. The Commission confidently declared that Cyprus's action extended further "the zone of monetary stability which is being established in Europe" and confirmed the ECU's increasing international stature.[35]

Yet the EMS was already lurching toward a major crisis. Throughout 1992 the mark rose steadily as high German interest rates attracted funds from the United States, where interest rates were low and the dollar continued to depreciate. As the mark climbed in value, weaker Community currencies fell to the floor of their ERM bands. Certain currencies—notably the lira and the pound—were inherently weak and ripe for devaluation. Dealers sensed that a realignment of the ERM was imminent. The Maastricht Treaty had itself encouraged speculation about an inevitable realignment or series of realignments before the advent of fixed exchange rates. Such speculation, in turn, tended to strengthen strong currencies and weaken weak ones.[36]

Of more immediate concern, the Bundesbank was less and less inclined to prop up weak currencies. In July and August, the Bundesbank spent a small fortune trying to keep the lira above its ERM floor. Convinced of the Bundesbank's unwillingness or inability to support the lira indefinitely, dealers moved large amounts of money out of the Italian currency and into the mark. Similar concerns about sterling led to massive sales of the pound and purchases of the mark. Ironically, the removal of exchange controls as part of the single market program contributed to the imminent crisis by making it possible to move money freely around the Community.

The evolution of the EMS into a fixed-rate regime exacerbated tension enormously. The frequency of realignments before 1987 (thirteen altogether) and absence of them afterward gave the impression that the EMS had turned into a quasi–currency union. Except in Germany and some other "core" currency countries, realignment became a dirty word, synonymous with political indecision and economic frailty. Britain had joined the ERM in October 1990 at a high benchmark central rate (2.95) against the mark; but it was politically impossible for the British government to contemplate realignment, especially with a general election in the offing.

Paradoxically, whereas the Maastricht Treaty had caused speculation about the inevitability of realignments before EMU, most governments feared that a parity change would affect their credibility, undermine confidence in the convergence criteria, contribute to an increase in inflation rates, and thereby make EMU harder to achieve. Realignments appeared to be incompatible with the treaty's convergence strategy and with the goal of EMU; as a tool of macroeconomic management, they seemed anachronistic at a time when the Community was moving toward a single monetary policy. For all of those reasons, governments unwisely but understandably endured mounting pressure in the ERM, often at a cost of high interest rates and declining competitiveness.

Matters came to a head in mid-September 1992, partly because of the negative result of the Danish referendum earlier in the summer and the unpredictability of the upcoming French referendum. First the Finnish markka, unofficially linked to the ERM, collapsed under the strain of huge speculative attacks. The Swedish krone, also unofficially linked to the ERM, was next. In the EMS, the Italian and British governments desperately shored up their ailing currencies, with noticeably unenthusiastic German support.

A finance ministers meeting in Bath on September 4–5, 1992, seemed an ideal opportunity to defuse the looming crisis and avert imminent disaster. Instead, the meeting ended in acrimony as Norman Lamont, the chancellor of the exchequer, blamed the Bundesbank for the Community's high interest rates, economic ills, and currency turbulence. Helmut Schlesinger, the Bundesbank president, promised only that Germany would not raise interest rates further. As for a possible realignment, Schlesinger neither proposed a devaluation of sterling nor suggested a new parity for the pound. Had he done so, it is doubtful in any case that Lamont would have accepted.

The surprise realignment of September 13, involving a 7 percent devaluation of the lira, did not affect the pound's parity in the ERM. More money flowed out of sterling, as dealers sought a safer haven and speculators renewed their attacks. On Tuesday, September 15, the pound closed just above its ERM floor. Reports of Schlesinger's support for a broader realignment made the pound's position untenable. Having spent billions trying to prop up the pound, the British government pulled sterling out of the ERM on "Black Wednesday," September 16. Italy, unable to stanch further speculative flows despite the Bundesbank's decision on September 13 to cut interest rates, followed suit.[37] In a preemptive move, Spain devalued the peseta by 5 percent against the remaining ERM currencies.

Denmark's rejection of the Maastricht Treaty aggravated but did not cause the ERM crisis. Similarly, opinion polls showing a possible French rejection of Maastricht in the September 20 referendum increased attacks against the franc, which were already acute. The French "yes," regardless of the margin, failed to stem the flow of funds out of the franc. Only concerted efforts by the French and German governments and central banks averted a disaster on September 22–23 and prevented a French devaluation.[38] Currency turbulence continued in late 1992 and early 1993, with the franc again under pressure, Spain and Portugal devaluing by 6 percent on November 23, and Ireland devaluing by 10 percent on January 30.

The currency crisis contributed to the contemporaneous Maastricht Treaty ratification debacle by undermining public confidence in the EMS and, by extension, in deeper European integration. With the pound outside the ERM and the Danish krone still inside but under growing pressure, public opinion in Britain and Denmark—already bitterly divided over Maastricht—hardened against ratification. Thus, the currency crisis could have undermined EMU by helping to hinder ratification in Britain and/or Denmark and, accordingly, preventing the treaty from being implemented.

Apart from affecting the vital question of ratification, what impact did the currency crisis have on EMU? By knocking Britain and Italy out of the ERM, the crisis made it highly unlikely that either country would rejoin on time to participate in EMU from the beginning of Stage III. Of course, Britain's participation was already doubtful for political reasons, Italy's for economic reasons. Elsewhere in the Community, the crisis shook confidence in the EMS but did not undermine the foundations of the system or seriously weaken intellectual and political support for EMU. Government officials pointed out that the crisis merely restored the EMS to its original state: a system of fixed *but adjustable* exchange rates. As the German ambassador in Washington pointed out, "Tensions arose because rates were not adjusted in time despite several years of divergent economic developments in several member states. These increasing divergences combined with the political uncertainty about [Maastricht] were bound to unleash speculation which forced an overdue adjustment."[39] Wim Duisenberg, president of the Dutch Central Bank, put it more bluntly: "What crisis? The problem was that we had forgotten how to realign." The situation in the EMS since September 1992, Duisenberg asserted the following January, was "one realignment that lasted four months."[40]

Duisenberg spoke too soon. The crisis peaked in July, not January, 1993. On July 29, when the Bundesbank decided not to make an eagerly awaited cut in interest rates, other EMS currencies—notably the franc—came under enormous pressure. Angered by French criticism of German monetary policy, the Bundesbank conspicuously failed to provide the massive assistance necessary to prop up the franc. After an emergency meeting, Community finance ministers announced that apart from the Dutch guilder, EMS currencies would float within a 15 percent band around their parity with the mark.

Most government officials and politicians defended the EMS tenaciously during the protracted crisis. Norman Lamont, who scored domestic political points by attacking the EMS and the Bundesbank immediately after "Black Wednesday," gave a qualified apology at a tense meeting of finance ministers on September 28, 1992. So strong was the consensus in favor of the EMS that Lamont signed a joint communiqué describing it as a "key factor of economic stability and prosperity in Europe."[41] Many concluded from the currency turmoil that EMU was the only solution. Not surprisingly, Commission Vice President Christopherson claimed at the height of the crisis that "only a single currency will put an end to [the] waves of speculation which we have witnessed over the last weeks."[42] The

OECD concurred, suggesting that "rather than casting doubt on the prospect for monetary unification, recent events should strengthen the EC members' resolve to conclude EMU as quickly as possible."[43]

Currency turmoil may have strengthened the rationale for EMU, but it drew attention to a serious weakness in the Maastricht strategy. Clearly, EMU would not happen by inertia, with the EMS transmuting itself into a currency union. As Maastricht stipulated, fixed exchange rates would only come about by political will and administrative fiat. In the meantime, semi-fixed exchange rates, free capital flows, and quasi-autonomous monetary policies would ensure further currency instability. Accordingly, Stage II seemed unnecessarily long, to the extent that it was necessary at all. Moreover, during Stage II the Bundesbank would continue to subordinate the EMS to German policy interests, possibly to the detriment of convergence between member states.[44]

Already in Stage I, Germany's high interest rates were forcing other ERM participants to pursue equally tight monetary policies, which exacerbated the Community's economic downturn and made the convergence criteria harder to meet. The Bundesbank's decision less than a week after the Maastricht summit to raise interest rates by 0.5 percent was widely denounced as an affront to the spirit of EMU and an egregious example of its blatant "Germany first" approach. Of course, the Bundesbank's duty was solely to Germany and not at all to the wider Community. Nevertheless, the persistence of high German interest rates in 1992, notwithstanding the small reduction of September 13, reinforced a perception that the Bundesbank sought to scuttle EMU. Inasmuch as the Bundesbank wanted to warn the Community, the message more than likely was that high inflation could not be tolerated and that a form of "monetary Darwinism"[45] would weed out the noncharter members of EMU.

Germans like to point out that their experience of hyperinflation in the early 1920s forged an anti-inflationary consensus, which accounts for the Bundesbank's preoccupation with price stability and determination to make it the primary objective of the ECB. The Bundesbank always argued that there was no trade-off between inflation and unemployment. As Karl-Otto Pohl insisted in 1977, well before becoming Bundesbank president, "inflation does not reduce unemployment. On the contrary, it is one of its major causes."[46] Economic theory and empirical evidence bears out the Bundesbank's point, except in the short term. But in the short term of 1992 and 1993, as the Bundesbank pursued a tough anti-inflationary policy that prolonged economic recession throughout the Community, unemployment rose alarmingly and dominated discussions at the June 1993 Copenhagen summit. Excessively high unemployment undoubtedly erodes support for EMU and creates the unfortunate impression that the ECB's primary objective of price stability will be pursued regardless of the Community's unemployment level.

The Maastricht Treaty's convergence criterion of price stability does not set an absolute inflation rate for prospective EMU participants, but it does stipulate that they must not exceed by more than 1.5 percent the rate of the Community's three best performers. Obviously, the Bundesbank wants to make sure that the targeted inflation rate is as low as possible. Ironically, it could be so low that Germany itself, struggling with post-unification inflationary pressures, might not pass the test.

As for the other convergence criteria, Germany may also miss the budgetary target. Unification increased public sector borrowing and pushed the country's deficit above 3 percent of GDP (the Maastricht reference point). High German interest rates, another result of unification and the deepening budget deficit, have spread recession throughout the Community and made the budget targets elusive for most member states. Although the European Council may use some discretion when applying the fiscal criteria, Germany is adamant (for the moment) that countries should be held to a strict interpretation of the rules.

Given the member states' current economic divergence, it is difficult to imagine a majority of them meeting the convergence criteria in 1996. By that time, of course, the Community may have four new, prosperous member states, thereby increasing the universe of potential EMU participants. Yet even with an expanded Community membership, how feasible is EMU without Germany and France? The obvious answer is that EMU will only come about if either Germany and France meet the convergence criteria—or if the convergence criteria are revised to meet changing circumstances in Germany and France.

Hence, there was renewed speculation in late 1992 and early 1993 about a two-speed EMU. Although Maastricht already differentiates between two groups of countries—those that will and will not participate in Stage III—at least the treaty allows all member states to become involved in decisionmaking. By contrast, informal ideas about a two-speed EMU hark back to the Dutch draft treaty—dismissed in September 1991 during the IGC—which restricted decisionmaking on EMU to its likely participants. A core group of countries, probably the original six member states minus Italy, could form a currency union and coordinate their economic policies closely, without regard for their partners in the slow lane.

The core countries' anger over Britain's abrupt departure from the ERM motivated some of the two-speed talk. Fearful of stoking anti-Maastricht sentiment in Britain and further jeopardizing ratification, Mitterrand, Kohl, and Delors quickly downplayed conjecture about a two-speed EMU. Nevertheless, French, German, and Commission officials undoubtedly considered contingencies for EMU in the event of a Danish and/or British rejection of the Maastricht Treaty. Even with Maastricht finally implemented, a fast-track EMU appeals strongly to core Community countries worried about the length of Stage II.

Despite the ratification crisis, currency turmoil, and economic recession, the near-completion of the single market program in December 1992 provided a much-needed boost for proponents of EMU. So did the December 1992 Edinburgh summit's agreement on the Delors II budgetary package. A protocol in the Maastricht Treaty called for the Community to establish a cohesion fund before the end of 1992 (which it did at Edinburgh) to help poor countries meet the convergence criteria. The cohesion fund may not actually help recipient countries meet the convergence criteria—the money is earmarked for environmental projects and trans-European networks—but it symbolizes Community solidarity and meets an important political condition for the achievement of EMU.[47] Nevertheless, with Europe in the grip of recession and the ERM in disarray, it is difficult to see EMU coming into being within the Maastricht Treaty time frame.

NOTES

1. Interview in *The Wall Street Journal,* October 29, 1990, p. 1.

2. Quoted in *The Economist,* March 9, 1991, p. 58.

3. SEA, preamble.

4. Kaiser, et al., *The EC: Progress or Decline?* (London: RIIA, 1983), p. 13.

5. Tomaso Padoa-Schioppa, ed., *Efficiency, Stability and Equity: A Strategy for the Evolution of the Economic System of the EC* (Luxembourg: OOP, 1987), p. 8.

6. Commission, *Economic and Monetary Union* (Luxembourg: OOP, 1990), p. 11.

7. Commission, *Economic and Monetary Union,* p. 14; and Commission, *One Market, One Money: An Evaluation of the Potential Benefits and Costs of Forming an Economic and Monetary Union* (Luxembourg: OOP, 1990), p. 9.

8. Commission, *From Single Market to European Union* (Luxembourg: OOP, 1992).

9. Padoa-Schioppa, *Efficiency,* pp. 3, 13.

10. Leon Brittan, speech to the British Chamber of Commerce in Germany, October 31, 1990.

11. See Commission, *One Market,* p. 10.

12. Bull. EC S/1–1976, p. 20.

13. Committee for the Study of Economic and Monetary Union, *Report on Economic and Monetary Union in the European Community* (the Delors Report), (Luxembourg: OOP, 1989), pp. 18–19.

14. COM(87)100.

15. Delors Report, p. 24.

16. Delors Report, p. 31; Niels Thygesen, "The Delors Report and European Economic and Monetary Union," *International Affairs* 4, no. 65 (Autumn 1989), pp. 637–652, 642–643.

17. Thygesen, p. 642.

18. Commission, *Economic and Monetary Union,* p. 21.

19. Hansard, 184/41, Cols. 470–9, January 24, 1991.

20. Quoted in *The Manchester Guardian Weekly,* July 7, 1991, p. 6.

21. Leon Brittan, Speech to the British Chamber of Commerce in Germany, October 31, 1990.

22. Commission, *Economic and Monetary Union,* p. 17.

23. Commission, *One Market,* p. 251.

24. Commission, *One Market,* pp. 28–29.

25. Peter Kenen, "Speaking Up for EMU," *Financial Times,* July 28, 1992, p. 15.

26. Martin Feldstein, "Europe's Monetary Union: The Case Against EMU," *The Economist,* June 13, 1992, pp. 19–22.

27. Commission, *Economic and Monetary Union,* p. 11.

28. Bull. EC 6-1988, 1.1.1-4, and 3.4.1.

29. Bull. EC 6-1989, 1.1.11.

30. Bull. EC 12-1989, Presidency Conclusions, point 1.1.11.

31. Bull. EC 6-1990, Presidency Conclusions, point 1.10.

32. Kenen, "Speaking Up," p. 15.

33. Paule de Grauwe, Daniel Gros, Alfred Steinherr, and Niels Thygesen, "Reply to Feldstein," *The Economist,* July 4, 1992, p. 67.

34. Quoted in *Eurecom* 4, no. 4 (April 1992), p. 1.

35. Quoted in *Eurecom* 4, no. 7 (July–August 1992), p. 4.

36. See *The Economist,* November 30, 1991, p. 16.

37. See "The ERM Crisis," in *The Financial Times,* December 12–13, 1992, p. 2.

38. See *The Financial Times,* November 20, p. 14.

39. Immo Stabreit, "The EMS," *Statements and Speeches* 15, no. 15 (September 30, 1992).

40. Quoted in *The Financial Times,* January 15, 1993, p. 2.

41. Council Press Release 8854/92, September 28, 1992, 1604th Council Meeting.

42. Speech to the European Institute, September 21, 1992.

43. OECD, *Financial Market Trends,* October 1992, p. 16.

44. See Peter Kenen, "EMU Reconsidered," paper prepared for a conference on European Economic and Political Integration, Meridian House, Washington, DC, February 1, 1993, p. 8.

45. "The ERM Crisis," *The Financial Times,* December 12–13, 1992, p. 2.

46. Quoted in *The Financial Times,* May 17, 1991, p. 18; Pohl inserted this phrase into the final communiqué of the 1977 G7 summit.

47. See Commission, *From the Single Act to Maastricht and Beyond: The Means to Match Our Ambition,* Bull. EC S/1–92; and Bull. EC 12-1992.

16

External Economic Relations

With a population of 340 million, the European Community is the world's biggest market. It is also the world's largest trading bloc and a formidable international economic actor. Most countries have diplomatic missions in Brussels accredited to the Community. The Commission negotiates on the Community's behalf in the General Agreement on Tariffs and Trade (GATT), participates in the work of the Organization for Economic Co-operation and Development (OECD), coordinates Western assistance to the countries of Central and Eastern Europe and the former Soviet Union, and has over one hundred diplomatic missions and offices around the world. The Commission president meets regularly with the president of the United States and other world leaders and attends the annual summits of the seven most industrialized countries (G7); commissioners frequently visit and receive government ministers from nonmember states to discuss trade, environmental, labor, and other economic issues.

Articles 110–116 of the EEC treaty endow the Community with ex-clusive competence for external trade subject to a cumbersome and some-times counterproductive decisionmaking procedure. Although the Com-mission has had responsibility for commercial policy since the early 1960s, technically the Common Commercial Policy (CCP) was not complete until the single market became fully operational, putting an end to long-standing quota restrictions and other controls that individual member states had im-posed against certain imports (mostly textiles, cars, and consumer elec-tronics) from third countries. Thus, the single market program meant, among other things, "putting in place the final elements of the CCP."[1]

The launch of the single market program focused international at-tention on the Community's growing economic importance. To the Com-mission's dismay, external reaction to the Community's internal economic development was far from favorable. "Fortress Europe" became a catch-phrase in the Unites States to signal concern about the implications of the 1992 program for nonmember states. The Community had given little thought to the external perception of the internal market program and responded to international criticism by emphasizing its commitment to free trade and open markets. Largely at Margaret Thatcher's urging, the heads of government issued a declaration at the December 1988 Rhodes summit on the "International Role of the European Community." In an effort to allay growing concern beyond the Community's borders, the European Council proclaimed that "the single market will be of benefit to Community and non-Community countries alike, by ensuring continuing economic growth. The internal market will not close in on itself. 1992 Europe will be a partner and not a fortress Europe."[2]

Yet the phrase "Partner Europe" lacked the resonance and appeal of "Fortress Europe." Nor were the Community's trading partners convinced that the post-1992 European market would be as accessible as the European Council promised. The contemporaneous Uruguay Round of the GATT seemed a fortuitous chance for the Community's trading partners to test Brussels' resolve to maintain a liberal international system and for the Community to leverage concessions from its trading partners based on the single market's purported benefits. The Rhodes declaration acknowledged the link between the single market and the Uruguay Round: "The internal market will be a decisive factor contributing to greater liberalization in international trade on the basis of the GATT principles of reciprocity and mutually advantageous arrangements. The Community will continue to participate actively in the GATT Uruguay Round, committed as it is to strengthen [sic] the multilateral trading system."

More than five years later, with the single market largely in place and the Uruguay Round still in progress, international concern about the Community's commitment to trade liberalization seemed vindicated. The Community's refusal to concede larger cuts in agricultural subsidies thwarted completion of the Uruguay Round at its scheduled deadline of December 1990. Of course, agricultural subsidies are not part of the single market program, and many other contentious issues complicated the Uruguay Round. But the Community's willingness to block a new trade agreement for the sake of agricultural subsidies epitomized pervasive Europrotectionism. According to Jeffrey Schott, a respected international trade analyst, "in most respects, EC interests in the Uruguay Round have centered on rulemaking in new areas such as services and trade-related intellectual property rights and institutional issues such as dispute settlement more than on liberalization of trade barriers. EC officials seem to be content with the status quo, so that they can proceed with their internal market reforms without the burden of also adjusting to external trade reforms."[3]

THE GENERAL AGREEMENT ON TARIFFS AND TRADE

Article 110 of the EEC treaty outlines the CCP's guiding principle: "To contribute, in the common interest, to the harmonious development of world trade, the progressive abolition of restrictions on international trade, and the lowering of customs barriers." To that end the Community has developed a network of multilateral, regional, and bilateral trading relationships involving almost every country in the world. At its core lies the Community's participation in the GATT, one of the international institutions launched in the immediate post–World War II period to promote multilateralism and nondiscrimination in global trade.[4] Negotiations for tariff reductions and other trade reforms take place in a series of rounds, the first seven of which, culminating in the Tokyo Round of 1973–1979, succeeded in reducing formal tariffs for most industrialized countries' manufactured goods to an average of only 5 percent.

Although "it is in the GATT that the Community has its highest profile," the Community itself is only "a de facto contracting party."[5] The Twelve, rather than the Community, are members of the GATT, but under the terms of the CCP the Commission negotiates on their behalf. Nevertheless, national governments seriously circumscribe the Commission's negotiating position: The Council of Ministers decides the Commission's mandate, the 113 Committee of national representatives watches over the Commission's shoulder as it negotiates, and the Council of Ministers—if necessary in the guise of the European Council—approves the final agreement. Thus, the Community's own description of the Commission as "the sole negotiator and spokesman on behalf of its members" is misleading, as is the claim that "the EC is able to take swift and effective decisions in the trade policy area."[6]

Discussions about the latest GATT round began in the early 1980s, largely at the United States' urging. Despite the success of the Tokyo Round, closet protectionism in the 1970s undermined the spirit if not the letter of the GATT. In an effort to preempt growing domestic pressure for overt protection of U.S. products, the Reagan administration called for a renewed round of GATT negotiations covering a broader range of economic activity. After lengthy preliminary discussions, government ministers launched the eighth round of GATT negotiations at a meeting in Punta del Este, Uruguay, in September 1986 and set a deadline of December 1990 for a new agreement.

The Uruguay Round was unique in a number of respects. First, the round began with ninety-two countries but subsequently involved nearly twenty more, while others waited impatiently to join. A realization by many Third World countries of the importance of trade liberalization, along with the emergence into the global economic system of the newly

Table 16.1 GATT Negotiations Involving the European Community

Name	Duration	Major Achievement
Dillon Round[a]	1960–1962	Tariff reductions of 20 percent on a wide range of industrial goods; compensated third countries for trade diversion caused by the formation of the EC.
Kennedy Round	1964–1967	Tariff reductions of about 30 percent on a wide range of industrial goods.
Tokyo Round	1973–1979	Improved legal framework for trade; addressed nontariff barriers.
Uruguay Round	1986–1993	Expanded GATT rules to cover agriculture and services; improved dispute settlement; further reduced tariffs

a. Four GATT conferences preceded the Dillon Round: the first Geneva conference (1947), conferences in Annecy (1949) and Torquay (1950–1951), and the second Geneva conference (1956).

independent countries of Eastern Europe and the former Soviet Union, accounts for the dramatic increase in GATT membership. Because a new agreement required unanimity and because many Third World participants were more assertive than in previous rounds, the Uruguay Round was especially arduous.

Second, the Uruguay Round had an unusually ambitious agenda. Whereas earlier rounds covered only trade in manufactured goods, the Uruguay Round also covered agricultural trade, intellectual property rights, and trade in services—which by the mid-1980s accounted for more than half the GDP of the economically advanced countries. In addition, the round sought to bring trade in textiles under GATT rules by phasing out the Multifiber Arrangement. The combination of over a hundred participants and a swollen agenda made a successful conclusion of the Uruguay Round doubly difficult to achieve. For instance, many Third World countries believed they had more to gain from liberalizing trade in farm products and textiles than from opening their markets to service industries and investment.

Third, the Uruguay Round was "the first big test of economic cooperation in the post–Cold War era."[7] The GATT was a crucial prop for the Western economic system during the Cold War. Moreover, the pervasive Soviet threat during the Cold War guaranteed U.S. preeminence in the GATT. Although the Uruguay Round began during the Cold War, the December 1988 midterm review coincided with the onset of reform in Eastern Europe, and the December 1990 ministerial meeting at which the Uruguay Round collapsed took place after the revolution in Eastern

Europe and as the Soviet Union began to crumble. U.S. Vice President Dan Quayle's linkage in January 1992 of a possible withdrawal of U.S. troops from Europe with the EC's intransigence in the Uruguay Round is understandable only in the context of the Cold War's end. By the same token, the end of the Cold War softened the impact of Quayle's threat, because Europeans were less convinced than at any time since the late 1940s of the need for a large U.S. troop presence.

At the beginning of the round, participants adopted a "standstill and rollback" clause, undertaking not to introduce any new restrictions inconsistent with GATT provisions during the negotiations and gradually to dismantle existing tariff barriers. The initial phase of the round saw the establishment of fifteen negotiating groups, covering everything from nontariff measures to safeguards to services. A Trade Negotiations Committee, to which a Group of Negotiations on Goods and a Group of Negotiations on Services reported, assumed overall responsibility for the talks. Most of the negotiations took place at the GATT secretariat in Geneva, with Arthur Dunkel, GATT's director-general, playing a pivotal role.

The inclusion of agriculture in the Uruguay Round put the Community on the defensive from the beginning. The CAP had already become a byword for protectionism, and the Community soon came under fierce pressure from the United States and the Cairns Group (an informal association of agricultural free-traders led by Australia) to curtail subsidies for agricultural production and exports. Third World countries insisted on progress on agricultural trade liberalization in return for concessions in other sectors. As Argentina's trade minister remarked when his country blocked an agreement at the midterm review in December 1988, "Argentina would not have much cause to modify its position in services if there was no agreement to liberalize trade in farm products."[8]

In 1987 the United States set the scene for a protracted quarrel with the Community by demanding the complete elimination of all trade-distorting measures within ten years. The EC was already alert to international efforts to curtail its agricultural export subsidies. Even before the Uruguay Round began, the Council of Ministers insisted that "the fundamental objectives and mechanisms both internal and external of the CAP shall not be placed in question."[9] External Relations Commissioner Willy de Clercq reiterated the point at the Punta del Este meeting in September 1986.[10] The irreconcilable positions of the United States and the Cairns Group, on the one hand, and the EC, on the other, caused the midterm review to end in acrimony. The row over agriculture affected other areas, with India blocking agreement on intellectual property rights and a number of South American countries threatening to reopen negotiations on tentatively agreed-upon issues unless the Community conceded more on farm trade.[11]

At the June 1989 Madrid summit, held six months after the midterm review, the European Council reiterated the importance of having a "successful conclusion of the multilateral negotiations under the Uruguay Round."[12] The heads of government also emphasized the need for an agreement on trade in goods, services, and intellectual property rights but avoided the contentious question of agriculture. By then it was obvious not only that agriculture was the linchpin of the Uruguay Round but that Washington and Brussels were monopolizing the agenda. As the United States intensified pressure on the Community to curb agricultural subsidies, the European Council "reaffirmed the Community's determination to oppose any recourse to unilateral measures which might jeopardize [the] international system"[13]—a clear reference to Section 301 of the 1988 U.S. Trade and Competitiveness Act.

The Uruguay Round made little progress after the midterm review, with all parties to the GATT avoiding commitments or concessions until the final ministerial meeting in December 1990. The EC sharply attacked Washington over the 1990 U.S. farm bill, which maintained domestic price supports and export subsidies for U.S. agriculture. Trans-Atlantic exchanges became especially sharp in 1990, as the Uruguay Round assumed a higher political profile in the United States and the EC. President Bush listed the round as a priority item at the July 1990 G7 summit in Houston. Indeed, the summit produced a feeling that the crisis had passed, thanks to a commitment by the leaders of the seven largest industrialized countries, plus the Commission president, to "substantial, progressive reductions in support and protection for agriculture."[14] The fact that Agriculture Commissioner MacSharry expressed satisfaction with the Houston text should have alerted the United States to its ambiguity.

When it came to translating the "Spirit of Houston" into concrete proposals, though, the Community failed to deliver. After several battles in the Commission and in the Council of Ministers, the Community eventually tabled an offer to reduce farm subsidies by 30 percent over ten years from 1986, a far cry from its trading partners' demand for cuts of 90 percent in export subsidies and 75 percent in other farm support over ten years from 1991–1992. Moreover, the EC insisted that any agreement to reduce farm subsidies and other supports would have to permit "rebalancing"— i.e., allowing the Community partially to offset cuts in some areas with increases in others, provided the overall trend in supports was downward.

A breakdown of agricultural talks in Geneva on November 10, only three days after the EC unveiled its offer, virtually doomed the looming Brussels ministerial meeting. Encouraging remarks by President Bush, Commission President Delors, and Italian Prime Minister Andreotti at their November 1990 Washington summit failed to dispel the gloom. As expected, the Brussels talks broke down largely because of the Community's refusal to make a more substantial offer to reduce agricultural subsidies and to reform the CAP. Ignoring criticism of the CAP, the Council of Ministers concluded that the debacle "was due to objective difficulties arising from the disparity between the ambitious goals which all the participants set themselves and the political possibilities of achieving them within the available timespan, on the basis of the technical preparation for the conference."[15]

Despite the Council's rationalization, most observers agreed that the ministerial meeting collapsed because of the Community's refusal to budge on agriculture. Yet it seemed extraordinary that the Community would allow the Uruguay Round to founder apparently for the sake of 10 million farmers, who between them account for only 3 percent of EC economic output. Clearly, the romantic appeal of agriculture and the political power of farmers in the Community should not be underestimated, nor should latent anti-Americanism. Many Europeans resented what they perceived as heavy-handed U.S. pressure to acquiesce in an agreement more advantageous to the United States than to the Community.

In the event, the Uruguay Round was not sufficiently high on the Community's agenda, notwithstanding official protestations to the contrary. Renato Ruggiero, the Italian trade minister, admitted as much in May 1990 when he accused both the Commission and Council of Ministers of neglecting the Uruguay Round in favor of the single market program and developments in Eastern Europe.[16] Ruggiero chaired the Council of Ministers during the Brussels fiasco in December 1990, by which time the Community was preoccupied with the imminent launch of the intergovernmental conferences on EMU and EPU.

The problem also lay in the complexity of the round and the balance of interests involved. Despite dire predictions about the consequences of the Uruguay Round's collapse, few politicians and businesspeople appreciated the urgency of a successful conclusion. Nor did everyone agree that a new trade agreement was in their best interests. That was true in the United States even more so than in the Community. Thus, on both sides of the Atlantic, political support for the kinds of concessions necessary to end the stalemate was undermined.

The Uruguay Round resumed in early 1991 and continued fitfully thereafter.[17] Like Bush a year previously, Prime Minister Major pressed at the London G7 summit in July 1991 for a political commitment to conclude the talks. At the November 1991 U.S.-EC summit, held under the auspices of the Transatlantic Declaration, both sides promised, once again, to reach accord before the end of the year. "For the first time," Delors claimed, "I am reasonably optimistic about the possibility of reaching an agreement. . . . This is a very important signal to the world economy."[18] Yet the following month the Community rejected a compromise proposal by Arthur Dunkel because it "called into question the very principles of the Community's agricultural policy."[19]

The first breakthrough came in May 1992, when the Community ended eighteen months of internal negotiations and finally reformed the

CAP. The reform's production and price reductions for various commodities, its provisions for direct income support rather than production-based subsidies for farmers, and its land set-aside incentives resuscitated the stalled Uruguay Round. MacSharry was predictably provocative: "Our international trading partners must recognize the magnitude of the step taken by the Community . . . and its contribution toward stabilizing international markets. [CAP reform] can provide the necessary impetus to conclude the Uruguay Round in the near future provided the other parties to these negotiations are prepared to be realistic, pragmatic, and reciprocate our contribution."[20]

Indeed, the Community's CAP reform sparked a renewal of negotiations that almost ended the impasse over agriculture in the Uruguay Round, but not before a simmering U.S.-EC dispute about oilseed subsidies boiled over in October and November 1992. Talks between both sides broke down in early November, inciting Washington to carry out a long-standing threat of retaliation by announcing punitive 200 percent tariffs on $300 million of EC agricultural exports (chiefly French white wine), effective December 5. The U.S. threat, and the election of a new U.S. president who promised less indulgence toward European subsidization, spurred EC ministers to settle their differences and negotiate a settlement. On November 20, following frantic trans-Atlantic "shuttle diplomacy" in which MacSharry played an uncharacteristic conciliatory role (doubtless because his term in the Commission was almost at an end), the Commission and the U.S. government reached a breakthrough agreement at Blair House in Washington on the oilseeds issue and other agriculture-related items.[21]

Under the terms of the agreement, the Community promised to limit the area of land devoted to oilseed production rather than the total amount of oilseeds produced. Up to 15 percent of that area (a total of 11 million acres) would be taken out of production in the first year and a minimum of 10 percent in future years. In the broader agriculture agreement, the Community agreed to cut the volume of subsidized exports by 21 percent over six years, starting in 1994. The United States accepted the principle of direct payments to compensate farmers who set aside 15 percent of their arable land as part of the earlier CAP reform. Finally, the United States agreed to a "peace clause" under which it will not demand GATT panel investigations of EC oilseed subsidies or EC export refunds as long as they conform to the final terms of the Uruguay Round.

Predictably, the French government characterized the Blair House agreement as a sellout to the United States and threatened to invoke the Luxembourg Compromise unless the Uruguay Round resulted in a favorable overall agreement. Yet the Luxembourg Compromise never had legal standing in the Community and has not been cited since the SEA. During the Maastricht referendum campaign in France, Elizabeth Guigou, the minister for European affairs, claimed that the Luxembourg Compromise was irrelevant and that France would work to ensure that it remained so. Gaullists rushed to the national veto's defense, however, forcing the government to announce that the Luxembourg Compromise "had not and will never be renounced by France."[22] At the crucial meeting of the Council of Ministers (or, possibly, the European Council), France could indeed have revived the national veto to placate its farmers. If so, France would definitively have destroyed the Uruguay Round and, by alienating its EC partners, seriously set back prospects for deeper European integration.

In the event, the expected showdown between the French government and French farmers, or between the French government and its Community partners, never materialized. Although prospects for a successful conclusion of the Uruguay Round looked bleak in 1993, an agreement was finally hammered out on December 15, the final deadline. The year had begun badly: President Clinton's affirmation of support for the GATT at his first meeting with John Major in February 1993 sounded like the platitudinous statements of every other statesman during the tortuous course of the negotiations. On the other side a statement that the Community is "entitled to expect its partners to make the substantial contribution that is required to arrive at a balanced overall agreement"[23] hardly suggested a conciliatory mood. Washington's and Brussels' preoccupation with agriculture during the first six years of the round blinded them to the complexity and seriousness of other issues and to the fact that an agreement depended on the consent of over a hundred additional parties. Only last-minute U.S. concessions to reopen the Blair House agreement and to remove the equally contentious audiovisual sector from the GATT package made a breakthrough possible. By ending the threat of French obstructionism in the Council of Ministers, the United States' capitulation let the Community off the hook.

In the early 1980s, a former deputy director-general of the GATT observed that "the structure of the EC decision-making process . . . is slow, hard to predict and has a protectionist bias."[24] The Community is not solely responsible for the failure of the Uruguay Round, but its performance bears out that observation and demonstrates the drawbacks of the CCP. According to the Community, "the Uruguay Round represents the forum for translating the external aspects of the single market into concrete advantages for its trading partners, particularly as concerns the future expansion of world trade in goods and the extension of liberalization rules to trade in services."[25] By those criteria, the external benefits of the single market program have yet to be realized.

THE EUROPEAN ECONOMIC AREA AND ENLARGEMENT

On October 22, 1991, after more than a year of arduous negotiations, the European Community and the EFTA member states (Austria, Finland,

Iceland, Liechtenstein, Norway, Sweden, and Switzerland) signed an agreement to establish the "European Economic Area," a huge internal market of nineteen countries and 380 million people accounting for 40 percent of global trade. It would be the world's largest and most lucrative commercial bloc. The putative EEA remained controversial even after the agreement's signing. No sooner was the ink dry than the Court of Justice ruled that a proposed EC-EFTA court to resolve EEA-related disputes would contravene Community law. The Court's ruling put the agreement back on the drawing board, from which it emerged again in February 1992.[26]

The signatories nonetheless hoped that the agreement would be ratified before the end of the year so that the EEA could come into existence at the same time as the single market, on January 1, 1993. But a narrow majority rejected the agreement in a referendum in Switzerland on December 6, 1992. After Denmark's rejection of the Maastricht Treaty, this was the second setback in seven months for a major Community initiative. Yet the Swiss referendum result was far less serious for the Community than the Danish referendum result. For one thing, the Maastricht Treaty meant much more for the development of European integration. For another, whereas the Maastricht Treaty could not be implemented unless ratified in each member state, a country's failure to ratify the EEA Agreement merely kept that country out of the enlarged single market. Thus, Switzerland's decision delayed but did not prevent the EEA from coming into existence, nor did it sway a majority of Liechtenstein's voters from endorsing the agreement in a referendum the following week.

The British government had promoted EFTA in the late 1950s as an intergovernmental alternative to the supranational Community. EFTA sought only to establish free trade in industrial goods, whereas the Community involved a high degree of economic, social, and political integration. Britain's application for Community membership in the early 1960s emphasized EFTA's limits and helped to ease friction between both bodies. EFTA's future seemed in doubt when Britain and Denmark eventually joined the Community in 1973, and the remaining EFTA countries negotiated free trade agreements with Brussels. Sweden had seriously considered applying for full Community membership in the late 1960s and early 1970s but decided against because of its traditional policy of neutrality. Blunt Soviet statements about the irreconcilability of neutrality with Community accession precluded an Austrian application during the same period.[27]

Formal EC-EFTA relations changed little during the next ten years. After a summit meeting in Vienna in May 1977, EFTA leaders called for closer cooperation with the EC on environmental, transport, and other issues. The Community responded positively, but no new initiative emerged. Only in the early 1980s, when both EFTA and the EC became increasingly concerned about the economic impact of new technologies, growing competition from the United States and Japan, and the drawbacks of a fragmented European market, did talks between them resume. Moreover, EFTA feared that the Community's high technology ventures and renewed interest in the internal market, launched in response to the rapidly changing international economic environment, would increase its members' economic vulnerability. Nor did the Community want to develop an internal market at the expense of a robust EC-EFTA trading relationship (EFTA was the EC's most important trading partner—more important than Japan and the United States combined).[28]

This was the background to the April 1984 meeting of Community and EFTA foreign ministers in Luxembourg, which resulted in a common declaration pledging closer cooperation on a range of issues leading eventually to a "European Economic Space" (EES). Despite the establishment of an EC-EFTA "High-Level Contact Group" and the conclusion in 1987 of two EC-EFTA conventions on trade and transport, the Luxembourg Declaration yielded disappointing results. EC-EFTA negotiations struggled to keep up with the single market program. Freer movement of goods, services, capital, and people in the Community heightened EFTA's fears of economic marginalization. At the risk of satellization, most EFTA countries voluntarily implemented the Community's single market legislation in order to remain competitive internationally.[29]

EFTA's insistence on a seat at the Brussels table provoked a "crisis" in May 1987 when Willy de Clercq, the external affairs commissioner, asserted the Community's sole decisionmaking authority and stressed the primacy of EC integration over EC-EFTA cooperation.[30] The disparity between both sides was glaringly obvious: EFTA had only 10 percent of EC's population, and its total GDP was less than Germany's alone. A number of EFTA countries reached the obvious conclusion and considered applying for membership. The economic impetus for accession was so strong that neutral Austria topped the list of impending applicants.

The EFTA countries met all the criteria for membership and enjoyed the advantages, from the Community's point of view, of having sound economies (thus probably becoming net contributors) and homogeneous "European" populations. Yet until it digested Iberian enlargement and implemented the single market program, the Community was uninterested in acquiring new members. Hoping to fend off applications from the EFTA countries, in a speech to the European Parliament on January 17, 1989, outlining the Commission's annual program, Jacques Delors reactivated the EES initiative and proposed "a new form of association, with common decision-making and administrative institutions."[31]

EFTA's enthusiastic response at its Oslo summit in March 1989 presaged intensive preparatory work to shape the hitherto vaguely defined EES. A high-level steering group, with five working groups covering the single market program, flanking policies (environment, transport, social policy, etc.), and legal and institutional issues, began work immediately. By October 1989 the steering group had established a basis for preliminary negotiations and identified the Community's willingness to concede "decision-shaping" and EFTA's demand for "decision-making" as one of the most contentious questions. After various procedural steps, both sides announced that negotiations to establish an EES would begin in mid-1990.[32] It was also in mid-1990 that, at Britain's behest, the expression "European Economic Area" replaced the silly-sounding "European Economic Space."[33]

The acceleration of EC-EFTA talks had not deterred Austria from opting for Community membership. As recently as 1988 the Soviet Union had repeated its long-standing reservations about Austria's accession but changed that position when reform swept Eastern Europe. Not wanting to miss a "historical opportunity," Austria applied to join the Community on July 1, 1989. Although Soviet opposition was no longer an issue, neutrality itself, to which Austrians had become deeply attached, remained a potential stumbling block. In its application, Austria pledged to accept the responsibilities of Community membership but clung to its international status of "permanent neutrality."[34] Although the Community ruled out further enlargement until after completion of the single market, Austria's application immediately raised disturbing questions about the compatibility of neutrality with the Community's commitment to an ever closer union.

Undoubtedly the Community's concentration on the IGCs contributed to the complexity of the EEA negotiations. Even without that distraction, the Community's chief negotiator described the talks as "the most complex negotiations which we have ever conducted on behalf of the EC."[35] On the internal market alone, the EFTA countries had to adopt approximately 1,400 existing Community acts covering over 10,000 pages of legislation. EFTA annoyed the EC by asking for numerous exemptions, but scaled back those demands in November 1990 in an effort to expedite an agreement. Yet the talks soon stalled over institutional arrangements in the putative EEA and only picked up after the EC agreed in mid-May to canvass EFTA opinion on draft legislation and to establish a panel of EC and EFTA judges to adjudicate EEA-related disputes.

By the fall of 1991 negotiations were again bogged down. Fishing rights, alpine trucking, and financial support for the Community's poorer member states posed almost insuperable obstacles to a final agreement. Spain and Portugal demanded generous access to Norwegian and Icelandic fishing grounds, Switzerland and Austria wanted to limit heavy-truck transit from Community countries, and Spain wanted a substantial increase in EFTA's initial offer to the Community's cohesion coffers. When the negotiations missed their third deadline, in September 1991, an exasperated Dutch presidency announced that an EEA agreement could prove impossible to reach and was in any case not a Community priority.

Clearly, the EFTA countries had more to lose from a complete breakdown of negotiations. Yet Switzerland and Iceland held out until the early hours of October 22 before accepting final offers on trucking and fishing, respectively. The Court of Justice's ruling against the EEA in December 1991 threatened to unravel the agreement completely, but renewed negotiations ended in February 1992 with a compromise over the legal mechanism to resolve EEA disputes. Both sides eventually signed the definitive agreement on May 2, 1992, after a last-minute revision of the Austrian truck-transit deal.[36]

At the beginning of the EEA negotiations in mid-1990, the EFTA countries—with the exception of EC applicant Austria—saw the putative agreement as a way to enjoy the benefits of the single market program without necessarily joining the Community. Two years later, at the end of the EEA negotiations, most of the EFTA countries saw the EEA as a staging post to full membership. What had happened in the meantime? First, although EFTA countries generally had outperformed their EC counterparts in the past, most of them stagnated economically in 1991 and saw far better prospects for improvement in the Community than outside it. Second, most EFTA countries were dissatisfied with the limited "decision-shaping" offered by Brussels and decided that full Community membership was the only way to acquire "decisionmaking" power. Third, EFTA countries feared exclusion from EMU. Fourth, no country wanted to be left outside the Community if its EFTA partners joined. Thus, Sweden applied for membership in June 1991, Finland in March 1992, and Switzerland in May 1992. Haunted by the specter of the 1972 referendum campaign, the Norwegian government delayed its application until November 1992. Iceland decided not to apply, largely because of concerns about its lucrative fishing zone.

With the end of the Cold War, neutrality virtually disappeared as an obstacle to Community membership. Some European neutrals were willing to abandon neutrality entirely; others clung to the label but conceded that it meant little in practice. In its opinions on Austria's, Sweden's, and Finland's applications, the Commission stressed the security and possible defense obligations of Community accession. At the Maastricht summit, the European Council asked the Commission to examine the implications of enlargement in the context of the new treaty. The Commission's report, presented at the Lisbon summit in June 1992, took a tough line on neutrality: Applicants would have to give "specific and binding assurances . . . with regard to their political commitment and legal capacity to fulfill their [CFSP] obligations."[37]

The Commission's report on enlargement also declared that "widening must not be at the expense of deepening." Accordingly, the European Council decided at Lisbon not to begin new entry negotiations until the member states had ratified the Maastricht Treaty and settled the

Delors II budgetary package.[38] However, Britain appeared eager to jump the gun on enlargement by beginning preliminary negotiations during its presidency in late 1992. This raised suspicion among other member states that Major, like Thatcher before him, favored widening over deepening. In the event, Britain was too preoccupied with the Maastricht Treaty ratification crisis to open exploratory talks with the applicant countries. Although formal enlargement negotiations were supposed to await ratification of the treaty, the heads of government decided at the December 1992 Edinburgh summit to begin negotiations with Austria, Sweden, and Finland in early 1993 and with Norway as soon as the Commission published its opinion on that country's application.[39]

The governments of Austria, Finland, Sweden, and Switzerland quickly declared their willingness to accept the terms of the Maastricht Treaty. Yet the treaty ratification crisis adversely affected opinion in those countries (and even more so in Norway), where support for Community membership was already far from unanimous. Apart from general concerns about loss of sovereignty and neutrality, each country had particular reasons to be wary of Community membership. Finns, Swedes, and Swiss fretted that the CAP would ruin their heavily subsidized agricultural sectors; Austrians and Swiss feared an additional influx of foreigners; Austrians worried about the anonymity of their bank accounts and the integrity of their tougher environmental laws; and Swedish snuff-takers (about 10 percent of the population) abhorred the Community's ban on snuff sales. The prominence of Community questions during the Austrian, Finnish, Swedish, and Swiss general elections in 1990 and 1991 demonstrated a high level of public interest in the issue.

Despite the applicant countries' commitments to the Maastricht Treaty, the concessions won by Denmark at the Edinburgh summit undoubtedly tempted them to seek similar opt-outs during the enlargement negotiations. But the Community was not inclined to make concessions to applicant countries, who lack the leverage Denmark had concerning ratification of the Maastricht Treaty. Under the circumstances, it is ironic that Denmark, in the Council presidency during the first half of 1993, presided over the opening round of the enlargement negotiations. It is also ironic that Nordic applicants seemed more enthusiastic than Denmark about European union, given Denmark's tendency to object to controversial aspects of the Maastricht Treaty on the dubious grounds of "Nordic solidarity."

The enlargement negotiations with Austria, Finland, Sweden, and Norway are bound to be difficult. By joining the EEA, those countries have adopted the bulk of existing Community legislation. Nevertheless, a host of contentious issues remain, including the CAP and the Common Commercial Policy, institutional representation, weighted voting in the Council of Ministers, participation in the non-Community "pillars" of the Union, and participation in the "European Social Community." If the negotiations progress satisfactorily, Austria, Finland, Sweden, and possibly Norway could join the Community in 1995, with shorter transition periods than for previous new members. But a much bigger and weightier "if" is whether the electorates in those countries will ratify the accession treaties. Opinion polls in the applicant countries have indicated that the prospect of Community membership is becoming less, not more, likely.

The current round of enlargement negotiations suggests that the EEA is destined for an early grave. Switzerland rejected the EEA, and four of the six remaining EFTA countries may soon be Community members. In that sense the EEA failed to meet Delors's initial objective of an alternative arrangement to Community enlargement. There is considerable speculation that the EEA may serve instead as an alternative to Community membership for the Central European countries, although it will be some time before those countries are able to implement the amount of Community legislation involved in the agreement.

ASIA

The EC-Japan relationship is the weakest side of the trilateral U.S.-EC-Japan relationship. Until recently, relations between the EC and Japan were almost exclusively economic, whereas both had robust political *and* economic relations with the United States. In 1990 the Japanese ambassador to the EC complained pointedly that during the previous year Jacques Delors had met the U.S. president five times but had met the Japanese prime minister only once.[40] Partly to assert an increasing political involvement in European affairs, Japan played an active role in the Eastern European aid effort. After the United States and the EC concluded the Transatlantic Declaration in November 1990, Japan pressed the Community for a similar accord.

Japan's weak political relationship with the Community is a function not only of its geographical distance from Europe but especially of Europe's fear of Japan's ability to produce and export inexpensive, dependable, high-quality consumer goods. The epilogue and prologue to the EC-Japan Declaration, eventually concluded by Prime Minister Kaifu, Commission President Delors, and Council President Lubbers in The Hague in July 1991, illustrate the extent of the Community's concern. French insistence on references to reciprocity and "balance," at a time when Japan's trade surplus with the Community grew sharply, delayed the declaration. Callous remarks about Japan and the Japanese by Edith Cresson, the French prime minister, made matters worse. Eventually, France accepted a Commission compromise calling for the EC and Japan to have "equitable access to their respective markets and to remove obstacles, whether structural or other, impeding the expansion of trade, on the basis of comparable opportunities."[41]

The declaration established an institutional framework for annual meetings between the Japanese prime minister, the Commission president, and the Council president, as well as regular meetings between Japanese ministers and EC commissioners. But those provisions, and the declaration's lofty rhetoric about "a deeper partnership based on the common ideals of freedom, democracy, and the rule of law," could not alter the reality of an unhealthy trade imbalance. Japan's expanding trade surplus, especially in electronics and cars, continued to alarm Brussels. Shortly after publicly issuing the joint declaration, the Commission and the Japanese government announced that they had concluded an export-restraint agreement—euphemistically called "Elements of Consensus"—to limit the number of Japanese cars entering the European market until the year 2000.

The agreement culminated two years of arduous negotiations within the Commission, among member states, and between the Community and Japan. Five Community countries—the UK, France, Italy, Portugal, and Spain—had long-standing quotas on Japanese car imports, which the single market program was about to bring to an end. To compensate the countries concerned, the Commission, under intense pressure from most European car manufacturers, proposed a post-1992 transitional period of voluntary restraints on Japanese car sales in the Community. By allowing direct imports from Japan of 1.23 million vehicles in 1999, compared with 1.24 million in 1989, the deal effectively froze until the end of the decade the level of direct exports of cars and light trucks from Japan to the EC.[42] After 1999, the Community car market will supposedly be fully liberalized. As a classic example of a voluntary export restraint in a sector where Japan has a strong competitive advantage, the EC-Japan auto agreement is a key element in the Community's "Japan strategy."[43]

The agreement was controversial, not only because of its blatant protectionism and insensitivity to the Uruguay Round but also because of the ambiguity surrounding its impact on cars produced by Japanese "transplants" in the Community. Located chiefly in the UK, these Japanese-owned factories have revolutionized car manufacturing in Europe and captured a substantial share of the market. The British government champions Japanese transplants and claims that the car agreement did not impose a ceiling on transplant production in the Community; strongly protectionist French and Italian car manufacturers detest transplants and reached the opposite conclusion; and the Commission sat on the fence by citing vague "working assumptions" for transplant output. Once the agreement became operational in 1993 and the protectionist demands of continental car makers increased, the market share of Japanese transplants became an even more politically explosive issue. National governments and sympathetic commissioners will inevitably increase pressure for an extension of the voluntary-restraint agreement before it expires at the end of the decade.

In the meantime, the fledgling political relationship between Japan and the EC continues to suffer from mutual misunderstanding and mistrust. Japanese investment in the Community, after soaring from $3.3 billion in 1986 to $14 billion in 1989, slowed considerably in the early 1990s.[44] But as the trade surplus widens further in Japan's favor, demands are on the rise from European industry for retaliatory measures against alleged "dumping" of Japanese products and for Community efforts to break down supposed "structural impediments" to entry into the Japanese market. As a result, relations between Brussels and Tokyo are unlikely to blossom into a strong political alliance in the near future.

Elsewhere in Asia, Communist China never shared the Soviet Union's squeamishness about the capitalistic European Community. China and the EC agreed to establish diplomatic relations in 1975 and signed a trade and economic cooperation agreement in 1978. So vigorous was their economic relationship that in 1985 China and the EC signed a new agreement to provide for more comprehensive cooperation. Three years later the Commission opened a delegation in Beijing.

The Community's cozy relationship with China came to an abrupt end in June 1989, when the Chinese government ruthlessly suppressed the pro-democracy student demonstrations in Tiananmen Square. Meeting in Madrid on June 26–27, the European Council condemned China's repression, suspended high-level bilateral meetings, postponed new cooperation projects, and cut existing programs.[45] Over a year later, the member states decided gradually to normalize relations with China, although the dilemma between upholding human rights and enhancing bilateral trade continued to confound the Community.

In the early 1990s the question of China's application for renewed GATT membership further vexed relations with the Community. China left the GATT in 1950 after the Communists took power but applied to rejoin in 1986. International condemnation of the Tiananmen Square massacre temporarily halted negotiations for China's GATT reentry. When they resumed, Taiwan's application for GATT membership complicated the issue. Taiwan's trading size and sustained economic growth in the early 1990s warrant its participation in the GATT, but many developing countries were reluctant to endorse its candidacy without China's approval. In return for allowing Taiwan to apply separately for GATT membership—albeit as an "autonomous customs territory," the formula used by Hong Kong and Macao when they joined the GATT with China's consent—the United States and EC promised China expedited consideration of its own GATT application.

The United States found the issue of Taiwan's GATT membership too sensitive politically, and fobbed it off on the EC. Martin Bangemann, the commissioner for industry and the internal market, told the Taiwanese government during a visit in April 1992 that the Community supported the island's GATT application.[46] Under the terms of a face-saving agreement eventually reached between China, the EC, and the United States, China will rejoin the GATT only minutes before Taiwan is admitted. But the question of when that will happen remains unresolved. Despite China's move to a free market system and, as a result, its extraordinary economic growth (notably in the south), the Community is unsure that China's trade policy is consistent with GATT principles.

In the meantime, the Community became involved in a number of trade disputes with China. One concerned a U.S.-China maritime agreement requiring trade between both countries to be carried exclusively in each other's ships. According to Community officials, this agreement contravened the nondiscrimination clause of the 1985 EC-China accord. The Community also complained that, on intellectual property, China gave U.S. companies better treatment than other foreign firms by awarding them retrospective rights. A more serious dispute involved a Community decision in June 1992 to impose quotas on imports of Chinese footwear as part of a scheme to harmonize rather than abolish national quotas in the single market.

The "three Chinas"—China, Taiwan, and Hong Kong—are members of the Asia Pacific Economic Cooperation group (APEC), a loose association that spans the Pacific from North America to Malaysia and includes some of the world's largest and fastest-growing economies: Brunei, Indonesia, Malaysia, the Philippines, Singapore, Thailand, the United States, Canada, Japan, Korea, China, Hong Kong, Taiwan, Australia, and New Zealand. Fearful that the single market would turn the EC into a closed trading bloc, Australia organized APEC in order to accelerate trade liberalization globally and eventually to promote political and security cooperation. APEC is a striking manifestation of Australia's recent efforts to identify more closely with the Asia-Pacific region, a development motivated by concern about increasing protectionism in the European Community, by the related fear of an Uruguay Round collapse (Australia and the Community clashed bitterly in the GATT over agricultural subsidies), and by a realization that most of Australia's trade is with other Asian countries (Australia is one of the few developed countries that runs a trade surplus with Japan, its biggest trading partner).

APEC's membership is too diverse to form a regional trading bloc modeled on the EC. Yet the six members of the Association of Southeast Asian Nations (ASEAN)—Indonesia, the Philippines, Thailand, Malaysia, Singapore, and Brunei—form a cohesive political group within APEC. Impressed by the EC's development but concerned about the Community's seeming equivocation about market liberalization, the ASEAN countries decided in February 1992 to establish a free trade area within fifteen years. The proposed Asian free trade association could also include Japan, the three remaining newly industrialized countries in the region (South Korea, Hong Kong, and Taiwan), and possibly Vietnam and Laos, which are eager to join ASEAN.

The ASEAN countries do not envision Australia and New Zealand as part of the regional free trade area. Ironically, ASEAN forms the core group within APEC, an organization that Australia founded in order to have a seat at the regional table. The 1992 decision to institutionalize APEC by establishing a secretariat in Singapore consolidated ASEAN's position at APEC's center and further undermined Australia's overall strategy in the region. Australia's political weakness vis-à-vis ASEAN is accentuated by APEC's failure to achieve concrete results since its inauguration in 1989.

Thus, ASEAN remains the most important economic and political group in the region. The Community has had relations with ASEAN since 1972. Three years later the Commission and ASEAN set up a working party to promote closer commercial, economic, and development cooperation. That led to a nonpreferential trade and economic cooperation agreement, which both sides have renewed every two years since the original agreement expired in 1985. The EC and ASEAN sought in the early 1990s to negotiate a new agreement that would improve upon their 1980 accord—a "bland statement of good intentions"[47]—by including provisions for trade dispute resolution and EIB lending. Progress stalled during Portugal's Council presidency in early 1992, however, over Indonesia's abysmal human rights record in East Timor, a former Portuguese colony that Indonesia annexed in 1975. An EC-ASEAN foreign ministers meeting in Manila in October 1992 ended indecisively because of Portugal's insistence that it is contrary to EC policy to upgrade relations with countries that have poor human rights records. Ironically, the proposed new agreement would contain human rights provisions that do not exist in the current agreement.[48]

India's economic reforms, intended to emulate Western market economies, open the prospect of closer trade relations with the Community. Accordingly, in December 1992 the Commission and the Indian government initiated a new framework cooperation agreement to replace the current economic and commercial cooperation agreement, taking into account the changing international system, the impact of the single market, and India's economic reforms.[49] The Community's dealings with Pakistan involve commercial and economic cooperation, science and technology, food aid, and refugee aid. Trade between the EC and Bangladesh is minimal, although the Community gave nearly 10 million ECU in aid to Bangladesh in 1992 to help accommodate refugees from Burma.[50]

LATIN AMERICA

The Community has extensive relations with individual Latin American countries and regional groupings, notably the Rio Group and Cartagena Agreement countries, and is keenly interested in the emergence of Mercosur, a customs union between Argentina, Brazil, Paraguay, and Uruguay that is due to begin in 1995. Spain and Portugal have taken the lead in promoting closer economic and political relations between the Community and their former colonies in Central and South America. Yet trade between the EC and Latin America continues to decline, and Community aid to the region (apart from development assistance to the Caribbean) remains small. Spain and Portugal pressed hard for an Ecofin decision in May 1992 to allow EIB lending in the region. The finance ministers set a ceiling of 250 million ECU annually over three years for EIB loans for projects to be agreed on a case-by-case basis.[51]

Modest though it was, the EIB agreement at least proved more substantial than the outcome of a highly publicized summit in Madrid in July 1992 between Iberian and Latin American leaders. Held five hundred years after Christopher Columbus arrived in the New World, Spain hoped that the summit would celebrate democracy in Latin America and strengthen Ibero-American relations. In the event, the suspension of Peru's constitution and an attempted coup in Venezuela earlier in the year, as well as Fidel Castro's personal domination of the event, underlined the fragility of Latin American democracy. Although claiming to be a bridge between Latin America and the Community, Spain and Portugal had nothing tangible to deliver at the summit.[52]

Yet Spain's bridge building across the Atlantic helped to restore diplomatic relations between Argentina and the Community, broken off in 1982 during the Falklands War. Argentina has unusually close family ties with Western Europe—more than a million Argentines are also citizens of EC countries—and conducts more trade than any other Latin American country with the Community. A gradual rapprochement in EC-Argentina relations led to a cooperation agreement in April 1990. The following July Argentina further improved its standing with the Community by restoring diplomatic relations with Britain.[53]

Spain's self-proclaimed role in the Community as a champion of Latin American interests suffered a serious setback in December 1992, when Madrid supported a Council of Ministers decision to set a tariff on banana imports from Latin America. The issue arose because, in the fragmented pre-1992 market, some member states discriminated against Latin American bananas and in favor of bananas from the African, Caribbean, and Pacific (ACP) countries, with which the Community has an extensive development assistance program. Realizing that the single market would allow unrestricted access of larger, cheaper Latin American bananas into the Community to the detriment of more expensive, poorer-quality ACP banana imports, EC agriculture ministers decided in December 1992 to convert the Latin American banana quotas into high tariffs.[54] The seven Latin American exporters involved—Costa Rica, Guatemala, Honduras, Nicaragua, Panama, Colombia, and Ecuador—already supply 60 percent of bananas consumed in the EC but could extend their share considerably in an unrestricted Community-wide market. Spain supported the Council's decision in order to protect its Canary Islands banana producers.

THE AFRICAN, CARIBBEAN, AND PACIFIC COUNTRIES

The row over bananas throughout 1992 pitted the Community's commitment to free trade against its strong support for the ACP countries. On the strength of a protocol in the EC-ACP development assistance convention that promises not to put ACP banana producers "in a less favorable situation than in the past or the present," the ACP countries lobbied hard for a guaranteed share of the Community's banana market. Although successful, the ACP countries may not always enjoy Community protection. The Council of Ministers' decision both shielded ACP banana imports and, by translating the Community's quotas against Latin American imports into tariffs, resolved a contentious issue in the Uruguay Round. However, such tariffs could be negotiated away in a future GATT round. ACP banana producers are well aware of the need to reduce costs and improve quality in anticipation of free trade in the Community's banana market.

Practically all products originating in the ACP countries have free access to the Community. Reciprocal arrangements are not compulsory; the ACP states must only give the Community most-favored-nation status. The Community's generous trade concessions to ACP countries are as old as the Treaty of Rome. Part IV of the Treaty (Articles 131–136) makes special provision for the Community's economic relations with its member states' colonies and former colonies. Initially most of these were French-African countries, with which the Community concluded the first and second Yaounde Conventions in 1963 and 1969.

Britain's impending accession to the Community in the early 1970s, together with Dutch and German pressure for a new Community approach to the Third World, led to a revision of the French-inspired principles underlying the Yaounde Conventions. Instead of a traditional donor-recipient relationship, the Community strove for a novel partnership with forty-six developing countries—including numerous British ex-colonies—in Africa, the Caribbean, and the Pacific. EC-ACP negotiations began in July 1973 and ended in February 1975 when both sides signed a new convention in Lomé, the capital of Togo.

The Lomé Convention included a development assistance package, a system of generalized preferences in trade, the export stabilization (STABEX) mechanism to guarantee ACP export prices regardless of fluctuations in world commodity prices, a host of innovative aid and technical assistance programs, and an EC-ACP institutional framework.[55] Most important, "Lomé was an immediate landmark, for the Nine had stepped into a front rank . . . vis-à-vis the Third World. In essence, the capital, technology, skills, and markets of the Nine—those elements so scarce in the South—were opened up to the ACP."[56] Successive EC-ACP agreements have extended the scope of the original Lomé Convention. The EC and sixty-six ACP countries signed Lomé IV, the most recent convention, in December 1989. Since then, Haiti, the Dominican Republic, and Namibia have adhered to the convention, bringing to sixty-nine the number of ACP states that are party to the agreement.

The Lomé Convention is the Community's showpiece development assistance program. But the Community's dealings with the heterogeneous and economically diverse ACP states have never been easy. Despite the much larger number of countries on the ACP side, the Community's immensely greater wealth and international influence, together with the inherent tension between ex-colonial powers and their ex-colonies, make for a difficult EC-ACP relationship. The Community complains that the ACP countries demand too much, and the ACP countries complain that the Community offers too little. Negotiations for successive Lomé Conventions in the recessionary 1970s and economically uncertain 1980s grew more and more edgy. The successful single market program, the faltering Uruguay Round, and unexpected developments in Eastern Europe further complicated the Lomé IV negotiations. The ACP states feared that the Community's preoccupation with the single market program, obduracy in the Uruguay Round, and increasing involvement in Eastern Europe meant that Brussels had little interest in Third World issues.

Despite arduous negotiations leading up to Lomé IV, the new convention "conveys in its structure a subtle balance of continuity and innovation."[57] Unlike the five-year duration of previous agreements, Lomé IV covers a period of ten years, from 1990 until 2000. Lomé IV retains its predecessors' relatively complex structure and comprehensive provisions but includes greater emphasis on human rights (and especially on women's rights), environmental protection, regional economic integration, and the need for overall, self-reliant, and self-sustained development. Provisions to help ACP countries manage their existing debt and avoid additional debt are another novelty in Lomé IV. Finally, the Community increased its aid to the ACP countries by 23 percent in Lomé IV.[58]

Although a new Lomé Convention will not be negotiated until the end of the decade, the deteriorating economic situation in most Third

World countries is already putting Lomé IV under enormous pressure. ACP states remain concerned about the Community's apparent introversion, not least because of the 1992 Maastricht Treaty ratification crisis. Nor does the economic recession in Western Europe in the early 1990s bode well for the future of EC overseas assistance. For the Community's ACP partners, the remainder of the 1990s looks distinctly bleak.

THE MEDITERRANEAN COUNTRIES

For historical, strategic, and economic reasons, the Community has always had a unique relationship with neighboring Mediterranean countries. To emphasize the importance of that relationship, the heads of government adopted a Global Mediterranean Policy (GMP) at their 1972 Paris summit. Although the Community had already concluded a variety of trade agreements with a number of Mediterranean countries, the GMP promised to deepen and broaden the Community's involvement in the region. Yet the grandiloquent GMP sounded more impressive than it really was. Economic recession later in the 1970s diminished the Community's ambitious plans for the Mediterranean Basin. The accession of Greece, Spain, and Portugal in the 1980s both strengthened the Community's Mediterranean orientation and strained its economic relations with nonmember Mediterranean countries by further restricting access to the Community marketplace for Mediterranean products.

Like the ACP countries, the nonmember Mediterranean countries feared the economic consequences of the single market program and the Community's generous economic assistance for the newly independent countries of Eastern Europe. In addition, the southern and eastern Mediterranean countries worried that the massive transfer of resources to Greece, Spain, and Portugal as part of the single market initiative (and, subsequently, as part of the effort to achieve EMU) would further widen the economic divide between member and nonmember Mediterranean states. The Community's preoccupation with Eastern Europe almost blinded Brussels to developments in the south, where economic and political instability also threatened the Community's security. Anxiety about a possible influx of immigrants from Eastern Europe finally drew the Community's attention to the reality of mass migration from the Mediterranean Basin. Appropriately, the Community turned its attention south as well as east during the Italian presidency in the second half of 1990.

Gianni de Michelis, the flamboyant Italian foreign minister, suggested that the Community launch a Conference on Security and Cooperation in the Mediterranean (CSCM), along the lines of the Conference on Security and Cooperation in Europe (CSCE). As a first step, the foreign ministers of Italy, France, Spain, and Portugal met their counterparts from five North African countries in October 1990. The ministers worked on a declaration of intent, setting out the principles for collaboration across the Mediterranean on political, economic, environmental, and cultural issues. Coming in the midst of the Gulf crisis, the meeting at least afforded an opportunity for the Community's Mediterranean member states to explore with neighboring Mediterranean countries the sources of conflict and insecurity in the region.

The proposed CSCM did not survive Italy's presidency, but it increased the tempo of Community involvement in the Mediterranean Basin. As a result, in 1992 the Community launched a "new Mediterranean policy" involving a "consistent political approach designed to help foster peace among the peoples of the region and their harmonious development."[59] Yet the Community's relations with most Mediterranean countries remained precarious. The situation in the Maghreb (Morocco, Algeria, and Tunisia) was especially sensitive. In October 1987 the Council rejected Morocco's application for Community membership on the self-evident grounds that Morocco was not a European country. Relations between the Community and Morocco deteriorated in early 1992 after the European Parliament voted down 463 million ECU in credit and aid under a cooperation agreement because of Morocco's poor human rights record. Morocco responded by freezing its agreement with the EC and jeopardizing a four-year fishing accord vital to Spain's large fleet. Manuel Marin, EC commissioner for development and fisheries, flew to Rabat to defuse the crisis. His success owed much to an EC foreign ministers' decision to explore a wide-ranging free trade agreement with Morocco, which could also include Algeria and Tunisia and help bind the Maghreb as a whole closer to the Community.[60] The June 1992 Lisbon summit endorsed the idea of a "Euro-Maghreb partnership" that would incorporate free trade, political dialogue, and economic, technical, cultural, and financial cooperation.[61]

Today, continued emigration from North Africa to the Community and increasing instability in Algeria emphasize the need for such action. The Community could absorb North African immigrants economically but not politically or culturally—hence the urgency of devising a coherent, comprehensive policy toward the Community's southern neighbors. Hence also the need for a common immigration policy (including a common policy on asylum for political refugees) based on the requirements of the internal labor market and backed by appropriate housing and social policies.[62]

At the other end of the Mediterranean, the Community's relations with Turkey are similar to its relations with Morocco but are further complicated by Turkey's ambiguous geographical position and its long-standing dispute with Greece. Like Morocco, Turkey is a source of mass emigration to the Community, has a dubious human rights record, and applied for

EC membership in 1987. The Commission's unfavorable opinion, published in December 1989, equivocated on the question of Turkey's European credentials but argued that, for various political and economic reasons, accession negotiations should not begin in the foreseeable future. Instead, the Commission advocated completion by 1995 of an EC-Turkey customs union, as stipulated in the 1963 association agreement.

Turkey based its membership application in part on its 1964 association agreement with the Community, which, like Greece's 1962 association agreement, anticipated eventual accession. The Commission had deliberated unfavorably on Greece's membership application in 1976, only to be overruled on political grounds by the Council of Ministers. Unlike Greece, however, Turkey could count on little sympathy from the Council of Ministers. Although of great strategic importance during the Cold War, even more so in the post–Cold War world, Turkey's huge Muslim population, chronic economic underdevelopment, and precarious attachment to democracy made it a weak candidate for EC entry. Not wanting to confront those issues head-on, other Community countries could hide behind Greece's de facto veto of Turkish membership.

Turkey's strategic value to the Community was especially obvious during the Gulf crisis. The Community responded by offering to help Turkey—as well as Jordan and Egypt—with approximately $2 billion worth of emergency aid. This offer alarmed Greece, but the new Conservative government, not wanting to jeopardize the country's effort to become a model Community member, did not attempt to block the Gulf assistance program. Perhaps to reward Greece, the member states put the contentious question of Turkey's occupation of northern Cyprus prominently on the Community's agenda in 1990. It was no coincidence that Cyprus delivered its long-expected application for Community membership on July 4, barely one week into the sympathetic Italian presidency (Malta followed suit later in July). Turkey denounced the Cypriot application because it purported to represent the entire island, including the part under Turkish rule. Thus, Turkey is in the invidious position of wanting to join the Community itself but seeking to block Cyprus's effort to do so.

Acute political problems aside, the Community's economic relations with Turkey are far from smooth. Negotiations between Brussels and Ankara to establish a customs union are dogged by disputes over copyright, dumping, textile quotas, and tariff and nontariff barriers. In any event, the customs union will exclude most Turkish farm produce and is unlikely to allow free movement of Turkish labor inside the Community. Nor will it extend to Turkey the single market's other benefits. For Turkey, therefore, the proposed customs union is an inadequate arrangement and an unacceptable substitute for full membership.

Political problems also overshadow the Community's economic relations with Israel, which are based on a 1975 free trade agreement that finally became fully operational in 1989. Israel desperately wanted to extend the free trade agreement with the EC, its main trading partner, but until the September 1993 Israel-PLO accord, political obstacles proved insurmountable. The Community is extremely critical of Israel's hard line in the Occupied Territories, and Israel objects to full EC participation in the Middle East peace process. Neighboring countries with which the Community has trade agreements dating from the 1970s—Syria, Egypt, Jordan, and Lebanon—also want closer economic involvement and would object to concessions to Israel. Although economically desirable, dealing with Israel and its neighbors on a pan-Mediterranean basis remains politically impossible pending a comprehensive peace settlement.

Thus, the Community's economic relations with nonmember Mediterranean countries are in considerable disarray. The Community is providing emergency assistance to Albania, Europe's poorest country; Yugoslavia, with which the Community had a cooperation agreement, has disintegrated; rivalry or outright hostility between Israel, Egypt, Lebanon, Syria, and Jordan block closer economic relations with the Community; Brussels ended all dealings with Libya because of that country's support for international terrorism; and the Algerian government's move in 1992 to stem Islamic fundamentalism by suspending elections is an irritant in its relations with the Community and could prevent the Community from concluding a free trade agreement with the Maghreb. The three remaining Mediterranean countries—Turkey, Cyprus, and Malta—are applicant states but are unlikely to join the Community before the end of the century.

NOTES

1. Commission, *Europe: World Partner* (Luxembourg: OOP, 1991), p. 11.

2. Bull. EC 12-1988, Presidency Conclusions, 1.1.10.

3. Jeffrey J. Schott, "The Single Market and the Uruguay Round: Implications for the Structure of World Trade," in U.S. Congress, House Committee on Foreign Affairs, *Europe, and the United States: Competition and Cooperation in the 1990s* (Washington, DC: Government Printing Office, 1992), p. 401.

4. See Jagdish Bhagwati, *Protectionism* (Cambridge, MA: MIT Press, 1989), pp. 40–42.

5. Commission, *World Partner*, p. 19.

6. *Ibid.*, p. 11.

7. Michael Aho and Bruce Stokes, "Managing Economic Interdependence: The European Challenge," in U.S. Congress, House Committee on Foreign Affairs, *Europe and the United States*, p. 350.

8. Quoted in *The Financial Times*, April 30, 1990, p. 22.

9. Bull. EC 3-1985, 2.2.12.

10. Bull. EC 9-1986, 1.4.2.

11. Bull. EC 12-1988, points 2.2.2–5; Finn Laursen, "The EC, GATT, and the Uruguay Round," in Leon Hurwitz and Christian Lequesne, eds., *State of the European Community: Policies, Institutions, and Debates in the Transition Years* (Boulder, CO: Lynne Rienner, 1991), pp. 378–381; Anna Murphy and Peter Ludlow, "The Community's External Relations," in Peter Ludlow, ed., *The Annual Review of European Community Affairs 1990,* (Brussels: CEPS, 1992), pp. 176–179.

12. Bull. EC 6 1989, Presidency Conclusions, point 1.1.13

13. *Ibid.*

14. G7 Summit Communiqué, Houston, July 10, 1990.

15. Bull. EC 12-1990, point 1.4.95.

16. See *The Financial Times,* March 24, 1990, p. 3.

17. For an account of the GATT negotiations in 1991 and 1992, see Finn Laursen, "The EC, the U.S., and the Uruguay Round," in Alan Cafruny and Glenda Rosenthal, *The State of the European Community: The Maastricht Debates and Beyond* (Boulder, CO: Lynne Rienner, 1993), pp. 245–264.

18. Quoted in *Eurecom* 4, no. 6 (June 1992).

19. Bull. EC 12-1991, 1.3.93.

20. Quoted in *Eurecom* 4, no. 6 (June 1992), p. 1.

21. Bull. EC 11-1992, point 1.4.83.

22. See Alec Stone, "Ratifying Maastricht: France Debates European Union," *French Politics and Society* 11, no. 1 (Winter 1993), p. 76.

23. Commission, *1992 Annual Report,* point 967.

24. Gardner Patterson, "The European Community as a Threat to the System," in William Cline, ed., *Trade Policy in the 1980s* (Washington, DC: Institute for International Economics, 1983), p. 242.

25. Commission, *World Partner,* pp. 14–15.

26. See Trevor C. Hartley, "The European Court and the EEA," *International and Comparative Law Quarterly* 41 (October 1992), pp. 84–88.

27. Frances Nicholson and Roger East, *From the Six to the Twelve: The Enlargement of the European Communities* (Harlow, England: Langman, 1987), pp. 136–142, 152–159.

28. See Finn Laursen, "The Community's Policy Toward EFTA: Regime Formation in the European Economic Space," *Journal of Common Market Studies* 28, no. 4 (June 1990), pp. 303–325.

29. See Clive Church, "The Politics of Change: EFTA and the Nordic Countries' Response to the EC in the Early 1990s," *Journal of Common Market Studies* 28, no. 4 (June 1990), pp. 401–30; Philippe Nell, "EFTA in the 1990s: The Search for a New Identity," *Journal of Common Market Studies* 28, no. 4 (June 1990), pp. 341–347; and Laursen, "Policy Toward EFTA," p. 315.

30. Bull. EC 5-1987, point 2.2.12.

31. Bull. EC S/1-1989, p. 17.

32. Laursen, "Policy Toward EFTA," pp. 320–325; and Church, "Politics of Change," pp. 408–410.

33. Rene Schwok, "EC-EFTA Relations," in Hurwitz and Lequesne, *Policies, Institutions,* p. 340, n. 1.

34. T. Wieser and E. Kitzmantell, "Austria and the European Community," *Journal of Common Market Studies* 28, no. 4 (June 1990), pp. 431–449.

35. Quoted in the *International Herald-Tribune,* February 15–16, 1992, p. 1.

36. Bull. EC 5-1992, 2.2.1

37. Commission Report on Enlargement, Bull. EC S/3-1992, p. 13.

38. Lisbon European Council, Conclusions of the Presidency, Bull. EC 6-1992, 1.3-4.

39. Edinburgh European Council, Conclusions of the Presidency, SN456/92, p. 5A.

40. *The Financial Times,* March 24, 1990, p. 3.

41. Bull. EC 7/8-1991, point 1.3.33.

42. The agreement is secret, but *The Financial Times* published details of it on September 23, 1991, p. 4, and September 26, 1991, p. 7.

43. See Dick K. Nanto, "The U.S.-EC-Japan Trade Triangle," in U.S. Congress, House Committee on Foreign Affairs, *Europe and the United States,* p. 361.

44. *The Financial Times,* November 13, 1992, Survey of Japan, p. 5.

45. Bull. EC 6-1989, Presidency Conclusions, point 1.2.24.

46. *The Financial Times,* April 26, 1992, p. 2.

47. *The Financial Times,* July 25, 1992, p. 3

48. Bull. EC 10-1992, point 1.4.33.

49. Bull. EC 12-1992, point 1.4.37.

50. Bull. EC 10-1992, 1.4.34.

51. Bull. EC 5-1992, point 1.2.29.

52. See *The Financial Times,* July 17, 1992, p. 1.

53. "Survey of Argentina," in *The Financial Times,* May 14, 1992, p. 3.

54. Council Press Release 10793/92, December 14–17, 1992, pp. 4–5.

55. See Frans A.M. Alting von Geusau, ed., *The Lomé Convention and the New International Economic Order* (Leyden: A. W. Sijthoff, 1977).

56. Pierre-Henri Laurent, "Decade of Divergence and Development," *The Annals of the American Academy of Political and Social Science* 440 (November 1978), p. 17.

57. Catherine Flaesch-Mougin and Jean Raux, "From Lomé III to Lomé IV: EC-ACP Relations," in Hurwitz and Lequesne, *State of the European Community,* p. 344.

58. See *The Courier* 120 (March–April), 1990.

59. Commission, *1992 General Report,* point 829.

60. Bull. EC 3-1992, point 1.2.202.

61. Bull. EC 6-1992, Presidency Conclusions, point 1.34.

62. See Edward Mortimer, "European Security After the Cold War," Adelphi Paper, September 1992.

17

The European Community in the Post–Cold War World

The Community conducted its external economic relations in the late 1980s and early 1990s in the context of the single market program and the Uruguay Round negotiations. In many cases political problems compounded difficult economic circumstances and contributed to tense bilateral and multilateral relations. Partly because of the close connection between external economic and political affairs, for more than twenty years member states have attempted to coordinate their foreign policies in European political cooperation and give the Community a foreign policy profile commensurate with its obvious economic importance. Although willing to collaborate within EPC and the Common Foreign and Security Policy, member states jealously guard their foreign policy making prerogatives, especially in the domain of "hard" security and defense. As a result, the Community has a convincing commercial policy, a tentative foreign and security policy, and only a putative defense policy.

The end of the Cold War posed enormous internal and external challenges for the Community. The most extreme concern, as Jacques Delors told the European Parliament in January 1990, was that "the Community, as a product of the Cold War, should die with the Cold War."[1] A more reasonable, although greatly exaggerated, fear was that Germany's preoccupation with unification and the Community's preoccupation with Germany would derail the single market program and the most recent initiative for EMU. The situation in Eastern Europe posed an immediate danger for the Community but also presented a unique opportunity. The danger was that widespread disorder in the disintegrating Soviet bloc, leading inevitably to massive migration, would sorely test Community solidarity;

the opportunity was to help neighboring countries develop economically and democratically and to foster a genuinely all-European integration. Eastern European countries looked to the Community for technical assistance, financial support, and export opportunities. The Community looked to the Eastern European countries for a chance to expiate the guilt of the previous forty years, when Western Europe prospered under U.S. protection while Eastern Europe withered under Soviet control.

Although a singular case, the war in Yugoslavia revealed the risk of massive instability in the East. A relatively small influx of Yugoslav refugees strained relations between member states, the recognition of new states sorely tested EPC, and a neighboring Community country (Greece) almost became embroiled in the conflict. Given the legal impossibility of Community-sponsored military action and the historical and political complications inherent in any Balkan crisis, the Community mustered an impressive set of responses—an "arms and military equipment embargo; suspension of financial protocols; suspension of trade and cooperation agreement and of various trade and aid benefits to Yugoslavia; trade concessions for Bosnia-Herzegovina, Croatia, Macedonia and Slovenia; convening of peace conference; facilitation of cease fires; dispatch of cease-fire monitors; diplomatic missions; and creation of both guidelines for recognition of new states and an arbitration commission for their implementation."[2] But given also the horror of the Yugoslav war, including well-publicized instances of "ethnic cleansing," murder, and rape, anything short of military intervention by the Community or its member states appeared hopelessly inadequate.

At least the Community's involvement in Eastern Europe and the Balkans demonstrated a commitment to greater international activism, particularly noteworthy as it came at a time of dynamic internal development and concern abroad about incipient isolationism. At the same time, the end of the Cold War put trans-Atlantic relations under additional strain. Washington encouraged Brussels to lead the international aid effort for Eastern Europe and to take the initiative in trying to resolve the Yugoslav war. Yet Washington clearly resented the Community's growing international profile and reveled in the Community's apparent inadequacy as an international political actor. A strong U.S. reaction against proposals in the intergovernmental conference on political union to merge the EC and the WEU, thereby possibly weakening NATO, demonstrated Washington's determination to maintain hegemony in Europe.

Thus, post–Cold War systemic change severely tested the Community's external political image and actions. The negotiations on political union manifested a commitment to greater international involvement, although the CFSP established limits beyond which member states would or could not collectively go. At the same time, assisting Eastern European reform, mediating the Yugoslav wars, and managing an increasingly difficult relationship with the United States challenged Community solidarity. Ultimately, however, these factors may have strengthened the Community's determination to become a more formidable international political actor.

FROM EPC TO CFSP

The dynamic of European integration, combined with increasing international complexity and interdependence, accounts for member states' efforts since the early 1970s to coordinate their foreign policies closely, first in the EPC procedure and subsequently in the more far-reaching CFSP. Member states launched EPC in response to the 1969 Hague summit's call for deepening at a time of widening, lest a larger Community become weaker. The heads of government also wanted to give the Community an international political profile equal to its growing economic importance. The metaphor most frequently used by academics and officials to describe the endeavor, then and since, is for "Europe to speak with one voice."[3]

Given the centrality of external affairs to state security and national sovereignty, governments are instinctively reluctant to cooperate in the foreign policy sphere. For that reason, it is hardly surprising that "Europe's" voice is often muted or that discordant notes are sometimes struck. The remarkable aspect of EPC is surely the extent to which member states automatically consult each other on most foreign policy issues and attempt to coordinate their international positions. But the gradual development of EPC and its slow transmogrification into CFSP means that the Community has an uneven capacity to influence external developments and lacks a global role commensurate with its economic weight. Although willing to collaborate within EPC and the CFSP, member states continue to retain certain foreign policy–related prerogatives, notably in the domain of "hard" security and defense.

The launch of *Ostpolitik* in the late 1960s provided a strong impetus to the development of EPC. So did the 1973 Middle East War, which strengthened the procedure further by giving member states a forum in which to exchange information and attempt to coordinate positions without directly affecting their vested national interests. The Nine's November 6, 1973, declaration on the Middle East was a milestone in member state foreign policy coordination and struck a decidedly pro-Arab tone. The Middle East continued to stimulate member state cooperation, especially through the "Euro-Arab dialogue." The so-called Venice Declaration of June 1980, in which the Nine recognized the special position of Palestine in the Arab-Israeli conflict, showed how closely member states coordinated on Middle East issues and how radical their joint position was.[4]

The Conference on Security and Cooperation in Europe (CSCE), which began in the early 1970s and culminated in the August 1975 Helsinki Final Act, helped enormously to forge a common Community identity and to promote EPC. The Community indicated at an early stage of the CSCE process that it would act as a group and be bound by CSCE commitments. The Community fared best as a group in negotiations on "Basket Two" (economic cooperation) and "Basket Three" (human rights) of the CSCE's activities. There was never an EC delegation in the CSCE, and the Community itself could not make proposals, but Commission officials, attached to the delegation of the country holding the Community presidency, participated fully in the negotiations. The presidency also adopts CSCE acts and declarations on behalf of the Community.[5]

The procedure for foreign policy coordination was initially based on the Luxembourg Report of 1970 and the Copenhagen Report of 1973. The reports identified four levels for conducting political cooperation:

- European summits
- Foreign ministers meetings "in EPC" (as distinct from in the Council of Ministers)
- Meetings of the Political (Davignon) Committee (foreign ministries' political directors)
- Meetings of working groups and the group of European correspondents (mid-level and junior officials)

Working groups address geographical and functional issues; the group of correspondents maintains close liaison between foreign ministries and prepares meetings of the Political Committee. A secure communications system (Coreu), for the exclusive conduct of EPC business, links the foreign ministries.

The Council presidency chairs meetings in EPC at all levels. There is no voting in EPC; instead, lengthy negotiations in a search for consensus create "informal pressures to agree."[6] According to a longtime participant, consensus is "one of EPC's fundamental rules . . . no one can be outvoted, but no one likes to be isolated. There is a strong tendency to follow the balanced opinion of the majority."[7] Unofficial and subtle linkages between EPC and other policy areas reinforce the "tendency" to follow along with the majority, although for most of the 1980s the Socialist Greek government had scant regard for EPC consensus building.

In the early 1980s, when the Community's external relations were every bit as problematical as its internal development, EPC's procedural limits became glaringly obvious. The onset of the "second Cold War"— the sudden heightening of East-West tension in the late 1970s after a decade of relatively benign relations—tested the Community's ability to act internationally. EPC proved an inadequate instrument, especially in response to sudden crises such as the Soviet invasion of Afghanistan in December 1979. Two years later, when General Jaruzelski imposed martial law in Poland, the member states met more promptly in EPC to try to coordinate their response. But it was not until March 1982 that the Community imposed limited sanctions against the Soviet Union.

A worsening East-West climate and member states' slow response to international crises led to a number of initiatives in the early 1980s to improve EPC and to broaden its agenda to encompass security and even defense issues. The 1981 London Report introduced minor procedural reforms but limited EPC discussions to "the political aspects of security." Hans-Dietrich Genscher, Germany's foreign minister, and Emilio Colombo, Italy's foreign minister, launched a joint initiative in November 1981 to strengthen the Community's institutional structure and to extend Community competence in external relations. Officially called the "Draft European Act," the Genscher-Colombo proposals sought to end the increasingly artificial distinction between EPC and EC external economic policy and to make it possible for the Ten "to act in concert in world affairs so that Europe will increasingly be able to assume the international role incumbent upon it."[8]

Community foreign ministers, who considered the proposals at the behest of the European Council, failed to find a way forward and could not concur on the relatively mild foreign and security policy proposals contained in the Draft European Act. Some member states were wary of developing a Community-based security structure that could have upset Washington; others (such as Ireland, Denmark, and Greece) faced domestic political constraints. Consequently, the foreign ministers' report to the June 1983 Stuttgart summit was a classic Community compromise. It resulted only in the "Solemn Declaration on European Union," a vague proclamation of the Community's international identity.[9]

The 1985 IGC gave member states a better opportunity to explore EPC reform and the possible development of a Community security dimension. The Political Committee considered foreign and security policy in a separate IGC working party. EPC's evolution since the early 1970s, a British and a joint Franco-German proposal submitted just before the Milan summit, and later proposals from Italy and the Netherlands formed the basis of its discussions. All member states agreed on the need to make the Community's external economic policy and the member states' foreign policies more consistent with each other. Other ideas included formalizing EPC in the Treaty of Rome, strengthening cooperation procedures, providing an EPC secretariat, and incorporating military and defense issues. Neutral Ireland shied away from going too far down the defense road, as did pacifist (though NATO member) Denmark and idiosyncratic (though also NATO member) Greece.

Title III of the SEA dealt exclusively with EPC. Procedural improvements included ending the distinction between foreign ministers' meetings "in EPC" and in the Council; associating the Commission fully with EPC; ensuring that the European Parliament was "closely associated with EPC"; creating a mechanism for convening the Political Committee or Community foreign ministers within forty-eight hours at the request of at least three member states; and establishing an EPC secretariat in Brussels. The SEA also stipulated that "the external policies of the European Community and the policies agreed in Political Cooperation must be consistent" and charged the presidency and the Commission with ensuring such consistency. However, Title III was not subject to judicial review.

Revolution in Eastern Europe and the Cold War's abrupt end brought security concerns to the top of the Community's agenda. The Community's sudden involvement in the Eastern European aid effort also emphasized the persistent divergence between EPC and external economic policy.[10] There was near-unanimity in the Community on the need to reform EPC; member states convened the IGC on political union largely for that reason. By developing a CFSP, member states and the Commission hoped to enhance European security at a potentially destabilizing time, boost the Community's international standing, and bind external economic and political policymaking more closely together.

The contemporaneous outbreak of the Gulf crisis in August 1990 focused additional attention on the importance of transforming EPC into a CFSP. Given the constraints of EPC, the Community reacted promptly and forcefully to news of the Iraqi invasion: Within two days it embargoed oil from Iraq and occupied Kuwait.[11] Yet the Community soon came in for criticism, especially in the United States, for its inability to do more. To some extent the Community was a victim of its own success. Prevailing Europhoria and pervasive discussion of a possible CFSP had raised false expectations about the Community's ability to take concerted international action, especially involving the use of force. In a speech to the European Parliament on September 12, 1990, Jacques Delors, who bore more responsibility than anybody else for raising such expectations, deplored the Community's inability to do more in the Gulf crisis.[12] As French Foreign Minister Roland Dumas remarked in January 1991, the outbreak of the Gulf War had clearly shown "that Europe does not have a common foreign policy."[13]

But the inadequacy of the Community's overall performance in the crisis revealed more than merely the limits of EPC. A marked divergence of opinion between member states on the advisability of using force against Iraq demonstrated the difficulty of their ever developing a common security policy in the Community.[14] Partly to emphasize Britain's sovereignty in national defense, Prime Minister Thatcher, coincidentally in Colorado with President Bush when the crisis erupted, immediately promised to join the U.S. military effort against Iraq. President Mitterrand repudiated France's previous policy of appeasing Iraq and enrolled in the international coalition but tried at the last moment to resolve the crisis with a unilateral diplomatic demarche. Chancellor Kohl was in the invidious position of wanting to participate in the coalition against Iraq but at the same time *not* wanting to raise European alarm about a new German forcefulness in international affairs. Kohl squared the circle by citing the German constitutional ban on sending troops outside the NATO area, offering instead to contribute financially to the war effort. Other Community leaders faced differing degrees of domestic uncertainty about the crisis. Their reactions varied from Spanish Prime Minister Felipe González's strong support for military action to Irish Prime Minister Charles Haughey's weak argument about the limits of "neutrality."[15]

To the extent that they wanted to cooperate militarily during the Gulf crisis, the Western European Union (WEU) provided a ready-made means for Community countries to do so. Nine Community countries—Britain, France, Germany, Belgium, the Netherlands, Luxembourg, Italy, Spain, and Portugal—made up the WEU, which, unlike NATO, could operate outside Europe. The WEU also had immense potential for long-term Community defense cooperation, not least because the United States was not a member. In 1984, during the height of the "second Cold War," the WEU's member states had revived the moribund organization in order to assert their security and defense identity. Three years later the WEU Platform on European Security emphasized the organization's commitment to European integration, especially in the context of the SEA.[16] With the Community striving for a CFSP as an element of political union and some member states simultaneously eager to cooperate militarily in the Gulf, the WEU inevitably returned to the fore.

France, then in the WEU presidency, invited all Community countries to attend a WEU meeting on August 21 to discuss possible military action in the Gulf. The meeting was held on the same day and in the same place as a meeting of Community foreign ministers to discuss political aspects of the crisis. But in an aide-mémoire on September 18, the Italian presidency of the Community went far beyond the short-term expediency of using the WEU in the Gulf crisis by suggesting a merger between the Community and the WEU.[17] Then, as later, Italy's proposal proved too radical for most Community countries. At the October 1990 Rome summit, the heads of government "noted a consensus to go beyond the present limits in regard to security" but could not agree on the putative CFSP's scope, content, and procedure, or the WEU's role in it. They were careful to state, however, that the CFSP would "be defined . . . without prejudice to the obligations arising out of the security arrangements to which Member States are party"—that is, without undermining NATO.[18]

As expected, the CFSP negotiations proved especially arduous during the IGC. The outbreak of war in Yugoslavia in June 1991 highlighted the difficulty of reconciling member states' notoriously discordant positions on security policy and defense. Three months previously, Delors had launched a carefully planned initiative to achieve a common defense policy for the Community.[19] Whereas most member states supported a Community defense identity, however, few supported a full-fledged defense policy. Neutral Ireland and pacifist Denmark especially bristled at the "D-word."

At least there was near-unanimity about using the WEU to develop a Community defense identity. But the precise relationship between the Community, the WEU, and NATO was difficult to decide. "Atlanticist" countries such as Britain, the Netherlands, and Portugal, staunch NATO supporters, traditionally shied away from Community initiatives that could weaken, or appear to weaken, the Atlantic Alliance. The end of the Cold War, doubts about NATO's future, and the United States' extreme sensitivity about its future role in Western Europe complicated the issue and increased the Atlanticists' determination to maintain a close link between the WEU and NATO. "Europeanist" countries—notably France—argued the contrary case, making the old point that a stronger European pillar would bolster the Alliance and the new point that, with the end of the Cold War, Europe needed to develop its own defense organization because the United States would quickly reduce its military involvement on the Continent. Germany sided instinctively with the Europeanists but, at least as long as Soviet troops remained in the eastern part of the country, opted pragmatically for the Atlanticists.

The compromise agreed to at Maastricht tilted more toward the Europeanists than the Atlanticists. The treaty allowed for "the eventual framing of a common defense policy, which might in time lead to a common defense." Although hedged with qualifications about a future defense policy, the unequivocal use of the "D-word" represented a new departure for the Community. The treaty also recognized the WEU as "an integral part of the development of the European Union," which may ask the WEU "to elaborate and implement [the Union's] decisions and actions . . . which have defense implications." A declaration on the WEU attached to the treaty explained the member states' intention to "build up WEU in stages as the defense component of the Union."

Inevitably, the declaration spelled out the WEU's relationship to NATO, citing the WEU's future development "as a means to strengthen the European pillar of the Atlantic Alliance." The treaty's language and the WEU declaration allowed both sides in the defense debate to claim victory. Yet a treaty commitment to review defense arrangements in 1996, along with the expiration of the WEU's own charter in 1998, suggest that the Community's defense identity will increasingly assume a Europeanist rather than an Atlanticist appearance.

As part of the defense agreement, WEU leaders decided on the second day of the Maastricht summit to grant Greece full membership.

Ireland's and Denmark's continuing nonmembership is institutionally awkward but politically convenient. Nevertheless, a number of unanswered questions remain, not least concerning the relationship between the WEU and the neutral states now negotiating Community membership and the relationship between the WEU and the Central and Eastern European countries (CEECs). Doubtless such issues will be high on the agenda of the Community's planned IGC in 1996.

Title V of the Maastricht Treaty, which contains the CFSP provisions, provides that on the basis of a unanimous decision the Council may refer to the WEU decisions and actions by the European Union that have defense implications. Title V also describes the objectives of the CFSP, strengthens the procedures for "systematic cooperation" between member states on international issues, and develops the concept of "joint action" by the European Union on foreign policy and security issues. By providing for unanimity on decisions of principle and majority voting on implementation, the treaty strikes a clumsy compromise on CFSP decisionmaking. The practical implications of the decisionmaking dispute became apparent during the IGC itself, with Germany arguing that the EC would never have recognized Croatia and Slovenia if unanimity was the rule and Britain claiming that unanimity was necessary to prevent Germany from forcing the Community's hand in the future.

It is difficult to say how the CFSP will operate in practice. A foreign ministers' report to the June 1992 Lisbon summit on the CFSP's likely development outlined only the purpose of joint action toward certain countries or groups of countries and "domains within the security dimension" subject to joint action. These include the CSCE process; disarmament and arms control in Europe, including confidence-building measures; nuclear nonproliferation issues; and economic aspects of security, in particular control of the transfer of military technology to third countries and control of arms exports. Despite the foreign ministers' report and ongoing work in Brussels to implement the CFSP successfully, it is hard to refute Reinhardt Rummel's conclusion that "too much attention has been attributed to the techniques of decision-making and to the implementation of policies. Problems seem to have been multiplied in this regard rather than reduced, while the attitudes of the policymakers have remained unchanged: The dominant foreign policy reflex in Western Europe is national, not communitarian, as conflict management in the Yugoslav civil war has amply demonstrated."[20]

EASTERN EUROPE AND THE FORMER SOVIET UNION

Called "Europe Agreements" to distinguish them from the Community's other association agreements, the December 1991 accords with Czechoslovakia,

Hungary, and Poland are the most advanced form of institutionalized relations between the Community and former Soviet bloc countries. The Europe Agreements seek to strengthen political and economic reform in "the Visegrad Three" countries (now the Visegrad Four, with Czechoslovakia having split into two sovereign states) and pave the way for eventual Community membership.[21] The Europe Agreements were "second-generation" agreements, intended to broaden the scope of bilateral Trade and Cooperation Agreements concluded in 1988 and 1989. Before negotiating those "first-generation" agreements, the Community had little formal contact with the countries of Eastern Europe. For ideological reasons the Soviet Union refused to recognize the Community and prevented its Eastern European satellites from negotiating badly needed trade accords with Brussels. Economic necessity finally forced Moscow to acknowledge the Community's existence in the late 1970s and to seek a bilateral agreement between the Community and the Soviet-dominated Council for Mutual Economic Assistance (CMEA). The Community regarded the CMEA as an unworthy interlocutor, declining to deal with it unless Brussels could also negotiate bilateral agreements with the Eastern European countries themselves.[22]

Relations between the Community and its Eastern European neighbors improved dramatically in 1984 when Mikhail Gorbachev came to power in the USSR. Gorbachev's obsession with economic reform throughout the Soviet bloc inevitably led him to make early overtures toward Brussels. By 1986 Willy de Clercq, the external affairs commissioner, was exploring the possibility of an EC-CMEA declaration and, under its auspices, bilateral trade agreements with individual Eastern European countries. Two years later, on June 25, 1988, Community and CMEA officials signed a joint declaration in Luxembourg, opening the way for a rapid conclusion of the more desirable and practical bilateral country accords.[23]

Gorbachev's ascendancy and the quickening pace of reform in Eastern Europe forced the Community to confront its glaring lack of an *Ostpolitik*. For nearly three decades the Community had prospered in a divided Europe, appropriating the name of the entire continent. Early intimations of change in the East prompted the Dooge Committee to preface its 1985 report on institutional reform with the lofty claim that "the Community has not lost sight of the fact that it represents only a part of Europe. Resolved to advance together, the member states remain aware of the civilization which they share with the other countries of the continent, in the firm belief that any progress in building the Community is in keeping with the interests of Europe as a whole."[24]

Yet the Community *had* lost sight of the fact that it represented only a part of Europe. For the Community's founding fathers, European integration was synonymous with *Western* European integration, centered on the Rhine. The Cold War not only provided a powerful impetus toward deeper European integration but also cut Eastern Europe irrevocably off from the West. Thereafter, the Community's easternmost border was firmly fixed on the Elbe. Thus, the emergence of the Eastern European reform movement in the mid-1980s, leading rapidly to the end of the Cold War, challenged the Community's assumptions about the meaning and definition of "Europe" and the potential scope of "European" integration.

Given the rapid pace of change in Eastern Europe in the late 1980s and the consequent shock of the Cold War's end, it is remarkable that the Community reacted so quickly and so well. The heads of government first discussed a concerted Community response at the December 1988 Rhodes summit.[25] Seven months later, at the G7 summit in Paris, the Commission agreed to assume responsibility for coordinating Western aid to Poland and Hungary, the politically most advanced countries in the region.[26] In December 1989 the Council of Ministers launched the Pologne-Hongrie: Actions pour la Reconversion Economique (PHARE) program "to support the process of reform in Poland and Hungary, in particular by financing or participating in the financing of projects aimed at economic restructuring . . . in particular in the areas of agriculture, industry, investment, energy, training, environmental protection, trade and services."[27] Although a specific Community initiative, PHARE soon became synonymous with assistance to Eastern Europe from the "G24" countries: the EC 12, the EFTA countries, the United States, Canada, Turkey, Australia, New Zealand, and Japan.

In July 1990 the Community decided to extend the PHARE program to Bulgaria, Czechoslovakia, East Germany, and Yugoslavia. Because of the brutal suppression of student demonstrations in Bucharest the previous month, Romania was not included. East Germany dropped out in October 1990, when it united with West Germany and thereby joined the Community, but in October 1991 the Community included the Baltic states in PHARE. In 1990 Brussels allocated 500 million ECU for PHARE; this amount increased to 785 million ECU in 1991 and 1 billion ECU in 1992.[28]

While developing the PHARE program, the Community concluded Trade and Cooperation Agreements with virtually all of the Eastern European countries.[29] Other Community assistance included emergency food aid and balance of payments loans. In addition, the Community played a prominent part in the French-sponsored European Bank for Reconstruction and Development (EBRD), which Mitterrand proposed at the extraordinary European Council in Paris in November 1989. The other G24 countries soon endorsed the idea of using public money from the West to help develop the private sector in the East. Representatives of numerous governments and public institutions from East and West approved the EBRD's statute at a ceremony in Paris in May 1990. Of the bank's 10 billion

ECU capital, the EC 12, the Commission, and the European Investment Bank contributed 51 percent; the United States, 10 percent; Japan, 8.5 percent; and the USSR, 6 percent. After a political wrangle about the bank's location and president, the EBRD began operating in London in April 1991 with the ill-fated Jacques Attali, a close friend and adviser of Mitterrand, at its head.[30]

Coping with the Eastern European challenge and coordinating the concerted G24 aid effort had a profound institutional, operational, and procedural impact on the Community. The Commission had to open delegations (embassies) in Eastern Europe, establish a PHARE operational service in Brussels, and reorganize internally. DG I (external relations) took the lead in dealing with Eastern Europe, but few of the other twenty-two directorates-general were unaffected. In particular, the Commission drew heavily on DG II (economic and financial affairs) and DG VIII (development assistance). Chairing G24 meetings at the official level imposed a huge administrative burden on the Commission.

The European Parliament experienced a similar upheaval. Eastern European parliamentarians made visits to Strasbourg, and MEPs journeyed to Eastern Europe; moreover, the European Parliament had the budgetary authority to allocate funds for PHARE and other Community assistance. Parliament's ability to block association agreements increased its political leverage when the Community began to negotiate such arrangements with Czechoslovakia, Hungary, and Poland. A reorganization of the European Parliament's staff and services reflected its enhanced involvement in international affairs as a result of the Community's emerging *Ostpolitik*. Parliament also produced a number of reports on developments in the Community's relations with the CEECs.[31]

By coordinating the G24 aid effort, the Commission raised its international profile considerably. The Commission's leadership of the G24 also intensified cooperation between Brussels and the member states and helped to close the conspicuous gap between EPC and the Community's external economic relations, for which the SEA provided.[32] Following the December 1989 Rhodes summit, the Belgian government pressed for more consistency between Community and member state policies toward Eastern Europe. A paper on Eastern Europe, prepared collectively by the Spanish presidency, the Commission, and the EPC secretariat for the June 1989 Madrid summit, set an important precedent in joint EC-EPC policymaking.[33] Thereafter, "the Community and its member states" became standard usage in EPC documentation.

Impressive though it was, the Community's response to developments in Eastern Europe had been improvised and understandably ad hoc. The rapid pace of events made it difficult for the EC, already coping with the impact of German unification, to devise a coherent strategy. The Community wanted to promote stability, democracy, and economic reform in the newly independent countries of the former Soviet bloc but was unable to respond positively to those countries' calls for membership. The Community was in a dilemma, a prisoner of its Cold War rhetoric. For thirty years it had bemoaned the division of Europe and advocated pan-European integration. It was hardly surprising that, with the sudden end of the Cold War, Eastern European countries used the Community's own rhetoric to advocate EC entry. Nor was it surprising that they cited the examples of Spain, Portugal, and Greece—which, like the countries of Eastern Europe, had sought Community membership to help consolidate democracy, improve their economies, and realize their "European" vocation. When Vaclav Havel, president of Czechoslovakia, called in a speech to the Polish Parliament in June 1990 for the two countries to "return to Europe," clearly he meant accession to the European Community.[34]

The model as well as the rhetoric of postwar integration strengthened the Eastern European countries' case for EC membership. Commenting on the fate of the former Soviet bloc, Jiri Dienstbier, foreign minister of Czechoslovakia, remarked in January 1992 that "we will be secure only if the relations among all European countries are, let's say, like the relations between Belgium and the Netherlands."[35] The strength and persistence of Eastern European aspirations for accession were strikingly apparent at a meeting in Prague in June 1991 to discuss Mitterrand's proposal for a "European Confederation." In his opening remarks, Havel stressed that "the Confederation should view [the EC] as its driving force and the model of its future . . . the nascent Confederation should . . . make way for [the democracies of Central and Eastern Europe] to join the EC, prepare them and be a mediator."[36]

Community leaders had no choice but to endorse their Eastern European counterparts' appeals for accession while arguing the impossibility of immediate enlargement. In his first speech to the UN General Assembly as foreign minister of united Germany, Hans-Dietrich Genscher proclaimed that "we want all democratic states to be able to accede to the Community."[37] But, like almost every other Community leader who expressed similar sentiments, Genscher realized that the Community could not expand eastward in the foreseeable future. The economic disparity between Western and Eastern European countries was too great to make enlargement feasible, and "an unspoken but nonetheless real fear of exodus from Eastern Europe caused by rising unemployment and higher prices is one obstacle to the early entry of Western-oriented countries like Czechoslovakia, Hungary, and Poland into the EC club."[38] Only Thatcher, hoping for a "weaker" Community, ignored the practical barriers to Eastern European accession.

By offering to negotiate association agreements with the Eastern European countries that fulfilled certain "fundamental conditions concerning democracy and a market economy,"[39] the Community hoped to stave off formal membership application. In August 1990, the Commission suggested that the Community conclude Europe Agreements with Czechoslovakia, Hungary, and Poland.[40] The agreements would have similar structures but different contents according to the needs of the individual countries.

Negotiations between the Commission and the three prospective associates took a full year to complete and pitted the member states' protectionist proclivities against their political rhetoric. When it came to granting the Eastern European countries liberal market access, a number of member states succumbed to domestic protectionist pressure—especially for steel, agriculture, and textiles—and blocked generous terms. "You cannot shed tears of joy for the people of Eastern Europe one day and the next tell them that you will not buy their products," an angry Jacques Delors remarked after a huge demonstration by French farmers protesting plans for greater Community access for Eastern European produce.[41] France eventually lifted its objections to meat imports from the three Eastern European countries after winning a Community commitment to try first to sell Eastern European meat on the Soviet market.[42]

Only when Hungary and Poland embarrassed the Community by threatening to walk out of the talks and Vaclav Havel warned that "right-wing authoritarian and nationalist forces" would exploit a failure to reach agreement[43] did the recalcitrant member states—notably France, Spain, and Portugal—come to their senses. Although denounced as "miserly and protectionist,"[44] the ensuing accords went far beyond the existing Trade and Cooperation Agreements by providing for a political dialogue and aiming for eventual free trade in a number of goods and products. The Europe Agreements also provided for the gradual adoption by Czechoslovakia, Hungary, and Poland of Community legislation, notably on the single market and competition policy. Most important for the new associates, the agreements recognized that the three countries' "final objective" was to join the Community and included arrangements to help "achieve this objective."[45] The Community signed an association agreement with Romania in December 1992 and with Bulgaria in February 1993.[46]

The Europe Agreement negotiations coincided with the IGCs and formally ended only six days after the Maastricht Treaty. The "Visegrad Three" were relieved that the IGCs did not raise insurmountable obstacles for prospective Eastern European applicants. If anything, the Maastricht Treaty's commitment to eventual EMU and deeper political integration sharpened the Europe Agreement countries' determination to join. Czechoslovakia, Hungary, and Poland were satisfied that they met the criteria for membership outlined in the Commission's June 1992 report on enlargement: geographical location (although the Commission conceded that it was impossible to define precisely Europe's eastern boundary); a democratic political system; a commitment to human rights; a functioning and competitive free market economy and an adequate legal and institutional framework; acceptance of the Community's *acquis;* and a willingness to participate in the CFSP and, possibly, a common defense policy.[47]

Nor are the three most politically and economically advanced Eastern European countries unduly concerned about the loss of sovereignty inherent in Community membership. Speaking just before the Maastricht summit opened, a Polish official remarked that his people were "now beginning to enjoy our freedom and independence" yet simultaneously attempting to join the Community.[48] Although unenthusiastic about surrendering any hard-won freedom, at least the official did not compare the Community to the old Soviet empire, as Thatcher and other Europhobes were then in the habit of doing.

In light of the Maastricht Treaty, Czechoslovakia, Hungary, and Poland saw the Europe Agreements as an important step on the road to full Community membership. Although acknowledging their present economic unpreparedness, they hoped to be ready to join the Community sooner rather than later. At a Community foreign ministers meeting in Luxembourg on October 5, 1992, the Czech, Hungarian, and Polish representatives proposed that accession negotiations begin in 1996 and end by 1999. Community foreign ministers were noncommittal, as were Major and Delors at a meeting with the Czech, Hungarian, and Polish prime ministers in London on October 28, 1992.[49]

Nevertheless, criticism within and outside the Community of the Europe Agreements' limited concessions—both political and economic—prompted the heads of government at the June 1992 Lisbon summit to ask the Commission to suggest ways of developing closer relations with the CEECs. The Commission's report, presented at the December 1992 Edinburgh summit, outlined a strategy for realizing the Europe Agreements' full potential and preparing the CEECs for "fuller participation in the process of European integration." Going beyond the Europe Agreements, the Commission called for a "European Political Area" and a Europe-wide free trade area. In order to boost confidence and stability in the CEECs, the Commission also advocated sending "a positive signal" to them "concerning the goal of eventual membership . . . under the right conditions." More unusually, the Commission recommended that the European Council establish "an Action Committee for Central and Eastern Europe inspired by the Monnet Committee and composed of eminent personalities from different parts of Europe."[50]

The Edinburgh summit welcomed the Commission's report but postponed decisions on its recommendations until the June 1993 Copenhagen summit.[51] At Copenhagen, the heads of government declared unequivocally "that the associated countries in Central and Eastern Europe which so desire shall become members of the European Union" and spelled out the candidates' membership requirement:

- Stability of institutions guaranteeing democracy, the rule of law, human rights, and respect for and protection of minorities
- Existence of a functioning market economy, as well as the capacity to cope with competitive pressure and market forces within the Union
- Ability to take on the obligations of membership, including adherence to the aims of political, economic, and monetary union

Further, the EC stipulated that "the Union's capacity to absorb new members, while maintaining the momentum of European integration, is . . . an important consideration in the general interest of both the Union and the candidate countries."[52]

Privately, most Community and member state officials concede that accession negotiations could begin before the end of the decade with the Czech Republic (the most economically advanced of Czechoslovakia's two successor states), Hungary, and Poland. Slovakia (Czechoslovakia's other successor state) is likely to join the remaining CEECs and be effectively condemned to perpetual associate status. The heads of government agreed at Copenhagen to accelerate the Community's efforts to open its markets and approved the trade concessions for the CEECs proposed in advance of the summit by the Council.

Inevitably, enlargement negotiations with the three Eastern European countries will be extremely difficult, with the Community's agricultural lobby and poorer member states perhaps blocking a successful conclusion. A Commission decision in November 1992 to impose antidumping duties on seamless steel tube imports from Croatia and three Eastern European countries, including Czechoslovakia, demonstrated the strength of protectionism in the Community. In addition, the accession of three new countries, enlarging the Community possibly to twenty member states by the end of the century, will have profound institutional repercussions, despite likely constitutional revisions as a result of the 1996 IGC.

There is no question of imminent Community membership for any of the former Soviet republics. The disintegration of the Soviet Union in December 1991—coincidentally, during the second day of the Maastricht summit—presented the Community with yet another challenge in the East. Two years earlier, the Community had concluded a Trade and Cooperation Agreement with the USSR, a "modest and prudent first step" in developing an economic and political relationship.[53] Apart from trying to encourage trade between the Community and the Soviet Union, Brussels sought to reassure Moscow that the Soviet Union would not be excluded from Gorbachev's metaphorical "common European house." In the following year, with German unification a reality and the Soviet Union descending into disorder, it was more important than ever for the Community to involve the USSR in a new European architecture. As a grudging host to several hundred thousand Soviet troops, Germany especially urged the Community to pursue a positive, constructive policy in the East. At the December 1990 Rome summit, Community leaders approved emergency food aid and an ambitious technical assistance program for the Soviet Union.[54]

Events in 1991 severely strained the Community's newly established relations with Moscow. Brussels protested against repression in the Baltic states in January 1991 and fretted about the apparent ascendancy of conservative Communists in the Kremlin. Yet the Commission opened an office in Moscow, just in time to observe at close quarters the failed military coup in August, Boris Yeltsin's triumph over Gorbachev, and the rapid dissolution of the USSR. With great regret, the Community watched Gorbachev go. On the day of his departure, the Community paid genuine tribute to Gorbachev's "great vision of a new Europe and a safer world," a vision that had helped to "end the partition of Europe and to bring down the German wall."[55]

The Community responded to the sensational circumstances of late 1991 and early 1992 by sending emergency food aid to Moscow and St. Petersburg and by immediately exploring options for longer-term economic assistance. The issue of diplomatic recognition of the Soviet successor states posed an immediate political problem for the Community. German pressure to recognize Croatia and Slovenia also obliged the Community to come up with acceptable criteria. Hence, after a contentious meeting on December 16, 1991, the foreign ministers of the Twelve adopted the "Guidelines on the Recognition of New States in Eastern Europe and the Soviet Union."[56] Demonstrating a desire for a pan-European approach to the emergence of new international entities in the East, the Community's criteria drew heavily on the CSCE's Helsinki Final Act (1975) and Charter of Paris (1991). Thus, the Community stressed the principle of self-determination, together with respect for human rights and the rule of law. In general, the Community promised recognition to "those new States which . . . have accepted the appropriate international obligations and have committed themselves in good faith to a peaceful process and to negotiations."[57]

The question of relations with the Soviet republics and the practical problems of promoting economic and political reform there reinforced the Community's need to develop a CFSP. Although the Maastricht Treaty had only just been signed, the situation in the newly independent states (NIS) of the former USSR presented an opportunity to implement immediately certain elements of a CFSP. On January 10, 1992, the foreign ministers of the Twelve discussed the possibility of opening combined Commission/member state diplomatic missions in some capitals of the former Soviet republics,[58] but nothing came of the idea.

The commission had better success with a January 1992 suggestion for new accords between the Community and the USSR successor states that would not go as far as the recently signed Europe Agreements with Czechoslovakia, Hungary, and Poland but would nonetheless promote economic reform and political stability. Six months later, the Commission presented to the Council draft directives for the negotiation of "Partnership and Cooperation Agreements" with the NIS. The Commission proposed "mixed agreements," to which the Community *and* the member states would be parties. As in the case of the Europe Agreements, the Commission envisaged a common structure for all Partnership and Cooperation Agreements but different contents for each partner.[59] Community foreign ministers approved the Commission's approach and advocated regional cooperation among the NIS, hoping the new states would avoid the temptation to erect barriers against each other. According to External Affairs Commissioner Andriessen, "the degree to which we are willing to help [the Soviet successor states] may be determined by their willingness to cooperate with each other."[60]

In pursuing Partnership and Cooperation Agreements with the former Soviet republics, the Community ran the risk of engendering an even stronger protectionist reaction in the member states. Although the proposed EC-NIS accords would not entail the same degree of market access as the Europe Agreements, they involved an element of openness potentially unacceptable to many member states. Nor were the independent states' arguments as persuasive as those of the Eastern European countries. For one thing, the NIS were physically more remote from Western Europe than the Community's immediate neighbors to the East. For another, the plight of the NIS had far less emotional appeal in Western Europe than has the fate of the recently liberated countries of Eastern Europe. Precisely because the Community had just granted liberal commercial concessions to Czechoslovakia, Hungary, and Poland and was ready to negotiate similar arrangements with Bulgaria and Romania, some member states felt that they had little left to offer anybody else without giving away the store. Nevertheless, events such as the August 1991 attempted coup and the September 1993 failed rebellion emphasize the need for a generous and bold Community approach to the former Soviet Union.

YUGOSLAVIA

In the summer of 1991, Europe's first post–Cold War conflict erupted in Yugoslavia. Since Marshal Tito's death in 1980, latent ethnic and nationalist tensions within and between Yugoslavia's constituent republics had become more and more manifest. The collapse of communism in Eastern

Europe and the end of the Cold War triggered Yugoslavia's implosion. Citing their right to "self-determination," Croatia and Slovenia proclaimed independence on June 25. The federal army immediately went to war with secessionist Slovenia and suffered a surprisingly swift defeat. This alarmed Serbia, Yugoslavia's dominant republic, which purged the army of federalists and launched a war of territorial expansion in neighboring Croatia, where a Serbian minority felt increasingly threatened by Croatia's assertion of independence and had already launched a civil war. The new round of fighting in Yugoslavia unleashed a ferocity last seen in Europe during World War II. More than any other event, Serbia's systematic destruction of Vukovar, a small town in central Croatia, symbolized the conflict's savagery and demonstrated the depth of Belgrade's ambition.[61]

A number of factors impelled the Community to attempt to mediate the Yugoslav conflict. One was an intangible but nonetheless real sense of European identity, solidarity, and shared destiny. Despite a claim by one of Europe's leading intellectuals that "the former Yugoslavia is not felt to be part of Europe at all . . . it is felt to be part of 'the Balkans': a distinct region, and a zone of dangerous instability,"[62] the end of the Cold War had instilled in the Community a sense of responsibility toward even remote corners of the Continent. Although the end of the Cold War had also caused confusion about the Continent's geopolitical boundaries, there was no doubt about the Balkans' inclusion in the "New Europe."

The Community's perceived failure during the Gulf War also compelled action in the Balkans. Smarting from U.S. allegations about the Community's ineffectual response to Iraq's aggression and with expectations still high about the Community's contribution to peace and stability in the New Europe, it would have been impossible for the Community to ignore an outbreak of fighting on the Continent. Moreover, many Commission and member state officials saw the Yugoslav crisis as a chance to shape a Common Foreign and Security Policy during the IGC then in progress. "This shows what the Community can achieve if it works together on foreign policy," Delors announced in June 1991 after the Community's first arbitration effort.[63]

The Yugoslav wars indirectly threatened the Community's own security, thereby making the development of an effective CFSP and a resolution of the conflict especially urgent. Apart from causing a mass exodus of refugees into nearby Community countries, the Yugoslav conflict could have aggravated instability in at least two dangerous directions. One was to the north, where the ultranationalist Russian opposition advocated military support for fellow Slavs in Serbia. On December 14, 1992, the moderate Russian foreign minister shocked his colleagues at a CSCE meeting by demanding that sanctions against Serbia be lifted and threatening retaliation if the West launched punitive strikes there. Half an hour later, the foreign minister retracted his extraordinary statement, which was supposed to show what could happen if President Yeltsin left office.[64] The bizarre event brought home to Western governments not only the volatility of Russian politics but also the extent of Russian nationalist support for Serbia.

The other direction in which the Yugoslav wars could have worsened an already tense situation was to the south, where Islamic indignation over the West's unwillingness or inability to protect Bosnian Muslims from Serbian attack fueled dangerous resentment. Arab countries contrasted the West's rigorous implementation of UN resolutions against Iraq with its failure to act militarily against Serbia; Islamic fundamentalists in the Middle East attempted to exploit their coreligionists' plight in the former Yugoslavia; and Turkey remained remarkably restrained despite intense internal pressure to help Muslims in Bosnia and Kosovo. Greek sympathy for Serbia and opposition to international recognition of Macedonia further threatened to ignite smoldering Greco-Turkish tensions.

As well as European solidarity, the legacy of the Gulf War, the contemporaneous effort to devise a CFSP, and the Yugoslav conflict's possible external repercussions, humanitarian goals motivated the Community's mediation efforts. Soon after the first shots were fired in Croatia in the summer of 1991, the breakaway republic became a living hell for many of its inhabitants. In April 1992 fighting spread to Bosnia, where both Serbia and Croatia wanted to expand but where mutual hatred of Serbia turned Bosnian Muslims and Croatian nationalists into temporary allies. Although all sides committed atrocities, Serbia's ruthless siege of Sarajevo, Bosnia's capital, seemed especially callous. Nightly news film of maimed and murdered Bosnians, victims of Serb sniper and artillery attacks, sickened the outside world. Evidence of Serb "ethnic cleansing" in Bosnia recalled Europe's nightmare of the early 1940s and made an even more compelling humanitarian case for Community intercession in the conflict.

Perhaps anticipating the bloodshed that would follow Yugoslavia's disintegration and aware of the fissiparous tendencies then emerging in the USSR, the Community's member states initially supported keeping the country together. At their October 1990 summit in Rome, the heads of government called for "preservation of the unity and territorial integrity of Yugoslavia."[65] Yet growing demands for independence in Slovenia and Croatia, bolstered by plebiscites in both republics that overwhelmingly endorsed self-determination, struck a sympathetic chord in the Community. Simultaneously, opinion in Western Europe became increasingly antipathetic toward Serbia's unreconstructed communist regime, which began to usurp the federal government. By June 1991, when U.S. Secretary of State James Baker warned in Belgrade that the United States would not recognize breakaway Yugoslav republics "under any circumstances,"[66] a number of Community countries were moving in the opposite direction. On June 25, Slovenia and Croatia declared independence; two days later, perhaps interpreting Baker's remarks as a green light, the federal army attacked Slovenia.

Coincidentally, a European Council opened in Luxembourg on June 27, the same day that fighting broke out in Yugoslavia. The Troika of Community foreign ministers (from the current, immediately preceding, and immediately succeeding presidencies) left Luxembourg on a dramatic overnight peace mission to Belgrade, returning to report to their Community colleagues before the summit's end. The foreign ministers' trip strikingly demonstrated the member states' concerns about the crisis and determination to broker a settlement. A remark by Hans van den Broek, foreign minister of the Netherlands and a member of the Troika, revealed the confidence and conviction that pervaded the Community's early peacekeeping efforts: "When we went on this mission to Yugoslavia, I really had the feeling that the Yugoslav authorities thought that they were talking to Europe, not just to a country incidentally coming by but to an entity whose voice counts."[67]

The sudden cessation of hostilities in Slovenia—the federal army withdrew in early July—seemed to vindicate the Community's involvement in the conflict. Similarly, the sight of white-uniformed EC peacekeepers in Slovenia briefly boosted the Community's international standing. Within a short time, however, the situation in Yugoslavia deteriorated dramatically. Slovenia had never been part of Serbia's expansionist plans; federalists in the Yugoslav army had precipitated fighting there. Nor did Slovenia include any minorities proclaiming their own "self-determination" and looking to neighboring republics for help. Thus, while the Community congratulated itself for acting promptly and successfully in Slovenia, the "real" war broke out in adjoining Croatia and later spread to Bosnia-Herzegovina.

The rapid escalation of the Yugoslav conflict in 1992 and 1993 suggests that the Community's involvement may have exacerbated rather than alleviated the situation there. To a great extent the Yugoslav wars were intractable: Decades of mutual animosity between Croats, Muslims, and Serbs had suddenly come to the fore. More to the point, the cruelty and fanaticism of Serb nationalists—in Bosnia, Croatia, and Serbia— seemed boundless. Thus, the Community's peacemaking potential was limited by the depth of hatred underlying the conflict and by the related fact that in Bosnia and Croatia the conflict was a complicated civil war compounded by a clear-cut case of outside aggression.

The instruments available to the Community included arbitration, inspection, diplomatic recognition or nonrecognition of the warring parties, diplomatic isolation, and economic sanctions and inducements. The Community could neither take nor threaten to take military action,

although individual member states and the WEU could. The utility of outside force in the Yugoslav war was in any case debatable. Estimates of the
large number of troops necessary to impose an effective cease-fire and the
casualties likely to have been incurred in doing so suggest that massive
military intervention was never a feasible option. Limited military measures might have helped to enforce economic sanctions, halt Serbian
shelling of Sarajevo and other Bosnian cities, or punish Serbs for perpe-
trating atrocities. Such action, however, was unlikely ever to end the war
entirely and could have provoked additional Serb retaliation against de-
fenseless civilians.

Other policy instruments were equally unlikely to halt hostilities
completely, but they may at least have ameliorated the conflict. Yet it is
difficult to refute the conclusion that the Community's intervention in Yugoslavia lacked the essential requirements of "timeliness, consistency, and
adequacy to the task at hand."[68] The most glaring Community weakness,
which affected the application and effectiveness of other policy instruments, involved diplomatic recognition of secessionist republics. Under
pressure from Germany, the Community recognized Croatia on January
15, 1992, although Croatia did not meet the Community's criteria for
diplomatic recognition. Community recognition of Croatia may have
helped to end Serbian aggression there, but at the cost of provoking war in
Bosnia. Meanwhile, Greece blocked Community recognition of Macedonia, at the cost of further increasing regional tension and almost igniting a
broader Balkan war.

A determination to maintain EPC cohesion accounted for the Community's inconsistency. Because of mounting domestic pressure, Germany
began to press for Community recognition of Croatia and Slovenia in the
fall of 1991. Few Community countries disputed Slovenia's right to self-
determination, but the fate of a large Serbian minority raised international
concern about Croatia's claim. Moreover, a majority of member states
doubted that fragmentation of the Yugoslav federation would ultimately
resolve the conflict. They feared as well that diplomatic recognition would
encourage, not discourage, Croatian and Serbian irredentism. Matters
came to a head at a foreign ministers meeting on December 16. After ten
hours of fierce debate, the foreign ministers drew up criteria for the recognition of new states in Yugoslavia and the former Soviet Union and established a commission under Judge Robert Badinter to evaluate requests
for recognition.[69] Germany wanted to recognize Slovenia and Croatia immediately but agreed not to act until January 15, regardless of the Badinter Commission's report.

Germany's unilateralism made nonsense of the Community's criteria and procedures for recognizing breakaway republics and, according
to Piet Dankert, the Dutch junior foreign minister, marked "a very unhappy beginning" for closer cooperation on foreign and security policy.[70]

Unable to change Germany's mind, and fearing a damaging split immediately after the Maastricht summit on a major international issue, the other member states agreed to go along. Despite an equivocal report from the Badinter Commission on the merits of Croatia's case, the Community succumbed to German pressure and recognized Slovenia and Croatia on January 15, 1992.[71]

The Community's recognition of Croatia triggered a predictable Serbian response. A member of the Serb National Organization in London found it "disturbing and astounding that the EC should recognize Croatia as an independent state. The fudging of [the Badinter Report] exposes the flippant hypocrisy of the EC . . . [due to] pressure from a bullying Germany for the sake of European unity."[72] In Serbia itself the Community lost all credibility as a neutral arbiter; in Croatia it lost a lot of leverage over the government.

The Badinter Commission had also called for a referendum in Bosnia on the republic's future. A boycott by the large Serbian minority ensured that the EC-inspired referendum would endorse Bosnian independence. The referendum result, together with EC recognition of Bosnia on April 6, triggered the bloodiest part of the Yugoslav wars, as local Serbs carved out separate enclaves and "cleansed" them of other ethnic groups. Soon there were widespread calls for Community action to prevent further Serbian atrocities. As if to illustrate the Community's continuing disarray, exactly a year after the Troika's June 1991 peace mission to Belgrade, President Mitterrand left the Lisbon summit on a secret visit to Sarajevo to dramatize the city's plight and to try to break the Serbian siege. Despite a decision at Lisbon to coordinate member states' policies more closely, Mitterrand embarked on his dramatic trip without telling his Community colleagues until the last moment.[73]

Notwithstanding Mitterrand's dash to Sarajevo, member states were so determined to maintain a semblance of solidarity during the Yugoslav wars that the heads of government decided at Lisbon not to recognize Macedonia. Paradoxically, the Badinter Commission had approved Macedonia's request for recognition, which the international community generally agreed would help rather than hinder peacekeeping efforts there. But Greece refused to recognize Macedonia unless the Yugoslav republic, having stolen "a historically Greek name and feeding long-nourished appetites for Greek Territory," dropped the word "Macedonia" from its title.[74] Greek hostility to the existence of a neighboring country called "Macedonia" dominated domestic politics in 1992 and 1993. Thus, Prime Minister Mitsotakis could argue not only that the Community should support Greece in order to maintain a common position on Yugoslavia but also that failure to do so would cause a Greek political crisis and result in a return of the detested Papandreou government. Indeed, Papandreou won the October 1993 general election largely because of dissatisfaction with Mitsotakis's economic policies.

The Lisbon decision soon seemed morally untenable but politically irrefutable. As Garret FitzGerald, the former Irish prime minister, pointed out, the Community's position was "all the more indefensible . . . [because] this Greek-imposed policy appears to be de-stabilizing one of the few areas of Yugoslavia that is peaceful, and is risking the internationalization of a conflict that has hitherto been confined to the territory of the old Yugoslav state."[75] FitzGerald called on the Irish government to reject the Lisbon decision, although he surely appreciated the difficulty of breaking ranks in EPC. The British presidency appointed a special ambassador to try to resolve the problem before the end of 1992, but to no avail. A demonstration by 1 million people in Athens on the eve of the Edinburgh summit strengthened the Greek's government's hand considerably. Preoccupied in any case with the Maastricht Treaty ratification crisis, the Delors II budgetary package, and enlargement, the heads of government dodged the embarrassing Macedonian issue, merely inviting their foreign ministers "to remain seized of this question."[76]

The Community's high hopes of mediation in Yugoslavia were an early victim of Serb implacability and of member state differences over the conflict. Initial Community intervention had resulted in the "Brioni Accords" of July 7, 1991, which committed all sides to a "peaceful and negotiated solution." The escalation of hostilities in Croatia prompted the Community to convene a peace conference on September 7 in The Hague and to apply intense pressure to ensure Serbian attendance. Delors's statement that the conference showed how far the Community had traveled down "the road to Political Union and in particular to a CFSP"[77] failed both to impress the combatants in Yugoslavia and to hide intra-Community strains over Croatian recognition. Serbian intransigence at the conference and belligerence in Yugoslavia made other member states more sympathetic toward Germany's case for recognizing Croatia and undermined the Community's arbitration efforts.

Community mediation fared little better in 1992. Persistent Serbian deception discouraged Lord Carrington, the EC mediator, to the point of resignation. A strong public reaction against Serbian atrocities in Bosnia redoubled the Community's diplomatic offensive, culminating in the joint UN-EC–sponsored London Conference of August 26, 1992.[78] Leaders of all six Yugoslav republics and a host of foreign ministers (including those of the UN Security Council countries) attended. The London Conference developed "peace principles," an "action program," and a negotiating framework for six working groups, which deliberated for the rest of the year in Geneva. The Geneva talks, in turn, ended at a conference in January 1993, at which Lord Owen (Carrington's successor) and Cyrus Vance (his UN counterpart) produced a comprehensive peace plan for Bosnia.[79]

Bosnian Muslims' unwillingness to accept a proposal that seemingly rewarded Serbian aggression, Bosnian Serbs' reluctance to cede control over any part of their recently acquired enclaves, and Croatia's determination to grab more territory in Bosnia doomed the painstakingly prepared Owen-Vance plan. At the June 1993 Copenhagen summit, Community leaders declared their refusal to accept "a territorial solution dictated by Serbs and Croats at the expense of the Bosnian Muslims."[80] However, such a solution to the Bosnian conflict seems increasingly likely, and the Community appears to have little option but to go along with it.

The Yugoslav situation was unique in many respects but nonetheless provided a useful lesson in the complexity of EC involvement in post–Cold War conflict resolution. The Balkans' history of "dangerous instability," which had dragged the great powers into World War I and which, as German unification reminded everyone, cast a long shadow over twentieth-century Europe, complicated the Community's response to the Yugoslav crisis. Yet it is an exaggeration to claim that "the permanent effort to maintain EC cohesion [during the Yugoslav conflict] prevented a Balkan war from turning into a European war. If parties to the conflict have largely been unable to enlist the support of one European country against another as they have done in the past, it is largely because of the EC's steadfastness."[81] Undoubtedly, Germany's support for Croatian independence in 1991 jogged memories of Nazi Germany's backing of fascist Croatia fifty years previously and sparked an ugly media reaction in France.[82] Similarly, France's instinctive sympathy for Serbia in 1991 echoed its support for Serbia during World War I. But the democratization of Germany (and Italy) since 1945, the demise of aggressive nationalism in Western Europe, and Western solidarity during the Cold War—to which the European Community certainly contributed—ensured that the Yugoslav war did not risk pitting Community countries against each other.

The impossibility of sending any German troops to Yugoslavia was a more pertinent legacy for the Community of recent Balkan and European history. The Gulf War had sparked a bitter controversy in Germany over the deployment of troops outside the NATO area. The Yugoslav crisis fueled further debate, but German atrocities in the Balkans during World War II definitively precluded the option of deploying troops there. Britain's "Northern Ireland syndrome" made the government in London extremely cautious about intervening militarily in Yugoslavia, apart from limited humanitarian assistance under UN auspices. Of the Community's three "great powers," only France appeared willing to take some form of military action, and it was not willing to act alone. Thus, the member states' reluctance to use force—whether or not force would have been effective—not only limited their range of policy instruments during the crisis but also hindered the development of a Community "defense identity" during the 1991 IGC on political union.

Far from reflecting well on the Community, the Yugoslav war emphasized deep foreign policy differences between member states and showed the limits of EC international action.[83] The Community's involvement also sapped popular support for European integration and contributed to the Maastricht Treaty ratification crisis. According to one poll, 82 percent of those who said they would vote against ratification in the French referendum claimed that the Community's inability to end the war in Yugoslavia affected their decision.[84] The Community's performance had a similarly debilitating effect in the United States. A rash boast in early July 1991 by Jacques Poos, Luxembourg's foreign minister and Council president-in-office, that "this is the hour of Europe, not the hour of the Americans,"[85] gave explosive ammunition to the Community's critics in the United States. The deputy editorial page editor of the *Wall Street Journal* could not resist the temptation to observe that the Community "looks less like the world's new superpower and more like a bloated Luxembourg."[86] However, some officials in the Community felt that the United States had set them up to take an inevitable fall over Yugoslavia.

Initial intervention in Yugoslavia may have "done more in two weeks to give the EC a sense of identity than two years of haggling among the twelve member states about the planned treaty on European union,"[87] but the Community's subsequent arbitration efforts seriously undermined its international standing and foreign policy effectiveness. Nor would the Community have performed better had the CFSP been in place earlier. The problem lay not simply in a lack of mechanism or structure but rather in profound historical differences compounded by a radical contextual change caused by the end of the Cold War. The Yugoslav crisis was a salutary lesson in the limits of European integration, specifically in the difficulty of sharing sovereignty in the sensitive areas of security and defense.

TRANS-ATLANTIC RELATIONS

In the altered international environment of the post–Cold War world, security and defense issues brought a new edge to U.S.-EC relations. Discussions in the Community in early 1991 about acquiring a security dimension and, ultimately, a military capability provoked an intemperate U.S. response, with warnings from Washington about the dangers of undermining NATO. At the same time, a series of events in 1991—notably the Gulf and Yugoslav conflicts—exposed weaknesses in the Twelve's fledgling foreign policy efforts and caused the United States to rethink the Community's ability to become a serious player in diplomatic and security affairs. Nevertheless, later in 1991 the United States seemed slightly alarmed, or at least discomfited, by the Community's rising political profile and forceful policy toward Eastern Europe. Despite a resounding victory in the Gulf War and the arrival of what one commentator called the "unipolar moment,"[88] the United States grew more and more concerned about losing leadership in Eastern Europe to the Community, an international *parvenu*.

The situation since the end of the Cold War complicated an already awkward trans-Atlantic relationship. From the U.S. perspective, the difficulty lay largely in the incremental, often untidy nature of European integration, which caused constant changes in the scope of the Community's agenda and in the character of its policy-formulating process. By contrast, bilateral, country-to-country relations were easily comprehensible: Both sides had a well-understood governmental structure and an easily identifiable set of issues. But in the case of the European Community, who exactly had decisionmaking power, and where precisely was the boundary between Community and member state competence?

The Treaty of Rome and its 1986 revision were obvious guides to the Community's competence and decisionmaking structure, and the United States had developed a procedure and an institutional framework to deal with the Community accordingly. The State Department, Commerce Department, Trade Representative's Office, and other U.S. government agencies had long been organized to manage Community business. Moreover, U.S. government officials involved in EC affairs, and the agencies for which these officials worked, understood that frequent nontreaty changes were endemic in the Community. For instance, the development of EPC in the early 1970s and the EMS in the late 1970s changed the Community's character considerably and caused a corresponding shift in Washington's official apparatus for the formulation and implementation of policy toward Brussels.

Yet other, less obvious changes in the Community's agenda and institutional structure were much more difficult for the United States to identify and respond to procedurally. This was especially true following the Community's revival in the mid-1980s. In terms of the Community's agenda, the most important changes were greater Community involvement in environmental policy, industrial policy, research, and science and technology. In terms of institutional structure, the changes have been most marked in the increasing assertiveness and growing authority of the European Commission.

For the United States, the resurgence of the European Commission was particularly perturbing. The name of the Commission itself evoked an unfavorable (and wholly wrong) image in Washington of all that is iniquitous about the Community: a bloated bureaucracy, an opaque administration, and an unaccountable authority. Who drafts proposals in the Commission? When are proposals circulated outside the Breydel? How can third countries express their points of view? The answers to those questions seemed to differ from one directorate-general to another.

Despite such changes in Community competence and institutional context, at least during the Cold War there was one constant: The European Community's agenda would never encompass military and defense issues. Of course, in the early 1970s the Community's member states launched EPC, a procedure for foreign policy coordination; a decade later, during a resurgence of East-West tension, some sought to extend EPC into the security domain. But Washington's hostile response, or some member states' anticipation of Washington's hostile response, helped restrict EPC deliberations to the "political and economic" aspects of security.

That state of affairs—frequent changes in the Community's competence (but no extension of it into military and defense issues) and institutional structure, and Washington's belated efforts to come to terms with them—might have continued indefinitely but for a number of contemporaneous developments toward the end of the 1980s. One was the striking success of the single market program and the possible extension of it into EMU; another was a realization by the Bush administration of an increasing financial constraint on U.S. foreign policy; and a third was reform and revolution in Eastern Europe.

The United States responded with a fundamental review in early 1989 of policy toward Europe. President Bush articulated the result in two speeches in May 1989, and Secretary of State Baker elaborated further in a famous speech in December of that year—one month after the fall of the Berlin Wall. The essence of the United States' "New Atlanticism" was a grim determination to preserve NATO regardless of the changes ahead, a grudging recognition of the CSCE's potential, and a genuine appreciation of the Community's importance as a political and economic anchor in an otherwise storm-tossed continent, despite exaggerated U.S. fears that the single market program would create a "Fortress Europe."

At the July 1989 G7 summit in Paris, Bush manifested Washington's newfound confidence in the European Community by encouraging the Commission to coordinate Western aid to Hungary and Poland.[89] The acceleration of reform in Eastern Europe further convinced the United States of the Community's political significance, not least as an essential underpinning for a united Germany, which Washington strongly supported. Simultaneously, however, the United States signaled that the Community would have to face up to its responsibilities also in the international trade arena. Thus in July 1990, at the G7 summit in Houston, the United States launched an offensive to pressure the EC to make key concessions on agriculture in the Uruguay Round of the GATT.[90]

This revision of U.S. policy and behavior toward the Community and a continuing surge of the Community's political importance in the late 1980s provided the background to the U.S.-EC Transatlantic Declaration of November 1990. The United States responded with alacrity to a proposal by the Irish prime minister, made during a visit to Washington in

February 1990 in his capacity as president of the Council of Ministers, for a formalized U.S.-EC relationship.[91] The appeal for the United States of such an arrangement grew throughout the year, as the Community reacted to the complete collapse of communism in Eastern Europe and the sudden inevitability of German reunification by calling for an IGC on political union in addition to the previously scheduled IGC on Economic and Monetary Union.

The "Declaration on U.S.-EC Relations," signed by U.S. President Bush, Council President Andreotti, and Commission President Delors in Washington in November 1990, was long on rhetoric and short on substance. Among the reasons for a solid U.S.-EC relationship, the declaration included a new factor: "the accelerating process by which the European Community is acquiring its own identity in economic and monetary matters, in foreign policy and in the domain of security." Yet apart from its general significance, the declaration's only tangible contribution to U.S.-EC relations was a strengthened framework for regular consultations to enable both sides to "inform and consult each other on important matters of common interest, both political and economic, with a view to bringing their positions as close as possible, without prejudice to their respective independence."[92]

As part of a process "to endow their relationship with long-term perspectives," the U.S.-EC declaration appeared to be a provisional measure pending the results of the IGCs, which were bound to affect Washington's policy toward the Community. The already well-known Delors Plan had set the agenda for the negotiations on EMU, the outcome of which was unlikely to cause much surprise in Washington. But the negotiations on EPU held out an entirely different prospect, both alarming and encouraging for the United States. Clearly, the key issues were the Community's apparent resolve finally to extend its agenda to include security and defense (alarming in Washington) and the possible institutional changes that would make the decisionmaking process more transparent and amenable to outside influence (encouraging in Washington).

No sooner had the Community signed the Transatlantic Declaration and launched the IGCs, however, than the GATT negotiations collapsed in Brussels in December 1990 over failure to resolve U.S.-EC trade disputes.[93] The talks broke down in a swirl of mutual recriminations, with the United States and the EC accusing each other of never having been serious about a successful conclusion. The EC especially objected to what seemed like excessive and high-handed U.S. demands for CAP reform. For its part, the United States saw the failure of the Brussels talks as evidence of the EC's intransigence and introspection. The EC seemed neither able nor willing to face up to its international responsibilities. In addition, some member states appeared to exploit a domestic reaction against Washington's conduct at the Brussels talks to entrench their uncompromising positions.

The fate of the GATT negotiations after December 1990 deepened U.S. disillusionment with the EC. U.S. fears in 1991 that the Community would become preoccupied with the IGCs, to the exclusion of pressing external obligations, seemed warranted. Nor did the Community's May 1992 agreement to reform the CAP give much cause for optimism.[94] Despite Community claims to the contrary, there was little in the reform package to remove the roadblocks to a successful GATT agreement. The unedifying squabble over agricultural subsidies in the early 1990s, therefore, was strikingly at variance with the U.S.-EC declaration's rhetoric about cherished common ties and values, mutual commitments to global economic progress, and greater trans-Atlantic solidarity.

Then again, Brussels' intransigence over agricultural subsidies could be interpreted as signaling the Community's coming of age internationally. Former U.S. Vice President Dan Quayle may have overstated the link between a successful outcome of the Uruguay Round and a continued U.S. commitment to NATO,[95] but the impact of the Cold War's end on U.S. influence in Western Europe was not lost on either the Community or its member states. The Community could afford to irritate the United States by stalling a GATT agreement precisely because Washington's political and military role in Western Europe was far less important in the post–Cold War era.

The member states' apparent acquiescence in U.S. pressure not to undermine NATO by developing an EC defense identity, exerted in the early stages of the IGC on political union, suggested that the United States continued to wield considerable diplomatic clout and that member states took seriously the threat of a U.S. military withdrawal from Europe. Indeed, the member states drew back from acquiring for themselves or the Community an independent defense capability and opted instead to use the WEU as a bridge between NATO and the EC. But their reasons for doing so were more diverse than simply succumbing to a U.S. demarche. Regardless of U.S. prodding, the member states themselves generally favored NATO's survival and could not agree about the form or content of an EC defense identity.[96]

The member states' differing and at times contradictory responses to the two major international crises during the course of the IGCs—the Gulf and Yugoslav wars—made it more difficult for them to agree on a Community-based security structure independent of the United States, even had they been willing to do so. By the same token, the Community's performance in both crises fueled doubts in Washington about Brussels' ability ever to fashion a coherent foreign and security policy. As for Washington's own reaction to the Gulf War, the speed and success with which it dispatched a massive expeditionary force briefly overcame the self-doubt and insecurity that had characterized the United States since the declinism debate of the mid-1980s.[97] The sudden upsurge of U.S.

triumphalism coincided with the Community's despondency over its own performance in the Gulf and was precisely the time at which Washington launched its demarche against the emergence of a European defense identity.

The United States' preoccupation with the post–Gulf War Middle East peace talks, U.S. awareness that the Balkan conflict was intractable, and Secretary of State Baker's unequivocal call in Belgrade for the survival of the Yugoslav state may help to explain Washington's willingness to allow the Community to take the lead internationally on mediating a Yugoslavia settlement. A more benign explanation is that, in keeping with its decision at the Paris G7 summit in 1989 about aid to Eastern Europe, the United States again allowed the Community to take the lead on a major international issue "in its own backyard." Whatever the reason, and whether or not the United States could have fared any better, the Community did not distinguish itself in Yugoslavia. Germany's push for recognition of Croatia and Slovenia in late 1991 and Greece's subsequent success in preventing recognition of Macedonia demonstrated the limits of Community involvement in the foreign policy sphere.

The United States' willingness to take a backseat to the Community on certain foreign policy issues was not in keeping with its character and was not easy for the Washington establishment to accept. A renewed U.S. assertiveness in the aftermath of the Gulf War victory, possibly coupled with anger over the Community's failure to negotiate a GATT agreement and dismay at its handling of the Gulf and Yugoslavia conflicts, caused Washington to seek a more prominent role in the provision of aid to the USSR. This issue came to a head in December 1991, when Secretary of State Baker surprised his European allies by unexpectedly announcing, in a speech at Princeton University, that the United States would host an international conference in Washington the following month to coordinate aid to the former Soviet republics.[98] Washington's insistence on participation and its sometimes churlish role in the Community-sponsored negotiations for a European Energy Charter further illustrated U.S. concern about losing the Eastern European initiative to the EC.

The EC did not react kindly to this approach. In classic Gallic, indeed Gaullist, style, President Mitterrand articulated the extreme European response to Baker's unilateral initiative on aid to the USSR by pointing out that the EC member states already provided the bulk of assistance and that the United States should instead come to Europe to coordinate the aid effort.[99] Mitterrand's uninhibited response went to the core of the "burden sharing" debate between Washington and Brussels over assistance to Eastern Europe and the disintegrating USSR, an issue on which U.S. passion ran particularly high. Washington saw the burden sharing debate in the context of the entire postwar period, during which the United States contributed heavily to Western Europe's reconstruction and security, and not only as a post–Cold War issue. Moreover, the United States was far from convinced that the EC had either the organizational or material resources to coordinate the aid effort.

Notwithstanding France's initial hostility to Baker's announcement in December 1991, the Council of Ministers endorsed the Community's participation in the Washington conference, but it took great care to coordinate the member states' positions beforehand and to affirm the Community's leading role in assisting the East. "The Community and its Member States," the Council announced in January 1992, "will participate in the Conference on the basis of a common position to be closely coordinated beforehand. . . . The [conference's] four working party co-chairmanships assigned to Member States or the Community will be held under a dual arrangement involving the Member States concerned and the Community."[100]

The row over assistance to the USSR coincided with the Maastricht summit. From the U.S. perspective, the outcome of the IGCs was satisfactory. As expected, the EMU negotiations generally led to an endorsement of the Delors Plan and a decision to establish a single currency by 1999 at the latest. The consequences of a single Community currency are not unfavorable for the United States. Speculation that the new ECU would likely challenge the dollar's role as a reserve currency failed to account for the inherent pressure on a reserve currency. Far from trying to prevent the ECU from becoming an international rival, the United States had no objection to such a development.

As for political union, the Maastricht Treaty formally altered the Community's competence and institutional framework in ways that were not disadvantageous to the United States. The extension of Community competence in areas such as environmental and industrial policy for the most part formalized the status quo. Moreover, the industrial policy provisions of the Maastricht Treaty were not as damaging to the United States as they might have been had certain member states, notably France, had their way. The treaty's foreign and security policy provisions pleased the United States by not establishing a separate EC defense identity, although, in the long term, the outcome of the EC-NATO-WEU debate tilts in favor of an independent EC defense position. In the meantime, like the EC member states themselves, the United States was curious to see how the CFSP, with its confusing mix of unanimity and majority voting before a common position could even be identified, would operate in practice. Finally, the institutional provisions of the treaty did not require a radical reappraisal of the U.S. foreign policy apparatus for dealing with EC affairs.

Given the United States' conceptual and operational difficulties with the Commission, it may seem paradoxical that the Commission's limited involvement in the Community's new CFSP was likely to benefit U.S.-EC relations. The Commission's previous lack of an overall foreign policy perspective and almost exclusive focus on economic issues had exacerbated trans-Atlantic trade disputes. In the long term, a more stable

U.S.-EC relationship may await the Commission's evolution into a full-fledged executive branch with responsibility for both the economic and political aspects of the Community's international relations. Until then, the Commission's limited involvement in CFSP, and Commissioner van den Broek's responsibility for "external political relations," are steps in the right direction. For the same reason, the United States will watch even more closely future negotiations on institutional reform in the Community, which are inevitable both in the context of further enlargement and in view of the pending 1996 IGC.

In the meantime, Washington's assertiveness in the Eastern European burden sharing debate and admonition of the EC over its handling of the war in Bosnia seemed to conflict with evidence in 1992 of the United States' growing preoccupation with domestic affairs at the expense of international interests. A faltering election campaign obliged President Bush to devote more time and attention to domestic economic problems. President Clinton's victory, and the large turnover of members of Congress, raised concerns abroad about the new administration's undisguised "America-first" bias. Yet such an outcome should not be confused with the reappearance of U.S. isolationism. The United States was bound to remain extremely active internationally, challenging the EC on a wide range of foreign economic and political issues.

Late in the Bush administration, the United States and the EC clashed bitterly over Community subsidies for oilseeds production. The dispute quickly escalated and virtually ensured that both sides would remain at loggerheads early in the Clinton administration. Washington's decision to retaliate against Community steel exporters and restrict EC bids on federal public procurement contracts portended an ugly trade war. U.S. resentment of Brussels ran deep, not least because of the Community's supposed emergence as a more committed actor in international affairs. Potentially serious differences over how best to assist the former Soviet Union and resolve the Yugoslav wars further strained the trans-Atlantic relationship. And in the background, threatening again to surge to the surface, was the vital political question of NATO's future. For all the rhetoric and historical significance of the Transatlantic Declaration and the importance of the Maastricht Treaty, U.S.-EC relations were under greater strain in 1993 than at any other time in the Community's existence.

NOTES

1. Jacques Delors, speech to the European Parliament, Bull EC. S1/90, p. 7.

2. Lily Gardner Feldman, "The EC in the International Arena: A New Activism," in *U.S. Congress, House Committee on Foreign Affairs, and the United*

States: Competition and Cooperation in the 1990s (Washington, DC: Government Printing Office, 1992), p. 401.

3. For an account of EPC's origins and development, see Christopher Hill, ed., *National Foreign Policies and European Political Cooperation* (London: Allen and Unwin, 1983); P. Ifestos, *European Political Cooperation: Towards a Framework of Supranational Diplomacy* (Aldershot: Avebury, 1988); Alfred Pijpers, et al., eds., *European Political Cooperation in the 1980s: A Common Foreign Policy for Western Europe* (The Hague: Martinus Nijhoff, 1988); and Martin Holland, *The Future of European Political Cooperation: Essays on Theory and Practice* (New York: St. Martin's. 1991).

4. See David Allen and Alfred Pijpers, *European Foreign Policy-Making and the Arab-Israeli Conflict* (The Hague: Martinus Nijhoff, 1984).

5. See Fraser Cameron, "The Future Relationship and Division of Responsibilities Between the EC and the CSCE," in Ian Cuthbertson, ed., *Redefining the CSCE: Challenges and Opportunities in the New Europe* (Helsinki: Finnish Institute of International Affairs, 1992), pp. 95–96.

6. William Wallace, "EPC: A New Form of Diplomacy," Royal Irish Academy conference paper, November 20, 1981, p. 12.

7. Franz Pfeffer, "The European Ten's Foreign Policy," unpublished paper, November 1983, p. 8.

8. "Draft European Act," Bull. EC 11-1981, point 3.4.1. For an academic appraisal of Genscher-Colombo, see Joseph Weiler, "The Genscher-Colombo Draft European Act: The Politics of Indecision," *Journal of European Integration* 4, nos. 2 and 3 (1983): 129–153.

9. Bull. EC 6-1983, point 1.6.1.

10. See Desmond Dinan, "EPC," in Leon Hurwitz and Christian Lequesne, eds., *The State of the European Community: Policies, Institutions, and Debates in the Transition Years* (Boulder, CO: Lynne Rienner, 1991), pp. 403–422.

11. Bull. EC 7/8-1990, 1.5.11.

12. OJ 3–393, Debates of the European Parliament, September 1990.

13. Quoted in *Le Monde,* January 15, 1991, p. 1.

14. See Pia Christina Wood, "EPC: Lessons from the Gulf War and Yugoslavia," in Alan Cafruny and Glenda Rosenthal, *The State of the EC: The Maastricht Years and Beyond* (Boulder, CO: Lynne Rienner, 1993), pp. 227–244.

15. See Trevor Salmon, "The Gulf and Yugoslavia: Dynamics of EPC for the Twelve and the Problems of Establishing Convergence," paper presented at the Eighth International Conference of Europeanists, Council for European Studies, Chicago, March 27–29, 1992.

16. See Alfred Cahan, *The Western European Union and NATO* (London: Brassey's, 1989).

17. The Italian proposal is reproduced in Laursen and Vanhoonacker, *Intergovernmental Conference*, p. 292.

18. Bull. EC 10-1990, Presidency Conclusions, 1.4.

19. Jacques Delors, speech at the Royal Institute for International Affairs, London, March 7, 1991.

20. Reinhardt Rummel, ed., *Toward Political Union: Planning a Common Foreign and Security Policy in the European Community* (Boulder, CO: Westview Press, 1992), p. 298.

21. Bull. EC 12-1991, 1.3.2.

22. See Peter Marsh, "The European Community and East-West Economic Relations," *Journal of Common Market Studies* 23, no. 1 (September 1984), pp. 1–13.

23. Bull. EC, 6-1988.

24. Ad Hoc Committee for Institutional Affairs Report to the European Council, March 1985, Bull. EC 3-1985, point. 3.5.1.

25. Bull. EC, 12-1988, 1.1.10.

26. Bull. EC, 7/8-1989, 1.1.1–6.

27. Council Regulation (EEC) 3906/89, December 18, 1989.

28. See Commission of the European Communities, *PHARE: Assistance for Economic Restructuring in the Countries of Central and Eastern Europe, an Operational Guide* (Luxembourg: Office of Official Publications, 1992).

29. Françoise de la Serre, "The EC and Central and Eastern Europe," in Hurwitz and Lequesne, *Policies, Institutions,* p. 304.

30. John Pinder, *The European Community and Eastern Europe* (London: RIIA, 1991), pp. 87–88.

31. See, for instance, "The Structure and Strategy for the European Union with Regard to its Enlargement and the Creation of a Europe-Wide Order," Report of the Committee on Institutional Affairs, May 21, 1992, EP 152.242/fin.

32. SEA Title III, Article 30.5.

33. Pinder, *Eastern Europe,* p. 34; de la Serre, "EC and Central Europe," p. 3.

34. Quoted in William Wallace, *The Transformation of Western Europe* (London: RIIA, 1990), p. 29.

35. Quoted in the *New York Times,* January 26, 1992, p. 10

36. Quoted in *The European,* June 14, 1991, p. 6.

37. *The Week in Germany,* September 27, 1991, p. 1.

38. Stanley Hoffmann, "The Case for Leadership," *Foreign Policy* 81 (Winter 1990–91), p. 30.

39. Bull. EC 4-1990, Presidency Conclusions, point 1.5-8.

40. COM/90/398, final, August 2, 1990.

41. Quoted in the *Washington Post,* October 10, 1990, p. B1.

42. See *The Financial Times,* October 1, 1991, p. 2.

43. Quoted in *The Guardian,* July 15, 1991, p. 4.

44. *The Financial Times,* May 2–3, 1992, p. 6.

45. Bull. EC, 12-1992, 1.3.2-4.

46. European Agreement with Romania, COM(92)511, December 21, 1992; European Agreement with Bulgaria, COM(93)45, February 18, 1993.

47. Commission report on enlargement, Bull. EC S/3-1992, pp. 11–12.

48. Quoted in *The Financial Times,* December 9, 1991, p. 3.

49. Bull. EC 10-1992, 1.4.6-7.

50. Commission of the European Communities, "Toward a Closer Association With the Countries of Central and Eastern Europe," December 2, 1992, SEC (92)2301 final.

51. Bull. EC 12-1992, Presidency Conclusions, point 1.76.

52. European Council in Copenhagen, June 21–22, 1993, Presidency Conclusions, SN 180/93, June 22, 1993.

53. Pinder, *Eastern Europe,* p. 75.

54. Bull. EC 12-1990, Presidency Conclusions, point 1.31.

55. EPC Press Release P. 135/91, December 25, 1991

56. EPC Press Release P. 128/91, December 16, 1991.

57. EPC Press Release P. 128/91, December 16, 1991

58. Council of Ministers Press Release, 4022/92, January 10, 1992.

59. See Information Note on "Partnership and Cooperation Agreements with the ex-USSR States," EC Delegation, Washington, D.C., P&PA/9/21/92.

60. Quoted in *The New York Times,* January 26, 1992, p. 10.

61. On the outbreak of war in Yugoslavia, see Misha Glenny, *The Fall of Yugoslavia: The Third Balkan War* (London: Penguin, 1992).

62. Conor Cruise O'Brien, "Hands Off: Why Europe Has Been Reluctant to Intervene," *The Atlantic* (November 1992), p. 36.

63. Quoted in *Le Monde,* June 28, 1991, p. 1.

64. *The New York Times,* December 15, 1992, p. A1.

65. Bull. EC 10-1990, Presidency Conclusions, point 1.8.

66. *The Washington Post,* June 25, 1991, p. A1.

67. Interview in the *International Herald Tribune,* July 1, 1992, p. 2

68. Catherine Guicherd, "The Hour of Europe: Preliminary Lessons From Yugoslavia," unpublished paper, Center for European Community Studies, George Mason University, p. 16.

69. EPC Press Release, P129/91, December 16, 1991.

70. Quoted in *The Financial Times,* January 16, 1992, p. 16.

71. EPC Press Release, P9/92, January 15, 1992.

72. D. Novakovic, letter to the editor, *The Guardian,* January 18, 1992, p. 2.

73. *Le Monde,* June 28, 1992, p. 1.

74. Embassy of Greece, *News From Greece,* 16/92, November 10, 1992, p. 1.

75. *The Irish Times,* August 14, 1992, p. 10.

76. Bull. EC 12-1992, Presidency Conclusions, point 1.74.

77. Quoted in *The Guardian,* September 4, 1991, p. 2.

78. Bull. EC 7/8-1992, point 1.4.17.

79. Bull. EC 1-1993.

80. European Council in Copenhagen, June 21–22, 1993, Presidency Conclusions, SN 180/93, June 22, 1993.

81. Guicherd, "The Hour of Europe," p. 16.

82. See, for instance, *Le Monde,* August and September 1991.

83. See Wood, "EPC: Lessons from the Gulf War and Yugoslavia", pp. 227–244. For an insider's account of the EC's failure in Yugoslavia, see Henry Wynaents, *L'Engrenage* (Paris: Denoel, 1993). Wynaents was a senior Dutch diplomat involved in the EC's peace efforts.

84. *Le Monde,* August 26, 1992, p. 1.

85. Quoted in *The Financial Times,* July 1, 1991, p. 1.

86. David Brooks, "A Superpower Europe? Forget It," *Wall Street Journal,* August 9–10, 1991, p. 10.

87. *The Guardian,* July 15, 1991, p. 4.

88. Charles Krauthammer, "The Unipolar Moment," *Foreign Affairs* 70, no. 1 (Winter 1990–91), pp. 23–33.

89. Bull. EC 7/8-1989, point 1.1.1–5.

90. *The New York Times,* July 12, 1990, p. A1.

91. *The Washington Post,* February 28, 1990, p. A1.

92. "Declaration on EC-US Relations," U.S. Department of State, November 11, 1990.

93. Bull. EC, 12-1990, 1.4.94.

94. Bull. EC 5-1992, point 1.1.138.

95. See *The Financial Times,* February 10, 1992, p. 1.

96. On the U.S. demarche, see John Newhouse, "The Diplomatic Round: A Collective Nervous Breakdown," *New Yorker,* September 7, 1991, p. 92.

97. See Paul Kennedy, *The Rise and Fall of the Great Powers: Economic*

Change and Military Conflict From 1500 to 2000 (New York: Random House, 1987).

     98. *The New York Times,* December 18, 1991, p. A1.

     99. *Le Monde,* December 21, 1991, p. 1.

     100. Council of Ministers Press Release, 4022/92, January 10, 1992.

Bibliography

Acheson, Dean. *Present at the Creation: My Years in the State Department.* New York: Norton, 1969.

Adams, William James, ed. *Singular Europe: Economy and Polity of the EC After 1992.* Ann Arbor, MI: University of Michigan Press, 1992.

Adenauer, Konrad. *Memoirs, 1945–1953.* Chicago: Regnery, 1966.

Allen, David, and Alfred Pijpers. *European Foreign Policy Making and the Arab-Israeli Conflict.* The Hague: Martinus Nijhoff, 1984.

Allen, David, Reinhardt Rummel, and Wolfgang Wessels. *European Political Co-operation: Towards a Foreign Policy for Western Europe?* London: Butterworths, 1982.

Alting von Geusau, Frans, ed. *The External Relations of the EC: Perspectives, Policies and Responses.* Lexington, MA: Lexington Books, 1974.

———, ed. *The Lomé Convention and a New International Economic Order.* Leiden, The Netherlands: A. W. Sijthoff, 1977.

Amin, A., and M. Dietrich, eds. *Towards a New Europe: Structural Change in the European Community.* Brookfield, VT: Edward Elgar, 1991.

Angarita, C., and P. Coffey. *Europe and the Andean Countries: A Comparison of Economic Policies & Institutions.* London: Pinter, 1988.

Arbuthnott, Hugh, and Geoffrey Edwards. *A Common Man's Guide to the Common Market.* London: Macmillan, 1979.

Archer, Clive, and Fiona Butler. *The European Community: Structure and Process.* New York: St. Martin's, 1992.

Bakhoven, A. E. *The Completion of the Common Market in 1992.* The Hague: Martinus Nijhoff, 1989.

Baldwin, R., C. Hamilton, and Andre Sapir, eds. *Issues in US-EC Trade Relations.* Chicago: University of Chicago Press, 1988.

Ball, George W. *The Past Has Another Pattern.* New York: Norton, 1982.

Bangemann, Martin. *Meeting the Global Challenge: Establishing a Successful European Industrial Policy.* London: Kogan Page, 1992.

Barfield, Claude E., and Mark Perlman. *Industry, Services, and Agriculture in the 1990s: The United States Faces a New Europe.* Washington, DC: American Enterprise Institute, 1992.

Barnouin, Barbara. *The European Labor Movement and European Integration.* London: Pinter, 1986.

Beije, Paul R., ed. *A Competitive Future for Europe? Towards a New European Industrial Policy.* London: Croom Helm, 1987.

503

Beloff, Max. *The United States and the Unity of Europe*. Washington, DC: Brookings Institution, 1963.

Bethlen, Steven, and Ivan Volgyer, eds. *Europe and the Superpowers: Political, Economic, and Military Policies in the 1980s*. Boulder, CO: Westview, 1985.

Bieber, Roland, Jean-Paul Jacques, and Joseph Weiler, eds. *An Ever Closer Union: A Critical Analysis of the Draft Treaty on European Union*. European Perspective Series. Luxembourg: Office for Official Publications of the European Communities, 1985.

Bliss, Christopher, and Jorge de Macedo. *Unity and Diversity in the European Economy*. London: Center for European Policy Research, 1990.

Brandon, Henry, ed. *In Search of a New World Order: The Future of U.S.-European Relations*. Washington, DC: Brookings Institution, 1992.

Brandt, Willy. *People and Politics: The Years 1960–1975*. Boston: Little, Brown & Co., 1978.

Brealey, Mark, and Conor Quigley. *Completing the Internal Market of the EC: 1992 Handbook*. Dordrecht, The Netherlands: Klewer, 1992.

Brinkley, Douglas, and Clifford Hackett, eds. *Jean Monnet: The Path to European Unity*. New York: St. Martin's, 1991.

Brittan, Leon. *European Competition Policy: Keeping the Playing Field Level*. Brussels: CEPS, 1992.

Bromberger, Merry, and Serge Bromberger. *Jean Monnet and the United States of Europe*. New York: Coward-McCann, 1969.

Brown, Neville L., and Francis G. Jacobs. *The Court of Justice of the European Communities*. London: Sweet & Maxwell, 1977.

Bruneau, Thomas C., Victor Da Rosa, and Alexandre Macleod. *Portugal in Development: Emigration, Industrialization, and the European Community*. Ottawa: University of Ottawa Press, 1991.

Brunt, Barry. *The Republic of Ireland*. London: Clapman, 1988.

Buckley, M., and M. Anderson. *Women, Equality and Europe*. London: Macmillan, 1988.

Bullock, Alan. *Ernest Bevin: Foreign Secretary, 1948–1951*. London: Heinemann, 1983.

Bulmer, Simon. *The Domestic Structure of EC Policy-Making in West Germany*. New York: Garland, 1986.

Bulmer, Simon, and Willie Patterson. *The Federal Republic of Germany and the EC*. London: Allen & Unwin, 1987.

Bulmer, Simon, and Wolfgang Wessels. *The European Council: Decision-Making in European Politics*. London: Macmillan, 1987.

Burgess, Michael. *Federalism and European Union: Political Ideas, Influences and Strategies in the European Community, 1972–1987*. London: Routledge, 1989.

Burstein, Daniel. *Euroquake: Europe's Explosive Economic Challenge Will Change the World*. New York: Simon & Schuster, 1991.

Butler, Michael. *Europe: More Than a Continent*. London: Heinemann, 1986.

Cafruny, Alan, and Glenda Rosenthal. *The State of the European Community: The Maastricht Debates and Beyond*. Boulder, CO: Lynne Rienner, 1993.

Cahan, Alfred. *The WEU and NATO: Strengthening the Second Pillar of the Alliance*. Washington, DC: Atlantic Council, 1990.

Calingaert, Michael. *The 1992 Challenge from Europe: Development of the European Community's Internal Market*. Washington, DC: National Planning Association, 1988.

Callaghan, James. *Time and Change*. London: Collins, 1987.

Canzoneri, Matthew, Vittorio Grilli, and Paul Masson, eds. *Establishing a Central Bank for Europe*. Cambridge: Cambridge University Press, 1992.

Capotorti, Francesco, Meinhardt Hils, Francis Jacobs, and Jean-Paul Jacques, eds. *The European Union Treaty: Commentary on the Draft Adopted by the European Parliament on 14 February 1984*. Oxford: Clarendon Press, 1986.

Cecchini, Paolo. *The European Challenge 1992: The Benefits of a Single Market*. Aldershot, England: Wildwood House, 1988.

Clarke, Michael. *British External Policy-Making in the 1990s*. Washington, DC: Brookings Institution, 1992.

Coffey, Peter, ed. *Main Economic Policy Areas of the EEC Toward 1992*. 3rd edition. Dordrecht, The Netherlands: Kluwer, 1990.

Colchester, N., and D. Buchan. *Europower: The Essential Guide to Europe's Transformation in 1992*. London: Times Books, 1990.

Collins, Michael. *Western European Integration: Implications for U.S. Policy and Strategy*. New York: Praeger, 1992.

Coombes, David. *Politics and Bureaucracy in the European Communities*. London: Allen & Unwin, 1970.

———. *The Power of the Purse: The Role of the European Parliament in Budgetary Decisions*. London: Allen & Unwin, 1976.

Cooney, Stephen. *NAM's Annual Report on the European Community Internal Market and Issues for U.S. Manufacturers*. Washington, DC: National Association of Manufacturers, Annual Series Since 1989.

Couve de Murville, Maurice. *Une Politique Etrangère, 1958–1969*. Paris: Plon, 1971.

Cox, Andrew, and Paul Furlong. *A Modern Companion to the European Community: A Guide to Key Facts, Institutions and Terms*. Cheltenham, England: Edward Elgar, 1992.

Crampton, Stephen. *1992 Eurospeak Explained*. Brussels: European Bookshop Ltd., 1990.

Cromwell, William C. *The United States and the Atlantic Pillar: The Strained Alliance*. New York: St. Martin's, 1992.

———, ed. *The Dynamics of European Integration*. London: Pinter, 1990.

Crouch, Colin, and David Marquand. *The New Centrism: Britain out of Step in Europe?* Oxford: Blackwell, 1989.

———. *The Politics of 1992: Beyond the Single European Market*. Cambridge, MA: Basil Blackwell, 1990.

Cutler, Tony. *1992 and the Struggle for Europe: A Critical Evaluation of the European Community*. Oxford: Berg, 1989.

Dahrendorf, Ralf, Theodore C. Sorensen, and Andrew Pierre, eds. *A Widening Atlantic? Domestic Change and Foreign Policy*. New York: Council on Foreign Relations, 1986.

Daiffill, John, and Massimo Beber, eds. *A Currency for Europe*. London: Lothian Foundation, 1991.

Danspeckgruber, Wolfgang, ed. *Emerging Dimensions of European Security Policy*. Boulder, CO: Westview, 1991.

Davidson, Paul, and J. A. Kregel, eds. *Economic Problems of the 1990s: Europe, the Developing Countries and the United States*. Brookfield, VT: Edward Elgar, 1991.

De Bassompierre, Guy. *Changing the Guard in Brussels: An Insider's View of the EC Presidency*. New York: Praeger, 1988.

De Cecco, Marcello, and Alberto Giovannini, eds. *A European Central Bank: Perspectives on Monetary Unification After Ten Years of EMS*. London: Center for European Policy Research, 1989.

De Gaulle, Charles. *Memoirs of Hope: Renewal and Endeavor*. New York: Simon & Schuster, 1971.

De Menil, Lois Pattison. *Who Speaks for Europe? The Vision of Charles de Gaulle.* London: Weidenfeld & Nicolson, 1977.

De Porte, Anton. *Europe Between the Superpowers: The Enduring Balance.* New Haven, CT: Yale University Press, 1979.

De Ruyt, Jean. *European Political Cooperation: Toward a Unified European Foreign Policy.* Washington, DC: Atlantic Council of the United States, 1989.

———. *L'Acte Unique Européen.* Brussels: Editions de l'Université de Bruxelles, 1987.

Delors, Jacques. *Le Nouveau Concert Européen.* Paris: Editions Odile Jacob, 1992.

———. *Our Europe: The Community and National Development.* London: Verso, 1992.

Deutsch, Karl. *France, Germany and the Western Alliance: A Study of Elite Attitudes on European Integration and World Politics.* New York: Scribner's Sons, 1967.

Deutsch, Karl, et al. *Political Community in the North Atlantic Area.* Princeton: Princeton University Press, 1957.

Dinan, Desmond. *Historical Dictionary of the European Community.* Metuchen, NJ: The Scarecrow Press, 1993

Drury, Robert, and Peter Xuereb, eds. *European Community Laws: A Comparative Approach.* Brookfield, VT: Dartmouth, 1990.

Dudley, James. 1992: *Understanding the New European Market.* Dearborn, MI: Financial Publications, 1990.

Edwards, Geoffrey, and Elfriede Regelsberger. *Europe's Global Links: The EC and Inter-Regional Cooperation.* New York: St. Martin's, 1990.

Edwards, Geoffrey, and Helen Wallace. *The Council of Ministers of the EC and the President in Office.* London: Federal Trust, 1977.

Ellwood, David. *Rebuilding Europe: Western Europe, America and Postwar Reconstruction.* London: Longman, 1992

Emerson, Michael. *The Economics of 1992.* Oxford: Oxford University Press, 1988.

Euromonitor Publications Limited. *The Single Market Handbook.* London: Euromonitor Publications Ltd., 1990.

European Access: The Current Awareness Bulletin to the Politics and Activities of the European Community. Comprehensive guide to current policies and activities in the EC, published six times a year by Chadwyck-Healey in association with the United Kingdom Offices of the European Commission.

Faulhaber, Gerald, and Gaultiero Tamburini. *European Economic Integration: The Role of Technology.* Boston: Kluwer, 1991.

Featherstone, K. *Socialist Parties and European Integration.* Manchester: Manchester University Press, 1988.

Featherstone, K., and D. Katsoudas, eds. *Political Change in Greece, Before and After the Colonels.* London: Croom Helm, 1987.

Featherstone, Kevin, and Roy Ginsberg. *The United States and the European Community in the 1990s: Partners in Transition.* New York: St. Martin's, 1993.

Federal Trust Study Group. *The EC and the Developing Countries: A Policy for the Future.* London: Federal Trust, 1988.

Feld, Werner. *The Future of European Security and Defense Policy.* Boulder, CO: Lynne Rienner, 1993.

———. *West Germany and the EC: Changing Interests and Competing Policy Options.* New York: Praeger, 1981.

Fennell, Rosemary. *The Common Agricultural Policy of the European Community.* London: Granada, 1979.

Folsom, Ralph H. *European Community Law.* St. Paul, MN: West, 1991.

Franklin, Michael. *Britain's Future in Europe.* London: RIIA, 1990.

Franklin, Michael, and Marc Wilke. *Britain in the EC.* London: RIIA, 1991.

Fratianni, Michele, and Juergen Von Hagen. *The EMS and EMU*. Boulder, CO: Westview, 1991.

Freeman, Christopher, Margaret Sharp, and William Walker. *Technology and the Future of Europe: Global Competition and the Environment in the 1990*. London: Pinter, 1991.

Freney, Michael, and Rebecca Hartley. *United Germany and the United States*. Washington, DC: National Planning Association, 1991.

Fritsch-Bournazel, Renata. *Europe and German Reunification*. Oxford: Berg, 1991.

Fursdon, Edward. *The European Defence Community: A History*. London: Macmillan, 1980.

Galtung, J. *Europe in the Making*. New York: Crane Russak, 1989.

Gautron, Jean-Claude, ed. *Les Relations Communauté Européenne: Europe de l'Est*. Paris: Economica, 1991.

Gazzo, Marina, ed. *Towards European Union*. 2 vols. Brussels: Agence Europe, 1985 and 1986.

George, Stephen, ed. *Britain and the European Community: The Politics of Semi-Detachment*. Oxford: Clarendon Press, 1992.

George, Stephen. *An Awkward Partner: Britain in the European Community*. Oxford: Clarendon Press, 1990.

———. *Politics and Policy in the EC*. 2nd ed. Oxford: Clarendon Press, 1991.

Gianaris, Nicholas V. *The European Community and the United States: Economic Relations*. New York: Praeger, 1991.

Giavazzi, Francesco, Stefano Micossi, and Marcus Miller, eds. *The European Monetary System*. Cambridge: Cambridge University Press, 1989.

Gillingham, John. *Coal, Steel and the Rebirth of Europe, 1945–1955*. Cambridge: Cambridge University Press, 1991.

Gimbel, John. *The Origins of the Marshall Plan*. Stanford: Stanford University Press, 1968.

Ginsberg, Roy. *Foreign Policy Actions of the European Community: The Politics of Scale*. Boulder, CO: Lynne Rienner, 1989.

Giovanni, Alberto, and Colin Mayer. *European Financial Integration*. London: Center for European Policy Research, 1991.

Goodman, John B. *Monetary Sovereignty: The Politics of Central Banking in Western Europe*. Ithaca, NY: Cornell University Press, 1992.

Goodman, S. F. *The European Community*. New York: St. Martin's, 1990.

Gowland, David, and Stephen James, eds. *Economic Policy After 1992*. Brookfield, VT: Dartmouth, 1991.

Goyder, D. G. *EC Competition Law*. 2nd edition. Oxford: Oxford University Press, 1993.

Green, Nicholas, Trevor Hartley, and John Usher. *The Legal Foundations of the Single European Market*. Oxford: Oxford University Press, 1991.

Gretschmann, K., ed. *EMU: Implications for National Policy-Makers*. The Hague: Martinus Nijhoff Publishers, 1993.

Griffith, Richard, and Alan Milward. *The Beyen Plan and the European Political Community*. Florence: European University Institute, 1985.

Grilli, Enzo. *The European Community and the Developing Countries*. Cambridge: Cambridge University Press, 1992.

Groom, A., and P. Taylor. *Functionalism: Theory and Practice in International Relations*. New York: Crane, Roussak, 1975.

Grosser, Alfred. *The Western Alliance: European-American Relations Since 1945*. New York: Vintage, 1982.

Guerrieri, P., and P. Padoan. *The Political Economy of European Integration: States, Markets and Institutions*. Savage, MD: Barnes & Noble, 1989.

Haas, Ernest. *The Obsolescence of Integration Theory.* Berkeley: University of California Press, 1975.

———. *The Uniting of Europe.* 2nd edition. Stanford: Stanford University Press, 1968.

Hackett, Clifford. *Cautious Revolution: The European Community Arrives.* New York: Praeger, 1990.

Haftendorn, Helga, and Christian Tuschhoff. *America and Europe in an Era of Change.* Boulder, CO: Westview, 1993.

Hagland, David G. *Alliance Within the Alliance? Franco-German Cooperation and the European Pillar of Defense.* Boulder, CO: Westview, 1991.

Hall, Graham, ed. *European Industrial Policy.* London: Croom Helm, 1986.

Hall, Peter A., Jack Haywards, and Howard Machin, eds. *Developments in French Politics.* New York: St. Martin's, 1990.

Hallstein, Walter. *Europe in the Making.* London: Allen & Unwin, 1972.

Hannequart, Achille, ed. *Economic and Social Cohesion in Europe: A New Objective.* London: Routledge, 1992.

Hanrieder, Wolfram. *Germany, America, Europe: Forty Years of German Foreign Policy.* New Haven, CT: Yale University Press, 1989.

Harrop, Jeffrey. *The Political Economy of Integration in the European Community.* 2nd edition. Aldershot, England: Edward Elgar, 1992.

Hathaway, Dale E. *Agriculture and the GATT: Rewriting the Rules.* Washington, DC: Institute for International Economics, 1987.

Heller, Francis H., and John Gillingham. *NATO: The Founding of the Atlantic Alliance and the Integration of Europe.* New York: St. Martin's, 1992.

Henig, Stanley, ed. *Political Parties in the European Community.* London: Allen & Unwin, 1979.

Hill, Christopher, ed. *National Foreign Policies and EPC.* London: Allen & Unwin, 1983.

Hine, R. C. *The Political Economy of European Trade: An Introduction to the Trade Policies of the EEC.* New York: St. Martin's, 1985.

Hodges, Michael. ed. *European Integration.* Harmondsworth: Penguin, 1972.

Hoffmann, Stanley, and Charles Maier, eds. *The Marshall Plan: A Retrospective.* Boulder, CO: Westview, 1984.

Hogan, Michael. *The Marshall Plan: America, Britain and the Reconstruction of Western Europe, 1947–1952.* Cambridge: Cambridge University Press, 1987.

Holland, Martin, ed. *The Future of European Political Cooperation.* New York: St. Martin's, 1991.

Horne, Alistair. *Harold Macmillan, 1957–1986.* New York: Penguin, 1989.

Hoscheit, Jean-Marc, and Wolfgang Wessels. *The European Council 1974–86: Evaluation and Prospects.* Maastricht: European Institute of Public Administration, 1988.

Howell, Patton R. *War's End: The Revolution of Consciousness in the European Community.* San Francisco: Saybrook, 1989.

Hufbauer, Gary Clyde, ed. *Europe 1992: An American Perspective.* Washington, DC: Brookings Institution, 1990.

Hufbauer, Gary Clyde. *The New Europe in the World Economy.* Washington, DC: Institute for International Economics, 1992.

Hughes, Kirsty. *European Competitiveness.* Cambridge: Cambridge University Press, 1993.

Hurwitz, Leon. *The EC and the Management of International Cooperation.* New York: Greenwood, 1987.

Hurwitz, Leon, and Christian Lequesne, eds. *The State of the European Community: Policies, Institutions, and Debates in the Transition Years.* Boulder, CO: Lynne Rienner, 1991.

Hyde-Price, Adrian. *European Security Beyond the Cold War.* London: RIIA, 1991.

Ifestos, Panayiotis. *European Political Cooperation: Towards a Framework for Supranational Diplomacy.* Aldershot, England: Avebury, 1987.

Jackson, Robert. *Europe in Transition.* New York: Praeger, 1992.

Jacobs, F. G., ed. *Yearbook of European Law.* Oxford: Clarendon Press (Annual).

Jacobs, F., R. Corbett, and M. Shackleton. *The European Parliament.* Boulder, CO: Westview, 1993.

Jeffries, John. *A Guide to the Official Publications of the EC.* 2nd edition. London: Mansell, 1981.

Jenkins, Roy. *European Diary, 1977–1981.* London: Collins, 1989.

———. *Life at the Centre.* London: Macmillan, 1991.

Joffe, Josef. *The Limited Partnership: Europe, the United States and the Burdens of Alliance.* Cambridge, MA: Ballinger, 1987.

Johnson, Peter, ed. *The Structure of European Industry.* Brookfield, VT: Edward Elgar, 1992.

Johnson, Stanley P., and Guy Corcelli. *The Environmental Policy of the EC.* London: Graham & Trotman, 1991.

Jopp, Mathias, Reinhardt Rummel, and Peter Schmidt, eds. *Integration and Security in Western Europe: Inside the European Pillar.* Boulder, CO: Westview, 1991.

Jouve, Edmond. *Le Général de Gaulle et la Construction de l'Europe (1940–1966).* Paris: Librarie Général de Droit, 1967.

Jovanovic, Miroslav N. *International Economic Integration.* New York: Routledge, 1992.

Karl Kaiser, et al., *The EC: Progress or Decline?* London: RIIA, 1983.

Keatinge, Patrick, ed. *Political Union. Studies in European Union.* Dublin: Institute of European Affairs, 1991.

Kennedy, Ellen. *The Bundesbank: Germany's Central Bank in the International Monetary System.* London: RIIA, 1991.

Kent, Penelope. *European Community Law.* London: Pitman, 1992.

Keohane, Robert O., and Stanley Hoffmann, eds. *The New European Community: Decision-making and Institutional Change.* Boulder, CO: Westview, 1991.

Kindersly, Richard, ed. *In Search of Eurocommunism.* London: Macmillan, 1981.

Kirby, Stephen, Terry McNeill, and Sally Harris. *Europe After the Gulf War: Reassessing Security Options.* Cheltenham, England: Edward Elgar, 1992.

Kirchner, Emil. *Decision-Making in the European Community: The Council Presidency and European Integration.* New York: St. Martin's, 1992.

Kissinger, Henry A. *The Troubled Partnership.* New York: McGraw-Hill, 1965.

———. *White House Years.* Boston: Little, Brown & Co., 1979.

Kitzinger, Uwe. *The Politics and Economics of European Economic Integration: Britain, Europe and the United States.* New York: Praeger, 1963.

Kramer, Alan. *The West German Economy, 1945–55.* Manchester: Manchester University Press, 1991.

Krause, Axel. *Inside the New Europe.* New York: Harper Collins, 1992

Kumcu, Erdogan. ed. *An Annotated Bibliography of the European Community.* Chicago: American Marketing Association, 1992.

Lacouture, Jean. *De Gaulle: The Ruler, 1945–1970.* London: Collins Harvill, 1991.

Laffan, Brigid. *Integration and Cooperation in Europe.* London: Routledge, 1992.

Laqueur, Walter. *Europe in Our Time: A History.* New York: Penguin, 1992.

Laursen, Finn, and Sophie Vanhoonacker, eds. *The Intergovernmental Conference on Political Union*. Maastricht: EIPA, 1992.

Lee, J. J., ed. *Europe in Transition: Political, Economic and Security Prospects in the 1990s*. Austin, TX: Lyndon Johnson School of Public Affairs, 1991.

Leigh, Michael. *European Integration and the Common Fisheries Policy*. London: Croom Helm, 1983.

Lepgold, Joseph. *The Declining Hegemon: The United States and European Defense, 1960–90*. New York: Praeger, 1990.

Levi, Lucio, ed. *Altiero Spinelli and Federalism in Europe and the World*. London: Lothian Foundation, 1991.

Levine, Robert A., ed. *Transition and Turmoil in the Atlantic Alliance*. New York: Crane Russak, 1991.

Liefferink, Duncan, and Philip Lowe, eds. *European Integration and Environmental Policy*. London: Belhaven Press, 1993.

Lindberg, Leon. *The Political Dynamics of Economic Integration* Stanford: Stanford University Press, 1963.

Lindberg, Leon, and Stuart Scheingold. *Europe's Would-Be Polity*. Englewood Cliffs, NJ: Prentice-Hall, 1970.

Lintner, Valerio, and Sonia Mazey. *The European Community: Economic and Political Aspects*. Brussels: European Bookshop Ltd., 1991.

Lipgens, Walter. *History of European Integration*. 2 vols. London: Oxford University Press, 1981 and 1986.

Lippert, Barbara, and Rosalind Stevens-Strohmann. *German Unification and EC Integration: German and British Perspectives*. London: RIIA, 1993.

Lister, Marjorie. *The European Community and the Developing World: The Role of the Lomé Convention*. Aldershot, England: Avebury, 1988.

Lodge, Juliet, ed. *The European Community and the Challenge of the Future*. London: Pinter, 1989.

———. *Political Union in Europe: The Crisis of Political Authority in the EC*. Cheltenham, England: Edward Elgar, 1992.

Ludlow, Peter. *Beyond 1992: Europe and Its World Partners*. Brussels: Center for European Policy Studies, 1989.

———, ed. *The Annual Review of European Community Affairs*. Brussels: CEPS, 1992.

———. *The Making of the European Monetary System*. London: Butterworths, 1982.

Mackenzie, Stewart, and John Alexander. *The European Community and the Rule of Law*. London: Stevens & Sons, 1977.

Macmillan, Harold. *At the End of the Day, 1961–1963*. New York: Harper & Row, 1973.

———. *Pointing the Way, 1959–1961*. New York: Harper & Row, 1972.

Maier, Charles S., ed. *The Cold War in Europe: Era of a Divided Continent*. New York: Markus Wiener, 1991.

Marjolin, Robert. *Architect of European Union: Memoirs, 1911–1986*. London: Weidenfeld & Nicolson, 1989.

Marsden, David, ed. *Pay and Employment in the New Europe*. Brookfield, VT: Edward Elgar, 1992.

Matthew, Alan. *The Common Agricultural Policy and the Less Developed Regions*. Dublin: Gill & Macmillan, 1985.

Mayne, Richard. *Federal Union: The Pioneers*. London: Macmillan, 1990.

———. *Postwar: The Dawn of Today's Europe*. New York: Schocken, 1983.

———. *The Community of Europe: Past, Present and Future*. New York: Norton, 1962.

————. *The Recovery of Europe: From Devastation to Unity.* London: Weidenfeld & Nicolson, 1970.

Mazery, Sonia, and Michael Newman. *Mitterrand's France.* London: Croom Helm, 1987.

McDonald, Frank, and Stephen Dearden, eds. *European Economic Integration.* New York: Longman, 1992

McGhee, George. *At the Creation of a New Germany: From Adenauer to Brandt: An Ambassador's Account.* New Haven, CT: Yale University Press, 1989.

McInnes, Colin. *Security and Strategy in the New Europe.* London: Routledge, 1992.

Meade, James Edward. *Negotiations for Benelux: An Annotated Chronicle 1943–56.* Princeton: Princeton University Press, 1957.

Mendes, A. J. Marques. *Economic Integration and Growth in Europe.* London: Croom Helm, 1987.

Mengozzi, P., and P. D. Duca. *European Community Law From Common Market to European Union.* Boston: Kluwer Academic Publishing Group, 1992.

Mennes, L.B.M., and Jacob Kol. *European Trade Policies and the Developing World.* London: Croom Helm, 1988.

Merlini, Cesare. *The Community and the Emerging Democracies: A Government Policy Report.* London: RIIA, 1991.

Michalski, Anna, and Helen Wallace. *The European Community: The Challenge of Enlargement.* London: RIIA, 1993.

Miller, Debra L. *EC 1992: A Commerce Department Analysis of European Community Directives.* Washington, DC: US Department of Commerce, 1989.

Milward, Alan. *The European Rescue of the Nation State.* Berkeley, CA: University of California Press, 1992.

————. *The Reconstruction of Western Europe, 1945–51.* London: Methuen, 1983.

Mitrany, David. *A Working Peace System.* Chicago: Quadrangle Books, 1966.

Molle, Willem. *The Economics of European Integration.* Brookfield, VT: Dartmouth, 1990.

Molle, Willem, and Ricardo Cappellin. *Regional Impact of Community Policies.* Brookfield, VT: Avebury, 1988.

Monnet, Jean. *Memoirs.* Garden City, NJ: Doubleday, 1978.

Montagnon, Peter, ed. *European Competition Policy.* London: RIIA, 1991.

Moreton, Edwina, ed. *Germany Between East and West.* Cambridge: Cambridge University Press, 1987.

Morgan, Annette. *From Summit to Council: Evolution in the EEC.* London: RIIA, 1976.

Morgan, Roger. *West European Politics Since 1945: The Shaping of the European Community.* London: Batsford, 1972.

Morgan, Roger, and Caroline Bray, eds. *Partners and Rivals in Western Europe: Britain, France, Germany.* Aldershot, England: Gower, 1986.

Nelson, Brian, David Roberts, and Walter Veit, eds. *The Idea of Europe: Problems of National and Transnational Identity.* Oxford: Berg, 1992.

Newhouse, John. *Collision in Brussels: The Common Market Crisis of 30 June 1965.* New York: Norton, 1967.

————. *De Gaulle and the Anglo-Saxons.* London: Deutsch, 1970.

Nicholson, F., and R. East. *From the Six to the Twelve: The Enlargement of the European Communities.* Harlow, England: Longman, 1987.

Nicoll, William, and Trevor Salmon. *Understanding the European Communities.* London: Philip Allen, 1990.

Noël, Emile. *Working Together: The Institutions of the EC.* Luxembourg: Office for Official Publications of the European Communities, 1988.

Nugent, Neill. *The Government and Politics of the EC.* 2nd edition. Durham, NC: Duke University Press, 1992.

Nuttall, Simon. *European Political Cooperation*. Oxford: Clarendon Press, 1992.

O'Nuallain, Colm, ed. *The President of the European Council of Ministers: Impacts and Implications for National Governments*. London: Croom Helm, 1985.

Padoa-Schioppa, Tomaso. *Efficiency, Stability and Equity: A Strategy for the Evolution of the Economic System of the European Community*. Oxford: Oxford University Press, 1987.

Palankai, Tibor. *The EC and Central European Integration: The Hungarian Case*. Boulder, CO: Westview, 1991.

Pelkmans, Jacques, and Alan Winters. *Europe's Domestic Market*. London: RIIA, 1988.

Perle, Richard. *Reshaping Western Security: The United States Faces a United Europe*. Lanham, MD: University Press of America, 1991.

Peterson, John. *Europe and America in the 1990s: Prospects for Partnership*. Brookfield, VT: Edward Elgar, 1992.

Pijpers, Alfred. *The European Community at the Crossroads*. Dordrecht, The Netherlands: Martinus Nijhoff, 1992.

Pijpers, Alfred, Elfriede Regelsberger, and Wolfgang Wessels, eds. *European Political Cooperation in the 1980s: A Common Foreign Policy for Western Europe?* Dordrecht, The Netherlands: Martinus Nijhoff, 1989.

Pinder, John. *European Community: The Building of a Union*. Oxford: Oxford University Press, 1991.

———. *The European Community and Eastern Europe*. London: RIIA, 1991.

Plender, Richard. *Plender and Usher's Cases and Materials on the Law of the European Communities*. 2nd edition. London: Butterworths, 1989.

Plumb, Lord. *Building a Democratic Community: The Role of the European Parliament*. London: Lothian Foundation, 1991.

Poidevin, Raymond, ed. *Origins of European Integration: March 1948–May 1950*. Brussels: Bruylant, 1986.

———. *Robert Schuman: Homme d'Etat, 1866–1963*. Paris: Imprimerie Nationale, 1986.

Political and Economic Encyclopedia of Western Europe. Brussels: European Bookshop Ltd., 1990.

Pomfret, Richard. *Mediterranean Policy of the EC: A Study of Discrimination in Trade*. London: Macmillan, 1986.

Pompidou, Georges. *To Reestablish a Truth*. Paris: Flammarion, 1982.

Pond, Elizabeth. *Beyond the Wall: Germany's Road to Unification*. Washington, DC: Brookings Institution, 1993.

Portes, Richard. *The EC and Eastern Europe After 1992*. London: Center for European Policy Research, 1990.

Pryce, Roy, ed. *The Dynamics of European Union*. London: Croom Helm, 1987.

Puchala, Donald J. *Fiscal Harmonization in the European Communities: National Politics and International Cooperation*. London: Pinter, 1984.

Quelch, John A., Robert D. Buzzell, and Eric R. Salama. *The Marketing Challenge of 1992*. Reading, MA: Addison-Wesley, 1989.

Ransome, Patrick, ed. *Towards the United States of Europe: Studies in the Making of the European Community*. London: Lothian Foundation, 1991.

Rasmussen, Hjalte. *On Law and Policy in the European Court of Justice*. Dordrecht, The Netherlands: Martinus Nijhoff, 1986.

Rassieri, Ruggiero. *Italy and the Schuman Plan Negotiations*. Florence: European University Institute, 1986.

Redmond, John, ed. *The External Relations of the European Community: The International Response to 1992*. London: Macmillan, 1992.

————. *The Next Mediterranean Enlargement of the EC: Turkey, Cyprus and Malta?* Aldershot: Dartmouth, 1993.

Reinicke, Wolfgang. *Building a New Europe: The Challenge of System Transformation and Systemic Reform.* Washington, DC: Brookings Institution, 1992.

Rosenberg, Jerry. *The New Europe: An A to Z Compendium on the European Community.* Washington, DC: Bureau of National Affairs, 1991.

Rosenthal, Glenda. *The Men Behind the Decisions.* Farnborough, England: Teakfield for Lexington Books, 1975.

Ross, George, Stanley Hoffmann, and Sylvia Malzacher. *The Mitterrand Experiment: Continuity and Change in Modern France.* Cambridge, England: Polity, 1987.

Rotfield, Adam D., and Walter Stutzle, eds. *Germany and Europe in Transition.* Oxford: Oxford University Press, 1991.

Roy, Jean-Louis. *1992: A Guide to the European Economic Community Charter.* New York: Collier Books, 1992.

Rummel, Reinhardt, ed. *Toward Political Union: Planning a Common Foreign and Security Policy.* Boulder, CO: Westview, 1992.

————, ed. *The Evolution of an International Actor: Western Europe's New Assertiveness.* Boulder, CO: Westview, 1990.

————, ed. *Western European Security Policy: Asserting European Priorities.* Boulder, CO: Westview, 1989.

Rusi, Alpo M. *After the Cold War: Europe's New Political Architecture.* New York: St. Martin's, 1991.

Sandholtz, Wayne. *High-Tech Europe: The Politics of European Cooperation.* Berkeley: University of California Press, 1991.

Sbragia, Alberta, ed. *Euro-Politics: Institutions and Policymaking in the "New" European Community.* Washington, DC: Brookings Institution, 1992.

Schmidt, Helmut. *The Path to European Union: From the Marshall Plan to the Common Market.* Baton Rouge, LA: Louisiana State University Press, 1962.

Schneider, Heinrich. *Austria and the EC.* London: RIIA, 1989.

Schoutheete, Phillippe de. *La Cooperation Politique Européenne.* Paris: Nathan, 1980.

Schuknecht, Ludger. *Trade Protection in the EC.* Philadelphia: Harwood, 1992.

Schwartz, Thomas A. *America's Germany: John J. McCloy and the Federal Republic of Germany.* Cambridge, MA: Harvard University Press, 1991.

Schwok, Rene. *U.S.-EC Relations in the Post-Cold War Era: Conflict or Partnership?* Boulder, CO: Westview, 1991.

Serfaty, Simon. *Fading Partnership: America and Europe After Thirty Years.* New York: Praeger, 1979.

————. *France, de Gaulle and Europe: The Policy of the Fourth and Fifth Republics Toward the Continent.* Baltimore: Johns Hopkins University Press, 1968.

Shackleton, Michael. *Financing the EC.* London: Pinter, 1990.

Sharp, Margaret. *Europe and the New Technologies: Six Core Studies in Innovation and Adjustment.* Ithaca, NY: Cornell University Press, 1986.

Sharp, Margaret, and Claire Shearman. *European Technological Collaboration.* London: RIIA, 1987.

Sharp, Paul. *Irish Foreign Policy and the European Community.* Aldershot, England: Gower, 1990.

Shonfield, Andrew. *Europe: Journey to an Unknown Destination.* London: Allan Lane, 1973.

Simonian, Haig. *The Privileged Partnership: Franco-German Relations and the European Community, 1969–1984.* Oxford: Clarendon Press, 1985.

Smith, Dale, and James Lee Ray, eds. *The 1992 Project and the Future of Integration in Europe.* New York: M. E. Sharp, 1992.

Smith, Michael, and Stephen Woolcock. *Redefining the U.S.-EC Relationship.* London: RIIA, 1993.

Smyser, W. R. *The Economy of United Germany: Colossus at the Crossroads.* New York: St. Martin's, 1992.

Spinelli, Altiero. *The Eurocrats: Conflict and Crisis in the European Community.* Baltimore: Johns Hopkins University Press, 1966.

Springer, Beverly. *The Social Dimension of 1992: Europe Faces a New EC.* New York: Greenwood, 1992.

Stares, Paul B., ed. *The New Germany and the New Europe.* Washington, DC: Brookings Institution, 1992.

Steinberg, James. *An Ever Closer Union: European Integration and Its Implications for the Future of U.S.-European Relations.* Santa Monica, CA: Rand, 1993.

Steinberg, Michael, ed. *The Technical Challenge and Opportunities of a United Europe.* Savage, MD: Barnes & Noble, 1990.

Stirk, Peter M.R. *European Unity in Context: The Interwar Period.* New York: Pinter, 1989.

Stirk, Peter, and David Willis, eds. *Shaping Postwar Europe: European Unity and Diversity, 1945–1957.* New York: St. Martin's, 1991.

Strasser, Daniel. *The Finances of Europe.* New York: Praeger, 1977.

Swann, Dennis. *The Economics of the Common Market.* 6th edition. Harmondsworth, England: Penguin, 1988.

Taylor, Paul. *The Limits of European Integration.* London: Croom Helm, 1983.

Thomsen, Stephen, and Stephen Woolcock. *Direct Investment and European Integration: Competition Among Firms and Governments.* London: RIIA, 1993.

Thomson, Ian. *The Documentation of the European Communities: A Guide.* London: Mansell, 1989.

Tovias, Alfred. *Foreign Economic Relations of the European Community: The Impact of Spain and Portugal.* Boulder, CO: Lynne Rienner, 1990.

───────. *The European Community's Single Market: The Challenge of 1992 for Sub-Saharan Africa.* Washington, DC: The World Bank, 1990.

Treverton, Gregory, ed. *Europe and America Beyond 2000.* London: RIIA, 1989.

───────, ed. *The Shape of the New Europe.* New York: Council on Foreign Relations, 1991.

───────. *America, Germany and the Future of Europe.* New York: Council on Foreign Relations, 1992.

Tsoukalis, Loukas. *Europe, America and the World Economy.* Oxford: Basil Blackwell, 1986.

───────. *The New European Economy: The Politics and Economics of European Integration.* 2nd edition. Oxford: Oxford University Press, 1993.

Tugendhat, Christopher. *Making Sense of Europe.* New York: Penguin, 1986.

Twitchett, Carol Cosgrove. *A Framework for Development: The EEC and the ACP.* London: Allen & Unwin, 1981.

Tykkylainen, Markku, ed. *Development Issues and Strategies in the New Europe.* Brookfield, VT: Dartmouth, 1992.

U.S. Congress, House Committee on Foreign Affairs. *Europe and the United States: Competition and Cooperation in the 1990s.* Washington, DC: Government Printing Office, 1992.

U.S. International Trade Commission. *1992: The Effects of Greater Economic Integration Within the European Community on the United States.* Initial report and series of follow-up reports. Washington, DC: USITC, 1989.

Urwin, Derek W. *The Community of Europe: A History of European Integration Since 1945*. New York: Longman, 1991.

Van Tartwijk-Novey, Louise. *The United States and the European Community*. Lanham, MD: Madison Books, 1992.

Van Ypersele, Jacques. *The European Monetary System: Origins, Operation and Outlook*. Chicago: St. James, 1985.

Von der Groeben, Hans. *The European Community: The Formative Years: The Struggle to Establish the Common Market and the Political Union (1958–1966)*. European Perspectives Series. Luxembourg: Office for Official Publications of the European Communities, 1987.

Vree, Johan K. de, Peter Coffey, R. H. Lauwaars, Max Jensen, Alfred Pijpers, and Edmond Volker. *Towards a European Foreign Policy: Legal, Economic and Political Dimensions*. Boston: Martinus Nijhoff, 1987.

Wall, Irwin M. *The United States and the Making of Postwar France, 1945–54*. New York: Cambridge University Press, 1991.

Wallace, Helen, ed. *The Wider Western Europe: Reshaping the EC/EFTA Relationship*. London: RIIA, 1991.

———. *Widening and Deepening: The European Community and the New European Agenda*. London: RIIA, 1989.

Wallace, Helen, and Wolfgang Wessels. *Towards a New Partnership: The EC and EFTA in the Wider Western Europe*. Geneva: EFTA, 1990.

Wallace, William, ed. *The Dynamics of European Integration*. London: Pinter, 1990.

———. *The Transformation of Western Europe*. London: RIIA, 1990.

Wallace, William, Helen Wallace, and Carole Webb. *Policy-Making in the European Community*. 2nd edition. New York: Wiley, 1983.

Weigall, David, and Peter Stirk, eds. *The Origins and Development of the European Community*. London: Pinter, 1992.

Welfens, P.J.J., ed. *European Monetary Integration: From German Dominance to an EC Central Bank?* Berlin: Springer-Verlag, 1991.

Wells, Sherrill Brown. *French Industrial Policy: A History, 1945–81*. Washington, DC: Office of the Historian, Department of State, 1991.

Werts, Jan. *The European Council*. Amsterdam: North Holland, 1992.

Wexler, Imanuel. *The Marshall Plan Revisited*. Westport, CT: Greenwood, 1983.

White, Theodore H. *Fire in the Ashes: Europe in Mid-Century*. New York: Sloan, 1953.

Wilke, Marc, and Helen Wallace. *Subsidiarity: Approaches to Power-Sharing in the EC*. London: RIIA, 1990.

Willis, Roy. *European Integration*. New York: New Viewpoints, 1975.

———. *France, Germany and the New Europe*. 2nd edition. Stanford: Stanford University Press, 1968.

Wilson, Thomas, and Estellie Smith. *Cultural Change and the New Europe: Perspectives on the European Community*. Boulder, CO: Westview Press, 1993.

Winand, Pascaline. *Eisenhower, Kennedy and the United States of Europe*. New York: St. Martin's Press, 1993.

Winter, Audrey. *Europe Without Frontiers: A Lawyer's Guide*. Washington, DC: Bureau of National Affairs, 1989.

Winters, Alan L., and Anthony Venables. *European Integration: Trade and Industry*. London: Center for European Policy Research, 1991.

Wise, Michael. *The Common Fisheries Policy of the EC*. London: Methuen, 1984.

Woods, Stanley. *Western Europe: Technology and the Future*. London: Croom Helm, 1987.

Woolcock, Stephen. *Trading Partners or Trading Blows? Market Access Issues in EC-US Relations*. London: RIIA, 1991.

Woolcock, Steven, Michael Hodges, and Kristin Schreiber. *Britain, Germany and 1992: The Limits of Deregulation.* London: RIIA, 1991.

Yannopoulos, George, ed. *Europe and America: 1992.* New York: Manchester University Press, 1991.

Young, Hugo. *One of Us: A Biography of Margaret Thatcher.* London: MacMillan, 1989.

Young, John W. *Britain, France and the Unity of Europe, 1945–1951.* Leicester, England: Leicester University Press, 1984.

───. *Cold War Europe: A Political History.* London: Routledge, 1991.

Zartman, William, ed. *Europe and Africa: The New Phase.* Boulder, CO: Lynne Rienner, 1992.

Ziring, Lawrence, ed. *The New Europe and the World.* Kalamazoo, MI: New Issues Press, 1993.

Zurcher, Arnold. *The Struggle to Unite Europe, 1940–1958.* New York: New York University Press, 1958.

OFFICIAL DOCUMENTS

This is a selected list of EC official documentation, published mostly by the Community's Office for Official Publications in Luxembourg.

Bulletin of the European Communities, official monthly record of events and policy actions for all institutions, published by the Commission.

Bulletin of the European Communities (Supplement), selected legislative or consultative documents, published at irregular intervals by the Commission.

COM Documents, proposals and amendments issued by the Commission (approximately 80 percent are published in the "C" series of the Official Journal of the European Communities). COM documents are annotated thus: The number in parentheses is the year; "620 final" means the final version of the 620th Commission document of that year.

Common Positions of the Council of Ministers (announced in the "C" series of the Official Journal of the European Communities).

Completing the Internal Market: Current Status Reports, updates on the 1992 legislative program, published twice a year.

Directory of Community Legislation in Force, published every June and December.

European Documentation, series of explanatory publications on EC policies published approximately five to seven times a year.

European Economy, published four times a year by the Commission's Directorate-General for Economic and Financial Affairs.

European File, series of small pamphlets outlining various aspects of EC development and policies, titles published approximately twenty times a year.

European Perspectives, academic monographs on EC-related subjects, published occasionally.

European Political Cooperation Documentation Bulletin, reproduces texts of the statements issued under EPC.

Fact Sheets on the European Parliament and the Activities of the European Communities, outlines Community policies, legislation, and activities, published by the Parliament and updated periodically.

General Report on the Activities of the European Communities, published annually by the Commission. Works published annually as addenda to the General Report:

The Agricultural Situation in the Community
Report on Social Developments
Report on Competition Policy.
Official Journal of the European Communities, legislation and other official acts of the EC, divided into four parts: legislation ("L") series, for regulations, directives, and other binding acts; communications ("C") series, for nonbinding decisions, resolutions, and notices supplement ("S") series, for public works and supply contracts; and annex, for plenary sessions of the European Parliament.
Opinions and Information Reports of the Economic and Social Committee (published in the "C" section of the Official Journal of the European Communities).
Panorama of EC Industry, describes over 150 sectors of manufacturing and service industries in the EC, published annually by the Commission.
Protocols, full texts of agreements between the EC and third countries, published by the Council.
Reports of Cases Before the Court, published by the Court of Justice in annual series, parts appearing at irregular intervals throughout the year.
Reports, Opinions, and Debates of the European Parliament (opinions are published in the "C" section of the Official Journal of the European Communities; EP debates are published in the Annex of the Official Journal).
Research on the Cost of "Non-Europe": Basic Findings (1988), a sixteen-volume study of the cost to the Community of not completing the single market program.
Review of the Council's Work, published annually by the Council of Ministers.
SCAD Bulletin, bibliographic guide published weekly by the Commission, lists wide range of EC documentation and articles from non-EC periodicals.
Statistical Office of the European Communities (Eurostat), produces various statistical publications arranged according to themes, including general statistics, economy and finance, foreign trade, and environment, among others.
Treaties Establishing the European Communities and Documents Concerning the Accessions to the European Communities, 2 vols. (1987), also includes text of the Single European Act and various resolutions and declarations.
Treaty on European Union (1992), text of the Maastricht Treaty.

Abbreviations

ACP	African, Caribbean, and Pacific Countries
AER	Assembly of European Regions
APEC	Asia Pacific Economic Co-operation
ASEAN	Association of Southeast Asian Nations
CAP	Common Agricultural Policy
CEECs	Central and Eastern European countries
CEEP	European Center of Public Enterprises
CEN	European Standardization Committee
CENELEC	European Electrotechnical Standardization Committee
CFI	Court of First Instance
CFSP	Common Foreign and Security Policy
CITES	Convention on Trade in Endangered Species
Coreper	Committee of Permanent Representatives
COST	European Cooperation in the Field of Scientific and Technical Research
CSCE	Conference on Security and Cooperation in Europe
DG	Directorate-General
EAGGF	European Agricultural Guarantee and Guidance Fund
EAP	Environmental Action Program
EBRD	European Bank for Reconstruction and Development
EC	European Community
ECB	European Central Bank
ECJ	European Court of Justice
ECSC	European Coal and Steel Community
ECU	European Currency Unit
EDC	European Defence Community
EDG	European Democratic Group
EDU	European Democratic Union
EEA	European Economic Area

EEC	European Economic Community
EEIG	European Economic Interest Grouping
EFTA	European Free Trade Association
EIA	Environmental Impact Assessment
EIB	European Investment Bank
EIF	European Investment Fund
EMI	European Monetary Institute
EMS	European Monetary System
EMU	Economic and Monetary Union
EN	European Norms
EPC	European Political Cooperation
EPP	European People's Party
EPU	European Political Union
ERM	Exchange Rate Mechanism
ERDF	European Regional Development Fund
ESCB	European System of Central Banks
ESPRIT	European Strategic Program for Research and Development in Information Technology
ETSI	European Telecom Standards Institute
ETUC	European Trades Union Confederation
Euratom	European Atomic Energy Community
GATT	General Agreement on Tariffs and Trade
IGC	Intergovernmental Conference
IMP	Integrated Mediterranean Program
IPPC	Integrated Pollution Prevention and Control
JET	Joint European Torus
MCA	Monetary Compensatory Amount
MEP	Member of the European Parliament
MFA	Multifiber Arrangement
MGQ	Maximum Guaranteed Quantity
MLF	Multilateral Force
NATO	North Atlantic Treaty Organization
OECD	Organization for Economic Cooperation and Development
OEEC	Organization for European Economic Cooperation
SAD	Single Administrative Document
SEA	Single European Act
TCDI	Group for the Technical Coordination and Defense of Independents
UNICE	European Union of Employers' Confederations
VAT	Value-added Tax
WEU	Western European Union

Index

521

About the Book and Author

Why is the European Community increasingly important? What is its purpose? How is it organized? Is it likely to "widen" or "deepen" before the end of the decade?

Anyone interested in contemporary Europe has contemplated these and a host of related questions. But few understand fully the Community's origins, activities, and operations, largely because the EC is a unique international entity that defies traditional evaluation and analysis.

This book—written in an accessible, straightforward style—cuts through the complexities of the EC and explains clearly the extent of European integration since World War II. Part I explores the Community's history and political development since the early 1950s, including the emergence of the European Union in the early 1990s. Part II describes and analyzes EC institutions. Part III assesses the Community's policies and programs, from agriculture to industry, from social affairs to science and technology.

Imaginative and interdisciplinary in approach, the book makes the EC comprehensible and whets the appetite for further research. It is essential reading for all who are interested in the emerging New Europe.

DESMOND DINAN is associate professor of history and director of the Center for European Community Studies at George Mason University and research fellow at the College of Europe (Belgium).